THE LIFE OF
RUTHERFORD BIRCHARD HAYES

VOLUME I

A Da Capo Press Reprint Series

THE AMERICAN SCENE
Comments and Commentators

GENERAL EDITOR: WALLACE D. FARNHAM
University of Illinois

THE LIFE OF RUTHERFORD BIRCHARD HAYES

NINETEENTH PRESIDENT OF THE
UNITED STATES

BY

CHARLES R. WILLIAMS

VOLUME I

DA CAPO PRESS • NEW YORK • 1971

A Da Capo Press Reprint Edition

This Da Capo Press edition of *The Life of Rutherford Birchard Hayes* is an unabridged republication of the first edition published in Boston and New York in 1914. It is reprinted by permission from a set of the original edition owned by the University of Virginia Library.

Library of Congress Catalog Card Number 79-87678
SBN 306-71714-X

Published by Da Capo Press
A Division of Plenum Publishing Corporation
227 West 17th Street, New York, N.Y. 10011
All Rights Reserved

Manufactured in the United States of America

THE LIFE OF
RUTHERFORD BIRCHARD HAYES

IN TWO VOLUMES

VOLUME I

Rutherford B. Hayes

THE LIFE OF
RUTHERFORD BIRCHARD
HAYES

NINETEENTH PRESIDENT OF THE
UNITED STATES

BY

CHARLES RICHARD WILLIAMS

WITH PORTRAITS AND OTHER ILLUSTRATIONS

VOLUME I

BOSTON AND NEW YORK
HOUGHTON MIFFLIN COMPANY
The Riverside Press Cambridge
1914

In Memoriam
WILLIAM HENRY SMITH
PATRIOT SCHOLAR FRIEND

PREFACE

THE *Life* of Mr. Hayes was to have been written by his most intimate personal and political friend, William Henry Smith. That was Mr. Hayes's hope and Mr. Smith's purpose. Soon after Mr. Hayes's death Mr. Smith began the contemplated work. His plan was to write not a simple biography, but a history to be called *The Life and Times of Hayes*.

From the beginning of Mr. Hayes's life to the time of his Administration as President, the slavery question, in its various ramifications and effects, had been the dominant concern of American politics and statesmanship. The policy toward the South pursued by Mr. Hayes when President practically marked the final passing of the question from national politics. "The first half of my active political life," Mr. Hayes wrote in his later years, "was first to resist the increase of slavery and secondly to destroy it. The second half has been to rebuild, and to get rid of the despotic and corrupting tendencies and the animosities of the war, and the other legacies of slavery." It was Mr. Smith's wish, therefore, more particularly, to trace the influence of slavery on American political development through the period of its aggressive demands, and onwards, until the problems left by the Civil War, which was its inevitable consequence, had been solved.

In spite of failing health, Mr. Smith, at the time of his death, in midsummer, 1896, had substantially completed a large proportion of his project. From his manuscript, what he had written relating to slavery was extracted, arranged in orderly sequence, and given to the public in 1903 under the title *The Political History of Slavery*. This is a praiseworthy contribution to American history, though unfortunately deprived of the fuller presentation of certain facts and forces which undoubtedly Mr. Smith would have given his work, could it have had the benefit of a final revision at his hands.

Mr. Smith had done much in assorting and arranging the countless Hayes papers. But of the actual biography of Mr. Hayes, he had written comparatively little. It was his dying

request to me — who rejoice in having been his son-in-law, and
in having been honored with his love and confidence — that I
should complete his undertaking. This request, which was seconded by Mr. Hayes's sons, I could not deny, though feeling
myself inadequately fitted by temperament and attainments for
the task. For many years, owing to the demands on my strength
of an exacting editorial position, it was possible for me to accomplish little. But since my grateful release from that position, in
the spring of 1911, I have been able to give my full time to the
work. This delay, I feel, has been every way to the advantage of
my effort. The further we are away from the exciting controversies of the culminating period of Mr. Hayes's public life, the
more impersonal and dispassionate can be our judgment.

The first chapter is substantially Mr. Smith's work. For
appreciable portions of other early chapters, also, I am indebted
to his pen. It did not seem necessary under the circumstances to
indicate these in the text.

All of Mr. Hayes's papers — and their number is myriad —
have freely and without restriction been placed at my disposal by
Colonel Webb C. Hayes. I may be permitted to say that I have
drawn my information entirely from the sources and that I have
relied for my conclusions hardly at all on what other men have
written of the period. It has been my purpose as far as possible
to allow Mr. Hayes to speak for himself, and so to reveal his
character and principles by his own utterances.

It is also proper for me to say that I approached my work with
many misgivings and prejudices, being by inheritance, by early
training, and by conviction, of the Democratic faith. I had
lightly accepted, without investigation or reflection, the common
Democratic assumptions regarding the disputed election. As
the result of my prolonged studies I have no hesitation in affirm-
ing my conviction, first, that under the Constitution the decision
of the Electoral Commission was the only possible decision; second, that the decision was not only legally right and sound, and
essential to the preservation of the integrity of state authority,
but that it was in accord with the eternal equities of the situation; and, third, that Mr. Hayes's large wisdom of administration was vastly more beneficial to the South, to the peace and
reconciliation of the country, than any course of conduct, that

can reasonably be thought of as possible to Mr. Tilden, could have been.

Most of my writing has been done here in the home made beautiful by the serene and happy life spent within its walls by Mr. and Mrs. Hayes. Something of the spirit of simple, wholesome, Christian living, which I have felt still pervading this great house, I trust I may have been able to impart to the pages of this labor of love.

CHARLES RICHARD WILLIAMS.

SPIEGEL GROVE,
FREMONT, OHIO, March 4, 1914.

CONTENTS

xii CONTENTS

ILLUSTRATIONS

THE ELECTORAL COMMISSION

THE LIFE OF
RUTHERFORD BIRCHARD HAYES

" *I would prefer to go into the war if I knew I was to die or be killed in the course of it, than to live through and after it without taking any part in it.*"

THE LIFE OF RUTHERFORD BIRCHARD HAYES

CHAPTER I

ANCESTRY AND EARLY YEARS

THE Hayes family is of Scotch origin. The name according to tradition first became known in the tenth century. In the reign of Kenneth II, the Danes entered the Frith of Tay with a large fleet. They were met by the Scottish king and a bloody battle was fought at Loncart, which, after a stubborn contest, resulted in the defeat of the invaders. The Danes attacked with such vigor as to compel the two Scottish wings to give way, but authorities differ as to who should have the honor of checking the rout. Sir Walter Scott says it was due to the intrepidity of Kenneth himself, while others attribute it to a farmer and his two sons.

The fight was cruell on both sides [runs the ancient chronicle] and nothing hindered the Scots so much as going about to cut off the heads of the Danes, ever as they might overcome them. Which maner being noted by the Danes, and perceiving that there was no hope of life but in victorie, they rushed foorth with such violence upon their adversaries, that first the right, and then after the left wing of the Scots was constreined to retire and flee backe, the middleward stoutly yet keeping their ground; but the same stood in such danger, being now left naked on the sides, that the victorie must needes have remained with the Danes, had not a renewer of the battell come in time, by the appointment (as is to be thought) of Almightie God.

For as it chanced, there was in the next field at the same time an husbandman, with two of his sons, busie about his worke, named Haie, a man strong and stiffe in making and shape of bodie, but indued with a valiant courage. This Haie beholding the king with the most part of the nobles, fighting with great valiancie in the middle ward, now destitute of the wings, and in great danger to be oppressed by the great violence of his enimies, caught a plowbeame in his hand, and with the same exhorting his sonnes to doo the like, hasted towards the battell, there to die rather amongest other in defense of his countrie than to remaine alive after the discomfiture in miserable thraldome and bondage of the cruell and most unmercifull enimies.   There was neere to the place of the battell a long lane fensed on the sides with ditches and walls of turfe, through the which the Scots which fled were beaten downe by the enimies on heapes.

Here Haie with his sonnes, supposing they might best staie the flight, placed themselves overthwart the lane, beat them back whome they met fleeing, and spared neither friend nor fo; but downe they went all such as came within their reach, wherewith diverse hardie personages cried unto their fellowes to returne backe unto the battell, for there was a new power of Scottishmen come to their succours, by whose aid the victorie might be easilie obteined of their most cruell adversaries the Danes: therefore might they choose whether they would be slaine of their own fellowes comming to their aid or to returne againe to fight with the enimies. The Danes being here staied in the lane by the great valiancie of the father and the sonnes, thought verely there had beene some great succors of Scots come to the aid of their king, and thereupon ceasing from further pursute, fled backe in great disorder unto the other of their fellowes fighting with the middle ward of the Scots.[1]

The king having thus vanquished his enemies, continues the chronicler, carried with him on his triumphal return the valiant Haie and his sons, who, as they entered Bertha, were received with little less honor than the king himself. Haie was ennobled and honors and lands were bestowed on him — "so much ground as a falcon would flie over at one flight" (a convenient but novel mode of land-surveying), which proved to be a tract of six miles in length and four in breadth, "in those parts where the river Taie runs by the town of Arrole over against Fife."[2] And "the king gave him armes three Scutcheons gules in a field of silver, a plowbeame added thereunto, which he used in stead of a battell axe, when he fought so valiantlie in defense of his owne countrie." Thus successfully launched upon the tide of prosperity, in time a descendant of this Haie was "decorated with the office of the Constableship of Scotland."

At Abbotsford are preserved the armorial bearings of the families of Rutherford and Hayes. The latter consist of a cross

---

[1] Holinshed's *Chronicles — The Historie of Scotland.*

[2] The falcon lighted on a stone, the chronicler says, "neere a village called Rosse." "The name of the Stone being called the falcons stone to this daie dooth cause the thing better to be beleeved."

between four stars, with the falcon crest, and for motto the single word, *Recte*. This has been and is the motto of the American family of Hayes.

The valor which won distinction for the farmer Haie under Kenneth has been notably emulated by the American descendants of the Scotch Hayes. They have never failed to respond to their country's calls. Both of Rutherford B. Hayes's grandfathers and three of his four great-grandfathers served in the armies of the Revolution, and the fourth great-grandfather was employed by Connecticut to collect funds to pay for army supplies.

George Hayes, from whom descended Rutherford Birchard Hayes in the sixth generation, came from Scotland as early as 1680, being then about twenty-five years old, and settled at Windsor, Connecticut, where early in 1683 his wife and infant children died. Through a second marriage, which took place August 29, 1683, at Windsor, he became the founder of the American family. His second wife was Abigail Dibble. In 1698 he removed to Salmon Brook, in that part of Simsbury now known as Granby, Connecticut. His name appears in the list of freemen in 1701, and in 1723 the town granted to "George Hays, Senor, 138 acres." He died at Simsbury September 2, 1725, leaving his widow and five sons and six daughters. All of these children married. Daniel Hayes, the oldest son, was born at Windsor, April 26, 1686. When about twenty-one he was captured by three Indians almost in sight of his home and taken to Canada, where he was held for over seven years. His fortitude in enduring hardship recalls traits of his distinguished descendant.

It was no uncommon experience for New England frontiersmen to be carried off to Canada by the Indians in hope of reward from the French. Early one autumn morning Daniel Hayes started into the woods, bridle in hand, to find his horse. He had not gone far, when suddenly three Indians sprang from hiding, seized him, bound his hands with the throat-latch of his bridle, and at once plunged into the wilderness toward Canada. The journey, lasting some thirty days, was full of suffering for the young captive. At night he lay on his back, with his arms and legs tied to trees and with slender sticks across his body the ends of which were under the sleeping Indians. Daytimes the party travelled rapidly, living on fish and game.

At the principal encampment on the Canadian border, the prisoner was delivered over to the head men, who, after deliberation, decided that Hayes should run the gantlet. The day for the test of endurance arrived, the lines were formed, and the young man, who understood well the risks, started upon the trial. Near the end of the ranks he saw a formidable warrior with raised club ready to fell him, and being too exhausted to take the chances of a blow, he bolted and sought safety in a wigwam at the door of which sat an aged squaw. She interposed for his protection and he became her "son" after the Indian custom of adoption, and was also made a member of the tribe. For five years (until her death) Daniel Hayes cared for this helpless old woman, supplying her with food and dragging her on a rude sled from place to place through the forests with much tenderness and cheerfulness. He did not cease to hope for relief, and at last the day of rescue came. A missionary priest visited the encampment and became attached to young Hayes; redeemed him, took him to Montreal, and apprenticed him to a kind-hearted Frenchman, who set him up as weaver and permitted him to retain a share of his earnings. When enough had been earned to remunerate him, the Frenchman put him in charge of a trusty Indian guide and turned his face homeward.

On a clear October morning, from the foot of Mount Holyoke the guide pointed out to Hayes a thin wreath of smoke in the distance, and then silently turned to retrace his steps through the forest. The young man "kneeled down and gave thanks to his God as he did aforetime," and then with buoyant step crossed the border-land to civilization, more eager, than if he had not been tried by adversity, to share in its responsibilities.

Daniel Hayes married at Simsbury, March 1, 1716, Martha Holcombe, who died the following year, leaving one son. He was admitted freeman in October, 1717. May 4, 1721, he married Sarah Lee, of Westfield, Massachusetts, by whom he had ten children. She died in 1738. January 2, 1723, the town of Simsbury granted him one hundred and twenty acres of land. About 1739 he married his third wife Mary, who survived him. He died at Salmon Brook, September 23, 1756, having had six sons and five daughters, of whom six died in infancy. Phelps, in his history of Simsbury, says that Daniel Hayes "was a prominent citizen often employed in public affairs, and during many years a pillar in the church at Salmon Brook."

Ezekiel Hayes, born at Salmon Brook, November 21, 1724, was the third child and second son of Daniel Hayes by his second wife. He was a prominent citizen and a large proprietor, and was known as "Captain" Hayes and "Scythe-Maker" Hayes. He removed early to New Haven, where he died October 17, 1807; but he lived at Branford, on Long Island Sound, from 1749 until after the Revolutionary War. He was twice married — first to Rebecca, daughter of John Russell, judge, and Speaker of the Assembly, and Sarah Trowbridge (whose grandmother was a Rutherford), by whom he had six children; and the second time, May 5, 1774, to Mrs. Abigail Hitchcock Brown, by whom he had four children. November 14, 1780, Captain Hayes was chosen collector of a tax for supplies for the American army under an act of the Connecticut Legislature. In 1798 he sold a cargo of scythes at Albany for a tract of land in the town of Romulus on Cayuga Lake.

The first Rutherford Hayes was the third child and second son of Ezekiel Hayes by his first wife, who, as just said, was a Rutherford by descent. He was born at Branford, July 29, 1756, and removed to Brattleboro, Vermont, in 1778, where he was a blacksmith, an innkeeper, and a farmer. At the time Mr. Hayes settled in Brattleboro the controversy was raging between those who supported the jurisdiction of New York and the friends of the new State of Vermont. He soon after married Chloe, daughter of Lieutenant Israel Smith, who was classed with the "Yorkers" of Cumberland County. The great body of the people of Brattleboro sided with New York, and Mr. Hayes probably sympathized with his neighbors. July 24, 1782, he was chosen ensign of the South Company of Brattleboro, commanded by Captain Artemus How in the Southern Regiment of Cumberland County. He was commissioned by Governor George Clinton. He received a grant of lands at Bainbridge, Chenango County, New York, as "recompense" for services and injuries suffered in sustaining the jurisdiction of that State.

Mr. Hayes was an active member of the Congregational

Church, maintained family worship, and extolled his trade as "a black business which brought in white money." At seventy he became a "total abstinence" man, fearing his example might be quoted against the cause of temperance. He is described as a round, corpulent old gentleman, with elastic, square step, of medium height, florid complexion, sandy hair, cheerful temper, and friendly, courteous manners. His laugh was hearty, as became one who found the world full of sunshine and good will.

The fourth child and second son of this marriage was named Rutherford, and was born at Brattleboro, January 4, 1787. He became a merchant's clerk at Wilmington, Vermont, and subsequently a member of the mercantile firm of Noyes, Mann & Hayes at Dummerston. He married at Wilmington, September 13, 1813, Sophia, daughter of Roger Birchard and Drusilla Austin. It is on record that at Dummerston he was "Captain of a militia company, a very handsome man, the flower of the Hayes family." He was an erect, slender, active man of popular manners and interesting in conversation, fond of fun, and much loved by all classes of people. In 1817 he removed to Ohio and became a farmer at Delaware.[1] He was a successful business man and a member of the Presbyterian Church. In the year 1822 there were many fatal cases of bilious and other fevers in central Ohio. Mr. Hayes was stricken, and after a brief illness died, on the 20th of July, in the very prime of life, leaving a wife, in delicate health, a son and a daughter. A posthumous child was born on the 4th of the following October, who was named Rutherford Birchard Hayes. Lorenzo, the elder son, was accidentally drowned three years later.

The family of the first wife of Captain Ezekiel Hayes was of sturdy English stock, independent, and God-fearing. John Russell, the American founder, was born in England about 1597. He was a glazier at Cambridge, Massachusetts, and was made a freeman March 3, 1636. He removed early to Wethersfield, Connecticut, following the eloquent Newtowne pastor, the Reverend Thomas Hooker, who sought in the Connecticut

---

[1] He had $8000 in gold when he arrived in Ohio. His intention had been to invest this at Cleveland; but, because of the prevalence of fever and ague there, he went on to Delaware and bought land. When this land was sold some thirty years later it brought less than Hayes paid for it.

Valley the freedom which was denied by the aristocratic government of Massachusetts. "The foundation of authority," said Mr. Hooker, "is laid in the free consent of the people," which sound democratic doctrine John Russell also held. He married for a second wife in Wethersfield, Dorothy, widow of the Reverend Henry Smith, and later removed to Hadley, where he died May 8, 1680, aged eighty-three years.

The elder of John Russell's two sons was born in England about 1626, and bore the same name. He graduated at Harvard College, studied for the ministry and was ordained as pastor of the church in Wethersfield about 1649. He continued in·this charge until the settlement of Hadley, whither he removed and continued in the ministry until his death, December 10, 1692. He was three times married — first, to Mary Talcott, second, to Rebecca Newbury, and third, to Mrs. Rebecca Whiting. At his house he concealed the regicides, Whalley and Goffe, for some time; which act of courage and Christian duty justifies the eulogy of the historian: "He feared not to do what he thought to·be right." One son by his first wife and one by his second wife survived him. Samuel Russell, son by the second marriage, was born November 4, 1660. He graduated at Harvard College in 1681 and became a minister. He married Abigail Whiting and was ordained in 1687 as pastor of the church in Branford,[1] Connecticut, and died June 25, 1731.

[1] Branford had been almost depopulated twenty years before by the removal of the larger part of the church and its minister, the Reverend Abraham Pierson, to New Jersey, where he had founded the town of Newark. During these twenty years there had been no settled minister at Branford, and Mr. Russell became the second father of the town. He was the son of the first minister of Hadley, Massachusetts, and had been a classmate of the Reverend James Pierpont in Harvard College in the class of 1681.

These two ministers, Russell, of Branford, and Pierpont, of New Haven, with the Reverend Samuel Andrews, of Milford, were alert for the public good and felt the need of a college nearer than Harvard. Ten trustees were chosen by the churches, including these three ministers. Sometime in 1700 a quorum of these trustees met in New Haven, and, that they might engage in some formal act by which they should acquire a legal control over the institution as its founders, they separated with the understanding that at their next meeting, appointed at Branford, they should come prepared to make a beginning by a gift of books. At this adjourned meeting, also in 1700, each member "brought a number of books and presented them to the body," and laying them on the table said, "I give these books for the foundation of a college in this colony." There proved to be about forty volumes in folio, and after the ceremony of presentation had been

Of Samuel Russell's nine children, the oldest was John Russell, who was born January 24, 1687. He graduated at Yale College in 1704, and four years later married Sarah Trowbridge. He was deacon in the church from 1733 to his death, was colonel of the militia, judge, member of the General Assembly forty-one sessions, clerk of that body fourteen years, and Speaker in 1751. He was the most conspicuous man in Branford, where he died July 7, 1757. The sixth of his eight children was Rebecca Russell, who became the wife of Captain Ezekiel Hayes, and the mother of the first Rutherford Hayes. She died May 27, 1773.[1]

Among the papers preserved at Spiegel Grove is a diary kept by Chloe Smith Hayes, which reveals whence some of the most striking traits of character of Rutherford B. Hayes were derived. He always had great admiration for this grandmother, which was justified by a long life as rich in usefulness as it was beautiful in simplicity. Her English ancestor, Lieutenant Samuel Smith, with his wife Elizabeth and four children, sailed for New England the last day of April, 1634, in the Elizabeth of Ipswich. They settled at Wethersfield, which town he represented in the Colonial Assembly for twelve years. He subsequently removed to Hadley, Massachusetts, where he held many public trusts and was often chosen to the General Court. His death is supposed to have occurred in 1680, in his seventy-eighth year.

His son John was slain by Indians, May 30, 1670, in Hatfield Meadows — "died fighting bravely while going to the rescue of Hatfield," leaving a widow and a son. The succession of John Smiths is unbroken until we come to April 2, 1739, when Israel

performed the trustees took possession of them and appointed their host, the Reverend Samuel Russell, of Branford, to be the keeper of the library. The books were chiefly theological works, most of them of an exegetical character; probably not one related to literature or science. The intellectual activity of the men who met at Branford is not to be estimated by the books there presented. They knew it was important that they should give something so that they might legally become the founders of the college, and gave what they could spare from their scanty libraries. Soon after the Branford meeting sundry other donations both of books and money were received "which laid a good foundation."

[1] George W. Noyes, of Wallingford, Connecticut, a descendant of Polly Hayes, traces, through the female branches of the Russell family, the Bradleys and Demings of Vermont; Admiral Foote, of Connecticut, and Mr. Street, the founder of the Yale School of Fine Arts. (MS. letter, April 6, 1870, at Spiegel Grove.)

HOUSE OF CAPTAIN EZEKIEL HAYES AT BRANFORD, CONNECTICUT

Smith, the father of Chloe, was born. The family was always one of influence and culture. One of Israel's brothers was a missionary to the Indians of Pennsylvania. He and another brother became Sandemanians ("I don't know as there is any such in the country now," Chloe Hayes writes in her diary, "nor do I know what their belief is"), and being loyalists, fled to Nova Scotia at the outbreak of the Revolution, but Israel was among the first to resist British aggressions. In 1776 he was made a member of the Committee of Safety for the county, in session at Westminster; April 22 he was appointed the agent for Brattleboro to the New York Convention; was a member of the convention at Windsor, June 4, 1777, which pledged "New Hampshire Grants or New Connecticut" to maintain "the present just war against the fleets and armies of Britain"; and later was employed to confer with Governor Clinton.

The attempted arrest of alleged British sympathizers forms an interesting episode in the enigmatical part taken by Vermont at this period of the contest with Great Britain. The intrigue with General Haldimand had become so bold as to scandalize the Whig cause, and it was deemed necessary to take decided action. Congress on November 27, 1782, declared it indispensable to the safety of the United States that traitorous intercourse between the inhabitants of Vermont and the enemy should be suppressed. It was understood that General Washington should cause the arrest of Luke Knowlton and Samuel Wells, the most notorious offenders, with a view to their punishment. He entrusted that delicate and confidential commission to Israel Smith, who, however, failed to find the men. In his report which was laid before Congress, he said that "Knowlton and Wells had received a letter from Jonathan Arnold, Esquire, at Congress, part of which was made public, which informed them that affairs in Congress were unfavorable to them, and would have them look out for themselves. What other information this letter contained he could not say." "I found in my march through the State," he added, "that the last-mentioned gentleman was much in favor with all the principal men in that State I had any conversation with." Mr. Arnold being present at the reading said he had never held any correspondence with the gentlemen mentioned and was surprised that such a notion prevailed with respect to him. But it was generally considered, remarked Mr. Madison, notwithstanding his denial of the correspondence, that he had, at least at second hand, conveyed the intelligence to Vermont. It was remembered that when the subject of arrest was first broached, Mr. Arnold suggested that the commander-in-chief should be directed to make a previous communication of his intentions to the persons exercising authority in the district, which General Washington took good care to omit.

Lieutenant Smith had four hundred and ninety-seven acres of land granted him for his services, and he was one of three commissioners appointed to take charge of the property of refugee Tories. He was reputed to be a partisan of New York in the controversy between that State and Vermont, but however that may be, he was by act of the Legislature of the latter State, in 1790, associated with Ira Allen and four others on a commission to treat with commissioners of New York as to a boundary line, and to remove certain obstacles which prevented the admission of Vermont into the Union — which was a recognition of his fairness. He subsequently removed from Brattleboro to Jericho, now Bainbridge, New York, where he was a farmer. His wife was Abigail, daughter of Isaac Chandler, of Enfield, Connecticut, and until 1774 they resided at South Hadley.

Chloe Smith, the eldest of eight children, was born at South Hadley, November 10, 1762. Married to Rutherford Hayes when she was seventeen, she became the mother of eleven children, and "lived to so great an age as to have left upon the memory of many surviving grandchildren and great-grandchildren the personal impression of her strong and resolute character, and her rugged Puritan virtues, tempered and softened by æsthetic gifts amounting almost to genius. It is to her that her posterity are fond of ascribing in vast measure whatever is best in their hereditary traits." [1] This portrait is given of her by a granddaughter: —

Her face was most expressive. Her forehead was low but full, and her hair was black to the last. Her complexion was dark. Her laugh was short and quick. She was not of a hopeful temperament, but was possessed of great force of will. . . . She had a vein of wit and dry humor. When grandfather would boast that he was not shifted about with every

[1] Howells.

THE HAYES HOUSE AT BRATTLEBORO, VERMONT

Home of Rutherford B. Hayes's Grandparents

new tide of opinion, she would remind him of the fact that in one hour he was converted from faith in colonization to rank abolitionism. Her word was law from which there was emphatically no appeal. At the wedding of one of the daughters it was proposed to omit the usual invitation to one of the humble neighbors, but grandmother said, "W——'s family will be invited."

For a description of the old homestead and some striking passages from a diary preserved there, the writer is indebted to a gifted descendant [1] who writes from the spot. Her letter brings vividly before us the scenes in which Chloe Smith Hayes lived and wrought, setting an example for her own and future generations. This is the letter: —

Six generations in direct line have lived upon or near the site of the house from which I write. It is a large, broad-fronted homestead, looking directly down the main street of the pretty village of West Brattleboro, Vermont; watching with dignified satisfaction the sweeping curve which its position forces upon the road. It was built for the village inn by my great-grandfather, and according to hearsay was a most popular house. Great-grandmother Chloe Smith, at the mature age of seventeen, married Rutherford Hayes, a few years her senior, and one of the treasures of the house is her diary. On the opening page is written: —

"My grandfather by my father's side was Deacon John Smith. His native place was Hadley. When Deerfield was destroyed by the Indians he was seven years old. In the morning he saw the smoke of the buildings that they had left burning. The inhabitants were carried captive to Canada. He (when he was married he went to South Hadley where it was a wilderness) was an eminent Christian and sustained that character to the day of his death. I have heard him say when he was converted it was a very dull time. After this was Whitefield's time. He used to speak of the great stir there was through New England — the first and second stir. It was not then called a revival, but a stir. My grandfather did not marry till he was more than thirty. He said his uncle from Wethersfield in Connecticut visited at his father's house and he slept with him. In the night he told him he had a daughter that would make him a good wife, and so it proved, he married his cousin Elizabeth."

After reading that we went down into the meadow behind the house, to where ancient slabs mark the graves of Deacon John Smith and Elizabeth his wife. Six generations ago! and among the numerous offspring, Great-grandmother Chloe stands out in bold relief. "How well I remember," said my mother one day at breakfast, "a scene that took place in this room. Two guests were discussing in loud tones, Lutherism and Calvinism. Grandmother left her seat at the head of the table,

[1] Miss Lucy Elliot Keeler, a great-granddaughter.

came toward the men, and striking the table with her hand said, 'Stop, every one of you; and without controversy, great is the mystery of godliness.' The men laughed and obeyed," added the narrator, "but how terrified my little heart was!"

Everything was turned Scriptureward in those days. Her grand-daughter came to show a pearl engagement ring, and was met with the reply, "And be sure you have the pearl of great price"; while to a grandson, bursting into the room with, "Oh, grandma, I'm engaged," came, "I hope you *are* engaged in religion."

Throughout the diary the verb "know" is spelt phonetically. One of her daughters once remonstrated, with this result: "I know that it is *know*, but I like *no* better!"

Her energy was phenomenal. Think of the balls to which all the countryside used to come, — the pies and puddings, meats and drinks, that had to be provided. After all were served great-grandmother herself must join in the festive dance; and at daybreak — at least twice in her life — did she take advantage of "being up and dressed so early" to start off on horseback with her husband for Bainbridge, New York. Only one recreation did she allow herself; that was worsted work. Bringing in a flower from the garden she would faithfully copy its form and colors upon her canvas; and so fascinating was this occupation that every Saturday night found her pushing her worsted work far under the bed, lest she be tempted to look at it on Sunday.

Looking into the absorbing diary, we find that "six daughters and three sons lived to marry and have families. None lived more than fifty miles from us until Rutherford moved to Ohio. In about five years he died, when he was thirty-five years old. His youngest child Ruther-ford [General Hayes] was named after his father and grandfather. That branch of our family is but *little known* by the other connections — they have *been at such a distance*." The italics in that sentence are my own.

In the antiquity room there are many relics of long past days. There is the little trunk, not large enough for a modern doll, in which great-grandfather brought hither his sole earthly possessions; the cradle in which all his children were rocked; spinning-wheels and cards, some of the famous worsted work, and best of all the old swinging tavern sign. This last was discovered a few years ago by one of the present genera-tion who found it under the attic eaves. It bears the inscription: —

R. Hays

Entertainment

— with a gorgeous painting of a jockey in yellow small-clothes and black top-boots, holding a spirited steed. Under the "R. Hays," and evidently the remains of earlier decoration, appear the dates "1775" and "1791." For more than one hundred years the old house has stood there, and to the initiated its doors open as freely and as widely as in the days of "auld lang syne."

The mother of Rutherford B. Hayes was of English descent. The founder of the American family was Thomas Birchard, who, in 1635, came from London in the Truelove to Roxbury, Massachusetts, with his wife Mary and six children. He was made a freeman at Boston, May 17, 1637, and a freeman of Hartford in 1639. He is afterward found at Saybrook, where he was Deputy to the General Court in 1650 and 1651. In a land sale in 1656 he is described as "of Martha's Vineyard." His only son, John Birchard, was born in England in 1628, came to America with his father, and afterwards became a proprietor of Norwich, where he was a man of considerable note. July 22, 1653, he married Christian Andrews, by whom he had fourteen children. She died, probably about 1680, and subsequently he married Mrs. Jane Lee Hyde. He was made a freeman at Hartford in October, 1663, Clerk of the County Court in 1673, Justice of the Peace in 1676, and Deputy to the General Court in 1691. He is the first schoolmaster of Norwich mentioned in the records, being engaged in 1677 for nine months of the year at £25 and provisions. He was one of the four original proprietors of the five-mile tract purchased at Owaneco, in 1692, where Lebanon was located, to which place he removed in 1698. He died November 17, 1702.

Of John Birchard's six sons who lived to maturity, the second was James Birchard, born July 16, 1665, who settled at Norwich West Farms, now Franklin. He married Elizabeth Beckwith, March 17, 1696, had ten children and lived to be eighty years old. His son John Birchard, born in 1704, was the father of Elias Birchard, born 1739, who was a Revolutionary soldier. "In June, 1775, Mansfield had a company of 98 men commanded by Colonel Experience Storrs with the Connecticut troops under General Putnam. This company participated in the battle of Bunker Hill, and with these brave volunteers was Elias Birchard, a Mansfield ancestor of R. B. Hayes." [1] The next year he served as a private in Captain Jonathan Brewster's company, Huntington's regiment, and later in Captain James Dana's com-

[1] *A Centennial Discourse*, p. 26, delivered in the First Congregational Church, Mansfield Centre, July, 1876, by the Reverend K. B. Glidden.

pany. Elias Birchard married Sarah Jacobs, January 25, 1758. Their oldest child, Roger Birchard, married Drusilla Austin, whose father, Daniel Austin, grandson of Anthony Austin, one of the first settlers of Suffield, Connecticut, was a Revolutionary soldier. They were the parents of Sophia Birchard, mother of Rutherford B. Hayes.

Descended from this long line of wholesome, conscientious, God-fearing men and women, it was quite in the order of nature that Rutherford B. Hayes should grow up to be a representative of the best type of Anglo-Saxon manhood. There was a unity in his private and official life, admirable in its sincerity and freedom from self-seeking; and at all times, in peace and in storm, an equanimity that belongs only to the finest nature — to the soul that has passed through the fire of discipline. Daily introspection, with him, as in the case of Chloe Smith Hayes, type of Puritan character, served only to stimulate to a more active and orderly discharge of duty, thus exemplifying Lord Bacon's wise aphorism, "Habit is the best magistrate." Complete mastery of the passions is acquired only when devotion to moral truth becomes the habit of the mind and the uniform guide in action.

The characters of men are often developed by fortune or by some unforeseen disaster. The sudden death of his brother-in-law, Rutherford Hayes, in July, 1822, changed the career of Sardis Birchard, then a young man, and developed the affections of a noble heart. Henceforth his sister and her children became his care. "At the time of my first recollections," wrote Rutherford B. Hayes in later years, "our family consisted of Mother, Fanny, Uncle Sardis, Arcena Smith, and myself. During these early years Uncle was regarded as the stay of the family and our protector and adviser in every trouble. He was appointed guardian of Fanny and myself and during all our lives has been a father to us." More faithful friend and protector widow never found for herself and children.

The family had been left well provided for, so far as means were concerned, in a comparatively new country. They lived in a new two-story brick house at the northeast corner of William and Winter streets, opposite the old brick Methodist meetinghouse, in Delaware, with ground sufficient for garden, trees, and lawn; and the income was derived from a fine farm, two miles north of the village, situated on the Olentangy, which Mr. Hayes had bought in 1816. The beauty and richness of Ohio as an agricultural State are nowhere surpassed, and the lands bordering the romantic Olentangy, favorite stream of the Indians, are among the most desirable. In those days the primeval forests had been invaded but not destroyed. In their depths the deer found security, while in early summer across vistas flashed the light of the cardinal bird, and the air resounded with the melody of the mockingbird, the catbird, the thrush, the bluebird, the redbird, the finch, and other songsters now seldom heard. In the autumn — it is well to recall the picture, then so familiar to a new people —

> "What gorgeousness, what blazonry, what pomp
> Of colors, bursts upon the ravished sight!
> Here where the maple rears its yellow crest,
> A golden glory; yonder where the oak
> Stands monarch of the forest, and the ash
> Is girt with flame-like parasite, a rolling flood
> Of deepest crimson."

It was here amid such scenes and influences that the childhood of brother and sister was spent — she, the elder, feeling all the responsibility of a protector. "She was loving and kind to me, and very generous," said the brother thirty years after, when reflecting on what he had lost in her death.[1] The great events in their childhood were connected with the farm on the banks of the Olentangy, to which visits were made three or four times a year. Sugar-making, cherry-time, cider-making, and nutting were the occasions of these long-looked-for and delightful trips. The tenants, who were always attentive to them, gave them colored eggs filled with sugar at Easter, and at other seasons pet birds, squirrels, rabbits, quail's eggs, turtle's eggs, and other curious gifts. They early began to go to school together. Fanny was easily the best scholar of her age, and was a favorite with all. "She read a great deal when she was a child," wrote her brother. "All the books we had were read by her before she was ten years old. Uncle gave her a history of England in two volumes,

[1] Frances Arabella, daughter of Rutherford and Sophia Birchard Hayes, was born at Delaware, Ohio, January 20, 1820; was valedictorian of her class at the seminary at Putnam, where she graduated; was married to William A. Platt, a prosperous business man of Columbus, September 2, 1839; died July 16, 1856, leaving three daughters and one son.

abridged, I think, from Hume and Smollett. She soon had it at
her tongue's end. She knew by heart the 'Lady of the Lake' and
a great part of 'Lalla Rookh' — gifts from Uncle Birchard —
almost as long ago as I remember anything about books. These
and a collection styled 'Original Poems,' containing 'The Last
Dying Speech and Confession of Poor Puss,' 'Tit for Tat,' and
other pieces of about equal merit, were our constant companions.
Finer poetry we have never seen since. When she was about
twelve she read all the plays of Shakespeare, and without any aid
from friends, so far as I know, selected those which are generally
esteemed the best, to be read again and again. This reading of
plays suggested the writing of plays, and she with my assistance
undertook to dramatize the 'Lady of the Lake.' I am sure
neither of us had ever heard of such a thing. This job, done on
joint account, occupied a good deal of our thoughts for a long
time. Our success was not very flattering. Long afterwards we
learned that it was a common thing to dramatize poems and that
the 'Lady of the Lake' had been upon the stage many years."

Two or three years before this attempt at dramatizing a
poem, Mrs. Hayes had been called to the bedside of Sardis Birchard, who was then ill at Lower Sandusky (now Fremont) where
he had embarked in business, and the children were left in the
care of a neighbor who thought it well for them to be in school.
The schoolmaster, Daniel Granger, "was a little thin, wiry, energetic Yankee, with black hair, sallow complexion, and piercing
black eyes; and when excited appeared to us a demon of ferocity.
He flogged great, strapping fellows of twice his size, and talked
savagely of making them 'dance about like a parched pea,' and
throwing them through the walls of the schoolhouse. He threw
a large jackknife carefully aimed so as just to miss the head of a
boy who was whispering near me. All the younger scholars were
horribly afraid of him. We thought our lives were in danger. We
knew he would kill some of us. Fanny and I begged Mr. Wasson
with many tears to take us out of school. But he knew Mr.
Granger to be a kind-hearted little man, and insisted on our
going. We then looked forward to mother's return as our only
hope."

In 1834 brother and sister made their first journey. In company with their mother they visited their relatives in Vermont

BIRTHPLACE OF RUTHERFORD B. HAYES AT DELAWARE, OHIO

and Massachusetts. The journey was made by stage-coach to Lower Sandusky (Fremont), thence by boat down the Sandusky River to Portland (now Sandusky), where they went on board the Henry Clay (built by the Pioneer Steamship Company of which General Peter B. Porter, of Black Rock, intimate friend and correspondent of the Kentucky statesman, was the leading spirit), on which they had a pleasant passage down Lake Erie. From Buffalo the route was by canal-boat to Schenectady, thence by railway to Saratoga, and thence by stage to Bennington.[1] "I recollect very little about Fanny during this trip," continues the memoir. "She was with her cousins the girls. I was with the boys. I recollect that I was proud to hear what was said about her. Grandfather Hayes and Grandmother and indeed all the kindred loved her. There were several superior girls among the Hayes cousins. In fact the observations I then made are the foundation of the notion I have often expressed that the Hayes women were far superior to the men. From this time I began to prize Fanny at her true value and to think of her as the joy of our little home circle. Whatever advantages other boys had over me, none had such a sister as mine." This girl had many accomplishments besides those named. Elsewhere in the memoir we are told that "when very young she was taught to ride, play chess, and shoot with a rifle. Although she was always a retiring, quiet, modest little girl, even so as to be a favorite with those whose sense of propriety swallows up every other virtue, yet in manly sports she was perfectly fearless and very successful. She rode gracefully and was the best rifle shot of any lady I ever knew. She was a skilled player at chess and indeed of many other games. She was small of her age as a girl, round, plump and healthy, neat in her dress, and of very winning manners. I do not remember," adds the brother with pardonable pride, "to have ever thought her beautiful until after she was married."

The time came when these two devoted friends had to separate. The sister went to finish her education at the seminary in Putnam, and the brother to an academy at Norwalk, Ohio, and later to Mr. Webb's school in Middletown, Connecticut; but she continued to take the liveliest interest in his studies. When

[1] Hayes, then in his twelfth year, kept a journal, still preserved, of this to him eventful trip.

studying Latin and Greek together at home, she often expressed regret that she was not a boy so as also to be permitted to attend college with him.

Mr. Isaac Webb, principal of Middletown Academy, recommended that young Hayes be fitted for entering Yale College, and he accompanied this recommendation with the following words, which must have gratified the mother's pride: "The conduct of your son has hitherto done honor to his mother and has secured our sincere respect and esteem. I hope and trust that he will continue to be a great source of happiness to you." That was written in August, 1838.[1] The advantages offered by an old institution like Yale were appreciated, but the distance from home was a serious objection. It was settled, therefore, that Rutherford should enter college in Ohio. He was examined for the freshman class at Kenyon College, Gambier, and was duly entered in November of that year. He was sixteen years old on the 4th of the preceding month.

[1] A month later Mr. Webb wrote Sardis Birchard: "Mrs. Hayes seems to have made a determination as to her son which I regret, but with which I have no right to find fault. Rutherford was doing so well in every respect, that I felt a strong desire for him to remain — for my own sake, as well as that of his companions and himself. Another year here, as I viewed the matter, might be made highly profitable to him. I hope to see the day when he shall become an active, useful man, and I am confident that any advantages afforded him will not be lost. He will carry with him our best wishes, with sincere friendship and respect, the just due of his integrity and worth."

CHAPTER II

IN COLLEGE AND LAW SCHOOL

COLLEGE days to young Hayes were very happy days. He devoted himself with zeal to his studies and bore his part in student activities. In the diary which he began to keep in his junior year and thereafter kept with tolerable regularity, he is unsparing in criticizing himself for shortcomings, and frankly confesses infractions of good resolutions. But there are abundant evidences of intellectual growth and of sound judgment in determining courses of action and in forming associations.[1] He is conscious that he excels in common sense, thanks to his heredity, and this he seeks to exercise in weighing all questions. June 17, 1841, we find this entry in his diary: —

I will devote the remainder of this page to mentioning some of the traits of character for which the hero of these etchings is most particularly remarkable. He has, in the first place, a very good opinion of himself, which can by no means be considered a failing, for if a man does not esteem himself, he would certainly be very silly to expect the esteem of others. But although he is so well convinced of the importance of self-esteem, there is, perhaps, no one more anxious to conceal it than he is. Again, there is no one who more heartily detests open flattery than he does, and yet, strange to say, it sounds very pleasant to his ears; it puts him in such good humor with himself, and, of course, with all about him, that he seems like another being while under its agreeable influence. He is so inconsistent as to wish to conceal this feature of his character; though he declares most positively that all men can be flattered, the only difference being, that some are more accessible to its approaches than others. At first sight, or I should rather say thought, it seems surprising that he should wish to conceal what he considers no disgrace, but it is only one of the thousand errings of poor human nature. He has his share, also, of that "great Caucasus" ambition, and as he loves to excel, it cannot be denied that he loves to have it known. It is no part of his creed that deception may be practiced to give others a high opinion of

---

[1] "Hayes, as a boy," said Stanley Matthews, "was notorious for having on his shoulders not only the levellest but the oldest head in college. He never got caught in any scrapes, he never had any boyish foolishness, he never had any wild oats to sow; he was sensible, not as some men are at the last, but sensible from the beginning."

his attainments, for common sense teaches that an undeserved reputation is of more injury than benefit.

I spoke above of his self-esteem. Now, I do not mean that he entertains an exalted opinion of his talents or acquirements, but merely that he thinks himself possessed of a good share of common sense, by which is meant a sound practical judgment of what is correct in the common affairs of life. He often betrays this peculiar kind of self-esteem by reflections like the following: "If I only had C.'s talents, what a figure I would make in this world." The reason of his entertaining so favorable an opinion of his common sense is that his family and relatives are somewhat remarkable for the possession of it, and he thinks it runs in the blood. Moreover, he has often been told (good authority) that he had a family share of this good quality.

Two days later we have the following: —

After studying my own disposition with a good degree of diligence, I am satisfied that the motives and desires which rule in my breast are, indeed, "past all finding out." There have been times when I exercised considerable firmness and decision, apparently without exertion; at other times, after making the best of resolutions, I find the strenuous will to carry them into effect almost entirely wanting. Considering my age and circumstances I do not think myself more deficient in this quality than other persons; but, be this as it may, I am determined from henceforth to use what means I have to acquire a character distinguished for energy, firmness, and perseverance. As I am now in the humor of writing I will put down a few of my present hopes and designs for the sake of *keeping* them *safe*. I do not intend to leave here till about a year after I graduate, when I expect to commence the study of law. Before then I wish to become master of logic and rhetoric and to obtain a good knowledge of history. To accomplish these objects I am willing to study hard, in which case I believe I can make, at least, a tolerable debater. It is another intention of mine, that after I have commenced in life, whatever may be my ability or station, to preserve a reputation for honesty and benevolence; and if ever I am a public man, I will never do anything inconsistent with the character of a true friend and good citizen. To become such a man I shall necessarily have to live in accordance with the precepts of the Bible, which I firmly believe, although I have never made them strictly the "rule of my conduct."

The traits of modesty and diffidence which at first seemed to stand in the way of success, are modified by an exertion of the will, but are preserved to beautify the character of the fully developed man.[1] His love of fun and humor and of manly sports

[1] "I recollect him as one of the purest boys I ever knew. — I never knew him to entertain for a moment an unmanly, dishonest, or demoralizing thought. And when we met in after life, in scenes which called for the highest manhood

was not abated by his hard study or his profound interest in serious questions, but was freely indulged. He never posed as *il penseroso*, but always appeared as one to whom life was joyous and full of sunshine. In childhood the beauties of nature had filled him with delight, and at every stage of his career this delight was as fresh as in youth. That he might not be betrayed by the sarcasm natural to him to comment on others to their prejudice or to wound their feelings, he early resolved to avoid speaking ill of any one. June 29, 1841, the diary has this entry: —

I make it a rule never to seek an opportunity to speak ill of any individual, and if it is my duty to blame, to do it in as mild terms as the subject admits of. I did not make this determination because I thought I was disposed to question the motives of others, or to censure without sufficient reason, but lest, by frequently indulging in remarks more severe than the occasion warrants, I may contract a habit of slandering my acquaintances which will grow stronger till the odious practice becomes a confirmed habit which cannot be shaken off. I saw a remark of Bacon on this subject which struck me as well worthy of remembrance. "There is," said he, "with the young and old, a prevalent habit of talking of persons rather than things. This is seldom innocent and often pregnant with many ills. Such conversation insensibly slides into detraction; and by dwelling on offenses we expose our own souls to contagion, and are betrayed into feelings of pride, envy, jealousy; and even when we speak in terms of commendation, we are sure to come in with a 'but' at the last, and drive a nail in our neighbor's reputation." My own experience furnishes me with abundant proofs of the truth of this sentiment; but by regarding my resolution with care I hope to deserve a name far better than the slanderer's. Another of the good resolutions referred to, is that while in the Society, I will do nothing calculated to produce disorder, or anything likely to have an evil tendency. My love of fun is so great and my perception of the ludicrous so quick, that I laugh at everything witty, and say all I can to add to the general mirth. Now this [is] agreeable enough at times, but the tendency to carry it to extremes is so great that I shall stop it entirely in future, if I can. My last resolution is, to act from no motives which I should be ashamed to avow.

This resolution to speak well of others became a habit, which in later life was mistaken by strangers for weakness of character. It was a part of the culture that formed the gentleman. Each year made the gifts of life richer to Hayes. It was with him as with Wordsworth, —

and patriotism, I found the man to be exactly what his boyhood had promised." (Letter of a college friend.)

"The everliving universe,
Turn where I might, was opening out its glories;
And the independent spirit of pure youth
Called forth at every season new delights,
Spread round my steps like sunshine o'er green fields."

Kenyon, like other colleges, had rival societies, in which Hayes took an active interest. The club for debating, however, was the one that claimed his chief attention, as here was intellectual collision and sharpening of wits, which should help him toward the goal of his ambition. And that goal he discloses in his diary in passages so striking as to be not only the record of an aspiration but the prophecy of his life achievement.

July 29, 1841. — In one little week I shall be a senior; a year, and then a graduate; but who can tell what changes a year may bring? Short as the three years since I entered college now seem, they have wrought great changes in my views of things and perhaps greater still in my anticipations and designs. I have always been ambitious, dreaming of future glory, of performing some virtuous or patriotic action, but it has been all dreams, and no reality. From my earliest recollection, I have thought I had great power in me, yet at the same time I was fully satisfied of my present insignificance and mental weakness. I have imagined that at some future time I could do considerable, but the more I learn, the more I feel my littleness.

Kenyon College, November 7, 1841. — I am now a member of the senior class; only one short year remains before the frail bark of my destiny will be tossing on the stormy waves of an untried sea. What will be its fate in the voyage of life, depends much on the exertions I am now making. I know I have not the natural genius to force my way to eminence; but if I listen to the promptings of ambition, "the magic of mind" I must have, and since I cannot trust to inspiration I can only acquire it by "midnight toil" and "holy emulation." My lofty aspirations I cannot conceal even from myself; my bosom heaves with the thought, they are part of myself, so wrought into my very soul that I cannot escape their power if I would. As far back as memory can carry me the desire of fame was uppermost in my thoughts, but I never desired other than honorable distinction, and before I would be "damned to eternal fame" I would descend to my grave unknown. The reputation which I desire is not that momentary eminence which is gained without merit and lost without regret; give me the popularity which runs after, not that which is sought for. For honest merit to succeed amid the tricks and intrigues which are now so lamentably common, I know is difficult, but the honor of success is increased by the obstacles which are to be surmounted. Let me triumph as a man or not at all.

Defeat without disgrace can be borne, but laurels which are not deserved sit like a crown of thorns on the head of their possessor. It is, indeed, far better to deserve honors without having them, than to have them without deserving them. Obscurity is an honor to the man who has failed in "the pursuit of noble ends by noble means." He can walk proudly forth before the face of nature and be conscious that he has not disgraced the image of his God. Although neglected and perhaps despised by his fellows, there is a monitor within whose approving smiles are more valuable than the plaudits of millions; the first sits upon her seat unalterable as the sun in his course, the other is more fitful than a summer's breeze. If an honorable man gains the applause of his countrymen, he is richly rewarded, for conscious of his own merit he feels that it is deserved, and knows that it is substantial because deserved.

I never desired other than honorable distinction. — The reputation which I desire is not that momentary eminence which is gained without merit and lost without regret. Give me the popularity which runs after, not that which is sought for. — For honest merit to succeed amid the tricks and intrigues which are now so lamentably common, I know, is difficult, but the honor of success is increased by the obstacles which are to be surmounted. Let me triumph as a man or not at all.

Surely much may be expected of the lad who at nineteen looks out upon life with so clear a vision and so lofty a purpose!

Notebooks still preserved afford evidence of the careful preparation made by the young student for society debates and public discussions. He set down on opposite pages the arguments on each side, weighed them and strove to reach a conscientious conclusion as to the side which merited approval. He had no illusions regarding the enervating methods pursued by far too many college students in preparing speeches for public exhibitions. Every college man will recognize the truth of the following analysis, which we find in the diary about the middle of Hayes's senior year: —

From this the currents of my thoughts naturally turned on the folly of college exhibitions. The student knows, that in obedience to the requisitions of the faculty, he must prepare an address to deliver before a mixed audience of friends and acquaintances, come what may. Pride and emulation prompt him to make every exertion, that his performance may be creditable to himself, and gratifying to his friends. If he is possessed of common modesty, he feels that he cannot write upon any subject such a speech as will, perhaps, be expected of him. The time approaches, and his piece must be written. Inability will not be received as an excuse. The terrors of college discipline are hanging over him, and when he finds there is no escape from the odious duty he puzzles his brain with the energy of despair for thoughts which he knows are not in it. After many fruitless endeavors to obtain a subject, as a last resort, he betakes himself to the advice of some elder friend who has passed the terrors of a first appearance in public. He soon receives the necessary information which his friend had received in the same manner and which has doubtless been handed down through many generations of collegians. The youthful orator takes his way with a light step and joyful countenance to the nearest library. Without a moment's hesitation he seizes the first of a long row of Reviews and rapidly glances over the table of contents. The object of his search being a good article on some subject which will "look well on the bill," he usually finds it without trouble. He bears off in triumph the volume containing his future eloquence, and, after carefully concealing it, hastens to his professor and gives him the subject he has chosen. The professor, anxious that his oration may speak well for his instructor, applauds his selection, and tells him of an article in a certain Review in which he will find some good ideas on his subject. The scholar feigns surprise that the subject has ever been written upon before, but *thinks* he will get the Review referred to. He returns to his room, adopts the train of thought furnished him by the Review, and, not infrequently, copies the language in which those thoughts are dressed. His oration is thus written; subject, sentiment, and language, all either borrowed or stolen. The composition, after having gone through the farce of correction, is committed, and finally delivered under circumstances anything but favorable to the display of practical good sense. If the evil ended with the exhibition, it would be comparatively slight; but after being praised and flattered for a performance of this kind, the student is anxious to retain the reputation he has acquired. Thus the folly must be repeated. Idleness, as well as inclination, prompts him to adopt this method of obtaining ideas; for he has now learned how easy it is to write without thought and gain applause without exertion. The habit is thus formed of seeking assistance from the productions of others, rather than relying on one's own powers. Large numbers [of] our college-bred men form their habits precisely in this way. It is not strange that they finally fall below those whose advantages being less were compelled to think and act for themselves from boyhood.

The temptation to avail ourselves of these cork jackets to buoy us up in our first attempts is, indeed, *great*. But if we would acquire the skill and strength necessary to stem the opposing tides of life, these artificial aids must be rejected. By their use vigorous original thinkers are never made; but this is what every one must be who wishes to become eminent.

Warm friendships spring naturally from genial associations and sound principles, and endure after one has left college and entered active life. Hayes's friends in college were wisely chosen, and they justified in after life the good opinion he formed of them. Of one who graduated before him he writes in his diary: —

The graduating class acquitted themselves with credit. My long-tried friend Trowbridge, for whose success I was most anxious, exceeded my fondest anticipations. The effect of his eloquence on me was indeed surprising. I am accustomed to feel strongly, how strongly words cannot tell, when one of my friends is gaining the palm of eloquence, but never before were tears drawn so copiously from my eyes as when the closing sentence of his oration passed his lips. I always thought him a persevering, strong-minded man, but I was then satisfied that he possessed the true fire of genius. With a fair field and good health he can be really great. His style of speaking is plain, strong, and to the purpose.[1]

Of a classmate he says: —

Guy M. Bryan fully retrieves the character of Texas. He is a Missourian by birth. He is a real gentleman, holds his honor dear, respects the feelings and wishes of others; is a warm and constant friend. He has good talents, though not a good scholar. He will, I trust, figure largely in Texas history. He is a true patriot.[2]

And though the two were on opposite sides during the Civil War, this opinion was in no whit modified, nor the warmth of friendship cooled.

One who was in college with Hayes gives us this portrait of him at Kenyon, which will serve for the man of later years, softened and toned by the experiences of life: —

Hayes was the champion in college in debate, class-section, and in the footpath; cheerful, sanguine, and confident of the future, never seeing cause for desponding; was a young man of substantial physique; in my whole acquaintance I never knew of his being sick one day, and so free from any weaknesses as to seem indefatigable. His greatest amusements were fishing and chess. In company he was humorous to hilarity; told quick, pungent stories, many of which I remember with laughter to this day; took things as they came; used to laugh at the shape of our boarding-house roast beef, but still ate. I do not think he had many intimate friends. Those with whom he was intimate were, and still are, the best men of my acquaintance. I don't remember a

[1] Rowland E. Trowbridge, of Michigan, served for several terms in Congress acceptably. He and Hayes were both members of the Thirty-ninth and Fortieth Congresses.

[2] Mr. Bryan filled many offices of distinction in Texas, and also served in Congress.

single man with whom he was intimate but that has been successful in his vocation.[1]

The four years of Kenyon were not passed without discussion of current political questions, and a showing of party colors. Hayes confides to his diary that he intends to be a lawyer and to let politics alone. His comments on a fellow collegian, who, in the prime of manhood, was one of the most public-spirited and useful of Ohio's distinguished citizens, — Lorin Andrews,[2] — express the bounds he had set for himself. He said: Andrews "was a warm supporter of General Harrison's; went to the birthday convention at Columbus, February 22, 1840, and came back a politician. Spent last summer stumping it. In my opinion he is a talented, energetic, honorable young man, and if he will let politics alone, will make a good lawyer." But Hayes could not wholly suppress his sentiments which, in common with those of his family, bore the Whig hue. And, as we shall more fully see in a subsequent chapter, he was even now an intelligent and interested observer of political currents.

The slavery question found entrance even within the precincts of Kenyon, but it did not move Hayes to take sides. In 1839 the students had "a glorious celebration" of the Fourth of July.

After dinner some speeches were made at the chapel in which some things were said which created a difficulty between a noble, warm-hearted Kentuckian[3] and the orator of the day. The sectional feeling which then existed was at once aroused. The members of the rival societies each espoused the cause of their own member, and a serious disturbance appeared unavoidable. After much useless disputing, Mr. Andrews of my class and Mr. Elliot proposed that we should take a short march to the tune of "Yankee Doodle." This was immediately agreed to, and the spirit-stirring notes of the favorite air recalled at

[1] Quoted in *The Great Commoner of Ohio*, p. 17, by Washington Gladden, D.D.

[2] Lorin Andrews was born in Ashland, Ohio, April 1, 1819. He actively engaged in the promotion of education. Princeton conferred on him the degree of LL.D. He was chosen President of Kenyon College in 1854. He was the *first Ohio volunteer* to the Union army in 1861; was elected colonel of the Fourth Regiment and served in West Virginia, where he died of typhoid fever, September 18, 1861. The news of his death was received with profound regret.

[3] Thomas M. Kane: studied law with an uncle in New Orleans, where he was admitted to the bar and began practice under the most favorable auspices. He was killed in a duel near New Orleans in the winter of 1846. The difficulty arose out of a dispute in a ballroom about positions!

once to the minds of the combatants the fact that we were all Americans, so that the dispute was amicably settled and we returned to college better friends than ever.

And Hayes patriotically adds : —

I trust all other sectional divisions and disputes may always be as fortunately ended as this.

Opportunity was afforded him on another occasion to display this sentiment, which was long remembered by Kenyon students. Two rival literary societies represented the sectional divisions — the Philomathesian whose members were from the free States, and the Nu Pi Kappa with a membership wholly Southern. The patronage from the South which had been liberal for many years gradually waned, until, in the winter of 1841, there were so few Southern students in the college that the members of the Nu Pi Kappa were apprehensive that the society would cease to exist for want of new members. This was a serious question with the members of the society.

I determined [the relation is by a classmate from the South] — I determined to open the subject to my intimate friend Hayes, to see if we could not devise some mode to prevent the extinction of a society, which was chartered by the State and had valuable property. We talked over the subject with all the feeling and interest with which we would now discuss the best means of bringing about an era of good feeling between the sections of the country. At last Hayes said, "Well, I will get 'old Trow,' Comstock, and some others to join with me, and we will send over a delegation from our society to yours, and then we can make new arrangements so that both societies can live in the old college." He and I then went to work to consummate our plan. Ten members of the Philomathesian joined the Nu Pi Kappa. A joint committee was then appointed from the two societies that reported a plan by which students could enter either society without reference to North or South.[1]

With all his steadiness of application to his classroom studies, to the exercises of the literary societies, and to courses of reading (of which more hereafter), Hayes constantly takes himself to task for not accomplishing more. We have an echo of this mood of mind, with, at the same time, a note of confidence in his mental powers, in an entry in the diary written just after his return from the midwinter vacation of his senior year : —

---

[1] "Recollections of Hon. Guy M. Bryan, of Texas," in *Account of Kenyon College*, pamphlet, p. 17.

Kenyon College, January 6, 1842. — I have just returned from home where I spent the holidays, frolicking with the girls and laughing most constantly either at my own folly or that of others. . . . But enough of this; two weeks of pleasure will suffice for this session and I am determined to apply myself to my studies more diligently than ever for the rest of the winter. Before another year rolls round I must make great progress. Within the last year my improvement has been rapid, yet I could have done much more had the *strenuous will* not been wanting. I am satisfied more and more by every day's experience, that if I would attain the eminence in my profession to which I aspire, I must exert myself with more constant zeal and hearty good will than I ever have before. The life of a truly great lawyer must be one of severe and intense application; he treads no "primrose path"; every step is one of toil and difficulty; it is not by sudden, vigorous efforts that he is to succeed, but by patient, enduring energy, which never hesitates, never falters, but pushes on to the last. This is the life I have chosen; I believe it is a happy one. Now is the time to acquire the habits which will enable me to endure its hardships, and if I make a right use of my present opportunities my after life will be as happy as it is laborious. While at home, I attended the United States Circuit Court and listened to the arguments of some of the first lawyers in the State. They did not equal my expectations, but some were indeed most excellent; yet none were so superior as to discourage one from striving to equal them. In fact, I never hear a speaker but I am encouraged to renew my exertions; if I listen to a poor one I am flattered to think of the favorable comparison which might be made between his efforts and my own, and when I hear a good one I always attribute his superiority to his industry rather than to his natural talents.

At last the four years of happy life and earnest endeavor drew to a close. Commencement came the first week in August, 1842, when Hayes lacked two months of completing his twentieth year. He was chosen valedictorian of his class. The theme on which he spoke was "College Life," and several contemporary accounts of the commencement exercises single out his speech for special commendation, as possessing merit quite unusual in such performances. One editor speaks of it as "chaste, beautiful and sublime, pure in diction and lofty in sentiment," and says it was delivered with captivating animation. "All who heard this oration," this editor says in conclusion, "pronounced it the best in every point of view ever delivered on the hill at Gambier." [1]

Graduation was followed by a few weeks of rest, and on October 17, 1842, Hayes began to read law in the office of Sparrow

---

[1] Mount Vernon *Democratic Banner*, August 9, 1842.

KENYON COLLEGE, GAMBIER, OHIO

Rutherford B. Hayes occupied the gable room at the extreme left of the picture. The room is now used by the students for social purposes

and Matthews at Columbus. The entrance to the portals of the legal profession, he confides to his diary after a few weeks of study, "is steep and difficult, but my chiefest obstacle is within myself. If I *knew* and could *master myself*, all other difficulties would vanish." Blackstone, Chillingworth, logic, and the study of German were engaging his attention, but society made claims upon him and general reading had attractions for him which he found it hard to resist. After a month of study we find him taking account of his progress in the following entry in his diary: —

Columbus, November 19, 1842. — Another week has passed, and a careful man should post his books every Saturday night to know how he stands with his customers. This is the rule for a business man. Is it of no importance to the student to know how he stands with his books, himself, and the world without? If dollars and cents are worthy a merchant's long train of accounts, are no memoranda needed by the student to ascertain how he has improved each hour as it passed? Shall he alone neglect to balance his books? No. No. To him "time is money" — nay, more than money; gold that's lost, renewed exertion may regain, but time once fled is gone forever. Then, let me give an impartial statement of what I have done, and what I have left undone, not only during the week past, but also during the whole month since I commenced the study of law.

I have read upwards of 750 pages of Blackstone, being an average of more than 150 pages per week. Also 50 pages of Chillingworth, an average of 10 pages per week. Also 150 pages of logic, an average of 30 pages per week. Five pages of German committed to memory — together with the general rules of grammar and construction which applied. Besides this I have read a good deal of what may be denominated *trash*, and which has been injurious; some 100 or 150 pages of Milton and Shakespeare may be reckoned as offset to a portion of the above-mentioned "trash." The quantity of information contained in the pages read, if once acquired, would be a sufficient reward for the cost in labor and time. If the *amount passed over* is only considered, my month's work has been a good one, and a large balance appears in my favor. But there is another element which should enter into this account — viz., the manner in which the work has been executed. In order to ascertain this it is necessary to say something of the end in view, and then we may speak of its attainment.

In studying Blackstone's "Commentaries," the object should be twofold, — legal information and mental discipline, — and success in the attainment of one of these ends implies success in the other. If mental discipline is totally neglected, little legal information will be acquired, and *vice versa*. The important powers to be disciplined, in studying a work like Blackstone, are the memory and attention. The other great powers of the mind — as apprehension, judgment, and reasoning — are of necessity called into action, but Blackstone's style is so clear that his meaning is seldom obscure, and he is so perspicuous in the statement of the reasons for what he says, and in his explanations, that great exertion is not requisite to comprehend him. As it is all plain reading the attention is the only power especially exercised; if this is well done the memory by natural consequence will be engaged. Thus much for what *should* be done, now to what *has* been done.

My attention has not been so exercised as to acquire the information and discipline which would satisfy my desires. And consequently I am *not satisfied* with my month's work in Blackstone.

My chief object in studying Chillingworth is to discipline the reasoning faculty. I found my task easier than I anticipated, and accomplished more than I expected to when I commenced. Yet I have not done as much as I *now* know I could have done. On the whole, this account balances.

In the study of logic, my object, being only to refresh my memory, was accomplished.

In German I have made respectable progress, but I must do better in future.

In my miscellaneous reading I have been injured by permitting myself to read newspapers. I must curb my propensity to this as I find it no benefit.

I am satisfied that for this month, I have been greatly deficient in many particulars. I have studied *long* enough each day and each week throughout the whole month. I have passed over sufficient ground. The deficiency is in the execution. My rules for the ensuing month shall be made out soon.

A week later we have this entry: —

The first volume of Blackstone has been finished since last Saturday and I have commenced the second with a full determination to read it with more attention than I have heretofore given to my law reading. German daily grows more interesting and I begin to long for the time when I can read it with facility. Chillingworth has been neglected for the ladies, not because I loved the society of the ladies better than his but because the tyrant necessity compelled me to abandon his great argument. I shall commence it again next week. My rules for the month are: —

First, Read no newspapers.

Second, Rise at seven and retire at ten.

Third, Study law six hours, German two, and Chillingworth two.

Fourth, In reading Blackstone's "Commentaries," to record my difficulties.

After ten months' office study, Hayes, in August, 1843, entered the Law School of Harvard University. Here he received

RUTHERFORD B. HAYES, 1845

Student at the Harvard Law School, from a Daguerreotype

the instruction of those eminent jurists and teachers, Judge Story and Professor Greenleaf — the greatest privilege a student could have. "Free from all the details, chicanery, and responsibilities of practice," said Richard Henry Dana, who was a student in the Dane Law School five years before Hayes, "we were placed in a library under learned, honorable, and gentlemanly instructors; and invited to pursue the study of jurisprudence as a system of philosophy." [1]

Hayes's diary shows the most faithful attendance on the lectures and keen enjoyment of all he heard and saw. He is not limited to the routine of the law, — the lectures, the clubs, and the practical work of the Moot Court, over which Judge Story presides to his great delight, — but he hears Longfellow, Bancroft, Sparks, and Dana in literature and history, and Webster, Choate, Adams, and Winthrop on the stump. Political questions and parties have an interest for him, as we shall see, which no resolutions can overcome. For them the law has a stronger affinity than any other calling possesses except possibly journalism. Excerpts from Hayes's diary will give us the drift of his thought and study: —

Cambridge, August 29, 1843. — Yesterday we heard the introductory remarks of our learned professors. After speaking of the object of our assembling, Judge Story proceeded to remark on the requisites of a finished legal character. He spoke at some length of the advantage and necessity of possessing complete control of the temper, illustrating his views with anecdotes of his own experience and observation. His manner is very pleasant, betraying great good humor and fondness for jesting. His most important directions were: "Keep a constant guard upon temper and tongue. Always have in readiness some of those unmeaning but respectful formularies as, *per ex.*, 'The learned gentleman on the opposite side'; 'My learned friend opposite,' etc. When in the library employ yourself in reading the titles, title-pages, and tables of contents of the books of reports which it contains, and endeavor to get some notion of their relative value. Read Blackstone again and again — incomparable for the beauty and chasteness of its style, the amount and profundity of its learning."

Cambridge, September 1. — I have now finished my first week in the Law School. I have studied hard and I am confident that my real gain is as great as I should have had in two weeks in an office. Our lectures have all the advantages of recitations and lectures combined, without

---

[1] Charles Francis Adams, *Richard Henry Dana : A Biography*, vol. i, p. 22.

their disadvantages. We have no formal lectures. Professors Story and Greenleaf illustrate and explain as they proceed. Mr. Greenleaf is very searching and logical in examination. It is impossible for one who has not faithfully studied the text to escape exposing his ignorance; he keeps the subject constantly in view, never stepping out of his way for the purpose of introducing his own experience. Judge Story, on the other hand, is very general in his questions, so that persons well skilled in nods, affirmative and negative shakings of the head, need never more than glance at the text to be able to answer his interrogatories. He is very fond of digressions to introduce amusing anecdotes, high-wrought eulogies of the sages of the law, and fragments of his own experience. He is generally very interesting, and often quite eloquent. His manner of speaking is almost precisely like that of Corwin. In short, as a lecturer he is a very different man from what you would expect of an old and eminent judge; not but that he is great, but he is so interesting and fond of good stories. His amount of knowledge is prodigious. Talk of many "irons in the fire"! Why, he keeps up with the news of the day of all sorts, from political to Wellerisms; and new works of all sorts he reads at least enough to form an opinion of, and all the while enjoys himself with a flow of spirits equal to a schoolboy in the holidays. So ho! the pleasures of literature are not so small after all!

September 16. — "Pleading and evidence," said Judge Story, "a lawyer should always have at his tongue's end. Chief Justice Marshall was the growth of a century. Providence grants such men to the human family only on great occasions to accomplish its own great ends. Such men are found only when our need is the greatest. Four great judges I have known in my time. I could not say that one was greater than another, but either was a head and shoulders taller than any man now living.

"When a young lawyer," said Judge Story, "I was told by a member of the bar at which I practiced, who was fifteen years my senior in the profession, that he wished to consult me in a case of conscience. Said he: 'You are a young man and I can trust you. I want your opinion. The case is this: I am engaged in an important cause; my adversary is an obstinate, self-willed, self-sufficient man, and I have him completely in my power. I can crush his whole case; it is in my hand, and he does not know it, does not suspect it. I can gain the case by taking advantage of this man's ignorance and overweening confidence. Now, the point is, Shall I do it?' I answered, 'I think not.' 'I think not, too,' he replied. 'I have determined to go into court to-morrow, show him his error, and set him right.' He did it. This was forty-five years ago, but I have never forgotten that act nor that man. He is still living, and I have looked upon him and his integrity as beyond all estimate. I would trust him with untold millions, nay, with life, with reputation, with all that is dear."

September 20. — I heard Mr. Jared Sparks lecture on "Colonial History." His style of writing and delivery are very plain, but his learning is varied and extensive, and his judgment good. He spoke of the learning, religion, and authors of Colonial times. As to what we call learning, there was next to none in the Colonies. The people were too busy in clearing land, making roads, and building churches to think of making great strides in literature. In the Northern Colonies common schools were early established; in the Southern, except South Carolina, they were neglected. The sons of the wealthy were sent to Oxford and Cambridge. So that at the South were more fine scholars and more ignorant citizens than in the North. . . . There was great religious intolerance in many Colonies. Rhode Island, under the auspices of Roger Williams, and Maryland, settled by Catholics, were exceptions and opened wide their arms to every sect and creed. The first author of distinction was Cotton Mather, a man of great talents, extensive reading, and retentive memory, but greatly deficient in good sense and stability. Unbounded credulity was his great failing. No tale was too marvelous for his ear. No ghost story came to his knowledge which was not speedily published to enlighten the wise and astonish the ignorant. Jonathan Edwards was a man of vast abilities, equal to the ablest men of his time, but much of his time and talents were spent in fruitless attempts to solve speculative difficulties in theology — "vain babblings — strifes of words — philosophy falsely so-called." Benjamin Franklin was the best writer who arose before the Revolutionary contest called to its aid pens able to contend with the minds of Europe. His works are the only American writings [that] deserved the rank of classic until within the last forty years.

Judge Story said: "A liberal allowance for a lawyer's library would be $10,000; for convenience merely $3000 would suffice; for necessity $300 might answer, and many eminent lawyers have commenced with less. My library was worth $300. All my means were contained in that and it exhausted all my means. The reports have quadrupled and elementary treatises are ten times as numerous now as in my day.

"Thomas Jefferson said: 'When conversing with Marshall I never admit anything. So sure as you admit any position to be good, no matter how remote from the conclusion he seeks to establish, you are gone. So great is his sophistry you must never give him an affirmative answer or you will be forced to grant his conclusion. Why, if he were to ask me if it were daylight or not, I'd reply, "Sir, I don't know, I can't tell."'

"A lawyer should never resort to petty tricks to increase his business. He should not leave 'a celestial bed to prey on garbage.' Courts will not unravel the threads that are good from the threads that are bad, but will leave the whole fabric exactly as it was woven."

September 26. — Judge Story in his lecture remarked that, as a body, lawyers, so far as his observations extended, were more eminent for

morality and a nice sense of honor than any other class of men. They
have the most important and delicate secrets entrusted to them; they
have more power of doing mischief, and are more instrumental in healing family dissensions, neighborhood feuds, and general ill-blood, than
any other profession. He considers the man who lays a wager on the
result of an election as more an enemy, or rather more dangerous to
public liberty, than the avowed adversary of our institutions. Wagers
tempt men to use corrupt means to gain power, and power corruptly
gained is sure to be corruptly used; the result is a continual sinking in
the scale, worse than despotism, for it is for the interest of despots to
make matters no worse, while corruption must increase to secure its
ends.

Throughout October the diary contains many pages of reflections upon the work in progress and the chances of success in
future. The young man notes the fact (October 2) that in two
days he will be twenty-one years old, and, after that event,
moralizes on the legal distinction between a minor "without
enough discretion to spend the millionth part of a mill" and a
citizen "wise and prudent enough to decide on matters involving
the wealth of Ind." "Whence the difference? Does the lapse of
a few short hours transform the headstrong and headlong child
of passion into the cautious, long-sighted disciple of experience,
soberness, and wisdom?" Questioning and refining congenial to
the legal mind in the atmosphere in which he lived; and perhaps
suggested by preparations for the first legal argument to be made
on the 22d and for participation in the Moot Court. "Reading
for authorities," he says, "is indeed like feeding on narcotics.
The stimulus is too great for the healthy stomach; agreeable and
exciting at first, but speedily followed by satiety and disgust."
His own defects are sharply criticized, the remedy for which is
found in "work, work, work."

October 25 we get a glimpse of one of the most interesting
personages of that age: —

I heard Mr. J. Q. Adams address the Whigs of Norfolk County, at
Dedham yesterday. His speech contained little politics but much abolitionism. Some of it was very good, much of it unreasonable and very
unfair. My opinion of the venerable but deluded old man was not all
changed. His speech was rather dry, contained some good hits, and
exhibited some good sparks of the internal fires, which, when aroused
into flame render him the impersonation of the "old man eloquent." I
do not wonder that he is regarded as a dangerous adversary in a mere

personal encounter. He is quick, sharp, fearless, and full of the wit and learning of all ages. He is not, at all times, an interesting or eloquent speaker, but when roused by repeated attacks, sneers, and taunts of his bitter foes, he is truly a most formidable man.

November 3. — Judge Story pronounces some highly wrought eulogies in the course of his remarks. In the last decision he said: "Sir James Mansfield was a very sensible, old-fashioned, common-law lawyer. He knew nothing but the common law. He cared for nothing else, and although a great judge yet he had not the grasp of mind for which Lord Ellenborough was distinguished. Brougham is a very able, clear-headed man, but not the greatest judge who ever sat upon the English bench. Tindale is an old-fashioned, common-law lawyer like Sir James Mansfield, but a strong man. Baron Parke is one of the ablest judges who ever sat upon the English bench, and perhaps the greatest lawyer now in England."

Cambridge, November 14. — For four or five days my attention has been withdrawn from my regular duties by the speeches I have listened to in reference to the subjects decided by the people at the election yesterday. I am not so easily enlisted in the excitements attending political discussions as I was prior to the election of General Harrison to the Presidency. I have not formed opinions upon any of the leading measures of public policy now proposed by the two great political parties which divide the country. I do not, therefore, take a very deep interest in the result of elections, but my desire to listen to some of the great lights of New England induced me to attend some of the meetings which have been held within a few days. The best speaker I heard at the Democratic meetings was George Bancroft, the historian. . . . He has none of those advantages of person and voice which contribute so much to the success of public speakers; but he has an elegant flow of language, a chaste style, and a well-stored mind, so that he is really one of the most interesting speakers I have heard.

R. C. Winthrop, M.C., from Boston, is a young man of fine attainments, a correct taste, and good natural ability. He appears to be much beloved, and is a very agreeable and effective speaker. He appears to be rapidly improving as a popular orator. Senator Choate is a strong man. His style of speaking is that of an impulsive, ardent, able, and practiced lawyer of the O'Connell stamp. Daniel Webster has been styled "the godlike," in derision. But if any man born of woman deserves the epithet, it is Daniel Webster. The majesty of pure intellect shines forth in him. In speaking he betrays no passion, no warmth, but all is cold and clear that falls from his lips. He *can*, indeed, be aroused, — Hayne learned that, — but he is habitually calm and passionless; yet there is a charm about the greatness of his intellect and grandeur of his mien which holds one suspended upon his lips.

Cambridge, November 15. — Francis [*sic*] Dana, Jr., of Boston, author of "Two Years Before the Mast," delivered a lecture before the Lyceum this evening on "American Loyalty." After having briefly adverted to the odium attached to the word "loyalty," and the reasons of it, he proceeded to draw the distinction between this principle or sentiment and patriotism: The first being the attachment and affection one has for the institutions and government of his country, the latter love of country. The French, for example, are the most patriotic people on the globe, and yet a people with less loyalty cannot be found under the whole heaven. The English are as loyal as they are brave and proud. The sentiment is a noble, high-minded one, consistent with the highest dignity, the greatest pride of personal character. He spoke of our want of it, the benefit of it, its conservatism; the evil tendency of its contrary. The two classes of men: Samuel Adams said: "Cousin John, you were born to build up; I was born to tear down."

To-day I argued my first cause in Moot Court, and though my success was not flattering, yet I see nothing to discourage a man in earnest in this matter, as I am. Greenleaf says you might as well attempt to abolish light as the principles of pleading. A clear statement of a man's case often wins the battle. "Commend me to the lawyer who can make a short, lucid statement of the grounds upon which rests his case."

November 27. — For the first time in my life I went to the theatre last week. I have been in Thespian societies, but never before in a regular theatre. I heard Mr. Macready play Hamlet. The part I suppose was well acted, but I take about as much pleasure in reading the play as I did in hearing it.

"Judge Parker [said Judge Story] was a good-natured, lazy boy when at college, became a good-natured, lazy lawyer, and made afterward a good-natured, lazy judge. He was universally beloved, always decided right, but gave miserable reasons for his opinions. While in the profession he used always to decide according to his own common sense, steering by the light of the Ten Commandments, and to advise his clients that that was the law."

December 21. — Judge Story delivered the most eloquent lecture I have ever heard, yesterday morning, on the duty of American citizens to adhere honestly and implicitly to the Constitution. The application was particularly directed to the abolitionists. "There is a clause in the Constitution which gives to the slaveholders the right of reclaiming a fugitive slave from the free States. This clause some people wish to evade, or are willing wholly to disregard. If one part of the country may disregard one part of the Constitution, another section may refuse to obey that part which seems to bear hard upon its interests, and thus the Union will become a 'mere rope of sand'; and the Constitution, worse than a dead letter, an apple of discord in our midst, a fruitful source of reproach, bitterness, and hatred, and in the end discord and civil war; till exhausted, wasted, embittered, and deadly foes have severed this Union into four, six, or eight little confederacies, or the whole shall crouch under the iron hand of a single despot. Such must inevitably follow the first success of those mad men, who even now are ready to stand up in public assemblies, and in the name of conscience, liberty, or the rights of man, to boast that they are willing and ready to bid farewell to that Constitution under which we have lived and pros-pered for more than half a century, and which I trust may be trans-mitted, unimpaired, from generation to generation for many centuries to come. It was the result of compromise and a spirit of concession and forbearance, and will end when that spirit dies from the hearts of this people. Let no man think to excuse himself from any duty which it enjoins. No mental reservation can save his honesty from reproach. Without perjury, no public officer can ever be false to his trust by refus-ing to execute the duties enjoined by that glorious instrument. In the case between the States of Pennsylvania and Maryland, I delivered the opinion at the solicitation of my brothers, who adopted unanimously my first draft."

Cambridge, January 4, 1844. — Judge Story delivered his last lecture for the term to-day. His parting advice was good, and his farewell to those who were about leaving the school feelingly eloquent. He spoke of the necessity of laying a deep and broad foundation in the elementary principles; [of] the distinction between a shrewd, ready practitioner and the man who regarded the law with the eye of reason and studied it in a spirit of philosophy. "The law," said he, "has been styled a jealous mistress. She will not share a divided heart. A lawyer must never become a political meddler if he wishes to have a lawyer's mind." He *never* knew a lawyer who had entered the political arena who ever recovered the power and temper which he had before possessed. He never knew a man — "you will never know a man" — whose devotion to his legal pursuits, if persevered in, has not been abundantly rewarded. "Keep out of politics till you are forty, and then you can, with the experience of forty years, direct your course for yourselves. I know that I now speak to those whose views of life are widely different from mine. I am glad that it is so. You have high hopes, ardent desires, boundless confidence, ambition, and energy. These are the feelings proper for youth. They are given you for wise purposes. If you felt as I feel, if you knew what I know, those efforts which will make life useful and render you a blessing to your age and country, if directed aright, would never be made. Ambition, energy, ardent desire would be nipped in the bud. To those who now leave the school I would say, you carry with you my best wishes. I may live to see some of you able advocates before me. I may hear of the success of others. You know not how I am rejoiced to hear of your success, and what a lively interest I take in your welfare. When I go from among you, the proudest inscription I would ask upon my tomb would be the fact that while I was professor in the law school

of Harvard College so many thousands graduated from it." Pshaw!
how my haste (indecent) spoils the old man eloquent.

Vacation was spent in reading, walking to Boston afternoons
for exercise, and in visiting. He "attended a meeting of Unita-
rians which was conducted a good deal like Methodist class meetings." After the usual opening exercises the pastor proposed for
consideration the following question, "Is life more to be dreaded
than death?" which a fat, jolly, grey-headed little man in a tone
full of good humor declared to be no question at all. He found
life beautiful and of all things the most desirable, whereas death
was the most fearful. A lawyer, somewhat advanced in years,
while arguing that life was a blessing, thought that death was a
blessing also. But such speculations were less to Hayes's taste
than the vigorous thought of the pastor, Dr. Walker: —

"Men complain that life is too short, and that the parts of which life
is made up are too long. Yet life is not made up of the weeks and months
which measure duration. Good actions and great thoughts are the
measures of life. A man of ninety may be a child, and the man [of]
thirty a veteran. It is not *how long* but *how much*, which turns the scale.
Wisdom bringeth grey hairs. There are periods in life when our energies
are aroused, great exertions are made, and a few hours at such a time
may have a more important and lasting effect upon our whole after life
than years of ordinary life. So, in the history of nations. There are
epochs characterized by great activity in developing the resources and
giving free scope to the energies of a people, which do more for their advancement in a few years than had been done in ages before. There are
some questions in the alternative, that not to decide in favor is to decide
against the thing under consideration. A man travelling a road comes
to one leading off and is in doubt whether to pursue it. Now, not to
decide for the new is to decide for the old. So, in matters of religion; to
hesitate is, for that time, at least, to decide against it. There are many
speculative difficulties which deter some men from deciding in favor of a
change of life, but these difficulties, many of them, never can be settled;
and if they could, it would not alter a man's practical conduct whichever
way they were settled, or if they remain unsettled. Speculation is not
life. We need not deliberate longer before we begin to act. We are not
expected to stop thinking because we have commenced acting. No man
is less able to deliberate because he has acted."

January 31. — To-day I attended a club composed of the members of
the Law School who are remaining here during the vacation. The subject debated was the admission of Texas into the Union. I advocated
the negative on constitutional grounds. Public speaking is no more

difficult than I expected to find it after so long a disuse. Connected trains of thought and logical reasoning must be the end of all my efforts. These are more useful and more difficult of attainment than fluency or grace of manner. No man of clear conceptions and logical habits of mind can fail to be fluent, and practice, careful practice, will remove those faults of manner which are to be avoided.

February 18. — Yesterday I returned from Vermont, after a visit of nearly two weeks to my grandmother, uncles, and cousins. They have not changed more since I last saw them about six years ago than is to be expected in the ordinary course of nature. Grandmother has been very industrious all her life. She is almost eighty and retains the use of her mental faculties in a good degree of perfection. Her good strong sense and great industry have made her very useful to all who have had any-thing to do with her. She bid me farewell, as she said, for the last time. I hope, however, to see her at least once again.

My uncle Austin Birchard is a most excellent man. His talents and industry, with the aid of better advantages for education in early life, would have given him a high rank in whatever pursuit he might have engaged. In fact, though deprived of early discipline, and shut out by deafness from one great source of improvement, he has, notwithstand-ing, acquired a reputation for political information and sagacity, and energy and success in his business, which belongs to few men in his section of the country. I enjoyed myself very much in his company. The reflection that constantly urged itself upon me, while conversing with him, was: "If Uncle could accomplish so much with so little encour-agement, and held back by his infirmity, what ought I not to accomplish with so great assistance and motive as I have always had?" Ah! there it is again. Ambition will peep out occasionally, philosophical as I have become; but Judge Story was right: ambition and confidence, high hopes, bright anticipations are proper inmates for the youthful breast. They furnish the incentives to exertion, without which we should be as useless as we would be miserable.

February 26. — The summer session of the Law School commenced to-day. One hundred and six students made their appearance. Profes-sor Greenleaf made the opening address. The only thing in it worthy of remark was his idea of a lawyer: "A lawyer is engaged in the highest of all human pursuits — the application of the soundest reason and purest morality to the ordinary affairs of life. He should have a clear head and a true heart, always acting at his fingers' ends." Moot cases were given out. Mine is to come up in three weeks. I have read the first chapters in Cruise and Kent. The respite afforded by the vacation seems to have had a very salutary influence. The law is quite interesting. I hope it may so continue. At all events I shall endeavor to profit by this session, as it may be my last in the school. . . . I must try to acquire greater mildness of temper and affability of manners. I cannot complain of nature. She has not been niggardly, but habit has somewhat changed the stamp of nature. Let me reform the habits — a task easily accomplished, and much will be done towards giving me the manners and sentiments of a true gentleman.

The rest of February and March were devoted to hard work, reading, preparing for two arguments, and attending lectures.

Dane's abridgement [Hayes quotes with approval] is a town meeting of legal principles without a moderator. — The law of real property is difficult, but I begin to see a little farther before me, and do not despair of some day becoming informed upon the subject. I read Blackstone first, then Cruise, and finally take up Kent. To me Kent appears the closest and most concise writer upon the subject. — The laws of nations and real property are not quite so interesting as a play of Shakespeare's, or a romance of Scott's, or a humorous tale of Dickens's, yet they are not the dryest of all dry things. Vacations are really useful; a short respite from study gives a real relish for the law.

He attended lectures by Professor Longfellow on the modern languages, and on Anglo-Saxon literature; and other lectures on anatomy.

Cambridge, May 12. — For many days I have been very busily engaged. The study of the law of real property, preparation for the performance of duties in clubs, the weather, and the political movements of the day, have, altogether, kept me from paying the proper attention to other affairs.

I heard Webster make a political speech in Faneuil Hall, Thursday evening. He supports the nominations of the Baltimore convention of May 2, Clay and Frelinghuysen. But his speech was poor for him. His course for the few months he remained in the Cabinet was a serious injury to his reputation.

I heard Walker preach twice to-day. What a powerful reasoner he is! How solemn and impressive are his appeals! His subject in the forenoon was taken from the 26th chapter of Proverbs, 16th and 17th verses: Cruelty for sport, false wit, ill-timed jests, sarcasm, ridicule, and all the means of wounding the feelings of a fellow creature wantonly. Let me bear it in mind. I need such admonition. This afternoon his argument was against the common notion: "We must consider *principles*, not consequences; *duties* are ours, events are God's." "We are not to be deterred from a course of conduct which we deem right out of fear of personal consequences, but in deciding upon the right, we are to look to the tendencies and consequences of our acts. The mischiefs which they may work to others may render bad that which by our theory is good. Christ is given as a model. Evils are to be removed as He would have removed them; not by fanaticism, by violence and bloodshed, but quietly, persuasively, with passionless serenity."

Cambridge, May 18. — We have had a little excitement here for a few days past, occasioned by a skirmish between some of the Southern law students, and the members of the senior class in college. It has resulted in a few slight bruises, the loss of a few soap locks, and the expulsion of one or two from each department. *Sic transit, etc.*

I am progressing slowly in the acquisition of the learning of real property. I shall be glad when this term is through. My health requires more attention than can be given it while engaged in study. In six weeks the vacation begins. Then I shall throw aside my books entirely for a season. Since I commenced the study of the law, I have taken no sufficient recreation.

June 12. — Judge Story has been lecturing for the last week on the Constitution. I will set down the principal things he mentions which I might otherwise forget.

He commenced with a short history of the Colonies, the Declaration of Independence, and the adoption of the Confederation. "The Congress of 1776 assumed powers, for they had none conferred on them by the people, which assumptions of power were acquiesced in, and thus ratified. Washington's commission was granted, alliances formed, armies raised, debts contracted, and other acts of sovereignty performed by this Congress, without a shadow of authority till the adoption of the Confederation in 1781.[1] The emergency required it.

"The principal acts of the first Congresses were done with Virginians for leaders, because that Massachusetts, the other leading Colony, was so deeply and so immediately interested. Thus Lee moved the Resolution of Independence, Jefferson wrote the Declaration, Washington led the armies; but John Adams carried the measure by his boldness and energy. He never spoke over twelve minutes — no one-hour rule was needed then. At the time of the Declaration, so doubtful were the members of Congress of the people's acquiescence, that they took every means of forestalling public opinion. And John Jay wrote to a friend: 'The measure is adopted; build bonfires on the hills; have rejoicings and assemblings that the public mind may be made safe.'[2]

"The Congress of 1777 issued paper money and sent a letter to

[1] "Whatever, then, may be the theories of ingenious men on the subject, it is historically true, that before the Declaration of Independence these Colonies were not, in any absolute sense, sovereign States; that that event did not find them or make them such; but that at the moment of their separation they were under the dominion of a superior controlling national government, whose powers were vested in and exercised by the general Congress with the consent of the people of all the States. . . . The Articles of Confederation . . . were not ratified, so as to become obligatory upon all the States, until March 1781." (Story's *Commentaries*, vol. I, pp. 202 and 203.)

[2] There are preserved in the handwriting of Jay resolutions adopted at White Plains, New York, July 9, requiring the publication of the Declaration "with beat of drum." (See Johnston's *Jay*, vol. I, p. 72.)

induce capitalists to take it, saying, 'Money will take to itself wings and fly away, but the faith of a nation will remain.'

"To show the weakness of considerations of honor and duty when opposed by interest, look at the unpaid officers and soldiers of the Revolution. Again, under the Confederation: Stay laws and all manner of laws were passed; conflicting interests were too strong for State pride. Marshall, Madison, Patrick Henry, and Washington were able for eight years to keep Virginia to the line of duty by only a majority of one, two, or three, in opposition to the demagogues whose power consisted in appeals to the passions, the distresses, etc., of the people. So strong was the feeling excited by the counter legislation on the subject of imposts that Massachusetts and Connecticut seriously contemplated the conquest and division of Rhode Island, who allowed all articles to come in duty free.

"The debates of the conventions of the States to ratify the Constitution are in a great measure lost. The debates in Virginia were the best reported, and the members of that convention say they are very incorrect. In Massachusetts no reports [were made] worth anything. The writings of those times are some of them to be found in the 'American Museum,' and the 'Federalist.' Greater and purer men than its authors never lived. I have heard Samuel Dexter, John Marshall, and Chancellor Livingston say that Hamilton's reach of thought was so far beyond theirs that by his side they were schoolboys — rush tapers before the sun at noonday. On the bank, Washington desired written arguments from the members of his Cabinet. Jefferson and Randolph opposed by reasons so cogent that Washington came to doubt. He sent for Hamilton, told him the state of his mind. Hamilton was surprised; said he had never dreamed of Washington's doubting; that, had he known that, he would not have written his report and recommended the course adopted. General Washington said he had not doubted till he saw Jefferson's and Randolph's arguments, and, said he, 'You must answer them or I cannot sign the bill.' Hamilton went to Mr. Lewis,[1] the first lawyer of Philadelphia who had no doubt of a bank's constitutionality, and asked him to listen to his argument, and tell him the errors and add suggestions of his own. They walked in Mr. Lewis's garden the whole afternoon. Hamilton went over his whole argument and, at sundown of the seventh day after General Washington had received the bill, they separated, satisfied that the argument was as strong as possible. That evening General Hamilton told his wife to give him a cup of strong coffee — said he should n't come to bed that night, as he was to write all night. That night he wrote the argument of eighty pages which contains all that has since been said, or can be said, in favor of the constitutionality of a bank, and *it is unanswerable*. All the departments of the Government have acquiesced in the decision made by General

---

[1] William Lewis. There is a reference to this incident in John C. Hamilton's *History of the Republic*, vol. IV, p. 247.

Washington. Mr. Madison regarded the question as settled in 1816. The Supreme Court with a majority of *Republican* judges — Marshall delivering the opinion — unanimously decided its constitutionality, in the case of Maryland."

Cambridge, June 13. — (The Final Interpreter.) The Judge [Story] first spoke of the opinion, sometimes expressed, that nothing is settled by precedent in constitutional questions. "If so, no one knows his rights or duties. The Executives, States, and Legislatures entertain different views of the same question at different times. Fifteen years ago New Hampshire thought and resolved that a Bank of the United States was constitutional. She now thinks and resolves the opposite. When I came into political life South Carolina maintained the highest constitutional doctrines. She prided herself on having always so stood. Now we know, etc., etc. We should soon be in the situation of old Judge Strong of this State in regard to our statutes: 'Yesterday the law was so, but I can't tell how it is to-day — I have n't yet heard what our Legislature has done.'

"It is a singular fact in relation to this matter, that the only questions which have been regarded as settled are those in which the powers exercised were *most doubtful; e.g.*, the power of removal in the Executive; it is nowhere given, nowhere implied by fair construction. It is really an incident to the power of appointment, but that power is in the President *and Senate*. There, then, should be the power of removal. But the first Congress determined otherwise. General Washington was so esteemed that they feared that it would look like a want of confidence in him to refuse him the power of removal. It passed the Senate by the casting vote of John Adams, the Vice-President. But this early decision has been held final by all strict constructionists. Again, the acquisition of foreign territory: Denied by President Jefferson, finally acquiesced in, now regarded as settled. The Post-Office question: the right to carry letters — is it exclusive in the general Government? This has been considered settled, but is now raised, and we shall be called to decide it the coming winter."

It is interesting to note how completely Judge Story, in the lecture reported above, and in his "Commentaries," [1] had separated from the Republican leaders who had expected him to expound the Constitution in harmony with their theories. He quotes Marshall in the case of Cohens *vs.* Virginia approvingly, and controverts Jefferson and Madison. "The judiciary of the United States," wrote Jefferson in bitterness of spirit in 1820, "is the subtle corps of sappers and miners constantly working underground to undermine the foundations of our confederated fabric.

---

[1] Book III, chap. IV.

They are construing our Constitution from a coördination of a general and special government to a general and supreme one alone." Jefferson would have had the judges dependent upon popular feeling, in which he had but followed George Mason, the most radical Virginia Democrat. "We ought to have the judiciary," said Mason, "under the check of the sovereign opinion of the people."

The vacation was spent at home in Columbus with relatives, where, Hayes records, he did not fall in love nor meet with other mishap. There in consultation with friends it had been decided that he should continue at Harvard until midwinter, after which he would return to Ohio and enter upon the practice of the law. He returned to Cambridge in August, several weeks before term began, and took up his studies again, now giving more time than formerly to literature and history. September 21, the diary is resumed: —

The ability to speak is so valuable to a lawyer that no time is misspent which is given to its attainment. Night before last I had an opportunity of listening to one of the best speakers I ever heard, J. M. Berrien, of Georgia. His natural advantages are great: a fine form, rather portly, an intellectual countenance with a most winning smile, and silvery voice, are but the external graces which adorn the man. He is an accurate, logical reasoner, fluent, warm, and entertaining. I never heard a speaker who could make abstract reasoning so interesting. Now, though I can never hope to equal him for want of his natural endowments, yet his habits of thought, power of expression, and winning manners, arising from sweetness of temper, can, in some degree, be acquired by continued study, attention, and effort. . . . First, knowledge of my profession; second, general information; third, the power of using my materials; and fourth, manners and temper suited to these acquirements.

Cambridge, October 1. — Professor Longfellow thinks that the fame of Goethe stands fairer in Germany now than it ever did before. Some of his writings certainly have an immoral tendency, while others are as pure and elevating as any that were ever written by uninspired pen. Goethe thought that so far as an author was careful of the moral principles of his work, so far was the perfection of the work likely to be lessened. He would prefer to write nothing immoral, but virtue must be sacrificed to literary excellence.

Judge Story considers Albert Gallatin and Hamilton the greatest financiers this country has ever produced. "Gallatin always said that he found in the Treasury Department nothing to alter. Hamilton had formed a system perfect in all its parts. Gallatin used to say that speakers — eloquent speakers — were too abundant in Congress; business men, good committee men, were too scarce. He was one of the greatest men of his time. Samuel Dexter, of whom Marshall said, 'a man of greater mind I never knew,' and Fisher Ames, one of the most fluent men who ever lived, called on Hamilton to get him to explain some of his financial plans. Hamilton conversed with them for three or four hours, going over the whole subject. After leaving the room, Ames said to Dexter, 'Hamilton is a man of most extraordinary power. Now, Dexter, to be plain with you, I have not understood one word Hamilton said for the last three quarters of an hour. How is it with you?' To which Dexter replied: 'Don't stop there; I have n't understood anything for the last two hours. I was in a thick fog — I could n't follow him.'"

November 18. — "The greatest speech Wirt ever made [said Judge Story] was in the case of the Cherokee Nation *vs.* The State of Georgia. The greatest speech Webster ever made was in the Dartmouth College case. Judge Marshall was affected to tears by the eloquent peroration of Wirt. He then said: 'I have not shed a tear before since Webster delivered his great speech in the Dartmouth College case. I then did not expect ever to shed another upon such an occasion.'"

Cambridge, January 1, 1845. — This is the beginning of the new year. In two or three weeks I shall leave the Law School, and soon after shall begin *to live.* Heretofore I have been getting ready to live. How much has been left undone it is of no use to reckon. My labors have been to cultivate and store my mind. This year, the character, the whole man must receive attention. *I will strive to become in manners, morals, and feelings a true gentleman.* The rudeness of a student must be laid off, and the quiet, manly deportment of a gentleman put on, not merely to be worn as a garment, but to become by use a part of myself. I believe I know what true gentility — genuine good breeding — is. Let me but live out what is within, and I am vain enough to think that little of what is important would be found wanting.

CHAPTER III

BEGINNING PROFESSIONAL LIFE — VISIT TO TEXAS

HAYES returned to Ohio early in 1845, and, having been admitted to the bar, March 10, at Marietta, established himself at Lower Sandusky (now Fremont) where his uncle, Sardis Birchard, was engaged in business. He formed a partnership with Ralph P. Buckland, whom he describes as "a sound lawyer, without ostentation or brilliancy, and of excellent principles, strict integrity, an inveterate politician (Whig, of course) — every way an estimable man." He continues his studies in law and literature, talks of love, and waits for clients — the usual experience of most young lawyers.

Two years of this routine, following immediately after the close and prolonged application of his student years, made heavy inroads on the young lawyer's vitality; and his friends became alarmed about his health. He himself was aware that a decided change in his mode of life was necessary. He was growing restless and despondent. He longed for active employment, for leadership. As a boy he had dreamed of a soldier's life, its perils and possible fame. The dream now came back to him, and on the first day of June he decided to volunteer for the Mexican War. He writes: —

I am induced to this by a mixture of motives. My friends, and those whose advice I was bound to listen to, have resolved that I shall leave the office for six months or a year to come, and I can think of no way of spending that time which is half so tolerable as the life of a soldier. If I can enjoy health I shall be most happy and receive benefit I am sure. I have no views about war other than those of the best Christians, and my opinion of this war with Mexico is that which is common to the Whigs of the North — Tom Corwin and his admirers of whom I am one. My philosophy has no better principle than that of the old woman who, while she mourned over her neighbor's calamity, was yet rejoiced to be able to witness the conflagration. Whatever doubts I might otherwise have of the morality of this feeling are entirely swamped in the love of enterprise which I share in common with other young men of my age.

Hayes promptly acted on this resolution by applying to influential friends for letters which might aid him in his purpose. One of these, Judge Ebenezer Lane, who had recently retired from the Ohio Supreme Court, responded in a letter which as clearly voices the repugnance of the intellectual class of the North to the war with Mexico as does the eloquent speech of Senator Corwin in the previous February. The virtues of an eminent man, the solicitude of an elder friend, and the conscientious convictions of a patriotic citizen are all reflected in the letter, which follows: —

While I earnestly deplore the occasion which leads you into another field of life, I can scarcely reconcile myself to the thought that you may participate in the scenes of this accursed war. I do not count the risks and perils: they are incident to a life of action; but I cannot look with patience or hope upon it, its authors, or its results.

Most willingly do I enclose the letter to Mitchell.[1] I only wish it might be used for a different purpose. If in any other form you believe I can be of service, do not fail to ask me. Wherever you are led may God bless and keep you, and give you back to us in restored health. May God lead you into other employments than that of fighting in a cause so foul.

Though grieved that one he esteemed should give support to an unjust war, still he would not withhold his endorsement of that one's character. The letter to Professor Mitchell follows: —

SANDUSKY, June 5, 1847.

MY DEAR SIR, — My friend R. B. Hayes, Esq., one of my professional brethren, of Lower Sandusky, is the bearer of this; — a graduate of Gambier and who received his law education at Cambridge, and has profited well by his opportunities. Among all my young friends in Ohio, there is none to whom I feel more closely attached than to Mr. Hayes; and none, whose character, attainments, position, aims, and professional prospects are higher than his.

I do not know precisely his views and wishes; but if it be in your power to aid him, I commend him to your kind offices, with entire confidence that he will amply justify the expectations and representations of his friends. — I am very respectfully,

E. LANE.

These are the words of a friend, to be sure, but also of a man of culture and affairs, who had achieved distinction in his

---

[1] The famous scientist, Professor O. M. Mitchell, a man of military experience, who was at that time in charge of the Adams Observatory.

profession, and who was revered by all classes for the purity of his life, and the uprightness of his character. They show what impression Hayes at twenty-five had made on a man of large experience of life, alike as to his qualities of mind and character and as to his professional prospects.

Armed with letters, Hayes journeyed to Cincinnati where he met "the leading military characters." Applicants for positions were very numerous, but Hayes wrote that his chances were good if he chose to press them.[1] This, however, he decided not to do. He had promised his friends to take the advice of physicians before committing himself. Dr. Mussey and Dr. Dresbach were consulted, and they both warned him that the Mexican climate would be perilous to him in the existing state of his health.[2] Judge Lane's letter, he writes his uncle, "has done more to satisfy me with the doctors' decision than anything else I have received or heard." Without great reluctance, therefore, he withdrew from the company he had provisionally joined and presently decided on a trip to New England. There, in the mountains and at the seashore, he spent the summer months, coming back to his desk the last of September with powers greatly refreshed. But by the end of another year the need of complete rest was again imperative, when a radical change of climate was resolved on. In December,1848, accompanied by his uncle, Sardis Birchard, he started for Texas on a visit to his classmate, Guy M. Bryan, the possessor of a vast estate in lands, who had already entered upon an honorable career in that newly acquired empire. Hayes gave himself up to the enjoyment of this trip. His cheerfulness and keen sense of the humorous are conspicuous whether on river steamboat, in crowded hotel, or in camp on the frontier.

The journey from Cincinnati to New Orleans by river consumed eight days, with many glimpses of the cities by the way, and with much enjoyment of the new phases of character which

[1] He hoped to be lieutenant in one of the two companies from Lower Sandusky, and went to Cincinnati with these companies, taking with him Benjamin Inman to be his substitute if the physicians advised against his purpose. Inman later became a prosperous farmer, and was a member of the Ohio Legislature when Mr. Hayes was elected President.

[2] Dr. Mussey gruffly said: "Go by all means; you may live six weeks in that climate with your trouble."

the chance of travel revealed. We have these pictures of life on
the steamboat, Moro Castle, in the diary: —

December 15. — I like this sort of life. Table equal to our best hotels.
Captain Scott more resembles a landlord with his smiles and jokes than
[the] haughty autocrat of a Western steamer. In the after part of the
cabin are four or five ladies with their children; one apparently an
unmarried lady and another a widow. The latter is the object of the
particular attentions of a fat, self-sufficient old nabob whom Uncle
styles "old soap grease." . . . Two ladies and two gentlemen generally
play cards in the after cabin. Next towards the bow another table of
social card players consisting of a loud-talking, boastful youngster (a
Jew Moses, of Cincinnati) whose garb and gab alike proclaim a volunteer officer, a good-natured, laughing Hoosier, [and] a third only remarkable for his height and the prodigious length of his arms. I noticed him
to-day at dinner; he reaches like a well-sweep to all parts of the table,
gathering and storing away an unheard-of quantity of provisions. Next
forward a table of chess or chequer players, with a few gaping lookers-
on. Next is a group of nondescripts, quite at a loss how to bestow themselves, some dozing listlessly in their armchairs, waiting patiently for
the next meal, others reading cheap tales of pirates, "love and murder,"
etc. Last group forward four professional gentlemen busy at poker for
money. I have read Warren's "Now and Then," Dickens's "Battle of
Life," and am now doing Cooper's "Bee Hunters." I read, play chess,
walk the deck, study the map, and chat occasionally. *Mem.* This is not
a talking boat.

December 20. — Yesterday heard frightful stories of cholera in New
Orleans. Reports dwindling away with every boat we meet. Saw General Taylor's residence, a neat, one-story, long cottage, porch all round,
on a pleasant hill. Saw an old white horse quietly feeding near the
house, supposed to be "Old Whitey." Baton Rouge is a fine town;
beautiful Statehouse building. At a sugar plantation land 250 barrels.
The overseer, on reading in the letter enclosing the bill of lading the
words "Dear Sir," broke out with great warmth: "Dear Sir! As if he
knew me!" After this exhibition of himself, I was not surprised to find
that he could not count the barrels.

New Orleans was reached December 21. Three days later passage was taken "on the fine ocean steamer Galveston bound for
the port of the same name." "General Worth and staff on board.
An exceedingly agreeable, fine-looking man; medium size, of a
plump, upright person, with good features, a bright, piercing black
eye (Bishop McIlvaine's), a bushy head of grey hair, affable and
easy in his manners." Christmas was spent on the Gulf, the chief
topic of conversation being the endless slavery question, and the

next day Galveston was reached, which presented a "glorious contrast to the disease and filth of New Orleans." One day more by river steamer brought the Ohioans to Bryan's plantation near the Brazos, where they were received with the warmth of true Southern hospitality — a hospitality which once enjoyed becomes a delightful memory. The house was "beautifully situated on the edge of the timber, looking out upon a prairie on the south, extending five or eight miles to the Gulf," with a large and beautiful flower-garden in front.

Social life here afforded no end of entertainment — balls and parties rapidly following one another, the guests riding ten, fifteen, and even twenty miles, arriving early in the afternoon, and remaining for nearly twenty-four hours, the great plantation house supplying room for all. "An exceedingly agreeable, gay, and polished company," we are told in the diary — "the ladies particularly noticeable for the possession of the winning qualities. Merriment and dancing until 4.30 A.M. — like similar scenes elsewhere." "Gentlemen breakfast from 10 till 11.30; all off by 12 o'clock." Several weeks passed in this delightful social intercourse, with frequent visits to neighboring plantations, hunting parties, and fishing excursions. Thus, January 25, 1849, the diary records: —

Ride with Uncle and Guy over Gulf Prairie to the mouth of the Bernard, to fish and eat oysters. A glorious day. Deer, cattle, cranes, wild geese, brant, ducks, plover, prairie hens, and the Lord knows what else, often in sight at the same time. The roar of the Gulf is heard for miles, like the noise of Niagara. Staked out horses with "lariats," eat old Sailor Tom's oysters, picked up shells, fished and shot snipe until 5 P.M., then rode home through clouds of mosquitoes, thicker than the lice or locusts of Egypt — like the hair on a dog's back. Notice the eagle's nest on the lone tree in the prairie, and reach home glad to get away from the mosquitoes.

Tuesday, January 30. — Ride with Mr. Perry over to Sterling McNeal's plantation. A shrewd, intelligent, cynical old bachelor, full of "wise saws and modern instances"; very fond of telling his own experience and talking of his own affairs. Living alone he has come to think he is the "be all" and "end all" here. The haughty and imperious part of a man develops rapidly on one of these lonely sugar plantations, where the owner rarely meets with any except his slaves and minions. Sugar hogsheads vary from 1100 to 1800 lbs. White and black mechanics all work together. White men generally dissolute and intemperate.

Returned, found Uncle Birchard returned from Oyster Creek with the trophy of a successful onslaught upon a tiger cat. Glorious weather. One little shower.

Monday, February 5. — Cold and clear. Forenoon spent with Stephen and the ladies — music and flirting. Afternoon rode up to Major Lewis's. Three agreeable young ladies; music, singing, and dancing — city refinement and amusements in a log cabin on the banks of the Brazos, where only yesterday the steam whistle of a steamboat was mistaken for a panther.

But parties and rides across the prairies to call upon ladies do not fill up the whole time. There are conversations with the able men who are laying the foundations of a new State, and a taste of the rough life in frontier towns. A grand tour was taken through northern and western Texas — the party of course travelling on horseback. The start was made February 7, "Guy mounted on a high Mexican saddle, covered with a red sheepskin, on Joel's mule, a grand beast; Uncle on a stout bright bay — 'Hotspur,' Guy's favorite horse; and I on a tall, gaunt, black, awkward, frisky piece of horseflesh, bought out of one of the Kentucky regiments sent to Mexico; — all with saddlebags, overcoats, and ropes for lariats."

The travellers find accommodations at the widely scattered plantations and are always welcome. Occasionally a "norther" keeps them indoors for a day, but for the most part they have bright skies and perfect weather. One night they pass at Colonel R.'s, a laughing joker of Indian blood, who had a lovely place on the banks of the Brazos — "keeps fine horses for racing and *always wins.*"

Monday, February 12, 1849. — Cold and clear. To-day rode over a high rolling prairie "most glorious to behold." . . . In the course of the day passed the house of the identical man whose chickens come up in the spring and *cross their legs to be tied,* so strong is the force of habit — their owner having moved once a year a day's journey (or week's) until he reached Texas, all the way from Kentucky!

February 17. — Clear and cold but bearable. Twenty-six miles to Colonel Chambers'. Through the village of Bastrop. First sight to-day of the green Colorado, with its picturesque hills and beautiful, widespread meadows. Ascend Guy's future home, one mile south of the village of B. He calls the hill on which he wishes to put his mansion,

"Bald Knob." It overlooks a lovely bottom, in horseshoe shape, of one thousand acres.

February 18. — Clear and bright, but still cool weather. Thirty-three miles to Austin over a fine rolling country. The last two days, pine and cedar in abundance — the country looking like one which suffers from the drouth; hills covered with small round pebbles, some places to the depth of four or five inches, under this layer a rich black soil. Austin is an inconsiderable village on the Colorado, with "large expectations." Governor's office, judges' rooms, etc., are little log cabins sixteen feet square; not more than one or two passable buildings in the city (?). Town full of discharged "Rangers," officers, and soldiers of the United States army, gamblers, and *others.* Costumes of every variety — Indian, Mexican, Christian, civil, military, and mixed. All armed to the teeth, fierce whiskers. Gaming and drinking very abounding in all quarters.

February 19. — Cloudy, but pleasant. "Surround" the city with Uncle afoot. Cross the lovely blue Colorado. The capitol is a low frame building on the top of a gravelly hill overlooking the village. The hotel consists of a number of log cabins, and is very comfortable, all things considered. The landlord is one of the famous "Rangers," — Captain McCulloch. General Harney is in town. In the evening, peep in upon a California meeting, held in the hall of the House of Representatives — a room with two ornaments, a map of the Holy Land, and another of the wanderings of the Jews. Called at the room of an old law student, of Delaware — Royal T. Wheeler, now a judge of the Supreme Court. His office as judge, "den" he calls it, being a log cabin about fourteen feet square, with a bed, table, five chairs, a washstand, and a "whole raft" of books and papers. Visit the Supreme Court: consists of three judges.

Tuesday, February 20. — Weather warm and balmy, but cloudy. Walk with Uncle over the Colorado to Barton Spring, named after the Barton who sent word to the commanding officer of a company of Regulars, sent out to guard the frontier, that if he did n't withdraw, *he* would let the Indians kill them! Spring is large but not unusually so. P.M. Ride to the top of Mount Bonvel north of Austin — a steep, high hill overlooking the valley and affording a fine view of mountain scenery, stretching off towards the northwest. Evening spent with Judge Wheeler, talking over old times.

Character sketches are not lacking.

Colonel K. was vain of his horsemanship and being Senator from San Patricio, and a candidate for United States Senator, took pains to exhibit his horsemanship by riding through the streets of Austin in every variety of posture; and was also voted a bore for making harangues, intended to be impressive and eloquent. To cut his comb, Williamson, of Washington County, nicknamed "Three-legged Willie," after one of Colonel K.'s efforts, rose and replied: "The gentleman from San Patricio is a great man; the gentleman from San Patricio is a very great man. He rides at a swift gallop through the streets of Austin, standing upright upon his horse — he is a great man; the gentleman from San Patricio is a very great man! He can swing himself from side to side of his horse when galloping at full speed — he is a great man. Mr. Speaker, the Senator from San Patricio is a very great man. I have seen him while riding swiftly, stoop from his saddle and pick up a dollar on the ground and safely regain his seat. Oh, Mr. Speaker, the gentleman from San Patricio is a great man! — he is a very great man!"

Replying [on another occasion] to a member from Galveston ["Willie" said]: "Galveston! What is Galveston? An isolated portion of the North American continent. Formerly, it was the haunt of the slave-dealer and the pirate, and now, it is the abode of the most graceless set of vagabonds that these two blue eyes ever looked upon!" Canvassing for the Legislature, his competitor, a military hero, boasted of the exploits he had performed in wars with the Comanches and Mexicans. Willie asked him how many he had killed. "Oh," said he, "that I cannot tell — it was in battle and I took good aim; but, come, Willie, how many men did you ever kill?" "I don't know," said Willie, "how many I have killed, but I've killed two that I got!" He had shot two men in duels.

Wednesday, February 21. — Misty and threatening, but no rain. Set out for San Antonio. Cross the Colorado and ride over a high dry prairie without much timber to San Marcos, on the beautiful stream of the same name, and the county-seat of Hays County. Visit the spring. The water spouts out of the foot of the mountain in streams of a foot in diameter.

Thursday, February 22. — Weather in the morning same as yesterday, clearing off in the afternoon. Ride twenty miles over a fine rolling country, looking old and cultivated with its orchards (mezquite trees), meadows, flocks and herds, but no houses, to New Braunfels. This is a German village of two or three hundred people at the junction of two of the most beautiful streams I ever saw, the Guadaloupe (pronounced Wah-loop) and the Comal. The water which flows from springs is so transparent the fish seem hanging in the air.

Saturday, February 24. — Off over high rolling prairies thirty-five miles to San Antonio. Stop at Mrs. Shelton's. Visit the Alamo with Mr. Bean; visit the graves of Walker and Gillespie. Find a party of California emigrants cooking in the room where Crockett fell.

Sunday, February 25. — Early in the morning go to mass at the Church of the Cracked Chimes. Mexican girls of all colors, with no bonnets, but shawls gracefully thrown over the shoulders, kneeling reverently on the ground floor. Attend Mr. McCulloch's church in the morning; sacrament administered, and a description of Christ's crucifixion by a ghost-like, consumptive gentleman from the North, with one foot in the grave, in the most elegant and impressive style imaginable. Singing by officers of the army. P.M. Walk about over this old ruined Spanish town — one or two American houses only. In front of one see General Worth walking about.

On his return to the North, in the early spring, Hayes found the cities of New Orleans and Cincinnati stricken with the cholera, and the citizens depressed with direful apprehensions. The summer was spent quietly in closing up his law partnership at Fremont [1] and in preparing to remove to Cincinnati.

---

[1] It was by reason of a petition presented to the County Court by Hayes about this time that the name of the town was changed from Lower Sandusky to Fremont.

CHAPTER IV

THE removal to Cincinnati was determined by considerations of health and by the hope of gaining a larger field of
effort. The climate of the northern part of the State caused
frequent throat trouble and excited apprehension of pulmonary
weakness. Moreover, Hayes had the feeling that he had fallen
into a rut, that he was not making the progress he was capable
of, that the somewhat narrow life of the county town was dead-
ening to ambition and restrictive of the wider outlook on life that
he craved. The travels in the East and the visit to Texas had
brought him home with renewed strength of body and with more
eager desire for professional activity and success. In this mood
he turned his eyes to Cincinnati, at that time not only the largest
city of the State, but also the leading city of the West, the centre
of the greatest business activity and of the highest culture. For
twenty years its growth had been the marvel of the whole country; its central situation, mild climate, and other natural advantages attracting to it able, energetic, and ambitious young men
from the older States, and industrious and worthy immigrants
from Germany and Great Britain, until in 1849 it numbered
118,000 people. Thirty years had passed since its incorporation
as a city. The increase of population from 1830 to 1840 was
ninety per cent, and for the next decade one hundred and fifty
per cent. Its accessibility to iron and coal mines and limestone,
the facilities offered for cheap transportation by canal, and river,
and railway to all points of the compass, and especially to the
vast territory stretching to the west and south, for the distribution of products, and the fruitfulness of the lands constituting
the great Mississippi basin, had made Cincinnati one of the
most important manufacturing cities in the Union.

Thus, Cincinnati had become the mart of an extensive com-
merce. Wharves crowded the river front for several miles, ware-

houses were built for the reception of the great staples of the South, and jobbers, packers, and manufacturers supplied in exchange the commodities of the North. Intimate social relations sprang up between the people of the two sections whose interests were now so closely connected. Merchants of Cincinnati had winter homes in New Orleans; and in midsummer, many planters of the Mississippi Valley sought recreation on the beautiful hills overlooking the Ohio, or found temporary homes on the shores of the Great Lakes. This intercourse influenced profoundly the politics of the Northwestern States, and retarded the growth of antislavery sentiments. Nay, more, to the shame of a class, be it said, policy led for a time to the suppression of free discussion.

Cincinnati was not merely a business centre. It had an intelligent and cultivated society, whose influence was widely extended. In 1837, Harriet Martineau, who was entertained in the best private houses, was charmed with the life of the city. If some whom she met were timid and awkward, most were well-bred, and the "spirit and sovereignty of the conversation were worthy of the people assembled." Each year added to the ethical as well as the material growth of this young city. Its schools became the pride of all; religious institutions were strongly supported; libraries were established; literary societies were formed; the fine arts were encouraged; and the press increased in excellence and influence. The surrounding country impressed visitors with its loveliness. Miss Martineau has described it as it was in 1837 — and as many recall it at a later period, before the exigencies of growth had destroyed the contour of the hills. The view was from the Montgomery Road: "It was of that melting beauty which dims the eyes and fills the heart, — that magical combination of all elements, of hill, wood, lawn, river, with a picturesque city steeped in evening sunshine, the impression of which can never be lost, nor ever communicated."

It was November 10, 1849, when Hayes left Fremont for Cincinnati. "Health and stimulus my principal motives," he confides to his diary. A visit of some weeks with his relatives at Columbus delayed his arrival at his new home until Christmas Eve. The first few days were spent in renewing old acquaintances, in making new, and in seeking an office. By January 8 he was established in an office with John W. Herron, "a good fellow by accounts and by appearance and 'sign' — as the hunters say." And "now," he adds, "for a period of waiting, patience, perseverance." He was full of hope and strong of purpose to succeed. The best houses were open to him; social life was attractive and congenial; and courts and bar were cordial in good will. There were at that time some hundred and seventy-five lawyers dividing the business — not a large ratio to the population of the district. Among them such men as Salmon P. Chase, Caleb B. Smith, Judge William Johnston, George E. Pugh, Alphonso Taft, George H. Pendleton, William S. Groesbeck, and Bellamy Storer were prominent. Hayes was prepared to be patient and to trust to his success in making friends for winning his share of business. His Kenyon College friend, Stanley Matthews, and Manning F. Force and George Hoadley, Jr., whom he had met at the Harvard Law School, were already well started in practice, and they gave him much encouragement.

But this period of waiting was not to be one of sitting with folded hands. The old habit of reading, study, and persistent self-examination was renewed. January 25 the diary says: —

I am now living again a student, with abundant leisure and few cares. Why may I not, by a few hours daily spent in systematic study, regain all I have lost in the last three or four unfortunate years spent or wasted at the North? Let me awake to my old ambition to excel as a lawyer, as an advocate. For style and language read Webster and Burke, Byron and Bulwer. The last two are strange names to be heard in a student's mouth, but to counteract the cramping effect of legal studies and practice and to give one that *copia verborum* and power of intense expression, which are so essential to success as a jury advocate, what are better? For mental discipline, read carefully and thoughtfully the most logical treatises on evidence, pleading, or kindred topics.

February 19 he wrote his uncle of his mode of life and prospects as follows: —

My office is in the "Law Building." The lower story is occupied by the express offices, an auction store, and a telegraph office; the upper stories by about eighteen lawyers, three or four architects, and a cooper or two, about one third of whom sleep in their offices or rooms adjoining. The rooms rent for about $10 per month each. Our office is one of the best, if not the best, in the building. In one corner of the room, about twelve feet square is partitioned off for a bedroom, in which are two husk mattresses on bunks the size of Mrs. B.'s lounge, a washstand, a bureau, and divers pegs on which hang divers dusty garments. In the morning about five o'clock, an Irishman (who is not a son of temperance) comes in, builds a fire, and sweeps out the office; about seven, more or less, the newsboy comes with the daily paper, and we get up, scratch open our eyes, read the news, and go to breakfast. My boarding-house is three squares off; a very respectable set of boarders; one Old School Presbyterian clergyman; four or five intelligent Scotch merchants, also Presbyterians, but not members of our preacher's church, and strong on doctrinal points; an agreeable lawyer and his lady (an old schoolmate of Fanny's); a young Methodist New Yorker who is always getting the worst of the argument from the Scotchmen; an insurance broker from Connecticut, very like John Pease, and with more sense than all the rest; two or three nondescripts; an old widow lady, great on homœopathy and Swedenborgianism, a son of hers, about forty, who echoes his mother's sentiments most dutifully; and myself.

While we are gone to breakfast, our Irishman and his wife make up the beds, bring water and brush off the dust, never omitting to arrange the books and papers on our tables *right wrong exactly*. After breakfast, I read law, student fashion, till noon, when one of us goes to the post-office, and then read news and letters, if there are any, until dinner. Every few days a forenoon is spent in court, if anything interesting is going on. Dinner at one o'clock. Remain in the office until near four, when we sally out to call on friends or ladies — in short, in search of *prey*. About half-past five I go to the gymnasium. . . . About half our evenings are spent in the office, one or two evenings a week with the ladies, and one or two at lectures, "Sons" [of Temperance], or something of that sort. Among the lawyers in this building are Judge Walker, Judge Road, Tom Gallagher, Gohlson & Minor, etc., etc., all clever and social. I attend church at Mr. Nicholson's (Episcopal). He is a very showy, dashing declaimer, once a Methodist, who draws large crowds of the younger sort. My Sunday resort is Mr. Jones's (who, by the way, often mentions you). There I find often some young lady (or now that George is East, his wife) with whom I go to church in the morning and return to dine (*mem.*, great Sunday dinners Mrs. Jones gets up), and in the afternoon to church again, or not, as suits the crowd.

I belong to a delightful little club composed of lawyers, artists, merchants, and teachers, which meets once a week — has debates, conversations (similar, I suppose, to those of the "Fremont Literary Association, H. Everett, Secretary"), essays, and oysters. All this looks well for enjoyment; but you would know the prospect of getting into business. This is not different from what I expected when I came here. All who stay and are found in their offices ready to do business, do get it. I think I can see some symptoms of work. About a week ago a substantial coal dealer accidentally stumbled in and gave me a five-dollar retainer to defend a suit for which I shall charge him twenty-five dollars when finished. Mr. Jones has given me a lot of notes which will probably have to be sued; if so, there is probably a hundred dollars more if I *succeed* in collecting them. It is a difficult affair, but I feel pretty confident of collecting them. I have two houses which wish to do for me what they can; at present, their business is in the hands of regular attorneys and they cannot change except by degrees and slowly. Their business would support me. Stem, Baker & Co., also speak good words for me occasionally.

In the months that follow the diary gives frequent evidence of diligent reading in law and literature, the attendance on lectures, and the making of acquaintances. After a month the young lawyer could see some hopeful signs of business. There is recurrence to the thought that the years spent in the North had been wasted. "Oh, the waste of those five precious years at [Lower] Sandusky!" he writes in one place. "Shall I ever recover what I have lost? I believe I can, and so will go on, high of heart and full of hope, determined to do whatever my hand findeth to do with my might." In these months there was assiduous reading of the law writers — "Starkie on 'Evidence,' with occasional sips of Greenleaf and reported cases; Kent on 'Negotiable Paper,' referring to our statutes and the decisions in Ohio; Story's 'Promissory Notes,' in connection with Ohio Reports." Besides this there was renewed study of logic and a return to German; Bulwer's "Schiller" reviving interest in the language and literature of the Fatherland.

The little club Hayes spoke of in the letter to his uncle was the Literary Club, which included in its membership some of the ablest men of the city. The club was famous in the years that followed for the number of eminent men who were members, and for having furnished to the Union armies a greater number of officers than perhaps any other society in the North. In the weekly meetings which Hayes was diligent in attending, he came in contact in a helpful and inspiring way with all that was best in the intellectual life of the city, and he made enduring friendships. March 3, 1850, he records: "Made my first speech in the club last night. So-so, but ratherish good, considering. Shall improve the privileges of the club in future to the fullest." That he kept his resolution is evidenced by many entries in his diary. But speaking at the club was not easy for him, nor was he entirely satisfied with his success. "I am not a good speaker, for such a body," he writes; "I must have the stimulus of an audience, or of a cause — an object — or I am a tame talker. This I shall try to mend for the sake of the exercise."

Subsequently, Hayes became a member of the Ohio Historical and Philosophical Society, and of other societies of a social and charitable nature. During the decade in Cincinnati he was also an active member of the Independent Order of Odd Fellows, which he had joined at Lower Sandusky, and for a part of the period, at least, of the Sons of Temperance. He was in frequent requisition for lectures before various lodges of the Odd Fellows, and the diary mentions with natural pride the applause and prominence that came to him therefrom. Hayes's interest in temperance led him to make his first efforts at distinctively public speaking. Of his first temperance speech, which was made November 18, 1850, at a Presbyterian church, he says: —

The remarks were extempore, being the first speech of the kind I ever made to a mixed audience. It is not very difficult, requires more preparation of the particular discussion, so as to fasten the heads of it in my mind, or a better knowledge of the subject without any previous preparation for the particular speech. In time I fancy I can make a decent temperance speech.

Two or three days later the diarist defines somewhat his temperance views — views which he continued substantially to hold throughout his life: —

I am a sincere but not extreme or violent friend of the temperance cause. I mean to prepare myself to speak on this subject by accumulating and arranging in my memory as many interesting facts, arguments, and statistics as I can; also by jotting down my own ideas on the subject as they occur to me. The learning to speak as well as the notoriety (not to speak of the good I may do) are objects worthy of the pains.

There was much of a public character to amuse, to entertain, and to instruct, as this was the period when Jenny Lind and Kossuth made captive with song and eloquent pathos all Americans; when the great figures of the stage were Charlotte Cushman, Edwin Forrest, James E. Murdoch, and James Henry Hackett; and when it was the fashion to attend the lectures of such men as Emerson, Agassiz, Mann, Lieber, Stockton, and

Beecher. We catch glimpses of these in the diary, and of the impression they made; as, for example: —

February 19, 1850. — Just returned from the lecture-room of the Young Men's Mercantile Library Association, where I heard a most eloquent and glorious lecture from Rev. Thomas Stockton — "Materialism, the Foundation of Irreligion, and Spiritualism the Corner-stone of Piety." Mr. Stockton certainly resembles Henry Clay in personal appearance as well as in genius.

In the spring of 1850, Emerson delivered a course of lectures which were well attended. Of his first lecture on "Natural Aristocracy" we are told that, "It was quaint and queer in expression, but suggestive and pithy — rather a series of disjointed thoughts on the same subject than a methodical, sustained chain of reasoning and discourse." "It strikes me that he shows himself a keen, close observer rather than a profound thinker." Hayes met Emerson and we have preserved the points of two conversations: —

Friday, May 24. — Called on Ralph Waldo Emerson at the Burnet House in company with Collins and Spofford, as a committee to invite Mr. Emerson to meet the Literary Club on some evening convenient to himself for the purpose of a free confab on literary men and matters. Mr. Emerson is above the middle height, a tolerable figure, but rather awkward; dresses in the plainly genteel style — black surtout and pants, black satin vest and cravat, common shoes. His head is not large, forehead low and narrow, hair cut short — a brown color, eyes a greyish blue, a rather large nose with deep lines from the nostrils on either side arching around the mouth, but not so as to give an unpleasant expression. Is agreeable in his manners and first address. Talks, as he speaks, freely, and in a somewhat quaint way.

He spoke of the clubs of London. Said he, "The clubs are London. One does not know London until he knows the clubs." He was introduced to the Athenæum as an honorary member. "Only thirteen strangers can be introduced at the same time — one from a nation. There are some twelve hundred members. And to a bachelor, his club is his all. It introduces him to an agreeable society of the first men in London, to a good library and reading-room — the best selected library in London, to good eating at cost prices. Entrance fee one hundred dollars, and thirty dollars per year. The bachelor's letters are sent to the club hall, a noble building. He meets his friends here, invites others to dine with him, gets the latest news, etc. . . .

"English gentlemen affect a slowness and hesitancy of speech. It is like the country — like a man just from his estate. To speak fluently is too like an attorney, which is thought low.

"Macaulay was not a successful debater. His best efforts were on the Reform Bill. He did not come into the debate until near its close. After he had spoken, all the speeches on the other side were in reply to him. Macaulay is the growth of the present state of society in England. He is a cockney. All the English are cockneys. He affects an elegance and youthfulness of style in his dress, which is unfitting in a man who has grey hairs. I have an old grudge against him because of his abuse of Bacon. He has abused all of England's noblest names. His History is a libel on the English character. No man is found who escapes him. Sidney and Hampden are not spared. His History has the merit of proceeding upon the principle that the history of a nation is not the history of its officers, but of its people — not an original notion with him, although Jeffrey very ungenerously gives him credit for it. Jeffrey knew that Carlyle had stated it long ago.

"I met Prince Albert in one of the clubs. Buckland was explaining to him some mechanism. He is a fine-looking man. I have said I never saw a good-looking German, but he is one."

Such are a few points he spoke of in a half-hour's chat. He has the common fault of his sect — Transcendentalists — of thinking that the hearty, earnest, sincere benevolence in the world is all centred in themselves; that all others are so bigoted as not to see the truth, or are too timid boldly to avow it; or, as Mr. Emerson said, "have too little pluck to avow it." He spoke of Henry Ward Beecher as one of the bold, hopeful reformers. Bushnell he wishes well, because he thinks well and hopes well for mankind.

Sunday, May 26. — This evening our Literary Club met and received a visit from Mr. Ralph Waldo Emerson. He, after being introduced to each member, sat down and began a free and easy conversation on literary men and things in England. Talked two and a half hours on all matters from letters to raising corn and pigs. A very pleasant man. A few items I give: —

"There are in London, it is estimated, seventy thousand persons who are considered 'good society'; and those who compose it find such a variety of persons, ideas, facts, important and trifling, always interesting in this great multitude, that the rest of the world is scarcely thought of. America is like Turkey or Hungary, interesting and talked of only when some particular circumstance makes it an object of notice. These people are therefore quite uninformed as to all the rest of the world — that is, the local peculiarities, politics, and geography which are usually known to travelled people.

"I spoke to Carlyle — thinking he would have none of this narrow cockneyism about him — of the future of the English race, and said that America was to be the seat of the English. With a continent, a quarter of the world at their command, to be peopled and improved by them, in America would be their history. Carlyle was restive, vexed, uneasy, could n't think of it. They see so much wealth, power, energy, and talent; they see the whole world passing in and out of their gates, that they cannot realize or imagine the possibility that there is any *outside* nation or people who shall ever be their rivals.

"In America there have been no creative, constructive, imaginative men. They do not come much oftener than once in two hundred years, and perhaps it is not our turn yet to have one. Wordsworth, Scott, and Shakespeare are creative men.

"Every author's writings are the transcript of his own life, emotions, etc., — it is autobiography thinly veiled. George Sand, the best living French novelist, has written nothing but her own confessions, veiled under the names and characters of her romances. Shakespeare had all emotions and passions — portrayed all in his dramas. . . .

"I never knew what people meant by 'Transcendental.' If it means those who believe with Plato in man's immortality, they should be called Platonists. But that does not describe the class to whom the term is applied — Coleridge and others. They are men who believe in themselves, in their own convictions, and rely upon them; these are the true men. I have some hope of such; they hope for themselves, they believe there is something more than this narrow scene in which we are to act. Men who are self-trusting, self-relying, earnest are called by the name Transcendentalists."

Mr. Emerson seemed quite puzzled, not to say vexed, when speaking of this subject. It was forced upon him by questions and suggestions.

"Macaulay is a man whose wares are all marketable. He is popular, simple, splendid in style. He has a prodigious memory, but to what end? What good does he do?"

Mr. Stephenson asked, "What good has Carlyle done?"

"Why, Carlyle [replied Emerson] has done the good which any man does who makes people think. He makes them *feel* their immortality; a man can't *think* without feeling that.

"Macaulay wrote a letter to his constituents dated 'Windsor Castle.' He happened to be there once a half-hour and took that opportunity to write the letter, or rather to *date* it, for he carried it with him ready written. It has been thrown up to him ever since. It was such a *faux pas*. A man like Macaulay, too, with such a sense of the proper.

"Children ought to have their imaginations cultivated; it must be done while they are young. Some things must be impressed on the mind when it is susceptible and tender, or they never can be. If children want to hear a story, tell it to them if you can, or get somebody that can do it, if you cannot. Give them the 'Arabian Nights,' attractive books; fill their minds with glorious thoughts. Let them early learn what they are, spiritual and immortal; and they must be, when men, such as they ought to be."

In a letter to his sister, Mrs. Platt, Mr. Hayes further discourses of Emerson: —

CINCINNATI, June 12, 1850.[1]

DEAR FANNY, — I do not think I shall visit you until the July term of the Circuit Court, when I suppose Uncle will also be at Columbus to look after his immortal lawsuit. . . .

I more than half suspect that you manifest an interest in Mr. Emerson more for the purpose of affording me an excuse to branch out on topics which have been uppermost in my circles the last few weeks than because of any great attractiveness you discover in the subject. I can say, as I heard Mr. Emerson say of Carlyle, that I have gossiped so much about him lately that I am almost ashamed to open my lips about him. His qualifications and peculiarities as a lecturer or essayist on miscellaneous subjects stand quite differently in my estimation from his opinions — not opinions either, but impressions or "inspirations" — in regard to religious subjects. On general subjects, such as "The Gentleman," "Eloquence," "England," etc., he is a charming, but not, in an equal degree, an instructive lecturer. He strikes me, contrary to my preconceived notions of him, as a close, keen observer rather than a profound thinker. There is no logic or method in his essays or lectures. A syllogism he despises. The force of a connected chain of reasoning, his mind seems incapable of appreciating. There is no such thing as one of his thoughts *following* from another. The natural result of this lack of logic is that one finds it next to impossible to grasp and hold fast what he says. When you leave the lecture-room you remember that he said many witty, sensible, pretty, and some deep things, but you feel at a loss where to begin in attempting to recall them. The whole lecture seems but a bead-string of suggestions, fancies, ideas, anecdotes, and illustrations, having no connection with each other except that they are upon the same subject. They are all either quaint, paradoxical, sensible, humorous, or have some other element which gives them interest if not positive value. They are expressed in a terse, singular style — Saxon but not at all Carlylish, and delivered in a subdued, earnest tone which is in perfect keeping with the style and thought.

Mr. Emerson is middle-aged, modest but self-possessed, of a good-humored, honest strain, which gives one a favorable impression of his heart and character. He gesticulates scarcely at all and awkwardly. I never knew one who could hold more undivided attention of his audience.

The matter of his lectures — the substance of them — is contained in a few leading ideas which pervade all his productions. The filling up — the seasoning — is, of course, new and different in different lectures, and his lectures are remarkable for being stuffed with thoughts; but still the great stratum which underlies and supports all he writes and says consists of a very few notions which are repeated and reappear over and over again, a thousand times in his various writings. Reading any one

[1] Mr. Hayes wrote at the head of this letter: "Carlyle said America had twenty millions of bores. Here is a specimen of my nationality."

book or even lecture will make you master of nearly all of them. They are such as the following: That men are born with a certain portion of magnetism, or Divinity in them, which determines their rank among their fellows. That man should have faith in this Divinity, faith in himself; that he, in fact, does have this faith in proportion to the amount of magnetism which belongs to him. That all uneasiness and striving is vanity. If a man strives after what is not in him he can never attain to it. If he appears to win it by effort he is after all a *sham*. He may deceive the world, but he does n't deceive himself, for when in the presence of another who has the true magnetism, *both* know and feel where the real power is. This is a sort of fatalism, but it is comfortable, it is satisfying to a man, whatever is his condition. I remember one of his sentences expressing this notion: "When you meet a man with the same tastes with yourself, but with greater magnetism, he will not only rule you but make you love your ruler." If your tastes are not the same, your strength does not work on the same level — you are not antagonists — you do not come in collision.

Mr. Emerson says Macaulay is a cockney, that his memory is a prodigy, like Jenny Lind's voice, but to what purpose is it? He is the greatest conversationalist in England except Charles Austin, an eminent advocate of London. Macaulay has no faith in high souls, high destiny. His History is a libel on English character. He touches no great name in history that he does n't daub, e.g., Penn, Sidney, Bacon, and others.

Disraeli is a fop. He has strung together in his novels things beautiful and true from the literatures of all languages. Like all his tribe he is a vender of old clothes, collected from a thousand backs, soaped and washed and varnished to look like new.

He is a worshipper of Carlyle, but says that in temper and manners, particularly to strangers, Carlyle is a bear.

Mr. Emerson was a Unitarian clergyman. Now he has some misty notions on religion resembling the German philosophy. He delivered three lectures, "Instinct and Inspiration," "Nature," etc., of which no one could make out anything definite or valuable. I *guess* at the ideas in this wise: (If what I say seems foolish don't suppose Emerson said the same, for he does n't *say* at all — he hints or intimates or walks round about what he *would* say, but don't say.) — The common distinction between mind and matter — there is nothing in it. Matter is *spirit with certain* attributes superadded, as color, weight, hardness, etc., etc. Spirit in the abstract, without these attributes, there is no such thing. Matter in the abstract, not based on spirit, is an absurdity. Matter and spirit are identical, in a certain sense; therefore spirit is the subtle essence which pervades all things. There is no *personal* creative God, but spirit which is diffused through all, which is a part of man and beast, is God. The highest manifestation of spirit is man. Man differs from mere matter in this: his spirit is self-conscious. Therefore man is *nearer* than any other object in nature to an impersonation of Deity.

And it may be said with more truth of man than of anything else, that he is God — that there is more God in him than in anything else. It is of the nature of spirit to be creative, to work itself out into material forms. This spirit is like an all-pervading yeast which ferments incessantly, working out new and constantly improving forms of what is called matter. Men die, but the spirit which was in their bodies takes to itself new attributes of a higher and more perfect nature, or mixes with the spirit of all things — with God — and goes on bubbling to all eternity, a drop in the great caldron of spirit which is at once God and the universe.

Now, in all this account of Mr. Emerson's theology (?) I have not said a word or used an illustration that I ever heard him use; but if I could comprehend what he would have said, if he had come down out of the clouds or up out of the mists, the notions I have given you are like those he would have expressed. The German philosophers, with Coleridge, Carlyle, Emerson, and others, are called by some Pantheists or Transcendentalists. Mr. Emerson hates those terms. He says Platonists would be more accurate, but yet not precisely so. He classes the writings of Plato, Mahomet, Confucius, the Bible, and the religious books of all nations, in the same category — all valuable as exhibiting the strivings of the human mind after a knowledge of Deity, or of themselves. He speaks of the feelings awakened by music, by the sight of boundless landscape, the ocean, the skies, etc., etc., as the longing of the spirit in us to mingle with the great ocean of spirit of which every being has a part.

The interest manifested by Hayes in the lectures of Emerson was characteristic of his catholic intellectual sympathies. He always read much and widely. He early made friends of the great authors, and the friendship was one that lasted him through life. In his student days he found time for extensive readinh outside of his courses of study. History and modern poetry hag most attraction for him at that period, but the older English poets also began to claim his attention. Near the beginning of his last year in college (at the age of nineteen) he writes: —

Kenyon College, December 10, 1841. — My reading heretofore has consisted chiefly of history, modern poetry, and such miscellaneous writings as chanced to fall in my way. I have it is true for a long time been an ardent admirer of Shakespeare and Milton, but till within a week I never tasted the sweet waters which are to be found in the authors of old English literature. I have as yet but just sipped the pure streams which flow from this source, but a single taste makes me love them. I first read Spenser, the father of English poetry. He has not the studied elegance of some modern writers, but his deficiency in polish and grace is more than compensated by the rich, vigorous flow of thought which runs through all his poems. Nature is painted as she is, not always beautiful or grand but ever charming from variety. Spenser has faults, but they are like spots on the sun which do not mar the beauty of his light, nor prevent the vivifying influence of his warmth. The tales of Spenser are of that romantic and marvelous kind which is usually found in the writings of the chivalrous ages when the Evil One employed magic spells to overcome the virtue of the good, and horrid monsters to subdue the bravery of the "trow Knights." In the "Fairy Queen" the master passions of the human bosom are drawn with a pencil of light. The meaner passions, envy, hatred, and jealousy, are represented as a "right jollie teem" drawing the "Queen of Darknesse" in her two-wheeled "carr" and driven by "Satanie" sitting on the beam, lashing them into a foam with his scourge of scorpion's tails. Ah! that some modern genius would show the deluded victims of passions, what a driver directs their course, and what a "jollie teem" is hurrying them to destruction. How quick they would lock the wheel, and cut the tugs to escape from the "faire crew" which madly rushes on! They would even risk life and limb in leaping from the "carr" of the damned one who drives. But no, our modern gentry are too busied culling the choice flowers of the "old poets" to think of benefiting their race. Instead of resorting to the same source from which they drew immortality, these are content to deck themselves with the cast-off drapery of another's creation.

A few days later he records the pleasure with which Scott's "Lord of the Isles" had set his heart tingling. He wishes he had the power of description there displayed. Then "the characters of our Revolutionary sires should be portrayed in colors whose brightness would eclipse the sun. The names of our heroes and sages would outlive 'the Bruce' in the affections of freemen." Before his graduation from college Hayes had read the principal English poets: Spenser, Shakespeare, Milton, Pope, Byron, Moore, Campbell, and Scott. In history, besides various compendiums, he had read Goldsmith's Rome and Greece, Gillie's Greece, Ferguson's Rome, Gibbon's "Decline and Fall," Milman's Jews, Bancroft, Marshall, Hume, Mackintosh, and others. He had the habit of noting in his diary striking passages from the authors he was reading. These quotations, which are very numerous, show an appreciation of what was finest in thought, loftiest in sentiment, and noblest in motive. A man does not write down great and inspiring words, unless these appeal to him; he does not record what is pure and ennobling in sentiment unless this strikes a responsive chord in his own bosom. "Who-

ever is a genuine follower of Truth," Hayes quotes in one place
from Burke, "keeps his eye steady upon his guide, indifferent
whither he is led, provided that she is the leader." There was a
principle of action which Hayes desired to make his own. His
frequent self-examination, his constant measuring of his achievements, not by what others had done or by what the world said,
but by his own ideal of conduct and effort, show how simply
and sincerely he strove to follow where Truth led the way.

There was no relaxation in general reading while he was a law
student at Columbus and at Cambridge. Much time was given
to German and satisfactory progress is recorded from time to
time. Shakespeare and Milton are read again, and at Cambridge a considerable course in ethics is undertaken. This
embraced Cicero's "Offices," Aristotle's "Ethics" in Gillie's
translation, Beattie's writings on morals, Paley's "Moral Philosophy," and Locke's "Essay on the Human Understanding."
Of Aristotle's "Ethics" Hayes writes: —

> Upon the whole, I have not learned so much from this volume as I
> should from the perusal of a modern book upon the same subject. I
> found many ideas which are to be found in later writers without any ac-
> knowledgment; much that was very sensible and little that was not so.
> Yet the impression upon my mind was not so enduring or strong as to
> render the whole my own.

Commenting on Paley's discussion of the moral sense Hayes
writes: —

> I cannot, at present, form an opinion upon this celebrated question,
> but incline to the belief in a moral sense to a certain extent. My posi-
> tion is, that all men naturally approve what they believe right; or per-
> haps better this, all men have a faculty, or by what other name it may
> be called, by which they are led to believe there is a moral quality in
> actions. This does not assert that men naturally approve what is
> right, for this would imply that men really know what is right, and all
> would then agree, which is confessedly false; but it only means that men
> have such a disposition that, if conscience was sufficiently enlightened,
> all would think alike upon *all important points* in casuistry. Now, this
> cannot be overturned by the arguments advanced against a moral sense
> which at the same time *discerns* and *approves* the right. First, all men
> do not approve the same acts. True; but *all* men do approve what
> they *believe* is right. Secondly, neither imitation, nor any principle of
> association by which certain acts done to third persons are judged of as
> if they affected ourselves, can account for the fact, that in all ages every

individual of every nation has exhibited the strongest evidence of possessing this disposition—to approve certain acts and disapprove of others. Nor can it be accounted for on our author's principles: that everything is to be judged of by its tendency, and is right because it is expedient. For men speak of this moral quality in many instances, when the act is of such a nature that they cannot say it is either expedient or the contrary; and acts are every day pronounced wrong which, to human foresight, are highly expedient.

This reasoning is by no means satisfactory to myself, but in my present circumstances I can give no better. I do believe that "honesty," according to the old adage, "is the best policy," as a general rule, or that which is *really* expedient is right; yet I do not believe that this expediency is the test of the morality of actions, or that an act is therefore right, which conduces to the greatest happiness, because of such tendency. But a safer rule would, it seems to me, be to say, *that is right which God commands or wills, because He wills it.* With this rule men would only be solicitous to know his will. While if the rule makes happiness the test, it will vary as greatly as do men's ideas of this greatest good, and the standard would really be made to depend on the whims, prejudices, and passions of men who are enough under the dominion of these, without constituting them guides. Virtue, he defines, the doing good to man, in obedience to the will of God, for the sake of eternal happiness. Why would it not be equally correct to say, "for the sake of eternal happiness, because God commands it"? Rewards and punishments appear to me additional *motives* to obedience, not the sole, nor even the "chiefest" inducements.

And of Locke's distinctive doctrine this judgment is expressed: —

I do not know what opinion to form about his doctrine of innate ideas. If I had heard nothing against it, I should adopt it. I cannot discover its weak points. His remarks about the idea of God are certainly correct. What two persons have the same notion of the Supreme Being?

Besides this course in solid reading Hayes was becoming acquainted with Addison, whom he found a pleasant companion, and he was not forgetting the poets, either English or American. Recording the purchase of a volume containing the poems of Drake, Prior, and Keats he says: "The poems I've not read, but Willis's observations give their chief characteristics, I suppose. If Willis would not strive so much after quaint forms of expression and would write with more shortness and perspicuity, I would be better pleased with the drippings of his pen."

In fiction Scott and Dickens were his favorite authors at this time. Writing March 3, 1844, Hayes says: —

"Form your habits so that every change must be for the better," says Paley. This I am trying to do, so far as reading aright goes. I read Chillingworth over and over again. For Saturday nights' reading the "Spectator" is my companion. Sunday the German Testament and Milton are my friends.

The good habit of reading was maintained during the first years of law practice spent at Fremont. In addition to the continued study of the law writers, time was regularly given to general literature. D'Aubigné's "History of the Reformation" was early read.[1] May 7, 1845, soon after he had established himself in practice, we have this entry in the diary: —

I am now fairly settled. Let me see how I will arrange my plans for study and business: — Read Greenleaf's "Evidence" and Story's "Agency," so as to finish them both in six weeks. Read a chapter in the Testament (German). One case a week in Smith's "Leading Cases" touching some topic of agency or evidence. Read a little Bacon and Burke. Study Livy an hour in the morning and logic at night. Poetry and light literature Sunday. Attend church regularly, and do all my business promptly. Now, of so much, some must many days be neglected. The order of the preference shall be: Latin, Evidence, Agency, German, Bacon, Logic, Burke, Smith's Cases; business first, always.

During the trip to Texas many novels of Scott, Bulwer, Dickens, and Cooper were read. And with the removal to Cincinnati study and general reading were resumed, as has already been noted, with quickened enthusiasm. Webster and Burke, Shakespeare and Milton, Byron and Bulwer, are sought again and again, while constantly the range of interest is widened. Mrs. Adams's letters are read with keen pleasure. Taylor's "Natural History of Society," Hawthorne's "Scarlet Letter,"

---

[1] "D'Aubigné constantly affirms that in his opinion, the Reformation was the immediate work of the Divine hand. Now it seems to me that Providence interferes no more in the greatest affairs of men than in the smallest, and that neither individuals nor nations are any more the objects of a special interposition of the Divine Ruler than the inanimate things of the world. The Creator gave to every creature of his hand its laws at the time of its creation; and whatever can happen in accordance with those laws He doubtless foresaw, and it cannot be supposed that his laws are so imperfect that special interpositions are necessary to render them capable of fulfilling their design nor that it is possible for them to be violated. The Reformation like other revolutions was agreeable to principles which have existed since the world began." (Diary, April 15, 1845.)

Emerson's "Essays," Humboldt's "Cosmos," Thackeray's "Pendennis," Ik Marvel's "Fresh Gleanings" ("a pleasant book, dreamy and spirituelle, mixed with the spice of close homely observation — a good hash — served with the relish of pure, undefiled old English"), John Forster's "Statesmen of the Commonwealth" and "Life of Sir John Eliot," and "Tristram Shandy," [1] are some of the books mentioned as being read in the first eighteen months of life in Cincinnati. All this was, of course, in addition to the reading of law and the study of German, the work for the Literary Club and the Odd Fellows, and the attendance on courses of lectures by Emerson, Agassiz, and others. But the young lawyer was by no means satisfied with what he had accomplished. Writing August 16, 1851, he says: —

I feel that I have read too much light reading, too little that is useful, instructive, solid, of late. I must give up my mental habits; become more energetic by tough reading. Let my lightest for a time be biographies and miscellanies such as [concern] the statesmen of Cromwell's time.

The same day he began the thorough reading of the life of William Ellery Channing, — "one of the noblest, purest men who ever lived," in his opinion, — from which he gained much inspiration; and two months later he writes: —

In general literature, read Burke, Shakespeare, and the standard authors constantly, and always have on hand some book of worth not before perused. Avoid occasional reading of a light character. Read always as if I were to repeat it the day afterwards.

In the years that followed to the outbreak of the war, while increasing business, a larger participation in public affairs, and the growing cares and responsibilities of domestic life left less leisure for general reading, still the principle just set forth continued to be consistently practiced. More of the standard books were constantly being added to the list read by him, like Pope's

---

[1] "*August 12, 1851.* — Finished Sterne's *Tristram Shandy* yesterday. An amusing book; it seems to me not a great one. Sterne's fame rests upon it. *Tom Jones, Gil Blas, Don Quixote,* etc., etc., are none of them books which I like. *Don Quixote* is by far the best; the rest are bawdy, show great knowledge of human nature in its lower developments, but not great, pure, high, eloquent, or holy. One thinks less hopefully of man and woman after reading them. I am now attacking *The Sentimental Journey* — another of the same ilk." (Diary.)

Homer and Burton's "Anatomy of Melancholy"; modern writers like De Tocqueville, Irving, Carlyle, Buckle, and Prescott were read, and comprehensive courses in American history and exploration were pursued. Shakespeare, Milton, Burke, and the Bible were never for long periods out of his hands.[1] In what spirit he read portions of the sacred Scriptures the following passage from his diary of Sunday, April 24, 1853, reveals: —

Have been reading Genesis several Sundays, not as a Christian reads for "spiritual consolation," "instruction," etc., not as an infidel reads to carp and quarrel and criticize, but as one who wishes to be informed and furnished in the earliest and most wonderful of all literary productions. The literature of the Bible should be studied as one studies Shakespeare, for illustration and language, for its true pictures of man and woman nature, for its early historical record.

The demands of the law, however exacting, into whatever fields of special research they rendered it necessary for Hayes to make excursions, were never allowed to monopolize all his thought and all his interest. Always he had an ear for other voices than those that spoke with such eloquence of evidence and agency, of constitutional limitations and the intricacies of real property; always he had an eye for something higher and finer than jury trials and arguments before the Supreme Court.

---

[1] The diary continues to make frequent mention of the books read. Now and then with comment. For example, December 17, 1859, we have this: "Have read *Recollections of Choate* this week. He was a 'remarkable man,' as Dickens says so many Americans are. I have heard him pour out in impetuous torrents his warm and wordy eloquence. It was no doubt most effective in compelling verdicts from juries, but never struck me as 'high art' or (the real thing) genuine nature. His best production, 'Eulogy on Webster,' at Dartmouth, is very beautiful. The lesson of his life — that is, the best suggestion one gets from it — is the importance and value of perpetual and persevering labor in any direction which one's judgment selects. Diction — verbiage — was his idol. He sacrificed pleasure, health, all to it. Well, it is important. Western lawyers, Cincinnati lawyers, do neglect too much what is termed learning, scholarship. Let me read and reread the best poets, as Shakespeare, Milton, Byron; the model prose writers, or speakers rather, as Burke, Webster. Addison does not interest me. He is smooth but, to me, dull. Choate, if this book contains his best, was not equal to Corwin, or Judge Johnston in wit, in shrewd and telling remark, in anecdote, or illustration. With vastly more reading and scholarship than Judge Johnston, with more magnetic power, with warmth and enthusiasm, he was not equal to the Judge in brains, in natural ability, in power of illustration, in wit, or in shrewd mastery of the prejudices and biases of juries. Judge Johnston as a thinker, as a man of intellect, is far his superior."

He continued always to drink copiously at the wells of English undefiled; to associate in spirit with the great souls of the race, speaking to the world in books that are not for an age but for all time. And so steadily he was growing stronger and wiser in unconscious preparation for the greater work yet to be done.

CHAPTER V

COURTSHIP AND MARRIAGE

YOUNG Hayes speaks of himself in one place as not a "ladies' man." But his diary affords abundant proof that from early manhood he found pleasure in woman's society. While he was in college he records how agreeable had been his vacation intercourse with the young ladies of his home neighborhood. In his early days of law study he laments that the ladies were taking too much of his time. At Cambridge, as at Gambier, the distractions of society were not allowed to interfere with his studies. But in the few years at Fremont, when he was making his first efforts at the bar, much time was given to the fair sex. He had expected, or rather had hoped, to marry early. While at Cambridge he records a whimsical wager with a fellow student that he should be married before he was twenty-five. The diary discloses that now and again he fancied himself becoming deeply interested in some young woman whose charms and graces he gallantly celebrates. But, as he writes, "reflection and observation prevented anything serious" resulting from these "incipient courtships"; and the more of life he saw, the more critical he became and the less inclined to yield to a sudden vision of captivating grace. "How crotchety one grows on that subject as years bring wisdom and experience," he says; and he records from time to time the marriage of some young woman on whom he had bestowed attention; wishes her all happiness, and rejoices that he had not pressed his suit.

The beginning of the year 1851 found him heart whole and fancy free. Perhaps not quite fancy free. The fair face and winning presence of the one destined to complete and bless his life were already much in his thoughts. She, Lucy Ware Webb, had just completed her course at the Wesleyan Woman's College at Cincinnati.[1] There had been some slight acquaintance between

[1] Mrs. Mary C. Wilber, wife of the president of the college and an instructor, wrote in after years of Lucy Webb's college life: "She was ambitious to excel in her studies, to do thorough work; was ever diligent, and marked 'perfect in

the two for more than three years. The first meeting had been when he was on a visit at Delaware, Ohio, in July, 1847, when she was "a bonnie schoolgirl of sixteen."[1] She was a girl of singular charm of personality who made an instant impression on every one she met. The young attorney was no exception. He recalled three years later how in his thought he had then contrasted or compared her graces with those of a young woman whom he at that time somewhat "affected." Chance and inclination gave Hayes many opportunities during his first year in Cincinnati to cultivate his acquaintance with Miss Webb. One of the first calls he made after going to Cincinnati was at Wesleyan College, and before the springtime was over he was aware that he "must keep a guard on his susceptibilities or he should be in beyond his depth." This fate, however, seemed to have no terrors for him, for his attentions were not relaxed.

In the following September, at the marriage of Dr. Little, at Delaware, Hayes and Miss Lucy Webb with another couple "assisted"; and Hayes, in describing the wedding reception, reveals how constantly his thoughts were occupied with "the bright eyes and merry smiles of that lovely girl." This preoccupation was intensified with the passing months, and it was not long before it became manifest to the young man that he was "in beyond his depth," and that the great river against whose current he had ineffectually striven was bearing him, no longer

deportment,' and thus she won immediately the respect and approval of her teachers, to whom she was a beloved, trusted young friend. She had the affection and confidence of her schoolmates, for the unfaltering courtesy, which marked her course in public life, was equally marked in her schoolgirl associations. She was of a hopeful nature, wore a sunny face; was gay in a conservative sense, enjoying all proper amusements like a bright, healthy, happy schoolgirl. But I do not believe she ever engaged in any pleasures inconsistent with her profession as a Christian. Her loyalty to principle was as notable when a student as when mistress of the White House. She possessed in a large degree the ofttimes dangerous gift of wit; was quick in repartee, but was careful in its exercise never to wound the feelings of others. She had a high sense of honor, and an abounding charity for the weaknesses and mistakes of those not well anchored in principle."

[1] Mrs. Webb had moved from Chillicothe to Delaware, Ohio, to be with her two sons while they were in college. Lucy was permitted to attend some of the classes with her brothers and to receive instruction from the professors. When the sons graduated in 1847, the family moved to Cincinnati, where the young men began their courses in medicine and Lucy entered the Wesleyan Woman's College.

resisting, to the main. May 23, 1851, after an evening with Miss Webb, he dwells in his diary on her graces of person and character and frankly confesses that he is ready to surrender. "So we go," he says. "Another bachelor's revery! Let it work out its own results."

The climax now was rapidly reached. Three weeks later the happy lover almost burst into song as he wrote of troth plighted and serene peace attained: —

Saturday, June 14, 1851. — Last night, Friday evening, — Friday no longer an ill-starred day in my calendar, — I went out on Sixth Street, passing up from Fourth on the west side of Race, when, just as I passed the corner of Race and Longworth, I saw a magnificent horse plunging and leaping like mad, with a buggy at his heels, along the sidewalk towards the corner I was passing. — Let every one look and jump for his life! At the moment I saw a lady, nearly at my side, in equal danger with myself. Involuntarily I threw my arms around her and hurried her back into the friendly protection of the receding doorway of the engine-house at the corner. She was alarmed, but accepted most graciously my apology and thanked me for my gallantry. Why do I speak of this? As a good omen, or what? It was almost as unpremeditated as another [act] which is the occasion of all this gossip. I went on my way rejoicing, an inch taller for this feat — of "arms," shall I say? — and *naturally* turned into the gate south side of Sixth, next house east of Dr. Presley's church, and soon was chatting gaily with my — since a goodly time — "received ideal" of a cheerful, truthful, trusting, loving, and lovable girl, who might have been the original in many points of Hawthorne's Phœbe — the sunbeam of the "House of the Seven Gables"; or of the fairy in Ik Marvel's revery over the anthracite, with the "deep eye reaching back to the spirit; not the trading eye, weighing your purse; nor the worldly eye, weighing your position; nor the beastly eye, weighing your appearance; but the *heart's eye*, weighing your soul! An eye full of deep, tender, earnest feeling. An eye which looked on once, you long to look on again; an eye which will haunt your dreams; an eye which will give a color, in spite of you, to all your reveries. An eye which lies before you in your future, like a star in the mariner's heaven, by which unconsciously you take all your observations."

Then he writes of the joy with which he listened "to her talk, 'soft and low' — tones and voice just matching that otherwise matchless eye." They spoke of a family they had known at Delaware, then living in a house near by, and went to call on them. They had "a queer, cordial welcome from the two old maids" and their brother. After their return, Miss Webb "compared

LUCY WARE WEBB (AFTERWARDS MRS. R. B. HAYES)

At the age of sixteen, from a Daguerreotype

the two spinsters to Dora's aunts in 'Copperfield'"; and then, "on a sudden impulse, unmeditated, involuntary," he declared his love, to her manifest surprise, and she confessed she "liked him very well," and "faith was plighted for life." No wonder the happy lover "went home to dream of it all again and again."

Lucy Ware Webb was the daughter of Dr. James Webb, of Chillicothe, where she was born August 28, 1831. Her father had died when she was two years old, at Lexington, Kentucky, whither he had gone to arrange for manumitting slaves of his inheritance, with the intention of sending them to Liberia. This was the year of the terrible cholera scourge and he remained at Lexington, his native place, to care for the poor slaves and to encourage friends, — as Henry Clay was doing at Ashland at the same time, —until he himself was stricken and died. He had served when a mere youth as a member of the Kentucky mounted riflemen in the War of 1812, participating in the campaign of General Harrison at Fort Meigs and Fort Stephenson.[1] His father, Isaac Webb, was a soldier in the Virginia line in the Revolutionary War, and after its close, in 1790, removed to Kentucky. The mother of Lucy, Mrs. Maria Webb, was the daughter of Isaac Cook, a Revolutionary soldier of Connecticut, who emigrated to the old Northwest Territory about ten years before Ohio became a State.[2]

It is an interesting and remarkable fact that Mrs. Lucy Webb Hayes, who won the hearts of the Union soldiers in field and

[1] The site of Fort Stephenson is now a public park in Fremont, containing the City Hall and the Birchard Library. The Harrison Trail winds through Spiegel Grove. A great white oak, under which young Webb bivouacked one winter night, is known as "Grandfather's Tree."

[2] This well-known pioneer is said to have been six feet two inches in height, slender and perfectly erect to the day of his death. His hair was fine, black, and usually combed straight back. His complexion was dark, his eyes black and pleasant. His step was quick and elastic; his manners genial. He had facility in writing verse, and wrote the Carriers' Addresses for New Year's Day for over thirty-five years for the Scioto *Gazette*, the *Galaxy*, and other publications. He held official positions of local importance for many years. He was appointed a justice of the peace by Governor Tiffin in 1803; in 1804 a judge of the Court of Common Pleas, to which office he was afterward elected by the Legislature — serving twenty-seven years. He was appointed brigadier-general of militia by Governor Worthington in 1816. He was repeatedly elected a Representative in the Legislature from Ross County, serving from 1819 to 1830.

hospital, and later, as wife of the President, gained the high respect and honor of the whole American people, numbered among her direct ancestors seven men that served in the Revolutionary armies, two grandfathers, three great-grandfathers, and two great-great-grandfathers.[1] Toward the close of the century some of these, who had received lands for services, emigrated to the West, settli.g in Ohio and Kentucky. After Dr. Webb's death, his wife and children freed the family slaves without conditions, and continued always to take interest in their welfare, repeatedly giving them needed assistance.[2]

Late in July, Miss Webb left Cincinnati for a long visit to friends in other parts of the State. Apropos of her departure Hayes writes: —

I do and shall feel quite lonely without her. Pouring out one's thoughts and feelings into the same kindly listening ear daily for a month is enough to endear the listener, even without the aid of sex, beauty, and sweetness to strengthen the tie. . . . My loving, of course, grows with intercourse; but, what is better for the permanency of the attachment, my good opinion, my *liking*, gains with every day's acquaintance.

[1] Captain Isaac Webb, of the Virginia line of the Continental army, and Isaac Cook, 3d, of the Connecticut line, grandfathers; Lieutenant-Colonel Isaac Cook, Jr., of the Connecticut line, Captain Matthew Scott, of the Pennsylvania line, and James Ware, of the Virginia line, great-grandfathers; Captain Isaac Cook (who was in his sixty-sixth year when the war began), father of Lieutenant-Colonel Isaac Cook, of Connecticut, and Brigadier-General William Thompson, of Pennsylvania, great-great-grandfathers. General Thompson was a native of Ireland. He emigrated to America, and settled at Carlyle, Pennsylvania. He was captain in the cavalry service during the French war and made the acquaintance of Arthur St. Clair at Quebec, with whom he served during most of the Revolutionary War. He resided for a time at Pittsburgh, and was one of the purchasers of old Fort Pitt when it was abandoned by the British. In June, 1775, he was appointed colonel of a regiment of riflemen, joined the American forces at Cambridge, and, November 10, had a skirmish with the British at Lechmere Point. Was appointed brigadier, March 1, 1776; soon after succeeded Lee in command at New York, and in April was ordered to Canada to join General Sullivan in command of that department. He was in command at Three Rivers, and was made prisoner with Colonel Irvine. After his exchange, which was painfully prolonged, he returned to the service. (*The St. Clair Papers*, vol. I, pp. 17–21, and 368 *et seq.*)

[2] Friends advised Mrs. Webb, who was left in moderate circumstances, to sell the slaves, inasmuch as they could not then be sent to Liberia, and it was unlawful to free them in Kentucky. She replied: "Before I sell a slave I will take in washing to support my family."

Miss Webb greatly disliked to write letters — a characteristic which she retained throughout her life; though her letters when she did write were bright and interesting. It was nearly a month before Hayes received a word from her. He did not even know part of the time where she was, and his diary shows his anxiety and impatience. August 16 he writes: "Not heard from L. yet. Do not know where she is even. Her mother is equally in the dark. She thinks letter-writing a horrible task — little less than martyrdom. I did feel vexed about it, but am clear of that feeling now." It was not easy, however, to keep the vexed feeling down at the long intervals between her infrequent letters. The quality of Hayes's letters to Miss Webb, during this first period of separation after the engagement, is shown by the following excerpt from a letter dated Cincinnati, August 21: —

To drive dull care away I have filled up my leisure hours reading (when not thinking of you) Sterne's works — the "Life, etc., of Tristram Shandy," and the "Sentimental Journey." This Mr. Sterne was a clergyman, witty and a shrewd observer of the worst parts of human nature. Such funny, dirty, worthless trash as delighted the good old times in which he wrote would now not be tolerated in decent society, except as picturing to one the manners of the olden time, and yet in the classic age of English literature a clergyman could write these books without serious damage to his reputation. When I see the immeasurable changes which a century or two have produced, it gives me heart to throw my little efforts in favor of the good projects of the age, however slow their apparent progress. Nothing great is accomplished in a day, but gradually the strong hours conquer all obstacles.

I have read another book — not yet finished — calculated to fill one with hope, "The Life and Works of Dr. Channing." The Doctor may be in error as to some doctrinal points, but the great features of his system are founded on the rock of truth. If ever I am made a Christian it will be under the influence of views like his. He says the test of Christianity is the state of the heart and affections, not the state of a man's intellectual belief. If a man feels the humility becoming one prone to sinfulness, looks above for assistance, repents of what he does that is wrong, aspires to purity of intention and correctness of conduct in all the relations of life, such a man is a *Christian*, for he adopts the spirit of Christ's teaching and imitates his example, — this, too, in spite of his faith, — whether it be Calvinistic, Unitarian, Universalist, or Papist. That I can comprehend. The half of the orthodox creeds I don't understand and can't fully believe.

When you feel lonely hereafter on a gloomy, country, summer Sunday, I would prescribe writing to your humble servant as a sovereign remedy.

Just take up a pen, — no matter how wretched a one, — dip it into the ink, — never mind its color or "consistency" (that's a word they use in speaking of glue), — and *write right* on; write the *blues*, or your sorrows, your hopes, or your fears, facts or fancies, fold up the sheet or sheets and mail them to me. They will find a willing reader; they will go to a sympathizing heart, one whose every pulsation will, if that be possible, be in harmony with your own. If there be one person in the world to whom I would unbosom my thoughts, my feelings, even my weaknesses and failings, that person is yourself. Nay, more, I believe *now* I could open to you any part of my own nature which I dare to look upon myself. For sooner or later it must all be known to you; and the more that is known of a true heart the better will a true heart love it. This proves the fallacy of Emerson's notion that the charm of the maiden is gone when her *consent* is known. For until that consent is known the lovers are both, in some sense, playing a game of deceit. Each wishes to conceal from the other supposed defects of whatever sort. But after the word is spoken and the spirit of genuine trustfulness awakened, *then* the discovery of trifling spots which do not reach the soul's purity is no longer to be dreaded. It only endears the loved one the more. There is a positive happiness in having something to overlook, to forgive, to set off against one's own shortcomings. To be linked to a perfect being in every sense would not be an equal and therefore not a happy union.

I can speak of your *perfections* and not exaggerate. Such, so great, and so many are the substantial and sterling qualities you own that whatever defects there may be are dwarfed by them, like spots on the sun, lost in the surrounding brightness. I do not fear the growth of your self-esteem or I might, as you advise me, be guarded in the expression of my sentiments and feelings, but if you have any failing it is *the lack of a rational self-confidence in small matters.* In important things I do not doubt that your fine sense of duty will always overcome easily any of those modest misgivings which sometimes annoy you.

Finally to his great joy Miss Webb returned in mid-October to the city, "looking more beautiful than ever," and manifestly endowed with "good health, that master blessing." In the months that ensued the entries in the diary are not numerous, but they are enough to indicate that in this case at least the course of true love ran smooth and with deepening current. Every allusion breathes of increasing content and fuller anticipation of happiness to come. December 5, noting the receipt of a Detroit paper containing the announcement of his college friend Trowbridge's marriage, Hayes writes: —

And speaking of good luck in such matters, I wonder who has fallen on a more precious prize than my own. She to-day happened accidentally to hear of a family in great distress — the father sick — the mother working from 3 o'clock A.M. until 12 P.M. for fifteen to twenty cents, making corsets. No help but a little girl of eight or nine years old; no wood, no furniture, no food, a bundle of straw in one corner. Lucy shed "some natural tears," but not stopping with tears, she stirred herself — got bedclothes, dishes, food, wood, medicine, etc.[1]

And with the beginning of the new year he prays Heaven's blessing on the "loved one whose nameless and numberless virtues and winning ways are growing into and around my heart."

For one reason or another the marriage was delayed until the very end of the year 1852.[2] It was celebrated December 30, Professor L. D. McCabe, of the Ohio Wesleyan University, performing the ceremony. "Thursday afternoon about 2 o'clock," the diary particularizes, "at the residence of Lucy's mother, on the south side of Sixth Street, between Race and Elm (No. 141), Cincinnati, Ohio. Present, sister Fanny and her daughter Laura, Uncle Birchard, Rogers and Andrews (Phi Zetas), Lucy's mother, two brothers, Uncle Isaac Cook, Aunt Lucy, and Will Scott, together with about thirty friends." Hayes was at this time entering on his thirty-first year, while his bride was nine years younger. A happy honeymoon was spent at Columbus in the household of the beloved sister Fanny.[3] Then a home was

---

[1] This incident foretokened the constant habit of Mrs. Hayes's life. No case of distress or need ever came to her knowledge that she did not seek instantly to alleviate it.

[2] There is evidence that the delay was borne with some impatience. In a letter to Miss Webb from Columbus, August 22, 1852, Hayes writes: "I have had a delightful summer vacation the last six weeks; have enjoyed myself as much as I ever did in the same length of time in my life, but yet I see how the pleasure could have been immeasurably increased. Do you grasp how? By simply having with me as my own dear wife the *loved* and I am sure *loving* one with whom I am now conversing. That was all that was wanting to fill the cup, and another summer shall not be passed by me without your sweet self as my own if I can help it. That glorious country house of Mr. Valette's [at Fremont] would have been enlivened, lively as it was, for me and for all so much if you could have been there with your sunny smile and sunnier heart to cheer it as Phœbe did the old 'house of seven gables.' And your songs — let me exhort you for the fiftieth time, as you love me (is there a stronger adjuration?) not to neglect the songs which can be sung anywhere, any time, without note or instrument. You do not know how all my happiest hours are associated in my memory with pleasant songs. With no musical taste or cultivation myself, I am yet so fond of simple airs that I have often thought I could never love a woman who did not sing them."

[3] Mrs. Laura Mitchell, writing soon after Mrs. Hayes's death, said of this time: "When my uncle brought her to us for the bridal visit, we children were

established with Mrs. Webb, and a life of conjugal felicity was
begun which through all the years that followed never knew
change except to increase in intensity and sweetness. After two
months of wedded bliss Hayes writes: —

February 27 : — Almost two months married. The great step of life
which makes or mars the whole after journey, has been happily taken.
The dear friend who is to share with me the joys and ills of our earthly
being grows steadily nearer and dearer to me. A better wife I never
hoped to have. Our little differences in points of taste or preference are
readily adjusted, and judging by the past I do not see how our tender
and affectionate relations can be disturbed by any jar. She bears with
my "innocent peculiarities" so kindly, so lovingly; is so studious in
providing for my little wants; is — is, in short, so true a wife that I
cannot think it possible that any shadow of disappointment will ever
cloud the prospect, — save only such calamities as are the common
allotment of Providence to all. Let me strive to be as true to her as she
is to me. Let me, too, be loving, kind, and thoughtful. Especially let
me not permit the passion I have to see constant improvement in those
I love, to be so blind in its eagerness as to wound a nature so tenderly
sensitive as I know I sometimes have done. This is, indeed, life! The
love of wedded wife! Can anything enjoyed on earth be a source of
truer, purer happiness — happiness more unalloyed than this? Blessings on his head who first invented marriage!

These two months are prophetic of the long life that is to follow. It will have many cares, many sorrows, large responsibilities, great honors. But through it all the golden thread of love
will run. There will be happiness and peace and rest and complete understanding whereof is born content at home, and so
there shall be the atmosphere in which the true man can grow to
his best estate.

The Hayeses continued to live with Mrs. Webb until the
spring of 1854. While with her, their first child, a son, was born
on November 4, 1853. To him was given the name of Birchard
Austin, in honor of the uncle. Mrs. Hayes spent the summers of
1853 and 1854 with relatives at Chillicothe, Columbus, and other
places of Ohio. When she returned to Cincinnati in the autumn

clamorous to appropriate her for our exclusive possession, glorying that in our
house only she was indeed 'Aunt Lu.' Very soon her name became the herald
to us all, and to our childhood friends, of happy, hilarious times. With later
years the joyful music of her dear name has softened and deepened into that
sweet, full chord of tenderness and love for which we have listened, since ever
she came to us, in all of our life's experiences of joy or sorrow."

RUTHERFORD B. AND LUCY W. HAYES

At the time of their marriage, December 30, 1852, from a Daguerreotype

of 1854, it was to go into a new home which Mr. Hayes had just bought. This was at number 383 Sixth Street, on the south side, west of Mound Street. Getting settled was attended with "all sorts of laughing over our loads of furniture — a good deal of it Lucy's mother's when she went to housekeeping — good but old." There was "a great sending of it back and forth for cleaning, varnishing, making as good as new," but at last everything was settled in comfortable and pleasant shape. Mrs. Webb, to whom Hayes was as devoted as to his own mother, became a welcome member of the household. She was a woman of great strength of character, combined with a sunny, hopeful disposition which always looked on the bright side of things. Here the family continued to live as long as a home was maintained at Cincinnati. Here was born March 20, 1856, the second son, who was named Webb Cook; and on June 24, 1858, the third son, who was named Rutherford Platt. Here all three boys were baptized Wednesday, June 8, 1859, in the presence of their near relatives. Here in tender and loving ministrations to their children in times of sickness, in mutual rejoicing as the little lives given into their keeping developed, in supporting and complementing each other in all their endeavors, husband and wife grew continually into closer and completer spiritual sympathy. Each was dependent on the other; each was necessary to the other. The diary contains many references to this deepening affection; [1] and makes many records in fond parental pride of the growth in body and character of the boys.

It was in this period also that Hayes was called upon to mourn the loss of his sister Fanny. The tie between these two had always been of the closest; their mutual love, devotion, and pride knew no bounds. There was complete sympathy between them in all the joys or the sorrows, the triumphs or the reverses, of either. "She loved me," Hayes wrote in his diary nearly a year after her death, "as an only sister loves a brother whom she imagines almost perfect, and I loved her as an only brother loves a sister who is perfect." To his sister Hayes first turned for advice

[1] For example, in September, 1853, writing of a visit among relatives, Hayes says: "This is the statistical summary of the summer. But its real enjoyment embraces many special things. I know my Lucy far better than before. We have been alone together among strangers, and I can't express how much deeper my love for her is."

or encouragement; of her he first thought when any good thing came into his life. His satisfaction was not complete till he could share it with her. To her he wrote more fully and freely than to any one else. To her house in Columbus — she was happily married before her twentieth birthday to William A. Platt, a man of substance and affairs — he made frequent visits in his college days and during his life at Fremont and Cincinnati. It was like a second home to him, and Fanny's children were almost as dear to him as his own. His first acute grief was when he sorrowed with her in January, 1851, over the death of her six-year-old son, Willie, — a bright and winsome lad, whom all had dearly loved. During the time of his engagement he had great joy in discovering a resemblance to his sister in the character of his betrothed. His marriage made no difference with the closeness of the relations between brother and sister. When in July, 1856, the end of things earthly came for her, the affliction fell upon Hayes with heart-breaking force. He writes: —

My dear only sister, my beloved Fanny is dead! The dearest friend of childhood, the affectionate adviser, the confidante of all my life, the one I loved best, is gone — alas! never again to be seen on earth. Oh, how we shall always mourn her loss! how we shall lament her absence at every family meeting! The pride of us all, the charm of every circle, and my own particular loss.

In his review of the year, on December 28, he writes: —

The most eventful, longest, and saddest year in its one great affliction that I have ever known. The void still remains. The wound does not heal. Not a day passes that this shadow does not darken some otherwise happy moments. I never am present at any scene of joyousness or festivity that Fanny's image is not present with its saddening influence. Oh, what a blessed sister she was! No other such loss could have happened to me. The long years of common experiences, joys, and sorrows, going back to the rosy period of life, bound her to me in a way that no acquaintance begun at a later period, however dear and close the relation, can equal. As we grow nearer the term of life, how sweet all the recollections of childhood become, and how dear those who can travel back to the same early memories!

CHAPTER VI

SUCCESS AT THE BAR

THE few years of practice at Fremont, Hayes looked back upon, as we have seen, as largely time wasted. There were occasions, indeed, while he was still at Fremont when the feeling that he was not using his powers to the best advantage came over him. But the hours of despondency and doubt were probably due more to physical than to psychical causes. He was not robust and his mental states took their color at times from his impaired bodily condition. We know, however, that in these years he made an excellent beginning in the practice of his profession, such, indeed, as to give older lawyers a decidedly favorable impression of his capabilities. This is shown by the letter of Judge Lane, given on a previous page, and by expressions in the letters of lawyer friends at Cincinnati whom he consulted in regard to the advisability of removing to that city. Moreover, in his diary, after a year and a half at Fremont, Hayes writes: "I have succeeded, in all the senses of that word, as well as I could desire in my professional career."

The change to Cincinnati was rather against the advice of Hayes's uncle, Sardis Birchard, to whose fostering guardianship he owed so much. But Hayes was confident that the event would prove the wisdom of his decision. He was conscious of the need of a larger arena to stimulate his powers to their best development. He began his professional life at Cincinnati in a very quiet way. He shared an office, it will be recalled, with another young lawyer, John W. Herron. Studying and reading and making acquaintances, the young man waited for business. He had been in Cincinnati six weeks before his first client appeared. This was a coal trader who gave him "a retainer of five dollars to defend a suit in the commercial court." In the next few months the references in the diary indicate that few clients sought his door. Late in November, 1850, when he had been in Cincinnati nearly a year, he writes: "I am now to work my way almost unaided.

Push, labor, shove, — three words of great power in a city like this. Two years must find me with a *living* and *increasing* business or I quit the city and probably the profession." Four months later he is in a despondent mood at his prospects — partly due as he admits to impaired health. Herron has just left him to enter another office as partner. He is alone, contrasting his aspirations with his accomplishments: —

I have now no prospects for good or glory immediately before me. . . . I fear I am wasting not [only] my substance, but what is even more, my mental endowments. Let me prick up a little of my ancient mettle and again at it. I see many of my early friends and acquaintances of no greater promise than mine evidently outstripping me in the race of life. Yet I feel that I am not inferior to them. The gift of continuance, aye, and health, I fear, are lacking. . . . My prospects here are in some points of view not dark, and in others not so bright as I could desire. I have made friends and with them acquired some position — some reputation — and yet I have next to no practice at all.

But Hayes's periods of despondency were never of long duration. Constitutionally he looked on the bright side of life. What we have just copied, he wrote in the gloom that precedes the dawn. The acquaintances he had been making, the faithful work he had been doing, had prepared the way, and the demands on his professional services began soon to increase. The patience his lawyer friends had warned him, on coming to Cincinnati, that he must exercise "until the tide should bring his turn around," was now to be rewarded. With the incoming of the year 1852 he was able to say: "So begins the new year. Rather prosperously with me. Money and friends more abundant than ever before." The year thus opening prosperously was to see Hayes engaged for the defense in several criminal cases of a very notable character — cases which gave him an opportunity to display his powers such as no previous cases had given. January 16 he made his maiden effort in the criminal court in the defense of a young man indicted for grand larceny. The man was convicted, but Hayes had done his part in such a way as to draw compliments from the court and the prosecuting attorney. So favorably was the judge impressed that he at once appointed Hayes to assist in the defense of Nancy Farrer, the poisoner of two families. Whereupon Hayes writes: —

It is *the* criminal case of the term. Will attract more notice than any other, and if I am well prepared, will give me a better opportunity to exert and exhibit whatever pith there is in me than any case I ever appeared in. The poor girl is homely — very; probably from this misfortune has grown her malignity. I shall repeat some of my favorite notions as to the effect of original constitution, early training, and associations in forming character — show how it diminishes responsibility, etc., etc. Must look over my Odd Fellow speech on Happiness. Study medical jurisprudence as to poisons; also read some good speech or poetry to elevate my style, language, thoughts, etc., etc. Here is the tide and I mean to take it at the flood — if I can.

His investigations brought to light many facts of the woman's heredity which made a strong presumptive case of insanity. But the community had been so horrified by the circumstances attending the poisoning that such a plea had little chance of success before a jury of the vicinage. Moreover, the repulsive face of the woman was enough to condemn her. She had a large and ugly mouth, a monstrous nose flattened at the tip, small eyes, deep-set and wide apart, shaded by heavy brows and glowering with malignant cunning. The very difficulties of the case only heightened the interest and zeal of the lawyer for the defense in preparing for the trial.

In the summer of 1851, a Mrs. Green living in the southern part of Cincinnati, who had recently been confined, was suddenly taken seriously ill, but lingered, alternately better and worse, until October 3, when she died. She was nursed during her confinement and subsequent illness by Nancy Farrer and an Italian woman named Brazilli. On her death the latter disappeared, and Nancy became a servant in the home of Elisha Forrest, a well-to-do merchant in Fulton, whose family consisted of himself, his wife, and three children. At the first meal cooked by Nancy, Mrs. Forrest was violently attacked and died in twenty-four hours. Two weeks later, her son John was attacked and died in thirty-six hours, and late in November another son, James Wesley, succumbed. Mr. Forrest and the third child also fell ill, but recovered. On the death of James suspicions were aroused and investigation resulted in the finding of arsenic and the label of the druggist from whom it was purchased. The druggist said he had sold the arsenic to Nancy Farrer to poison rats. In the stomachs of the victims arsenic was found sufficient to cause death in each case. When the *post mortem* of the boy James was held, Nancy was present, but neither her countenance nor manner gave indication of conscious guilt. Three indictments were found against Nancy for poisoning Mrs. Forrest and her children, and a joint indictment against her and Mrs. Brazilli for the murder of Mrs. Green. In the following February, Nancy was tried on the indictment for the murder of James Wesley Forrest, the last victim of these tragedies.

The trial lasted ten days and throughout absorbed public attention. Mr. Hayes fought every inch of ground for the prisoner, but his principal plea was that she was not a free moral agent. He proved that her origin, training, and associations were vicious; that her father had died of *delirium tremens*, and that her mother was insane, professing to be a Mormon prophetess. Nancy made similar professions. She said to her counsel one day that the Italian woman poisoned Mrs. Green and taught her how to use arsenic. It was clear that her motive was not gain nor revenge, for her victims were her friends and benefactors. The only plausible theory was, that it was insane love of power.

The ruling of the court was, as it had been in similar cases, that insanity must be proved affirmatively when pleaded as an excuse for crime. The medical experts were asked whether they believed the prisoner knew right from wrong. On their declaration that they so believed the jurors were charged to find according to the facts. The assumption, that if a person knew right from wrong, insanity was not proved, Hayes confronted with the opinion of Dr. Bell, of the McLean Asylum, who asserted that insane persons generally knew right and wrong; and with an impressive discussion of the tendency of hereditary traits, which science has since much emphasized. He illustrated his theory by telling the pathetic story of Mary Lamb, impelled against her will to slay her father and mother, and added: —

Awful as are the tragedies which she [Nancy Farrer] has been the instrument — as I believe, the unconscious instrument — of committing, their horrors sink into insignificance when compared with the solemn and deliberate execution by reasoning, thinking men of such a being as she. On the subject of insanity I have asked more than is sustained by the weight of judicial opinion even in this country. But I suppose that when the facts and principles of any science come to be so well established that they are universally recognized and adopted by the most intelligent as well as the most conservative members of the profession which deals with that science, it is in strict harmony with the expansive and liberal rules of the common law that courts should also recognize and adopt those facts and principles. The calamity of insanity is one which may touch very nearly the happiness of the best of our citizens. We all know that in some of its thousand forms it has carried grief and agony unspeakable into many a happy home; and we must all wish to see such rules in regard to it established as would satisfy an intelligent man if, instead of this friendless girl, his own sister or his own daughter were on trial. And surely to establish such rules will be a most noble achievement of that intelligence and reason which God has given to you, but which he has denied to her whose fate is in your hands.

The deep impression made on the jury by this argument was evident from the fact that they were out three days before they brought in a verdict of guilty. Failing in his motion for a new trial, Hayes carried up the case to the Supreme Court. In his argument on insanity before that court, he said: —

There is no fact more essential to crime than the possession of reason. The existence of this fact the law properly presumes. But if that presumption is denied, if there is evidence tending to overthrow it, why not apply to that evidence the same humane maxim which is extended to every other presumption of the law? The only answer I find to this inquiry is, that the safety and protection of society require this departure from principle; that otherwise the defense of insanity would be successfully interposed in cases where in truth, depravity, not insanity, was at the bottom of the crime. It is needless to remark in reply that every presumption for the protection of innocence is liable to be used as a shield for guilt. The question is still to be answered, Why is the defense of insanity to be treated as odious by the law? Is it so peculiarly liable to abuse that fundamental rules are to be changed to guard society against it? On the contrary, I believe it has been shown by those who have investigated the subject, the danger is in the opposite direction; that until a recent period there were ten insane and therefore innocent persons who suffered punishment, to one criminal who escaped on the pretext of insanity; and that now, in view of the state of the law and the prejudices of the community, injustice is more frequently done to the insane accused than to the public.

I admit that cases are occurring frequently in which this defense is set up and the accused acquitted where there is, in truth, very little that looks like permanent and real insanity. But what are these cases? Are they cases of feigned insanity, cases in which the jury are deceived and acquit the accused because they are deceived? Far from it. They are cases in which verdicts of acquittal are rendered against the rigorous requirements of the law, because the juries are satisfied that the acts charged are such as good men and good women might commit, acts which do not evince "a heart regardless of social duty, and fatally bent on mischief." They are cases in which the accused has suffered some great wrong for which the law provides no adequate remedy. Cases like that of young Mercer, at Philadelphia, who slew the seducer; the Irish girl lately at Newark who killed the man who had betrayed, ruined, and deserted her; and the Ohio girl at Milwaukee who did the same thing. In all these cases the defense was insanity, and the verdict acquittal; but the verdict would have been the same on any other plea. Nobody is deceived by the defense. Insanity is set up because under that defense more conveniently than under any other the story of the wrong suffered by the accused can be spread before the jury. The general sense of the community approves these verdicts of acquittal, because it is felt that the best person in the community might, under the same circumstances, commit the same acts; because there is no other redress for such a wrong; because, finally, the slain deserves his fate.

We submit that the defense of insanity is not to be regarded as odious in the law because of these cases. The same verdict would be rendered in the same cases if the plea of self-defense were set up, if under that plea the circumstances of provocation could as well be got before the jury. Laying this class of cases out of view and how often is it that juries are deceived by feigned insanity? I suppose there may have been such cases, but I have not met with them. But cases of the other sort are but too easily found. The famous case of the negro Freeman in New York, convicted but insane beyond all question, will be remembered; but we need not travel from home for examples. In our own reports (12th Ohio) is the case of a man convicted in this county — the case of Clark convicted on the opinion of the sheriff and other experts against the opinion of Dr. Ackley. At the time of that conviction very painful doubts were felt by many as to its justice; and after the execution of Clark the *post-mortem* examination demonstrated that he was totally irresponsible. His brain was softened to the consistency of lard, and the opinion of Dr. Ackley was confirmed. I submit, in view of facts like these, that the presumption against insanity is not so necessary to the safety of society that a greater amount of evidence should be required to overthrow it than is requisite to overthrow other similar presumptions of law.

Hayes's plea was successful. The judgment of the lower court was reversed in an opinion, fully sustaining his leading positions, four in number, which has since been accepted as good authority.

On the principal points the court held: That it is not enough to charge the jury that "the only insanity which exonerates from criminal responsibility, is the inability to distinguish right from wrong, as to the act charged, at the time of its commission"; but it must be remembered that sanity signifies a freedom of will to avoid a wrong, no less than the power to distinguish between right and wrong — without which capacity no responsibility attaches.

An application was next made for an inquest of lunacy, which found Nancy Farrer of unsound mind. "She will now go to a lunatic asylum," writes Hayes in his diary, "and so my first case involving life is ended successfully. It has been a pet case with me; has caused me much anxiety, given me some prominence in my profession, and indeed was the case which first brought me practice in this city. It has turned out fortunately for me — very, and I am greatly gratified that it is so."

Before the argument on appeal in the Nancy Farrer case, which was in December, 1853, he had been retained in two other murder cases, the most prominent of which — that of the State of Ohio *vs.* James Summons — he took to the Supreme Court in January of the same year, when he made his first oral argument before that court. It was pronounced by Thomas Ewing "the best first speech" he had ever heard in the Supreme Court. The conclusion of this argument was in the following words: —

We are not here to plead merely for James Summons. He is bankrupt in fortune and character, broken in health and intellect, and bereft of almost every rational hope in life. Occasional fits of *delirium tremens* and repeated attacks of epilepsy have reduced him almost to imbecility, and the little remnant of existence which a reversal of this judgment will spare to him has perhaps very little value. Nor are we here to plead for those little ones who derive their being through him and who are growing up to bear his name. Nor even for the sake of his aged father, already crushed to the earth, and who has such claims to our sympathy and regard. Nor for his mother, who has clung to him through all these years of sorrow and shame with a devotion at once so touching and so sublime! But we are here earnestly to beg of this court — very respectfully to ask, to demand of this court that fundamental rules upon which depend the liberty and life of every citizen, long established and solemnly guarded, shall not now be disregarded, nor broken down merely in order that James Summons may perish. We are here, in the language of the great lawyer of our day — we are here, in the language of Mr. Webster — "to hold up before this unfortunate man the broad shield of the Constitution," and if through that he be pierced and fall, he will be but one sufferer in a common calamity.

The plea presented to the court will best be understood by some statement of the case. In July, 1849, Summons was arraigned on two indictments charging murder in the first degree, committed by poisoning with arsenic the tea of which his mother, father, and other relatives partook; two of them with fatal effect. The chief witness was a servant girl, who brewed the tea; and it was conceded that without her testimony no conviction could be had. Summons was first tried in May, 1850, when after seven days' hearing, the jury failed to agree. He was tried again in June, and after ten days' hearing the jury again failed to agree. At these two trials the servant girl, Mary Clinch, testified. Before the third trial in April, 1851, she died, and her testimony was then supplied by a witness who undertook to give it from memory, aided by notes taken at the former trials. The jury again disagreed. At the fourth trial in April, 1852, the testimony of Mary Clinch was supplied in the same manner as before. The trial resulted in conviction, the jury accompanying the verdict with a recommendation to executive clemency. From this sentence an appeal was taken by writ of error to the Supreme Court. The ground of reversal mainly relied upon, was that the District Court erred in permitting the testimony of Mary Clinch to be given to the jury from memory, by any witness, and especially by the actual witness who was alleged to be legally incompetent.

Pending the discussion and determination of these questions, four of the five judges of the court as first constituted retired, and new judges took their places. Twice did a majority of the court determine to reverse judgment against the prisoner; twice was this determination recalled, and finally, by a majority of the new judges, the sentence was affirmed.

During all this time Summons protested his innocence; and his father and mother, who drank of the poisoned tea, declared their belief in his innocence. The Governor on petition of the judges of both the District and the Supreme Courts commuted the sentence to imprisonment for life.

In April, 1853, Hayes made his first argument in the United States Circuit Court, Justice McLean presiding, in association with Thomas Ewing and George E. Pugh, in a case involving an important question. It arose under a motion to enjoin the Junction Railway Company, from Sandusky to the Maumee River, from crossing Sandusky Bay by means of a causeway and draw-bridge, on the ground that this would be injurious to navigation, and consequently in violation of rights guaranteed by the Ordinance of 1787. It was also doubtful whether under its charter the railway company could claim a *prima-facie* right to cross the bay, even leaving apart the general question of interference with navigation. The people of Fremont, with Sardis Birchard in the lead, were much aroused on the subject, fearing that the obstruction of the bay would do their town irreparable damage. Hayes made a very thorough study of the law and the authorities bearing on the question, being engaged in the preparation of the case at intervals for several months. Practically all the work of preparing the bill on which the injunction was asked fell on him. He was thoroughly convinced, in the light of the previous decisions of the United States courts, that the causeway and drawbridge would be a legal nuisance; but looking at the whole subject of transportation and the growing importance of railways in the economy of life, he had doubts whether larger utilities would not be secured by allowing the construction of the bridge, rather than by seeking to preserve absolutely uninterrupted water communication in the bay. But his doubts did not lessen the zeal with which he sought to establish what he believed to be legal rights; even if there was failure in securing all that was claimed, the contest, he believed, would result in minimizing the obstruction. Mr. Pugh was associated with him in the case from the start. On Hayes's advice, when the time drew near for appearing in court, Mr. Ewing, who at that time was one of the leaders of the Ohio bar, was also engaged. To him the bill, affidavits, and case as already prepared by Hayes were submitted and he pronounced them perfect. Hayes had neglected nothing that would tend to strengthen the position for which he was contending, which was, indeed, characteristic of the thoroughness with which he regularly prepared his cases.

Some time after Herron left Hayes, another young lawyer, named McDowell, came to share the office. Hayes's geniality, his love of books, and his eagerness for intellectual growth attracted men of similar tastes to him. His office was the frequent resort of older members of the bar, in whose conversation Hayes found pleasure and profit, and of members of the Literary Club who came to discuss things uppermost in the world of literature, science, and politics. On January 1, 1854, Hayes entered into partnership with R. M. Corwine and W. K. Rogers under the firm name of Corwine, Hayes & Rogers. The last named left Cincinnati to make his home in Minnesota in 1856, when the firm style became Corwine and Hayes. The firm was reasonably prosperous and Hayes continued in the partnership until December, 1858. When he withdrew from the firm, several thousand dollars were due him as his share of the earnings of the partnership.

In March, 1855, Hayes was associated with Salmon P. Chase and Timothy Walker in saving a slave girl named Rosetta Armstead from a return to the South. The case excited great popular interest, as did all slave cases at the time, especially as it involved a conflict between federal and state jurisdiction. The point was that Rosetta had not fled to Ohio, but had been brought there, and so was not amenable to the Fugitive Slave Law. Her master, a clergyman named Henry M. Dennison, of Louisville, had entrusted her to a friend to take to Richmond, Virginia. This man left the boat at Cincinnati and proceeded by way of Columbus, where he was detained over Sunday. Here the girl was brought before the Probate Court on a writ of *habeas corpus* and was adjudged to be free. The court appointed Lewis G. Van Slyke as her guardian. Meanwhile Mr. Dennison appeared on the scene. He had a talk with Rosetta, Mr. Van Slyke and others being present, and gave her a choice of returning with him or of remaining free. When she chose the latter, he bade her good-bye, adding that he should probably never see her again. In spite of all this he obtained a warrant for her arrest from United States Commissioner John L. Pendery, of Cincinnati, to which city she was thereupon brought by the marshal. Her guardian at once obtained a writ of *habeas corpus* from Judge Parker, of the Court of Common Pleas of Hamilton County. After thorough argument by Messrs. Chase, Walker, and Hayes for Rosetta, and by Messrs. Pugh and Flynn for the master, the court ordered the girl set free, holding that a state court on a writ of *habeas corpus* had a right to inquire into the legality of the detention of persons by a United States marshal, and deciding that "under the constitution of Ohio the alleged right of transit with slave property through the State did not exist."

But no sooner was Rosetta restored to the custody of her guardian than she was rearrested on the warrant issued by Commissioner Pendery, who now heard argument on the whole question. Popular excitement ran high, and the court-room was thronged. In this case the chief legal argument was made by Mr. Hayes who, Mr. Chase says, "acquitted himself with great distinction."[1] He denounced Mr. Dennison's conduct in "despising his pledged word and suing out a writ that she was a fugitive as worse than the most ultra fanaticism of those classed as abolitionists"; and he argued: "The parol manumission the claimant made of her is good in Ohio — good in law, good in morals. A slave court says that acts of manumission may be inferred from the 'acts and conduct of the master.' The acts of Mr. Dennison at Columbus were impliedly and expressly to the liberation of Rosetta." He then analyzed the Fugitive Slave Law and showed that, even waiving the parol manumission, the law did not apply to the case of Rosetta. She had not fled from her master; she had made no effort to escape. She had been brought into the State with her master's consent, by his agent. He reminded the commissioner of the opinion of a Southern Judge of the United States Supreme Court under the Law of 1793 (which was similar in language to the Law of 1850) which said: "If a slave go from one State to another with the consent or connivance of the master, it is not an escape under the fugitive slave clause." The argument was heard with close attention by the commissioner, while the audience followed it in profound silence to the close, when there was an outburst of prolonged applause; while his fellow lawyers pressed about him with their congratulations. He had not spoken in vain. The commissioner held the case under advisement for nearly a week, when he reached the same conclusion that had already been reached by the state courts, and set the girl at liberty, when no further effort was made to restore her to bondage.[2]

At the end of five years in Cincinnati, Hayes writes: "I cannot

[1] Warden's *Life of Chase*, p. 345.
[2] This was not the only fugitive slave case in which Hayes's activity was aroused. Recalling this period later in life, he wrote: "My services were always freely given to the slave and his friends in all cases arising under the Fugitive Slave Law from the time of its passage until such cases were ended by the War of the Rebellion."

but look back with a feeling of gratification, not to say pride. I told Uncle that in five years I believed that he and every other friend I had would be glad that I had gone to Cincinnati. It is enough to fill me with pleasant feeling that I am sure that my hope has been realized." Two years later he looks back with satisfaction over the "business, success in life, etc.," of the previous twelvemonth. Again, after two years he says: "I am now fairly established as a lawyer, with a good reputation and flattering prospects"; and Christmas Eve, 1859, just ten years after his arrival in Cincinnati, he writes: "Without any extraordinary success, without that sort of success which makes men giddy sometimes, I have nevertheless found what I sought — a respectable place. Good!"

CHAPTER VII

INTEREST AND ACTIVITY IN POLITICS

L IKE all normally constituted young Americans of his time,
Hayes began early to be an interested observer of political
movements, though in his student days he looked askance at
young men who were inclined to dabble in politics. He came
of sturdy Whig ancestry, and so, naturally, his sympathies were
with the Whig cause, and his political heroes were men who had
been most faithful and efficient in its proclamation and defense.
The great campaign of 1840 roused him, boy of eighteen as he
was, to a high pitch of enthusiasm. His deep interest is revealed
by his diary in which he wrote a consecutive history of the campaign, beginning it in June, and making additions from time to
time as the memorable contest advanced, until in November he
was able to record the success of Harrison at the polls. This account of the campaign is remarkable for its clearness of insight
and its maturity of judgment. It is difficult to realize that it is
the work of a lad in his sophomore year at college. After describing the causes which contributed to Van Buren's declining
popularity, and giving an account of the Harrisburg Convention,
the young historian proceeds: —

In this State (Ohio) many who had before been supporters of Van
Buren came out publicly and declared their intention to go for Harrison.
About this time the Baltimore *Republican*, a Van Buren print, sneer-
ingly said of General Harrison: "Give him a pension of two thousand
dollars and a barrel of hard cider and he will be content to live in a log
cabin the remainder of his days." Great use was made of this by the
Harrison party. They styled themselves the "Log Cabin and Hard
Cider Party." In February and March, '40, log cabins began to be
built for council houses for the Harrison party.

A convention was held on the 22d of February in this State (Columbus) to respond to the nomination and nominate candidates for state
officers. Large and spirited meetings were held in the different counties
nominating delegates to "the Convention." All knew that the State
was aroused, but as the weather was bad, the roads almost impassable,
few expected that there would be much of a "turn out," but the day

came and with it the greatest convention in many respects ever held; there was no plan or system, but each delegation bore as their emblem whatever their caprice dictated. Log cabins, hard cider, canoes, boats (all kinds) were brought with thousands of mottoes. At this convention it was, that political songs were first sung to any great extent; and this was the first of that series of great conventions for which this campaign will be remarkable. Number present 20,000.

Then follow comments on the results of the various state elections, the enthusiasm and confidence of the writer rising as the summer, with its shouting, singing, marching hosts, its vast concourses of people, and its ringing oratory, passed into autumn. Early in October Hayes writes: —

The Van Buren party know that nothing but success in this State can save them. They are accordingly straining every nerve. Johnson, Allen, and others are stumping it over the State. Mr. Corwin (candidate for Governor) has also been before the public.

October 20 the election of Corwin is noted with exclamations of delight and the narrative is brought to an end early in November with these sentences: —

The long agony is over. The "whirlwind" has swept over the land, and General Harrison is undoubtedly elected President. I never was more elated by anything in my life. His majority in this State, about sixteen acres or 23,000. Kentucky and everywhere else is going fine. Glorious! Up on the Reserve, Birney and Van Buren ran about alike. Ha-ha!

With the election of Harrison, Hayes's interest in politics temporarily subsided; and yet only relatively. An entry in the diary of September 6, 1841, when he was on vacation at Columbus, while disclaiming interest, shows that the young man was closely following the current of public affairs and forming his opinions thereon. He writes: —

The grogshop politicians of this goodly city have been in a constant ferment for a few weeks past because of the veto of the Bank Bill by President Tyler. The Van Buren men who opposed him so strenuously last fall now laud him to the skies for his integrity and firmness in disregarding his party relations for the sake of the Constitution. On the other hand, his former friends, the old Whigs, stigmatize him as a traitor to his principles for disregarding the wishes of a majority of his supporters. For myself I do not consider the professions of the Van Buren men sincere, nor do I think the harsh denunciations of the Whigs as very becoming the original supporters of Harrison and Tyler. It is only by remaining united that they can continue to advance the great interests of the country, and they should be careful how they hazard all by casting loose from John Tyler for a conscientious discharge of duty. I was never more rejoiced than when it was ascertained that Harrison's election was certain. I hoped we should then have a stable currency of uniform value, but since Tyler has vetoed one way of accomplishing this, I would not hesitate to try others. So much for politics in which I have ceased to take an interest. My hopes and wishes were all realized in the election of old General Harrison and I am glad to be able to say that I am now indifferent to such things.

Doubtless, in common with most of his countrymen, Hayes later modified his opinion of Tyler. It is worthy of special note that Hayes was most interested "in a stable currency of uniform value." We shall find him much later in life doing valiant service in that cause.

In the next two years we hear nothing from Hayes in regard to politics. But at Cambridge, November 14, 1843, in telling of the political speeches that he had heard, he says: "I am not so easily enlisted in the excitements attending political discussions as I was prior to the election of General Harrison to the Presidency." But as the excerpts from the diary summarizing Judge Story's lectures, given in a preceding chapter, show, Hayes was quick to catch and retain whatever the great jurist had to say that bore on the political development of the country, thus unconsciously revealing his abiding interest in the subject. And while he was not "easily enlisted," as he thought, in election controversies, yet within a month we find him saying: "Literature and politics fill the current of my thoughts." But he decides that he has not the ability to win literary honors, while "mere political honors, as such, are too dearly purchased at the price of tranquil enjoyment, fine feelings, and a fair fame." The passage shows, however, into what regions the young man's day dreams were taking him. A month later he records Story's advice: "Keep out of politics till you are forty. Then you can with the experience of forty years direct your course for yourselves."

Hayes was past forty and had had ample experience of life before he entered the arena of national politics as an aspirant for public office. But every national campaign before that time found his sympathies, and, in many of them, his voice, enlisted on the Whig or Republican side. In 1844 the young man of twenty-two, while not so moved as he had been four years before, was profoundly interested in the fortunes of Henry Clay, whom all good Whigs not only believed in but even devotedly loved. How deep Hayes's feelings were, how bitter his disappointment at the news of defeat, is revealed by the diary on November 9, 1844: —

> Politics have filled all minds for the last ten days. . . . The result of the Presidential election has disappointed me greatly. I would start in the world without a penny if by my sacrifice Henry Clay could be chosen President. Not that the difference to the country is likely to be very great, in my opinion, but then to think that so good and great a man should be defeated! Slandered as he has been, it would have been such a triumph to have elected him. But it cannot be.

These words correctly reflect the feelings of unnumbered thousands of the American people of that day whose political idol and ideal Clay had long been.

The diary fails to record one incident which shows more clearly than his words how deeply young Hayes's feelings were enlisted. Under the auspices of the Henry Clay Club of Boston, a great demonstration occurred which was attended by Hayes, his uncle Sardis Birchard, and an acquaintance from Delaware, Ohio. As the procession passed the Tremont House, Hayes, observing that different States were represented, remarked that only an Ohio delegation was lacking. He disappeared, but soon returned with a rude banner bearing the word "Ohio" in bold letters with which he joined the procession. Ohio men continued to drop in behind the standard until, when Boston Common was reached, the Ohioans numbered twenty-four, and were received with cheers.

About the campaign of 1848 the diary contains very meagre information. But enough is given to show that Hayes had caught the infection of Whig enthusiasm for Taylor. He records having made a trip to Xenia to hear Corwin speak, and he sums up the campaign by saying: "Work like a trooper for old Zack and enjoy the victory."

In 1851, Hayes began to take some part in the local politics of Cincinnati. He attended ward and county meetings, and at the County Temperance Convention he displayed his usual good sense by speaking in opposition to the plan of forming a separate temperance party. The meeting decided against his views, but he was well satisfied with his speech. He "found it an easy thing to speak in such bodies. The thing is energy, brevity, and sound positions; clearness in argument and control of temper. A little joking may do, enough to show one's good nature and give an impression of cleverness (in the American sense) is well, but any more fun-making than this does not succeed in such businesslike bodies." To this sensible ideal of public speaking, thus early evolved, Hayes remained loyal throughout his career. His political speeches were always distinguished for their plainness, their clearness of argument, their directness of appeal, and their pervasive common sense. It was in the state campaign of 1851 that Hayes made his first attempts at political speaking. He found it "a very easy kind of talking." He summarizes his experience as follows: —

The first half or three quarters with my speaking faculties should be spent in calm, dispassionate, sensible talk. I then seem to have established a sort of relationship or sympathy with my audience and also to have acquired a warmth which enables me to branch out into humorous and impassioned speaking with tolerable success. I think I have made a very favorable impression. I spoke first twenty minutes, next about forty-five, next an hour, and so on until I reached an hour and three quarters.

In the Presidential contest of the next year, Hayes was found among the workers for General Scott. He had seen Scott on the occasion of his visit to Ohio in the spring of 1851, and had been favorably impressed with his appearance. "He will do for President,"[1] was his judgment then.

[1] "*April 9, 1851:* — Monday morning, the 7th, saw General Scott for the first time. Great crowds of people thronged the streets leading to the landing. The general came down the river on the Pittsburgh packet. The uncertainty in the time of his arrival prevented there being anything like a formal reception. The old general stepped out in the forepart of the boat, dressed in full military costume, with a yellow plume in his chapeau, etc., etc. Was cheered, and bowed gracefully, as he ascended from the deck and made his way to the carriage. Great numbers crowded toward him and seized his hand, and one Irishman even embraced him. Monday evening, there was a class graduated by the Law School at College Hall. General Scott was present. The orator of the evening, B. Storer, alluded to General Scott, which brought the house down. The general then made a neat little speech, saying that he could not venture to call himself a lawyer, — that he had only practised six months, — but he had felt the benefit of his law studies in every week of his life, and, addressing the class, he added: 'You will find yourselves benefited by your studies here whatever may be your subsequent

But he was not at all sanguine of Whig success; and his favorable impression of Scott did not deepen with the advance of the canvass. As early as June 28 he wrote to his uncle expressing doubt of Scott's chances, but declaring his purpose to do all he could in his behalf. The letter, which throws much light on the political condition of the time, follows: —

The preliminaries of the great political play of 1852 are concluded. The old stagers have been killed off, and new actors are upon the boards. There is a sad satisfaction in the political taking-off of Webster. The Presidency could add nothing to his greatness, and the refusal of the Southrons to support him, though very mortifying, carries with it a lesson that may prove useful to younger men who have ambition. The same may be said of Cass, barring emphasis on the greatness. No one ever made the mistake to believe him a great statesman. He never was true to republican principles, to freedom. He deserved his defeat in 1848, and his rejection now by the barons he served, is cause for gratulation.

As to these new actors: Now that light is thrown on the proceedings at Baltimore, it does not seem difficult for me to foretell who will win the plaudits of the multitude in the last act. But the favor will not go by merit, or as we would wish. The advantage is with the leaders of our hereditary enemy — more 's the pity. The times are out of joint; the Whig leaders proved unequal to the task of setting them right, and our opponents prosper because the Democratic party is a party of spoilsmen who work in harmony, each hoping for a share. Not so with the Whigs. They are hopelessly divided. The continued possession of the offices did not prove a centripetal force sufficient to bind them together. The Southerners who can contribute a few electoral votes insisted on abandoning ancient principles, and on making the faithful enforcement of the Fugitive Slave Law a test of party loyalty, which weakens the party in the North where we must look for the votes to elect our candidate. Scott *is* our candidate and we must do the best we can for him under the circumstances. There is a fighting chance — this much I say to revive your enthusiasm. Of course, I shall take part in the canvass as you wish. "My mother whips me and I whip the top."

Hayes spoke frequently during the campaign, dwelling on past differences of the parties rather than on the new subserviency to

careers. I wish you all success in your profession. May your career in it be longer and more brilliant than mine was. Accept an old soldier's prayer for your success.'

" He is a noble-looking man for a soldier, — six feet four inches high, well-proportioned, — keen, clear, grey eye; dignified and commanding in person, his hair a little thinned on the top of his head and slightly grizzled with age. He'll do for President." (Diary.)

slavery of both, on the successful military career of General
Scott, and on what Ohio needed to secure good local government.
The last topic he treated with a thoroughness and plainness prophetic of his future career. But he felt that he was fighting in a
losing cause. September 24 he writes: —

I have made some political speeches, neither very good nor very bad;
enough to satisfy me that with a motive, and my heart in the work, I
could do it creditably. I would like to see General Scott elected President. But there is so little interest felt by the great body of thinking
men that I shall not be surprised at his defeat; indeed, my mind is prepared for such a result. The real grounds of difference upon important
political questions no longer correspond with party lines. The progressive Whig is nearer in sentiment to the radical Democrat than the
radical Democrat is to the "fogy" of his own party; vice versa. Politics
is no longer the topic of this country. Its important questions are
settled — both on the construction of the Constitution and the fundamental principles which underlie all constitutions. Consequently the
best minds of the country will no longer be engaged in solving political
questions, in meditating on political subjects. Great minds hereafter
are to be employed on other matters; or if upon political or semi-
political questions it will not be upon those which are to determine
who are to govern, to hold office, etc. Government no longer has its
ancient importance. Its duties and its powers no longer reach to the
happiness of the people. The people's progress, progress of every sort,
no longer depends on government. But enough of politics, henceforth
I am out more than ever.

A few days later (October 14) he is still less confident of the
outlook: —

My hopes of a successful result in the approaching Presidential election are waxing feeble "by degrees and beautifully less." I shall speak
a few times before the election, and then farewell for a time — I hope
for a long time — to politics, with its excitements, its disappointments,
and all the distracting and dissipating cares and thoughts which belong
to it.

November 3, when it was known that the Whigs had suffered a
crushing defeat, Hayes wrote to his uncle, who had been much
more hopeful of success, the following letter of jocose consolation: —

"Whom the Lord loveth He chasteneth." Very consolatory text that
is. I trust you will apply it to your own case with proper unction; I am
doing so with a good deal of success. — You have heard of the philosopher who endeavored to extract sunbeams from cucumbers. Well, we

Whigs may as well do the same thing in this wise: your town I see by the reports did well. So did my ward, and my town and county tolerably fair. You may reckon that as sunbeam number one. Not a very bright beam, it is true, but then you must consider it comes from a cucumber! Another ray of comfort is, we are beaten so preposterously that we can't lay our defeat to any neglect or blunder on the part of any of Scott's friends. No prudence or sagacity, no industry or expense, could have averted the result; there is, therefore, no self-condemnation. Count this beam number two. Our Waterloo is so huge that we are not kept several days dangling in suspense between the heaven of success and the pit of despond, but are compelled to make one big plunge which is over before we have time to shiver with apprehension, and we are rejoiced to find ourselves not killed after all but alive and kicking. This will do for glimmer number three. I will give but one more; that is, that the Locofoco majority is so great that they must needs divide and so again be conquered. As Judge Matthews said to me a few days ago, speaking of a legislative body, if we have only two majority we can rely upon it, but if it is twenty some men will think for themselves and we are beaten by divisions. Well, well, it's all over now. No great odds anyhow; hope you take it with your usual philosophy.

Finally on the same day Hayes in his diary dismisses the defeated general in these words: —

My candidate, General Scott, is defeated by the most overwhelming vote ever recorded in this country. A good man, a kind man, a brave man, a true patriot, but an exceedingly vain, weak man in many points. General Scott no doubt deserves defeat if weakness and undue anxiety to be elected can be said to deserve such treatment. I have long anticipated such a result. Should have felt more sure of it but for my diffidence in my own judgment and reliance on that of others; henceforth I shall trust more to my own opinions in these matters.

These paragraphs afford an admirable reflection of Hayes's equipoise and political sagacity. He kept a clear head and a steady judgment even in the heat of partisan advocacy. His own ardent wishes did not blind him to the signs of the times. He was able to keep the other side in view, to weigh its chances and to estimate the sources of its strength. He could see also the weak places in the battle line to which he himself was contributing what strength he had.

Hayes was roused into activity by the Kansas-Nebraska measure. He had been a layman hitherto, interested in all public questions and taking his share in discussing them as occasion offered, but henceforth he was a leader in organizing sentiment

to defeat the consummation of the intent underlying that measure, and in preparing the antislavery Whigs for a new departure in party action. He had a just opinion of the sentiment in
the South, as the following letter to his uncle, of June 5, 1854,
shows: —

I agree with you as to the proceedings at Washington. A deed has
been done by Congress that promises no end of evil to the country.
The President, in flagrant violation of his pledge, made it an administration measure. Does this mean that Pierce, jealous of the growing
power of Douglas, decided to exceed him in a show of zeal in anticipation
of 1856? Be that as it may, his agents here have been very industrious
in disseminating the information among Democrats that the Administration has rewards for the faithful and scourges for those who fail in
fealty at this time. Timothy C. Day's wit has less of the Attic flavor
and more of irony than usual when speaking of the Democratic leaders,
but he has been unsound for several years. W. M. Corry's Democracy
you cannot question, yet his comments to friends on the Kansas-Nebraska business leave a tang in his mouth. A split is probable. Disney's
career is certain to close with this Congress. Able as he is, he cannot
stem the tide that has set in. It is now remarked that he has been an
exponent of Southern rather than of Northern opinion; of the school of
Cass and Buchanan, that placed the power of the Government under
the absolute dominion of the South.

Who shall blame the South for accepting what the Northern Democrats offered freely? I shall not, for one. My censure is reserved for those
who, reared in the atmosphere of freedom, have needlessly struck down
restriction and brought in strife. It is different in the South. There
party lines are obliterated in the defense of the institution that is at
once the foundation of their social order and of their business system.
They leave no one in doubt as to their views; they do not resort to double
dealing. Their public men do not pander to Northern sentiment for
the Presidency. They play for the possession of power, and when won
they use it to strengthen their position. Since their disappointment at
the results of the Mexican War; since California was admitted as a
free State, they have cast about for some means of restoring the sectional equality in the Senate. Why they should place such emphasis
on this, except as a matter of pride, one cannot understand, since they
control the Senators of a number of Northern States, and never fail
to command a majority in that body on any proposition that relates
to slavery.

The Southern people have been educated to believe in the superiority
of their social system; in the primacy of the State; in an undefined
obligation of the Constitution to protect their peculiar property everywhere. This belief is so universal, so far as my observation goes, that
I am not surprised they present a solid front. They do not anticipate

a solid North. Shall we not have it? The danger is great. We must meet it. Just what course we shall take, is as yet undecided. Our Whigs cling to the old party name and traditions. Can we make them a unit on this question? In the North without doubt. But — ?

But in the state political contest of 1855, Hayes took no active part, though he had gone as a delegate from Hamilton County to the State Republican Convention. He notes that the campaign is on, but says that he is not engaged in it and is reasonably indifferent as to results. The next year, however, he threw himself with great ardor into the new Republican movement. He was earnestly in favor of Frémont, "for free States and against new slave States"; and as he reviewed the campaign after it was over he could say: "I took a part which satisfies me in the great struggle for liberty." [1] But here again he had no illusions — no false hopes of success. He could, as four years before, calmly consider the chances of immediate success, and see that they were not flattering; while at the same time he had confidence that the movement which was beginning must contain the principles of ultimate triumph. It was actuated by the spirit of liberty; it embodied the consciousness of the "irrepressible conflict"; it was evidence of a quickened and quickening public conscience. It might not win now; but sooner or later win it must. Writing October 30, when the campaign was practically completed, Hayes says: —

I feel seriously the probable defeat of the cause of freedom in the approaching Presidential election. Before the October elections in Pennsylvania and Indiana, I was confident Colonel Frémont would be elected. But the disastrous results in those States indicate and will probably do much to produce his defeat. The majorities are small, — very small, — but they discourage our side. I shall not be surprised if Colonel Frémont receives less than one hundred electoral votes. But, after all, the good cause has made great progress. Antislavery sentiment has been created and the people have been educated to a large extent. I did hope that this election would put an end to angry discussion upon

[1] Years afterward, he wrote: "I was an earnest and active Republican 'from the start' and aided in the organization of the party in Ohio in 1855. An antislavery Whig before that date, I took no interest or part in the Know-Nothing movement, to which I was opposed on principle; but believing slavery to be the one great evil and crime of the country, I enlisted in the first party which was organized to oppose it with any prospect of success, with my whole soul in the work. I supported Frémont in 1856 zealously, hopefully, ardently, joyously."

this exciting topic, by placing the general Government in the right position in regard to it, and thereby securing to antislavery effort a foothold among those who have the evil in their midst. But further work is to be done and my sense of duty determines me to keep on in the path I have chosen — not to dabble in politics at the expense of duty to my family and to the neglect of my profession, but to do what I can consistently with other duties to aid in forming a public opinion on this subject which will "mitigate and finally eradicate the evil." I must study the subject, and am now beginning with Clarkson's history of the "Abolition of the Slave Trade."

A few days later Hayes finds encouragement in the history of the abolition of the slave trade by England. After four years of effort the question first came to vote in the House of Commons in 1791.

Pitt, Fox, Burke, Windham, Sheridan, and almost all of the great men of that day spoke eloquently for the cause of justice and humanity, but on the division the motion of the friends of abolition was lost by 88 to 163!! Look at those figures, faint-hearted Republicans, and take courage! After twenty years of defeats, disappointments, and disheartening reverses the cause triumphed gloriously in 1807 — 283 to 16!! ... How similar the struggle to that now going on here! The same arguments pro and con, the same prejudices appealed to, the same epithets of reproach, the same topics. On one side, justice, humanity, freedom; on the other, prejudice, interest, selfishness, timidity, conservatism; the advocates of right called "enthusiasts," "fanatics," and "incendiaries." ... In short, the parallel between that struggle and this is complete thus far. I shall be content if it so continues to the end.

The election of day after to-morrow is the first pitched battle. However fares the cause, I am enlisted for the war.

Verily he was "enlisted for the war"; and the war involved a greater effort and a larger sacrifice than he had any conception of when he recorded this determination. Through the four years that ensued the ferment was working; more and more it was becoming apparent to thoughtful men that the country could not continue half slave and half free; the times were ripening fast for the long and bitter struggle — still scouted as altogether impossible — which should redeem liberty and should save our nation as by fire.

Meanwhile, in his sphere and according to his opportunities, Hayes was doing what he could, while not neglecting his profession, to form public opinion on the all-absorbing topic. He had been forced by circumstances to relinquish the view he had held in 1852 that "politics is no longer *the topic* of this country," that all the "important questions were settled." Here loomed a question — long becoming more acute, more exigent of solution — of supreme importance. And Hayes now saw its importance — its possibilities of disaster; not fully, to be sure, but with increasing clearness of vision.

It was in these years that Hayes had his first experience in public office, but in an office strictly in the line of his professional work. His progress as a lawyer, as we have already seen, while not specially striking or sensational, had been steady and continuous; and his success had been of the solid and substantial sort which at the same time won the respect of his fellow lawyers and inspired confidence in the community at large. He had appeared in many important cases on which the popular attention had been fixed, and he had done his work with such zealous thoroughness and painstaking devotion to the interests of his clients as to leave on the public mind an altogether favorable impression of his powers and trustworthiness.   Early in December, 1858, the office of City Solicitor became vacant through the death of its incumbent. It fell to the City Council to fill the vacancy. The Council, consisting of thirty-four members, was pretty evenly divided among Republicans, Democrats, and Americans. Seven men were placed in nomination, Hayes last of all. The leading Republican candidate was Caleb B. Smith, afterwards a member of Mr. Lincoln's Cabinet, but the Americans were opposed to him. They preferred Hayes. Eighteen votes were necessary to a choice. On the first ballot Smith had twelve, Hayes only four votes. With succeeding ballots Hayes's vote increased, while Smith's fell off, till on the seventh ballot Hayes had seventeen votes, thus lacking only one of an election. Five more ballots were taken with the same result. But on the thirteenth ballot, a young Irish attorney, Dennis J. Toohy, a Democrat representing the Thirteenth Ward, broke the deadlock by casting his vote, much to the consternation of his Democratic associates, for Hayes.[1]

[1] William Disney, one of the candidates before the Council, writing of this incident in the Cincinnati *Commercial Gazette*, January 31, 1893, says: "So it was that Hayes was taken from private life, and without his solicitation was placed in his first public office. His luck followed him to the end of his days."

Hayes entered at once upon the duties of this office, which thus unexpectedly, and without solicitation on his part, had been conferred on him. The press greeted his selection with words of cordial commendation, and the impression made by his first appearance in the Council Chamber (literally his first appearance, for though he had been in the city eight years he had never before entered the Council Chamber) satisfied the Council that no mistake had been made in his election. "The duties of my new office," he wrote his uncle, "are all in the line of my profession. The suits of the city, advice to all officers in legal matters, etc., etc., occupy my attention. The litigation of a city like this is very important and of great variety. My assistant will attend to the less important matters, leaving me free to devote to the leading cases all my time. The amount of business is not large — at least not too large; not so perplexing I think as my old place." So well did he meet expectations that at the city Republican Convention the next spring he was, under suspension of the rules, unanimously nominated for the post he was filling. His popularity in the city was revealed by the election, his majority being greater than that of any other man on the ticket, and exceeding the majority for the head of the ticket — the candidate for Mayor — by one hundred and ninety-eight votes. This evidence of Hayes's popularity, as well as his continued display of ability in meeting the requirements of his office, attracted to him the attention of his fellow Republicans in other parts of the State. When the Republican State Convention began to assemble at Columbus in June, a movement was started with the view of nominating him for the Supreme Bench. Men from the northern part of the State were especially active in this. But Hayes was very well satisfied with the position he already held. The salary was $3500, and the duties agreeable. He had no desire to leave the active practice of the law for the bench. As soon, therefore, as he heard of what was going forward at Columbus he notified his friends on the ground that he could not consent to be a candidate.

But while he refused to consider a place on the state ticket, Hayes was by no means a mere disinterested observer of the progress of the political campaign of that year. He was eager for the growth of Republican sentiment and was doing what he could to stimulate it. The American party, while working with the Republicans in local affairs, was not yet wholly fused with it. Hayes had no affiliation with the American party at any stage of its development, but he had seen the wisdom of treating its adherents in a conciliatory spirit in the hope that the third party might disappear — merged in the growing party of freedom. When it was arranged that Mr. Lincoln, whose great debate with Douglas had made him peculiarly the prophet of the new Republicanism, should speak at Cincinnati in September, Hayes was apprehensive lest the orator might say something which would tend to mar the existing harmonious relations between Americans and Republicans. He undertook on his own responsibility to get a hint of warning to Mr. Lincoln in a letter, interesting not only for this main fact, but also because it shows incidentally the doubt then prevailing in Ohio as to Mr. Lincoln's exact political standing. The letter, which was dated September 14, and addressed to A. P. Russell [1] at Columbus, follows: —

> I am not a member of any executive committee and am not "one in authority" except in the humble capacity of "a sovereign." As a private, I write to make a suggestion, which I hope you will see carried to the right person. Mr. Lincoln is to speak here the last of this week (I am sorry it was not a week later, after our ticket is in the field); and all honest Americans as well as Republicans are waiting to give him a rousing reception. My suggestion is that Mr. Lincoln be informed of the facts in regard to our position here, so that he may not give a too strictly partisan cast to his address. We go by the name of "Opposition Party," and injury might be done if party names and party doctrines were used by Mr. Lincoln in a way to displease the American element of our organization. The Americans are liberal, however, and very generally sympathized with Mr. Lincoln in his contest with Douglas, although perhaps not subscribing to all his views. I understand Mr. Lincoln was an old Clay Whig, of Kentucky parentage, and with a wholesome dislike of Locofocoism. These qualities with a word of caution as to our peculiar position will enable him to make a fine impression here.
>
> If our ticket is formed without a rumpus, we are confident of carrying a majority for all. I write, supposing you will see Mr. Lincoln at Columbus. Dennison seems to be a full match, if not an overmatch, for his competitor. — Sincerely,
>
> R. B. HAYES.
>
> P.S. The Douglas meeting was largely attended, but was not a success. It rather injured than strengthened the "Party of Permanency."

[1] Author of *Half Tints, Library Notes, A Club of One,* and other charming books, and at that time Secretary of State.

Hayes attended the Lincoln meeting in Fifth Street Market, and he gives us his impression: —

Mr. Lincoln has an ungainly figure, but one loses sight of that, or rather the first impression disappears in the absorbed attention which the matter of the speech commands. He is an orator of an unusual kind, so calm, so undemonstrative, but nevertheless an orator of great merit. It is easy to contrast him after the manner of Plutarch, but his like has not been heard in these parts. His manner is more like Crittenden's, and his truth and candor are like what we admire in the Kentuckian, but his speech has greater logical force, greater warmth of feeling.

Clearly, Hayes did not see in the speaker the next President, or he would have set that down in his comments.

CHAPTER VIII

EVENTS were moving rapidly toward the great crisis in our
nation's life. How rapidly, contemporary opinion shows,
hardly one of the actors in the scene conceived. It is easy
enough to see now upon what rocks the ship of state was surely
drifting, but the abounding optimism of the American people
blinded them to the drift, and kept them hopeful that the rocks,
of which they could not help now and then to have an indistinct
and fleeting vision, would dissolve into thin air as they were approached. North and South had drawn apart further than either
knew. Minor differences between them, in their institutions,
their manners, their attitude to life, had existed for generations.
But out of these alone serious dispute could never have arisen.
Lapse of time and increasing commercial and social intercourse
would surely have modified them, or at least have made each
section tolerant of the other's views. Even the larger differences
of constitutional interpretation and of protection or free trade,
acute and exasperating as they might be at times, had in them
no potency of disintegration and disruption.

The one great source of difference, which no compromise long
could lay, which gave force and effect to all other differences, —
emphasizing their importance, using them to create prejudice
and antagonism, — was the existence of slavery. Against this
all the forces of civilization were steadily working; against this
the moral sentiment of Christendom was arraying itself with
ever-increasing clearness of view and determination of purpose.
Gradually more and more of the people of the North were coming to look upon slavery with horror and detestation. While
all but comparatively few believed that the rights of the slave
States, as guaranteed by the Constitution, should be maintained, yet the open sympathies of vast numbers were with the
slaves that escaped from bondage; and if they did not aid them

in their flight, they put no obstacle in their way and rejoiced when they had crossed the border beyond reach of recapture. And the more certainly, as we can now see, that slavery was doomed, the more arrogant the slaveholders of the South became in their political demands; the more determined they were that the power of the general Government should be exercised for the protection of their institution; that the slave power should be coequal with the forces of freedom in settling the public domain beyond the Missouri and in establishing new States.

It was the repudiation by Congress of the Missouri Compromise that created the Republican party; it was the struggle in Kansas, with the National Administration aiding the slave power, and the Dred Scott decision that caused its rapid growth. However careful its leaders might be to proclaim, as they did proclaim, their rejection of abolitionist intention or views and their purpose steadfastly to respect and maintain the integrity of the constitutional safeguards protecting slavery, yet it was clear to all that the new party was the party of freedom; the new party recognized, or rather embodied, the growing abhorrence of slavery; the new party had its face clearly set toward a future — sometime sure to come, its coming to be hastened in all legitimate ways — when all men should be free. The instinct of friends and enemies alike of the new movement was unerring in recognizing the words of Abraham Lincoln, "I believe this government cannot permanently endure half slave and half free," [1] and the phrase of William H. Seward, "It is an irrepressible conflict," [2] as expressing the true and dominant sentiments of the new force in American politics. But, in spite of the frequent threats of fiery Southern orators and journalists, neither leaders nor followers then had any serious notion that the conflict would result in attempted disunion and the unspeakable woes of civil war. Not till States had actually revolted, had set up a separate government, had put armies in motion, had fired upon the national flag, did men cease to dispute over even the right of the Federal power to send the national troops into rebellious States and to preserve the national life by force of arms.

[1] At Springfield, Illinois, June 17, 1858.
[2] At Rochester, New York, October 25, 1858.

During this period, when the nation was anxiously watching the progress of events in Kansas, when the determination of the slave power to exact its uttermost demands was leading to the hopeless division of the Democratic party, when the excited agitation of uncompromising abolitionists was stimulating John Brown to his abortive attempt to incite a slave insurrection, Hayes had no clearer prevision of the tremendous fate impending over the country in the immediate future than the great mass of his fellow citizens. He recognized the Frémont campaign as the first battle in the contest for freedom; he gloried in the part he had taken in that campaign; he registered a vow, as we have seen, that he was enlisted for the war; he continued steadfastly to do what he could to create public opinion in favor of larger liberty and against the encroaching spirit of the slave power; and he looked forward hopefully to the political combat of 1860 for a long step forward toward the prevalence of the principles he held dear. But he had no premonition of the approaching cataclysm. During the years 1859 and 1860 life passed agreeably with him. His work as City Solicitor was pleasant and not too arduous. Domestic and social relations were all that could be desired. His influence in his party was increasing; his position in the community was one of recognized leadership; his duties afforded him ample leisure for reading and for the society of his friends.[1] In the midsummer weeks of 1860 he was able to lay work aside and in company with his wife to take a delightful trip down the St. Lawrence to Quebec and the Saguenay and on to Boston and other Eastern points. A year later the events of this journey were recalled with peculiar interest in the midst of mountain campaigning in western Virginia.

Some weeks before this trip, the day after the divided Democrats at Baltimore had made their nominations for the Presidency, Hayes recorded in his diary his estimate of the political

---

[1] "You ask what I am doing. Not working hard, not working much. I earn my salary, I am sure, and am therefore conscience-clear. I have read a good deal this winter, — more than usual, — some history, some poetry, some religion, biography, and miscellaneous matter; but no novels and no politics. I am intending to go into politics and novels as soon as I finish three or four books that I have now on hand. I never enjoyed life better. Barring two or three anxious weeks on the boys' accounts, this has been a happy winter." (Letter to Sardis Birchard, February 4, 1860.)

probabilities. Four tickets in the field, he observes, was a new thing in his day. He continues: —

My Republican friends are confident that Lincoln and Hamlin will be elected by the people. I have a good deal of apprehension on the sub-. ject. I fear the election will go to the House. — Let me cipher. There are 303 electoral votes; 152 are required for a choice. We may count for Lincoln the States carried by Frémont in 1856; — eleven States, 114 electoral votes. Add Minnesota, 4 votes, — 118 votes certain. Pennsylvania (27), Oregon (3), probably, — 148. Four more votes necessary to elect him. If California, New Jersey, Illinois, or Indiana should go for Lincoln, the vote of either State added to 148 would elect.

Hayes thought New Jersey and Illinois might both be counted as probable for Lincoln, his chance depending on there being "a small defection in favor of Bell and an equal or larger defection from Douglas." With these two States counted for Lincoln his electoral vote, Hayes figured, would probably be 167. Hayes figured that Bell was certain of 39 votes, from Kentucky, Tennessee, Louisiana, and Maryland. He did have exactly that number, though Virginia, which Hayes had counted as only probable, contributed her vote to the total in the place of the two last States given in Hayes's list as certain. Douglas, Hayes thought, was sure of no votes, but likely to get the votes of Indiana, California, Missouri, and Delaware. (He did get the 9 votes of Missouri and 3 from New Jersey.) While Breckinridge, Hayes thought, was sure of 45 votes. "On the whole," Hayes concludes, "I think Lincoln's chances the best, but not a moral certainty; — that Bell or Breckinridge will be next."

On Hayes's return from his Eastern trip he entered into the canvass, but not at first with great spirit; which indicates clearly that up to this time he had no foreboding of the consequences with which the campaign was pregnant. September 30, in a letter to his uncle, Hayes wrote: —

I have made a few little speeches in the county townships, and shall make a few more. I cannot get up much interest in the contest. A wholesome contempt for Douglas, on account of his recent demagoguing, is the chief feeling I have. I am not so confident that Lincoln will get votes enough, as many of our friends. I think his chances are fair, but what may be the effect of fusions in such anti-Republican States as New Jersey and Pennsylvania, is more than I can tell, or confidently guess until after the state elections. In this county the fight is doubtful, but probably against us.

A few days later he speaks of the lively election canvass and
says that he has enjoyed it well. The meetings were "prodigious"
and the chances improving. There is no further reference to the
campaign until election day. The October elections had practically determined the result, and Hayes is no longer in much
doubt. He writes: "The election is quiet, but the voting active.
All right, of course." On the same day Hayes made in his diary
the first entry touching politics since the one in June after the
Baltimore Convention — an entry which shows that the violent
threats of the Southern leaders had begun to impress him as
possibly more than campaign rhetoric: —

The Southern States are uneasy at the prospects of Lincoln's election
to-day. The ultra South threatens disunion, and it now looks as if South
Carolina and possibly two or three others would go out of the Union.
Will they? And if so what is to be the result? Will other slave States
gradually be drawn after them, or will the influence of the conservative
States draw back into the Union or hold in the Union the ultra States?
I think the latter. But at all events I feel as if the time had come to test
the question. If the threats are meant, then it is time the Union was
dissolved or the traitors crushed out. I hope Lincoln goes in. All now
depends on New York. The October election settled Pennsylvania and
the other doubtful States.

The rejoicing over the triumph of Lincoln at the polls was
soon dampened by the ominous clouds gathering forebodingly
along the southern horizon. The threats of disunion began rapidly to be carried out. The North was in dismay for the time
being. Everywhere efforts were made to ward off the coming
disaster by conciliation, concessions, and compromises. Men
were loath to contemplate the idea of the National Government
exercising coercion upon a revolting State; so pervasive still was
the notion that in the American Commonwealth the constituent
parts were in some of the essential elements of government
greater than the whole. Only gradually did the loyal people of
the North come to a clear apprehension of the fundamental
truth, that the first duty of every government is self-preserva-
tion, by all means, not only against alien foes but domestic
enemies. It seems difficult now to understand that men ever
could so long have disputed over the right of the National Government to coerce a rebellious State. On December 19, a meeting
was held at the Opera House in Cincinnati in the interest of

public peace. Speeches were made denying the constitutional right of secession, but counselling moderation and kind treatment; and resolutions to the same effect were adopted. The resolutions, at the same time, denounced the "uncandid discussion of the slavery question as the chief cause of the political evils of the day"; declared with all emphasis against state laws intended to defeat the execution of the Fugitive Slave Law; expressed abhorrence of any efforts to excite the slaves to insubordination; and, finally, expressed confidence in the "efforts of candid men to counteract the evil spirit so long spreading in the land and to preserve our glorious Union."

It is known that Hayes, while he took no active part in this meeting, was in sympathy with the spirit of conciliation which actuated it. But he no longer entertained hopes that the emergency could be met by compromise. The time for that was past. January 4, 1861, he writes in his diary: —

South Carolina has passed a secession ordinance, and Federal laws are set at naught in the State. Overt acts enough have been committed — forts and arsenal taken, a revenue cutter seized, and Major Anderson besieged in Fort Sumter. Other cotton States are about to follow. Disunion and civil war are at hand; and yet I fear disunion and war less than compromise. We can recover from them. The free States alone, if we must go on alone, will make a glorious nation. Twenty millions in the temperate zone, stretching from the Atlantic to the Pacific, full of vigor, industry, inventive genius, educated and moral, increasing by immigration rapidly, and above all free — all free — will form a confederacy of twenty States scarcely inferior in real power to the unfortunate Union of thirty-three States which we had on the first of November. I do not feel gloomy when I look forward. The reality is less frightful than the apprehension which we have all had these many years. Let us be temperate, calm, and just, but firm and resolute. Crittenden's compromise! No, no. Windham, speaking of the rumor that Bonaparte was about to invade England, said: "The danger of invasion is by no means equal to that of peace. A man may escape a pistol however near his head, but not a dose of poison."

Three weeks later Hayes writes again; preferring with many moderate men of all parties that the States bent on the suicidal course of secession should be allowed to have their way: —

Six States have "seceded." Let them go! If the Union is now dissolved it does not prove that the experiment of popular government is a failure. In all the free States, and in a majority if not in all of the slaveholding States, popular government has been successful. But the experiment of uniting free and slaveholding States in one nation is, perhaps, a failure. Freedom and slavery can, perhaps, not exist side by side under the same popular government. There probably is an "irrepressible conflict" between freedom and slavery. It may as well be admitted and our new relations may as well be formed with that as an admitted fact.

Monday, February 11, Mr. Lincoln began his memorable progress from Springfield to Washington. A committee from Cincinnati met Mr. Lincoln's party at Indianapolis to give it welcome and to escort it to the Ohio metropolis. Mr. and Mrs. Hayes were of this committee. Mr. Lincoln's speeches and conversation gave Hayes great confidence in the new President. He writes his uncle: "He is in good health, not a hair grey or gone, in his prime, and fit for service, mentally and physically. Great hopes may well be felt." In another letter Hayes gives details of the Cincinnati reception: —

The reception given to the President-elect here was most impressive. He rode in an open carriage, standing erect with head uncovered, and bowing his acknowledgments to greetings showered upon him. There was a lack of comfort in the arrangements, but the simplicity, the homely character of all was in keeping with the nobility of this typical American. A six-in-hand with gorgeous trappings, accompanied by outriders and a courtly train, could have added nothing to him; would have detracted from him, would have been wholly out of place. The times are unsuited to show. The people did not wish to be entertained with a display; they did wish to see the man in whose hands is the destiny of our country.

You will read the speeches in the papers, and search in vain for anything to find fault with. Mr. Lincoln was wary at all times, wisely so I think, and yet I hear no complaint. Our German Turners, who are radical on the slavery question and who are ready to make that an issue of war, planned to draw from him some expression in sympathy with their own views. They serenaded him and talked at him, but they were baffled.[1] In private conversation he was discreet but frank. He believes in a policy of kindness, of delay to give time for passions to cool, but not in a compromise to extend the power and the deadly influence of the slave system. This gave me great satisfaction. The impression he made was good. He undoubtedly is shrewd, able, and possesses strength in reserve. This will be tested soon.

Meanwhile Hayes's term of office as City Solicitor was drawing to a close. It would end Monday, April 8. The day for the

[1] Cf. Francis F. Browne, *The Life of Abraham Lincoln*, p. 385.

city election was April 1. Hayes was a candidate for reëlection, but he had little hope of success. The Democrats and the Know-Nothings, who still had a considerable following in Cincinnati, had united in the naming of a city ticket, which they were supporting with much earnestness. Combined they could command a decided majority over the Republicans. Hayes wrote to his uncle, March 17: —

> Our chance is that there will be some slip or mistake which will upset the union. I shall go under with the rest, but expect to run ahead of the ticket. Of course I prefer not to be beaten, but I have got out of the office the best there is in it for me. . . . Yes, giving up Fort Sumter is vexing. It hurts our little election, too; but I would give up the prospect of office, if it would save the fort, with the greatest pleasure.

There was no slip or mistake to "upset the union," and three days before the election, Hayes again writes his uncle, who was solicitous for his success, in these words: —

> You are more anxious that I should be reëlected than the occasion calls for. I philosophize in this way: I have got out of the office pretty much all the good there is in it — reputation and experience. If I quit now, I shall be referred to as the best, or one of the best Solicitors, the city has had. If I serve two years more, I can add nothing to this; I may possibly lose. I shall be out of clients and business a little while, but this difficulty will perhaps be greater two years hence; so you see it is no great matter; still I should prefer to beat and with half a chance I should.

The election turned out quite as Hayes expected. The entire Republican ticket was routed, but Hayes received more votes than any of his fellows in defeat.

Hayes lost no time in making new arrangements for the future. Frederick Hassaurek had just been appointed by the President Minister to Bolivia. He left a good law practice, largely among the Germans. Hayes arranged to take this in partnership with Leopold Markbreit, Hassaurek's brother-in-law, "a bright, gentlemanly, popular young German," and the day after his term of office expired he had moved into his new quarters and was already at work.

The reduction of Fort Sumter and the call of the President for seventy-five thousand volunteers practically put a stop to idle controversy in the North as to the right of the Government to defend and to recover its own. The effect everywhere was

electric. Party cries were drowned for the time in patriotic
shouts. The minority that still could not, in spite of the imperative logic of events, escape from the logical coil in which their
views of States' rights had involved them, could make no head
against the vast majority eager to spring to the rescue of the
threatened Republic. Hayes writes in his diary: —

Sunday evening, April 14, the news of Lincoln's call for seventy-five
thousand men [was] received here with unbounded enthusiasm. How
relieved we were to have a Government again! I shall never forget the
strong emotions, the wild and joyous excitement of that Sunday evening.
Staid and sober church members thronged the newspaper offices, full
of the general joy and enthusiasm. Great meetings were held. I wrote
the resolutions of the main one. Then the rally of troops, the flags floating from every house, the liberality, harmony, forgetfulness of party
and self — all good. Let what evils may follow, I shall not soon cease
to rejoice over this event.

The meeting to which Hayes refers was held in the hall of the
Catholic Institute, Monday evening, April 15. The room was
packed long before the hour and hundreds were turned away.
Speeches of glowing patriotism were made by Thomas J. Gallagher, the chairman, and by Judge Storer, Judge Dickson,
Judge Stallo, Edward F. Noyes, and others. The resolutions
written by Mr. Hayes were read by him as chairman of the resolutions committee and adopted by the meeting with enthusiastic
unanimity. They were as follows: —

Resolved, That the people of Cincinnati, assembled without distinction of party, are unanimously of opinion that the authority of the
United States, as against the rebellious citizens of the seceding and disloyal States, ought to be asserted and maintained, and that whatever
men or means may be necessary to accomplish that object the patriotic
people of the loyal States will promptly and cheerfully furnish.

Resolved, That the citizens of Cincinnati will, to the utmost of their
ability, sustain the general Government in maintaining its authority,
in enforcing the laws, and in upholding the flag of the Union.[1]

In a letter to his uncle, written earlier in the day on which this
meeting occurred, Hayes says: —

We are all for war. The few dissentients have to run like quarter
horses — a great change for two weeks to produce. As the Dutchman
says: "What a beeples!" Poor Anderson, what a chance he threw away.

[1] Cincinnati *Gazette*, April 16.

The Government may overlook it or even whitewash it, but the people and history will not let him off so easily. I like it; anything is better than the state of things we have had the last few months. . . . Mother thinks we are to be punished for our sinfulness, and reads the Old Testament vigorously. Mother Webb quietly grieves over it. Lucy enjoys it and wishes she had been in Fort Sumter with a garrison of women. Dr. Joe is for flames, slaughter, and a rising of the slaves.

In the days that followed Hayes's thoughts were constantly upon the national crisis. He decided not to "think of going into this first movement." He would wait and see. He went to Columbus, April 19, to help his brother-in-law, Dr. James D. Webb, to obtain an appointment as surgeon to one of the first regiments. The next day he writes his uncle: —

I have joined a volunteer home company to learn drill. It is chiefly composed of the Literary Club; includes Stephenson, Moline, John Groesbeck, Judge James, McLaughlin, Beard, and most of my cronies. We wish to learn how to "eyes right and left," if nothing more. A great state of things for Christian people, and then to have old gentlemen say as you do, "I am glad we have got to fighting at last." Judge Swan and Mr. Andrews and the whole Methodist clergy all say the same. Shocking! One thing: don't spend much on your house or furniture henceforth. Save, save, is the motto now. People who furnish for the war will make money, but others will have a time of it. Mother thinks it is a judgment on us for our sins. Henry Ward Beecher, who is now here, says it is Divine work — that the Almighty is visibly in it.[1]

May 12 he writes to the same correspondent: —

The St. Louis and other news revives the war talk. We are likely, I think, to have a great deal of it before the thing is ended. Bryan writes me a long, friendly secession letter — one-sided and partial, but earnest and honest; perhaps he would say the same of my reply to it. I wish I could have a good talk with you about these days. I may be carried off by the war fever, and would like to hear you on it. Of course, I mean to take part, if there seems a real necessity for it, but I am tempted to

[1] April 23, he wrote his uncle: "No doubt the accounts sent abroad as to the danger we are in from Kentucky are much exaggerated. Kentucky is in no condition to go out immediately. If the war goes on, as I think it ought, it is probable that she will leave us, and that we shall be greatly exposed, but she has no arms, and almost no military organization. Even their secession Governor is not prepared to precipitate matters under these circumstances. We are rapidly preparing for war, and shall be on a war footing long before Kentucky has decided what to do. . . . A great many gentlemen of your years are in for the war. One old fellow was rejected on account of his grey hair and whiskers. He hurried down street and had them colored black, and passed muster in another company."

do so, notwithstanding my unmilitary education and habits, on general enthusiasm and glittering generalities; but for some pretty decided obstacles, I should have done so before now.

A few days later his plans are practically decided on, and he writes to his uncle: —

You say nothing about my going into the war. I have been fishing for your opinion in several of my late letters. Unless you speak soon, you may be too late. My new business arrangement, and my prospects, bad as times are, are evidently good. Whenever other lawyers have business, I shall easily make all that is needed; but still, as Billy Rogers writes me, "This is a holy war," and if a fair chance opens, I shall go in; if a fair chance don't open, I shall, perhaps, take measures to open one. So don't be taken by surprise if you hear of my soldiering. All the family have been sounded, and there will be no *troublesome* opposition. In view of contingencies, I don't like to leave home to visit you just now. I shall be able to leave money to support the family a year or two, without reckoning on my pay. Events move fast these days.

Since writing the foregoing, Judge Matthews called, and we have agreed to go to Columbus to lay the ropes for a regiment. There are a thousand men here who want us for their officers.

The talk with Judge Matthews (Stanley Matthews), when the decision to enter the service was formed, is the subject of an entry in the diary under date of May 15: —

Judge Matthews and I have agreed to go into the service for the war, — if possible into the same regiment.[1] I spoke my feelings to him which he said were his also, viz., that this was a just and necessary war and that it demanded the whole power of the country; *that I would prefer to go into it if I knew I was to die or be killed in the course of it, than to live through and after it without taking any part in it.*

These concluding words, underscored as they were written, are the solemn and deliberate expression of a high and holy patriotism. Not with the rashness of sudden impulse, when flags were flying and martial music filled the air with its intoxicating strains, but with ample weighing of possibilities, with full

[1] Secretary Chase, who was the personal friend of both men and knew their worth, offered to obtain colonelcies for Matthews and Hayes. They preferred to enter the service with lower rank and win their way upward. The regiment, of which they became respectively lieutenant-colonel and major (the Twenty-third Ohio Volunteer Infantry), was the first Ohio regiment enlisted for three years or the war, and the first whose field officers were appointed by the Governor. The field officers of the three-months regiments had been elected by vote of the men themselves.

May 15, 1861

    Judge Matthews and ~~myself~~ I have agreed to go into the service for the war. if possible into the Same Regiment. I spoke my feelings to him which he said were his also viz that this was a just and necessary war and that it demanded the whole time of the Country. That I would prefer to go into it —— I knew I would to die or be killed in the course of it, than to live through and after it without taking any part in it.—

19th
    We find a good deal of difficulty in getting new Companies or Regiments accepted for the war, but we shall persevere —

understanding of what the cost might be, Hayes made his choice and determined his course. In this he was a type of thousands of his fellow countrymen. The country was in peril. Better death in helping to save it than life with the consciousness of having turned a deaf ear to its summons when its need was dire and friends and neighbors were springing gladly to its rescue!

CHAPTER IX

STEPS were at once taken by Hayes and Matthews to carry their resolution into effect. They put themselves in communication with the Governor, who personally knew of their worth and ability. But the State's quota of troops seemed already to be full, and for some weeks no new regiments were accepted. "We find a good deal of difficulty," Hayes writes in his diary May 19, "in getting new companies or regiments accepted for the war, but we shall persevere." And a week later a letter to his uncle says: —

I have been watching the enlistments for the war during the last week with much interest, as the chance of our enterprise for the present depends on it. If twenty regiments enlist out of the twenty-six now on foot in the State, there will be no room for ours. If less than twenty go in for three years, we are safe. Until the news of the advance into Virginia arrived, and the death of Colonel Ellsworth, there was a good deal of hesitation in the various camps. The natural dissatisfaction and disgust which many felt, some with, and some without, adequate cause, were likely to prevent the quota from being filled out of the three-months men. But now all is enthusiasm again. Of course, I like to see it, but for the present, it probably cuts us out. Well, we shall be ready for the next time.

Early in June, however, the Governor was able to make the two men an offer, which they were prompt to accept. The history of the next few weeks is fully recorded by diary and letters:

June 7. — I received a dispatch from Governor Dennison asking me if I would accept the majority in a regiment of which William S. Rosecrans was to be colonel and Judge Matthews lieutenant-colonel. I read it to Lucy, consulted with my old law partner, who happened to be visiting Cincinnati, and thereupon replied that I would accept as proposed. Late in the afternoon of the next day I received a dispatch from the Governor addressed to Judge Matthews and myself directing us to report to the adjutant-general at Columbus Monday morning. Not being able to find Judge Matthews in the city, on the next day (Sunday P.M.) I rode out to his residence in Glendale, took tea with him and his family, and rode into the city, arriving a few minutes before 9 P.M. I bid good-bye to my family and at 9.30 P.M. we took the cars by way of Dayton for Columbus.

June 10. — Monday morning we went to the Governor's office and learned that the Governor had made up a regiment composed of companies chiefly from the extreme northern and northeastern part of the State, the field officers being all from Cincinnati, to be the Twenty-third Regiment, Ohio Volunteer Infantry, for the service of the United States during the war. This regiment was to be organized under General Order No. 15, issued by the Adjutant-General of the United States, May 4, 1861, and was the first regiment in Ohio in which the regiment did not elect its own field officers. We feared there would be some difficulty in reconciling the men to officers not of their own selection. . . . All the captains came into the Governor's office soon after we entered, in a state of some excitement, or at least some feeling, at finding themselves placed under strangers from a distant part of the State. We were introduced to them. Colonel Rosecrans, unfortunately, was not present, having not yet arrived from some military service at Washington. . . . A little acquaintance satisfied us that our captains were not disposed to be unreasonable; that their feeling was a natural one under the circumstances, and that all ill-feeling would disappear if we showed the disposition and ability to perform our duties. Captain Beatty, however, would not be content. He had been a Senator in the Legislature, was fifty-five or sixty years old, and not disposed to go under young men. We took a hack out to Camp Jackson,[1] four miles west of Columbus on the National Road. Several companies were mustered into service by Captains Simpson and Robinson the same day. Colonel E. A. King, of Dayton, was under state authority in command of all the soldiers, some twenty-five hundred in number, not mustered into service. As rapidly as they were mustered in, they passed under Colonel Matthews as the ranking field officer in United States service. Luckily Captain Beatty was not ready for the mustering officer and we succeeded in getting Captain Zimmerman's fine company in his place. Ditto Captain Howard in place of Captain Weller. Our mustering was completed June 11 and 12. We were guests of Colonel King (for rations) at the log headquarters and slept at Platt's.[2] Both good arrangements. Wednesday evening [June] 12, we got up a large marquee — fine, but not tight, and that night I had my first sleep under canvas — cool but refreshing.

June 13. — Colonel William S. Rosecrans appeared and assumed the command. Our regiment was paraded after retreat had been sounded. The long line looked well, although the men were ununiformed and

---

[1] Name soon after changed to Camp Chase.
[2] Mr. Hayes's brother-in-law.

without arms. We were lucky in having a band enlisted as privates at Ashland. Colonel Rosecrans is a spirited, rapid talker and worker and makes a fine impression on officers and men. . . . There are many good singers in camp, and as we are not reduced to order yet, the noises of the camp these fine evenings and the strangeness have a peculiar charm. How cold the nights are! I am more affected as I look at the men on parade than I expected to be—not more embarrassed. I am not greatly embarrassed, but an agreeable emotion, a swelling of heart possesses me. The strongest excitement was when I saw the spirit and enthusiasm with which the oath was taken. Our captains impress me as a body most favorably.

June 16. — Colonel Rosecrans and Matthews having gone to Cincinnati and Colonel King to Dayton, I am left in command of camp, some twenty-five hundred to three thousand men — an odd position for a novice, so ignorant of all military things. All matters of discretion, of common judgment, I get along with easily, but I was for an instant puzzled when a captain in the Twenty-fourth, of West Point education, asked me formally as I sat in tent for his orders for the day, he being officer of the day. Acting on my motto, "When you don't know what to say, say nothing," I merely remarked that I thought of nothing requiring special attention; that if anything was wanted out of the usual routine I would let him know.[1]

Early the next week Colonel Rosecrans returned and set vigorously to work organizing the regiment. The very evening of the day he returned, a dispatch came from Washington announcing his appointment to the rank of brigadier-general, and ordering

---

[1] Hayes himself failed to record one incident of these early days in camp which showed his tact and good sense in dealing with the men. Mr. McKinley described it in a speech before the Ohio Grand Army the year of Mr. Hayes's death. "I saw General Hayes," he said, "for the first time in June, 1861. He had been commissioned as major of the Twenty-third Ohio Volunteer Infantry, in which was the company to which I belonged. I remember — and it was the first incident that attracted my attention to the new major — that when the regiment was taken to the arsenal to receive its arms, it was proposed to give to the regiment a lot of old-fashioned muskets, which we believed — and we knew all about it, of course — were unsuitable for service at the front. And that entire regiment, after receiving them, stacked them about the arsenal and returned to their camp, refusing to accept the muskets offered by the State. I suppose if that had occurred later in the war, every company in the regiment would have been put in arrest; but Matthews and Hayes went from company to company, and addressed the young men in a most patriotic appeal. I remember well and vividly the speech of young Hayes. He said it was not so much the weapons that we were to use in the war as it was the spirit with which we used the best weapons that were given us by the Government to sustain the Government of the United States. We took our guns, and it was but a little while until we had very much better ones."

him to western Virginia to take command of Ohio troops moving in that direction. "I shall never forget," Hayes wrote, "how his face shone with delight as he read the dispatch."

June 20. — Yes, the loss of our colonel did trouble us. Matthews does not yet wish the responsibility of command. With a few weeks' experience, I would prefer his appointment; in fact, I would anyhow, but we are casting about, and the Governor will consult our wishes. Our present preference is either Colonel Scammon or Colonel George W. McCook — the latter, if he would take it. It will probably be satisfactory. If the new man is competent, he will be a very mean man if he does not get on well with us.[1]

The next day Colonel Eliakim Parker Scammon was appointed to command the regiment, and June 30, Hayes writes his wife: —

Our colonel is fond of pleasantry, amiable and social. He enjoys the disposition of Matthews and myself to joke, and after duty, we get jolly. But he has not a happy way of hitting the humors of the men; still, as we think him a kind-hearted, just man, we hope the men will learn to appreciate his good qualities, in spite of an unfortunate manner.

A few days later the diary says: —

Colonel Scammon is a gentleman of military education and experience; intelligent and agreeable, but not well fitted for volunteer command; and I fear somewhat deficient in health and vigor of nerves. We shall find him an entertaining head of our mess of field officers. After some ups and downs we have succeeded in getting for our surgeon my brother-in-law, Dr. Joseph T. Webb. Our field officers' mess consists of Colonel Scammon, Lieutenant-Colonel Matthews, Dr. Webb, and myself.

July 23. — We are in the midst of the excitement produced by the disastrous panic near Washington. We expect it will occasion a very early movement of our regiment. We shall, perhaps, be ordered to the Kanawha line. We certainly shall, unless the recent defeat shall change the plan of the campaign. . . . The Washington affair is greatly to be regretted; unless speedily repaired, it will lengthen the war materially. The panic of the troops does not strike me as remarkable. You recollect the French army in the neighborhood of the Austrians were seized with a panic, followed by a flight of many miles, caused merely by a runaway mule and cart and "nobody hurt." The same soldiers won the battle of Solferino a few days after. But I do think the commanding officer ought not to have led fresh levies against an enemy entrenched

[1] Letter to Mrs. Hayes.

on his own ground. Gradual advances, fortifying as he went, strikes me as a more prudent policy. But it is easy to find fault. The lesson will have its uses. It will test the stuff our people are made of. If we are a solid people, as I believe we are, this reverse will stiffen their backs. They will be willing to make greater efforts and sacrifices.

We worked late last night getting our accoutrements ready. In the hurry of preparations to depart, I may not be able to write you before I go. Good-bye.[1]

July 24. — Our regiment was reviewed by the Governor and Major-General Frémont. It was a gratifying scene. The Colonel (Frémont — I must always think of the man of '56 as the "Colonel") looked well. How he inspires confidence and affection in the masses of people! The night before I was introduced to him at the American. He is a romantic, rather, perhaps, than a great, character. But he is loyal, brave, and persevering beyond all compare.

July 25. — Last night I went into Columbus to bid good-bye to the boys; on the road met Lucy, Laura, and Mother Webb; advised them to return. After we were at home (Platt's) Lucy showed more emotion at my departure than she has hitherto exhibited. She wanted to spend my last night with me in Camp Chase. I took her out. We passed a happy evening going around among the men, gathered in picturesque groups, cooking rations for three days at the camp fires. Early in the morning, as she was anxious Mother Webb should see the camp before I left, I sent her in by a hack to return with Mother Webb, which she did, and they saw us leave the camp. I marched in with the men afoot — a gallant show they made as they moved up High Street to the depot. Lucy and Mother Webb remained several hours until we left. I saw them watching me as I stood on the platform at the rear of the last car as long as they could see me. Their eyes swam. I kept my emotions under control enough not to melt into tears. . . . A pleasant ride to Bellaire. Stayed in the cars all night.

The loyal people of western Virginia were in the vast majority. They had refused to be carried out of the Union by the ordinance of secession, but had organized a new government. Thereupon Confederate forces had been sent across the mountains and McClellan had fought his brief and successful Rich Mountain campaign. After the Bull Run disaster McClellan was summoned to Washington and General Rosecrans was left in command of the Union force along the line of the Baltimore and Ohio Railroad. The three-months men were leaving for home and the long-time regiments were coming in to take their places. The

[1] Letter to Sardis Birchard.

purpose in view was to drive the remaining Rebel troops from the State, to check the rising secession feeling, and to sustain and protect the Union people. Hayes's regiment reached Clarksburg July 26. The next day he wrote his wife: —

Our second day, from Bellaire to this place, was an exceedingly happy one. We travelled about one hundred and thirty miles in Virginia, and with the exception of one deserted village of secessionists (Farmington) we were received everywhere with an enthusiasm I never saw anywhere before. No such great crowds turned out to meet us as we saw from Indianapolis to Cincinnati assembled to see Lincoln; but everywhere, in the corn and hay fields, in the houses, in the roads, on the hills, wherever a human being saw us, we saw such honest, spontaneous demonstrations of joy as we never beheld elsewhere. Old men and women, boys and children — some fervently prayed for us, some laughed, and some cried; all did something which told the story. The secret of it is, the defeat at Washington, and the departure of some thousands of three-months men of Ohio and Indiana led them to fear they were left to the Rebels of eastern Virginia. We were the first three-years men filling the places of those who left. It was pleasant to see we were not invading an enemy's country, but defending the people among whom we came. Our men enjoyed it beyond measure. Many had never seen a mountain, none had ever seen such a reception. They stood on top of the cars, and danced and shouted with delight. We got here in the night. General Rosecrans is with us. No other full regiment here. We march to-morrow up the mountains. All around me is confusion — sixteen hundred horses, several hundred wagons, all the preparations for a large army — our own men in a crowded camp putting up tents. No time for further description.

P.S. — Colonel Matthews showed me a letter from his mother received at the moment of his leaving. She said she rejoiced she was the mother of seven sons all loyal and true, and that four of them were able to go to the war for the national rights. — The view from where I sit is most beautiful, long ranges of hills, a pleasant village, an extensive sweep of cultivated country, the fortified hill where an Indiana regiment proposes to defend itself against overwhelming odds, etc., etc.

The Twenty-third Ohio was a model regiment, composed of intelligent men who faced danger without dismay, and who submitted cheerfully to thorough discipline. The march from Clarksburg to Weston was made in rainstorms over muddy roads. The first night many of the men, too tired to put up tents, threw themselves on the ground and slept none the less soundly. The glorious scenery on the west fork of the Monongahela was recompense for the toil endured, and the men had great sport picking

blackberries which covered the hills in profusion.[1] There were
rumors of an army under General Robert E. Lee moving westward with the avowed purpose of driving Rosecrans — the
"Dutch General" as the Rebel press designated him — into the
Ohio River, and Rosecrans with characteristic energy was preparing for the conflict. He had only eleven thousand men to
guard and hold the country, but reënforcements were promised
by the Governor of Ohio.

The Twenty-third was in the enemy's country at Weston, and
local tribunals having been suppressed or discontinued, the quar-
rels of the citizens were settled by the major, who held a sort of
police court. No punishment more severe than a bread-and-
water diet was inflicted. Details were made for the apprehension
of guerrillas who infested the mountains, picking off our soldiers
or plundering and oppressing Union men. July 30, Hayes writes
his wife: —

We are in the loveliest spot for a camp you ever saw — no, lovelier
than that; nothing in Ohio can equal it; it needs a mountainous region
for these beauties. We do not know how long we shall stay, but we
suppose it will be three or four days. We have had two days of marching
— not severe marching at all, but I saw enough to show me how easily
raw troops are used up by an injudicious march. Luckily we are not
likely to suffer that way. We are probably aiming for Gauley Bridge
on the Kanawha where Wise is said to be fortified. General Rosecrans
is engaged in putting troops so as to hold the principal routes leading
to the point.

The people here are divided; many of the leading ladies are secessionists. We meet many good Union men; the other men are prudently
quiet; our troops behave well.

August 8. — Our regiment is divided for the present. One half under
Colonel Matthews has gone forty-four miles south. We remain in charge
of a great supply depot, and charged with keeping in order the turbulent
of this region. The Union men are the most numerous, but the other
side is the more wealthy and noisy. . . . We are so busy that we do not
complain much of the tediousness of camp life. We are now constantly
hearing of the approach of General Lee from eastern Virginia with a force
large enough to drive us out and capture all our stores, if one fourth that
is told is true. He is said to be about seventy-five miles southeast of
us in the mountains. Whether there is truth in it or not, I have no doubt

[1] " This is the land of blackberrying. We are a great, grown-up, armed black-
berry party and we gather untold quantities." (Letter, July 30, to Sardis Birchard.)

that troops will be urged into this region to hold the country. At any rate, as it is on the route to east Tennessee, and on a route to cut off the railroads from the southwest, I am sure there ought to be a splendid Union army assembled here. I suppose it will be done.[1]

August 17. — We are kept very busy, hunting up guerrillas, escorting trains, etc., etc. Attacking parties are constantly met on the roads in the mountains, and small stations are surrounded and penned up. We send daily parties of from ten to one hundred on these expeditions, distances of from ten to forty miles. Union men persecuted for opinion's sake are the informers. The secessionists in this region are the wealthy and educated, who do nothing openly, and the vagabonds, criminals, and ignorant barbarians of the country; while the Union men are the middle class — the law-and-order, well-behaved folks. Persecutions are common, killings not rare, robberies an everyday occurrence. Some bands of Rebels are so strong that we are really in doubt whether they are guerrillas or parts of Wise's army, coming in to drive us out. The secessionists are boastful, telling us of great forces which are coming. Altogether, it is stirring times just now. Lieutenant-Colonel Matthews is nearly one hundred miles south of us with half our regiment, and is not strong enough to risk returning to us. With Colonels Tyler and Smith, he will fortify near Gauley Bridge on Kanawha.[2]

August 18. — We have received word that the enemy in force is coming towards us through the mountains to the southeast, and have been ordered to prepare three days' rations, and to be ready to march at a moment's notice, to attack the enemy. I am all ready. We are to go without tents or cooking utensils. A part of Colonel Moor's Second German Regiment are to go with us. Markbreit is among them. They reached here last night. It will be a stirring time if we go, and the result of it all, by no means clear. I feel no apprehension — no presentiment of evil.[3]

Buckhannon, August 21. — On Sunday night, August 18, about 12 o'clock, we were ordered to quietly pack and march rapidly to this place. Some of our men had just returned from long scouting expeditions. They were weary with marching over the hills in rain and mud, and here was another march without sleeping. It was borne cheerfully — the men supposing it was to meet an enemy. We find this a lovely spot — superior in some respects to the scenery about Weston. We have a beautiful camp about one and one half miles from the village. Here we have parts of five regiments — all but this from Cincinnati. Men are constantly arriving, showing the rapid concentration at this point of a large body of troops. We are ignorant of its purpose, but suppose it to be for service.[4]

---

[1] Letter to Sardis Birchard.
[2] Letter to Sardis Birchard.
[3] Letter to Mrs. Hayes.
[4] Letter to Hayes's mother.

August 22. — It is a cold, rainy, dismal night. We are all preparing for an early march. . . . All are cut down to regulation baggage — many trunks will stop here. A tailor sits on one end of my cot sewing fixings; all is confusion. The men are singing jolly tunes. Our colonel takes his half-regiment, the left wing, and half of McCook's Germans, and we push off for the supposed point of the enemy's approach. We shall stop and camp at Beverly awhile, and then move as circumstances require.[1]

Beverly, August 24. — We marched from Buckhannon, as I wrote you, but the rain stopped; the air was delicious, the mountain scenery beautiful. We camped at night on the hills without tents. I looked up at the stars and moon — nothing between me and the sky, and thought of you all. To-day had a lovely march in the mountains; was at the camp of the enemy on Rich Mountain and on the battlefield. Reached here to-day. . . . The Guthrie Grays greeted us hospitably. Men are needed here and we were met by men who were very glad to see us for many reasons. We go to the seat of things on Cheat Mountain perhaps to-morrow.[2]

Beverly, Va., August 25, 1861. Sunday A.M. — Supposing I might have to go on towards Cheat Mountain this morning I wrote you a very short note last night. I now write so soon again to show you how much I love you and how much my thoughts are on the dear ones at home. I never enjoyed any business or mode of life as much as I do this. I really feel badly when I think of several of my intimate friends who are compelled to stay at home. These marchings and campings in the hills of western Virginia will always be among the pleasantest things I can remember. I know we are in frequent perils — that we may never return and all that, but the feeling that I am where I ought to be, is a full compensation for all that is sinister, leaving me free to enjoy as if on a pleasure tour. I am constantly reminded of our trip and happiness a year ago. I met a few days ago in the Fifth Regiment, the young Moore we saw at Quebec. . . . We saw nothing prettier than the view from my tent this morning. McCook's men are half a mile to the right, McMullen's Battery on the next hill in front of us, the Virginia Second a half mile in front, and the Guthries to the left. We, on higher ground, see them all; then mountains, meadows, and streams — nothing wanting but you and the boys.

Sunday evening. — Just got orders to go to Huttonsville. Look on my map of Virginia and you will see it, geography style; but the beautiful scenery you will not see there. We are to be for the present under General Reynolds — a good officer, and then General Benham or General Rosecrans — all good. The soldiers are singing so merrily to-night. It is a lovely, sweet, starlit evening. I rode over to Colonel Sondershoff (I think that is the name of McCook's soldierly and gentlemanly

---

[1] Letter to Mrs. Hayes.   [2] Letter to Mrs. Hayes.

lieutenant-colonel) to tell him about the march, and from his elevated camp I could see all the camps "sparkling and bright." I thought of the night you walked with me about Camp Chase. Good-night.[1]

Somewhere in Tygart's Valley, near Cheat Mountain Pass, Virginia, August 26, 1861; Monday evening, 8.30 P.M. After a march of 18 miles. — You will think me insane, writing so often and always with the same story — delighted with scenery and pleasant excitement. We are camped to-night in a valley surrounded by mountains on a lovely stream under great trees, with the Third Ohio, Thirteenth Indiana, one half of Mc-Cook's Ninth, and the Michigan Artillery, which mother remembers passed our house one Sunday about the last of May, and McMullen's Battery all in sight. Our General Reynolds makes a good impression. We are disposed to love him and trust him. We expect to remain here, and hereabouts, until the enemy, which is just over the mountain, either drives us out, which I think he can't do, or until we are strong enough to attack him. A stay of some weeks, we suppose.[2]

French Creek, August 30. — "The best laid schemes of mice and men," etc., especially in war. That beautiful camp at the head of the valley where we were to stay so long had just been gotten into fine order when the order to leave came: "Make a forced march to French Creek by a mountain path, leaving tents, baggage, and knapsacks to be sent to you." We obeyed and are yet alive. A queer life. We are now as jolly as if we never saw trouble or hardship. Two nights ago and three nights ago we lay in the rain in the woods without shelter, or blankets, and almost without food, and after such hard days' toil that we slept on the mountains as soundly as logs. All the horses used up, Uncle Joe's "Birch" among the rest, except my pretty little sorrel "Webby," which came through better than ever. Let me describe my kit: Portmanteau, containing two pairs of socks, one shirt, a towel containing bread and sugar, a tin cup, a pistol in one holster and ammunition in the other, a blanket wrapped in the India rubber you fixed, and a blue (soldier's) overcoat. Seven miles we made after 2.30 P.M. on a good road to Huttonsville, then by a bridle path part of the way [and] no path the rest, following a guide six miles over a steep, muddy, rocky mountain. At the foot of the mountain I put Captain Sperry, who was footsore, on "Webby," and pushed ahead afoot. I could see we would not get over the mountain to a stream we wished to camp on until after night unless we pushed. I put on ahead of the guide and reached the top with Lieutenant Bottsford, the keen-eyed snare-drummer, Gillett (Birch remembers him, I guess), a soldier, and the guide alone in sight.

We waited till the head of the column came in sight, got full instructions from the guide, directed him to wait for the column and leaving him — reënforced, however, by the silver-cornet player — we hurried down. In half an hour it was dark as tar. I led the little party, blundering sometimes, but in the main right, until we could hear the river; long before we reached it, all sound of the column was lost and the way was so difficult that we agreed they could not get down until daylight. We got to the river at 9.15 with three matches and a Fremont *Journal* to kindle fire with, no overcoats and no food. It was a wet night. Did n't we scratch about to get dry kindling, and were n't we lucky to get it and start a great fire with the first precious match? . . . The head of the column got down to us, to our surprise, at 10 P.M. McMullen gave up at 11 P.M., halfway up the mountain, and the Germans were below him. The next day we toiled on, thirteen and one half hours' actual marching over the hills to this place, thirty miles. About three hundred of our men reached here at 8 P.M.; dark, muddy, rainy, and dismal — hungry, no shelter, nothing. Three companies of the Fifth, under Captain Remley (part of Dunning's Continentals) were here. They took us in, fed us, piled hay, built fires, and worked for us until midnight like beavers, and we survived the night. Our men will always bless the Cincinnati Fifth.

Those who seemed unable to keep up, I began to order into barns and farmhouses about six o'clock. The last six miles was somewhat settled. I took care of the rear. In the morning we found ourselves in a warm-hearted Union settlement. We got into a Presbyterian church. We made headquarters at a Yankee lady's and fared sumptuously. But McMullen and the Germans were still behind. They got in twenty-four hours after us in another dark, wet night. Dr. Joe was in his glory. He and I took [charge] of the Germans. They were completely used up. The worst-off we took into a barn of Mrs. Sea. I mention the old lady's name for she has two sons and a son-in-law in the Union army of Virginia, and gives us all she had for the Germans. We got through the night's work about midnight, and to-day have enjoyed hugely comparing notes, etc., etc. Our tents reached us just now and I am writing in mine. The colonel was used up. Joe and I are the better for it. The move is supposed to be to meet the enemy coming in by a different route.[1]

Sutton, or Suttonsville, Virginia, September 5, 1861. — We are in another camp of fine views. This is the last stronghold of our army as we advance toward the enemy. We are now part of an army of from six to eight thousand, and are pushing towards an advancing enemy stronger in numbers, it is said. Some time will perhaps elapse before we meet, but we are pretty certain to meet unless the enemy withdraw. This I think they will do. I like the condition of things. Our force, although not large, is of good regiments for the most part. . . . General Rosecrans is in command in person, with General Benham of the regular army to second him. We are camped on both sides of Elk River, connected by a beautiful suspension bridge; camps on high hills, fortifications on all

---

[1] Letter to Mrs. Hayes.

the summits — "gay and festive" scene, as Artemus Ward would say, especially about sundown, when three or four fine bands are playing in rivalry. Elk River empties into the Kanawha, so that the water now dripping from my tent will pass you perhaps about a fortnight hence. The clearest, purest water it is, too. From the tops of the high hills you can see the rocks in the river covered by ten or twenty feet of water. Nothing finer in Vermont or New Hampshire.

... We got to-day papers from Cincinnati, the *Times* of the 28th and the *Commercial* of the 2d. Think of it — only three days old. It has rumors that General Rosecrans is captured — well, not quite. He is in good health and the Twenty-third Regiment is his especial guard. No force can get him here without passing my tent.

Among the interesting things in camp are the boys. You recollect the boy in Captain McIlrath's company? We have another like him in Captain Woodward's. He ran away from Norwalk to Camp Dennison, went into the Fifth, then into the Guthries, and as we passed their camp he was pleased with us and now is a boy of the Twenty-third. He drills, plays officer, soldier, or errand boy, and is a curiosity in camp. We are getting dogs, too, some fine ones. Almost all the captains have horses, and a few mules have been "realized" — that's the word — from secessionists.[1]

The forced marching of the troops, which Rosecrans led in person to the Gauley River, was a very severe test of the endurance of new recruits. On Sunday before the battle of Carnifex Ferry we learn from the diary that Hayes rode in nineteen hours a distance of between fifty and sixty miles, crossed a stream with more water than the Sandusky at Fremont over thirty times, — wet above the knees all the time, — and had no sleep for thirty-six hours; and on Tuesday, the day of the battle, the troops marched seventeen miles, drove the enemy's pickets out of Summerville, followed them nine miles to Gauley River where General Floyd was entrenched behind formidable works on a high hill, with a precipitous side for his front, and both flanks protected by the bluffs of the river. Rosecrans had with him less than eight regiments. His army was divided. Receiving word that General Wise was threatening to cut off General J. D. Cox, who was on the Kanawha with a small force, he left the larger part of his army under General Reynolds in a strong position at Cheat Mountain Pass to engage the attention of General Lee, and moved by forced marches to the relief of General Cox.

[1] Letter to Mrs. Hayes.

Floyd was in his way at the crossing of the Gauley at Carnifex Ferry, and, without pausing, he prepared to carry the entrenchments. The first brigade under the unfortunate General Benham of the regular army was directed to move with caution against the enemy's front. That officer, after driving in the outpost, dashed ahead with his brigade through the woods, and suddenly found himself in close proximity to Floyd's works. He could not safely withdraw and the regiments in his brigade engaged the enemy for several hours, at a disadvantage, until darkness put an end to the contest. Major Hayes, with four companies of the Twenty-third, after an exhausting struggle over cliffs and through dense masses of mountain laurel, got under fire, but he had no opportunity to display the qualities of his command. His men went in with enthusiasm, but night soon intervened.[1]

The troops were withdrawn from the woods and posted in the order of battle behind ridges, preparatory to renewing the assault in the morning, but in the grey of the morning it was ascertained that the enemy had withdrawn across the river during the night and had destroyed the ferryboat to prevent rapid pursuit. General Rosecrans complimented Hayes and his detachment for what was done; and attributed the hasty retreat of the enemy in part to their belief that his detachment had uncovered their rear and flank. General Rosecrans's loss was twenty killed and about one hundred wounded. Colonel Lowe, of the Twelfth Ohio, was killed, and Colonel Lytle and Captain Stephen McGroarty, of the Tenth, severely wounded. The courage and steadiness of the Ohio men was widely commented on, and at Columbus a salute was fired in their honor.

The disappointment in the Union ranks over the escape of Floyd was intense, but as this movement caused Wise also to withdraw, a junction between the forces of Rosecrans and Cox was effected without loss. Rosecrans again went in search of the enemy, but with a force entirely inadequate for the work before him. An attack by a portion of Lee's army on the Cheat River stronghold occupied by Reynolds had been repulsed and the Confederate general now hoped to cut off Rosecrans's

[1] Cincinnati *Commercial*, September 18. Report by Captain W. D. Bickham, of General Rosecrans's staff.

communications in the rear on the Kanawha and then over-whelm him in front. But the "Dutch general" was not to be caught, and the Confederates withdrew from western Virginia. It was conceded that he had outgeneralled Lee.[1]

The first letter after this affair to his family by Major Hayes, adds some particulars: —

Gauley River, eight miles south of Summerville, September 11, 1861. — We have had our first battle and the enemy has fled precipitately. I say "we," although it is fair to say that our brigade, consisting of the Twenty-third, the Thirtieth (Colonel Ewing), and Mack's battery, had little or nothing to do except to stand as a reserve. The only exception to this was four companies of the Twenty-third, Captains Sperry, Howard, Zimmerman, and Woodward, under my command, who were detailed to make an independent movement. I had one man wounded and four others hit in their clothing and accoutrements. You will have full accounts of the general fight in the papers. My little detachment did as much real work, hard work, as anybody. We crept down and up a steep, rocky mountain, on our hands and knees part of the time, through laurel thickets almost impenetrable, until dark. At one time I got so far ahead in the struggle that I had but three men. I finally gathered them by a halt, although a part were out all night. We were over half an hour listening to the cannon and musketry wait-ing for our turn to come.

You have often heard of the feelings of men in the interval between the order of battle and the attack. Matthews, myself, and others were rather jocose in our talk, and my actual feeling was very similar to what I have when going into an important trial — not different, nor more in-tense. I thought of you and the boys and other loved ones, but there was no such painful feeling as is sometimes described. I doubted the success of the attack and with good reason and in good company. The truth is our enemy is very industrious and ingenious in contriving ambuscades and surprises and entrenchments, but they lack pluck. They expect to win and often do win by superior strategy and cunning. Their entrench-ments and works were of amazing extent. During the whole fight we rarely saw a man. Most of the firing was done at bushes and logs and earth barricades. We withdrew at dark — the attacking brigades having suffered a good deal from the enemy, and pretty severely from one of those deplorable mistakes which have so frequently happened in this war — viz., friends attacking friends. The Tenth and Twenty-eighth (Irish and Second German of Cincinnati) fired on each other, and charged doing much mischief. My detachment was in danger from the same cause. I ran upon the Twenty-eighth, neither seeing the other until within a rod. We mutually recognized, however, although it was a "mutual

[1] See Pollard, *The Lost Cause*, chap. IX.

surprise." It so happened, curiously enough, that I was the extreme right man of my body and Markbreit the left man of his. We had a jolly laugh and introductions to surrounding officers, as partners, etc., etc. The enemy were fairly panic-stricken by the solid volleys of McCook's Ninth and the rifled cannon of Smith's Thirteenth. The Tenth suffered most. The enemy probably began their flight by a secret road soon after dark, leaving flag, ammunition, trunks, arms, stores, etc., but no dead or wounded.[1]

The test made this season between the Southern and the Western soldiers justified the opinion that the former were inferior in the qualities that make good soldiers. Their skirmishers were not good marksmen, and they flinched from close contests. The Ohio and Indiana men proved themselves the best shots and the steadiest fighters. Hayes, September 14, wrote: —

The enemy are no match for us in fair fighting. They feel it and so do our men. . . . The letters, diaries, etc., etc., found in Floyd's trunks and desks, show that their situation is desperate. Thousands are in the army who are heartily sick of the whole business. We retook a large part of the plunder taken from Colonel Tyler, as well as prisoners. The prisoners had been well treated — very. The young men in Floyd's army, of the upper class, are kind-hearted, good-natured fellows who are unfit as possible for the business they are in. They have courage, but no endurance, enterprise, or energy. The lower class are cowardly, cunning, and lazy. The height of their ambition is to shoot a Yankee from some place of safety.

Hayes had attended to all of the legal business for General Rosecrans in addition to his regimental duties, and September 19, General Rosecrans appointed him judge-advocate-general. He accepted the appointment as the order of his superior, though it was against his preferences. He writes in his diary: —

I dislike the service, but must obey, of course. I hope to be relieved after a few weeks' service. In the meantime I will try to qualify myself for an efficient discharge of my new duties. I agree with General Rosecrans that courts-martial may be made very serviceable in promoting discipline in the army.

While Hayes was attached to headquarters he was allowed when practicable to remain with his regiment. He moved about

---

[1] " Where I was a few balls whistled forty or fifty feet over our heads. The next day, however, with Captain Drake's company I got into a little skirmish with an outpost, and could see that the captain and myself were actually aimed at, the balls flying near enough, but hurting nobody. The battle scared and routed the enemy prodigiously." (Letter to Mrs. Hayes, September 15.)

from camp to camp wherever the duties of his new position demanded his presence. From General Cox's camp on Sewell Mountain, "September 27 (Saturday or Friday, I am told)," he wrote his wife: —

We are in the midst of a very cold rainstorm — not farther south than Lexington or Danville, and on the top of a hill or small mountain. Rain for fifteen hours, getting colder and colder, and still raining; in leaky tents, with worn-out blankets, insufficient socks and shoes, many without overcoats; this is no joke. I am living with McCook in a good tent, as well provided as anybody in camp; better than either General Cox or Rosecrans. I write this in General Cox's tent; he sits on one cot reading, or trying to read, or pretending to read, Dickens's new novel "Great Expectations." McCook and General Rosecrans are in the opposite tent over a smoke, trying to think they are warmed a little by the fire under it. Our enemy far worse provided than we are, and no doubt shivering on the opposite hill, now hidden by the driving rain and fog. We all suspect that our campaign in this direction is at an end. The roads will be miry, and we must fall back for our supplies. My regiment is fourteen miles back on a hill — when clear we can see their tents. Just now my position is comparatively a pleasant one. I go with the generals on all reconnaissances, see all that is to be seen and fare as well as anybody. We were out yesterday P.M. very near to the enemy's works; were caught in the first of this storm and thoroughly soaked. I hardly expect to be dry again until the storm is over.

Up Gauley River, Camp Sewell, October 3. — We are in the presence of a large force of the enemy — much stronger than we are, but the mud and floods have pretty much ended this campaign. Both the enemy and ourselves are compelled to go back to supplies soon. I think, therefore, there will be no fight. We shall not attack their entrenchments now that they are reinforced, and I suspect they will not come out after us. Donn Piatt just peeped in. He always has funny things. I said, quoting Webster, "I still live." "Yes," said he, "Webster — Webster; he was a great man; even the old Whigs about Boston admit that!" And again, speaking of the prospect of a fight he said, "This whistling of projectiles about one's ears is disagreeable. It made me try to think at Bull Run of all my old prayers; but I could only remember, 'O Lord, for these and all thy other mercies, we desire to be thankful.'"

We shall soon go into winter quarters at posts chosen to hold this country — Gauley Bridge, Charleston, etc., etc. Who will get into a better place is the question. We all want to go to Washington or to Kentucky or Missouri. We are in General Schenck's Brigade, and hope he will make interest enough to get us into good quarters. There is much sickness among officers and men. My health was never better than during these four months. . . .

I am still on General Rosecrans's staff, but having just finished an extensive tour of court-martial, am again in camp with my regiment in good order. It is like going home to get back. Still this practising on the old circuit after the old fashion, only more so, — an escort of cavalry and a couple of wagons with tents and grub, — has its attractions. I shall get out of it soon, but as a change, I rather enjoy it.[1]

Camp Lookout, Monday, October 7, 1861. — Our campaign is closed — no more fighting in this region unless the enemy attack, which they will not. We are to entrench at Mountain Cove eight miles from here, at Gauley Bridge, twenty miles off, and Summerville about the same. These points will secure our conquest of western Virginia from any common force and will let half or two thirds of our army go elsewhere. I hope we shall be the lucky ones to leave here.

The enemy and ourselves left the mountains about the same time — the enemy first and for the same reason, viz., impossibility of getting supplies. We are now fourteen miles from Mount Sewell and perhaps thirty from the enemy. Our withdrawal was our first experience in backward movement. We all approved it. The march was a severe one. Our business to-day is sending off the sick, and Dr. Joe is up to his eyes in hard work. We have sixty to send to Ohio. This is the severest thing of the campaign. Poor fellows — we do as well as we can with them — but road wagons in rain and mud are poor places. . . .

Don't worry about the war. We are doing our part, and if all does not go well, it is not our fault. I still think we are sure to get through with it safely. The South may not be conquered, but we shall secure to the nation the best part of it. We hope to go to Kentucky. If so we shall meet before a month. Our regiment is a capital one. But we ought to recruit; we shall be about one hundred to one hundred-fifty short when this campaign is ended.

To-morrow is election day. We all talked about it to-day. We are for Tod [2] and victory.

Tuesday morning, 6 A.M., October 8. — Your election day. This wet, dirty letter and its writer have had considerable experience in the last twenty-four hours, and since the above was written. In the first place we have had another bitter storm — and this cold, raw morning, we shiver useless near the fires. At one time yesterday I thought I should have to take back a good deal of what I said in the letter I had just started to Cincinnati. I was at the hospital three quarters of a mile from camp, helping Dr. Joe and Captain Skiles put the sick into the wagons to be transported to Gallipolis and Cincinnati, when firing was heard and word came that the enemy in force had attacked our camp. The doctor and I hurried back leaving Captain Skiles to look after the sick. All the army, seven regiments (5000 to 6000 men) were forming in line of battle. I joined my regiment and after waiting a half hour or so we were ordered to quarters with word that it was only a scouting party driving in our pickets. This was all in a rainstorm. The poor fellows in hospital, many of them panic-stricken, fled down the road, and were found by Dr. Joe on his return three or four miles from the hospital. Three of our regiment got up from their straw piles, got their guns and trudged up the road and took their place in line of battle. The behavior of the men was for the most part perfectly good. The alarm was undoubtedly a false one — no enemy is near us.

We shall go if the sun come out seven miles nearer home to Mountain Cove, and begin to build quarters and fortifications for a permanent stronghold. This brings us within an easy day's ride of the navigable waters of the Kanawha. Thence a steamboat can take us in about a day or so to Cincinnati — pretty near to you. Telegraph also all the way; — speaking of telegraph makes me think I ought to say, Captain Gaines (our Prosecuting Attorney) has done as much, I think more, useful service, dangerous too, than any other officer in western Virginia. The history of his company protecting the telegraph builders would be a volume of romantic adventures.[1]

HEAD-QUARTERS 23D REG'T., O. V. INF., U.S.A.,
MOUNTAIN COVE, SIX MILES ABOVE GAULEY BRIDGE,
October 9, 1861.

DEAR BROTHER, — We are now near, or at the point, where an entrenched camp for winter quarters is to be established. It will command the main entrance to the head of the Kanawha Valley, and can be held by a small force — it is within a day's ride of navigable waters connecting with Cincinnati, and telegraphic communications nearly complete. From half to two thirds of the men in western Virginia can be spared as soon as a few days' work is done; indeed, green regiments just recruited could take charge of this country, and release soldiers who have been hardened by some service. Our regiment is second to no other in *discipline*, and equal in *drill* to all but two or three in western Virginia. We think it would be sensible to send us to Kentucky, Missouri, or the seacoast for the winter. We can certainly do twice the work that we could have done four months ago, and there is no sense in keeping us housed up in fortifications, and sending raw troops into the field. In Kentucky, disciplined troops — that is, men who are obedient and orderly — are particularly needed; a lot of lawless fellows plundering and burning would do more hurt than good among a Union people who have property. We have met no regiment that is better than ours, if any so good. Now, the point I am at is, first, that a large part of the soldiers here can be spared this winter; second, that for service, the best ought to be taken away. With these two ideas safely lodged in the minds of the powers that be, the Twenty-third is pretty sure to be withdrawn. If you can post the Governor a little, it might be useful.

We are pleasantly associated. . . . My connection with General

[1] Letter to Mrs. Hayes.

Rosecrans's staff, I manage to make agreeable by a little license. I quarter with my regiment, but am relieved from all but voluntary regimental duty. I think I have never enjoyed any period of my life as much as the last three months. The risks, hardships, separation from family and friends are balanced by the notion that I am doing what every man, who possibly can, ought to do, leaving the agreeable side of things as clear profit. My health has been perfect. A great matter this is. We have many sick, and sicknesses on marches and in camp are trebly disturbing. It makes one value health. We now have our sick in good quarters and are promised a ten days' rest. The weather to-day is beautiful, and I don't doubt that we shall get back to good condition in that time.[1]

October 9. — Captain Zimmerman and I have just returned from a long stroll up a romantic gorge with its rushing stream. . . . We found the scattered fragments of a mill that had been swept away in some freshet last winter, and following up came to the broken dam, and near by a deserted house — hastily deserted lately; books, the cradle and child's chair, tables, clock, chairs, etc. Our conjecture is that they fled from the army of Floyd about the time of the Carnifex fight. We each picked up a low, well-made, split-bottom chair and clambered up a steep cliff to our camp. I now sit in the chair. We both moralized on this touching proof of the sorrows of war, and I reached my tent a little saddened — to find on my lounge, in my tidy, comfortable quarters, your good letter of October 1. . . . Tell Mother Webb not to give up. In the Revolution they saw darker days — far darker. We shall be a better, stronger nation than ever, in any event. A great disaster would strengthen us; and a victory, we all feel, will bring us out to daylight. . . . I feel as you do about the Twenty-third, only more so. There are several regiments whose music and appearance I can recognize at a great distance over the hills, as the Tenth, Ninth, and so on; but the Twenty-third I know by instinct. I was sitting in the court house at Buckhannon one hot afternoon, with windows up — a number of officers present, when we heard music at a distance. No one expected any regiment at that time. I never dreamed of the Twenty-third being on the road, but the music struck me like words from home. "That is the band of my regiment," was my confident assertion; true of course. We have lost by death about six, by desertion four, by dismissal three, by honorable discharge about twenty-five to thirty; about two hundred are too sick to do duty, of whom about one fifth will never be able to serve. I was called to command parade this evening while writing this sheet. The line is much shorter than in Camp Chase, but so brown and firm and wiry that I suspect our six hundred would do more service than twice their number could have done four months ago.[2]

¹ Letter to William A. Platt.   ² Letter to Mrs. Hayes.

CHAPTER X

IN WINTER QUARTERS — GUERRILLAS

THE work of suppressing the Rebellion did not go forward without disappointments, without hardships and disasters as well as successes, and the newspapers were filled with complaints, with censorious comments on the incapacity of officers in the field, and of those administering the Government, and with appeals for relief of suffering soldiers. The general in command of the fighting men in western Virginia came in for his share. Rosecrans was not the first commander to suffer because of the dereliction or incapacity of quartermasters in the prompt distribution of supplies. The forced marches rendered necessary by the attempts of the enemy to recover West Virginia caused a good deal of sickness. Fault was found with Rosecrans for his march from Clarksburg. Ought he to have remained there to preserve the health of his troops, leaving Cox on the Gauley to be cut off by an overwhelming force, as he probably would have been if not supported? His movement beyond the Gauley failed because General Lee had also made a flank movement and joined Floyd and Wise. Rosecrans had not the force to attack Lee, and it was good generalship to fall back so as not to have a long stretch of impassable road behind him. In letters to his wife, Hayes comments sanely on the injustice being done to the President and others charged with responsibilities, and on the conditions of soldier life: —

October 17. — I am practising law again. My office is pleasantly located in a romantic valley on the premises of Colonel Tompkins of the Rebel army. His mansion is an elegant modern house, and by some strange good luck it has been occupied by his family and escaped uninjured while hundreds of humbler homes have been ruined. Mrs. Tompkins has kept on the good side of our leaders and has thus far kept the property safe. The Twenty-third is seven miles or so up the valley of New River. I was there last evening. Dr. Joe has been sick a couple of days, but is getting well. Very few escape sickness, but with any sort of care it is not dangerous. Not more than one case in a hundred has thus far proved fatal. Colonel Matthews has gone home for a few days.

You will see him, I hope. If he succeeds in one of the objects of his trip, I shall probably visit you for a few days, within six weeks or so. Our campaign here is ended, I think, without doubt. We hear stories which are repeated in your papers which look a little as if there might be an attempt to cut off our communications down the Kanawha, but I suspect there is very small foundation for them. We are strongly posted. No force would dare attack us. To cut off supplies is the most that will be thought of, and any attempt to do that must meet with little success, if I am rightly informed about things.

We have had the finest of fall weather, for several (it seems many) days. The glorious mountains all around us are of every hue, changing to a deeper red and brown as the frosts cut the foliage. I talk so much of the scenery you will suspect me to be daft. In fact I never have enjoyed nature so much. Being in the open air a great part of each day and surrounded by magnificent scenery, I do get heady I suspect on the subject. I have told you many a time that we were camped in the prettiest place you ever saw. I must here repeat it. The scenery on New River and around the junction of Gauley and New River where they form the Kanawha is finer than any mere mountain and river views we saw last summer. The music and sights belonging to the camps of ten thousand men add to the effect. Our band has improved and the choir in McIlrath's company would draw an audience anywhere. The companies, many of them, sound their calls with the bugle which with the echoes heighten the general charm.[1]

Camp Tompkins, October 19, 1861. — I got your letter of last Sunday yesterday. You can't be happier in reading my letters than I am in reading yours. . . . Don't worry about suffering soldiers and don't be too ready to give up President Lincoln. More men are sick in camps than at home; sick are not comfortable anywhere, and less so in armies than in good homes. Transportation fails, roads are bad, contractors are faithless, officials negligent or fraudulent, but, notwithstanding all this, I am satisfied that our army is *better fed, better clad, and better sheltered than any other army in the world.* And, moreover, where there is a want it is not due to the General or State Government, half as much as to officers and soldiers. The two regiments I have happened to know most about, and to care most about, McCook's Ninth and our Twenty-third, have no cause of complaint. Their clothing is better than when they left Ohio and better than most men wear at home. I am now dressed as a private and I am well dressed. I live habitually on soldiers' rations and I live well. No, Lucy, the newspapers mislead you. It is the poor families at home, not the soldiers, who can justly claim sympathy. I except, of course, the regiments which have bad officers, but you can't help their case with your spare blankets. Officers at home begging better be with their regiments, doing their appropriate duties.

[1] Letter to Mrs. Hayes.

Government is sending enough if colonels, etc., would only do their part. McCook could feed, clothe, or blanket half a regiment more any time, while alongside of him is a regiment, ragged, hungry, and blanketless, full of correspondents writing home complaints about somebody. It is here as elsewhere. The thrifty and energetic get along and the lazy and thoughtless send emissaries to the cities to beg. Don't be fooled with this stuff. I feel for the poor women and children in Cincinnati. The men out here have sufferings but no more than men of sense expected, and were prepared for, and can bear. I see Dr. S. wants blankets for the Eighth Regiment. Why is n't he with it, attending to its sick? If its colonel and quartermaster do their duties as he does his, five hundred miles off, they can't expect to get blankets. I have seen the stores sent into this State and the Government has provided abundantly for all.

It vexes me to see how good people are imposed on. I have been through the camps of eight thousand men to-day, and I tell you they are better fed and clothed than the people of half the wards of Cincinnati. We have sickness, which is bad enough, but it is due to causes inseparable from our condition. Living in open air, exposed to changes of weather, will break down one man in every four or five, even if he was clad in "purple and fine linen and fared sumptuously every day." As for Washington, McClellan and so on, I believe they are doing the thing well. I think it will come out all right. Wars are not finished in a day. Lincoln is perhaps not all that we could wish; but he is honest, patriotic, cool-headed, and safe. I don't know any man that the nation could say is, under all the circumstances, to be preferred in his place. As for the new Governor, I like the change as much as you do. He comes in a little over two months from now.

A big dish of politics. I feared you were among croakers and grumblers — people who do more mischief than avowed enemies to the country. It is lovely weather again. I hope this letter will find you as well as it leaves me.[1]

Camp Tompkins, October 21, 1861. Monday morning before breakfast. — Dr. Clendenin goes home this morning and I got up early to let you know how much I love you. . . . The doctor will give you the news. I see Colonel Tom Ford has been telling big yarns about soldiers suffering. They may be true — I fear they are — and it is right to do something; but it is not true that the fault lies with the Government alone. Colonel Ammon's Twenty-fourth has been on the mountains much more than the Guthrie Grays, for they have been in town most of the time; but nobody growls about them. The Twenty-fourth is looked after by its officers. The truth is, the suffering is great in all armies in the field in bad weather. It can't be prevented. It is also true that much is suffered from neglect, but the neglect is in no one place. Government is in

[1] Letter to Mrs. Hayes.

part blamable, but the chief [blame] is on the armies themselves, from generals down to privates. It is certainly true that a considerable part of the sick men now in Cincinnati, would be well and with their regiments if they had obeyed orders about eating green chestnuts, green apples, and green corn. Now, all these men ought to be helped and cared for, but in doing so it is foolish and wicked to assail and abuse as the authors of the suffering any one particular set of men. It is a calamity to be deplored and can be remedied by well-directed labor, not by indiscriminate abuse. I am filled with indignation to see that Colonel Ewing is accused of brutality to his men. All false. He is kind to a fault — all *good* soldiers love him; and yet he is published by some lying scoundrel as a monster. I'll write no more on this subject. There will be far more suffering this winter than we have yet heard of; try to relieve it, but don't assume that any one set of men are to be blamed for it. A great share of it can't be helped. Twenty-five per cent of all men who enlist can't stand the hardships and exposures of the field, if suddenly transferred to it from their homes, and suffering is inevitable to all.[1]

The Potomac divided the hostile forces of the United States and the Confederacy in the vicinity of Leesburg for several months without a serious conflict between them. The purpose of the Confederates was to cross into Maryland and flank the army defending Washington. To prevent this threatened danger, McClellan had kept a strong force well in hand. Late in October an attempt was made to ascertain the strength of the enemy in front. The reconnaissance on the 20th, made in considerable force under Colonel Devens, was supported on the morning of the 21st by a larger force commanded by Colonel Edward D. Baker, who was placed in charge by General Stone. The order to cross was definite, but no adequate provision of boats had been made for the safe return of the troops in case of disaster. The enemy, under cover of the woods, sharply attacked Colonel Baker's force. The Union soldiers fought with great intrepidity, but they were outnumbered, and were at the mercy of the attacking party as they had no means of recrossing the river. The loss of life was great considering the numbers engaged.[2] Colonel Baker fell while cheering his men, pierced by six bullets. His loss alone was a disaster to the cause, as it created a feeling of discouragement highly injurious at this time. Somebody had blundered, and the

---

[1] Letter to Mrs. Hayes.
[2] The Union force numbered 2100, of which 944 were returned as "killed, wounded, and missing." The Confederate loss was 300.

popular indignation was so great as blindly to embrace the innocent with the guilty. The battle of Ball's Bluff stands out as one
of the darkest incidents of the war. This brief recital will explain
the reference to Colonel Baker in the following: —

Camp Tompkins, October 29. — We hear that Lieutenant-Colonel
Matthews, who left for a stay of two weeks at home, about the 18th,
has been appointed colonel of the Fifty-first Regiment. This is deserved.
It will, I fear, separate us. I shall regret that much, very much. He is
a good man of solid talents, and a most excellent companion. Well, if
so, it can't be helped. The compensation is the probable promotion I
shall get to his place. I care little about this. As much to get rid of the
title "Major" as anything else, makes it desirable. I am prejudiced
against "Major." Doctors are majors, and (tell it not in Gath) Dick
Corwine is major. So, if we lose friend Matthews there may be this
crumb, besides the larger one of getting rid of being the army's lawyer or
judge, which I don't fancy.

Colonel Baker, gallant, romantic, eloquent, soldier, senator, patriot,
killed at Edwards Ferry on the upper Potomac! When will this thing
cease? Death in battle does not pain me much. But caught, surprised in
ambush again after so many warnings! I do not lose heart. I calmly
contemplate these things. The side of right with strength, resources,
endurance, must ultimately triumph. These disasters and discouragements will make the ultimate victory more precious. But how long? I can
wait patiently if we only do not get tricked out of victories. I thought
McClellan was to mend all this. "We have had our last defeat; we have
had our last retreat," he boasted. Well, well, patience. West Pointers
are no better leaders than others.[1]

CAMP TOMPKINS, VIRGINIA, October 29, 1861.
TUESDAY MORNING AFTER BREAKFAST.

MY DEAR BOY, — If I am not interrupted I mean to write you a
long birthday letter. You will be eight years old on the 4th of November — next Monday, and perhaps this letter will get to Cincinnati in
time for your mother or grandmother to read it to you on that day. If
I were with you on your birthday I would tell you a great many stories
about the war. Some of them would make you almost cry and some would
make you laugh. I often think how Ruddy and Webby and you will
gather around me to listen to my stories — and how often I shall have
to tell them — and how they will grow bigger and bigger as I get older,
and as the boys grow up, until if I should live to be an old man they will
become really romantic and interesting. But it is always hard work for
me to write, and I can't tell on paper such good stories as I could give
you if we were sitting down together by the fire.

I will tell you why we call our camp Camp Tompkins. It is named

[1] Diary.

after a very wealthy gentleman named Colonel Tompkins who owns the farm on which our tents are pitched. He was educated to be a soldier of the United States at West Point, where boys and young men are trained to be officers at the expense of the Government. He was a good student and when he grew up he was a good man. He married a young lady who lived in Richmond and who owned a great many slaves, and a great deal of land in Virginia. He stayed in the army as an officer a number of years, but getting tired of army life he resigned his office several years ago, and came here and built an elegant house and cleared and improved several hundred acres of land. The site of his house is a lovely one. It is about a hundred yards from my tent, on an elevation that commands a view of Gauley Bridge, two and a half miles distant, — the place where New River and Gauley River unite to form Kanawha River. Your mother can show you the spot on the map. There are high hills or mountains on both sides of both rivers, and before they unite they are very rapid and run roaring and dashing along in a very romantic way. When the camp is still at night, as I lie in bed, I can hear the noise like another Niagara Falls.

In this pleasant place Colonel Tompkins lived a happy life. He had a daughter and three sons. He had a teacher for his daughter and another for his boys. His house was furnished in good taste; he had books, pictures, boats, horses, guns, and dogs. His daughter was about sixteen, his oldest boy was fourteen, the next twelve, and the youngest about nine. They lived here in a most agreeable way until the Rebels in South Carolina attacked Major Anderson in Fort Sumter. Colonel Tompkins wished to stand by the Union, but his wife and many relatives in eastern Virginia were secessionists. He owned a great deal of property which he feared the Rebels would take away from him if he did not become a secessionist. While he was doubting what to do and hoping that he could live along without taking either side, Governor Wise with an army came here on his way to attack steamboats and towns on the Ohio River. Governor Wise urged Colonel Tompkins to join the Rebels; told him, as he was an educated military man, he would give him command of a regiment in the Rebel army. Colonel Tompkins finally yielded and became a colonel in Wise's army. He made Wise agree that his regiment should be raised among his neighbors, and that they should not be called on to leave their homes for any distant service but remain as a sort of home guards. This was all very well for a while. Colonel Tompkins stayed at home and would drill his men once or twice a week. But when Governor Wise got down to the Ohio River and began to drive away Union men, and to threaten to attack Ohio, General Cox was sent with Ohio soldiers after Governor Wise.

Governor Wise was not a good general or did not have good soldiers, or perhaps they knew they were fighting in a bad cause; at any rate, the Rebel army was driven by General Cox from one place to another until they got back to Gauley Bridge near where Colonel Tompkins lived. He had to call out his regiment of home guards and join Wise.

General Cox soon drove them away from Gauley Bridge and followed them up this road until he reached Colonel Tompkins's farm. The colonel then was forced to leave his home, and has never dared to come back to it since. Our soldiers have held the country all around his house.

His wife and children remained at home until since I came here. They were protected by our army and no injury done to them. But Mrs. Tompkins got very tired of living with soldiers all around, and her husband off in the Rebel army. Finally a week or two ago General Rosecrans told her she might go to eastern Virginia, and sent her in her carriage, with an escort of ten dragoons and a flag of truce over to the Rebel army about thirty miles from here, and I suppose she is now with her husband. I suppose you would like to know about a flag of truce. It is a white flag carried to let the enemy's army know that you are coming not to fight but to hold a peaceful meeting with them. One man rides ahead of the rest about fifty yards carrying a white flag — any white handkerchief will do; when the pickets, sentinels, or scouts of the other army see it, they know what it means. They call out to the man who carries the flag of truce and he tells them what his party is coming for. The picket tells him to halt, while he sends back to his camp to know what to do. An officer and a party of men are sent to meet the party with the flag of truce, and they talk with each other and transact their business as if they were friends, and when they are done they return to their own armies. No good soldier ever shoots a man with a flag of truce. They are always very polite to each other when parties meet with such a flag.

Well, Mrs. Tompkins and our men travelled till they came to the enemy. The Rebels were very polite to our men. Our men stayed all night at a picket station in the woods along with the party of Rebels who came out to meet them. They talked to each other about the war and were very friendly. Our men cooked their suppers as usual. One funny fellow said to a Rebel soldier, "Do you get any such good coffee as this, over there?" The Rebel said, "Well, to tell the truth, the officers are the only ones who see much coffee, and it's mighty scarce with them." Our man held up a big army cracker, "Do you have any like this?" and the Rebel said, "Well, no — we do live pretty hard"; and so they joked with each other a great deal.

Colonel Tompkins's boys and the servants and tutor are still in the house. The boys come over every day to bring the General milk and pies and so on. I expect we shall send them off one of these days and take the house for a hospital or something of the kind. And so you see Colonel Tompkins did n't gain anything by joining the Rebels. If he had done what he thought was right everybody would have respected him. Now the Rebels suspect him, and accuse him of treachery if anything occurs in his regiment which they don't like. Perhaps he would have lost property, perhaps he would have lost his life if he had stood by the Union. But he would have done right and all good people would have honored him.

And now, my son, as you are getting to be a large boy I want you to resolve always to do what you know is right. No matter what you will lose by it, no matter what danger there is, always do right. I hope you will go to school and study hard, and take exercise too, so as to grow and be strong; and, if there is a war, you can be a soldier and fight for your country as Washington did. Be kind to your brothers and to grandmother and, above all, to your mother. You don't know how your mother loves you and you must show that you love her by always being a kind, truthful, brave boy; and I shall always be so proud of you. Give my love to "all the boys" and to mother and grandmother.—Affectionately,

Your Father.[1]

The promotion and relief from court duty both came promptly.

October 31. — A dispatch from Adjutant-General Buckingham announces my promotion to lieutenant-colonel *vice* Matthews, and James M. Comly as major.[2]

Camp Tompkins, Virginia, November 2, 1861. — I am about to return to my regiment six or eight miles up New River at Camp Ewing. I shall probably be comfortably settled there to-night. . . . We had a noisy day yesterday. A lot of Floyd's men (we suppose) have got on the other side of the river with cannon. They tried to sink our ferryboats to prevent our crossing Gauley River at the bridge (now ferry, for Wise destroyed the bridge). They made it so hazardous during the day that all teams were stopped; but during the night the ferry did double duty, so that the usual crossing required in twenty-four hours was safely done. Both sides fired cannon and musketry at each other several hours, but the distance was too great to do harm. We had two wounded and thought we did them immense damage. They probably suffered little, or no less, but probably imagined that they were seriously cutting us. So we all see it. Our side does wonders always! We are not accurately informed about these Rebels, but appearances do not make them formidable. They can't attack us. The only danger is that they may get below on the Kanawha and catch a steamboat before we drive them off. I wish you could see such a battle. No danger, and yet enough sense of peril excited to make all engaged very enthusiastic. The echoes of the cannon and bursting shells through the mountain defiles were wonderful. I spent the day with two soldiers making a reconnaissance—that is to say, trying to find out the enemy's exact position, strength, etc. We did some hard climbing, and were in as much danger as anybody else, that is, none at all. One while the spent rifle balls fell in our neighborhood, but they had n't force enough to penetrate clothing, even if they should hit. It's a great thing to have a rapid river and a mountain gorge between hostile armies![3]

[1] Letter to Birchard A. Hayes.   [2] Diary.
[3] Letter to Mrs. Hayes.

November 3, Sunday. — Yesterday and to-day it has been rainy, stormy and disagreeable. I came up to my regiment yesterday as lieutenant-colonel. The men and officers seemed pleased with my promotion. . . . A. M. Flicklin, of Charlottesville, Virginia, a brother-in-law of Mrs. Colonel Tompkins, came with her bearing a flag of truce. He stayed with us last night. He is an agreeable, fair-minded, intelligent gentleman of substance, formerly, and perhaps now, a stage proprietor and mail carrier. He says he entertains not the shadow of a doubt that the Confederate States will achieve independence. He says the whole people will spend and be spent to the last before they will yield. On asking him, "Suppose, on the expiration of Lincoln's term, a States' rights Democrat shall be elected President, what will be the disposition of the South towards him?" he replied hesitatingly, as if puzzled, and seemed to feel that the chief objection to the Union would be removed. So it's Lincoln, Black Republican, prejudice, a name, that is at the bottom of it all. His account of things goes to show that great pains have been taken to drill and discipline the Rebel troops, and that their cavalry are especially fine.[1]

Camp Ewing, November 5. — We are having stirring times again. The enemy has got a force and some cannon on the other side of New River and are trying to shell such of our camps as lie near the river bank. We are just out of reach of their shot. McCook, in sight of us below, is camped in easy range, and they are peppering at him I hear their guns every two or three minutes as I write. He does n't like to move, and probably will not until they do him some serious harm. They fired all day yesterday without doing any other mischief than breaking one tent pole. A ball or shell would hardly light before his men would run with picks to dig it up as a trophy. It is probable that we shall cross the river to attempt to drive them off in a day or two. You will know the result long before this letter reaches you.[2]

Camp Ewing, November 9. — I wish you could see how we live. We have clothing and provisions in abundance, if men were all thrifty, food enough and good enough in spite of unthrift. Blankets, stockings, undershirts, drawers, and shoes are always welcome. These articles or substitutes are pretty nearly the only things the soldiers' aid societies need to send. India rubber or oil-cloth capes, or the like, are not quite abundant enough. Our tents are floored with loose boards taken from deserted secession barns and houses. For warmth we have a few stoves, but generally fires in trenches in front of the tents or in little ovens or furnaces formed by digging a hole a foot deep by a foot and a half wide and leading under the sides of the tent — the smoke passing up through chimneys made of barrels, or sticks, crossed cob-house fashion, daubed with mud.

---

[1] Diary.   [2] Letter to Mrs. Hayes.

There is not much suffering from cold or wet. The sickness is generally camp fever — a typhoid fever not produced I think by any defect in food, clothing, or shelter. Officers who are generally more comfortably provided than the privates suffer quite as much as the men — indeed, rather more in our regiment. Besides, the people residing here have a similar fever. Exposure in the night and to bad weather in a mountain climate to which our men are not accustomed seems to cause the sickness, irrespective of all other circumstances. . . .

I never was healthier in my life. I do not by any means consider myself safe from the fever, however, if we remain in our present location, higher up in the mountains than any other regiment. If I should find myself having any of the symptoms I shall instantly come home. Those who have done so have all recovered within a week or two, and been able to return to duty. I do not notice any second attacks although I suppose they sometimes occur. Other regiments have had more deaths than we have had, but not generally a larger sick list.

Our men are extremely well behaved, orderly, obedient, and cheerful. I can think of no instance in which any man has ever been in the slightest degree insolent or sullen in his manner towards me. During the last week the enemy have made an attempt to dislodge us from our position by firing shot and shell at our camps from the opposite side of New River. For three days there was cannonading during the greater part of daylight of each day. Nothing purporting to be warfare could possibly be more harmless. I knew of two or three being wounded, and have heard that one man was killed. They have given it up as a failure and I do not expect to see it repeated. . . .

The newspapers do great mischief by allowing false and exaggerated accounts of suffering here to be published. It checks enlistments. The truth is, it is a rare thing for a good soldier to find much cause for complaint. But I suppose the public are getting to understand this. I would not say anything to stop benevolent people from contributing such articles of clothing and bedding as I have described. These articles are always put to good use.[1]

November 10. — Went with Colonel Scammon, Captain Crane, and Lieutenant Avery to Pepper-box Knob and looked over into enemy's camps on south side of New River; thence with Avery to Townsend's Ferry — the proposed crossing place. Most romantic views of the deep mountain gorge of New River near the ferry. Climbed down and up the hill by aid of ropes. Two Rebel soldiers got up an extempore skiff just opposite where our men were getting our skiffs and crept down the cliffs. They came over and were caught by our men as they landed. They were naturally surprised and frightened. A third was seen on the other bank who escaped. So our scheme is by this time suspected by the enemy.[2]

[1] Letter to Hayes's mother.
[2] Diary.

November 13. — We left all baggage early in the morning except what the men could carry and started down to Gauley to pursue Floyd, or rather to attack him. Had a good march down to Gauley — the whole Third Brigade under General Schenck. Weather warm as summer — almost hot. Crossed New River at a ferry near its mouth worked by Captain Lane and his good men, thence down left bank of the Kanawha to the road from Montgomery's Ferry to Fayetteville, thence about two miles to Huddleston's farm where we bivouacked among briars and devil's needles; officers in corn fodder in a crib. The band played its best tunes as we crossed New River, Captain Lane remarking, "I little hoped to see such a sight a week ago when the enemy were cannonading us." About 10.30 o'clock General Schenck got a dispatch from General Benham saying Floyd was on the run and he in pursuit, and urging us to follow. At midnight the men were aroused and at one we were on the way.[1]

November 14. — *Thursday.* — A dark, cold, rainy morning; marching before daylight in pitchy darkness. (*Mem.:* Night marches should only be made in extremest cases; men can go farther between daylight and dark than between midnight and dark of next day, and be less wornout.) We stopped in the dark, built fires and remained until daylight; when we pushed on in mud and rain past enemy's entrenchments on Dickinson's farm to Fayetteville where we arrived about eight or nine A.M. After passing enemy's works the road strewed with axes, picks, tents, etc., etc., — the débris of Floyd's retreating army. Fayetteville, a pretty village, deserted by men and by all but a few women. We quartered with Mrs. Manser; her secession lord gone with Floyd. We heard, P.M., of General Benham's skirmishers killing Colonel St. George Croghan to-day — colonel of Rebel cavalry and son of Colonel George Croghan of Fort Stephenson celebrity. Died in a bad cause, but Father O'Higgins of the Tenth says he behaved like a Christian gentleman. Colonel Smith wears his sword — shot through the sword-belt.[2]

November 15. — General Benham's brigade returned from the pursuit of Floyd. He runs like a quarter horse. One of the servants says that when Floyd was here (Fayetteville) Mrs. Manser said she hoped he would n't leave. He replied, "I assure you, madam, I'll not leave Cotton Hill until compelled by death or the order of the Secretary of War," and, added the darky, "the next I saw of him he was running by as fast as he could tar."[3]

November 17. — I was sent in command of one hundred men of the Twenty-third and one hundred of Twenty-sixth six miles towards Raleigh to Blake's to watch a road on which it was thought Colonel Jenkins's Rebel cavalry might pass with prisoners and plunder from Guyandotte.

---

[1] Diary.　　　　[2] Diary.　　　　[3] Diary.

We bivouacked on the snow in fence corners — ice half-inch thick — and passed the night not uncomfortably at all. A party of Rebels from Floyd's army met us here with a flag of truce. Had a good little chat with several of them. They did not seem at all averse to friendly approaches. It seemed absurd to be fighting such civil and friendly fellows. I thought they were not so full of fight as our men — acted sick of it. One youngster, a lieutenant in Phillips's Legion, T. H. Kennon of Milledgeville, Georgia, wanted to buy back his little sorrel mare, which we had captured — a pleasant fellow. They were after Croghan's body.[1]

Fayetteville, Virginia, November 19 (Tuesday), 1861. — We are housed comfortably in a fine village deserted by its people, leaving us capital winter quarters. Floyd intended to winter here, but since his retreat we are left in possession. We have had severe marching — two nights out without tents, one in the rain, and one on the *snow*. We stood it well, not a man sick of those who were well — and the sick all improving, due to the clear, frosty weather. Dr. Joe is reading with much satisfaction the news of the success of our fleet. It is most important. We are hoping to stay here for the winter if we do not leave Virginia. It is much the best place we have been in. All or nearly all the people gone, fine houses, forage, healthy location, etc., etc. . . . . We are now entirely clear of the enemy. I met a party of Georgians yesterday with a flag of truce — had a good friendly chat with them. They are no doubt brave, fine fellows, but not hardy or persevering enough for this work. They really envied us our healthy and rugged men. They are tired of it, heartily.[2]

Fayetteville, Virginia, November 25. — I rode yesterday over Cotton Hill and along New River, a distance of thirty miles. I was alone most of the day, and could enjoy scenes made still wilder by the wintry storm. We do not yet hear of any murders by "bushwhackers" in this part of Virginia, and can go where we choose without apprehension of danger. We meet very few men; the poor women excite our sympathy constantly. A great share of the calamities of war fall on the women. I see women, unused to hard labor, gathering corn to keep starvation from the door. I am now in command of the post here, and a large part of my time is occupied in hearing tales of distress and trying to soften the ills the armies have brought into this country. Fortunately a very small amount of salt, sugar, coffee, rice, and bacon goes a great ways where all these things are luxuries, no longer procurable in the ordinary way. We try to pay for the mischief we do in destroying corn, hay, etc., etc., in this way.[3]

Fayetteville, Virginia, November 29, 1861. — We are to stay here this winter. Our business for the next few weeks is building a couple of forts

---

[1] Diary.   [2] Letter to Mrs. Hayes.   [3] Letter to Hayes's mother.

and getting housed 1500 or 2000 men. . . . The village was a fine one, pretty gardens, fruit, flowers, and pleasant homes. All natives gone except three or four families of ladies. . . . We are in no immediate danger here of anything except starvation, which you know is a slow death and gives ample time for reflection. All our supplies come from the head of navigation on the Kanawha over a road, remarkable for the beauty and sublimity of its scenery, the depth of its mud, and the dizzy precipices which bound it on either side. On yesterday one of our bread wagons with driver and four horses missed the road four or six inches and landed (landed is not so descriptive of the fact as *lit*) in the top of a tree ninety feet high after a fall of about seventy feet. The miracle is that the driver is here to explain that one of his leaders "hawed" when he ought to have "geed." We are now encouraging trains of pack mules. They do well among the scenery, but unfortunately part of the route is a Serbonian bog where armies whole might sink if they have n't, and the poor mules have a time of it. The distance, luckily, to navigable water is only sixteen to twenty miles. If however the water gets low the distance will increase thirty to forty miles, and if it freezes, why then we shall be looking to the next thaw for victuals. We are to have a telegraph line to the world done to-morrow, and a daily mail subject to the obstacles aforesaid, so we can send you dispatches showing exactly how our starvation progresses from day to day. On the whole I rather like the prospect. We are most comfortably housed and shall no doubt have a pretty jolly winter. There will be a few weeks of busy work getting our forts ready, etc.; after that I can no doubt come home and visit you all for a brief season.[1]

December 13. — Another beautiful winter day — cold, quiet, sun strong enough to thaw all mud and ice. No ice on streams yet that will bear a man. Building redoubts at either end of town. Since I came to Virginia in July I have not shaved; for weeks at a time I have slept in all clothes except boots — occasionally in boots, and sometimes with spurs; a half-dozen times on the ground without shelter; once on the snow. I have worn no white clothing (shirts, drawers, etc.) for four months, no collar or neckerchief or tie of any sort for two months, and have not been the least unwell until since I have taken winter quarters here in a comfortable house. Now I have a slight cold.[2]

December 16. — Rode with Colonel Scammon to Townsend's Ferry; that is we rode to the top of the cliffs on New River, thence with six men of Company B we scrambled down by the path to the river, perhaps by the path three quarters of a mile. A steep rocky gorge, a rushing river, the high precipices, all together make a romantic scene. It was here we intended to cross with General Schenck's brigade to cut off Floyd's

---

[1] Letter to Laura Platt, a niece.   [2] Diary.

retreat. Boats were prepared, four skiffs brought from Cincinnati, but the river rose just as we were about to cross, making it impossible. It has always been a question since whether the enemy were aware of our purpose and would have opposed our crossing. I supposed that so much work preparing could not have escaped their notice, and that they were ready for us. Opposition on such a path would have been fatal. From all I saw at the ferry I am inclined to think they knew nothing of our purpose. There are no signs of pickets or ambuscades to be found on this side. The distance from the river to the village is only two miles and we could probably have taken it and held it. The bold enterprises are the successful ones. Take counsel of hopes rather than of fears to win in this business.[1]

December 21. — It is rumored that Great Britain will declare war on account of the seizure of Slidell and Mason. I think not. It will blow over. First, bluster and high words; then, correspondence and diplomacy; finally, peace. But if war, what then? First, it will be a trying, a severe, and dreadful trial of our stuff. We shall suffer, but we will stand it. All the Democratic element, now grumbling and discontented, must then rouse up to fight their ancient enemies, the British. The South too, — will not thousands there be turned towards us by seeing their strange allies? If not, shall we not with one voice arm and emancipate the slaves? A civil, sectional, foreign, and servile war — shall we not have horrors enough? Well, I am ready for my share of it. We are in the right and must prevail.[2]

December 23. — I have just heard by telegraph of the birth of my fourth son. In these times, boys are to be preferred to girls. . . . Yes, we are in winter quarters — most comfortable quarters. I have to myself as nice a room as your large room, papered, carpeted, a box full of wood, and with a wild snowstorm blowing outside to make it more comfortable by contrast. We have had eighteen days of fine weather to get ready in, and are in pretty good condition. We have our telegraph line running down to civilization — get Cincinnati papers irregularly from four to ten days old. I have enjoyed the month here very much. Busy fortifying — not quite ready yet, but a few more days of good weather will put us in readiness for any force. The enemy are disheartened; the masses of the people want to stop. If England does not step in, or some great disaster befall us, we shall conquer the Rebellion beyond doubt, and at no distant period.[3]

The close of the year saw the Union forces in control of the situation in western Virginia. The Rebels had been beaten and forced back at every point. The President in his annual message

---

[1] Diary.   [2] Diary.   [3] Letter to Sardis Birchard.

could say: "After a somewhat bloody struggle of months, winter closes on the Union people of western Virginia, leaving them masters of their own country."

New Year's Day, 1862, in the mountains of Virginia dawned bright and clear, following twenty-six fine days in December. The conditions favoring military operations kept Hayes and his command on the alert to check any advance of the enemy. Winter quarters remained at Fayetteville, but there was much arduous campaigning in the surrounding region and plans were made for pushing farther to the south. The diary and letters continue to tell the story of events: —

Camp Union, Fayetteville, Virginia, January 2. — Major Comly reports finding about 120 muskets concealed in and about Raleigh; also twelve or fifteen contrabands arrived. What to do with them is not so troublesome yet as at the East. Officers and soldiers employ them as cooks and servants. Some go on to Ohio. Nobody in this army thinks of giving up to Rebels their fugitive slaves. Union men might, perhaps, be differently dealt with — probably would be. If no doubt of their loyalty, I suppose they would again get their slaves. The man who repudiates all obligations under the Constitution and laws of the United States is to be treated as having forfeited those rights which depend solely on the laws and Constitution. I don't want to see Congress meddling with the slavery question. Time and progress of events are solving all the questions arising out of slavery, in a way consistent with eternal principles of justice. Slavery is getting deathblows. As an "institution" it perishes in this war. It will take years to get rid of its débris, but the "sacred" is gone.[1]

A few weeks later there is an advance in opinion. The slow progress made in suppressing the "insurrection" leads to reflections on the most certain way to end the conflict: —

I am gradually drifting to the opinion that this Rebellion can only be crushed finally by either the execution of all the traitors or the abolition of slavery. Crushed, I mean, so as to remove all danger of its breaking out again in the future. Let the border States, in which there is Union sentiment enough to sustain loyal State Governments, dispose of slavery in their own way; abolish it in the permanently disloyal States — in the cotton States — that is, set free the slaves of Rebels. This will come, I hope, if it is found that a stubborn and prolonged resistance is likely to be made in the cotton States. President Lincoln's message, recommending the passage of a resolution pledging the aid of

[1] Diary.

the general Government to States which shall adopt schemes of gradual emancipation, seems to me to indicate that the result I look for is anticipated by the Administration. I hope it is so.[1]

January 3. — Charles, an honest-looking contraband, six feet high, stout-built, thirty-six years old — wife sold South five years ago — came in to-day, from Union, Monroe County. He gives me such items as the following: "Footing boots, $9 to $10; new boots, $18 to $20; shoes, $4 to $4.50; sugar, 25 to 30 cents; coffee, 62½ cents; tea, $1.50; soda, 62½; salt, $24 a sack; bleached cotton domestic, 40 to 50 cents. . . . Companies broken up in the Rebel armies by furloughs and sickness. Rich men's sons get discharges. Patrols put out to keep slaves at home. They tell slaves that the Yankees cut off arms of some negroes to make them worthless and sell the rest in Cuba for $2500 each to pay cost of the war. — 'No Northern gentlemen fight; only factory men thrown out of employ.' They [the negroes] will fight for the North, if they find the Northerners such as they think them. They 'press' the poor folks' horses and teams, not the rich folks'. The poor folks grumble at being compelled to act as patrols to keep rich men's negroes from running off. When I came with my party, eleven of us, in sight of your pickets, I hardly knew what to do. If you were such people as they had told us we would suffer. Some of the party turned to run. A man with a gun called out 'Halt!' I saw through the fence three more with guns. They asked, 'Who comes there?' I called out, 'Friends.' The soldier who had his gun raised dropped it and said, 'Boys, these are some more of our colored friends,' and told us to come on, not to be afraid, that we were safe. Oh, I never felt so in my life. I could cry, I was so full of joy. And I found them and the Major [Comly] and all I have seen so friendly, such perfect gentlemen, just as we hoped you were, but not as they told us you were." [2]

But the Unionists living within the military lines of the Confederate Government had to pay dearly for the fugitives who made their way to the Union forces. Numbers of them were murdered, all were robbed, and marked for future depredations. A court was held at Huntersville in January, and the magistrates were compelled to levy a tax upon the people to pay for the slaves who had recently run away from Pocohontas County.[3]

January 4. — Major Comly calls his camp at Raleigh "Camp Hayes." It rained last night as if bent to make up for the long drouth. Foggy this morning, warm and muddy enough to stop all advances. — Besides, yesterday, the Twenty-sixth Regiment was ordered from here to Kentucky. Two other regiments go from below. Ten regiments from

[1] Diary, March 27, 1862.   [2] Diary.   [3] Wheeling *Intelligencer.*

New York in same direction. Such an immense force as is gathering ought to open the Mississippi River, capture Memphis, New Orleans, and Nashville before the heat of summer closes operations on that line. Oh, for energy—go-ahead! With horses here we could do wonders,[1] but such a rain as last night forbids any extensive movements.[2]

Hayes had hoped that his regiment would be transferred to Kentucky or to some other field. The service in the mountains of Virginia was important, but it was unsatisfactory because it offered no opportunity for his regiment to be made part of a great army and to participate in large movements. The desire for a wider field was natural; but when a fellow officer expressed the opinion that the Twenty-third Ohio was unfairly treated he repelled the imputation: "Don't think our position an insignificant one. We make more captives and do more than any regiment I have yet heard of in Kentucky."

January 7. — Since writing you a deep snow has fallen, postponing indefinitely all extensive movements southward. We shall have a thaw after the snow, then floods, bad roads for nobody knows how long, and so forth, which will keep us in our comfortable quarters here for the present at least. I shall not leave for home in less than three weeks. . . . I sent Laura some letters written by lovers, wives, and sisters to Rebels in Floyd's army. The captured mails on either side afford curious reading. They are much like other folks, these Rebel sweethearts, wives, and sisters. I trust we shall crush out the Rebellion rapidly. The masses South have been greatly imposed on by people who were well informed. I often wish I could see the people of this village when they return to their homes. On the left of me is a pleasant cottage; the soldiers, to increase their quarters, have built on three sides of it, the awkwardest possible shanty extensions; one side has a prodigious stone and mud chimney, big enough for great logs ten feet in length. On three of the prominent hills of the village, considerable earthworks have been built; there are no fences in sight, except around the three buildings occupied by leading officers. Such is war. — One young lady writing to her lover, speaks of a Federal officer she had met, and laments that so nice a gentleman should be in the Union army.[3]

[1] Hayes recurs to this idea about cavalry in a letter to his brother-in-law, William A. Platt, January 28: "We are a good deal in the field just now, and have made some good moves lately, considering the weakness of our force, and that we had but forty cavalrymen. I see in the papers a good deal said about 'too much cavalry accepted.' If we had only five hundred now, we could do more injury to the enemy than has yet been done by the Port Royal expedition."

[2] Diary.

[3] Letter to Mrs. Hayes.

January 7. — The day before Christmas Private Harrison Brown, Company B, stole a turkey from a countryman who came in to sell it. I made Brown pay for it fifty cents, and sent him to the guardhouse over Christmas. I hated to do it. He is an active, bright soldier, full of sport and lawless, but trusty, brave, and strong. He just came in to offer me a quarter of venison, thus "heaping coals of fire on my head." He probably appreciated my disagreeable duty as well as any one, and took no offense.[1]

January 12 (Fayetteville). — We are letting a good many of our soldiers go home now that the snow, rain, and thaw have spoiled the roads. Joe [2] seems worried that we are not holding somebody's horses in the "Grand Army" (a foolish phrase) in Kentucky. We are, or rather have been, having our share of enterprises toward the jugular vein of rebeldom — the Southwest Virginia Railroad — and have captured prisoners and arms in quantity. I was out beyond Raleigh (Camp Hayes) last week and returned the day before yesterday. Such consternation as spread among the Rebels on the advance of our troops was curious to behold. The advance party went fifty miles from here. People proposed to go as far up as Dublin Depot. Regiments were sent for to Richmond; rumor said two bodies of Yankees one thousand strong were approaching, one on each bank of New River. The militia of five counties were called out, and a high time generally got up. There are many Union men south of here who kept us well posted on Rebel movements. Major Comly is left at Raleigh, and I feel somewhat apprehensive about him. Since the Twenty-sixth has been recalled I am in command of the post here. I shall send home a sabre captured by Company G on the late trip up New River towards the railroad. It is one of a dozen taken, which belonged to a company of Richmond cavalry commanded by Captain Caskie. . . .

You will send Joe off as soon as it is safe for him to go. I am always amused with his talk on one subject. He is resolved to consider our regiment as a much abused and neglected one. We were in about the only successful campaign made last summer. We have the best winter quarters in the United States. He thinks we can't be favorites of General Rosecrans because he don't send us away to Kentucky or somewhere else! And so on. Joe seems to feel as if something was wrong about the regiment; as if he would like to leave it, etc., etc. Now, if he is not satisfied with it, I will do all I can to get him a place in another regiment. Don't let him stay in this on my account. I am liable to leave it at any time, and I really don't want anybody in high position in the regiment who is dissatisfied, and particularly, if he is a friend or relation of mine. I feel a duty in this matter. The happiness of several hundred men is affected more or less, if one of the prominent officers allows himself to be habitually out of sorts about things. You may show this to Joe.

---

[1] Diary.   [2] His brother-in-law, Dr. Joseph T. Webb.

Don't let there be any misunderstanding. I prefer greatly, that Dr. Joe should be our surgeon, but if he feels that he can't return to western Virginia, or go anywhere else that the chances of war may take us without feeling injured and soured, then my preference is that he do not come. . . . I ought not to trouble you with this, but it is written, and you will not think me unkind, will you? [1]

January 14. — My old veteran, Orderly Gray, says it makes his flesh creep to see the way soldiers enter officers' quarters, hats on, just as if they were in civil life! — The Twenty-sixth Regiment left to-day. Spent the afternoon looking over a trunkful of old letters, deeds, documents, etc., belonging to General Alfred Beckley. They were buried in the graveyard near General Beckley's at Raleigh. Some letters of moment showing the early and earnest part taken by Colonel Tompkins in the Rebellion. The general Union and conservative feeling of General Beckley is shown in letters carefully preserved in his letter-book. Two letters to Major Anderson full of patriotism, love of the Union and of the Stars and Stripes — replies written, one the day after Major Anderson went into Sumter, the other much later. His (General Beckley's) desire was really for the Union. He was of West Point education. Out of deference to popular sentiment he qualified his Unionism by saying, "Virginia would stay in the Union as long as she could consistently with honor." [2]

January 15. — Two more contrabands yesterday. These runaways are bright fellows. As a body they are superior to the average of the uneducated white population of the State, who are unenterprising, lazy, narrow, listless, and careless of consequences to the country, if their own lives and property are safe. Slavery leaves one class, the wealthy, with leisure for cultivation — for intellectual enjoyment. They are usually intelligent, well-bred, brave, and high-spirited. The rest are serfs. . . . I discharged three suspected persons heretofore under arrest; all took the oath. Two I thought too old to do mischief. One I thought possibly honest and gave him the benefit of the possibility. [3]

January 17. — We hear of the resignation of Cameron and Welles. What does this mean? I think we must gain by it. I hope such men as Holt and Stanton will take their places. If so, the nation will not lose by the change. [4]

January 18. — All important movements everywhere are stopped by the rain and mud already. Still further "postponement on account of the weather." How impatiently we look for action on Green River; at Cairo! As to the Potomac, all hope of work in that quarter seems to be abandoned. Why don't they try to flank the Rebels — get at their

---

[1] Letter to Mrs. Hayes.   [2] Diary.   [3] Diary.   [4] Diary.

communications in the rear? But patience! Here we are in a good position to get in the rear via two railroads. Suppose two, or even three or four bodies of men were to start, one by way of Lewisburg for White Sulphur Springs and Jackson Depot; one via Peterstown and Union east side of New River for Central Depot; one via Princeton and Parisburg, right bank of New River for Dublin; and another via Logan Court House for some point lower down on the railroad. . . .

The scenery of New River is attractive. The river runs in a deep gorge cut through the rocks to a depth varying from one thousand to two thousand feet. The precipitous cliffs are occasionally cut through by streams running into the river. The rapid rushing river and brawling mountain streams furnish many fine views. The "Glades," a level region near Braxton and Webster Counties, where streams rise, and a similar region, called the "Marshes of Cool," are the battle grounds of this part of western Virginia. Braxton and Webster are the haunts of the worst Rebel bushwhackers of the country. Steep mountains, deep gorges, and glens afford them hiding-places. They are annoying, but not dangerous except to couriers, mail carriers, and very small parties. They shoot from too great a distance at large parties to do much harm.[1]

Rumors of activity in other parts of the country penetrate the mountain district and are joyfully received. "What we want," Hayes wrote, January 19, "is greater energy, more drive, more enterprise, not unaccompanied with caution and vigilance." A few days later came the news of Thomas's great victory over Zollicoffer at Mills Springs. The only dash to the satisfaction this gave was the first report that Colonel Robert McCook, of the Ninth Ohio, was dangerously wounded. "Later: — not seriously but gloriously wounded."

I am delighted with the Kentucky victory, and particularly that my friend McCook and his regiment take the honors. We were good friends before the war, but much more intimately so since we came into service.[2]

[1] Diary. The following agreement captured by Colonel Hayes's men explains the guerrilla "principles." It is given here *verbatim et literatim* : —

"We the undersigned do heartily constitute ourselves into a company of guerillas, known by the name of the flat top copperheads, for the purpose of defending our immediate country, our Western Va. against the invation of the Yankeys. We Bind ourselves By Every obligation of honor and patternage, to obey the command of our officers and to be true and faithful to the confederate states of America, and to be true to our selves and families and serve for the during term of six months Except sooner discharged. March 26th, 1862." (Signed by C. F. Foley, Captain, and over eighty others.)

[2] Letter to Mrs. Hayes.

January 22. — Three prisoners brought down last night. Captain McVey, a bushwhacking captain, armed with sword and rifle, was approaching a Union citizen's house to capture him, when the Union man, hearing of it, hid behind a log, drew a bead on "secesh" as he approached, called out to him to lay down his arms, which "secesh" prudently did, and thereupon the victor marched him to our camp at Raleigh. Another prisoner, a son of General Beckley, aged about sixteen. Why he was taken I don't understand. He carried dispatches when the militia was out under his father, but seems intelligent and well disposed. Disliking to see one so young packed into a crowded guardhouse (thinking of Birch and Webb, too), I took him to my own quarters and shared my bed with him last night.[1]

January 24. — Alfred Beckley, Jr., left with a pledge to return if he failed to get exchanged for young Henderson of Company H, Twenty-third, the captured scout.[2]

The release of the favorite scout was obtained by young Beckley.[3] When Hayes was at Raleigh again some time after this event, he writes: —

Mrs. General Beckley called with another lady. Mrs. Beckley, in tears, said her husband was at home, and had concluded to surrender himself; that she had n't seen or heard from him for three months; hoped we would n't send him to Columbus, etc. In his letter, he pledged his honor not to oppose the United States, and to behave as a loyal citizen. I called to see him; found him an agreeable old gentleman of sixty; converses readily and entertainingly. Told an anecdote of General Jackson capitally. He said Old Hickory's hair bristled up, his eyes shot fire, and his iron features became more prominent as, in a passion, raising both hands, he said (speaking of a postmaster Beckley wished to retain in office and who had himself taken no active part against General Jackson, but whose clerks had been against the general): "What if the head is still when both hands are at work against me?" — shaking his hands outstretched and in a towering passion. The lieutenant then subsided in the presence of such wrath. General Beckley thinks western Virginia is given up to us, and that his duty is to go with his home — to submit to the powers that be. I agreed to his views generally, and told him I would recommend General Cox to assent to his surrender on the terms proposed.[4]

---

[1] Diary.   [2] Diary.

[3] "He left Richmond February 23. He is called 'Cleveland' by his company, from the place of his enlistment. Others call him 'the pet lamb,' from his delicate and youthful appearance. He is a quiet, observing, enterprising youngster — slender, sickly-looking, amiable; runs all risks, endures all hardships, and seems to enjoy it. A scout in fact, he is in constant danger of being taken for a spy." (Diary, March 14.)   [4] Diary.

But this lenity was not approved. In due course an order was received requiring General Beckley to be arrested and taken to Wheeling. His wife and family felt grieved enough. The general said he recognized the propriety of it and did not complain.

January 30. — People constantly come who are on their way to Ohio, Indiana, or other Western States. Many of them young men who are foot-loose — tired of the war. No employment, poor pay, etc., is driving the laboring white people from the slave States. Mr. Ellison and his wife and little boy are here to see their son John R. who is a prisoner in our guardhouse to be sent to the government prison at Columbus as a prisoner of war. They seem glad to find their son safe out of the Rebel ranks and not at all averse to his going to Columbus as a prisoner of war. Their only fear seems to be that he will be exchanged into the Rebel army again.[1]

Having obtained leave of absence Hayes started for Ohio February 1. On his way down the Kanawha, he visited General Cox at Charleston. "A good talk — a sound man — excellent sense. Heard the church bells at Charleston, the first for six months. A home sound." The weeks of absence were pleasantly spent at home with visits to Columbus, Delaware, and Fremont. The last day of February found Hayes again at Fayetteville. Then followed several weeks of bad weather, snows and heavy rains and bottomless mud, which rendered military movements exceedingly difficult, if not impossible. The Twenty-third Regiment was soon all concentrated at Raleigh, where several companies had been since early in the winter under Major Comly. Small detachments were constantly sent out to scour the surrounding hills for bushwhackers, of whom many were captured. Virginians, fleeing from the Confederate draft, were received and helped on their way to the North and West. The regiment was drilled whenever "falling weather" (to use the locution of the mountains) did not forbid, and preparations were made for a forward movement toward the East Tennessee and Virginia Railroad as soon as roads and weather permitted. About the middle of March General Frémont was placed in command of the Mountain Department. The brigade of which the Twenty-third Regiment was part belonged to the division of General J. D. Cox which constituted the extreme right wing of Frémont's

[1] Diary.

army. The Twenty-third Regiment occupied at Raleigh the most advanced position when spring opened. The brigade was under command of Colonel Scammon; and Hayes was in command of his regiment. The men of the brigade were in fine condition for service — nearly all were well and strong. They had learned their trade; they marched with the elastic step and the precision of veterans; they had faith in themselves and confidence in their leaders. Open-air life was so exhilarating that Hayes often felt that indoor life was unworthy of manhood. "How the blood leaps and thrills through the veins as we race over the hills," he says. "Physical enjoyments of this sort are worth a war. How the manly, generous, brave side of our people is growing. With all its evils war has its glorious compensations."

Fayetteville, March 11. — The last of the Twenty-third quartered in Fayetteville is gone. Camp Hayes, Raleigh, headquarters henceforth. Heard of the evacuation of Manassas. How did they do it undisturbed? *What was McClellan doing?* A great victory over the combined forces of Van Dorn, Price, McCulloch, and McIntosh reported to have occurred in Arkansas.[1]

March 12. — A bright warm day. I go to Raleigh, bidding goodbye to Fayetteville. We entered Fayetteville either the 13th or 14th of November; four months in one home — not unpleasant months considering the winter weather of this region. Rode to Raleigh on my new bright bay; a good ride; reached Raleigh just as our regiment was forming for dress parade; eight companies in line — looked large. Was greeted warmly. I gave them the news of the evacuation of Manassas and the victory in Arkansas. Three cheers given for the news, three more for General Curtis, and three for the Colonel (?). All seemed pleased to be again together. How well they looked! The band is in capital condition. How I love the Twenty-third! I would rather command it as lieutenant-colonel than to command another regiment as colonel.[2]

Raleigh, March 16. — I am here in command of nine companies of the Twenty-third, one section (two guns) of an artillery company (thirty men), and one company of cavalry. We are quartered in the court house, churches, and deserted dwellings. It is near the spurs of the Alleghany Mountains, which about twenty miles from here are filled with militia. A few regulars and bushwhackers are just in front of us. We are kept on the alert all the time. . . . As a general rule, we get the

[1] Diary.   [2] Diary.

better of the bushwhackers in these affairs. There is no hesitation on our part in doing what seems to be required for self-protection.[1]

March 18. — A queer prisoner brought in from New River by Richmond. — Richmond who is a resolute Union citizen was taken prisoner at his house by three Rebels — two dragoons and a bushwhacker. One of the dragoons took Richmond behind him and off they went. On the way . . . Richmond drew his pocket knife slyly from his pocket, caught the dragoon before him by his hair behind and cut his throat and stabbed him. Both fell from the horse together. Richmond cut the strap holding the dragoon's rifle, took it and killed a second; the third escaped, and Richmond ran to our camp.[2] — Jesse Reese, brought in as a spy by Richmond, says he is a tailor; was going to Greenbrier to collect money due him. Says he married when he was about fifty; they got married because they were both orphans and alone in the world.[3]

March 19. —'About noon a gentleman rode up and inquired for the colonel commanding. He turned out to be Clifton W. Tayleure, a local editor formerly of Baltimore *American,* lately of Richmond *Enquirer.* Left Richmond a week ago to avoid the draft. All between eighteen and forty-five to be drafted to fill up the old regiments; all between sixteen and eighteen, and forty-five and fifty-five, to be enrolled as home guards to protect the homes and guard the slaves. He is a South Carolinian by birth, lived there until he was fifteen; came North; has been a "local" in various cities since; has a family in Baltimore; went to Richmond to look after property in August last; could n't get away before; got off by passes procured by good luck, etc., etc.; is a Union man by preference, principle, etc. This is his story. He is about thirty-three years of age, of prepossessing appearance, intelligent, and agreeable. Gives us interesting accounts of things in the capital of secession. Says the tradespeople are anxious for peace, ready for the restoration of the old Union. He seems to be truthful. I shall give him a pass to General Cox, there to be dealt with as the general sees fit.[4]

---

[1] Letter to Sardis Birchard. — Men that promised to keep the peace had nothing to fear. Hayes issued this notice: "No citizen who remains peaceably at home and who neither directly nor indirectly gives aid or comfort to the enemies of the United States will be molested in person or property by the troops under my command." Many of the people of the region played fast and loose with both sides. "None of the people," Hayes says, "are perfectly reliable. They will do what is necessary to protect their property."

[2] "Abram Bragg and William C. Richmond with other Union men never sleep at home. They hide up on the hills during the night. This they have done for two months past." (Diary, March 28.) Dr. Webb in a letter narrates the same incident, saying in conclusion: "There is no mistake about this; he came to camp with their two guns. His knife and coatsleeve is covered with blood. Richmond is a trump, and two hundred such men would clear out this country of Rebels."

[3] Diary.

[4] Diary. — In 1885, Mr. Hayes received an interesting letter from this gentle-

March 20. — Frémont at the head of our department — the Mountain District, western Virginia and east Tennessee. Good. I admire the general. If he comes up to my anticipations we shall have an active

man, at that time temporarily sojourning in London. Mr. Tayleure details the incidents attending his capture while, as correspondent of the Richmond *Enquirer*, he was seeking to reach General Jenifer's headquarters. Fleeing from a bushwhacker he says: "I found myself upon the Raleigh turnpike and in the immediate presence of a squad of foot-soldiers belonging to the Twenty-third Ohio. I put a bold face on it and saluting the sergeant was passing on — eastward, when he quite courteously halted me, and asked me my name, where I was from, and whither I was going. I gave my name, stated I was a noncombatant from Richmond, and that I was a physician hurrying to a wounded patient. 'Of course you have the password?' he inquired. I had not; and the man apologetically told me it was then his duty to report with me at headquarters. There was no resisting, and in a short time I stood before — Colonel Hayes of the Twenty-third Ohio. You were so courteous to me, my dear General, so considerate when, in reply to a question of yours, I replied I was a soldier, and begged to be excused from answering, that you quite disarmed my hostile prejudices and inspired me with much respect for you instead. I have never forgotten, shall never forget, your kindness on the occasion. I pardon even the member of your staff who induced me to drink some bad whiskey; it flattered my pride to deal in that sort of magnanimity; but in *your* case, I stood debtor to your generous dealing, and was glad to remember the debt. One of your staff with whom I slept that night in a dismantled house tried to shoot me as 'a spy'; another interfered and saved my life. I am uncertain or not whether it was *you*, who thus interposed. It was you, however, who next day restored my horse to me, and with no other check upon me than the parole of a gentleman, sent me forward to Brigadier-General Scammon, whom I only remember as a bigoted Catholic. From thence I was sent to Major-General Cox (whom I then thought one of the handsomest men I had ever seen), and by General Cox was paroled to report to army headquarters in Baltimore, where, in obedience to my parole, I remained. The exposure, difficulties, and dangers I encountered in keeping my parole, I should not like again to encounter. I am now a grey-haired old man, not distant I hope from the eternal rest I desire, and thinking to-day of the danger I had passed through, the dear good people I had met, and been glad to meet, your own name, with the pleasant memories it suggests, recurred to my mind. . . . I would have written you long ago, but you were high in power, or on the line of political advancement, and I was afraid my motives would be mistaken; now, however, that I am temporarily absent from my native land (I am a Southerner), and you out of power, — temporarily, I hope, — I think I may venture to thrust myself upon your attention, and to salute you with my best wishes and with my highest respect."

Mr. Hayes wrote Mr. Tayleure, quoting in his letter the paragraph from his diary given in the text. Mr. Tayleure replied gratefully with further reminiscences of the experience of 1862, especially about General Scammon, and added: "I don't know whether or not General Scammon is alive, but I must say to you that I was as much annoyed at his manner, as I was impressed with your courtesy and confidence. It would have given me pleasure to outwit General Scammon. I would have died rather than betray *your* trust. When you were President and my countrymen of the South were saluting you, the 'amen' which my heart pronounced was as sincere a response as manhood could ask of truth."

campaign. . . . Colonel Scammon returned, also Major Comly, to Fayetteville. They send no news and bring no newspapers. Thoughtless fellows! No, I must not call the colonel fellow. He put down a country-man who came in with, "Are you the feller what rents land?" Colonel Scammon: "In the first place I am not a feller. In the second place, take off your hat; and in the third place, I don't rent land. There is the door." [1]

March 22. — We are all feeling very hopeful. We expect to move soon and rapidly, merely because Frémont is commander. I do not see but this war must be soon decided. McClellan seems determined, and I think he is able to force the retreating Manassas army to a battle, or to an equally disastrous retreat. A victory there ends the contest, I think. We shall be months, perhaps years, getting all the small parties reduced, but the Rebellion, as a great peril menacing the Union, will be ended. . . .

You ought to see what a snowstorm is blowing. "Whew!" I had a tent put up a few days ago for an office; before I got it occupied, the storm came on, and now it is split in twain. . . . Our regiment was never so fine-looking as now. It is fun to see them. No deaths, I believe, for two months, and no sickness worth mentioning. Chiefly engaged in hunting bushwhackers. Our living is hard — the grub, I mean, and likely not to improve; salt pork and crackers. The armies have swept off all fresh meats and vegetables; a few eggs once in a great while. [2]

March 24. — The recent victories convince a great many in the region south of us, that the game is up. On the other hand, the Government at Richmond is making desperate efforts to get out under arms nearly the whole population of military age. Many are running away from drafting. Being the extreme outpost, we see daily all sorts of queer characters. They sometimes come in boldly; sometimes, with fear and trembling. I am often puzzled what to do with them, but manage to dispose of them as fast as they come. An odd, laughable incident occurred to Joe the other day. You know his fondness for children. He always talks to them and generally manages to get them on his knee. Stopping at a farmhouse, he began to make advances toward a three-year-old boy who could scarcely talk plain enough to be understood. The doctor said, "Come, my fine little fellow, I want to talk with you." The urchin with a jerk turned away saying something the doctor did not comprehend. On a second approach, the doctor made it out — "Go to Hell, you damn Yankee!" This from the little codger was funny enough. [3]

April 13. — A year ago to-day Sumter was taken. Great events, great changes since then. The South was eager, prepared — "armed

[1] Diary.   [2] Letter to Mrs. Hayes.
[3] Letter to Sardis Birchard.

and equipped." The event found the North distracted, undecided, unarmed, wholly unprepared, and helpless. Then came the rousing up of the lion-hearted people of the North. For months, however, the superior preparation of the South triumphed. Gradually the North — the nation, got ready. And now the victory over Beauregard and at [Island] No. 10, following Fort Donelson, put the Nation on firm ground while the Rebellion is waning daily.[1]

Camp, south of Raleigh, April 22. — The ugly chap on the enclosed bill is Governor Letcher, of Virginia. He is entitled to our lasting gratitude. He is doing more for us in this State than any two brigadiers I can think of. He has, in all the counties not occupied by our troops, little squads of volunteers busily engaged in hunting up and "squadding in," as they call it, all persons capable of military duty. Thousands who wish to escape this draft, are now hiding in the mountains, or seeking refuge in our lines. Meantime, the rascals are plundering and burning in all directions, making friends for the Union wherever they go. The defeat of the enemy in eastern Virginia [will] send this cob-house tumbling very fast.

We left Raleigh last week, and have been struggling against storms and freshets ever since. To-day it has snowed, rained, sleeted, and turned off bright but gusty a dozen times. Camp muddy, tents wet, but all glad to be started.

I have for the present an independent command of the Twenty-third Regiment, a section of McMullen's Battery, and a small body of horse. We are the advance of Frémont's column. We are directed to move by "easy marches" forward south, the design being, I suppose, to overtake us in full force by the time we meet any considerable body of the enemy. We meet and hear of small bodies of enemy now constantly, but as yet nothing capable of serious resistance.[2]

[1] Diary. [2] Letter to Sardis Birchard.

CHAPTER XI

CONSTANT rains delayed the forward movement. April 29 found Hayes's command only nine miles from Raleigh. Foley's band of guerrillas was causing much annoyance, and on that day Hayes dispatched Lieutenant Bottsford with Company C on ahead, sixteen miles, to run Foley to earth. The next day Hayes moved forward twelve miles and received word from Bottsford "that he found Foley's nest, but the bird gone." By 6 o'clock, May 1, Hayes had his command in motion toward Princeton, twenty-two miles to the south, which was reached at 5 P.M. In a letter to his wife, written the next day, Hayes gives a graphic account of the exciting day's experiences: —

Princeton, Mercer Co., Virginia, May 2, 1862. — I reached yesterday this town, after a hard day's march of twenty-two miles through deep, slippery mud and a heavy rain, crossing many streams which had to be waded — one waist-deep. The men stood it bravely and good-humoredly. To-day, only twelve are reported as excused from duty. Our advance company (C) had a severe battle.[1] Seventy-five of them were attacked by two hundred and forty of Jenkins's Cavalry (now Jenifer's) [dismounted] with seventy-seven of Foley's guerrillas. The battle lasted twenty minutes, when the Rebels fled, leaving their killed and wounded on the ground. One of our men was killed outright, three mortally wounded, and seventeen others more or less severely injured. The whole regiment came up in a few moments, hearing the firing; did n't they cheer us? As I rode up, they saluted with a "Present arms."

[1] " The company was in line ready to move off to return to camp, when they saw a party of bushwhackers coming down the road who called out (Captain Foley called): 'Don't fire. We're Richmond's men.' Immediately after, a volley was fired into our men from all sides. They were surrounded by three hundred 'secesh.' Finding the attack so heavy, Company C was ordered by Lieutenant Bottsford to take shelter in the log house where they had quartered. They kept up such a spirited fire that the enemy retreated, leaving four dead, four mortally, four more dangerously, wounded. All these we got. Captain Foley had his shoulder broken. The enemy fled in confusion. This was a splendid victory for Lieutenant Bottsford and Sergeant Ritter (Company C) and Sergeant Abbott (Company I)." (Diary, May 1.)

Several were bloody with wounds as they stood in their places; one boy limped to his post who had been hit three times; as I looked at the glow of pride in their faces, my heart choked me; I could not speak, but a boy said, "All right, Colonel, we know what you mean." The enemy's loss was much severer than ours.

We pushed on rapidly, hearing extravagant stories of the force waiting for us at Princeton. Prisoners, apparently candid, said, we would catch it then. We would have caught Lieutenant-Colonel Fitzhugh and his men, if our cavalry had had experience. I don't report to their prejudice publicly, for they are fine fellows, gentlemen, splendidly mounted and equipped. In three months they will be capital, but their caution, in the face of ambuscades, is entirely too great. After trying to get them ahead, I put the Twenty-third in advance and the cavalry in the rear, making certainly double the speed, with our footmen trudging in the mud, as was made by the horsemen on their fine steeds. We caught a few and killed a few. At the houses, the wounded Rebels would be left. As we came up, the men would rush in, when the women would beg us not to kill the prisoners or the wounded. I talked with several who were badly wounded. They all seemed grateful for kind words, which I always gave them. One fine fellow, a Captain Ward, was especially grateful.

This work continued all day; I, pushing on; they, trying to keep us back. The fact being that General Heth had sent word that he would be in Princeton by night with a force able to hold it. As we came on to a mountain a couple of miles from Princeton, we saw that the Rebels were too late; the great clouds were rolling to the sky — they were burning the town. We hurried on, saved enough for our purposes, I think, although the best buildings were gone. The women wringing their hands and crying and begging us to protect them, with the fine town in flames around us, made a scene to be remembered. This was my May day. General Heth's forces got within four miles; he might as well have been forty. We are in possession, and I think I can hold it. Joe and Dr. McCurdy had a busy day. They had secesh wounded as well as our own to look after. Dr. Neal, of the Second Virginia Cavalry (five companies of which are now here in my command), a friend of Joe, assisted them.

Saturday morning. — I intended to send this by courier this morning, but in the press of business, sending off couriers, prisoners, and expeditions, I forgot it. Telegraph is building here; anything happening to me will be known to you at once. It now looks as if we would find no enemy to fight.

The weather, yesterday and to-day, is perfect. The mountains are in sight from all the high grounds about here, and the air pure and exhilarating. The troubles of women, who have either been burnt out by secesh or robbed of chickens and the like by us, are the chief thing this morning. One case is funny. A spoiled, fat Englishwoman, with great pride and hysterics, was left with a queer old negro woman to look after her wants. Darky *now* thinks she is mistress. She is sulky — won't work, etc., etc. Mistress can't eat pork or army diet. There is no other food here. The sight of rough men is too much for her nerves! All queer. We are now eighty-five miles from the head of navigation in time of flood and one hundred twenty-five in ordinary times; a good way from "America," as the soldiers say.

May 2. — The cavalry yesterday took the Bluff Road and came into the road from Princeton to Giles Court House — five miles. They came across tracks leading to Princeton. Soon saw soldiers, opened fire and had a fusillade of wild firing, the enemy fleeing to the mountains. It was the Forty-fifth Virginia coming to reënforce Princeton.[1]

May 3. — The Forty-fifth Regiment had marched twenty miles through the rain to reach here, were very tired and straggled badly. They were regularly stampeded — panic-stricken and routed; they report *three* killed in one party of stragglers. They had a cannon drawn by six horses, but our men "yelled so" and "fired so fast" that it was no place for cannon, so they wheeled about and fled with it. All queer. Company C killed eleven. Colonel Jenifer burned Rocky Gap (four houses) and continued his flight towards Wytheville. The Rebels report us two thousand cavalry and eight thousand infantry!! Got our tents to-day; got into a good camp overlooking the town.[2]

May 6. — I have been rather anxious to-day. We heard from contra-bands and others that the Narrows [of New River] was deserted except by a small guard for property and tents. Major Comly, with companies H, I, and K, and Captain Gilmore's cavalry, was dispatched to the point eighteen to twenty-two miles distant. No tidings yet, although a courier ought to have reached here before this time if they and he trav-elled rapidly. I suggested that, if necessary to secure property, they go to Giles Town.

In the meantime I hear that a foraging party of six of our men as guards under Corporal Day, with three battery men and a wagon, has been taken by a large party of cavalry on the Tazewell Road — ten miles. Jenifer's cavalry have gone to Tazewell, got their horses and are now in the saddle ready to cut off our men. Oh, for an enterprising cavalry force!

I have looked for a messenger since 5 o'clock from Major Comly. At midnight received a message from Major Comly that the party finding the Narrows deserted and all property gone, had gone on to Giles and taken it completely by surprise, capturing some prisoners and a large amount of stores — two hundred and fifty barrels of flour and every-thing else. Very lucky, and Colonel Scammon therefore approved of the whole expedition, although it was irregular and in violation of the letter of orders. The enemy just out of Giles were at least eleven

---

[1] Diary.   [2] Diary.

hundred and had forces near to increase it to fifteen hundred. Our party was only two hundred and fifty! The colonel, fearing the capture of our little party ordered me to proceed at daylight with two companies Second Virginia Cavalry and the rest of Twenty-third Regiment to reënforce Giles.[1]

Giles Court House, or Parisburg, May 7, 6.30 p.m. — Just reached here from Princeton after a fatiguing march of twenty-eight miles. Found the major very glad to see us. All anxious, hearing reports of Forty-fifth [Virginia] reënforced by Thirty-sixth or Twenty-second with artillery, etc., etc. Now, all safe if we are vigilant. The country after the road strikes New River is romantic, highly cultivated, and beautiful. Giles Court House is [a] neat, pretty village with a most magnificent surrounding country both as regards scenery and cultivation. The people have all been secesh, but are polite and intelligent. When Major Comly, Captain Gilmore, and Captain Drake entered town, the people were standing on the corners, idly gossiping; — more numerous than the invaders. They did not at first seem to know who it was. Then such a scampering, such a rushing to the streets of women, such weeping, scolding, begging, etc., etc. Spent the night posting pickets and arranging against an attack, so as to prevent a surprise. At midnight a citizen came in saying the enemy were preparing to attack us — the Forty-fifth and Twenty-second — when he was at their camp, twelve miles from here at Cloyd Mountain. I doubled the pickets, dressed myself, and kept about quietly all the rest of the night.[2]

Parisburg, May 8. — No attack or approach last night. Passed out at daylight a mile and a half in direction of enemy. Selected my ground in case of an approach of the enemy. Talked with Mr. Pendleton, Colonel English. Find more intelligence and culture here than anywhere else in Virginia. To-day Sergeant Abbott found a Rebel picket or scouting party on the mountain overlooking the village, peering into us with a field-glass. A reconnaissance to-day discovered three regiments in line, marching coolly and well to the front as our men crossed Walker's Creek, ten or twelve miles from here. They are said to have three pieces of artillery and some cavalry. We get no reënforcements to-day and hear of none on the way. I have asked for artillery two or three times and get none. No message, even, to-day. It is a great outrage that we are not reënforced. We are losing stores all the time, which the enemy slips away — not [to] speak of the possibility of an attack by an overwhelming force. Shameful! Who is to blame? I think we shall not be attacked, but I shall have an anxious night.[3]

The reconnaissance penetrated the enemy's country to within ten miles of the railway which it was so important to cut. But

---

[1] Diary.   [2] Diary.   [3] Diary.

the Confederate Government fully realized the necessity of preventing the destruction or the interruption of this most important line of communication to the West. Reënforcements had been hurried forward to General Heth and Generals Williams and Humphrey Marshall were not far away. The Confederate commander was pushing on in force and with artillery to retake Parisburg and drive the little body of Union men back into the mountains. Hayes's call for aid was not heeded until too late. It is doubtful, indeed, whether sufficient men could have arrived in time to prevent the necessity of a retreat in the face of the forces the Confederates were bringing against the town. The position in the midst of a hostile region was too far from the base of supplies to make it tenable, with the number of troops in General Cox's division. May 9 was an anxious day for Hayes and his little command. An attack by a superior force was known to be imminent, before which, unless reënforcement came, a retreat was inevitable.

At the first streak of dawn Saturday morning Hayes was up and out on the picket line. Hearing six shots fired in the direction of the enemy, he was sure the attack was coming. He hastened back to camp and got his men in motion. The cavalry was sent to the front; Captains Sperry and Drake were ordered to skirmish before the enemy and check their advance; while the rest of the regiment formed to support them. The entire force was led by Hayes to the ground he had already selected beyond the town. Presently the enemy was seen approaching, four regiments or battalions strong, in line of battle.

The artillery soon opened on us [wrote Hayes in his diary that afternoon]. The shell shrieked and burst over [our] heads; the small arms rattled and the battle was begun. It was soon obvious that we would be outflanked. We retreated to the next ridge and stood again. The men of the Twenty-third behaved gloriously. The men of Gilmore's cavalry ditto. The men of Colonel Paxton's company not so well. I was scratched and torn on the knee by a shell or something, doing no serious injury. I felt well all the time. The men behaved so gallantly! And so we fought our way through town — the people rejoicing at our defeat — and on for six hours until we reached the "Narrows" five and one half miles distant. The time seemed short. I was cheered by Gilmore's cavalry at a point about three and a half miles from Giles Court House, and we were all in good humor. We had three men killed, a number wounded — none severely, and lost a few prisoners. In the "Narrows" we easily checked the pursuit of the enemy and held him back until he got artillery on to the opposite side of New River and shelled us out. Reached here [Adairs, ten and one half miles from Giles] about 1 P.M. safely. A well-ordered retreat which I think was creditable.

Hayes was very proud of the conduct of the Twenty-third Regiment in this masterly retreat. To Mrs. Hayes the day after the battle he wrote: —

The Twenty-third looked gloriously after this. We got off by a miracle. We lost one killed, one wounded badly, and a host slightly. Applause was never so sweet as when right in the midst of the struggle Gilmore's cavalry gave me three cheers for a sharp stroke by which I turned the column out of range of the enemy's guns which with infinite trouble he had placed to sweep us.[1]

The enemy lost thirty-one killed and seventy-two wounded. The retreating force had the best of the fighting notwithstanding the enemy had artillery. "Never was a man prouder of his regiment," said Hayes, "than I of the Twenty-third. I keep thinking how well they behaved."

The command remained at Adairs one day and then moved back a short distance to a strong position at the mouth of East River, where it was joined by the rest of the brigade under Colonel Scammon. In the retreat Hayes's force had been obliged to abandon the stores captured at Parisburg and had lost also its tents, except those belonging to headquarters. The supplies were inadequate, owing to lack of transportation, the brigade

[1] In a letter (February 14, 1884) from Edward E. Henry, — a member of the regiment in 1862, — is this reference to the retreat: "Since the day of the Giles Court House raid (and many other tight places) — the 'Narrows' — where you asked McIlrath to take his company and keep back the enemy a short time and he answered: 'Colonel, if I take my men up among those rocks I can never get them out in God's world'; so well we remember your reply, 'Company A, will you follow me?' With a shout we followed you without fear of those shells and came back all right."

"Colonel Hayes in the whole affair has shown himself an able commander and fully established the confidence of every man in the Twenty-third Ohio Regiment, and while he exhibits the true gentleman in every respect, he is a noble, brave officer, and the men under him are willing to follow him under every circumstance." (Cincinnati *Commercial*, May 28.)

The Cleveland *Leader*, May 29, had a letter from a member of Company A describing the retreat from Parisburg. It said Hayes showed himself ready for any emergency and adds: "Our regiment to a man are ready to follow Lieutenant-Colonel Hayes wherever he chooses to lead. He has the entire confidence of the regiment."

was without bread, and but for the bacon procured in the neighborhood would have suffered. Meanwhile General Cox was advancing from Fayetteville. He reached Princeton the morning of the 16th. Hardly had camp been pitched when General Humphrey Marshall appeared with a greatly superior force and drove him out. The next day General Cox returned the compliment. But he was convinced that with the forces at his command it was impossible to hold so advanced a position, and he sent word to Colonel Scammon's brigade to fall back and join him at Princeton. The retrograde movement was continued to Flat Top Mountain, about seventy miles from the farthest point reached by Hayes, where camp was established in a secure position.

Hayes was greatly chagrined for the time at the retreat. He thought the issue should have been tried with Williams and Marshall at Princeton after the whole division had got together. But with fuller knowledge of the situation this mood changed. Moreover, as he had led the advance and had covered the retreat during the whole movement, he could not fail to be satisfied with his share in it.[1] General Frémont complimented him for "energy and courage," and also noticed the "gallantry" of the Twenty-third. Two companies of Paxton's cavalry and the Thirty-fourth Ohio had behaved badly, and the fleeing men had reported the army routed and Hayes fatally wounded. The report caused many days of intense anxiety to Mrs. Hayes. This was finally relieved by a dispatch from Hayes which reached Cincinnati about a week after the battle at Parisburg. From Flat Top Hayes wrote reassuringly: —

Flat Top Mountain, May 25. — Dr. Joe has a letter from McCabe in which he speaks of your anxiety on my account. I hope that it has not been increased by my dispatch. You will always hear the precise truth from me. You may rely on it that you hear exactly the state of things. It would be idle to say that we have been in no danger, or that we are not likely to be in peril hereafter; but this is certain that there is not

[1] "We got off very well, having the best of all the fighting, losing very little property in the retreat, and conducting it in good order. General Cox and staff narrowly escaped capture. My command had a narrow escape. With any common precautions we should have been captured or destroyed, but luckily I had mounted pickets two miles further out than usual and got notice of the trap in time." (Letter to Sardis Birchard, May 20.)

half the danger for officers in a regiment that can be trusted to behave well, as there would be in a regiment of raw troops. Besides, the danger on this line is much diminished by a victory which one of our brigades under Colonel Crook gained day before yesterday at Lewisburg. He routed the army under General Heth, which drove me out of Giles, captured their cannon, etc.

May 26. —Your excellent letters of 17th and 19th came this morning — only a week in getting to me. I wrote you yesterday by the soldiers, Corporal West and Harper, but I must give you another by the sutler who goes in the morning, just to show how much I think of you and your letters. We are now at rest on a mountain-top with no immediate prospect of anything stirring. We stand for the moment on the defensive, and are not likely to be disturbed. We have been having exchanges of wounded and prisoners with the enemy. They have behaved very well to our men, and were exceedingly civil and hospitable in our negotiations with them. They feel a good deal discouraged with the general prospect, but are crowding our small armies with Banks and Frémont pretty severely. All will be well if we carry the pivots at Richmond and Corinth. Enough of this.

I still feel, just as I told you, that I shall come safely out of this war. I felt so the other day when danger was near. I certainly enjoyed the excitement of fighting our way out of Giles to the Narrows as much as any excitement I ever experienced. I had a good deal of anxiety the first hour or two on account of my command, but not a particle on my own account. After that, and after I saw we were getting on well, it was really jolly, we all joked and laughed and cheered constantly. Old Captain Drake said it was the best Fourth of July he ever had. I had in my mind Theo. Wright singing the Star-Spangled Banner; "the bombs bursting in air" began before it was quite light, and it seemed to me a sort of acting of the song, and in a pleasant way, the prayer would float through my thoughts, "In the dread hour of battle, O God be Thou nigh."

A happy thing you did for the soldiers, good wife.[1]

---

[1] Letter to Mrs. Hayes. This is in allusion to the gracious incident described by Mrs. Hayes in her letter as follows: " Our hospitals are all full of sick and wounded. A great difference can be seen between the sick and wounded. The sick appear low-spirited, downcast, while the wounded are quite cheerful, hoping soon to be well. I felt right happy the other day, feeling that I had made some person feel a little happier. Going down to Mrs. Herron's, I passed four soldiers — two wounded and two sick. They were sitting on the pavement, in front of the office where their papers were given them; they were just in from Camp Dennison, too late to get their tickets to Chicago. I passed them, and then thought, well, anyhow, I will go back and ask them where they are going. A gentleman, whom I saw there was with them, said he had just got in from Camp Dennison, and found they were too late to get their tickets for that evening. I asked, ' Where will you take them? ' He said, he did not

Flat Top, May 30. — A hot summer day. A very singular thing happened this afternoon. While we were at supper, 5.30 P.M., a thunderstorm broke out. It was pretty violent. Avery and Dr. McCurdy got up a warm discussion on electricity. As the storm passed away, we all stepped out of the tent and began to discuss the height of the clouds, the lapse of time between the flash and the thunder. While we were talking, Avery having his watch out and I counting, there came a flash and report. It seemed to me that I was struck on the top of the head by something the size of a buckshot. Avery and McCurdy experienced a severe pricking sensation in the forehead. The sentinel near us was staggered as by a blow. Captain Drake's arm was nearly benumbed; my horse Webb (the sorrel) seemed hit; over a hundred soldiers felt the stun or pricking; five trees were hit about a hundred yards off and some of them badly splintered. In all the camps something similar was felt. But no harm done! [1]

June 2. — General McClellan telegraphs that he has had a "desperate battle"; a part of his army across the Chickahominy is attacked by "superior numbers" — they "unaccountably break"; our loss heavy, the enemy's "must be enormous"; "enemy took advantage of the terrible storm"; all of which is not very satisfactory. General McClellan's right wing is caught on the wrong side of a creek raised by the rains — loses its "guns and baggage" — a great disaster is prevented. This is all, but it will demonstrate that the days of Bull Run are past. [2]

June 4. — News that Frémont has pushed over into the Valley of Virginia and is regaining what Banks lost. The battle at Richmond seems more favorable. [3]

June 5. — Rained most of the day. Want of exercise these rainy days begets indigestion, indigestion begets headache, blue devils, ill nature, sinister views, and general disgust. Brightened up a little by news that

know, but must get them to the nearest place, as they were very weak. Some one had told him the Herrie House was the nearest. I said, 'Doctor' (the wounded man had told me he was his family doctor and had come to take him home), 'if you will take them to my house, I will gladly keep them and have them taken to the cars. There is the street car which will take you near my house.' He was very thankful, and we put sick and wounded on, and I started them for Sixth Street, while I finished my errand, took the next car, and found my lame man hobbling slowly along. We fixed them in the back parlor. The doctor I asked to stay also, to take care of them. He said he could not thank me enough; that he was a stranger here, and was almost bewildered as to what to do or where to take them. Mary was up early, and we had a cup of coffee for them before five. I thought of you in a strange country, wounded and trying to get home; the cases were not exactly alike, but if any one was kind to you, would I not feel thankful?"

[1] Diary.   [2] Diary.   [3] Diary.

General Pope has taken 10,000 men and 15,000 stand of arms from Beauregard's retreating army. It looks as if Beauregard's army was breaking up. — Later, news of the taking of Memphis and Fort Pillow.

General Cox read me a letter from General Garfield in which he speaks of the want of sympathy among army officers with the cause of the war; that they say Seward, Chase, and Sumner are more to blame than Davis and Toombs! General Sherman said he was "ashamed to acknowledge that he had a brother (Senator John Sherman) who was one of these damned Black Republicans." [1] These semi-traitors must be watched. Let us be careful who become army leaders in the reorganized army at the end of the Rebellion. The man who thinks that the perpetuity of slavery is essential to the existence of the Union is unfit to be trusted. The deadliest enemy the Union has is slavery — in fact, its only enemy.[2]

June 12. — On this mountain the weather is colder than Nova Zembla, and since the enemy left us we have been in a state of preparation to go ahead, which means do-nothingness so far as soldiers are concerned. I have now an expedition out under Major Comly — not important enough for a regimental commander, so I am here in inglorious idleness. A day's life runs about thus: At 5 A.M. one or the other of our two Giles County contrabands, Calvin or Samuel, comes in hesitatingly and in a modest tone suggests, "Gentlemen, it is 'most breakfast time"; about ten minutes later, finding no results from his first summons, he repeats, perhaps with some slight variation; this is kept up until we get up to breakfast, that is to say, sometimes, cold biscuit cooked at the hospital; sometimes, army bread, tea, and coffee, sugar; sometimes, milk, fried pork; sometimes, beef, and any "pison" or fraudulent (?) truck in the way of sauce or pickles or preserves (!) — good peaches sometimes — which the sutler may chance to have. After breakfast there is a little to be done; then a visit of half an hour to Brigade Headquarters, Colonel Scammon's; then a visit to Division ditto, General Cox's, where we gossip over the news, foreign and domestic, all outside of our camps being foreign, the residue domestic; then home again, and novel-reading is the chief thing till dinner. I have read "Ivanhoe," "Bride of Lammermoor," and [one] of Dickens's, and one of Fielding's the last ten days.

P.M. Generally ride with Avery from five to ten miles, and, as my high-spirited horse has no other exercise, and, as Carrington (Company C boy) is a good forager and feeds him tip-top, the way we go it is locomotive-like in speed. After this, more novel-reading until the telegraphic

---

[1] Some months later a similar report reached John Sherman who promptly called his brother's attention to it. (Cf. *The Sherman Letters,* letters of September 23 and October 1, 1862.)

[2] Diary.

news and mails, both of which come about the same hour, 5.30 P.M.
Then gossip on the news and reading newspapers until bedtime —
early bedtime — 9 P.M. We have music, company drills — no room for
battalion drills in the mountains — and target practice with other little
diversions and excitements, and so "wags the world away." . . .

Keep up good heart. It is all coming out right. There will be checks
and disappointments, no doubt, but the war goes forward. We are
much better off than I thought a year ago we should be — a year ago!
Then we were swearing the men in at Camp Chase. Well, we think
better of each other than we did then and are very jolly and friendly.[1]

June 13. — Put up our tents on new camping-ground on Brammer's
farm one and one half miles on Pack's Ferry Road.[2]

June 16. — Last night walked with Captain Warren down to General
Cox's headquarters. Talked book. The general is a reader of the best
books — quite up in light literature; never saw the Shakespeare novels;
must try to get him "Shakespeare and his Friends." . . . The extracts
from Richmond papers and Jeff Davis's address to the soldiers indicate
that the Rebels are making prodigious efforts to secure the victory in the
approaching struggle. I trust our Government will see that every man is
there who can possibly be spared from other quarters.[3]

June 22. — Inklings and hints of matters before Richmond are more
encouraging. But these delays of McClellan are very wearisome.[4]

June 25. — Dined with General Cox. He has a plan of operations
for the government forces which I like: To hold the railroad from Memphis through to Huntsville, Chattanooga, Knoxville, [and] southwest
Virginia to Richmond; not attempt movements south of this except by
water until after the hot and sickly season. This line is distant from
the enemy's base of supplies — can therefore by activity be defended
and gives us a good base.[5]

June 27. — Read the account of the disaster on White River, Arkansas, to the gunboat Mound City. The enemy sent a forty-two pound
ball through her boilers and a horrible slaughter followed, scalding and
drowning one hundred and fifty men!

General Pope appointed to the "Army of Virginia," being the combined forces of Frémont, Shields, Banks, and McDowell, now in the
Valley of Virginia. Sorry to see Frémont passed over, but glad the

---

[1] Letter to Mrs. Hayes.

[2] Diary. — The regiment had been without tents since the retreat three weeks
before, except barely enough for the officers. "The men build shelter of bark,
rail pens, and the like. I call this 'Woodchuck Camp.'" (Diary, June 6.) Much
of the time it was extremely cold. But the men bore it all uncomplainingly.

[3] Diary.   [4] Diary.   [5] Diary.

concentration under one man has taken place. General Pope is impulsive and hasty, but energetic, and, what is more important, patriotic and sound — perfectly sound. I look for good results.[1]

June 30. — We have rumors of "tremendous fighting" before Richmond — that we have achieved a success, etc. What suspense until the truth is known.[2]

July 3. — General Cox is trying to get our army transferred to General Pope's command in eastern Virginia. The dispatches received this afternoon fill me with sorrow. We have an obscure account of the late battle or battles at Richmond. There is an effort to conceal the extent of the disaster, but the impression left is, that McClellan's grand army has been defeated before Richmond! If so, and the enemy is active and energetic, they will drive him out of the Peninsula, gather fresh courage everywhere, and push us to the wall in all directions. Foreign nations will intervene and the Southern Confederacy be established!

Now for courage and clear-headed sagacity. Nothing else will save us. Let slavery be destroyed and this sore disaster may yet do good.[3]

July 6. — I knew you would be troubled when Frémont was relieved from duty, and perhaps still more when you hear of McClellan's repulse before Richmond. These things appear to postpone the termination of the war, but are such disasters as must be looked for in such a contest. We must make up our minds that we have a heavy work, and that reverses must frequently occur. *We* have no right to complain of our lot. We have a beautiful and healthy camp — with the enemy in front strong enough to keep us busy holding our position, without much danger of losing it. It is the common opinion that if the reverse before Richmond has been serious, we shall be sent to eastern Virginia, and I may add, that it is the universal wish that we may see some of the movements that are going on there. . . .

Don't get down-hearted about the war and our separation. It will all come right, and then how happy we shall be — happier than if we had not known this year's experience.[4]

July 7. — The news of to-day looks favorable. McClellan seems to have suffered no defeat. He has changed front — been forced (perhaps) to the rear; sustained heavy losses, but his army is in good condition; and has probably inflicted as much injury on the enemy as it has suffered. This is so much better than I anticipated that I feel relieved and satisfied. The taking of Richmond is postponed, but I think it will happen in time to forestall foreign intervention.[5]

Flat Top Mountain, July 10. — I think you would enjoy being here. We have a fine cool breeze during the day; an extensive mountain scene,

[1] Diary.   [2] Diary.   [3] Diary.
[4] Letter to Mrs. Hayes.   [5] Diary.

always beautiful but changing daily, almost hourly. The men are healthy, contented, and have the prettiest and largest bowers over the whole camp one ever saw. They will never look so well or behave so well in any settled country. Here the drunkards get no liquor, or so little that they regain the healthy complexion of temperate men. Every button and buckle is burnished bright, clothes brushed and washed clean. . . . We have dancing in two of the larger bowers from soon after sundown until a few minutes after nine o'clock. By half-past nine all is silence and darkness. . . . Occasionally the boys who play the female partners in the dance exercise their ingenuity in dressing to look as girlish as possible. In the absence of lady duds they use leaves, and the leaf-clad beauties often look very pretty and always odd enough.

We send parties into the enemy's lines which sometimes have strange adventures. A party last Sunday, about forty miles from here, found a young Scotchman and two sisters, one eighteen, and the other fourteen, — their parents dead, — who have been unable to escape from rebeldom. They have property in Scotland and would give anything to get to "the States." One officer took one girl on his horse behind him, and another the other, and so escaped. They were fired on by bushwhackers, the elder lady thrown off, but not much hurt. They were the happiest girls you ever saw when they reached our camp. They are now safe on the way to Cincinnati, where they have a brother.[1]

Camp Green Meadows, July 14. — We came here yesterday. It is a fine camp, but warm and summery compared with Flat Top. There is no noticeable scenery in view from camp, but we are near New River, at the mouth of Blue Stone River, where the scenery is truly grand. I rode down there this morning to enjoy it. We marched fifteen miles yesterday — the happiest gang of men you ever saw. We are nearer the enemy, and have more of the excitement incident to such a position than at Flat Top. I am in command here, having six companies of the Twenty-third, Captain Gilmore's cavalry (the men who behaved so well when we fought our way out of Giles), a section of McMullen's artillery, besides two squads of the First and Second Virginia Cavalry. Every one seems to be happy that we are out by ourselves; besides, Major Comly with the other four companies Twenty-third is only five miles from us. . . . I sent off Captain Drake and two companies with a squad of cavalry just now, to effect a diversion in favor of Colonel Crook, who is threatened by a force said to be superior to his own. The captain is instructed to dash over and "lie like a bulletin" as to the immense force of which he is the advance, then to run back double-quick — risky but exciting. . . . Don't worry about the country — "it's no good." We can't help it if things go wrong. We do our part and I am confident all will come right. We can't get rid of the crime of centuries without suffering.[2]

[1] Letter to Hayes's mother.   [2] Letter to Mrs. Hayes.

July 15. — Captain Drake with Companies H and I returned this morning. The mounted men crossed the ford just above Blue Stone on New River. . . . They learned that the only enemy in Monroe is probably the Forty-fifth, some cavalry, and artillery, and they have withdrawn from the river towards Centreville or some other distant part of the country. All others gone on towards the Narrows or railroad.

At nine o'clock I took four companies and the band and went to Pack's Ferry where the men went in swimming. Crossed 262 of them in the flying bridge, which swings from side to side of the river by force of the current alone. The bow (whichever way the boat goes) is pulled by means of a windlass up the stream at a small angle. . . . The scenery is of the finest. The river is a clear, beautiful river. Strange, no fish except catfish, but they are of superior quality and often of great size.

The enemy shows signs of activity in Tennessee again. Our men will have a hard time during the next two or three months, trying to hold their conquests. We will have our day when cold weather and high water return, not before. — About Richmond there is much mystery, but supposed to be favorable.[1]

Camp Green Meadows, July 17.—I am not satisfied that so good men as two thirds of this army should be kept idle. New troops could hold the strong defensive positions which are the keys of the Kanawha Valley, while General Cox's eight or ten good regiments could be sent where work is to be done. Barring this idea of duty, no position could be pleasanter than the present. I have the Twenty-third Regiment, half a battery, and a company of cavalry under my command stationed on the edge of Dixie; part of us here, fourteen miles, and part at Pack's Ferry, nineteen miles from Flat Top and Colonel Scammon's and General Cox's headquarters. This is pleasant. Then we have a lovely camp, copious cold water springs; and the lower camp is on the banks of New River — a finer river than the Connecticut at Northampton — with plenty of canoes, flatboats, and good fishing and swimming. The other side of the river is enemy's country. We cross foraging parties daily to their side; they do not cross to ours, but are constantly threatening it. We moved here last Sunday the 13th. On the map you will see our positions in the northeast corner of Mercer County on New River near the mouth of and north of Blue Stone River. Our camps five miles apart — Major Comly commands at the river, I making my headquarters here on the hill. We have pickets and patrols connecting us. . . .

It is now a year since we entered Virginia. What a difference it makes. Our camp is now a pleasanter place with its bowers and contrivances for comfort than even Spiegel Grove. And it takes no ordering or scolding to get things done. A year ago, if a little such work was called for, you would hear grumblers say, "I did n't come to dig and chop, I could do that at home. I came to fight, etc., etc." Now, springs are opened, bathing-places built, bowers, etc., etc., got up as naturally as corn grows; no sickness either. About 815 to 820 men; none seriously sick and only eight or ten excused from duty. All this is very jolly. We have been lucky with our little raids in getting horses, cattle, and prisoners — nothing important enough to blow about, although a more literary regiment would fill the newspapers out of less material. We have lost but one man killed and one taken prisoner during this month. There has been some splendid running by small parties occasionally; nothing but the enemy's fear of being ambushed saved four of our officers last Saturday. So far as our adversaries over the river goes they treat our men taken prisoners very well. The Forty-fifth, Twenty-second, Thirty-sixth, and Fifty-first Virginia are the enemy's regiments opposed to us; they know us and we know them perfectly well. Prisoners say their scouts hear our roll calls and that all of them often enjoy our music.[1]

Camp Green Meadows, July 18. — I am really jolly over the Rebel Morgan's raid into the Blue-Grass region of Kentucky. If it turns out a mere raid, as I suppose it will, the thing will do great good. The twitter into which it throws Cincinnati and Ohio will aid us in getting volunteers. The burning and destroying the property of the old-fashioned conservative Kentuckians will wake them up, stiffen their sinews, give them backbone, and make grittier Union men of them. If they should burn Garrett Davis's house he will be sounder on confiscation and the like. In short, if it does not amount to an uprising it will be a godsend to the Union cause. It has done good in Cincinnati already. It has committed numbers, who were sliding into secesh, to the true side.[2]

July 20. — Morgan's gang, or Rebels encouraged by him, have got into Warrick County, Indiana. This is the first successful (if it turns out successful) invasion of free soil. I regret it on that account. I wished to be able to say that no inch of free soil had been polluted by the footsteps of an invader. However, this is rather an incursion of robbers than of soldiers. I suppose no soldiers have yet set foot on our soil.[3]

Camp Green Meadows, July 23. — I to-day received a dispatch from Captain Clements that I have been appointed colonel of the Seventy-ninth Regiment to be made up in Warren and Clinton Counties. I shall make no definite decision as to acceptance until I get official notice of it. I suppose it is correct. I shall much hate to leave the Twenty-third. I can't possibly like another regiment as well, and am not likely to be as acceptable myself to another regiment. If there was a certainty of promotion to the command of the Twenty-third I would certainly wait for it. . . . I begin to fear another winter in these mountains. I could stand it after two or three months' vacation with you in Ohio, but to go straight on another year in this sort of service is a dark prospect.

[1] Letter to Sardis Birchard.   [2] Diary.   [3] Diary.

Altogether, much as I love the Twenty-third, I shall probably leave it. I shall put off the evil day as long as I can, hoping something will turn up to give me this regiment, but when the decision is required I shall probably decide in favor of the new regiment and *a visit to you and the boys.* I know nothing of the Seventy-ninth except that a son of the railroad superintendent, W. H. Clements, is to be major. I knew him as a captain in the Twelfth — a well-spoken-of youngster. It will be a sad day all around when I leave here.[1]

Hayes with a strong force of infantry, artillery, and cavalry, went on an errand of mercy over New River into Monroe County, the night of July 25, to rescue the wife and four children of Archibald Caldwell, a Union man who had been kept away from home and persecuted for his loyalty. He succeeded in getting them from under the noses of the heavy forces of the enemy and returned to camp the next day without loss or accident. The cavalry marched almost fifty miles in twelve hours; the artillery, with a mountain howitzer, twenty-five miles in nine hours; the infantry thirty-six miles in fourteen hours' marching time and twenty hours altogether. Horses fell down, men fell down, Caldwell got faint-hearted and wanted to give it up, but the commander persisted. At half-past one a house was reached where after much difficulty it was ascertained that no Rebels were on the road in front. Thereupon the cavalry was ordered to push on rapidly the remaining seven miles to Mrs. Caldwell's house and fetch away the family. The rest of the force was ordered to bivouac and no pickets were posted. The position was secure and Hayes himself watched till daybreak while the weary men slept. In spite of the risk and hardship Hayes calls it "a pretty jolly expedition."

Camp Green Meadows, August 6, 1862. — This has been a day of excitement and action. Before I was out of bed a courier came saying our pickets on New River above Blue Stone were probably cut off — that firing had been heard near them, and none had come in to the picket station. I ordered Companies C and E to go down and look them up, supposing some small party of the enemy had attempted to cut them off. Before the companies could get away another courier came reporting that the enemy in force — 3000 to 4000 — had passed down New River on the other side; of course this was to attack the ferry. I sent word to the ferry and to Flat Top; directed the men to put one day's rations in

1 Letter to Mrs. Hayes.

haversacks, forty rounds of ammunition in boxes, and fill canteens. Then word came that the force was smaller than supposed, and no cannon. I dispatched Flat Top (Colonel Scammon) to that effect and that reënforcements were not needed. Soon after a courier came from [the] ferry that the enemy in large force were firing cannon, rifled, at them. I sent this to Flat Top; then called up Companies E, C, and K to go to reënforce the ferry. I sent the band to give them music and told the men: "Fighting battles is like courting the girls — those who make the most pretensions and are boldest usually win; so go ahead, give good hearty yells as you approach the ferry, let the band play, but do not expose yourselves. We all know you are brave; keep together and keep under cover. It is a bushwhacking fight across the river. Don't expose yourselves to show bravery. We know you are all brave." The men went off in high spirits. — A courier came from Blue Stone saying the enemy were at the ford with a cannon in some force. I sent Company I down there to watch them and hinder them if they attempted to cross. Under what he deemed obligatory written orders Major Comly destroyed the large ferryboat. Soon after, the enemy ceased firing and made a rapid retreat. They ran their horses past the ford at Blue Stone. Whether they left because they heard our band and reënforcements coming, or because *they saw the Major had done their work,* is problematical. . . .

A singular and almost fatal accident occurred about 5.30 p.m. In the midst of a severe thunderstorm the guard tent was struck by lightning. Eight men were knocked flat; cartridge boxes exploded, muskets were shattered, etc. The eight were all badly hurt, but dashing cold water on them they revived. They were playing "seven-up." They thought it was [a] shell. One said as he came to, "Where are they? Where are they?" Another spoke up repeating the question — "Where is Colonel Hayes? Where is the Colonel?"[1]

August 9. — Am planning to go to the salt well and destroy it, also to catch "Old Crump" if he is at home. Jacobs, of Company G, a scout, went up yesterday to Crump's Bottom and reports favorably. All safe now. Curious, quiet fellow, Jacobs. He takes no grub, wears moccasins, passes himself for a guerrilla of the Rebels, eats blackberries when he can't get food, slips stealthily through the woods, and finds out all that's going.

Old Andy Stainwault, a fat, queer-looking old fifer with a thin voice, and afflicted with a palpitation of the heart! (a great coward, otherwise a worthy man), was one of the first men who reached here from the ferry after the attack of Wednesday. He was informed that the enemy was in great force. I asked him if they fired their cannon rapidly. "Oh, yes," said he, "very rapidly — they fired twice before I left the camp."

Sad news. The dispatch tells us that "General Bob McCook was murdered by guerrillas while riding in front of his brigade in Tennessee."

[1] Diary.

He always said he did not expect to survive the war. He was a brave man, honest, rough, — "an uncut diamond," — a good friend of mine. We have slept together through several stormy nights. I messed with him in his quarters on Mount Sewell. Would that he could have died in battle! Gallant spirit! Hail and farewell.[1]

Camp Green Meadows, August 10. — Your letter of the 2d came last night; a great comfort it was. Several things last night were weighing on me, and I needed a dear word from you. I had got a reluctant permission to send a party to attempt to destroy the salt works at the Mercer Salt Well twenty-five miles from here, over a rough mountain country full of enemies, and uncertain who might be at the well. I started the party at 6 P.M. to make a night march of it to get there, and do the work and get fairly off before daylight. Captains Drake and Zimmerman were in command with twenty of Gilmore's gallant cavalry and one hundred thirty of our best men. I had got all the facts I could before they left, but after they were gone three hours, a scout I had given up, came in with information that the works were strongly guarded. I slept none during that night, and then, too, the sad news that McCook was murdered was in the evening dispatches, casting a deep shadow over all. It needed your letter to carry me through the night. I was out at early dawn walking the camp, fearing to hear the gallop of a horse; time went on slowly enough, but it was a case where no news was good news; if they had run into trouble, the word would have returned as fast as horseflesh could bring it. By breakfast time, I began to feel pretty safe; at eight, I visited the hospital and talked cheerfully to the sick, feeling pretty cheerful really; about half-past nine, Captain Drake rode in; the fifty miles had been travelled, and the secesh salt well for all this saltless region was burned out root and branch. Three horses were badly wounded; many had their clothes cut, but not a man was hurt. They reached the well at 2 A.M. — found it in full blast — steam on, etc., etc., received one feeble volley of rifle balls and the thing was done. . . .

As I am writing a messenger from headquarters comes with a significant order headed "secret." I am ordered to place all things in readiness to move on thirty minutes' notice, . . . any time after to-morrow at three o'clock P.M. This means what? I suspect a move to the east by way of Lewisburg and White Sulphur Springs; it may be a move to eastern Virginia, it may be toward Giles and the railroad again.[2]

August 12. — I send this morning to J. C. Dunlevy the following dispatch: "I am glad to hear that the Seventy-ninth is likely to be promptly filled without drafting. If so I shall join it as soon as leave can be obtained." So I am committed![3]

---

[1] Diary. — "Robert L. McCook, who entered the service at the head of the first German, or Ninth Ohio Regiment. He was murdered while sick on a cot in an ambulance. The incident caused widespread sorrow and excitement."

[2] Letter to Mrs. Hayes.   [3] Diary.

CHAPTER XII

ANTIETAM CAMPAIGN — WOUNDED AT SOUTH MOUNTAIN, SEPTEMBER 14, 1862

ABOUT the middle of August, General Cox's division was ordered east of the mountains. It remained there for two months, taking part in the memorable battles of South Mountain and Antietam. Hayes's letters and diary continue to give details.

ON STEAMER MONITOR, KANAWHA RIVER,
EVENING, August 18, 1862.

DEAR WIFE, — I am four hard days' marching,[1] and a few hours' travel on a swift steamer nearer to you than I was when I last wrote you, and yet I am not on my way home. You will see in the newspapers, I suppose, that General Cox's division (the greater part of it) is going to eastern Virginia. We left our camp Friday, the 15th, making long and rapid marches from the mountains to the head of navigation on this river. We now go down to the Ohio, then up to Parkersburg, and thence by railroad eastwardly to the scene of operations. My new regiment fills slowly, I think, and it may be longer than I anticipated before I shall be called for at Cincinnati, if at all. There is talk of an order that will prevent my going to the new regiment, but I think it is not correctly understood, and the chance, it seems to me, is, that I shall go home notwithstanding this change of place. Our men are delighted with the change. They cheer and laugh, the band plays, and it is a real frolic. During the hot, dusty marching, the idea that we were leaving the mountains of West Virginia kept them in good heart. . . .

[1] "The weather was extremely hot, and the pace trying, but our officers were very considerate, ordering frequent rests, and directing wagon masters and all others in charge of transportation to aid in carrying men who were disabled and tired. In this there was none more considerate than Colonel R. B. Hayes. He made personal effort to mingle with the men marching, often walking that some footsore soldier might ride, and when words of cheer seemed to fail in their purpose, the clear, ringing order would be given, 'Let us hear from the band.' Right nobly the band would respond and the most encouraging strains were found in the tune, 'We are so glad to get out of the wilderness'; at this the men would cheer and push on with more life." (MS. by Captain John S. Ellen.)

The Twenty-third marched, August 15, twenty-four miles; August 16, twenty-four and one half miles; August 17, twenty-two and one half miles; August 18, by noon, sixteen miles.

August 19. Evening ; same steamer on the Ohio River. — We have [had] a particularly jolly day. The river is very low, and at many of the bars and shoals, we are compelled to disembark and march the troops around. In this way we have marched through some villages and fine farming neighborhoods in Meigs County. The men, women, and children turned out with apples, peaches, pies, melons, pickles (Joe took to them), etc., in the greatest profusion. The drums and fifes and band all piped their best; the men behaved like gentlemen and marched beautifully. Was n't I proud of them? How happy they were. They would say, "This is God's country." So near you and marching away from you! That was the only sad point in it for me. Only one man drunk so far; his captain put him under arrest; he insisted on an appeal to me, and on my saying, "It's all right," he was sober enough to submit, saying, "Well, if the Colonel says it's right, it must be right," so he made no trouble.[1]

Washington, August 25. — We arrived here after ten days' marching and travelling this morning. We go over to Alexandria in an hour or two to take our place in General Sturges's army corps of General Pope's command. Colonel Scammon leads the First Brigade of General Cox's division in the new position. If the enemy press forward, there will be fighting. It is supposed they are trying to push us back. Reënforcements are pouring in rapidly.

In case of accident, Joe and I will be reported at the Kirkwood House in this city. I feel a presentiment that all will be right with us. If not, you know all the loving things I would say to you and the dear boys. My impression is that the enemy will be in no condition to hurry matters fast enough to get ahead of the new legions now coming in. They must act speedily or they are too late.[2]

Washington, August 26. — Here all arrangements connected with army matters are perfect. An efficient military police or patrol arrests all men and officers not authorized to be absent from their regiments, and either returns them to their regiments or puts them under guard and gives notice of their place. A good eating-house feeds free of expense and "sleeps" all lost and stray soldiers. An establishment furnishes quartermasters of regiments with cooked rations at all times. Fine hospitals, easily accessible, are numerous. The people fed and complimented our men (chiefly the middling and mechanical or laboring classes) in a way that was very gratifying. We felt proud of our drill, and healthy brown faces. The comparison with the new, green recruits pouring in was much to our advantage. Altogether Washington was a happiness to the Twenty-third.[3]

Camp near Upton's Hill, near Falls Church, on the road to Manassas, August 30. — Nearly all day we have heard cannon firing as is supposed

---

[1] Letter to Mrs. Hayes.   [2] Letter to Mrs. Hayes.   [3] Diary.

in [the] direction of Manassas Junction. It is believed that General Jackson is fighting Pope. The firing was heard yesterday a considerable part of the day. We all listen, look at the couriers — anybody moving rapidly attracts a thousand eyes. For a long time the thing was not very much attended to; now it gets exciting. We feel anxious. We wish to know whether the battle is with us or with our foes. It is now 5 or 5.30 P.M. The decision must come soon. It is not a bright nor a dark day. It is neither hot nor cool for the season — a fair fighting day. The only report we hear is that a Union man eight miles out says we got possession of Manassas yesterday, and that the Rebels to-day are trying to get it back — that they have been repulsed three times. . . . Anxious moments these! I hear the roar as I write.

7.30 P.M. — A lovely, quiet sunset — an exhilarating scene around us — the distant booming growing more faint and more distant apparently till at early dark it died away. With us or with our foes? — It is said . . . that Jackson made a speech saying that they must win this fight; that it would decide the fate of the Confederacy! Well, we wait. The suspense is less dreadful since the cannon no longer roars.

9.30 P.M. — No news. This I interpret to mean that there has been no decided victory, no decided defeat — a drawn battle. Why not mass to-night all the thousands of troops to overwhelm Jackson to-morrow? It could have been done in time to have flogged him to-day. He is *the* Rebel chieftain. His destruction destroys the Rebel cause.[1]

August 31. — This Sunday evening the reports from the battlefield are less favorable than the morning rumors. There is talk of "no result"; . . . that our army has fallen back four miles to Centreville. . . . No firing all day to-day. This evening, after dark, firing of heavy guns was heard for a few minutes, apparently in the same place as before.[2]

September 1. — About five o'clock this P.M., heavy firing began in the old place; said to be near Centreville or at Bull Run. A fierce rainstorm with thunder set in soon after, and for the last two hours, there has been a roaring rivalry between the artillery of earth and heaven. It is now dark, but an occasional gun can still be heard. The air trembles when the great guns roar. The place of the firing indicates that our forces still hold the same ground, or nearly the same, as before. It is queer; we really know but little more of the fight of two or three days ago, than you do; in the way of accurate knowledge perhaps less, for the telegraph may give you official bulletins. We have seen some, a great many of our wounded, some five or six hundred of the enemy taken prisoners, and a few of our men paroled. Some think we got the best of it; some otherwise. As yet, I call it a tie. I am very glad to be here. The scenes around us are interesting, the events happening are most important. You can hardly imagine the relief I feel on getting away from the petty warfare

---

[1] Diary.   [2] Diary.

of western Virginia. Four forts or field works are in sight, and many camps. The spire of Fairfax Seminary (now a hospital), the flags on distant hills whose works are not distinguishable, the white dome of the Capitol, visible from the higher elevations, many fine residences in sight, all, all make this seem a realization of the pride and pomp of glorious war. The roar of heavy artillery, the moving of army wagons, carriages, and ambulances with the wounded, marching troops and couriers hastening to and fro, fill up the scene. Don't think I am led to forget the sad side of it, or the good cause at the foundation. I am thinking now of the contrast between what is here and what I have looked on for fifteen months past. . . .

I just got an order that I must be especially vigilant to-night to guard against surprise, or confusion in case of alarm. I don't know what it indicates, but that I have done so often in the mountains that it is no great trouble. So I go to warn the captains.[1]

Tuesday, September 2. — A clear, cold, windy day, bracing and northern. No news except a rumor that the armies are both busy gathering up wounded and burying the dead; that the enemy hold rather more of the battlefield than we do. . . . The impression I get is, that we have rather the worst of it, by reason of superior generalship on the part of the Rebels.

9.30 P.M. — New and interesting scenes this evening. The great army is retreating — coming back. It passes before us and in our rear. We are to cover the retreat if they are pursued. They do not look or act like beaten men; they are in good spirits and orderly. They are ready to hiss McDowell. When General Given announced that McClellan was again leader, the cheering was hearty and spontaneous. The camps around us are numerous. The signal corps telegraphs by waving lights to the camps on all the heights. The scene is wild and glorious this fine night. Colonel White of the Twelfth and I have arranged our plans in case of an attack to-night. So to bed. Let the morrow provide for itself.[2]

Wednesday, September 3. — No alarm last night. Enemy quiet in front. A little firing near Chain Bridge, supposed to be feeling of our positions. It is rumored that the main body is going up the Potomac to cross. . . .

P.M., *after supper.* — I am to-night discouraged — more so than ever before. The disaster in Kentucky is something, but the conduct of men, officers, generals and all, in the late battles near Bull Run, is more discouraging than aught else. The Eastern troops don't fight like the Western. If the enemy is now energetic and wise, they can take great advantage of us. Well, well, I can but do my duty as I see it.[3]

On the same day Hayes wrote to his uncle, Sardis Birchard, as follows: —

[1] Letter to Mrs. Hayes. [2] Diary. [3] Diary.

We had decidedly the advantage in the fighting of Thursday and Friday — 28th and 29th. At the close of the 29th, Jackson was heavily reënforced, and worsted us on Saturday. Saturday evening our reënforcements reached General Pope and we were about equal in the subsequent skirmishing. I get some notions of the troops here as I look on and listen, not very different from those I have had before. The enemy here has a large force of gallant and efficient cavalry. Our cavalry is much inferior. The Rebel infantry is superior to ours gathered from the cities and manufacturing villages of the old States. The Western troops are, I think, superior to either. The Rebels have as much good artillery as we have. We have largely more than they, but the excess is of poor quality. In generalship and officers they are superior to us. The result is we must conquer in land warfare by superior numbers. On the water we have splendid artillery, and are masters. High water, deep rivers, heavy rains, are our friends.

General Sigel is a favorite with the troops. Generals Banks and Schenck are praised by them. General McDowell is universally denounced. General Pope is coldly spoken of. General McClellan is undoubtedly a great favorite with [the] men under him. Last night it was announced that he was again in command at this, the critical region now. Everywhere the joy was great, and was spontaneously and uproariously expressed. It was a happy army again. There is nothing of the defeated or disheartened among the men. They are vexed and angry — say they ought to have had a great victory — but not at all demoralized. I speak, of course, only of those I see, and I have seen some of the most unfortunate regiments. . . . Unless the enemy gets decided and damaging advantages during the next fortnight, it is believed we can push them back with heavy loss, and with a fair prospect of crushing them. . . .

We see that a strong Rebel force occupies Lexington, Kentucky. All the river towns are threatened. This is our dark hour. We will weather it, I think. Generalship is our great need. . . . I shall stay with the Twenty-third. I saw Haynes [1] and told him I supposed we were cut out by the order. I care nothing about it.

---

[1] William E. Haynes, of Fremont, then a captain in the Eighth O.V.I., to whom had been offered the command of the Hundredth O.V.I. The "order" referred to was issued from the War Department and forbade any transfer, resignations, or leave to officers serving in the Army of the Potomac, which worked against new regiments' having the benefit of the experience of officers promoted from old regiments. Writing of this to his mother, September 1, Hayes said: "I suppose it is settled that old officers can't go to the new regiments. This settles my chance for the Seventy-ninth also. All right, as far as I am personally concerned. The rule is a bad one — a very bad one, so bad, that it will, perhaps, be changed, but it is no hardship to me personally. I see no regiments here that I would prefer to the Twenty-third. General Cox's six regiments from Ohio are among the crack troops of the army in the opinion of everybody. Colonel Scammon distinguished himself the other day, and will, I doubt not, be a brigadier." For the present Captain Haynes was under the objectionable rule, but

P.S. Since writing I have been in a caucus of the major-generals. It is curious, but a large number of truthful men say Sigel is an accomplished military scholar, but such a coward that he is of no account on the battlefield. Funny! We don't know all about things and men from the newspapers.

Thursday, September 4. — A cheerful, bright morning and a sound sleep dispel the gloom resting on my mind as to the future. During the night a courier came to my tent saying that two thousand of our wounded are in the hands of the enemy and are starving. The enemy is in bad condition for food. Siege guns were put in the fort on our right (Ramsey) during the night. The preparations are advancing which will enable us to hold the post and "save Washington."

10 A.M. The rumor is that the enemy is directing his course up the Potomac, intending to cross into Maryland. We now hear cannon at a great distance in a northern direction.

About 4.30 P.M. The enemy began to fire at our cavalry picket about three miles out. Wagoners rolled in; horsemen ditto in great haste. The regiments of General Cox's division were soon ready — not one quarter or one third absent or hiding, or falling to the rear, as seems to be the habit in this Potomac army, but all, all fell in at once. The Eleventh, Twelfth, Twenty-third, Twenty-eighth, Thirtieth, and Thirty-sixth Ohio can be counted on. After skedaddling the regiment of cavalry who marched out so grandly a few hours before, the firing of the enemy ceased. A quiet night followed.

Cincinnati is now threatened by an army which defeated our raw troops at Richmond, Kentucky. Everywhere the enemy is crowding us. Everywhere they are to be met by our raw troops, the veterans being in the enemy's country too distant to be useful — a queer turning the tables on us; and yet if they fail of getting any permanent and substantial advantage of us, I think the recoil will be fatal to them. I think, in delaying this movement until our new levies are almost ready for the field, they have let the golden opportunity slip; that they will be able to annoy and harass, but not to injure us; and that the reaction will push them further back than ever. We shall see.[1]

September 6. — Left Upton's at 7.30 A.M., marched through Georgetown and Washington . . . towards Leesboro' road—a very dusty, hot, oppressive day.[2]

Sunday, September 7. — Left the suburbs of Washington to go on the Leesboro' road about twelve to fifteen miles. Road full of horse, foot,

November 3 his resignation was accepted to enable him to accept promotion, and November 10, 1862, he was promoted to be lieutenant-colonel of the Tenth Ohio Cavalry in which regiment he served with distinction.

[1] Diary.   [2] Diary.

and artillery, baggage and ambulance wagons; dust, heat, and thirst. "The Grand Army of the Potomac" appeared to bad advantage by the side of our troops. Men were lost from their regiments; officers left their commands to rest in the shade, to feed on fruit; thousands were straggling — confusion and disorder everywhere. New England troops looked well; Middle States troops badly; discipline gone or greatly relaxed.

On coming into camp Major-General Reno, in whose corps we are, rode into the grounds occupied by General Cox's troops in a towering passion because some of the men were taking straw or wheat from a stack. Some were taking it to feed to horses in McMullen's battery and to cavalry horses; some in the Twenty-third Regiment were taking it to lie upon. The ground was a stubble-field in ridges of hard ground. I saw it and made no objection. General Reno began on McMullen's men. He addressed them, "You damned black sons of b——." This he repeated to my men and asked for the colonel. Hearing it, I presented myself and assumed the responsibility, defending the men. I talked respectfully, but firmly; told him we had always taken rails, for example, if needed to cook with — that if required we would pay for them. He denied the right and necessity, said we were in a loyal State, etc., etc. Gradually he softened down. He asked me my name. I asked his, all respectfully done on my part. He made various observations to which I replied. He expressed opinions on pilfering. I remarked in reply to some opinion substantially, "Well, I trust our generals will exhibit the same energy in dealing with our foes that they do in the treatment of their friends!" He asked me, as if offended, what I meant by that. I replied, "Nothing; at least I mean nothing disrespectful to you." (The fact was I had a very favorable opinion of the gallantry and skill of General Reno; and was most anxious to so act as to gain his good will.) This was towards the close of the controversy, and as General Reno rode away the men cheered me. I hear that this, coupled with the remark, gave General Reno great offense. He spoke to Colonel Ewing of putting colonels in irons if their men pilfered! Colonel Ewing says the remark "cut him to the quick"; that he was "bitter" against me. General Cox and Colonel Scammon (the latter was present) both think I behaved properly in the controversy.[1]

September 8. — Camp near Leesboro', Maryland. Nothing new this morning. Men from Ohio all in a talk about General Reno's abusive language. It is said that when talking with me he put his hand on his pistol; that many standing by began to handle their arms also. I am sorry the thing goes so far.[2]

[1] Diary.

[2] Diary. — After Mr. Hayes had returned to private life at Spiegel Grove, General Jacob D. Cox (September 4, 1882) wrote him, enclosing an extract from the *History of the Twenty-first Massachusetts Volunteers*, containing a reference to the Reno incident grossly reflecting on the Western soldiers, and asked him to put

Camp northwest of Brookville, Maryland, September 10. — We are now about twenty-five or thirty miles northwest of Washington, about thirty

the facts in a letter which Major E. C. Dawes (formerly of the Fifty-third Ohio) would lay before the Massachusetts Military Historical Society, of which he was a member, for the purpose of having the error corrected. The *History* declared: "The Fourth Division (under General Cox) waged war on the Pope principle, plundering the country unmercifully, the President's regiment being fully as bad as the rest in this respect"; — and more quite as unwarranted. In his letter General Cox said: "As to discipline on the march, my remembrance is clear that it was much better than that of troops about us. . . . We were warmly compli-mented by McClellan, Burnside, and Reno himself on the soldierly bearing and discipline of the command." He urged General Hayes to write out his recollec-tions of the incident, adding: "It is not worth while to let such things pass into history uncontradicted"; but General Hayes declined. His reply is characteris-tic: —

(Private)   FREMONT, OHIO, 8th Sept. 1882.

MY DEAR GENERAL, — Your note of the 4th inst. came during a brief absence from home. I appreciate your kindness and your kindly suggestions. After sleep-ing over it, I am not inclined to depart from my custom in dealing with attacks upon me. The extract you send seems to be an inexcusable assault on your com-mand and on me personally. To give a correct relation of the Reno altercation would be to disparage an officer who died in battle a few days after the affair, and who cannot now give his side of the controversy.

One of the brigades of the division was commanded by General Crook and an-other by General Scammon, both regular army officers, conspicuous for strictness of discipline. General Scammon was, at the time, still colonel of the Twenty-third. The regiment on that march repeatedly reported, as I was glad to do, not a single absentee on the first roll-call immediately after the halt.

The altercation in its general facts was as you recall it. But the occasion of it was this: The regiment halted to bivouac in a stubble-field. The men got bun-dles of straw, or possibly of wheat unthreshed, from a stack in a field to lie upon. General Reno saw it. I was temporarily absent. The general, as you say, "in a rough way" accosted the men, and as I returned I heard his language, and re-torted *in behalf of my men* — not in my own at all, for he had said nothing to me. Hence the row between us.

I was told while I was lying wounded that General Reno was greatly pleased by our vigorous attack, and that he had paid us a high compliment, expressing grat-ification that our difficulty had gone no further than it did.

Now, excuse my suggestion. Let officers tell the story whose names are not called in question in the note referred to — say General Scammon, General Crook, and yourself. I am grateful for your attention to this misrepresentation, and hope you will not differ widely from me as to the correctness of the course I take. — Sincerely,

                                                    R. B. HAYES.

GENERAL J. D. COX.

General Cox wrote General Crook, as General Hayes suggested, and received a letter corroborating his statement of the good discipline and conduct of his divi-sion. Crook also said: "I heard at the time something with reference to a con-troversy between Generals Reno and Hayes, but if ever I knew what it was about I have forgotten it. In this matter it seems as if the statement of General Hayes

miles from Baltimore, in Maryland. The army is gradually moving up, to operate against the Rebels who have crossed the Potomac. We march about eight to twelve miles a day. General Cox's division always near the front, if not in front. We are now in front. Captured a Rebel patrol last night. . . . Order is coming out of chaos. The great army moves over three roads, five or eight miles apart. Sometimes we march in the night and at all other hours, moving each subdivision about six or eight hours at a time in each twenty-four hours. Some large body is moving on each road all the time. In this way the main body is kept somewhere in the same region. General Burnside is our commander. I have not yet seen him. He was cheered lustily, I am told, yesterday when he met his troops below here. His Yankee regiments are much the best troops we have seen East. "The Grand Army of the Potomac" suffers by comparison with General Cox's or General Burnside's men. It is not fair, however, to judge them by what we here see. They are returning from a severe and unfortunate service which of necessity has broken them down.

We march through a well-cultivated, beautiful region, poor soil but finely improved. I never saw the Twenty-third so happy as yesterday. More witty things were said as we passed ladies, children, and negroes (for the most part friendly) than I have heard in a year before. The question was always asked, "What troops are these?" or, "Where are you from?" The answers were, "Twenty-third Utah," "Twenty-third Bushwhackers," "Twenty-third Mississippi," "Drafted men," "Raw Recruits," "Paroled prisoners," "Militia going home," "Home Guards," "Peace Men," "Uncle Abe's Children," "The Lost Tribes," and others "too numerous," etc. Nearly all the bands are mustered out of service. Ours, therefore, is a novelty. We marched a few miles yesterday on a road where troops have not before marched. It was funny to see the children. I saw *our boys* running after the music in many a group of clean, bright-looking, excited little fellows.[1]

Frederick, Maryland, September 13, 1862, A.M. — Yesterday was an exciting but very happy day. We retook this fine town about 5.30 P. M., after a march of fourteen miles and a good deal of skirmishing — cannon firing and uproar and with but little fighting. We marched in just at sundown, the Twenty-third a good deal of the way in front. There was no mistaking the Union feeling and joy of the people, — fine ladies, pretty girls, and children were in all the doors and windows, waving flags and clapping hands; some "jumped up and down" with happiness. Joe enjoyed it and rode up the streets bowing most gracefully.

should be conclusive." General Scammon was out of the country at the time of this correspondence, and while General Cox was waiting to procure his statement, so much time elapsed that the original purpose of correcting the misstatements through the Massachusetts Military Historical Society was abandoned.

[1] Letter to Mrs. Hayes.

The scene as we approached across the broad bottom lands in line of battle, with occasional cannon firing and musketry,—the beautiful Blue Ridge mountains in view and the fine town in front, — was magnificent. It is pleasant to be so greeted. The enemy had held the city just a week. "The longest week of our lives"; "We thought you were never coming"; "This is the happiest hour of our lives," were the common expressions. It was a most fatiguing day to the men. When we got possession of the town — before the formal entry — men lay down in the road, saying they could n't stir again. Some were pale, some red as if apoplectic. Half an hour after they were marching erect and proud, hurrahing for the ladies! Colonel Moor, Twenty-eighth, of Cincinnati, was wounded and taken prisoner in one of the skirmishes yesterday. The enemy treat our men well — very well. We have of sick and wounded five hundred or six hundred prisoners taken here.[1]

By crossing the Potomac east of the Blue Ridge, and threatening Washington and Baltimore, General Lee expected to cause the Union troops to withdraw from the south bank where their presence endangered his communications. Having accomplished this result, he proposed to move into western Maryland, establish communications with Richmond through the Shenandoah Valley, and, by threatening Pennsylvania, induce McClellan to follow and thus draw him from his base of supplies. He hoped to detain the Union army on the northern frontier until the approach of winter should render its advance into Virginia difficult if not impracticable. Thus the Confederate commander had a comprehensive plan which he pursued with energy. He had supposed that the advance upon Frederick would lead to the evacuation of Martinsburg and Harper's Ferry, thus opening the line through the Valley. This not having occurred he entrusted to General Jackson the task of seizing those points, and detached from his army a strong force for that purpose on the 10th of September.[2] The Union forces marched leisurely, and were lingering at Frederick on the 13th, the day on which the Confederates had obtained possession of the Loudoun, the Bolivar, and the Maryland Heights, and were investing Harper's Ferry. Knowledge of this movement coming to McClellan through an

---

[1] Letter to Mrs. Hayes.
[2] General Halleck estimated Lee's entire strength at 97,000 men, over one third of whom were sent against Harper's Ferry; and McClellan's force at 90,000 — an overestimate in both cases. Lee claimed that he had less than 40,000 at Antietam, probably an underestimate.

intercepted order, he began to push forward with greater rapidity, and sent word to Colonel Miles in command at Harper's Ferry that he would send relief.

To accomplish this it was necessary to force the passage of the South Mountain Range and gain possession of Boonsborough which was already occupied by the enemy. The main army moved along the National Road which crosses the mountain by Turner's Pass, while a detachment under General Franklin was directed to carry Crampton's Pass, some six miles below, which afforded the most direct route for the relief of Harper's Ferry. The mountain near Turner's Pass is about one thousand feet in height. Its slopes are precipitous, rugged, and wooded, and form a strong natural military barrier. Here the enemy's troops were in considerable force, with artillery bearing upon all the approaches to their position. On the morning of the 14th, General Pleasanton, on making a reconnaissance with cavalry, brought on an engagement. The division of General Cox, of Reno's corps, coöperating with Pleasanton, moved up the mountain by the old Sharpsburg Road to the left of the main road, the First Brigade — Scammon's — being in advance with Hayes's regiment in front. The Second Brigade under Colonel Crook marched in column of reserve, and in supporting distance. Hayes was directed to follow a mountain path, and get around the enemy's right and attack and take a battery of two guns supposed to be posted there.[1] He went with a guide by the right flank up the hill, Company A deployed in front as skirmishers. Soon after nine o'clock he saw a strong force of the enemy approaching him from the opposite hill. He formed hastily in the woods and pushed on through bushes and over rocks toward the enemy, who fired a heavy volley wounding and killing some. It being difficult to hold men under such a hot fire, Hayes ordered a charge, which his men, with a yell, made in gallant style. The enemy gave way, but soon re-formed and began another furious fire. Hayes again ordered a charge, and the Twenty-third this time drove them out of the woods, halting at a fence near the edge of the woods, from which position they kept up a brisk fire on the Rebels who had taken shelter behind

---

[1] Hayes said: "And if I find six guns and a strong support?" Colonel Scammon replied: "Take them anyhow!"

BATTLE OF SOUTH MOUNTAIN, MARYLAND, SEPTEMBER 14, 1862

Where Colonel Hayes was severely wounded

stone walls and fences beyond a cornfield near the summit of the hill.[1]

Just as Hayes had given the command to charge a second time, he felt a stunning blow and found that a musket ball had struck his left arm immediately above the elbow, fracturing the bone. Hayes, fearing an artery might be severed, asked a soldier near him to tie his handkerchief around his arm above the wound; but a few minutes after, weak and faint from loss of blood, he was forced to lie down. He lay about twenty feet behind the line held by his men and could form a pretty accurate notion of the progress of the fight and could still direct his men. Presently, seeing something going wrong, he staggered to his feet and began to give directions. But returning faintness compelled him again to lie down. The enemy's fire was occasionally very heavy — balls passed near his face and hit the ground all around him. Men fell or were carried to the rear, but the line of the Twenty-third did not waver. Being informed that there was danger of the enemy flanking him on the left, he directed Captain Drake to wheel his company so as to meet the threatened attack. This movement caused the whole line to fall back a few yards, thus leaving him between his own men and the enemy. Later, there being a lull in the firing, he called out, "Halloo, Twenty-third men, are you going to leave your colonel here for the enemy?" In an instant half a dozen men sprang forward to carry him off the field. This brought on renewed firing, when he ordered the men back to cover. A little later Lieutenant Jackson came and insisted on taking him out of range of the enemy's fire. He laid him down behind a log and gave him a canteen of water, which revived him. When the firing again slackened,

[1] The Reverend C. E. Manchester, who had served in the Twenty-third, in an address at Broadway M.E. Church, Cleveland, the Sunday after Mr. Hayes's death, said: "On the morning of the famous battle of South Mountain in Maryland we were sent out to reconnoitre. After a quiet, almost noiseless march through the woods, we came face to face with a larger body of the enemy. They were behind a stone wall, and we were in the edge of the woods with a cleared space between us and them. Bullets pattered about us like raindrops on the leaves. It was a pivotal moment. Could we stand such odds? Then we heard the voice of Colonel Hayes saying: 'Men of the Twenty-third, when I tell you to charge, you must charge. You must not flinch if hell yawns before you. Charge bayonets!' We were up and at them, met by a cloud of bullets that brought down many a brave fellow. Among the rest, Colonel Hayes was wounded and borne from the field."

Hayes was carried back up the hill where his wound was dressed by Dr. Webb. The command now devolved upon Major Comly. The enemy suddenly opened fire from the left, and the regiment changed front on the first company, thus effectually meeting the change of tactics. Soon after, the remainder of the brigade came up, when a united charge up the hill with bayonets dislodged the enemy and put the crest in possession of the Union troops.[1] From this vantage-ground the contest was continued until the enemy were driven from the mountain. The victory was won at heavy cost to the Twenty-third. The severely wounded included Lieutenant-Colonel Hayes, Captain Skiles (who lost an arm), Captain Hunter, Lieutenant Ritter (leg amputated), and Lieutenants Hood, Naughton, and Smith. The loss of the regiment altogether was nearly two hundred, of whom almost one fourth were killed on the field or afterwards died of their wounds. The colors of the regiment were riddled, and the blue field almost completely carried away by shells and bullets.[2]

This recital shows the valor of Hayes and his men, which won the admiration and praise of the officers in chief command. They made three bayonet charges during the day, in each of which the enemy were driven with heavy loss. In one of these charges the Twenty-third was pitted against the Twenty-third North Carolina, whose flagstaff the Ohio regiment bore away in remembrance of the day. In his diary Hayes makes this record: "While I was lying down I had considerable talk with a wounded Confederate soldier lying near me. I gave him messages for my wife and friends in case I should not get up. We were right jolly and friendly. It was by no means an unpleasant experience."

Colonel Hayes was taken to the residence of Captain Jacob Rudy in Middletown, where he remained until convalescent. The night after the battle he received this message from Colonel

[1] General J. D. Cox in his report says: "The Twenty-third Ohio having reached the crest on the left, established itself there in spite of a most vigorous resistance on the part of the enemy." (*War Records*, vol. XIX, p. 459.) General Cox on the death of General Reno succeeded to the command of the corps, Colonel Scammon to the command of the division, and Colonel Ewing to the command of the brigade.

[2] "Of the many good men who fell that day in our command, there was none more regretted than our brave, bright, and youthful Sergeant-Major Reynolds. His remains were found the morning after the battle at a point in advance of any position held by our troops." (MS. by Captain John S. Ellen.)

Scammon: "I was sorry to hear of your wound. Take care of yourself, and get well as soon as you can. Our brigade and division did *splendidly*. We can say this between ourselves. General Cox sends his best regards and sympathy." The feeling of gratification over the victory of South Mountain was moderated by the death of General Reno, who was shot near sunset while in front, observing the operations of his corps. He was a brave and capable officer.

The Twenty-third Regiment under Major Comly gave a good account of itself in the battle of Antietam which immediately followed. The wounded of the heroic troops who took part in the battles of South Mountain and Antietam were nursed by the citizens of Middletown and Frederick with a tenderness, said Hayes, "as if they were their own brothers." The Rudys, with whom he himself found refuge, gave him every attention. "Here I lie," he records, September 18, "nursing my shattered arm, 'as snug as a bug in a rug,'" but impatient for the arrival of Mrs. Hayes. She reached Washington Sunday morning, September 21. A diligent and anxious search was made through the Washington hospitals, and then at Frederick. At last, when hope was almost exhausted, a wounded soldier of the Twenty-third Regiment directed the searching party to Middletown. As may be supposed the reunion was most joyful. To his uncle Hayes wrote, September 26: —

Lucy is here and we are pretty jolly. She visits the wounded and comes back in tears; then we take a little refreshment and get over it. I am doing well. Shall perhaps come home a little sooner than I expected to be able to. I am now in a fix. To get me for the Seventy-ninth some of its friends got an order to relieve me from the Twenty-third from the War Department. So I am a free man and can go or come as I see fit. I expect, however, to remain with the Twenty-third.[1]

[1] The New York *Herald* in April, 1877, printed a long letter from Middletown, Maryland, in which its correspondent gives many reminiscences of Mrs. Rudy and her daughter of Colonel Hayes's sojourn under their roof. Miss Ella Rudy said: "Though he suffered constantly and got little sleep for a week and longer, he was always cheerful. He not only would n't be cross — he would n't allow any extra trouble to be taken on his account. Mother used to ask him if she could not 'do something' for him. He always thanked her, but said no; he did n't need anything, he was doing very well. The only thing he did have changed was his bed." It was a corded bed. He asked to have boards substituted for the cords so that the mattress would lie level. Mrs. Rudy said: "We fell in love with him directly. He did n't talk much, but what he said was to the point.

The prospect of immediate promotion to the command of his old regiment decided Hayes against going to the Seventy-ninth if the order relieving him could be rescinded. General Cox interested himself in the matter and to good purpose. The following letter was very welcome to its recipient: —

CAMP NEAR ANTIETAM, October 2.

MY DEAR COLONEL, — Your request to have the order revoked discharging you for the purpose of allowing you to take the colonelcy of the Seventy-ninth Ohio, has been forwarded by me through army headquarters to the War Department, recommending that your request be at once granted, and I trust this will be done. I regard the order as a conditional one, based upon your taking command of the Seventy-ninth, and the condition failing, I incline to think the order itself inoperative. I have so expressed myself and hope to see you soon in command of the gallant old Twenty-third. Comly will take good care of it in your absence. Your wound I deeply regret in itself, but coming as it did, as the seal and signet of your glory at South Mountain, I don't know but you are to be congratulated upon it. Trusting you will have a speedy and thorough recovery, I remain,

Ever your sincere friend,

J. D. Cox.

LIEUT.-COLONEL R. B. HAYES,
    Twenty-third Ohio Volunteers.

The order was revoked by the War Department. On October 15, Colonel Scammon received his appointment as brigadier-general and Hayes became colonel of the Twenty-third, Comly, lieutenant-colonel, and Captain McIlrath, major, and the happy family remained unbroken except as the shot and shell of the enemy thinned the ranks. How Hayes was esteemed at home is shown by an editorial of the Cincinnati *Commercial* which appeared about this time: —

There is not in all the bright and honored roll of our citizen soldiers, one of whom the people of Hamilton County have better reason to be proud than Colonel R. B. Hayes. His name has been frequently used

He never used harsh language toward the Rebels, and never liked to hear others do so. He spoke generously of the Southern officers, and of the bravery of their men. His manners were remarkably mild. It was the same with Mrs. Hayes. As soon as he was out of danger, she used to spend a part of every day in the hospitals, visiting Rebels and Union men alike. She took grapes to them, and any other delicacies she could get, and sometimes she would read to those who liked to hear her. She had a great many favorites, but she was attentive to all, and admired by everybody." — Friendly relations were maintained between the Hayes and Rudy families for many years.

within a few days in connection with the representation in Congress of the Second District; and it is due to truth to say that the district is fortunate, indeed, if it contains a more able, excellent, popular man. His capacity as a civilian has been shown in a successful career at the bar; and it is well known that he is a clear-sighted, strong, honest man, with deep convictions, earnest purposes, and an unblemished record. He entered the army early in the war, and has been faithful, alert, brave, and energetic in the discharge of his duties as an officer. In the several engagements in which he has participated, he handled his men with skill and without bravado performed a heroic part.[1]

This further record (made by Colonel Comly) relating to the Twenty-third at this time is of interest: —

President Lincoln arrived from Washington October 1, and remained several days, visiting the battlefields of South Mountain and Antietam, and reviewing the victorious troops. In so doing he rode along in front of the line, accompanied by generals McClellan and Burnside, with several of their staff officers. He rode a white horse, and his pantaloons had worked up nearly to the top of his boots, presenting a comical appearance. When he arrived at that portion of the line where the Twenty-third was stationed, General Burnside pointed towards the regiment, making some remark, when President Lincoln immediately turned his horse and rode over towards the colors of the regiment. General Burnside called his attention to the flag which was at salute. The color sergeant then raised the flag and held it horizontally, to show how it had been riddled by bullets and shells. The President seemed much affected by the account which General Burnside gave him of the loss which the regiment had sustained in the two battles, and particularly at South Mountain.

The healing of Hayes's wound made rapid progress and October 4 he was able to write his mother as follows: —

My birthday — forty years old — a good, happy day, pleasantly and sadly spent looking over the battlefield and visiting the graves of our gallant dead with Lucy. We leave here to-morrow, go to Baltimore and thence via Harrisburg and Cleveland to Fremont, and expect to reach Columbus about the last of next week, — say the 10th or 11th. My arm is doing well, will be all right in a month or six weeks.

Hayes was with his family and friends in Ohio on leave during October and most of November, where he was an interested observer of the progress of events. He was not disheartened by the Union reverses nor by the result of the elections. To Sardis Birchard, November 12, he wrote: —

[1] *Commercial*, October 1, 1862.

The elections don't worry me. They will, I hope, spur the Administration to more vigor. The removal of McClellan, and the trial of Buell and Fitz-John Porter; the dismissal of Ford, and substituting Schenck for Wool, all look like life. General Burnside may not have ability for so great a command, but he has energy, boldness, and luck on his side. Rosecrans, too, is likely to drive things. All this is more than compensation for the defeat of a number of our politicians by the politicians of the other side. As to the Democratic policy it will be warlike, notwithstanding Vallandigham and others. Governor Seymour has made a speech in Utica since his election indicating this. Besides, that party *in power* must be a war party.

Meanwhile, early in October, General Cox and his division had been ordered back to West Virginia. The Twenty-third Regiment marched to Hancock to take the cars for Clarksburg. At Hancock it was ordered to go in hot pursuit of Stuart's cavalry, which was reported to be making a raid in Pennsylvania. No enemy was discovered and the following day (October 13) the Twenty-third returned to Hancock, having eaten breakfast in Pennsylvania, dinner in Maryland, and supper in Virginia. The next day the regiment was transported to Clarksburg, from which point it marched to the Kanawha, passing over almost exactly the same route by which it moved on its first arrival in western Virginia fifteen months before. The regiment went into quarters at Camp Maskell, on the south side of the Kanawha, two miles below Gauley Bridge and in sight of the falls. There Hayes joined his regiment November 30, his wound well healed, but his arm not yet fully restored to its normal strength. The next day he wrote his wife: —

We are on the south side of the Kanawha — same side as the Eightyninth — at the ferry below, and in sight of, the falls, two miles below Gauley Bridge. There, do you know where we are? It is a muddy (bad, slippery mud) place, and as it rains or sleets here all winter, that is a serious objection. Now you have the worst of it. In all other respects, it is a capital place. Beautiful scenery, — don't be alarmed, I won't describe, — no guard or picket duty, scarcely; good water and wood, convenient to navigation, no other folks near enough to bother, and many other advantages. The men are building cabins without tools or lumber (sawed lumber, I mean), and will be at it some weeks yet before we look like living. It was jolly enough to get back with the men, all healthy and contented; glad to be back in western Virginia by themselves. They greeted me most cordially. It was like getting home after a long absence. The officers all came in, twenty-four in number, and around the wine, etc., you saw packed, talked over the funny and sad things of the campaign; few sad, many funny. We resolved to build a five hundred dollar monument to the killed, to be put in cemetery ground at Cleveland. . . .

The Eighty-ninth were camped on this ground. When the Twenty-third moved up alongside of them, the officer of the day in the Eighty-ninth was heard by some of our men telling in his camp that they were near an old regiment now, and that they must be watchful at night or the Twenty-third would steal whatever they wanted. That night, cook-stoves, blankets, a tent from over the sleepers' heads, and a quantity of other property mysteriously disappeared from the Eighty-ninth, notwithstanding their vigilance. Our men sympathized; our camp was searched, but, of course, nothing was found. After the Eighty-ninth moved, men were seen pulling out of the river stoves and other plunder by the quantity. The Eighty-ninth surgeon was a friend of Captain Canby. He called on the captain a few days ago and was surprised to find his cooking-stove doing duty in Captain Canby's tent. The best of it was, the Eighty-ninth appeared to take it in good faith.

Camp Maskell, December 14. — Very glad, indeed, the bag is found; glad you read the article of Dr. Holmes in the *Atlantic Monthly.*[1] It is indeed a defense pat for your case. I knew you would like it. You must keep it. When we are old folks it will freshly remind us of a very interesting part of our war experience. If the enchanted bag contains my spurs, and if they are both alike (which I doubt), you may send them to me when a good chance offers. The pair I now use are those worn by Lorin Andrews, and given me by McCook. I don't want to lose them. — The fine weather of the past week has been very favorable for our business and we are getting on rapidly. The river is so low that a cold snap would freeze it up, and leave us "out in the cold" in a very serious way — that is, without the means of getting grub. . . .

One of our new second lieutenants, McKinley [William McKinley, Jr.], a handsome, bright, gallant boy, got back last night. He went to Ohio to recruit with the other orderly sergeants of the regiment. He tells good stories of their travels. The Twelfth and Thirtieth sergeants stopped at second-class hotels, but the Twenty-third boys " splurged." They stopped at the American and swung by the big figure. Very proper. They are the generals of the next war.[2] . . .

[1] "If you were only here, would n't I like to read *My Hunt after the Captain.* Don't laugh any more. Really, the learned doctor was more bothered and out of his wits than your wife; once within ten miles, then back again to Philadelphia. I shall send you the number, for fear you do not get it. This has pleased me a great deal. Let me know how you like it." (Letter from Mrs. Hayes, December 4.)

[2] The report of Lieutenant-Colonel Comly after the battles of South Mountain and Antietam, on which Colonel Hayes recommended the promotion of young McKinley, is worth reading in this connection: " Commissary Sergeant McKinley

P.S. Three months ago to-day, the battle of South Mountain. We celebrated it by climbing the mountain, on the other side of the river, to the castle-like looking rocks which overlook the falls of the Kanawha. Captains Hood, Zimmerman, Canby, Lovejoy, and Lieutenant Bacon were of the party. Hood and I beat the crowd to the top. Hood, the worst wounded, up first. When I saw him shot through that day, I little thought I would ever see him climbing mountains again.[1]

Camp Maskell, December 20. — Another serious reverse. Burnside's repulse at Fredericksburg is bad enough, as it looks from my point of view. It would seem as if neither party in eastern Virginia was strong enough to make a successful invasion of the territory of the other, which is equivalent to saying that the Rebellion can there sustain itself as long as it stands on the defensive. I don't like two things in this campaign of General Burnside: First, it looks as if his first delay opposite Fredericksburg was an error. Second, to attack an enemy of equal (or nearly equal) strength behind entrenchments is always an error. This battle is a set-off for Antietam. That forced the Rebels back across the Potomac. This forces us back across the Rappahannock. We suffer, I fear, a larger proportionate loss. I suspect the enemy lost but little comparatively. Now remains our last card — the emancipation of the slaves. That may do it. Some signs of wavering are pointed out by the correspondents, but I trust the President will now stand firm. I was not in a hurry to wish such a policy adopted, but I don't now wish to see it abandoned. Our army is not seriously weakened by the affair at Fredericksburg and very slight events will change the scale in our favor. Push on the emancipation policy, and all will yet go well. Our partisanship about generals is now rebuked. General McClellan has serious faults or defects, but his friends can truly claim that if he had retained command this disaster would not have occurred. The people and press would perhaps do well to cultivate patience. It is a virtue much needed in so equal a struggle as this. If the people can hold out we shall find the right men after a while.[2]

showed ability and energy of the first class, in not only keeping us fully supplied with rations throughout the fight, but in having them fully prepared for eating also. We had plenty when everybody else was short. He delivered them to us under fire in two instances, with perfect method and coolness."

[1] Letter to Mrs. Hayes.   [2] Letter to Sardis Birchard.

CHAPTER XIII

THE beginning of 1863 found the Twenty-third in comfortable log cabins at the camp near the falls of the Kanawha. The name was changed from Camp Maskell to Camp Reynolds. Ditches had been dug under Hayes's direction which thoroughly drained the camp, a good parade ground was made, and the regiment was settled down to easy winter service. General Ewing had just been sent south with several regiments, and the command of the brigade had devolved upon Colonel Nelson H. Van Vorhes, of the Ninety-second Ohio. This was a new regiment which had seen no service and Colonel Van Vorhes was fresh from civil life. But his commission was issued a few weeks before Hayes's promotion, and so despite Hayes's abundant experience Van Vorhes outranked him. Hayes could not fail to feel the injustice of being made the subordinate of an untried officer, but he writes in his diary: "It is according to rule and I shall cheerfully submit. . . . I am here to do my duty wherever I am placed, and I mean to do it fully and cheerfully wherever the credit goes." The command of Van Vorhes was of short duration. Barely a week passed before Hayes was appointed to the command of the First Brigade of the Second Kanawha Division, consisting at first of his own regiment, the Eighty-ninth Ohio, and two small bodies of cavalry.

The last week in January Mrs. Hayes with the two eldest boys joined her husband for a two months' visit and shared his quarters — a double log cabin with two rooms eighteen by twenty feet in size. The next two months passed very pleasantly. On this visit and on subsequent visits to the army, Mrs. Hayes by her beauty, charm of manner, tact, and assiduous kindness in caring for the comfort of the soldiers in camp and hospital, won their admiration and gratitude, which were manifested on every suitable occasion as long as she lived.[1] About the middle

[1] One instance of Mrs. Hayes's kindness the men of the Twenty-third never

of March, Hayes was ordered to garrison Charleston. He established headquarters at Camp White, directly across the river from the city, having the Twenty-third Regiment with him. The other parts of his brigade were stationed at various points on the river above and below, but all within easy reach. March 22, Hayes writes his uncle: —

We seem intended for a permanent garrison here. We shall probably be visited by the Rebels while here. Our force is small, but will perhaps do. My command is Twenty-third Ohio, Fifth and Thirteenth Virginia, three companies of cavalry, and a fine battery. I have some of the best, and, I suspect, some of about the poorest, troops in service. They are scattered from Gauley to the mouth of Sandy on the Kentucky line. They are well posted to keep down bushwhacking and the like, but would be of small account against an invading force. We have three weak but very good regiments, Twenty-third, Twelfth, and Thirty-fourth Ohio, some — a small amount of — good cavalry and good artillery, and about three or four regiments of indifferent infantry. So we shall probably see fun, if the enemy thinks it worth while to come in.

Hayes believed that the general conditions were favorable for a vigorous prosecution of the war. March 24 he writes in his diary: —

In the North a reaction favorable to the war is taking place. The peace men — sympathizers with the Rebels, called Copperheads or Butternuts — are mostly of the Democratic party. They gained strength last fall by an adroit handling of the draft, the tax law arrests, the policy favorable to the negro, and the mistakes and lack of vigor in

tired of relating. There was in the regiment an unsophisticated country lad named James Saunders who never suspected when his comrades played jokes on him. Soon after Mrs. Hayes's arrival in camp and before it was generally known, one of the boys said to Jim, who was lamenting the sad condition of his blouse: "Did n't you know there is a woman at the colonel's quarters whose business it is to mend the boys' clothes?" "I'll go this afternoon," Jim said, "and have my blouse doctored." The boys waited in high glee for his return. He soon reappeared in shirt-sleeves. The boys asked what happened. Jim replied: "I told the colonel that I heered there was a woman there to do sewing for the boys, and as my blouse needed mendin' and buttons sewed on, I had come to get it done. He kind o' smiled, and turned to the woman settin' there and asked her if she could fix the blouse for me, and she said she could as well as not, as she had nothing special on hand. So I took it off and left it, the colonel tellin' me to call 'round this afternoon and git it. You all seem to laugh, but I don't see anything funny." The boys broke into a loud chorus of laughter, and one of them said: "Jim, don't you know that that woman is the colonel's wife?" "I don't care; she's a lady anyhow, and I am goin' to git my blouse, just as she told me to." He did go, and was again received in that manner which made him forget himself and his awkwardness, and his blouse was restored to him in perfect repair.

prosecuting the war. This led to overconfidence, and a more open hostility to the war itself. The soldiers in the field considered this "a fire in the rear," and "giving aid and comfort to the enemy"; they accordingly by addresses and resolutions made known their sentiments. Loyal Democrats, like John Van Buren [and] James T. Brady, begin to speak out in the same strain. A considerable reaction is observable. The late acts of Congress, the conscription, the financial measures, and Habeas Corpus Act give the Government great power and the country more confidence. If the conscription is wisely and energetically administered there is much reason to hope for good results. In the meantime the Rebels are certainly distressed for want of provisions. The negro policy does n't seem to accomplish much. A few negro troops give rise to disturbances where they come in contact with our men and do not as yet worry the enemy a great deal.

Camp White was fortified so as to enable the small garrison to hold out against a largely superior force in case of attack. Jenkins and his men made a sudden foray upon Hurricane Bridge where the Thirteenth Virginia of Hayes's brigade was stationed. They were repulsed and started for Point Pleasant. They attempted to seize two steamboats from Charleston, firing on them from ambush from both sides of the river. But the captains refused to stop, running the gantlet of the musketry and so kept on their way. Thereupon the Rebels proceeded down the river to Point Pleasant, taking all the horses and cattle they could find, and captured the town. But they held it only a few hours when they were driven out and retreated up the river. Meanwhile, on the report reaching Charleston that the steamers had been fired on, Colonel Comly had been sent down the river with five companies of the Twenty-third to defend Coalsmouth. From there he was ordered to go on down the river to prevent Jenkins's men from recrossing to the south side. But the Rebels crossed before Comly could get to them. The Jenkins "raid was a failure," writes Hayes. "He lost about one hundred fifty men while in this region and accomplished nothing."

Nothing disturbed the monotony of garrison life for many weeks. Mrs. Hayes with her mother and all the boys visited the camp in June and remained two weeks. The visit was saddened by the death of the youngest boy, then eighteen months old. In July a movement was made against Raleigh, the troops going up the river by boat to Loup Creek and then marching toward Fayetteville. Raleigh was reached July 14, and the enemy was found to be strongly entrenched at Piney River. "It was deemed unsafe," writes Hayes, "to assault in front, and finding it would take much time to turn the position, it was resolved to leave without attempting to storm the works. During the night the Rebels kindly relieved us by running away." The next day the Rebel camp was destroyed and General Scammon's command started back to Fayetteville, which was reached on the 16th. There the telegraph brought word of John Morgan's raid in Ohio. The famous leader was reported to be at Piketon moving east to destroy the Union stores at Gallipolis and to escape across the river at that point. It was expected that he would reach Gallipolis on the morning of the 18th. Hayes conceived the idea that it would be possible to march to Loup Creek that night, take steamers there in the morning, and arrive at Gallipolis in time to give Morgan a warm welcome. He telegraphed to his quartermaster at Charleston, asking if there were steamers available. The instant reply was that two were there. Hayes ordered these started at once for Loup Creek. General Scammon was inclined to doubt the feasibility of the plan when Hayes asked permission to carry it out. The men had marched seventeen miles in the hot sun that day and were in no condition for a forced night march. It was doubtful whether if they embarked they could reach the Ohio in time to be of service. But Hayes was so much in earnest in pressing his plan that Scammon finally accepted it and prepared to go with four regiments and McMullen's battery, Hayes having command of the Twenty-third Ohio and the Thirteenth Virginia. Hayes at once went to the camp where the men were busy cooking their suppers and told them what it was proposed to do. They received the word with a shout of pleasure, and crying, "We are off for God's country," made hasty preparations for the march. They marched steadily till near midnight when they rested for two hours or so. Just after daylight, as they were approaching Loup Creek, they saw the steamers rounding the river bend. Boats and men reached the landing at almost the same time. The embarkation took place without delay. The tired men threw themselves upon the decks and slept most of the day as the steamers moved down the river.

The next morning bright and early the steamers were at Gallipolis. The troops quickly disembarked and prepared to receive

Morgan, who was reported to be within five miles of the town. Presently, however, word was brought in by scouts that he had veered off and was making up the river as though with the intention of seeking to cross at Pomeroy. The troops at once returned to the steamers which started up the river to Pomeroy, arriving there the next morning. Militia were in force here. About noon Morgan came. The Twenty-third went out to meet him, and finding him in force sent back for the Thirteenth Virginia, and the two regiments formed in line of battle and threw out skirmishers. Morgan's men dismounted and did the same. The Rebel commander evidently expected to find only militia. On seeing the well-defined skirmish line he held a brief consultation with his officers. Doubt was dispelled as to the character of the forces confronting him when the battle line appeared. Seeing that the Federal troops were "regulars and not militia," — to use the Rebel's words, — Morgan refused battle and hurried off with some loss. One man in the Twenty-third was wounded slightly in the hand.

Morgan started across country for Buffington Island. Hayes's men reëmbarked and the steamers started around the long bend of the river, reaching the island at daylight the next morning. Here Morgan was attacked by General Judah's cavalry assisted by the gunboats and by Hayes's command. There was "not much fighting by the Rebels," Hayes records, "but great confusion, loss of artillery, etc." Many of Morgan's men surrendered; the remnant fled up the river seeking some place to cross. Hayes's steamers started up the river and guarded the fords at Lee's Creek, Belleville, and Hocking. The next day they went back to Gallipolis, Hayes recording: "Morgan's army gone up. We got over two hundred prisoners. Everybody got some. No fight in them. The most successful and jolly little campaign we ever had." It is probably not to be wondered at that there was "no fight in them" after their long and arduous raid and running fight of a fortnight across two States. Lieutenant Abbott with ten men captured a hundred of Morgan's men and a whole company of our militia. Morgan's men, being without horses or food and completely exhausted, were seeking some regulars to surrender to. They saw Union troops approaching and sent out a flag of truce with instructions to surrender if the troops were

regulars; to demand their surrender if they were militia. They
proved to be militia, who promptly gave up their arms to the
Rebels. Not long after, Lieutenant Abbott and his handful of
men were met, and when Morgan's men found them to be regulars they surrendered, prisoners and all, and were marched into
camp.[1] Hayes had a right to be happy over the success of this
little campaign. While the cavalry that pursued Morgan so long
and far deserved the lion's share of the credit for annihilating the
Rebel army, and the militia and gunboats did their part, there
can be little doubt that Morgan would have got across the Ohio,
with the most of his force, at least, at Pomeroy, if the troops
from the Kanawha had not been there to intercept him.

Hayes got back to Camp White with the Twenty-third on
July 22. The Thirteenth Virginia was left at Point Pleasant.
During his absence General Scammon's cavalry had gone from
Raleigh on a raid into Virginia to cut the East Tennessee
and Virginia Railroad. They penetrated the enemy's country as
far as Wytheville, where they had a desperate encounter, and

---

[1] A similar capture is recorded in the following report: —

ON BOARD STEAMER B. C. LEVI, 20 July, 1863.

COLONEL HAYES, — We have the honor to submit the following report: On
Friday, July 19, we were going from Racine, Ohio, to Buffington Island; when
within about four and one half miles of the latter place, two armed citizens (we
supposed them to be militiamen) came riding toward us at full speed. They halted
and informed us that they had just seen two hundred Rebel cavalry on the road
leading to Oldtown, and that they were advancing on the place. We had met a
company of militia a short distance back, and proposed that these two citizens
ride on and bring them up. They went in pursuit of the company of militia, but
returned with only one man, a private in the Eighth Kentucky U.S. Cavalry.
We now advanced cautiously toward the Oldtown Road, and when within a short
distance of said road, overtook one Captain Seeson. We now numbered six, all
told. When within sight of the road leading to Oldtown, we saw the column of
Rebel cavalry advancing. It was our intention to fire, which we were preparing
to do, when the column halted, and the man in advance drew his rammer, tied a
white handkerchief to it, and rode forward. When he came up, he stated that
they were one hundred and forty-five of Morgan's command of Confederate
cavalry, and wished to surrender, making the remark, "Boys, we have captured
lots of you, but you have got us this time." The terms of the surrender were
"unconditional"; we accepted them, went forward, disarmed the Rebels, and
having no transportation for arms, threw them by the roadside. We then
escorted the column to General Hobson's quarters, near Buffington Island, where
we were relieved. — Very respectfully,

ALFRED ARTHUR,
D. H. KIMBERLEY,
Co. A, 23d O.V.I.

sustained severe losses. But the raid did great damage to the Rebels, as the following letter to Sardis Birchard of August 6 shows: —

I think it probable that we shall remain in West Virginia. The enemy has become alarmed by our movements against the Tennessee Railroad, and has been strengthening their posts in front of us until now we have twice our numbers watching us. To keep them out of mischief, it is more likely that our force will be increased rather than diminished. A gunboat has come up to help us within the last half-hour. Our Wytheville raid did the Rebels more harm than was reported — five thousand suits of clothing, over four thousand new arms, and quantities of supplies were burned. I think they will not attempt to drive us out in their present scarcity of men and means.

The next few months were spent in garrison duty at Camp White. Excerpts from letters and diary will show the progress of events: —

Camp White, August 25. — I keep my cavalry moving as much as possible; the infantry has little to do. The prisoners taken and deserters coming in all talk in a way that indicates great despondency in Dixie. If the movements of Rosecrans on Chattanooga, Burnside towards Cumberland Gap, and Gilmore at Charleston are reasonably successful, the Rebellion will be nearer its end by the middle of October than I have anticipated. A great contrast between the situation now and a year ago when Lee was beating Pope out of the Valley and threatening Washington. Beat the peace men in your elections and the restoration of the Union is sure to come in good time.[1]

Gallipolis, September 24. — Lucy arrived here safely last night. We shall go up the Kanawha to-morrow. I hope that Rosecrans will be able to hold Chattanooga after all. If he does, this struggle will be a most serious disaster to the Confederacy, even if they have gained the battle, as a mere military result.[2]

September 30. — To-day I explained to the Twenty-third Order No. 191 respecting the reënlistment of veteran volunteers. I told them I would not urge them to reënlist; that my opinion was that the war would end soon after the inauguration of a new President or of Lincoln for a second term — say within one year after the expiration of their present term i.e., June, 1865, — unless foreign nations intervened, in which case they would all expect to fight again. About sixty (60) reënlisted.[3]

[1] Letter to Sardis Birchard.   [2] Letter to Sardis Birchard.
[3] Diary.

October 19. — You are a prophet. Brough's[1] majority is "glorious to behold." It is worth a big victory in the field. It is decisive as to the disposition of the people to prosecute the war to the end. My regiment and brigade were both unanimous for Brough. Lucy will go to Chillicothe and home this week. She will fix up mother, gather the chickens and return in two or three weeks, if all things look well, for the winter.[2]

November 7. — I am asked if I would not be gratified if my friends would procure me promotion to a brigadier-generalship. My feeling is that I would rather be one of the good colonels than one of the poor generals. The colonel of a regiment has the most agreeable position in the service and one of the most useful. "A good colonel makes a good regiment," is an axiom. Two things make me sometimes think it desirable to have the promotion, viz., the risk of having a stupid brigadier put over me and the difficulty and uncertainty of keeping up my regiment, — that is, the risk of losing my colonelcy.[3]

Camp White, December 4. — We are threatened with a Rebel invasion again; if they don't come after us, it looks now as if we should go after them. When this is over, our men will generally go home, and I am pretty likely to go also. About the last of this month or early in January, if matters go well, I shall probably visit you.[4]

Four days later Hayes started with his command under General Scammon for a campaign to Lewisburg, to coöperate with General Averell in an attack on the railroad at Salem. There were four days of hard marching after leaving the boats at the head of navigation. The outposts of the Rebels were encountered twelve miles out from Lewisburg and were driven back through the town. The next day the army started back for the Kanawha. Many of the men of the Twenty-third, having been so long in camp at Charleston, had discarded their heavy service shoes for closer-fitting footgear. The marching in the mild weather soon made them footsore and they threw away their shoes. But on leaving Lewisburg a cold rain set in which presently turned to snow. To add to their discomfort they had no shelter at night. The last day and night they marched nearly all the time to keep warm, singing to keep up their spirits. Before leaving Charleston Hayes had been urging the men to reënlist. Now the men kept shouting, "Show me the man who wants us to reënlist," or "Show me the d——d fool who will

---

[1] Union candidate for Governor of Ohio. [2] Letter to Sardis Birchard.
[3] Diary. [4] Letter to Sardis Birchard.

reënlist." But when the boats were reached, Hayes telegraphed to Camp White to have rousing fires kindled in all the quarters and hot coffee and supper ready against the arrival of the men. Then, when they were refreshed by the good cheer, he spoke to them again, urging them to reënlist. A ball in the interest of the Sanitary Commission was to be given Christmas Eve at Cleveland. By leaving next morning, December 19, men could get there in time. All that reënlisted should have an immediate furlough. The appeal was not in vain; many reënlisted and the next day two companies started on furlough for Ohio. A few days later Hayes was able to record that about three hundred had reënlisted and that his regiment could now fairly be called a veteran regiment. It was, indeed, the first regiment of Ohio to be entitled to that distinction. This was due to the zeal and earnestness with which Hayes had exhorted the men to continue in the service.

Hayes's headquarters remained at Camp White till the last of April, 1864. Mrs. Hayes and the two younger boys were in camp with him till that time and the oldest boy for the last month and a half, when Hayes and Mrs. Hayes returned from a month's visit in Ohio. During the winter most of the men went home on furlough; new recruits were added to the regiments and received much drill. Early in February, General Scammon and two members of his staff were surprised at night on a steamboat a few miles up the river from Point Pleasant and captured. Of this incident Hayes wrote his uncle: —

The capture of General Scammon and two of his staff will postpone my coming a few days — only a few days, I hope. I must be cautious what I say, but to you I can write that his capture is the greatest joke of the war. It was sheer carelessness, bad luck, and accident. Everybody laughs when he is alone, and very intimate friends laugh in concert when together. General Scammon's great point was his caution. He bored us all terribly with his extreme vigilance. The greatest crime in his eyes was a surprise. Here he is caught in the greenest and most inexcusable way.

General Crook was placed in command of the Kanawha forces, much to Hayes's satisfaction, and preparations were made for a vigorous campaign, as soon as the weather permitted, by much the same route as that taken by General Cox's army in the spring of 1862 and by General Scammon's cavalry in 1863, to reach the East Tennessee and Virginia Railroad, burn the bridges and destroy the tracks. With the coming of settled weather in the last of April, General Crook's command was materially strengthened. April 20, Hayes wrote his uncle: —

It now seems certain that we are to take an active part in the summer's campaign. We expect to see some of the severe fighting. The Rebel troops in our front are as good as any, and we shall attempt to push them away. My brigade is three large regiments of infantry, containing a good many new recruits. They have been too much scattered (at ten or twelve places) to be properly drilled and disciplined. Still, we have some of the best men in service. Of course, if they should make a falter in action, I will be a good deal exposed, otherwise, not so much as heretofore. Still I have no misgivings on my own account, and even if I had, you know my views of such things well enough to know that it would not disturb me much.

A week later Hayes bade good-bye to wife and boys, and the great raid was begun.

CHAPTER XIV

1864 — ADVANCE AND RETREAT — CLOYD MOUNTAIN

GENERAL FRANZ SIGEL was in command of the Department of West Virginia and was the immediate superior of General Crook. But the latter had been in direct communication and consultation with General Grant, who originated the plan for the West Virginia campaign. Sigel was to move up the Shenandoah Valley simultaneously with Crook's advance from the Kanawha. Crook was to reach the railway, do all the damage he could, subsisting as much as possible on the country, and withdraw when he could no longer maintain himself to Lewisburg, whence he was expected to be able to effect a junction with Sigel if that general was successful in pushing forward to Staunton. General W. W. Averell, in command of Crook's cavalry division of about two thousand men, was sent from Charleston by way of Logan Court House to strike the railway at Saltville. He was to burn the saltworks if possible and march east to Dublin destroying the railroad as he went. Crook with the rest of the army proceeded by way of Fayetteville and Raleigh to Princeton. His army was in three brigades and numbered 6155 men. Hayes commanded the First Brigade, consisting of the Twenty-third and Thirty-sixth Ohio and parts of the Thirty-fourth Ohio, mounted infantry, and the Fifth and Seventh Virginia Cavalry, all dismounted. To deceive the enemy as to his point of attack, Crook had ordered a demonstration made from Beverly, and had sent the Fifth Virginia to Lewisburg. So well did his plan succeed that he met no opposition until he reached Princeton, where a small force of cavalry was encountered and driven off. McCausland's brigade had gone from there only the night before to meet Crook at Lewisburg, leaving their tents standing. These were burnt and Crook pushed on south by the shorter but more difficult Rocky Gap Road,[1]

[1] "At Princeton we found and captured without a shot an elaborate earth fort, beautifully sodded on its side and marked with sod 'Fort Breckinridge.' The boys soon changed the lettering to 'Fort Crook.'" (Russell Hastings, MS. Memoirs.)

avoiding the easier route by way of the New River Narrows by which the Rebels now expected him.

Two days' march from Princeton brought the Union forces on May 8 to Shannon's Bridge, on the northwestern slope of Cloyd Mountain. Here it was reported that General A. G. Jenkins was in force on the summit of the mountain. The next morning, with the Second Brigade and two regiments of the Third, Crook ascended the mountain to the left of the road. When he reached the summit he discovered the enemy three quarters of a mile away entrenched on a wooded spur opposite to and commanding the road where it leaves the mountain. As soon as the Union forces appeared, the Rebel artillery opened vigorously. Crook sent the Second Brigade to the left to turn the enemy's right flank, and with the two regiments of the Third joined the rest of his command which was already descending the slope. The Second Brigade had many bushy ridges and deep gullies to pass and was some time in getting into position. Meanwhile the First Brigade (Hayes's) was ordered to the left of the road to join on to the right of the Second Brigade, and the Third to form on the right of the First. Hayes's brigade found great difficulty in reaching its position. The woods were so dense and the acclivities so precipitous that the officers had to abandon their horses and proceed on foot. Finally about noon position was reached at the foot of the mountain in the edge of a forest, where the lines were hastily formed. Between the forest and the base of the hill on which the Rebels were posted stretched a meadow several hundred yards in width. The hill was skirted by a muddy stream two or three feet deep. As soon as the firing on the extreme left indicated that the Second Brigade was in position, General Crook ordered the other two brigades to charge.

Across the meadow Hayes's men went under a galling fire of musketry and artillery, never wavering, plunged through the stream, and dropped down for a moment's rest under cover of the hill. Then up the steep hill they rushed, Hayes in the van, undeterred by the fierce volleys of musketry and grape which wrought sad havoc in their ranks — up the hill and over the breastworks yelling like demons, as at South Mountain. The fight continued for a time at close range, but the impetuosity of the Union charge at last bore all before it; the Rebel line began to waver and fall back, and soon broke in confusion and was in full retreat toward Dublin Depot, five miles away. Two miles from the railway the fleeing Rebels were met by reënforcements, five hundred men that had just arrived by train from Morgan's army at Saltville, and a fresh stand was made. Hayes with part of his brigade and two guns of McMullen's battery was in close pursuit. The guns were at once brought into play, and Hayes ordered his men to charge, "yelling like devils." The enemy was quickly routed and the day was won. Crook's losses were 107 killed, 508 wounded, and 28 missing. He captured 230 prisoners, — not including wounded men, among whom was General Jenkins, — two guns,[1] and many small arms. Crook estimated the Rebel losses in dead and wounded at about a thousand, saying, "We buried over two hundred of the enemy's dead." But the report of General McCausland, who assumed command when Jenkins was disabled, gives the total Rebel loss, killed, wounded, prisoners, and missing, as 538.

At Dublin Depot many public stores were captured. The rest of the day was spent in burying the dead and caring for the wounded. From lack of transportation two hundred of the more severely wounded had to be left in charge of surgeons and with abundant supplies near the battlefield. The Rebels retreated eastward toward New River Bridge, and the next morning our

---

[1] "The battery was captured, and the Twenty-third Ohio, having fortunately passed over it, claimed it as their own. A young recruit of Company B passing by one of the guns took off his cap and with an Indian war-whoop jammed it into the muzzle. . . . Some few members went back to these guns after the enemy had been thoroughly routed and found them in the possession of a corporal's guard of the Pennsylvania Buck Tails. They claimed they had charged and captured them. The boys tried to persuade them they were in the wrong; that the Twenty-third had passed over the battery a few moments after the Buck Tails had turned tail and run away. The guard would not allow any one to pass. Our boys thought they might have to capture the guns again by force, when the boy recruit, without cap, came back. He took the case in at once, and in the most respectful tone said: 'Mr. Corporal, may I go to that gun and get my cap?' The corporal was considerably nonplussed and said: 'No one can touch those guns. We have had charge of them ever since we captured them, and shall continue to hold them.' The boy said: 'Well, Mr. Corporal, if I cannot go to the gun, won't you please run your hand into that gun on the left of the battery, and there you will find my cap, which I jammed in there while you were skedaddling back into the woods.' The cap was found with '23d Ohio' on the front, and that corporal's guard, amidst the jeers of the Twenty-third boys, melted away." (Russell Hastings, MS. Memoirs.)

army followed destroying the railway as it moved. The Rebels had crossed the river and posted their artillery so as to command the approach to the bridge. Crook's artillery was placed in position at advantageous points on the west side of the river and an artillery duel, which made much noise and caused little damage, continued for two hours. Meanwhile a company was sent to burn the bridge. In spite of the continuous firing of the enemy this was successfully accomplished by lighting fires in freight cars and pushing them out upon the bridge. Soon cars and bridge were burning fiercely. The band of the Twenty-third played and all the men hurrahed as the flames crept to the top of the high bridge leaping from timber to timber. Within two hours this great bridge, four hundred feet long, had tumbled into the river and disappeared.[1]

Crook had accomplished the main purpose of his raid in burning the bridge. At Dublin he had seen dispatches from Richmond reporting the repulse of General Grant, and he decided that he had best direct his course at once toward Lewisburg. The afternoon after the bridge was destroyed he marched twelve miles down the river to Pepper's Ferry and crossed to the east side and the next day reached Blacksburg. From here the army moved back over Salt Pond and Peter's Mountains by way of Union to Alderson's Ferry on the Greenbrier River, reaching there on May 15. The four days' march was full of hardship. A cold, dreary rain fell most of the time, the roads were seas of mud, provisions and forage were scanty, horses gave out, and wagons had to be abandoned, and the enemy's cavalry appeared from time to time, and, though always repulsed, caused some anxiety.

At Union, General Averell had joined Crook. His movement had been almost barren of results. After a most arduous march of eight days through the mountains he drew near to Saltville only to learn that it was strongly held. Without venturing an attack he moved on to Wytheville, where, on the afternoon of

---

[1] "One spectacle you would have enjoyed. The Rebels contested our approach to the bridge for two or three hours. At last we drove them off and set it on fire. All the troops were marched up to see it — flags and music and cheering. On a lovely afternoon the beautiful heights of New River were covered with our regiments watching the burning bridge. It was a most animating scene." (From letter, May 19, to Mrs. Hayes.)

May 10, he attacked a force under General Morgan which he believed to be considerably larger than his own. The fight was maintained till dark without decisive result. Averell, hopeless of winning, moved rapidly east,[1] crossed New River, the 12th, destroyed the railway for several miles east, burning the shops at Christiansburg, and started north to overtake Crook. It took two days to get all of Crook's command across the Greenbrier by the ferry, the high water making fording impossible. By May 19 the whole army had reached Meadow Bluff — having spent nine days in making a march which with good weather would have been made in four. The Fifth Virginia was there with supplies, and the men were soon rested and recuperated from their three weeks of continuous marching, fighting, and exposure.[2] The first day in camp Hayes wrote his uncle: —

MEADOW BLUFF, GREENBRIER COUNTY,
WEST VIRGINIA, May 19, 1864.

DEAR UNCLE, — We are safely within what we now call "our own lines" after twenty-one days of marching, fighting, starving, etc., etc. For twelve days we have had nothing to eat except what the country afforded. Our raid has been, in all respects, successful. We destroyed the famous Dublin Bridge and eighteen miles of the Virginia & Tennessee Railroad, and many depots and stores; captured ten pieces of artillery, three hundred prisoners, General Jenkins and other officers among them, and killed and wounded about five hundred, besides utterly routing Jenkins's army in the bloody battle of Cloyd Mountain. My brigade had two regiments and part of a third in the battle. The Twenty-third lost one hundred killed and wounded. We had a severe duty, but did just as well as I could have wished. We charged a Rebel battery, entrenched on a wooded hill, across an open, level meadow three hundred yards wide,[3] and a deep ditch, wetting me to the waist,

---

[1] "I see the papers call this 'Averell's raid.' Very funny! The cavalry part of it was a total failure. General Averell only got to the railroad at points where we had first got in. He was driven back at Saltville and Wytheville." (From letter, May 25, to Mrs. Hayes.)

[2] Lieutenant-Colonel Comly in his diary, May 19, says: "Have not had my clothes off since the 29th of April. Slept outdoors in the rain considerably, and have been a great deal short of food. No grumbling, however, in the command. About four hundred miles marched." — Hayes in his diary says: "One of the most interesting and affecting things is the train of contrabands, old and young, male and female, one hundred to two hundred, toiling uncomplainingly along after and with the army."

[3] General Crook in his report says the meadow was "from one fourth to one half mile wide"; Lieutenant Comly, "five hundred or six hundred yards in width." Hayes's estimate, therefore, is evidently very conservative.

and carried it without a particle of wavering or even check, losing, however, many officers and men, killed and wounded. It being the vital
point, General Crook charged with us in person. One brigade from the
Army of the Potomac (Pennsylvania Reserves) broke and fled from the
field. Altogether, this is our finest experience in the war, and General
Crook is the best general we have ever served under, not excepting
Rosecrans. Many of the men are barefooted, and we shall probably
remain here some time to refit. We hauled in wagons to this point over
two hundred of our wounded, crossing two large rivers by fording and
ferrying and three high ranges of mountains. The news from the outside world is meagre and from Rebel sources. We almost believe that
Grant must have been successful from the little we gather.

Meanwhile Sigel had advanced up the Shenandoah Valley
according to the original plan. At New Market, May 15, his
progress was disputed by General Breckinridge, and his forces
were utterly routed and sent flying down the Valley to Strasburg.
General Grant was so dissatisfied with Sigel's performance that
he at once put General Hunter in his place. General Hunter
promptly assumed the offensive and began to advance on Staunton, at which point General Crook's forces were ordered to join
him. Crook's losses in the recent raid had been made good by
fresh arrivals, but he was still deficient in equipment, some of
his men being barefooted. Camp was broken up at Meadow
Bluff May 31, and the march across the mountains by the route
of the present Chesapeake and Ohio Railroad was begun. The
Virginia Central Railroad was struck at Goshen and from there
eastward many miles of the road were demolished. The men,
Hayes wrote in his diary, "turn over rails and ties and tumble
them down the embankment; burn culverts and ties as far as
possible. The railroad can be destroyed by troops marching
parallel to it very fast."[1] The Rebels made attempts to impede
the advance of the army, but they were in too small force to
offer serious resistance. June 5, Hunter routed the enemy at

---

[1] "On this march we became experts at destroying railways, the brigade in one
day tearing up twelve miles and breaking and bending all the iron rails. We drew
the spikes, placed the ties some fifteen feet apart so the rails when piled upon
these ties would rest at their ends and with no support in the middle. Under the
middle a fire was kindled, the heat would soften the iron, and the rails would bend
by their own weight. These rails would have to be sent to the mills and rolled
before they could again be used. One day the soldiers bent some rails in the
shape of U.S. and twisted others around trees, and it is said these rails are to be
seen there to this day." (Russell Hastings, MS. Memoirs.)

Piedmont and the following day took possession of Staunton, capturing many prisoners and supplies. Here Crook joined him June 8,[1] and obtained shoes for his barefoot men. The next day nine officers and one hundred and sixty men of the Twenty-third Ohio, along with many others whose terms had expired, were sent back under Colonel Moor, guarding a train and refugees and contrabands by Buffalo Gap to Beverly, to be mustered out. The band played "Home, Sweet Home" as their old comrades bade them a final good-bye and turned their faces to the north.

After destroying all public supplies and workshops and much of the railroad at Staunton, Hunter moved on up the Valley in four columns, his advance line skirmishing with the Rebels almost constantly, but steadily driving them back. At Lexington the enemy was in force with artillery well posted, and the bridge across the North River burnt. While our artillery and Hayes's brigade in front kept the Rebels engaged, General Averell crossed the river several miles above the town and Crook's Second Brigade was sent to cross about two miles above to attack the town on the flank. As soon as the Rebels discovered this movement they promptly retired. Hayes's brigade was the first to enter the town. At Lexington, for reasons which appear hardly satisfactory, Hunter lingered for two whole days. He destroyed all public stores and burnt the house of ex-Governor Letcher and the Virginia Military Institute. This was not approved by many of the officers, among whom were Crook and Hayes.[2] June 14 the forward movement was resumed. The

1 "We reached the beautiful Valley of Virginia yesterday over North Mountain and entered this town this morning. General Hunter took the place after a very successful fight on the 6th. We seem to be clear of West Virginia for good. We shall probably move on soon. Our march here over the mountains was very exciting. We visited all the favorite resorts of the chivalry on our route, White Sulphur, Blue Sulphur, Warm, and Hot Springs, etc., etc. Lovely places some of them. I hope to visit some of them with you after the war is over." (Letter to Mrs. Hayes, from Staunton, June 8.)

2 "You wrote one thoughtless sentence — complaining of Lincoln for failing to protect our unfortunate prisoners by retaliation. All a mistake, darling. All such things should be avoided as much as possible. We have done too much rather than too little. General Hunter turned Mrs. Governor Letcher and daughters out of their home at Lexington and on ten minutes' notice burned the beautiful place in retaliation for some bushwhacker's burning out Governor Pierpont. And I am glad to say that General Crook's division officers and men were all disgusted with it. . . . You use the phrase 'brutal Rebels.' Don't be cheated in that

scattered forces of the enemy were driven back without difficulty, and two days later the army had crossed the Blue Ridge
near the Peaks of Otter, had struck the railway at Liberty, and
had moved eastward toward Lynchburg, destroying the road as
it went. Meanwhile a detachment of two hundred picked men
from Averell's cavalry division had made a circuit of Lynchburg,
doing considerable damage, but bringing back little definite
information. Rumors came to Hunter that Breckinridge was
holding Lynchburg with twenty thousand men. But he advanced
cautiously all day June 17, skirmishing constantly. Near night-
fall Crook's Second Brigade had a sharp engagement and drove
the Rebels back to within three miles of the town. The First
Brigade went at double-quick for a mile or two to the support of
the Second and bivouacked that night in close promixity to the
Rebel lines.[1] All night long trains could be heard arriving in
Lynchburg, bringing reënforcements. The next morning Hunter
made an effort to capture the city and some lively fighting
occurred, in which Hayes's command had its share, but he
became convinced that with the constantly arriving reënforcements under Early the Rebel army was far superior to his. Had
he not delayed at Lexington, or had he even pushed forward

way. There are enough 'brutal Rebels,' no doubt; but we have brutal officers and
men, too. I have had men brutally treated by our own officers in this raid. And
there are plenty of humane Rebels. I have seen a good deal of it on this trip.
War is a cruel business and there is brutality in it on all sides, but it is very idle
to get up anxiety on account of any supposed peculiar cruelty on the part of
Rebels. Keepers of prisons in Cincinnati as well as in Danville are hard-hearted
and cruel." (Letter to Mrs. Hayes, from Charleston, West Virginia, July 2,
1864.)

[1] "About dark we (First Brigade) were filed off and lay in line of battle until
about eight, waiting for orders to make a night attack. About this time our skirmishers noticed a force camping alongside of them. Too dark to see who it was.
One of our officers asked: 'What brigade is that?' 'Gordon's brigade of Early's
division. Who do you uns belong to?' — 'The same,' said the officer, who found
that if he did not already belong to them, there was danger that he would
shortly. After waiting some time for the order to charge, we were ordered into
camp, where we were within pistol shot of the enemy's camp. . . . Soon after
going into position we could hear a sudden challenge, then a shot, then a shower
of bullets from the enemy's line came whistling over our heads. Then our skirmishers opened fire and for an hour or two they blazed away at each other every
opportunity. This is a most murderous style of amusement, and pretty soon
they commenced shouting: 'What are you uns firing at we uns for?' — 'What
did *you* shoot for, then, you d——d scoundrels?'" (MS. Diary of Lieutenant-
Colonel Comly.)

more boldly and vigorously on the 16th, there is little doubt that he could have captured Lynchburg.[1] Now his duty was to save his army and get back as quickly as possible within our lines.

His ammunition was too nearly exhausted to permit him to venture on retracing his steps by the Shenandoah Valley, as Early could easily have got in his rear or fallen on his flank by the numerous gaps through the Blue Ridge. His only recourse was to retreat with his scantily provisioned army westward and across the mountains to the Kanawha. Early considerately held off from making a strong attack on the 18th, Hunter throughout that day maintaining a bold front. But as soon as night came, Hunter drew off his forces and marched rapidly to Liberty. Early followed in force with cavalry and infantry, and between Liberty and Buford Gap caused our forces much annoyance though inflicting small injury. The Rebel cavalry kept up the pursuit as far as the Catawba Mountains. Hunter's army followed the line of the railway four miles beyond Salem, destroying bridges and track as thoroughly as the hasty march permitted. Then it turned to the north, crossed the mountains to New Castle, and pushed on night and day by Sweet Sulphur and White Sulphur Springs to Meadow Bluff; where supplies were expected to be found. But the officer left in charge of that post with four hundred men had become alarmed at a guerrilla demonstration and had retired with the trains to Gauley Bridge. Finally two days later a provision train was met near Mountain Cove and the starving men were fed. The retreat was begun the night of June 18; the supply train was reached the forenoon of June 27. In the nine days and nights the army had marched over two hundred miles, throughout the time with insufficient supplies, many of the men going hungry for days. The men bore the

---

[1] "Had General Hunter moved by way of Charlottesville, instead of Lexington, as his instructions contemplated, he would have been in a position to have covered the Shenandoah Valley against the enemy, should the force he met have seemed to endanger it. If it did not, he would have been within easy distance of the James River Canal, on the main line of communication between Lynchburg and the force sent for its defense. I have never taken exception to the operations of General Hunter, and I am not now disposed to find fault with him, for I have no doubt he acted within what he conceived to be the spirit of his instructions and the interests of the service. The promptitude of his movements and his gallantry should entitle him to the commendation of his country." (U. S. Grant, "Report" July 22, 1865, *Official War Records*, vol. xxxiv, part i, p. 20.)

fatigue and hunger uncomplainingly but many dropped out exhausted by the way,[1] and wandered off into the mountains seeking food. The night of the 27th the army camped in old Camp Ewing, near Gauley Bridge. The ambulances were emptied and sent back along the line of march to pick up sick and exhausted men. The army passed on by easy marches to Charleston, arriving there July 1. Meanwhile from Camp Piatt, ten miles above Charleston, June 30, Hayes wrote his uncle: —

Back home again in the Kanawha Valley. Our raid has done a great deal; all that we at first intended, but failed in one or two things which would have been done with a more active and enterprising commander than General Hunter. General Crook would have taken Lynchburg without doubt. Our loss is small. The Twenty-third has nobody killed. My brigade loses less than one hundred. Our greatest suffering was want of food and sleep. I often went asleep on my horse.[2] We had to go night and day for about a week to get out.

We are all impressed with the idea that the Confederacy has now got all its strength of all sorts in the field, and that nothing more can be added to it. Their defeat now closes the contest speedily. We passed through ten counties where Yankees never came before; there was nothing to check us even, until forces were drawn from Richmond to drive us back.

There are rumors that we are to go East soon, but nothing definite is known. We hope we are to constitute an independent command under General Crook. We have marched in two months past, about eight hundred miles; have had fighting or skirmishing on our front forty days of the time. My health and my horse's (almost of equal moment) are excellent.

Two days later from Charleston he wrote again: —

We are told this morning that General Crook is to have the command of the "Army of the Kanawha," independent of all control below Grant.

[1] "Marched all the next day, still without a bite to eat. It is incredible that men should endure so much, but the glorious old regiment did not even grumble. Once in a while a man would drop out silently, exhausted, but not a word of complaint. One curious thing I noticed: when daylight came, the men always seemed in some sort refreshed by it, as if they had taken a meal." (MS. Diary of Lieutenant-Colonel Comly.)

[2] "In this condition we marched, the men dropping down frequently asleep in the road. They were waked and started again. I myself went to sleep walking a number of times. Dr. Barrett went to sleep standing up, and was near being left behind. Captain Warren was left once in the same way and did not wake until nearly the whole column had passed." (MS. Diary of Lieutenant-Colonel Comly.)

If so, good. I don't doubt it. This will secure us the much-needed rest we have hoped for and keep us here two or three weeks. My health is excellent, but many men are badly used up. . . .

I do not feel sure yet of the result of Grant's and Sherman's campaigns. One thing I have become satisfied of. The Rebels are now using their last men and last bread. There is absolutely nothing left in reserve. Whip what is now in the field and the game is ended.

But there was to be short rest for the worn and weary soldiers. Their presence was urgently demanded east of the Alleghanies. As soon as Hunter and his army were well in the mountains, Early started with a large force for the Shenandoah Valley which was now left unguarded. He reached the Potomac, meeting slight resistance (Sigel, of course, running away from Martinsburg at the first alarm), passed over into Maryland, defeated Lew Wallace, who with an inferior force had bravely sought to check his advance at Monocacy, and advanced to the very fortifications of Washington, reaching there July 11. Meanwhile the scanty forces at the National Capital had been reënforced with veterans sent by Grant from Petersburg. Early soon saw that the capture of Washington was impossible, and the night of July 12 retired rapidly and succeeded in crossing the Potomac to Leesburg, Virginia, with all the plunder his raiders had gathered in Maryland. Then followed three weeks of perpetual fighting, raiding, marching, and countermarching in the lower Shenandoah Valley and in western Maryland, with frequent changes of commanders of departments and corps, with clashings of authority and conflicting orders, resulting in dissipating the strength of the Union forces and giving the alert and clear-headed Early almost constant success.[1] At last (August 5) Grant solved the perplexing situation by insisting on a consolidation of the Middle, Washington, Susquehanna, and West Virginia Departments and placing General Sheridan with an adequate army in command. Then began the brilliant campaign in the Valley which finally crushed the Confederate strength in that quarter.

[1] See Grant's *Memoirs*, chap. LVII.

CHAPTER XV

MEANWHILE at Charleston the men [1] were being refitted as rapidly as possible and started east; by steamers to Parkersburg, and by the Baltimore and Ohio Railway to Martinsburg. The water in the Kanawha and the Ohio was so low that only the smallest steamers could be used, and even so the men had frequently to disembark and march around the shallows. It was July 14 when Hayes with Crook reached Martinsburg. Major-General Wright was in command of the troops pursuing the retreating Early, who was making for Snicker's Gap and Ferry. Hunter and the other department commanders were supposed to be coöperating with him. But no one seemed to know exactly what to do or what was being done. Grant was too far away to keep in close touch with affairs and Halleck shirked responsibility. July 18, Hayes was sent up the west bank of the Shenandoah with his full brigade and a battery to strike the Rebels on the flank and to unite with Wright's command at Snicker's Ford, it being supposed that Wright would by that time have driven Early before him and be in possession of the ford. But Wright's advance under General Crook had been unable after a sharp engagement to dislodge the Rebels. The night of the 18th, having driven the Rebel outposts before him, Hayes camped at Bull Skin Creek, ten miles or so from Harper's Ferry and about the same distance from Snicker's Ford. The cannonading at the latter place had been distinctly heard, but the result of the fighting he did not know. A night of much anxiety was passed, and the next morning Hayes proceeded cautiously up the river, presently meeting the enemy's skirmish line which vigorously contested his progress. Then, leaving two regiments to guard the train, he pushed on with the Twenty-third and Thirty-sixth Ohio, skirmishing with Bradley Johnson's cavalry

---

[1] The Twelfth Ohio was here consolidated with the Twenty-third.

till he was within six miles of the ford. Rodes's infantry division was sent to meet him and the enemy was then in such force as to compel him to retire. He came near being surrounded, but fought his way back, moving the regiments hand over hand, to the camp of the previous night.

The next day Hayes retired to Charlestown, where he received orders from Crook (who had been promoted to brevet major-general and was in command of the Army of West Virginia in the field) to join him at Snicker's Ford; Early having abandoned that position and retreated toward Winchester. He made the junction with Crook the following day, and Crook with his full command advanced to Kernstown beyond Winchester. His forces, much less numerous than the army he was pursuing, were no match for Early, who turned (July 24) and fiercely attacked. There was sharp fighting, but the contest was too unequal to be long sustained.

At the first fire Crook's dismounted cavalry, along with some infantry, broke to the rear and fled to Martinsburg, accompanied by many-tongued rumor. Hayes's brigade was in the thickest of the fight. His brigade was formed in line of battle on the left of Colonel Mulligan's division. The orders were to advance and charge the enemy, gradually wheeling to the right, so as to take the enemy, who were believed to be passing around the Union right, on the flank. There were signs that the Rebels were in the hills on both sides of them, thus having the Federal forces in a trap. But the advance movement was made rapidly and in good order. It had not proceeded far before the enemy in large force, in two lines of battle, preceded by a strong line of skirmishers, moved rapidly over the ridge of hills on the Union left and opened fire on flank and rear. An effort was made to change front to meet this attack, but the fire was so heavy and destructive that the left was doubled back in confusion on the right of the brigade. Hayes soon formed a new line behind a stone fence, at right angles to the original direction, the right resting near the point reached by the right of the brigade when the enemy attacked on the left. Fire was opened on the enemy and his course checked long enough to enable a great part of the wounded to be got to the rear. It was now discovered that the enemy, with his greatly superior force, enveloped the troops on Hayes's right and that these had been driven back. Colonel Mulligan was mortally wounded while rallying his regiment, the Twenty-third Illinois. Hayes moved his brigade back in good order, and was directed by General Crook in person to hold the enemy in check long enough to enable one of his batteries, which was very much exposed, to withdraw, and then to fall back slowly, bearing to the right of Winchester going north.[1]

Hayes had a horse shot under him and he was struck in the shoulder by a spent ball. His brigade sustained a loss of four hundred. But he brought his men off in good order, the Twenty-third covering the retreat,[2] and reached Bunker Hill in safety, where the army bivouacked. After a few hours' rest, the retreat was continued to Martinsburg, where the Rebels again appeared and were beaten back. Then the retreat was continued across the Potomac and the camp was pitched July 26 near the Antietam battle ground.[3] Two days later Crook's army was back at Hall-town, where it was joined by the Sixth and Nineteenth Corps with General Wright, who took command of the combined

[1] Official Report of Colonel R. B. Hayes, *War Records*, vol. xxxvii, pp. 311–12. The total loss of Crook's army was 1185. — "We reached here to-day after two nights and one day of pretty severe marching — not so severe as the Lynchburg march — and one day of very severe fighting at Winchester. We were defeated by a superior force at Winchester. My brigade suffered most in killed and wounded and not so much in prisoners as some others. . . . This is all a new experience — a decided defeat in battle. My brigade was in the hottest place and then was in condition to cover the retreat as rear guard, which we did successfully and well for one day and night. Of course, the reason — the place for blame to fall — is always asked in such cases. I think the army is not disposed to blame the result on anybody; the enemy was so superior that a defeat was a matter of course if we fought. The real difficulty was, our cavalry was so inefficient in its efforts to discover the strength of the enemy that General Crook and all the rest of us were deceived until it was too late. We are queer beings. The camp is now alive with laughter and good feeling. More so than usual — the recoil after so much toil and anxiety." (Letter to Mrs. Hayes, from camp near Sharpsburg, July 26, 1864.)

[2] "Hayes covered retreat with our regiment, marching in hollow square. Cavalry followed us very closely. Once after dark Hayes set a trap for them. We halted in edge of woods, and lay down and waited until they came within a few yards, when the whole line rose and fired a blizzard right into them. They did not follow us so closely after that." (MS. Diary of Lieutenant-Colonel Comly.)

[3] "Not many signs existed of a great battle having been fought there. Some fences showed the bullet marks, and in Sharpsburg the marks of shells were found, but the fields were all in cultivation as though no trampling host had ever passed over them." (Russell Hastings, MS. Memoirs.)

forces.[1] The next day, on learning that McCausland had crossed the Potomac with his cavalry and was pushing north on a plundering raid to Pennsylvania, General Wright transferred his whole army to the Maryland side of the Potomac, and the next few days were spent in a series of apparently aimless marches, under a blistering midsummer sun, alike maddening to officers and disastrous to men. The irritation is shown by brief entries in Hayes's diary as: "July 31, Men all 'gone up,' 'played out,' etc. Must have time to build up or we can do nothing. Only fifty to one hundred men in a regiment came into camp in a body." [2] While in camp at Monocacy, August 4, ninety recruits for the Twenty-third Regiment arrived. Among them was a "bounty-jumper" named Whitlow, who was at once recognized. He had enlisted in the Twenty-third at Charleston the previous winter as a Confederate deserter; had deserted with his arms shortly before the spring campaign opened; and had been captured in the Rebel ranks at Cloyd Mountain. He was to have been tried there, but he made his escape on the homeward march. Now he was promptly arrested, tried by drumhead court-martial, and condemned to be shot. The sentence was executed at sundown in the presence of the entire brigade, formed in hollow square.

General Sheridan took command of the four consolidated departments and of the Army of the Shenandoah, August 5. Grant had proposed that General Hunter should remain at the head of the department and that General Sheridan should have command of the forces in the field. But General Hunter, with an unselfishness and patriotism that cannot be too highly praised, suggested that the situation would be simplified by his retirement and voluntarily made way for Sheridan's full control. Sheridan's army consisted of the Sixth and Nineteenth Corps under Generals Wright and Emory respectively, General Crook's Army of West

[1] Wright had been called back to Washington as soon as Early appeared to be retreating up the Shenandoah, Grant believing that he was returning to Richmond and desiring to have the Sixth Corps sent to him. As soon as it was seen that Early had no idea of going south, except as he was driven, the orders to Wright were changed.

[2] Lieutenant-Colonel Comly the same day wrote: "Nobody knows what we are marching for. It seems as if some man in a delirium was sending us up and down from sheer restlessness." Hunter a few days later told Grant that he had been so bewildered by contradictory orders from Washington that he had lost all trace of the enemy. See Grant's *Memoirs*, chap. LVII.

Virginia, which usually acted as the left wing, and ample cavalry under General Torbert, with Merritt and Averell as division commanders. The troops were mostly veterans under officers of proved ability and bravery. The whole army made something like forty thousand men, but it was impossible to bring the entire force into the field, as so many men had to be employed on detached service, protecting the railways, convoying trains, and guarding fords and supply depots. During the next five weeks Sheridan's operations consisted principally of offensive and defensive manœuvring for certain advantages which the enemy sought to counteract.[1] He hoped to keep Early in the northern part of the Valley and to bring on a decisive engagement somewhere in the region of Winchester. But Early was well informed of what was going on in Sheridan's camps about Harper's Ferry, and presently began slowly to retire up the river. As soon as Sheridan had his forces well in hand he started after Early, the Sixth Corps on the right, Crook's army on the left, the Nineteenth Corps in the centre, all within supporting distance, and his cavalry protecting the flanks and skirmishing in advance of the main line. In this way with numerous skirmishes he went up the Valley about forty miles to Cedar Creek, where he found that Early had just passed and established himself in a strong position at Strasburg. Here Sheridan's army remained for three days, when reports reached the commanding general that heavy reënforcements for Early were arriving from Richmond. These reports were confirmed by a dispatch from General Grant, who consequently directed Sheridan to exercise the greatest caution and to act for the time being on the defensive. The configuration of the Valley offered no good line of defense south of Halltown, four miles from Harper's Ferry. Sheridan therefore decided to fall back to that point. The movement was at once begun and successfully carried out, though the Rebels followed closely and attacked frequently; and a strong line was formed at Halltown which was maintained for a week, with Early and his reënforced army close at hand and daily combats on the picket line or by sorties. The retrograde movement was a source of much apprehension and condemnation in the North and there was a clamor of the critics for Sheridan's displacement. But the troops were

[1] Sheridan's *Memoirs*, chap. XXIII.

not in the least disturbed by it; rather their confidence was increased by the masterly manner in which they felt that they were being handled.[1] While near Strasburg, August 14, Hayes wrote Sardis Birchard: —

> You see we are again up the famous Valley; General Sheridan commands the army; Generals Early and Breckinridge are in our front; they have retired before us thus far; whether it is for the purpose to follow and force a battle, I don't know; the effect is to relieve our rail from Rebels. My health is excellent. Our troops are improving under the easy marches. We shall get well rested doing what the Sixth and Nineteenth Corps of the Potomac (who are with us) regard as severe campaigning.

One reason that influenced Sheridan in his cautious policy was the intimation he had received from Washington of the disastrous effect a defeat might have in the Presidential campaign then in progress. Everywhere the Republicans were exceedingly apprehensive. The belief was widespread that the Administration had not measured up to the requirements of the great emergency. The principal effort of the Republican leaders of the political

[1] "Notwithstanding we have been falling back from one position to another for a week past the men have not only not lost confidence, but have gained steadily, and are now ready to do anything Sheridan and Crook may order. These indications are not to be despised. Troops know when they are properly handled." (Lieutenant-Colonel Comly's MS. Diary, under date of August 22.) August 23, Hayes wrote Mrs. Hayes from camp near Charlestown: "Winchester is a noble town. Both Union and secesh ladies devote their whole time to the care of the wounded of the two armies. Their town has been taken and retaken two or three times a day several times. It has been the scene of five or six battles and many skirmishes. There are about fifty Union families. Many of them 'F.F.' But they are true as steel. Our officers and men all praise them. One queer thing, the whole people turn out to see each army as it comes and welcome their acquaintances and friends. The Rebs are happy when the secesh soldiers come, and *vice versa*. Three years of this sort of life have schooled them to singular habits. — I have heard heavy skirmishing ever since I began to write. Now I hear our artillery pounding, but I anticipate no battle here, as I think our position too good for Early to risk an assault and I suppose it is not our policy to attack them. . . . I believe you know that I shall feel no apprehension of the war being abandoned if McClellan is elected President. I, therefore, feel desirous to see him nominated at Chicago. Then no odds how the people vote, the country is safe. If McClellan is elected, the Democracy will speedily become a war party. A great good that will be. I suspect some of our patriots having fat offices and contracts might then, on losing them, become enamored of peace! I feel more hopeful about things than when I saw you. This Presidential election is the rub; that once over without outbreak or other calamity and I think we save the country."

campaign in Ohio was directed to obtaining the nomination of the most popular citizens for the various offices. This was looked to particularly in the Congressional districts. Hayes, while on the march, had given a reluctant consent to the use of his name, on the assurance that it was necessary to make the Second District safe.[1] He got word of his nomination just before the army began to advance to Strasburg, and notes the fact without comment in his diary. When the army got back to Halltown he received a letter from William Henry Smith in behalf of his constituents entreating him to come home and make speeches in his district. In the midst of arduous camp duties and with the sound of hostile artillery sounding in his ears, Hayes immediately wrote this characteristic reply: —

> CAMP OF SHERIDAN'S ARMY,
> August 24, 1864.
>
> FRIEND SMITH, — Your favor of the 7th came to hand on Monday. It was the first I had heard of the doings of the Second District Convention. My thanks for your attention and assistance in the premises. I cared very little about being a candidate, but having consented to the use of my name I preferred to succeed. Your suggestion about getting a furlough to take the stump was certainly made without reflection.
>
> An officer fit for duty who at this crisis would abandon his post to electioneer for a seat in Congress ought to be scalped. You may feel perfectly sure I shall do no such thing.
>
> We are, and for two weeks have been, in the immediate presence of a large Rebel army. We have skirmishing and small affairs constantly. I am not posted in the policy deemed wise at headquarters, and can't guess as to the prospects of a general engagement. The condition and spirit of this army are good and improving. I suspect the enemy are sliding around us towards the Potomac. If they cross we shall pretty certainly have a meeting. — Sincerely,
>
> R. B. HAYES.

Mr. Smith never felt that he had any cause to regret writing the letter to which this reply — destined to become famous in the Presidential campaign of 1876 — was made. It was his belief, which he shared with many good and wise men, that failure to reëlect Mr. Lincoln, or failure to elect a Congress with a decided

---

[1] "As to that candidacy for Congress, I care nothing at all about it — neither for the nomination nor for the election. It was merely easier to let the thing take its own course than to get up a letter declining to run and then explain it to everybody who might choose to bore me about it." (Hayes to Sardis Birchard, July 10, 1864.)

Union majority, would be more disastrous than the loss of a battle, as either result would probably lead to a fatal peace. Hence the presence among the people of men with the smell of the smoke of battle on their garments might save the campaign to the party of the Union.[1] There were abundant facts to show how desperate the political situation was at this period.

Early did not dare attack Sheridan's strong position at Halltown in force. There were daily engagements, sometimes approaching the importance of battles, between detachments of the two armies, and the interchange of hostile courtesies was for a time almost continuous on the picket lines.[2] Early started a strong force as if to cross into Maryland, but this was intercepted by Torbert's cavalry. The last of August, as the Union cavalry was moving to the south threatening the Rebel right flank, Early began to retire slowly up the Valley, Sheridan promptly following him. August 30, Hayes was in camp near Charlestown where he wrote his uncle: —

We have had no general engagement, but a world of small affairs the last week. I think the enemy are giving it up. We are slowly pushing them back up the Valley. General Sheridan's splendid cavalry do a great share of the work; we look on and rest. This has been a good month for us. We are a happy army.

[1] "With a full understanding of the importance of your services in the position you now occupy, you have been chosen to represent the loyal sentiment of this district, from a conviction that courage, ability, and a single-hearted devotion to the country, are qualities as necessary in the legislative assemblies of the nation as on the battlefield. The conflicts to be fought there, though free from danger of ball and steel, are fully as essential to the welfare of our country, and as honorable as the more bloody fields of strife." (From letter, signed Thomas H. Weasner, President, and Harry C. Armstrong, Secretary of Convention, notifying Hayes of his nomination.)

[2] "The skirmish lines kept up a constant firing until they finally agreed to stop firing and each hold their line where it was then established; though before this happened short truces of peace were agreed upon. Between the two lines was a promising cornfield, full of luscious corn just fit for roasting-ears. One day when I was on the line about midday I noticed a white handkerchief shaken and a voice called out: 'Hullo, Yank! Let's stop firing for dinner and go down to the cornfield for roasting-ears!' This, after some talk of 'honor bright,' 'true as Indian,' etc., was agreed to, and the two lines met in the cornfield, exchanged lies and newspapers, carried back the corn-ears, roasted them, and had dinner. When dinner was all through, one of our boys shook a handkerchief calling out: 'Hullo, Johnny Reb, are you all through?' The reply was: 'Yes, say when you are ready.' And each skirmisher found his hole in a hurry, and at the word 'ready!' bang went the rifles all along the line." (Russell Hastings, MS. Memoirs.)

Camp of Shericani Alley near Charleston Va

Aug 24. 1862

Friend S.

I see it is likely McClellan will be nominated. If they don't load him down with too much treasonable peace doctrine, I shall not be surprised at his election. I can see some strong currents which can easily be turned in his favor, provided always that his loyalty is left above suspicion. I have no doubt of his personal convictions and feelings; they are sound enough, but his surroundings are the trouble.

For several days the manœuvring for position continued. Hayes's brigade, on September 3, held the extreme left wing of Sheridan's line near Berryville. Grant was vigorously occupying Lee's attention, and Lee had directed Early to return to Richmond a part of the troops with which he had recently been reënforced. Thereupon Early started back Kershaw's division to go by Berryville and Ashley's Gap, supposing the way was clear. But near Berryville, late in the afternoon of September 3, Kershaw encountered Hayes, who had no idea of letting him pass. The Rebels came on as though with the expectation of sweeping all before them, but the Ohio veterans, unconfused by the stampede of certain companies of recent recruits, stubbornly stood their ground, and after a long and fierce engagement, involving considerable loss, the Rebels were defeated and forced back to Early's main line.[1] Three days later Hayes wrote of this fight to Sardis Birchard: —

CAMP OF SHERIDAN'S ARMY,
NEAR BERRYVILLE, VIRGINIA,
September 6, P.M., 1864.

Saturday evening (3d Sept.) my brigade and two regiments of the other brigade of the Kanawha Division fought a very fierce battle with

---

[1] "It was a magnificent fight. . . . After dark every shell-burst looked like a belch of fire. It was indescribable. . . . There was an immense amount of firing, but the darkness saved us from many casualties. . . . One sad thing happened to me. As I rode up and down the line almost too dark to see, I saw three men going to the rear, one limping and one each side holding him up. This was a common dodge for getting away, if there were any sneaks. I rode up angrily, and recognized a big Irishman who had come a short time before as a substitute. I ordered him back to the regiment. 'But, Kur-r-nel, I'm wounded,' he said with a long roll on the r. 'No, you're not wounded,' I said angrily. 'You and these other two men are trying to sneak out of the fight in the dark. Go back!' He came alongside as I sat on my horse. 'Give me your hand, Kur-r-nel!' I let him take my hand, not knowing what he meant. 'Feel,' said he, and he stuck my hand into a hole in his shoulder which it scarcely filled. The hot blood spirted up my arm to the shoulder. I drew back in horror, shocked beyond measure. 'You poor fellow, poor fellow! forgive me! Go back to the doctor, quick!' He started away and fell dead almost instantly." (Lieutenant-Colonel Comly's MS. Diary.)

a division of South Carolina and Mississippi troops under Kershaw. We whipped them handsomely after the longest fight I was ever in. Took seventy-five officers and men prisoners and inflicted much severer loss than we suffered. Prisoners say it is the first time their division was ever flogged in a fair fight. My color-bearer was killed and some of the best officers killed or wounded. We have fought nine times since we entered this Valley and have been under fire when men of my command were killed and wounded probably thirty or forty times since the campaign opened. I doubt if a brigade in Sheridan's army has fought more; none has marched half as much. I started with two thousand four hundred men; I have now less than twelve hundred, and almost none of the loss is stragglers.

I hope they will now get Sherman's army to Richmond. It will be taken if they do it promptly; otherwise, I fear, not for some time.

McClellan would get a handsome soldiers' vote if on a decent platform; as it is, he will get more than any other Democrat could get.

I am glad you feel as you do about my safety. It is the best philosophy not to borrow trouble of the future. We are still confronted by the enemy. I can't help thinking that the fall of Atlanta will carry them back to Richmond. What a glorious career Sherman's army has had! That is the best army in the world. Lee's army is next. There is just as much difference between armies, divisions, and brigades as between individuals. Crook, I think, has the best and the worst divisions in this army; of the one you can always count upon that it will do all that can be expected, and of the other, that it will behave badly.

For the next few days the army remained practically at rest holding the lines already established. On September 8, Crook's command was sent around to the extreme right and stationed at Summit Point.[1] From there Hayes wrote Sardis Birchard, September 12: —

We have had no severe fighting since the 3d. The frequent rains have filled the Potomac so it is no longer fordable. I look for no attempt now

[1] From this point, writing to Mrs. Hayes September 9, Hayes said: "Speaking of politics. It is quite common for youngsters, adopting their parents' notions, to get very bitter talk into their innocent little mouths. I was quite willing Webb should 'Hurrah for Val' [Vallandigham] last summer with the addition, 'and a rope to hang him.' But I feel quite different about McClellan. He is on a mean platform and is in bad company, but I do not doubt his personal loyalty and he has been a soldier, and what is more, a soldier's friend. No man ever treated the private soldier better. No commander was ever more loved by his men. I therefore want my boys taught to think and talk well of General McClellan. I think he will make the best President of any Democrat. If on a sound platform I could support him. Do not be alarmed. I do not think he will be elected. The improved condition of our military affairs injures his chances very materially. He will not get so large an army vote as his friends seem to expect. With reasonably good luck in the war, Lincoln will go in."

on the part of the Rebels to get over the river, and think there will be
very little fighting unless we attack. We are gaining strength daily.
Our policy seems to be not to attack unless the chances are greatly in
our favor. Military affairs wear a much better look. Our armies are
rapidly filling up. I should not be surprised if Grant should soon find
himself able to make important moves.

I like McClellan's letter. It is an important thing. It is the best evidence to Europe and the South that the people intend to prosecute the
war until the Union is reëstablished. Still, if things continue as favorable as they now are, I think Lincoln will be elected.

I see that Mr. Long is not renominated. I supposed he would be, and
that my election over him was quite a sure thing. Against Mr. Lord,
the result will depend on the general drift matters take. I am not going
to take it to heart if I am beaten. "It's of no consequence at all," as
Mr. Toots would say. Mr. Lord's wife and family are particular and
intimate friends of ¦my wife and family. His wife is a sister of Stephenson's wife. Divers friends of his and mine will be in a worry how to vote,
I suspect.

Hayes was quite right in his surmise of the commanding general's policy. Sheridan proposed not to strike until he was sure
that he could deliver an effective and decisive blow. Meanwhile,
in response to Lee's urgent demand, Early had finally got Kershaw's division off for Richmond, both Lee and Early evidently
believing that events had shown that Early's regular force was
sufficient to handle Sheridan. Sheridan got definite information
of the departure of Kershaw the evening of September 16. He
decided that the time had come to strike, and he began his preparations for an immediate advance, intending to throw a large
force into Newton, to the south of Winchester, beyond Early's
right flank. But a dispatch that night from General Grant summoned him to Charlestown the next day for a conference.[1] Grant
had come with a carefully made plan of campaign for Sheridan in
his pocket, which, however, he never took out nor referred to,
when he heard Sheridan's clear exposition of the situation of
affairs, grasped the plan of operations he had formed, and caught
the enthusiasm of his confidence in its success. He simply gave
Sheridan the laconic direction: "Go in!"

Sheridan, on his return to his headquarters near Berryville,

---

[1] "*Saturday, September 17.* Waited with the regiment at Charlestown while
train loaded at Harper's Ferry. General Grant here to-day to visit Sheridan.
Passed through our camp. Had only one orderly — nobody else — with him.
Not much like McClellan, that!" (Comly's MS. Diary.)

learned that Early had sent two of his divisions (Rodes's and Gordon's) north to Martinsburg. Thereupon he determined to attack directly in front, hoping to crush Ramseur and then turn and strike the divisions farther north. But Early at Martinsburg the morning of the 18th heard of Grant's visit to Sheridan, and, apprehensive that it portended some aggressive movement, at once began to withdraw his troops from Martinsburg and get them within supporting distance of the rest of his army. At 3 A.M., September 19, Sheridan's forces began to move into position for the great battle of the Opequon. The cavalry was to advance on both flanks and seize the fords across the Opequon Creek; the Sixth and Nineteenth Corps were to cross the Opequon at the Berryville Pike, after Wilson's cavalry had captured the crossing and driven the Rebels from the gorge beyond, to form in battle line on the open ground at the head of the defile, and press the attack upon the Rebel main line; Crook's command (now sometimes unofficially known as the Eighth Corps, from the addition to it of the remnant of that corps) was to march from Summit Point eight miles to the rear of the main position and be held in reserve. Sheridan purposed, if all went as he hoped, to send Crook to the left toward Newton to cut off Early's retreat.

But things did not go quite as he had hoped. Wilson's cavalry successfully seized the crossing, passed rapidly up the long defile, surprised and captured Ramseur's outworks at the head of it, and held their ground till the infantry pressed through to their support. It took much longer, however, for the two corps to pass through the defile and get in line of battle than Sheridan had counted on, and during this precious time the divisions of Rodes and Gordon were hastening from near Stephenson's Depot and Bunker Hill, whither they had been returned the day before from Martinsburg, to the field of battle; while Wharton's division under Breckinridge remained at Stephenson's to contest the Federal advance from that quarter.[1] While the cavalry on both flanks was continuing to do effective work, it was late in the forenoon before the infantry corps were ready to press forward.

---

[1] It was gradually driven back by Merritt's cavalry, and in the afternoon when the final charge was made held position to the left of Gordon's division and nearer Winchester.

By that time Rodes and Gordon were both in position, Rodes on Ramseur's immediate left and Gordon to the left of Rodes. The Confederate line was in strong position along elevated ground about two miles east of Winchester, stretching from Abraham's Creek on the south to Red Bud Run on the north, a distance of something over two miles. Beyond both streams the cavalry forces were operating. Between the Rebel position and Sheridan's line lay a mile or so of undulating farmland, dotted here and there with patches of wood and undergrowth, but for the most part open meadow and cornfields already ripe for the harvest. The Union lines were formed under heavy artillery fire, and their advance shortly before noon was met with obstinate resistance. For an hour or so the battle raged furiously. Some slight gain was made by the Sixth Corps on the extreme left, but for the most part the Confederates held their position, and Rodes detecting a weak place, where the Sixth and Nineteenth Corps joined, charged and repulsed our line. Russell's reserve division was sent to drive back the charging foe and brilliantly executed its commission, though at the cost of its able leader's life.

A lull in the engagement followed while the broken divisions of Ricketts of the Sixth and Grover of the Nineteenth Corps were rallied, and the whole line was reëstablished in nearly the same position as at the first advance. Not hearing from Torbert, who was to drive the outposts of the enemy before him on the extreme right, join with Averell at Stephenson's Depot, and sweep on against the Confederate left, Sheridan somewhat reluctantly — for he disliked to give up his original plan — decided to order up Crook's command and put it into action at the right of the Nineteenth Corps and to act as a turning column on the enemy's left flank.

Meanwhile Crook's army, or the Eighth Corps, was waiting, expectant, in a clover-field some two miles distant. The battle line was in view and the firing of small arms could be distinctly heard. The day was bright and every aspect of nature beautiful. Crook and Hayes, with the members of their staffs,[1]

---

[1] The staff of Colonel Hayes was constituted as follows: Lieutenant-Colonel Joseph T. Webb, surgeon; Captain Russell Hastings, adjutant-general; Lieutenant William McKinley, aide; Lieutenant O. J. Wood, aide; Lieutenant A. W. Delay, quartermaster and commissary; Lieutenant B. A. Turner, ordnance.

lay in the clover, chatting, laughing, and exchanging jokes. Crook looks up with a smile: "I cannot find a four-leaved clover, so I suppose we shall have to go in." Hayes responds: "I saw the moon over my left shoulder, so I suppose we must go in"; and another officer adds: "One of my socks is on wrong side out, so I suppose we must go in"; [1] and thus the joke goes around. And sure enough, the moment for them to enter the combat is near at hand. Sheridan's headquarters and signal station are in plain sight. The flags are fluttering out the commander's orders with impetuous rapidity. Presently a staff officer is seen to mount a horse and start rapidly in their direction. The men spring to their feet; the officers tighten their sword-belts; Crook, looking through his field-glass, says, "It is Tony Forsyth, and he is coming to tell us to go in." The officer alights from his panting horse, salutes General Crook, and delivers Sheridan's order. The Army of West Virginia marched as rapidly as possible through the long defile, impeded with ambulances, wounded men seeking the field hospitals, and panic-stricken cowards straggling to the rear. Once out of the defile, it took position to the right of the Nineteenth Corps. Here General Sheridan joined Crook, his face shining with the fire of battle.

The situation is explained in a few words, and then Crook is ordered to take one division and make a détour to the right to find the enemy's left. He is "then to strike and carry all before him at all hazards. Let there be no question as to this movement being a success." The duty of the Sixth and Nineteenth Corps now was to hold the enemy desperately occupied until the Eighth Corps could execute the turning movement with which Sheridan hoped to decide the combat.[2]

Crook selected the Second Division, under Colonel Duval, to perform the arduous and hazardous feat of swinging around on the enemy's left flank. He knew that the *élan* with which the veterans of this division entered battle carried with it a force more important than numbers. The line of march was along the line of Red Bud Run, the Second Division north of the stream, the First

---

[1] June 7, on the march to Staunton, Hayes writes in his diary: "The General (Crook) found a four-leaved clover yesterday. I saw the moon over my right shoulder. Funny how a man of sense can think even for a moment of such follies."

[2] *Harper's Monthly*, vol. 30, p. 199.

Division south, in supporting distance. Hayes's brigade formed the extreme right. The Second Division marched through deep gullies and tangled thickets, over wooded hills and across open fields for a mile, then westward over the same kind of country for a half mile, and then southward in the direction of the firing and the supposed left flank of the enemy.[1] The march had consumed an hour and a half and it was now about half-past three. Meanwhile Torbert's cavalry, operating on the right flank, had driven the opposing infantry and cavalry before him, had joined with Averell, and was ready to coöperate with Crook's command in turning the Rebel left. Just before Crook's Second Division got fairly around, the First Division under Colonel Thoburn made a gallant charge driving the enemy back. The arrival of the Second Division completed the work. The Second Division reached its position under cover of a dense cedar thicket, where it halted and formed with the First Brigade (Hayes's) in advance. Throwing out a light line of skirmishers, the division moved rapidly to the front repelling the enemy's cavalry. At the same time the Union cavalry emerged from the woods on the right. Advancing thus under a scattering fire across two or three open fields, Hayes's men reached the crest of a slight elevation. Off diagonally to the left was seen the enemy's infantry line, which at once began a brisk cannonade. On now under a galling fire Duval's division rushed at double-quick to a thick fringe of underbrush, through which it quickly dashed, when for the first time the character and strength of the enemy's position were revealed. His front was covered by a stone wall, while his left rested on an almost impassable morass created by Red Bud Run. It was nearly waist-deep, with thick soft mud at the bottom, while its surface was closely overgrown with moss nearly strong enough to support a man. The banks of the slough were overgrown with tangled thickets; beyond, the ground was rough and uneven; the whole was covered by a Rebel battery.

To cross the morass seemed impossible; to cross it under fire was, indeed, rushing into the jaws of death. The whole line hesitated for a moment. The well-known voice of Hayes, ringing distinct and clear, said, "Come on, boys," as he spurred his horse into the morass and, regardless of the bursting shells, pushed

[1] Russell Hastings, MS. Memoirs.

ahead; with his horse sometimes down and sometimes up, he rode, waded, and dragged his way through.[1] His horse stuck fast.[2] He dismounted and floundered on, the first man over. When his feet struck firm ground, he found he was protected from the battery by the bank above him. He greeted the first man [3] that followed him with lifted cap and hearty hand-grasp. The men inspired by Hayes's example quickly followed, many directly in his path, others seeking narrower and less difficult places to right and left. It was a task of almost incredible difficulty even if grape and canister from the Rebel battery had not been playing upon them. Men were killed; others, wounded, sank helpless into the thick, slimy mud. Only a few hundred got over. Lines and organizations were completely broken, and the men of the different regiments and brigades were mingled into one great throng; but no time was lost in re-forming. "Now, men," shouted Hayes, "up the bank and at them." Up they went, and, supported by the cavalry, Crook's whole command, now united, though still a disorganized mass, "cheering as they went, rushed on, heedless of the destructive fire of shot, shell, canister, and musketry that thinned their ranks, and which would have driven back in disorder troops less determined, all seemingly intent on one grand object, the total and complete rout of the enemy." [4]

[1] Hayes crossed at the widest point. The width here he says in his official report was twenty to thirty yards. Later in life he estimated it as forty to fifty yards, in which estimate others agreed. General Hastings's estimate was still higher. — In his diary, April 5, 1887, Hayes wrote: "Captain James M. Craig, formerly sergeant of Company H, Twenty-third, came yesterday. He seemed by his dress and general appearance not to be a favorite of fortune. I recall him as a tall, fine-looking soldier — a brave and faithful officer. He was wounded at Cloyd Mountain, also twice at Sheridan's victory of Winchester after crossing the slough. He crossed (then a lieutenant of Company F) soon after I did. He describes the slough as fifty yards wide, and up to his shoulders, with a soft deep mud at the bottom. . . . Craig with a few joined me under the bank; the bank or hill up to the enemy's rifle pits was twenty to twenty-five feet high. We were there protected from the enemy's shot until enough joined us to rush up the hill. Not more than three hundred got over the slough."

[2] The horse, lightened of his rider, struggled out, and Hayes mounted him again. But he had been mortally wounded while in the slough and soon gave out.

[3] There is some doubt as to who this man was; it was an officer of the Thirty-sixth Ohio. Captain B. F. Stearns and Lieutenant Jacob Reasoner both claimed the distinction. A letter from the latter, written September 18, 1887, is so circumstantial in its description of the crossing and so manifestly conscientious in statement of details as to throw the weight of probability in his favor.

[4] Official Report of General Crook, *War Records*, vol. XLIII, part I, p. 362.

But some of the best men of the whole army, Colonel Comly declared, were in that line, and there was no "give-back" to it. "They never looked behind them." [1]

They met several checks in passing over the space to the enemy's works, being swept by a cross-fire from the battery in front and from the Star Fort in flank. A number of men of General Gordon's command, under cover of a stone fence on the right, poured in a most galling enfilading fire. The Thirty-sixth Ohio and the Fifth Virginia of Hayes's brigade drove them from cover in confusion, when the cavalry charged and captured them.[2] Whenever a body of the enemy had been dislodged by the infantry, the cavalry charged, capturing the fleeing soldiers. The gallantry of this attack on the flank of the enemy is vividly portrayed in a description written shortly after the battle by an officer of the Nineteenth Corps.[3] He says: —

To our right we heard a mighty battle yell which never ceased for ten minutes, telling us that Crook and his men were advancing. To meet this yell there rose from the farthest sweep of the isolated wood, where it rounded away toward the Rebel rear, the most continuous wail of musketry that I ever heard. It was not a volley nor a succession of volleys, but an uninterrupted explosion without a single break or tremor. As I listened to it I despaired of the success of the attack, for it did not seem to me possible that any troops could endure such a fire. The captain of our right company, who was so placed that he could see the advance, afterward described it as magnificent in its steadiness; the division which accomplished it moving across the open fields in a single line without visible supports, the ranks kept well dressed in spite of the stream of dead and wounded which dropped in the rear, the pace being the ordinary quickstep and the men firing at will, but coolly and rarely. At this moment the whole army assumed the offensive.

[1] Account by Colonel James M. Comly, in Cincinnati *Commercial*.

[2] This wall according to the account of General Hastings, cited above, was on the famous historical Hackwood Farm, where General Braddock camped in 1755 before taking up his fatal march for Fort Duquesne, accompanied by young George Washington. Gordon's soldiers, behind the stone wall and stationed in a large stone building and an ancient log house, poured into the ranks of Hayes's command such a galling fire as to call for a determined effort to dislodge them. In accomplishing this the Thirty-sixth Ohio especially lost many men.

[3] Captain J. W. DeForest, *Harper's Magazine*, vol. 30. In referring to this account in a letter to Sardis Birchard, Hayes said: "When you read on the 199th page the writer's account of our battle yell as we advanced, and of the Rebel musketry which met it, you will remember that I led the advance brigade of the advance division, and that perhaps the happiest moment of my life was then, when I saw that our line did n't break and that the enemy's did."

At the critical period of this forward movement General Crook was riding up and down the line, as was his wont in battle, silent, but by his presence inspiring the men with heroism. It was then that Colonel Duval fell, wounded, and was succeeded in command of the Second Division by Hayes, who was everywhere exposing himself with reckless daring. As he was the first over the slough, so he had been in advance of the line half the time since. His adjutant-general — Captain Russell Hastings — had been severely wounded, men were dropping all around him; but he rode through it all as though he bore a charmed life.[1]

Other brave men were on that line, a short distance from the enemy's works, lying under the terrific cross-fire, and waiting for a demonstration from the left which should enable them to charge the works. They waited wearily, minutes seeming hours, but the expected help did not come. Something must be done, as the concentrated fire was cutting up the charging column. Selecting some Saxony rifles in the Twenty-third Ohio (pieces of seventy-one calibre, with a range of twelve hundred yards), Comly ordered Lieutenant McBride to creep forward to a little knoll and kill the enemy's artillery horses, which were in plain sight. They crept up like Indians, keeping under cover as much as possible. At the first shot a horse dropped. Almost immediately another was killed. A panic seized the artillerists and they began to limber up. The infantry took the alarm and a few men ran from the entrenchments. Then the whole Union line rose, and with a tremendous yell rushed for the breastworks. The Confederates of Gordon's and Breckinridge's divisions, without stopping to fire another shot, rushed out pell-mell, and were captured

[1] Cincinnati *Commercial.* — "Several years after the close of the war I met General Gordon, who commanded the Confederate left on that afternoon. He pointed with pride to a scar on his cheek, and said, 'I am indebted to Hayes's boys for this beauty spot.' He further said: 'When we first saw you coming over the hills, we rather laughed the movement to scorn, knowing of this morass on our left; but when on you came, plunging into the morass as though it was mere pastime, we began to wonder of what metal such men were made. One of my staff remarked "they must be devils," and as you rose to the brink of the hill away went my boys as though the devil was after them. After that charge my men always spoke of your corps as Crook's devils.' He further said: 'At Fisher's Hill, three days afterwards, when Crook played the same trick on us, turning our left, our men, as soon as they saw you charging down the mountain-side, passed the word along the line, "Here come Crook's devils again, we had better be getting out of this," and away they went.'" (Russell Hastings, MS. Memoirs.)

by that terrible cavalry which had been hanging like a cloud on the Union flank waiting its opportunity. Eight battle-flags were captured, and a large number of prisoners, probably two thirds of the whole number captured in the battle. The "greybacks" soon looked as numerous as the "blue coats." The enemy's artillery in the Star Fort was obliged to stop firing and fall back, and the battle was at an end. About this time the Sixth Corps emerged from the woods in the rear, and started forward in magnificent style, lines all well dressed, and everything in striking contrast with the shattered appearance of the Eighth Corps.[1] Crook, triumphant, and accompanied by the gratified Sheridan, moved forward through Winchester (his command the first to enter the town), and as far as Milltown, two miles south on the Strasburg Pike, where his army went into camp as the shades of night were gathering, having thus passed from the extreme right of the infantry line to a point beyond the extreme left.[2] The Sixth and Nineteenth Corps did not pass through Winchester until the following day.

And thus ended the battle of Opequon, which sent Early "whirling through Winchester," which finally redeemed the lower Shenandoah Valley from Confederate control, and relieved Maryland and Pennsylvania from all apprehension of further incursion. The victory, despite its cost in loyal blood, filled the north with exultant jubilation and added to the increasing despondency of the South. Grant ordered a salute of one hundred guns. Lincoln sent a congratulatory dispatch. Sheridan's policy of caution was vindicated. He was once more the popular hero, to grow in favor till Appomattox. His promotion immediately followed, while he pressed on up the Valley to make Early's disaster complete.

[1] Comly's MS. Diary.
[2] Official Report of Colonel R. B. Hayes of the movements of the Second Division. *War Records,* vol. XLIII, part I, p. 402.

CHAPTER XVI

FISHER'S HILL AND CEDAR CREEK

THE next day the victorious army advanced to the neighborhood of Strasburg. Early had occupied a very strong position two miles to the south on Fisher's Hill, a precipitous bluff, along the front of which runs a brawling stream, called Tumbling Run. His right was perfectly protected by the north fork of the Shenandoah, just beyond which the Massanutten Range sprang abrupt. The Valley here is at its narrowest, about three and a half miles wide. Along the bluff formidable earthworks had been constructed, when Early retreated up the Valley in August. These were now strengthened, especially in the more open country on the Confederate left beyond the Valley Pike to the base of the steep, cedar-covered North Mountain.

A brief survey of the position satisfied Sheridan that a direct assault would involve very serious losses besides being of doubtful success. He decided to repeat the manœuvre which had won the day before, namely, to turn Early's left by sending the gallant Crook and his hardy veterans to scale North Mountain and pass along its side through the dense cedar growth. At a council of officers that afternoon Sheridan outlined his plan. Crook approved, but General Wright doubted its practicability, in which he was supported by Emory. Wright wished to assault the works in front, and was confident he could carry them. As for the flanking movement, "a goat could not climb over that mountain, much less armed men." [1] Crook quietly expressed his ability to execute the manœuvre and said: "If the Sixth and Nineteenth Corps will advance from the front when they hear my guns, the battle can be won with very little loss of life." The discussion grew warm, when Sheridan adjourned the council

---

[1] This was Early's opinion, too. General Gordon, so Hayes records later in life, suggested to Early that his position was not safe, that his left flank had been turned once and might be again. But Early, or some one for him, replied, "Nothing but a crow could go up there."

to meet at his quarters in the evening. At the evening meeting Colonels Thoburn and Hayes, Crook's division commanders, were present and joined in the support of General Sheridan's plan. As to the practicability, Hayes said the men of his division had been climbing the mountains of West Virginia for three years and could do almost any feat.[1] He was confident he could take his division along the mountain-side to the desired point with perfect success. The discussion was animated, but Sheridan decided on the flanking movement.

Success depended on complete secrecy, as Sheridan's army lay in full view of the Confederate signal station on the Massanutten Mountain. To escape observation, in the night of September 20 Crook's command was moved into heavy timber north of Cedar Creek, where it lay concealed all the next day, Wednesday. Early continued industriously strengthening his works while Sheridan spent the day in gradually moving his army to the right, driving the Confederates from two or three advantageous points that they still held north of Tumbling Run. Wednesday night Crook's troops were brought across Cedar Creek and hidden in a wood behind Huff's Hill, where they lay until daylight. Then, protected by ravines and woods, they were marched beyond the right of the Sixth Corps, which was directly in front of Early and a little to the right of his centre. Then Ricketts's division was pushed out so as to confront the enemy's left, where with Averell's cavalry it would be in position to swing round and join Crook when the critical moment came.

While this movement of Ricketts absorbed the enemy's attention and he was expecting the attack from that quarter, Crook passed unobserved into the heavy forest of the mountain-side. Hayes's division was in the van, and Crook and Hayes rode together at the head of the column. Presently the way became so steep and difficult that officers had to dismount and proceed on foot. Hayes alone, who was riding a team horse he had picked up on the way from Winchester, which could go anywhere a man could, remained on his horse. It was hard climbing, but the men pressed eagerly forward. By half-past three they had passed

---

[1] An old fifer in the Thirteenth West Virginia Regiment used to say, "I was born on the mountain-side, have always stood sidewise with one foot higher than t'other ever since I can remember." (Russell Hastings, MS. Memoirs.)

beyond the enemy's left, when they began to descend the mountain by the left flank. As they reached the edge of the timber the enemy discovered them and opened with their batteries, but it was too late. Crook's men threw off knapsacks, rations, some of them coats even, and sprang to the charge with the same wild yell which had startled Gordon's men at Opequon three days before. All before them gave way in panic and ran like sheep in utter confusion. Ricketts swung in on their left about a mile from the base of the mountain and Wright's and Emory's corps rushed to the assault in front across Tumbling Run, up the frowning bluff and over the breastworks, all with such daring and impetuosity that almost before the Confederates could realize what had happened their rout was complete [1] and they were once more madly whirling up the Valley before Sheridan's exultant army. Sheridan with the main army followed rapidly after the fleeing Rebels for fifteen miles that night. Crook's corps, weary with its strenuous all-day exertion, culminating in its furious charge, returned to the point where impedimenta had been divested and camped for the night. The next three days it spent

---

[1] "The rout was utter and complete. Nothing but inability to run any longer prevented us from capturing the enemy's train. We were in sight of it when it moved out. Our cavalry on this occasion, being in command of Averell, did as much of nothing as it was possible to do; with Sheridan's cavalry, we should have captured the enemy's wagon train, and the greater part of his force. As it was, the success was beyond that of any battle I have been in. Piece after piece of artillery was abandoned as we got in rear; it could not be brought off. Some of the officers (brave fellows) stood at their guns, serving them with their own hands, until dragged off by our men. One of these, a Virginian, and a splendid fellow, told me that some of his men had insisted, early in the day, that there were men moving among the thickets of cedar on the mountain, and that they bothered him about it so, that he finally sent a shell up there to satisfy them, but that nothing came of it. He was told that the shell went through the color guard of one of our regiments, knocking the Enfield out of the hands of one of the corporals of the guard. 'The devil it did! Well, I thought it was a mistake. We supposed a goat could n't climb up that mountain, yet we had a picket up there, and expected to hear from it, if any disturbance occurred. The men were so uneasy that I kept watching; could n't see a sign of anything; I was just turning away, when suddenly it seemed as if that mountain just belched out Yankees at us. There was n't a spot that was not covered by blue coats and bayonets. I sprang to the gun, there, myself, and began firing as fast as it could be loaded; but it was no use. By the time I would get your range and be ready to fire, you would be a hundred yards below, and running like devils for our works!' This officer was seized and dragged from his gun as he was in the very act of discharging it into the masses of our men who were piling all around him. He was well cared for by our men who admired his pluck." (Comly's MS. Diary.)

with the rest of the army in pursuing the demoralized Confederates up the Valley. There were frequent small engagements with the Rebel rear guard which made desperate efforts to save Early's train.[1] Harrisonburg was reached Sunday and Crook's army went into camp for a much enjoyed respite of several days.[2] Here the next day Hayes wrote his uncle of the eventful week's experience: —

You have heard enough about our great victories at Winchester and Fisher's Hill. I will say only a word. No man can see or know what passes on all parts of a battlefield. Each one describes the doings of the corps, division, or what-not, that he is with. Now, all the correspondents are with the Sixth and Nineteenth Corps and the cavalry command. General Crook has nobody to write him or his command up. They are, of course, lost sight of.[3]

[1] "And succeeded pretty well, although a number of wagons were burnt. Every little while we saw fresh fires, as parts of the train would be abandoned and sacrificed, until we thought they could not have much left." (Comly, *ut supra*.)

[2] "It is understood that the infantry will not pass this point, although the cavalry is to go as far as Staunton. The men are all jolly; laughing and gossiping and telling stories and reading the illustrated papers, which follow us closer than our own trains, except the ones that carry our ammunition. Sheridan keeps them on time. I noticed a group of our men reading a very affecting account from one of the pictorials (accompanied by an illustration) of a dog standing sentinel over a dead Confederate soldier, when one of the listeners spoke up eagerly, 'Who got that dog?' Every soldier who can get one, has a pet dog. Some of them have lambs or sheep which they take a deal of trouble in leading on the march. One had a rooster which he carried. They would rush in a body after a rabbit or a coon, no matter what was going on. They are all crazy after children, petting them and 'hovering' them as tenderly as mothers." (Comly, *ut supra*, September 26.)

[3] Comly, in his diary, September 21, speaks in a similar strain of the partial reports of the correspondents: "The peculiarity of the correspondent is, that he seems to think all the fighting is done by the corps he happens to be with. This curious hallucination is said to be produced by the bread and butter at corps headquarters. The difficulty with us is, that General Crook will not keep any of this bread and butter on hand; or, if he does, it is not eaten by correspondents. The other corps are mostly Eastern troops, while ours are Western. And, if our own Cincinnati papers will not send correspondents with us, it is too much to expect of Eastern papers to do so. The consequence is, that it is only when the official dispatches are published that we are heard of; by that time the Eastern papers have decided the question, and the public are convinced that the fighting has all been done by the Eastern troops. Our Western papers, having no correspondents of their own with us, copy the accounts of the Eastern press, and our friends at home have the veracious intelligence that the Sixth and Nineteenth Corps have won a glorious victory, *General Crook's command being in reserve!* So, in the account of this battle, which we read to-day in the Baltimore *American*, we are placed in reserve, supporting the Nineteenth Corps through the

At Winchester at noon the Sixth and Nineteenth Corps had been worsted. In the afternoon General Crook (who is the brains of the whole thing) with his command turned the Rebel left and gained the victory. The cavalry saved it from being lost after it was gained. My brigade led the attack on the Rebel left, but all parts of Crook's command did their duty. The Sixth Corps fought well; the Nineteenth failed somewhat, and the cavalry was splendid and efficient throughout. This is my say-so. My division entered the fight on the extreme right of the infantry — Merritt's splendid cavalry on our right and Averell still further on our right. We ended the fight on the extreme left. The Rebels retreated from our right to our left, so that we went in at the rear and came out at the front — my flag being the first into and through Winchester. My division commander was wounded late in the fight, and I commanded the division from that time. It is the Second — General Crook's old division.

At Fisher's Hill the turning of the Rebel left was planned and executed by General Crook against the opinions of the other corps generals. My division led again. General Sheridan is a whole-souled, brave man (like Dr. Webb), and believes in Crook, his old class- and room-mate at West Point. Intellectually, he is not General Crook's equal, so that, as I said, General Crook is the brains of this army.

The completeness of our victories can't be exaggerated. If Averell had been up to his duty at Fisher's Hill, Mr. Early and all the rest would have fallen into our hands. As it is, we have, I think, from the two battles five thousand Rebel prisoners unhurt, three thousand wounded, five hundred killed, twenty-five pieces of artillery, etc., etc. In the Fisher's Hill battle the Sheridan cavalry [Torbert's] was over the mountains going around to the rear. This, as it turned out, was unfortunate. If they had been with us instead of Averell there would have been nothing left of Early. General Averell is relieved. I lost one orderly; my adjutant-general — Captain Hastings — and field officers in all regiments wounded.

The next day Hayes wrote his uncle again: —

ONE HUNDRED MILES SOUTH OF THE POTOMAC,
September 27, 1864.

Our work seems to be done for the present. The cavalry and small scouting parties are after the scattered and broken army. It looks as if we should after [a] while return towards the Potomac. We are resting in the magnificent Valley of Virginia. A most happy campaign it has been. Our chance to act has been good and it has been well improved.

action; when the truth is, we had the extreme right — the post of honor — the place where the hardest fighting was done, and the most of the enemy killed and wounded — the place where three fourths of all the prisoners were captured, and the place where the enemy was first driven from his line of works, forcing the whole line to fall back in confusion, or to be surrounded."

My immediate command is one of the very finest and has done all one could desire. There are five or six brigadier-generals and one or two major-generals, sucking their thumbs in offices at Harper's Ferry and elsewhere, who would like to get my command, — one came out here yesterday to ask for it, — but General Crook tells them he has all the commanders he wants and sends them back. There is not a general officer in General Crook's army and has not been in this campaign.

Things look well in all directions. Lincoln must be reëlected easily, it seems to me. Rebel prisoners — the common soldiers — all talk one way. "Tired of this rich man's war — determined to quit if it lasts beyond this campaign."

While the army was lying at Harrisonburg, Lieutenant Meigs, Sheridan's engineer officer, was perfidiously killed, within the Federal lines and less than three miles from camp, by men dressed as Union soldiers. Sheridan, who was much attached to the brilliant young officer, regarding the murder as a culminating atrocity of the guerrilla warfare continually waged upon his men on detached service by the inhabitants of the Valley, ordered the burning of all the houses within an area of five miles. Hayes, even at the time when indignation was hot at guerrilla enormities, did not believe in the righteousness of this act (as an entry in the diary shows), which involved the cruel suffering of innocent people. Probably even the warmest admirer of the great commander would find it hard now to justify the act.[1] Sheridan in retiring down the Valley, which he began to do October 6, was thoroughly executing Grant's order to destroy all provisions and forage so that "a crow in flying from Staunton to Winchester must carry his rations."[2] Hayes's old regiment had a share in this arduous and distressing work of desolation, which was not at all to the taste of Colonel Comly.[3] Early followed Sheridan

---

[1] The severity of the order was mitigated in its execution. "When a few houses in the immediate neighborhood of the scene of the murder had been burned Custer was directed to cease his desolating work." (Sheridan's *Memoirs*, vol. II, p. 52.)

[2] "Great droves of cattle and sheep are going past us north. Everything eatable is taken or destroyed. No more supplies to Rebels from this Valley. No more invasions in great force by this route will be possible." (Hayes to Mrs. Hayes, from Harrisonburg, Virginia, October 2, 1864.)

[3] "*Saturday, October 8.* — The Twenty-third sent across the Shenandoah to rake in cattle and stock, and burn all supplies capable of furnishing aid and comfort to the armies of the enemy — to burn mills, destroy barns, having supplies in them, etc. To rejoin command at Strasburg. I demanded written orders — not liking to burn things. Had a very hard march across mountains and

closely, his cavalry, which had been reënforced and placed under the command of the energetic but boastful General Rosser, constantly harassing the Union rear. Wearying of this, Sheridan halted for a day at Fisher's Hill and Strasburg and ordered Torbert and Custer to go out and whip Rosser or be whipped by him. The Union generals preferred the former alternative and they proceeded to secure their choice in most brilliant style under the eyes of the commanding general and his staff.[1] Two days later Sheridan established himself on high ground north of Cedar Creek, and Early occupied his old position at Fisher's Hill. The Sixth Corps was started toward Manassas to be sent to Petersburg, but, on indication of Early's renewed confidence, it was called back and took position to the right and a little in the rear

valleys, most of the way without any road; forded the Shenandoah four times — waist-deep and very cold. Brought in over fifteen hundred nice cattle; lost over two hundred crossing the river; also twelve or fifteen horses. Routed several guerrilla camps. Killed a Captain Brown. We had several narrow escapes, my regiment being entirely alone on that side of the river, and with all those cattle to guard and bring safe to camp. The people were much enraged against us, and there were many pitiful scenes that fairly broke my heart, but 'orders is orders,' as Colonel Scammon's orderly used to say. We executed the order as carefully and tenderly as possible, burning and destroying only what we were imperatively ordered to do. Of course, it is the right thing to destroy the enemy's supplies in this Valley, but I hate none the less to have such a duty to perform. It does not seem real soldierly work. We ought to enlist a force of damned scoundrels for such work. Once during the day, the enemy got between us and our army, in strong force, and there was quite a little battle in front of us. (Rosser's division of cavalry.) It looked bilious for us with all those cattle. I struck back into the mountains at as rapid a pace as possible, with our menagerie, and made a large circumbendibus over toward Massanutten Mountain. We found a ford and got safely into camp. Sheridan sent word to us, thanking us, and we were ordered into camp near his headquarters, Hayes, with the rest of the brigade being at the rear, guarding against Rosser's cavalry." (Comly's MS. Diary.)

[1] "*Monday, October 10.* — Custer licked Rosser beautifully. Captured eleven pieces of artillery and three hundred-fifty prisoners, and destroyed his ambulances and wagon train. The Richmond papers said the *horsemen* in the Valley were to be called out, and *cavalry* sent in their places; so Rosser was sent. Yesterday our cavalry run him out from a little beyond Strasburg to a little place called Edenburg, capturing and destroying all his artillery (one piece escaped), train, and ambulances, and breaking up his command. Send us more cavalry, gentlemen. Sheridan, who has a boisterous sort of humor, said yesterday, when he rode out, that he was 'going to see this new saviour of the Valley'; and when he came back past our camp, he was laughing and swearing, and said: 'By —— Custer's got everything he had on wheels. The last we saw of him, he was going over Rude's Hill with only one piece of artillery left, and that was going so fast that only one wheel touched the ground!'" (Comly, *ut supra*.)

of the Nineteenth Corps. The latter occupied the centre while
Crook's command held the extreme left, his First Division under
Colonel Thoburn holding a hill in the angle formed by the junction of Cedar Creek with the Shenandoah, and his Second Division under Hayes lying a short distance behind the First, connecting closely with the Nineteenth Corps. Over on the extreme
right, between the Sixth Corps and North Mountain, Custer's
cavalry was posted, strongly protecting that flank. Powell was
at Front Royal with his cavalry guarding against a Rebel advance by way of the Luray Valley, and the fords of the Shenandoah were picketed.[1] Sheridan's forces were busy at Fisher's
Hill; both armies were making reconnaissances in force with
varying fortunes. October 15, Hayes wrote Sardis Birchard: —

> We are resting. Early, reënforced, came up a few days ago, evidently
> thinking a good part of our army had gone to Grant. Finding his mis-
> take, he moved back to his old fortifications on Fisher's [Hill], and is
> now there digging and chopping like mad. What we are to do about it,
> I can't tell. It must be serious business for the Rebels to feed an army
> there now.

It was a serious business to feed the army after the havoc
wrought by Sheridan. Early was conscious that he could not long
maintain himself so far from his base. Through reënforcement
his army was again about as strong as before the recent disasters.
Lee had written him: "The enemy must be defeated. I rely on
you to do it." He was eager to retrieve his fallen fortunes. Moreover, he was laboring under the illusory notion that a large
part of Sheridan's army had been detached and was on its way
to Grant. Sheridan did not believe Early would be so rash as to
bring on a general engagement. There was a difference of opinion
between him and Grant as to what should be the future policy of
his army. It was important to discuss the subject with Stanton
and Halleck, and October 15 Sheridan started for Washington
with cavalry escort through Manassas Gap to Rectortown and
then with two of his staff by rail, reaching his destination the
morning of the 17th. General Wright, of the Sixth Corps, was
by virtue of seniority left in command. He was made somewhat

---

[1] Crook had recognized the weakness of the protection of the fords, and had
asked for a cavalry force there. This had been ordered sent, but for some reason
seems not to have arrived by the night of the 18th.

solicitous by a dispatch caught from the Rebel signal station which implied that Longstreet was on his way to join Early. The dispatch had overtaken Sheridan at Front Royal, and while he thought it likely to be a ruse (as in fact it proved to be), he sent Torbert's cavalry — which he had brought with him to begin a raid toward Charlottesville — back to Wright, and he himself went on his way, haunted, despite his judgment, with apprehension lest the intercepted dispatch might be true.

Early, of course, knew nothing of Sheridan's absence. But the consideration noted above made him eager to attack, and he and his able lieutenants were seeking to devise a plan which might have promise of success. Finally, Tuesday, October 18, Early decided to adopt the tactics which had been used against himself by Sheridan at Winchester and Fisher's Hill with so disastrous results. This plan[1] was to send Gordon with a heavy force, by a difficult and circuitous route, which involved fording the Shenandoah twice and passing around the Massanutten Mountain by a rugged footpath, to turn the Union left while Rosser engaged the Union right and the rest of Early's force attacked directly in front. The plan was well conceived and brilliantly executed. Gordon started at eight o'clock that night and reached his position at early dawn without incident. The Union camp had gone to rest that night in perfect security, a reconnaissance of the afternoon having brought back reassuring news, confirmation of which General Wright proposed to obtain by another reconnaissance under General Grover from the right early the next morning. But before dawn broke the Rebels, without sending out skirmishers, advanced, in full battle line, capturing or driving in the Union pickets and falling suddenly in front and flank on Crook's First Division.

The surprise was complete, and the division, not more than fifteen hundred strong, fell back in considerable disorder [2] to the

---

[1] The plan was suggested by General Gordon and Captain Hotchkiss, topographical engineers, who from Three Top Mountain had made a careful study of the Federal lines and the approaches thereto.

[2] "Is it any wonder that this small division of infantry (First Division of Crook's command) and the brigade of the Nineteenth Corps still further to the rear were swept backward pell-mell by the onset of Early's whole army except one division — an onset which drove not only the Nineteenth Corps, but the irreproachable Sixth about four miles to the rear after they had full notice by

Second Division (likewise with about fifteen hundred men present), which had been quickly roused and got in line by Hayes. In this movement Crook's artillery, under the brave and alert Captain du Pont, did admirable work in checking the Rebel advance and got off with the loss of seven guns. "When the enemy's line had reached within easy range of the Second Division" — to quote an account written shortly after the battle by Colonel Comly and submitted for correction to Crook and Hayes — "an order came from General Wright to move up by the right flank and close upon the Nineteenth Corps whose left was a short distance to Hayes's right. About the same time the provisional brigade [Kitchings's] on the left — which had come up as train guard, and did not belong anywhere in particular — commenced falling back. (They did some good fighting during the day.) And fugitives from the First Division and a brigade of the Nineteenth Corps, which had been hurried into the woods on our right when the fight opened, came pouring back through the interval between Hayes's division and the Nineteenth Corps. General Wright's order, in the noise, was misunderstood by a part of the line and it commenced falling back slowly. As soon as it was understood the line halted in a belt of woods near the pike."

When Hayes saw his men wavering he rode down the line in front, imploring them to stand their ground. The ground was steep, his horse on a gallop; suddenly, out of the bank of fog obscuring the whole field, came a blaze of musketry and Hayes's horse fell pierced by twenty balls. Hayes himself was unscathed, but from the speed of his horse he was thrown violently to the ground where for a brief space he lay stunned. He was badly bruised and one ankle, which had caught fast in the stirrup, received a severe and painful wrench. When he recovered full consciousness the Rebel line was close upon him, but he managed to

the alleged 'disgraceful flight' of the Eighth Corps and plenty of time to form? It 'bangs Banaker' to understand why it is that historians of regiments, brigades, even army corps, find it so disgraceful in one poor little division of infantry, a mile or more from support, and with little warning, to fall back, somewhat nimbly, from an attack which sent two stately corps and more, four miles to the rear, after the fullest possible notice." (Letter of General James M. Comly to Major John M. Gould, dated "Toledo, Ohio, January 8, 1884.") This letter was written to correct erroneous statements as to the action of Crook's command.

regain his feet and escaped unhit to his men in the woods, where he mounted his orderly's horse.[1] Presently the whole line was

[1] Some of his retreating men, who had seen him fall and not rise immediately, carried word to the rear that Hayes had been killed. In an informal address before the Loyal Legion at Cincinnati, March 6, 1889, Mr. Hayes in recounting incidents of this battle said: —

"It happened that my family was better known than other families were in the command to which I belonged, as my wife had been frequently with us in camp. About that time a very interesting circumstance had occurred in my family, at home, in Ohio. A child had been born. We had been having some victories that were notable, at the battle of Winchester and Fisher's Hill, and then the news came of this incident at my home. I let it be known that I had a new boy at home and that I should call him George Crook, after our corps commander. . . . At night, the reporters, who had got together at the telegraph headquarters, were sending off accounts of the battle. The colonel commanding the First Division of Crook's corps had been killed; the colonel commanding the Second Division, which was myself, had been killed, and so on, making out a large list. These reporters liked a good butcher's bill, you know. A gentleman, a captain of my command, who had seen me on horseback all of the latter part of that battle, said to them: 'Why, you are not sending off word that Colonel Hayes is dead?' 'Oh, yes, it has gone off long ago; he was killed in the morning. We have seen men who saw him killed.' 'Well,' said he, 'that is not so; I saw him until dark.' — You know Sheridan had carried out his promise to those stragglers; you remember his promise to them? As he met them he said, Buchanan Read has it, 'a terrible oath.' Do you remember what that terrible oath was? He said: 'Boys, turn back; face the other way. I am going to sleep in that camp to-night or in hell.' Those were the words with which Sheridan turned them back. —

"Well, that captain was a man of sense, a good man to have about when anything was going on. He sat right down at the instrument and telegraphed to my wife, at Chillicothe, Ohio. 'The report that your husband was killed this morning is untrue. He was wounded, not dangerously, and is safe.' The next morning, or the next but one after the battle, the carrier took the daily paper to my wife as usual. . . . Her uncle saw the paper coming, and hurried into the room, and before she could take it up, he grabbed it and quietly put it to one side, a little disturbed. He had heard what was in it. . . . Just at that moment it so happened that the telegraph boy came with the dispatch from the captain of my command, giving the message that I have recited. When that was read, the relief came.

"Rather an interesting incident grew out of the sending of that dispatch. As soon as I learned of it, I inquired for the name that was signed to the dispatch. It was given to me, and I at once inquired for persons of that name. I found a reporter of the New York *Herald* of that name. 'Did you send that dispatch?' I asked him, for I desired to thank him for this good act. 'No,' said he; 'I should have been very glad to have done it, but I did not send it.' I found four persons of the same name. The first name was not known, but I found four of the same surname. Each one resolutely denied sending it, and for thirteen years I continued to inquire, telling about it in circles, hoping to find that man, and one time about thirteen years afterward, when I was telling about it in the White House to some gentlemen from West Virginia, one of them said: 'Why, I know who that man is; it is so-and-so, of our village.' It turned out to be a quiet man

engaged and, taken front and flank, fell steadily back. An obstinate and successful stand was made by Crook's command to save the headquarters trains of Sheridan and Crook where Colonel Thoburn, the First Division commander, and other brave officers were killed.

"From this point" — to resume Colonel Comly's narrative — "the whole of Crook's line fell slowly back, fighting stubbornly, finding themselves after this on the left of the Sixth which had seemingly been thrown to the left, via the rear of the Nineteenth as the train moved out." The Union lines fell back some three or four miles through Middletown, where they made a stand and constructed hasty barricades of rails, whereupon many of the soldiers who had had no breakfast lighted fires and brewed coffee. The Rebels were in full possession of the Union camps which men and officers lingered behind to plunder. Early was seeking to re-form his lines for another advance.

Meanwhile the greatest reënforcement possible to the Union army was hurriedly approaching from Winchester — a single man, to be sure, but better than a legion, General Sheridan. He had left Washington by special train Monday noon after six hours in the city, the uncertainty of the situation he had left at Cedar Creek giving him no respite from anxiety; had spent that night at Martinsburg, and had ridden to Winchester Tuesday. There reassuring word from Wright had sent him to bed with a light heart. Wednesday morning at daybreak a picket had wakened him with a report of firing. He knew of the reconnaissance to be made that morning by General Grover and he thought it came from that. Even a second report some time later that the firing still continued did not change his opinion as to its character. But he had breakfast hastened and about half-past eight set forth with his escort toward Cedar Creek, nearly twenty miles south. He had not gone far when his trained ear taught him that a general engagement was on and his men were falling back. He quickened his pace, and soon panic-stricken fugitives were met, telling dire tales of disaster as they fled by. Nearer the field the men were resting by the roadside brewing coffee. They cheered

who had not told it to me, and made no fuss about it, but at home had told it. So, thirteen years after the battle of Cedar Creek, I found the man who sent that dispatch, and I have been very fond of him ever since."

as he passed, and many of them, abandoning their coffee, fell in behind him and started back to their commands. It is all a familiar story but of undying interest — how everywhere the young commanding general's appearance revived the spirits of his men and infused in them fresh courage and confidence. Here is Comly's description of the arrival of Sheridan at Crook's command: —

Crook was lying a rod or two over to our left. Hayes and I were together with our commands. He was badly bruised by his fall when his horse was killed under him, and had several slight wounds besides. He was teasing me and grumbling because we did not advance, instead of waiting for the enemy.

Suddenly there is a dust in the rear, on the Winchester road, and almost before we are aware, a fiery-looking, impetuous, dashing young man in full major-general's uniform, and riding furiously a magnificent black horse, literally "flecked with foam," and no poetic license about it, reins up and springs off by General Crook's side.[1] There is a perfect

[1] Hayes, in the Loyal Legion address quoted in the last preceding note, said, speaking of Sheridan's account of the battle in his *Memoirs* : —

"He [Sheridan] says that passing up the pike, sometimes on one side, and sometimes on the other, coming to Cedar Creek, he struck first the division of Getty of the Sixth Corps; that he passed along that division a short distance, when there arose out of a hollow before him a line consisting entirely of officers of Crook's Army of West Virginia and of color-bearers. The army had been stampeded in the morning, but these people were not panic-stricken. They saluted him, but there was nothing now between the enemy and him and the fugitives but this division of Getty's. Said he, 'These officers seemed to rise right up from the ground.' This was twenty-four years afterward, but he recollects it perfectly well except names. Among them, however, he recollects seeing one, Colonel R. B. Hayes, since President of the United States, and drops the story there, leaving the impression that there were no men there — no privates, no army — simply some color-bearers and some officers. The fact is that in the hollow, just in the rear, was a line of men, a thousand or twelve hundred probably, and they had thrown up a little barricade and were lying close behind it. He came up and saw these officers and did not see the men, or seems not to have seen them; but I had no idea at the time that he did not see the private soldiers in that line. . . . We had then been, I suppose, an hour or an hour and a half in that position. We had learned that General Sheridan was in Winchester, and the moment he found out there was a battle on, and that disaster had befallen his men, we knew that he would come as rapidly as the horse could bear him to the scene of the trouble. We were confident of another thing — that we were strong enough, if any commander would take charge of our army, to completely overwhelm the army that had driven us in the morning. In the first place they had marched that night and were worn out, and we had slept well until they disturbed us early in the morning. We were comparatively rested, therefore, and when Sheridan came there was along the whole line a thrill of joy and satisfaction, for we knew that when he came victory was not far off.

"I do not, of course, mention this by way of criticism. It only shows that the

roar, and everybody recognized Sheridan. He talks with Crook a little while, cutting away at the tops of the weeds with his riding-whip. General Crook speaks half a dozen sentences that sound a great deal like the whip, and by that time some of the staff are up. They are sent flying in different directions. Sheridan and Crook lie down and seem to be talking, and all is quiet again, except the vicious shells of the different batteries and the roar of artillery along the line. After a while Colonel [James W.] Forsyth comes down in our front and shouts to the General: "The Nineteenth Corps is closed up, sir." Sheridan jumps up, gives one more cut with his whip, whirls himself around once, jumps on his horse, and starts up the line. Just as he starts he says to the men: "We are going to have a good thing on them now, boys!" It don't sound like Cicero or Daniel Webster, but it doubled the force at our end of the line.

And so he rode off, a long wave of yells rolling up to the right with him. We took our posts, the line moved forward — and the balance of the day is already history.

It was between three and four when Sheridan had reëstablished his line and was ready to attack. In the whirl of preparations for the aggressive movement, when the tension must have been the greatest, he had thought of the honor and glory of Crook's command on which the disaster of the morning had first fallen. "When I reached the Valley Pike," said Sheridan, "Crook had reorganized his men, and as I desired that they should take part in the fight, for they were the very same troops that had turned Early's flank at the Opequon and at Fisher's Hill, I ordered them to be pushed forward; and the alacrity and celerity with which they moved on Middletown demonstrated that their ill-fortune of the morning had not sprung from lack of

wisest and best and bravest of men cannot see all that occurs in a battle, and this has led me very often to regret to see the accounts that we sometimes see in print. We hear that such an organization behaved badly, from a person who perhaps knows nothing of the situation of that organization. Soldiers, it seems to me, should be careful to be very charitable toward their neighbors. It is so difficult to put ourselves in their places. Suppose you had been with that division where Colonel Thoburn was killed, which was surprised in the morning — would you have done better? And so with three fourths — I don't know but nine tenths — of the unpleasant controversies that we see in the magazines and newspapers between soldiers. The practical lesson that I would draw from all this loose talk that I have been giving you, is that battles cannot be known in their entirety, from beginning to end, from one end of a long line to another, by any one man. No one is authorized to say that in some distant part of the field there was bad behavior or inexcusable behavior. There may have been disaster, but if I had been there with my favorite troops the same disaster would perhaps have occurred."

valor." [1] "At one of the pauses in this forward movement," by which Early's victorious army of the morning was utterly routed and driven in wild disorder from the Union camp, Comly writes, "our command was delayed at a very high rail fence (I can hardly believe such a fence was left, but it was), Crook was on his horse and had passed the fence when Hayes climbed up, and by holding to one of the stakes and standing on the rider was more elevated than Crook, and could use his glass more effectively. He was able thus to give Crook some important information, which I did not hear. But the result was that Hayes mounted his horse and dashed to the front at a headlong gallop, ahead of his infantry. I have learned since that he found Captain du Pont, who was moving down the pike, and under his immediate orders Captain du Pont passed through Middletown at a swinging trot, with his own battery, going to the front. Hayes, being very well mounted, and free to 'cut across,' got ahead out of sight, and on the eminence near where our camps had been, found General Sheridan, entirely alone, using his glass in the most excited manner. As soon as he saw Hayes he yelled at him: 'If I had a battery here we could knock h—ll out of their train and capture all their artillery!' Hayes answered: 'All right, General; I've got just what you want, coming as fast as it can!' He galloped back to Du Pont, who immediately started all his horses at a gallop, and came down the pike like a whirlwind. The first shell he fired lit in the very midst of a narrow place where the head of the enemy's retreating column had got gorged by attempting to pass too many abreast. General Hayes has described the scene to me vividly, and it is enough to make one get up and give three cheers all alone by himself to think of it as he describes it — shell after shell dropping in the thickest of the throng, drivers cutting traces and scampering out of it, teams, ammunition, caissons, and cannon abandoned and left literally *piled up* by the gorge."

No wonder that Early was in the depths of despair at this third overwhelming disaster, coming as it did when he had thought the day was his, and that he should report to Lee his willingness to lay down his command. And no wonder the North was wild with delight at disaster turned, by one man's splendid audacity and confidence in his men, into a glorious triumph.

[1] Sheridan's *Memoirs*, vol. II, p. 89.

Promotions were showered upon the redoubtable army. Sheridan, Crook, Hayes, Comly, and many others received well-merited recognition, in some cases long and unjustly withheld.

Two days after the battle Hayes wrote his uncle very briefly of the great victory and of his share in the battle: —

Early, reënforced by a division or two of Longstreet's corps, was foolish enough to attack us again on the 19th. It was a foggy morning, and the attack before daylight. One of General Crook's divisions (the First) was doubled up and our whole army flanked out of its position in confusion. But after daylight, order was gradually restored, and in the afternoon, General Sheridan attacked in turn — retook all we had lost and utterly ruined Early. It was done easily and with small loss. The fact is, all the *fight* is out of Early's men. They have been whipped so much that they can't keep a victory after it is gained. This is the last of fighting on this line, I am confident. My horse was killed under me instantly, dashing me on the ground violently; luckily, I was not much hurt. I was hit also fairly in the head with a spent ball. Narrow escape! The Rebs got my saddle, pistol, etc.

General Max Weber, a "veteran of European reputation," and one of the senior brigadiers in our service, came out yesterday with the intention of taking command of this division. General Crook sent him to Hagerstown, Maryland, to await orders!

In a letter to Mrs. Hayes, October 27, Hayes added about the battle: —

Some of the foolish fellows in the Sixth and Nineteenth Corps, feeling envious of our laurels in previous battles, have got the Eastern correspondents to represent the rout of Crook's corps as worse than theirs, etc., etc. There is not a word of truth in it. A sentence in General Sheridan's dispatch was no doubt *intended to correct this, in a quiet way :* "Crook's corps lost seven pieces of artillery, the Nineteenth, eleven, and the Sixth Corps, six." We were attacked before them and of course under more unfavorable circumstances and yet we lost no more. In fact *I* lost nothing. My division fell back, but brought *everything* we had — our *two cows*, tents, and everything. Of course we lost no artillery, but did save an abandoned piece of the Nineteenth Corps.

The battle of Cedar Creek was the end of the active campaigning in the Shenandoah Valley. There were many minor engagements with small detachments of the enemy, especially with Rosser's cavalry and Mosby's raiders, but Early had had enough and Lee had no further hopes of a victory in that quarter. The Union forces began to settle down to guard and routine duties.

CHAPTER XVII

END OF THE WAR — BREVET MAJOR-GENERAL

AFTER a few days Sheridan began to withdraw his army down the Valley, so as to be nearer his base of supplies, and to send the divisions that he no longer needed to Grant. Finally, after several changes of camp, Crook was established in winter quarters at Cumberland, Maryland, where Hayes named his camp Camp Hastings, in honor of his gallant adjutant-general, who was still hovering between life and death on his bed of pain at Winchester. October 11, the Ohio state election had occurred, when Hayes was elected to Congress in the Second District by a majority of 2455.[1]

The Ohio men in Sheridan's army had voted that day, and nearly unanimously for the Union ticket. November 9 came the general election, when with almost as great unanimity the Ohio men in the Valley had cast their ballots for Lincoln. In that election General Sheridan voted for the first and perhaps the last time, and Lieutenant William McKinley, Jr., voted for the first time. Hayes records in his diary that he "went with Generals Sheridan and Crook and Colonel Forsyth to the polls of Thirty-fourth Regiment. All vote for Lincoln. Sheridan's maiden vote." Later in life Hayes gave a fuller description of this event, saying: —

Sheridan had never voted, as he was an army officer, but he understood that, under the laws of Ohio, an Ohio soldier could vote. He learned that the polling-place was at my headquarters, so he came over the day before and talked about it. Next day he came with General Forsyth, of Toledo, and General Crook. I passed the word around that

[1] "I suppose you are pleased with the result of the election. Of course I am on *general* reasons. My *particular* gratification is much less than it would be, if I were not so much gratified by my good luck in winning 'golden opinions' in the more stirring scenes around me here. My share of *notoriety* here is nothing at all, and my *real* share of merit is also small enough, I know; but the consciousness that I am doing my part in these brilliant actions is far more gratifying than anything the election brings me." (Letter to Mrs. Hayes, October 21.)

Sheridan and Crook would vote about nine o'clock, and five thousand soldiers and two brass bands were on hand. The polling-place was a wagon, and three non-commissioned officers were judges and two young fellows clerks. I said I would vote first, so as to show Crook and Sheridan how it was done. I stepped up and said: "My name is Rutherford B. Hayes; I vote in Hamilton County, Ohio, in the Fifteenth Ward, Cincinnati." All this was put down. Then Sheridan stepped up. He was a little embarrassed under the gaze of all the men. He looked at the judge, the judge stared at him. "Your name, sir!" said the judge, with infinite dignity. Sheridan spoke up, "Philip H. Sheridan." "In what State do you vote?" asked the judge, impressively. "In Ohio." "In what county?" "Perry County." "In what ward or township, sir?" asked the judge, with solemnity. "My father lives in Reading Township," Sheridan replied, in an embarrassed way, for it was all new to him. Then General Crook stepped forward, pulling his mustache nervously, as was his habit. He gave his name, and said he lived in Dayton, Montgomery County. "What ward, sir?" asked the judge. "I don't know," General Crook said; "I always stopped at the Phillips House, though." "Oh, call it the First Ward," I said, and down it went that way. In speaking with Sheridan afterward, he said, with feeling: "This is my first vote: I don't ever expect to vote again, but I did want to vote for Old Abe."

Letters from Hayes to his uncle give interesting glimpses of his life during these closing months of that eventful year. Thus, from Camp Russell, near Kernstown, November 20, he wrote: —

We have had no battle for a month, and it is a week yesterday since I heard Rebel firing! This is wonderful. It is now six months since I could say the same. We do not feel settled here, but are getting very comfortable. It is *probable* that we shall have a rest sometime this winter, but not yet certain. The Sixth and Nineteenth Corps may be needed at Richmond or somewhere, but I think the Army of West Virginia will do guard duty merely. What an interest the country now feels in Sherman; it looks as if he might strike some vital blows.

A few days later came word of his promotion to brigadier-general. After the battle of Cedar Creek, great injustice had been done to Crook's command by the newspaper correspondents, who had represented the brave veterans, that had done such heroic and effective service at Opequon and Fisher's Hill, as becoming utterly demoralized by the morning rout. Sheridan commiserated with Crook at this misrepresentation, saying that no army had suffered more from that cause; and, commenting on the fact that its divisions had been led throughout the campaign

by colonels, he declared to Hayes that from the date of the battle
of Cedar Creek he should be a brigadier-general. If conspicuous
bravery and sound military judgment ever merited reward, they
did in the case of Hayes. When the announcement of the promotion reached the camp, Hayes was overwhelmed with congratulations, and General Crook presented him with shoulder straps
that he himself had worn, of which Hayes was justly proud. The
commission dated from October 19, the day of the battle of
Cedar Creek, and the reason for the promotion, as officially
announced, was "For gallant and meritorious services in the
battles of Opequon, Fisher's Hill, and Cedar Creek."

Writing of this and of other topics of current interest to his
uncle, December 12, Hayes said: —

The campaign in the Valley is closed. The Rebel infantry has all
been withdrawn; our own is leaving rapidly; it goes to Grant. The destination of Crook's command is not yet known. It probably waits news
from Sherman. I shall ask for leave of absence as soon as we get orders
to go into winter quarters, which may come any day.

I have been promoted to brigadier-general. The honor is no great
thing, it having been conferred, particularly at the first part of the war,
on all sorts of men for all sorts of reasons; but I am a good deal gratified,
nevertheless; it is made on the recommendation of General Crook, approved by Sheridan. This, at the close of such a bloody campaign, is
something; besides, I am pleased that it seems so well received by officers and men of the command. It has not yet been officially announced,
and will not be for perhaps a week or so.

I am very glad Governor Chase is Chief Justice. I had almost given
up his appointment. I received letters from Judge Swayne's friends
urging me to write in his behalf. I heard nothing of the kind from the
friends of Governor Chase. I suppose they felt safe. I replied to Mr.
Perry and others that I was for Chase.

It seems I have a place at West Point at my disposal. It is quite
encouraging to know that my district abounds in young Napoleons. I
hear of a new one almost every mail. The claim of one is based largely
on the fact that he has two brothers in the service. I happen to know
that they (both officers) have been so successful in finding soft places in
the rear, that neither of them, after more than three years' service, has
ever been in a battle.

I begin to feel very anxious about Sherman. His failure would be a
great calamity in itself. Besides, it would bring into favor the old-fogy,
anaconda style of warfare. Boldness and enterprise would be at a dis-
count. If he has made a mistake, it is in not moving with more celerity.

We ought to have another draft without delay; or rather, another call for troops, to be followed by a draft if volunteering failed to produce the required number within a reasonable period.

Not only had Hayes reason for gratification in his promotion, but he had cause for great pride in the valor, the confidence in him, and the efficient service of the men of his brigade, during the almost continuous marching and fighting of this memorable battle year. The severest service was during Hunter's raid from Staunton through Lexington to Lynchburg, and the retreat over the mountains to the Kanawha. The most disastrous service was in the defeat at Kernstown, near Winchester, July 24. The most conspicuous service was in the brilliant flank movements at Opequon and Fisher's Hill. The brigade during these campaigns marched over all of the ranges of the Alleghany Mountains four times, and crossed all the different ranges of the Blue Ridge twice. The diary of Colonel Comly shows that the Twenty-third Ohio Regiment — and this may be considered as showing the character of the service of the whole brigade — was engaged in battles, affairs, or skirmishes, of greater or less importance, on nineteen days in the month of June; that in July, August, September, and October it was under fire at some point in every five miles of distance in the Shenandoah Valley from Harper's Ferry to Harrisonburg. Twenty-six officers of the regiment were present for duty at the beginning of the campaign. Twenty-three out of the twenty-six were either killed or wounded. At the close of the year the three officers who escaped unhurt were commended to army headquarters for conspicuous bravery in action.

The number of men of the rank and file who were killed or wounded was in almost as great proportion as the casualties among the officers. The total number of men and officers enrolled in the regiment first and last during its service was 2230. Of this number 159 were killed or mortally wounded, and 408 others were wounded. The deaths from disease were 131, including 39 deaths in Confederate prisons. The Twenty-third Regiment was one of the 300 regiments out of the 2047 of the Union armies which sustained the heaviest losses in battle.[1] Its largest loss was at South Mountain and Antietam — nearly all that it had suffered till this last year of the war. And in this year the

---

[1] Colonel William F. Fox, *Regimental Losses in the Civil War*, p. 377.

Twenty-third met with no special disaster. Its losses simply indicate its severe and hazardous service throughout the long summer and autumn. Only seven Ohio regiments of infantry and two of cavalry lost more officers than the Twenty-third, and six regiments suffered an equal loss in killed and wounded. Only about one regiment out of fifteen of all that Ohio sent to the field saw as hard service as the Twenty-third. Hayes himself was wounded in battle six times and had four horses shot under him. Of all the Presidents from Washington to Wilson, twelve were officers in the regular or volunteer service. None of these besides Hayes was wounded except James Monroe, who as a young lieutenant was wounded at the battle of Trenton.

From Stephenson's Depot, December 20, Hayes wrote his uncle: —

We broke camp at Camp Russell yesterday at early daylight, and marched to this place on the railroad from Harper's Ferry towards Winchester. It rained, snowed, blew, and friz again; awful mud to march in and still worse to camp in; but to-day it is cold, and none of us got sick, so far as I know. Our First Division took cars to join Grant. It is said we shall follow in a day or two. This is not certain, but I shall not be surprised if it is true. I prefer not to go, and yet one feels that it is almost necessary to be present at the taking of Richmond. I am content, however, to go. I believe in pushing the enemy all winter, if possible. Now that we have a decided advantage is the time to crowd them. Things look as if that were to be the policy. I like the new call for troops. What good fortune we are having. If Sherman takes Savannah, and then moves north, this winter will be the severest by far that our Rebel friends have had.

As soon as winter quarters were comfortably established at Camp Hastings, Hayes obtained leave of absence for twenty days, which he spent in a happy and well-earned visit to his family and friends in Ohio. He was back at his post by February 10 and soon immersed in preparations for the spring campaign. Within a few days occurred the sensational capture of Generals Crook and Kelley, while quietly sleeping at their headquarters in Cumberland. At three o'clock in the morning of February 21, a company of Confederate soldiers under Lieutenant McNeill, of Early's army, quietly entered the town, overcame the headquarters guard, and went directly to the room of General Crook and, without disturbing anybody else in the house, ordered him to dress and accompany them. General Kelley and his adjutant were captured in the same way. "It was done so quietly," reported Major Robert P. Kennedy, "that others of us, who were sleeping in adjoining rooms to General Crook, were not disturbed." [1] The alarm was given in a few minutes by a watchman, and a party dispatched in pursuit, but the captors were too fleet. The unfortunate officers were lodged in Libby Prison.

When General Hayes realized the situation, he dispatched an officer, who was personally acquainted with Secretary Stanton, to Washington to explain the affair and ask that an effort be made to procure an early exchange for General Crook. The Secretary of War was in a furious mood, and declared that Crook and Kelley deserved to rot in prison for being captured. When the officer pressed his suit, he was threatened with arrest for being in Washington without permission. He was glad to take the first train leaving the Capital. Hayes then addressed General Grant a letter and dispatched it by special messenger to City Point. This appeal met with kind and sympathetic attention. An exchange for General Crook was procured. He was placed in command of a division of cavalry in Sheridan's corps and bore a conspicuous part in its brilliant movements. A letter from Hayes to his uncle (of March 24) contains additional particulars: —

Crook was all right with Grant, but Stanton was angry. Grant, however, rules matters where he really attempts it. Stanton refused to make an effort for a special and privileged exchange. Grant had it done. Crook stopped at headquarters of the army, and was invited by General

[1] *War Records*, vol. XLVI, p. 470. — Writing of this incident to Mrs. Hayes, February 21, General Hayes said: "You will be sorry to hear that the Rebs got General Crook this morning. A party of perhaps fifty or so dashed into town in the night — went direct to the hotels where General Crook (the Revere) and General Kelley (the St. Nicholas) quartered, took them prisoners and hurried off. All possible pains to recapture them have been taken, but I have no confidence of success. No special blame will attach to any one, I suppose. General Kelley commanded the post and had such guards posted as he deemed necessary — the same, I suppose, he has had for the last year or more. The picket post was not blamable, I think, at least not flagrantly so. It is a very mortifying thing to all of us. I have been in the habit of staying at my camp out a mile or so, and so was not looked for. The fact was I had received an order to get quarters in town, and was in town that night at General Duval's headquarters. But he having left, as everybody knew, a week before, his quarters were not searched; — a narrow chance for me. The only other officer taken was Captain Melvin, adjutant-general of General Kelley. The only possible danger to General Crook is the chance of his attempting to escape and failing."

Grant to stay and take an important active command before Richmond. Crook told him he wanted to be restored to the Department of West Virginia, if only for a day, to show the public that he was not in disfavor. It was accordingly so arranged. He returned here, took command, came out to my camp and had a happy meeting with the men. The next day he left to report to General Grant. It is supposed he will take the cavalry of the Army of the Potomac. It is probably better for his reputation that it is so.

Letters of Hayes in March and April give details of his last weeks of army service: —

Camp Hastings, March 16, 1865. — I have very little care or responsibility. My command is exclusively a fighting command. I have nothing to do with guards, provost, or routine duty connected with posts. Mine is the only movable column west of Winchester; if an enemy threatens any place, I am to send men there when ordered. My time is wholly occupied drilling and teaching tactics and the like. My brigade furnishes details for guard and provost when needed, but I am not bothered with them when on such duty. My regiments are all large; nearly four thousand men in the four, of whom twenty-five hundred are present at least. . . . We like Hancock very well. He behaved very handsomely with Crook's staff, and all of the troops and officers which were particularly favorites with Crook. We were all left in our old positions, although some pressure was brought against it.

I see gold is tumbling. If no mishap befalls our armies, the downward tendency will probably continue. Then *debtors* must look out. It will not be so easy to pay debts when greenbacks are worth eighty to ninety on the dollar. My four years are up about the first of June.[1]

New Creek, West Virginia, April 5, 1865. —The victories at Richmond are breaking up all our arrangements in this quarter. I am assigned to a new command, mostly of West Virginia troops,[2] including cavalry,

---

[1] Letter to Sardis Birchard.

[2] Hayes, the day after this letter was written, issued the following address to the men from whom his new command now separated him: —

HEAD-QUARTERS SECOND BRIGADE,
FIRST DIVISION, DEPARTMENT WEST VIRGINIA,
NEW CREEK, W. VA., April 6th, 1865.

To the Officers and Men of the First Brigade, First Division, Department West Virginia.

It is with very great regret that I have been compelled to part with the officers and men of the First Brigade. With many of you I have been associated in the service almost four years, with three of the Regiments of the Brigade more than two years, and with all the Regiments during the memorable campaign of 1864. The battle of Cloyd Mountain, the burning of New River Bridge, and the night march over Salt Pond Mountain under Gen'l Crook in May — the days and

infantry, and artillery, and am ordered to take my little army by mountain routes to some point west of Lynchburg, or to Lynchburg, and unite with somebody there. It is almost an impossible thing to do on account of want of supplies in a destitute country over awful roads. I hope it will be given up. My headquarters, while getting ready, are to be here. I hope the plan will be given up, and that I shall go to the Valley with the other troops. I am very busy getting ready. I go down to Cumberland to-night and will return in the morning.[1]

New Creek, West Virginia, April 8, 1865. — The glorious news is coming so fast that I hardly know how to think and feel about it. It is so just that Grant, who is by all odds our man of greatest merit, should get this victory. It is very gratifying, too, that Sheridan gets the lion's share of the glory of the active fighting. The clique of showy shams in the Army of the Potomac are represented by Warren. We do not know the facts, but I suspect Warren hung back, and after the Potomac fashion, did n't take hold with zeal when he found Sheridan was to command. So he was sent to the rear! General Crook wrote me the day before the battle that the *men* were in superb condition and eager for the fray, but that some of the *generals* were half whipped already. No doubt he meant Warren. Crook commanded the advance of Sheridan's attack. No doubt his strategy had much to do with it.

Personally, matters are probably as well as they could be, considering that "we are in the hands," as Joe says, "of the Yankees." The fall of Richmond came the day before we all left Camp Hastings. We had a glorious time; all the men gathered, all the bands, and Chaplain Collier

nights of marching, fighting, and starving on the Lynchburg Raid in June, — the defeat at Winchester and the retreat on the 24th and 25th of July — the skirmishing, marching, and countermarching in the Shenandoah Valley in August — the bloody and brilliant victories in September — the night battle at Berryville — the turning of the Enemy's left at Sheridan's battle of Winchester, the avalanche which swept down North Mountain upon the Rebel stronghold at Fisher's Hill, the final conflict in October, the surprise and defeat of the morning and the victory of the evening at Cedar Creek — these and a thousand other events and scenes in the campaign of 1864 form part of our common recollections which we are not likely ever to forget. As long as they are remembered we shall be reminded of each other and of the friendly and agreeable relations which so long existed between us.

It is very gratifying to me that I was allowed to serve with you until we received together the tidings of the great victory which ends the Rebellion. Whatever may be your fortune, I shall not cease to feel a lively interest in everything which concerns your welfare and your reputation. Under the able and gallant officer who succeeds me — under whom we have served together with so much satisfaction — I am confident that your future will be worthy of your past. As an organization and as individuals you have my most fervent wishes for your happiness and success.

R. B. HAYES, Brig.-Gen'l.

[1] Letter to Sardis Birchard.

and I talked. I did not then, of course, say good-bye, but I said about all I would have said if just parting. The Thirty-sixth is about as near to me — the officers possibly more so — than the Twenty-third. I am in command of all sorts now — a good regiment of cavalry, the old Pennsylvania Ringgold Cavalry, two batteries of Ohio men, one of them Captain Glassie's (the old Simmonds Battery), one of the veteran West Virginia regiments, Second Veterans, and a lot of others of less value. It was intended to send me in command of about five thousand men — quite a little army — by mountain routes towards Lynchburg. We are still preparing for it, but I have no idea *now* that we shall go.

I wish to remain in service until my four years is up in June. Then I shall resign or not as seems best. If matters don't suit me I'll resign sooner.[1]

New Creek, West Virginia, April 12, 1865. — I am just beginning to fully realize and enjoy our great victories. I am more glad to think my fighting days are ended than I had expected. Grant deserves his great victory. Crook, too, had a conspicuous place. It was his immediate command which captured the wagon trains, Armstrong guns, prisoners, etc., which figure so largely in Sheridan's reports.

I am still preparing for my expedition, but I am confident it is given up and will never be undertaken; it is rendered useless. I think it not improbable that there will be an extra session of Congress; if so I go out of service then, of course. I am pretty well pleased with matters now.[2]

New Creek, West Virginia, April 16, 1865. — My mountain expedition is given up. If I go at all from here, it will be directly up the Valley to occupy Staunton. In any event, I think I shall see no more active campaigning.

I have been greatly shocked by the tragedy at Washington! At first it was wholly dark. So unmerited a fate for Lincoln! Such a loss for the country! Such a change! But gradually, consolatory topics suggest themselves. How fortunate that it occurred no sooner! Now the march of events will neither be stopped nor changed. The power of the nation is in our armies, and they are commanded by such men as Grant, Sherman, and Thomas, instead of McClellan, Hooker, etc. Lincoln's fame is safe. He is the darling of history evermore. His life and achievements give him titles to regard second to those of no other man in ancient or modern times. To these, this tragedy now adds the crown of martyrdom.[3]

The same day in a letter to his wife Hayes gave fuller expression to his feelings and apprehensions at the receipt of the news of the overwhelming calamity at Washington: —

[1] Letter to Mrs. Hayes.   [2] Letter to Sardis Birchard.
[3] Letter to Sardis Birchard.

When I heard first, yesterday morning, of the awful tragedy at Washington I was pained and shocked to a degree I have never before experienced. I got on to the cars, then just starting, and rode down to Cumberland. The probable consequences, or rather the possible results, in their worst imaginable form, were presented to my mind, one after the other, until I really began to feel that here was a calamity so extensive that in no direction could be found any, the slightest, glimmer of consolation. The nation's great joy turned suddenly to a still greater sorrow. A ruler tested and proved in every way, and in every way found equal to the occasion, to be exchanged for a new man whose ill-omened beginning made the nation hang its head. Lincoln for Johnson! The work of reconstruction, requiring so much statesmanship, just begun! The calamity to Mr. Lincoln; in a personal point of view, so uncalled-for a fate! — so undeserved, so unprovoked! The probable effect upon the future of public men in this country, the necessity for guards; our ways to be assimilated to those of the despotisms of the Old World. And so I would find my mind filled only with images of evil and calamity, until I felt a sinking of heart hardly equalled by that which oppressed us all when the defeat of our army at Manassas almost crushed the nation.

But slowly, as in all cases of great affliction, one comes to feel that it is not all darkness; the catastrophe is so much less, happening now, than it would have been at any time before, since Mr. Lincoln's election. At the period after his first inauguration; at any of the periods of great public depression; during the pendency of the last Presidential election; at any time before the defeat of Lee, such a calamity might have sealed the nation's doom. Now the march of events can't be stayed, probably can't be much changed. It is possible that a greater degree of severity in dealing with the Rebellion may be ordered, and *that* may be for the best.

As to Mr. Lincoln's name and fame and memory, — all is safe. His firmness, moderation, goodness of heart; his quaint humor, his perfect honesty and directness of purpose, his logic, his modesty, his sound judgment, and great wisdom; the contrast between his obscure beginnings and the greatness of his subsequent position and achievements; his tragic death, giving him almost the crown of martyrdom, elevate him to a place in history second to none other in ancient or modern times. His success in his great office, his hold upon the confidence and affections of his countrymen, we shall all *say* are only second to Washington's; we shall probably *feel* and *think* that they are not *second* even to his.[1]

---

[1] A year later Mr. Hayes wrote: "The truth is, if it were not sacrilege, I should say Lincoln is overshadowing Washington. Washington is formal, statue-like — a figure for exhibition. But both were necessary to complete our history. Neither could have done the other's work." (Letter (April 15, 1866) to Sardis Birchard.)

General Hayes participated in the grand review, and afterwards spent several days, in Washington. He was accompanied by Mrs. Hayes, and the reunion with old friends was all that they had anticipated. He sent in his resignation to take effect just four years from the time he enlisted. His appointment of brevet major-general, for "gallant and distinguished services during the campaign of 1864," dated from March 13, 1865. From Washington he returned to New Creek, where he remained in command until mustered out.[1] Twenty-one years later Hayes records in his diary the following modest reflections on his military service: —

May 13, 1886. — I read with emotion that brought tears to my eyes the following, in the semiweekly (New York) *Tribune,* in a notice of the second volume of General Grant's "Memoirs": —

"In the fighting before Petersburg,[2] Grant had under his command General Rutherford B. Hayes [of whom he says]: 'His conduct on the field was marked by conspicuous gallantry as well as the display of qualities of a higher order than that of mere personal daring. This might well have been expected of one who could write at the time he is said to have done so: "Any officer fit for duty who at this crisis would abandon his post to electioneer for a seat in Congress, ought to be scalped." Having entered the army as a major of volunteers at the beginning of the war, General Hayes attained by meritorious service the rank of brevet major-general before its close.' "

We are in the habit in the family of calling flattering mention, particularly of Lucy, "Aaron's beard." This is a particularly agreeable specimen of "A.B." I am more gratified by friendly reference to my war record than by any other flattery. Of course I know that my place was a very humble one — a place utterly unknown in history. But I am also glad to know that I was one of the good colonels. I was not promoted to brigadier-general until after the close of the active operations in 1864. I never fought in battle as a general. An important command was arranged for me by General Hancock in the spring of 1865,

---

[1] To Sardis Birchard: —

May 20, 1865.

Private Underhill, Twenty-third Ohio V.I., will take my private horse, a large white horse, to Fremont. He was formerly in a government wagon train, but was too high-spirited, and was exchanged for my private horse. He has been in many battles, and is a capital war horse.

R. B. HAYES.

This horse, "Old Whitey," lived, a pensioner, for nearly fifteen years after his establishment at Spiegel Grove. He was buried near the base of Cemetery Knoll in the grove, a great boulder marking his grave.

[2] This is, of course, the blunder of the *Tribune.* Grant (*Memoirs,* vol. II, p. 340) is speaking of Sheridan's campaign in the Shenandoah Valley.

but the sudden collapse of the Confederacy at Appomattox put an end to the war just as I was preparing and concentrating my forces for an expedition from the Baltimore and Ohio, at or near Clarksburg, with Lynchburg and the Southwest Virginia and Tennessee Railroad as my objective.

The delay in my promotion to brigadier-general was due mainly to myself. Early in political life I had made it a rule never to seek office. When I went in the army, feeling that I lacked the military education necessary for command, my aversion to office-seeking was intensified by the consideration that to seek and get a place beyond my capacity might lead to disaster and failure which would involve the lives of the men under me. I therefore firmly resolved to seek no promotion — no place — and I used absolutely no effort at any time to get ahead. With political, family, and social influences I could, perhaps, have begun higher in rank, and probably could a year or two earlier have been made a general. My feeling, often expressed, after my promotion to colonel was, "I prefer to be one of the good colonels to being one of the poor generals." So decided was this that I often considered the question of declining promotion to the brigadier-generalship, and have sometimes regretted that I ever accepted it.

As a colonel or lieutenant-colonel I commanded a brigade, important posts with infantry, cavalry, and artillery, and in battle repeatedly commanded a division. Brigadier-generals and even major-generals, it was said, were sent to the Army of West Virginia in the Shenandoah Valley in 1864, when all its brigades and divisions were commanded by colonels, but the War Department which had sent them was persuaded by Sheridan and Grant to recall them. I may feel without undue personal vanity that, though unknown as a general, I was one of the good colonels in the great army. This fortunate (for me) sentence of our great commander proves this. I think with pleasure of two other facts pointing the same way. After I left my old command in the spring of 1865 and assumed duties elsewhere, without my knowledge a meeting was called in the camps near Winchester of Ohio troops, with Colonel Devol of [the] Thirty-sixth Ohio as chairman, and with entire unanimity they passed resolutions touching my conduct and character as a soldier, and recommended me for Governor of Ohio to the Republican convention then about to meet at Columbus. When I heard of it I peremptorily refused my assent. Having just been elected to Congress I could not, without the approval of my constituents, leave the place they have given me.

In 1871, on the anniversary of the battle of Cedar Creek, October 19, a meeting of the Society of the Army of West Virginia was held at Wheeling. It was the first regular meeting of the society in pursuance of an adjournment of a general meeting held the year previous at Moundsville, West Virginia. A constitution and by-laws were adopted, and the officers were elected. I was not present at either meeting, and had nothing at all to do with either. I was, however, pleased to learn that I was elected first President of the Society of the Army of West Virginia.

(See Report of the Ninth Reunion of the Army of West Virginia at Portsmouth, p. 8.)

At the time of my promotion to brigadier-general I was greatly pleased. (1) It came as a recognition in the field of my conduct during the fiercest and bloodiest campaign of the war. (2) It relieved me of the apprehension I had often painfully felt that I was liable for want of work to lose my splendid brigade and division and to be put under some incompetent political brigadier.

After Grant's commendation, words of eulogy of Hayes's soldiership by a civilian would be superfluous. A simple résumé of the important battles in which he bore a worthy part is more impressive than laudatory phrases: —

1. He commanded the regiment which led the attack and successfully opened the battle of South Mountain, where he was severely wounded.

2. He commanded the brigade which led the assault and carried the works of the enemy in the fierce battle of Cloyd Mountain, where the Rebel General Jenkins was defeated and killed.

3. He commanded one of the two brigades which covered the retreat that saved Crook's army after the defeat at Winchester, July 24, 1864.

4. He commanded one of the two brigades selected by Sheridan to lead in repeated attacks on Early's lines in the Shenandoah Valley in August, 1864.

5. He commanded one of the two brigades which fought at Berryville, September 3, and by great gallantry saved the day.

6. He commanded the brigade which led the flank attack which turned Early's left and defeated him in Sheridan's great victory at Opequon, September 19. And it was while marching to secure position to strike the enemy that Hayes performed one of the daring feats of the war: charged through an almost impassable morass upon a battery.

7. He commanded the division of Crook's army which led the way in scaling North Mountain, and, striking Early on the left flank, made certain the victory of Fisher's Hill, September 22.

8. He commanded one of the divisions which retained its organization and gained great distinction in the battle of Cedar Creek, October 19.

9. In more than fifty engagements, large and small, he always displayed personal daring, self-possession, and efficiency.

CHAPTER XVIII

MR. HAYES had resigned his commission in the volunteer service in June, 1865, and returned to Ohio. The summer months were spent for the most part in Fremont and among friends and relatives in various parts of the State. It was not till October that he returned to his old home in Cincinnati and reëstablished himself there. Meanwhile, a state campaign for the election of Governor and other state officers, including the Legislature which would elect a United States Senator, was in progress. General J. D. Cox was the Union candidate for Governor. Mr. Hayes was not content to be a silent participant in the canvass, but offered his services to the campaign managers and made many speeches which contributed their share to the triumph in October of the Union ticket.

While still in the field in the Shenandoah Valley, engaged in almost daily fighting, and without taking any part in the canvass, he had (as already recorded) been nominated and elected to Congress in the Second Ohio District — a part of Hamilton County (Cincinnati). Congress assembled at the regular time, early in December. This was the famous Thirty-ninth Congress. In the period that had elapsed since the expiration of the Thirty-eighth Congress, on March 4, history had rapidly been making. The final overthrow of the Confederate forces and the complete downfall of the Confederate Government had been signalized; the foul assassination of the great Lincoln had plunged the nation into gloom and mourning; Andrew Johnson had succeeded to the Presidency, and, by virtue of his authority as commander-in-chief of the military forces of the Republic, had by proclamation instituted measures for the rehabilitation of the rebellious States. The action of the President and the results accomplished thereunder in the Southern States had been watched by the loyal people of the North with intense interest and with many misgivings.

The growing sentiment was that the President was moving too precipitately; that the States which had sought with all their resources to destroy the Union should not be allowed to resume their "proper practical relations," to use Mr. Lincoln's phrase, in the Government, until guaranties against possible future efforts to secede had been established.

The great task of the Thirty-ninth Congress, therefore, was to solve the tremendously important problem of reconstruction. This was made all the more difficult by the obstinate insistence of the President on the adequacy of the method of readjustment he had proposed and pursued, and by the rapidly developing alienation of the President from sympathy and coöperation with the leaders in Congress of the party to which he owed his election. The longer the dispute continued the more determined the President became in his attitude, and the less inclined to compromise grew the spirit of the controlling element in Congress. But it is unnecessary to follow in detail the progress of this historic controversy.

The Thirty-ninth Congress contained an unusual number of able and experienced legislators. The delegation from Ohio was particularly strong. Mr. Hayes in his diary (December 1, 1865) records his impressions of his Ohio colleagues on the occasion of their first caucus: —

A caucus of the Ohio Union delegation held at Mr. Delano's room to-night. Present: Ashley, Bingham, Buckland, Bundy, Clark, Delano, Eggleston, Garfield, Hayes, Hubbell, Lawrence, Plants, Schenck, Shellabarger, Spalding, and Welker. Absent: Eckley. It was our first and a very agreeable meeting.

We agreed to oppose the admission of any delegate from the Rebel States for the present.

Ashley is a large, good-natured, popular style of man — full of good humor. Shellabarger, a sober, gentlemanly, able man. General Garfield, a smooth, ruddy, pleasant man; not very strong. Clark, disposed to talk rather too much. Lawrence, ditto, and not quite happy in his views. Delano, clear and correct. Hubbell, talky. Schenck, Delano, Spalding and Shellabarger, in the order I name them, strike me, judging by to-night, as the strongest men. Bingham and Ashley said so little that I can't place them.

General Schenck gave notice that he would propose an amendment on the first opportunity by which Representatives would be based on suffrage. All seemed to acquiesce. On General Schenck's suggestion,

I offered the resolution, with educational test or condition added. Adopted, with two negatives, viz., Ashley and Shellabarger.[1]

Of the general Republican caucus Mr. Hayes writes the next day: —

The general caucus to-night a pleasant thing. Mr. Morrill, of Vermont, an intelligent merchant, — who put the vote "*contrary-minded* will say no," — presided. Thad Stevens made the important motions. A committee of seven reported resolutions, to be submitted to the Senate and House, providing for the appointment of a Joint Committee of fifteen, nine from the House, six from the Senate, to report as to the status of the Rebel States and whether they were in a condition to be represented; and in the meantime all members from these States to be kept out. [The caucus] adopted on a test vote the Ohio idea [Mr. Hayes's resolution relating to representation based on suffrage, adopted the night before by the Ohio delegation]. Stevens angry — resisted — threatened to leave the caucus. Finally carried his point, as stated, namely, a Joint Committee of fifteen.

"The Ohio idea" was embodied by Mr. Hayes in the following resolutions: —

Resolved, That it is the sense of the caucus that the best if not the only mode of obtaining from the States lately in rebellion guaranties which will be irreversible is by amendments of the national Constitution.

Resolved, That such amendments to the national Constitution as may be deemed necessary ought to be submitted to the House for its action at as early a day as possible, in order to propose them to the several States during the present sessions of their Legislatures.

---

[1] Of the leaders in Congress Mr. Hayes gave his impression in a letter to Mrs. Hayes of December 7: "Thus far the noticeable men on our side of the house are Thad Stevens, Judge Kelley, and Roscoe Conkling, and on the Democratic side, James Brooks. — Stevens is over seventy — sharp-faced, grim-looking. The only blemish in his puritanical severe appearance is a brown wig. He is witty, cool, full of and fond of 'sarcasms,' and thoroughly informed and accurate. He has a knack of saying things which turn the laugh on his opponent. When he rises every one expects something worth hearing, and he has the attention of all. You remember his speech on confiscation. He is radical throughout except I am told he don't believe in hanging. He is leader. Judge Kelley, of Philadelphia, talks often — has studied rhetoric and elocution, and I am told is theatrical overmuch, but so far his little short speeches have been exceedingly well delivered. Roscoe Conkling, of New York State, delivers measured sentences in a grave, deliberate way that is good. James Brooks, former Know-Nothing leader, speaks pleasantly and is the leader of the Democrats; has, of course, to talk for buncombe. Delano has talked a little, and is a good specimen of the lively, earnest style of Western talkers. No doubt abler men have not yet showed themselves — Banks and others. The House is a more orderly and respectable body so far than

Resolved, That an amendment, basing representation on voters instead of population, ought to be promptly acted upon, and the judiciary committee is requested to prepare resolutions for that purpose, and submit them to the House as soon as possible.

In the event, the "Ohio idea" substantially prevailed. What Mr. Hayes's trend of thought was at this period in regard to universal manhood suffrage is revealed by an entry in his diary of January 10, 1866: —

Caucus decided against the bill of Kelley [enfranchising the negroes in the District of Columbia] preferring *qualified* to *universal* suffrage. Universal suffrage is sound in principle. The radical element is right. I was pleased, however, that the despotism of the committees and of the older members was rebuked. The suffrage bill ought not to have been pressed in advance of other and far more important business. The rights of the majority as against committees and leaders have gained. Much confusion and some feeling. Mr. Stevens quite angry. Said he would vote against qualified suffrage. Preferred no bill at all! The signs of harmony are more hopeful.

Again, April 15, 1866: —

The policy is to leave to the States the question of suffrage, but in the District [of Columbia] and the Territories it is for Congress to lay down the rule. Now, colored people are citizens of the United States. In some States they are allowed to vote; in some they are not. And in the places where all the States are interested it is right to treat all citizens alike. When they come to form State Governments I leave it to the people to say — as in Colorado.

Besides, in the District and in Territories they have no political power.

My decided preference [is] suffrage for all in the South, colored and white, to depend on education. Sooner or later in the North also; say, all *new* voters to be able to write and read.

February 26 Mr. Hayes wrote his uncle: —

I don't know whether I have written to you since the veto or not. [The veto of the Freedmen's Bureau Bill.] Many of our good men still hope that we may retain the President; but it is a very faint hope, scarcely more than a wish that he may return "to the bosom of the family." The general impression is, however, that Rebel influences are now ruling the White House, and that the sooner Johnson is clear over the better for us. Almost all are for going forward with business and measures in the usual and proper way, without excitement or abuse.

I had expected. The reading of the President's Message was an imposing thing. The members, all attentive, looked like the thing we imagined."

A few days later [March 4] he wrote to the same correspondent: —

We are still not clear as to the chances of harmony with the President. He no doubt differs, and has all along avowedly and openly differed, with us on some important matters. At the time of his unfortunate talk on the 22d [February], he seemed to be surrounded and possessed by all manner of evil influences. He now seems to feel that he was misled and is really anxious to conciliate. If he signs [the] Civil Rights Bill and the Tennessee Resolution, which will both pass soon, the chances are that a complete rupture will be avoided. Otherwise, otherwise. It is an interesting time to be here, and I enjoy it very much now — the last three weeks more than ever before. My ever hopeful temper is a good thing in these perplexing and exciting times.

March 17, to General M. F. Force, Mr. Hayes wrote: —

I could argue with you on the wisdom and justice of what Congress is doing with our erring sisters, if I knew exactly your points. The truth is Congress has done next to nothing yet on that subject and can give good reasons for not having yet done anything. The position held by the majority is this: The Rebel States having gone into insurrection and lost their lawful State Governments, it is for the lawmaking power of the nation to say when (or whether) such new State Governments have been set up as ought to be recognized. Is not this sound? Granting this, ought we to recognize any State Government which does not *undertake*, at least, to afford adequate protection to Union people and freedmen? And further, is there evidence showing such State Governments except in Tennessee and possibly Arkansas?

These citations are sufficient to show that Mr. Hayes was in full sympathy and accord with the dominant influences in Congress and in the country. as to the proper mode of dealing with the refractory States. He did not approve of the extreme radicalism, the uncompromising bitterness of expression, of Thaddeus Stevens, the dominating leader in Congress of the Republican majority. That was alien to his temper of mind and disposition. But he was convinced that hostages for the future must be required of the "erring sisters" before they could be allowed to sit as equals about the common hearthstone. His votes, both during this session and subsequent sessions of Congress, on all the important resolutions and measures dealing with the reconstruction problem were uniformly given with the majority of his party.[1]

[1] How deeply he felt the imperative necessity of making the adoption of the

But he took no part in the prolonged debates that these subjects evoked. He was without experience in legislative work; he was of the opinion that Congressmen were inclined to talk too much; and he found himself in a body of men most of whom had had years of congressional service. It was not in accord with the fundamental qualities of his character or his desire to push himself forward or to seek to make himself conspicuous. But in his relations with his fellow Congressmen and in committee work his sound good sense and his calm judgment made him a wise counsellor and an efficient member. The impression made upon his colleagues in Congress was well expressed later by General·Garfield in conversation with the well-known newspaper correspondent, Ben: Perley Poore. He said that when Mr. Hayes entered the House he was firmly "resolved not to make the mistake of talking too much and he became the most patient listener in the Capitol. Yet when it was known that he advocated the passage of a bill, it was pretty sure to pass. 'Hayes says it's all right' was a valuable endorsement."

It was in the activity of the Committee on Library, of which he was chairman, that he found his most congenial employment. This was a joint committee, the other House members being William D. Kelley, of Pennsylvania, and Calvin T. Hulburd, of New York. The Senate members were Messrs. Howe, of Wisconsin, Fessenden, of Maine, and Howard, of Michigan. In this period, and largely through the efforts of Mr. Hayes, the Library space was vastly expanded, the Smithsonian Institution's collection of books and papers was transferred to the Library of Congress, and the valuable Peter Force collection of Americana was

Fourteenth Amendment a condition precedent to the readmission of Representatives of the rebellious States in Congress, is shown by a letter to Murat Halstead, editor of the Cincinnati *Commercial,* dated February 2, 1866, commenting on an editorial of January 30: "You say: 'We would not make the adoption of the amendment a condition precedent to the admission of the Southern Representatives.' I move a reconsideration of that opinion. The amendment never can be got except as a condition. The South will never give up its power if admitted with it. I would be disposed, I think, to let in the loyal Tennesseeans when their State adopts it. The Rebel States will always be represented (during our day, at least) by repudiators — by men willing to assume every sort of claim payable South. Twenty-two Senators added to the twelve or fifteen now there, and the political power of four millions and a quarter negroes in the House and the Electoral College, is a serious thing. It deserves reconsideration — that idea of yours."

purchased by the Government.[1] One of the functions of the committee also was to pass upon works of art which the Government was importuned to purchase. Mr. Hayes possessed too good taste[2] to be influenced by the confidence of artists or the enthusiasm of their friends in behalf of feeble or meretricious performances. He exerted his influence in favor of selecting artists of known and established reputation to execute government commissions.

Mr. Hayes also served on the Committee on Private Land Claims; and throughout his career in Congress he was attentive and assiduous in serving the interests of his constituents that were committed to his care and in protecting claimants of pensions from greedy attorneys.

In the summer of 1866 Mr. Hayes was renominated for Congress by acclamation and in October was reëlected by an increased majority, though the Republican majority in the other Cincinnati district was considerably reduced. The election followed a strenuous canvass in which Mr. Hayes took an active part. Ohio being one of the "October States," and members of its delegation having been conspicuous in the dispute with the President, both parties made the strongest effort possible to win popular approval. Success in the October States would foreshadow and strengthen the result in the majority of the States in November. Speakers of national reputation came from other States to assist the local orators, and everywhere the respective

---

[1] In January, 1893, Mr. Ainsworth R. Spofford, long Librarian of Congress, wrote: "As chairman of the Committee on the Library of Congress on the part of the House, Mr. Hayes took a lively interest in its affairs. When the great historical collection of Peter Force, the Washington printer and journalist, was offered to the Government in 1866, his keen appreciation of the value of its stores was evinced in the committee, which unanimously recommended its purchase, and this rich library of books, pamphlets, manuscripts, and newspaper files was secured to the nation. The knowledge and experience then acquired of historical documents were of much value to him in later years, when he aided in securing for the State of Ohio the manuscript papers of Governor St. Clair; and it also helped him in his always vigilant and zealous collection of the materials of history for his own large private library."

[2] Mr. Spofford records of Mr. Hayes while President: "Once, he asked me to take him to see a noted historical picture — Carpenter's 'Emancipation Proclamation' — then newly presented to Congress, on the artistic merits of which opinions were much divided. After standing before it a few minutes, taking in the effect, he turned and said to me: 'Well, Spofford, it is bitter bad, is n't it?' and in this caustic judgment candor compelled me to concur."

RUTHERFORD B. HAYES, 1866
While Member of Congress, 1865–1867

merits of the President's policy and the policy of Congress, including the newly submitted Fourteenth Amendment, were exhaustively debated and fervidly advocated. Even a cursory reading of the speeches of that campaign gives one a vivid impression of the intensity of feeling which then stirred the hearts of men.

Mr. Hayes was constantly in the campaign the last few weeks before the election. A speech made by him in the Seventeenth Ward of Cincinnati on September 7 was widely circulated as a campaign document. It presented a calm review of the pending issues and a judicious defense of the Fourteenth Amendment. After a brief introduction Mr. Hayes declared: —

There are now only two plans of reconstruction before the country. The plan of those who supported the war measures of Mr. Lincoln's Administration, which may be called the Union plan, and the plan which originated with those who opposed the war measures of Mr. Lincoln, and which may be called the Rebel plan. There was another plan before the country which in some of its features was like the Union plan; in others it resembled the Rebel plan; and it had some provisions peculiar to itself. This plan, which may properly be called the Administration plan, never had many supporters outside of the influence of the executive patronage, and has now been, as I shall hereafter show, for all practical purposes abandoned.

He then proceeded to show by quotation from Mr. Johnson's speeches, made before his election as Vice-President and immediately after he succeeded to the Presidency, how different were the earlier views of the President as to the proper treatment of the rebellious States from those for which he now stood sponsor. He reviewed the action of President Lincoln in reorganizing certain States, and summarized the results accomplished under the application of Mr. Johnson's policy in these words: —

From this it appears that the result of what is usually called the President's policy in dealing with the people of the rebellious States, is, that in all of those States except West Virginia and Tennessee, which repudiated his policy, loyal men have been compelled to take back seats, while the places of honor and of political power have been filled by Rebels. . . .

We often hear from unthinking or uncandid people that Congress prevents ten States from having their due representation in Congress. Even General Dix said something of this sort at Philadelphia. Senator Hendricks, of Indiana, strongly partisan as he is, is compelled to admit, in the elaborate speech he lately delivered at the capital of his State, and I quote his words, that "Rebels are not excluded by the action of the present Congress; they stand excluded by the law." If every man duly elected from the Rebel States, claiming to have been loyal, was admitted to a seat in Congress, more than nine tenths of those States and of their people would still be wholly unrepresented. There is much talk of taxation without representation. The truth is that those people deprived themselves of representation by going into the Rebellion, and now, actuated by the same spirit as they were then, they continue to deprive themselves of that right by refusing to obey the law.

Certain conditions were required of these people. They comply with some of them. As to this essential condition — obedience to the law of the country — they refuse compliance; they become exacting; they become arrogant; they say, by their conduct, to the Government and to the loyal people of the country: "We are the conquerors; we make conditions; it is for us to dictate terms. If you wish the proper relations between us and the Union to be fully restored you must change your law. We will not consent to be represented in your Congress except by men whom you call traitors. If you want your Union restored we demand that you repeal the law which prescribes the loyal oath. You must allow Rebels to take part in the work of restoration." . . .

The rebellious people of the South having, with such great unanimity, refused to elect Senators and Representatives to Congress who were qualified according to law as the Administration plan required, the question at once arose: Who shall yield — the nation or the Rebels; the victors or the vanquished? The peace party of the North, under the same influences which controlled it during the war, promptly took sides with the Rebels. By their votes and speeches in Congress they denounced the loyal oath, declared it to be tyrannical and unconstitutional, and began, in the usual way, an agitation looking to its repeal. The Union party was equally prompt and explicit in taking sides against the Rebels and in favor of the law. Upon the first opportunity after the meeting of Congress in December last, Mr. Hill, a Union member of the House from Indiana, submitted this resolution: —

"*Resolved*, That the Act of July 2, 1862, prescribing an oath to be taken and subscribed by persons elected or appointed to office under the Government of the United States before entering upon the duties of such office, is of binding force and effect on all departments of the public service, and should in no instance be dispensed with."

A Democrat from Ohio, Mr. Finck, moved that it be tabled, which was disagreed to — yeas 32, nays 126 — and the resolution was passed — every Union man save one voting for it and every Democrat voting against it. Among those voting for the resolution were Mr. Raymond, General Rousseau, and all the other members who subsequently became known as the special friends of the President. What course the President himself would pursue was not for a long time clearly apparent. There were passages in his speeches and veto messages during the winter and spring, which, taken by themselves, indicated a purpose on his part to stand by the loyal oath. The same speeches and messages, however, contained repeated and violent attacks upon Congress for refusing representation to eleven Southern States, when it was perfectly well known by him and by the country that, with a few exceptions, those States had elected no members of either House qualified to take their seats, unless the loyal oath was repealed or disregarded. Besides, we heard neither from him or his supporters any complaint of the refractory spirit of the Rebels, which has prevented them from yielding a cheerful obedience to the law. All complaints and accusations were aimed at Congress. . . .

The speeches and messages of the President on these bills [the Freedmen's Bureau and Civil Rights Bills] indicated his conversion to the Rebel plan of protecting Southern Unionists and freedmen — that is, that they were to have such protection only as might be granted by the laws of the Rebel States, administered by Rebel officials. This left but one important step to take to completely commit his Administration to the Rebel plan of restoration, namely, to abandon the condition that Representatives and Senators from the Rebel States must be, in the President's words, "unmistakably and unquestionably loyal." This step he has never ventured clearly and publicly to take. But the Philadelphia Convention settled that question. The fatal step has, in fact, been taken. The Rebels know that they are to have their own way. The nation is to yield. Nothing will keep Rebels out of Congress but the election by the people of men determined to maintain and enforce Mr. Lincoln's loyal oath. The Philadelphia Convention on this subject passed the following resolution: —

"*Fourth* — We call upon the people of the United States to elect to Congress none but men who admit the fundamental right of representation, and who will receive to seats *loyal* Representatives from every State *in allegiance* to the United States, and submit to the consideration of each House to judge of the election returns and qualifications of its own members."

This resolution is intentionally ambiguous, but it will deceive nobody who does not wish to be deceived. The peace men and Rebels, who were a large majority of that convention, openly declare that a "*loyal* Representative" is one who is ready *now* to support the Constitution of the United States, and that no inquiry should be made as to his loyalty during the Rebellion. They say that the word "loyal" refers to the present or the future, not to the past. In this sense it was adopted by the convention, and accepted by the President and his friends. If votes can be gained by claiming that it refers to past loyalty — to loyalty during the Rebellion — no doubt the claim will be made; but the simple truth is, under that resolution, Mr. Stephens, late Vice-President of the Rebel Confederacy, and about seventy other Rebels, intend to obtain seats in the Congress of the United States.

The last remaining feature of the Administration plan of dealing with the people of the rebellious States having thus been abandoned, let us examine briefly the Rebel plan. It has the support, in all its parts, of the men who during the war were peace men at the North, and Rebels at the South. It has the advantage of being consistent with itself and with the previous history of its authors and friends. Those who in the North opposed the war were, during the whole struggle, in very close sympathy with the people engaged in the Rebellion; their sympathy for the loyal white people was not strong, and they were bitterly hostile to the loyal colored people both North and South. Their plan is in harmony with all this. According to it, the Rebels are hereafter to be treated in the same manner as if they had remained loyal. All laws, state and national, all orders and regulations of the military, naval and other departments of the Government, creating disabilities on account of participation in the Rebellion, are to be repealed, revoked, or abolished. The rebellious States are to be represented in Congress by the Rebels they have chosen, without hindrance from any test oath. All appointments in the army, in the navy, and in the civil service, are to be made from men who were Rebels, on the same terms as from men who were loyal. The people and governments in the rebellious States are to be subjected to no other interference or control from the military or other departments of the general Government than exists in the States which remained loyal. Loyal white men and loyal colored men are to be protected alone in those States by state laws, executed by state authorities, as if they were in the loyal States.

The Union party objects to this plan, because it is wrong in principle, wrong in its details, and fatally wrong as a precedent and example for the future. It treats treason as no crime, and loyalty as no virtue. It restores to political honor and power in the Government of the nation men who have spent the best part of their lives in plotting the overthrow of that Government, and who, for more than four years, levied public war against the United States. It allows Union men in the South who have risked all, and many of whom have lost all but life, in upholding the Union cause, to be excluded from every office, state and national, and in many instances to be banished from the States they so faithfully labored to save. It abandons the four millions of loyal colored people, who lost the protection which owners give their property, when they were made free to save the nation's life, to such treatment as the ruffian class of the South, educated in the barbarism of slavery and the atrocities of the Rebellion, may choose to give them. It leaves the obligations of the nation to her creditors, and to the maimed soldiers and to the widows and orphans of the war, to be fulfilled by men who hate the cause in which those obligations were incurred. It claims to be a plan which restores the Union without requiring conditions, but in conceding to the conquered Rebels the repeal of laws important to the nation's welfare, it grants a condition which they demand, while it denies to the loyal victors conditions which they deem of priceless value.

Instead of this mode of dealing with the people of the rebellious

States, the Union party presents a plan which, also, has the merit of being in perfect harmony with the opinions and history of that party during the whole war. We have already seen that the leading objects of desire with the Union party have been: —

1. The removal of every relic of slavery from the Federal Constitution, and from the institutions and laws of all the States.

2. That loyalty should be respected and treason made odious.

3. That the national obligations to the patriotic people who furnished men and means to crush the Rebellion should be faithfully fulfilled.

The Union party undertakes to accomplish these objects by an amendment of the national Constitution. No other form of guaranty has any title to be called irreversible. The constitutions and laws of the States and the resolutions of conventions afford no security to the nation. They are as changeable as the wishes and purposes of the men who make them. The creditor who takes security does not leave it in the possession and control of his doubtful debtor, but places it in his own safe and keeps the key himself. The nation, accepting pledges from the States lately in rebellion, will place them in the national Constitution, where they will remain until removed by the nation's consent.

Mr. Hayes proceeded thereupon to a careful analysis, exposition, and justification of the several clauses of the Fourteenth Amendment, clearly setting forth the need for each and its adequacy to meet that need, and ended his speech with this impressive paragraph: —

This is a short and imperfect presentation of the Union plan of restoration. The chief objection to it remains to be considered. It is said that the South will never accept of these terms, but, on the contrary, will require the nation to change its laws, so that her seventy Rebel Senators and Representatives, soon to be increased, by her full negro representation, to eighty or ninety, will be admitted without question to the Congress of the United States. This presents the sole issue. The Rebels say, "Peace, harmony, and restored union you can have by giving up your just demands, and yielding to the unjust requirements of the South"! This is the old familiar story. For many years the people of the North believed it. For the sake of harmony and union they yielded to every arrogant demand until, at last, they learned that every concession was the parent of increased arrogance, and new threats of discord and disunion. Their manhood and sense of justice were at length aroused, and in opposition to slavery extension and slavery dictation, they elected Abraham Lincoln President. The slaveholders rebelled and, during four years, waged against their own Government a war of unparalleled atrocities. Overthrown and beaten in that war, prostrate and utterly helpless at its close, they now assume the air and bearing of conquerors, and propose to dictate terms. The Seward-Johnson party advises the people, for the sake of peace and union, to submit to this demand. The Union party is prepared to make great sacrifices in the future as in the past for the sake of peace and for the sake of union, but submission to what is wrong can never be the foundation of a real peace or a lasting union. They can have no other sure foundation but the principles of eternal justice. The Union men therefore say to the South, "We ask nothing but what is right, we will submit to nothing that is wrong." With undoubting confidence we submit the issue to the candid judgment of the patriotic people of the country, under the guidance of that Providence which has hitherto blessed and preserved the nation.

It is hardly necessary to recall that the people voted by large majorities to sustain Congress, and that the breach between Congress and the President became irreconcilable.

During the midwinter recess, 1866, Mr. Hayes, accompanied by his wife, went with other members of Congress and their wives to New Orleans. The object of the trip was both social and political. The Congressmen wished to see for themselves the conditions in the South, to meet and talk with Southern leaders on their own ground. Stops were made at Knoxville, Chattanooga, Nashville, and Memphis, and two days were spent at New Orleans. In all these cities receptions, banquets, and other social attentions were showered on the party and speeches were made by the men of both sections, mostly in a friendly and patriotic spirit. Mr. Hayes's impressions of the people he met were altogether agreeable. Writing to his uncle from Memphis (December 26, 1866) Mr. Hayes says: —

We are thus far on our way to New Orleans, with everything thus far the very pleasantest possible. I last night experienced a new sensation. I went with General Howard to a meeting of colored people and made them a short talk. Their eager, earnest faces were very stimulating.

We meet the leading Rebels everywhere. The Rebel officers are particularly interesting. I get on with them famously. I talk negro suffrage and our extremest radicalism to all of them. They dissent, but are polite and cordial.

Two days later he again wrote, from New Orleans, that "one of the pleasant points in this trip is making the acquaintance of the leading Rebel officers." There was endless interest in comparing with them experiences during the dreadful fighting days. It is evident, while his views as to the governmental policy demanded at the time were not changed, that his understanding of Southern sentiment was enlarged and his sympathies with

Southern needs widened. It is evident, too, that he left a favorable impression on the minds of the men he met in New Orleans; for in the first months of his service as Chief Magistrate, when his Southern policy was fiercely denounced by ex-Senator Ben Wade (who had also been of the visiting party of 1866), the New Orleans *Democrat* recalled "the liberal tone and bearing" of Mr. Hayes at the time of the visit and contrasted it with "the coarse and narrow-minded truculency" displayed by Senator Wade. "It was, indeed," the paper continues, "a great relief to get away from—— [Wade] and to enjoy the agreeable and pleasant companionship of his congressional colleague, the then General R. B. Hayes, who, in all his intercourse with our people, manifested a cordial sympathy and fraternity toward them, and a delicacy and tact in the choice of topics of conversation which impressed most favorably and kindly all with whom he was brought into intercourse."

The second session of the Thirty-ninth Congress was throughout tense and strenuous. The Republican majority continued to override the vetoes of the President in legislating for the reconstruction of the Southern States, and coming to distrust the President almost absolutely, — more, indeed, than a review at this time seems quite to justify, — provided for a meeting of the Fortieth Congress on March 4, 1867, immediately on the expiration of the Thirty-ninth.

Throughout this session and the opening session of the Fortieth Congress, Mr. Hayes acted consistently though unobtrusively in support of the measures and policies of his party.

CHAPTER XIX

FIRST TERM AS GOVERNOR

THE first suggestion of General Hayes's fitness to be Governor of Ohio was made by his old brigade in a meeting at Winchester, Virginia, in April, 1865, just after he had been transferred to a new command under Hancock.[1] The complimentary resolutions in which this suggestion was embodied were gratifying to the general as a renewed and emphatic expression of the confidence of his men in their commander, but he gave the suggestion itself no serious thought. He was already elected to Congress. If the war was over, he would resign and take his seat; he had no wish to seek, or to permit his friends to seek for him, the nomination for any other office.[2]

But conditions were changed two years later. General Cox, whose military qualities and success were of the highest character, had disappointed his friends as Governor. After a year's experience at Columbus it was apparent to him, as well as to the party, that his renomination would be inadvisable; especially as under the able leadership of Messrs. Thurman, Pendleton, and Vallandigham, the Democrats had been winning ground against the extreme radicalism of the Reconstructionists represented by Senator Wade, and were preparing to make an aggressive campaign. As early as January 8 the Democrats met in state convention at Columbus, adopted a platform, written by Mr.

[1] The meeting was held April 20. The resolutions adopted by it were published in the Cincinnati *Commercial* of May 3, and were as follows: —

"*Resolved*, That we propose Brigadier-General R. B. Hayes, of Hamilton County, as the Union candidate for the next Governor of Ohio.

"*Resolved*, That General Hayes, in addition to possessing the ability and statesmanship necessary to qualify him, in an eminent degree, for Chief Magistrate of the great State of Ohio, is a soldier unsurpassed for patriotism and bravery, he having served four years in the army, earning his promotion from a major in one of the Ohio regiments to his present position."

[2] "General R. B. Hayes respectfully declines to permit his name to be used as a candidate for the nomination of Governor of Ohio by the Union State Convention." (Editorial paragraph in Cincinnati *Commercial*, May 12, inserted at Mr. Hayes's request.)

Vallandigham, denunciatory of the congressional mode of reconstruction and of negro suffrage, and nominated their most popular leader, Allen G. Thurman, for Governor.

Republican party leaders were at once on the alert to choose a candidate who would be most likely to make a winning contest, and General Hayes was urged to announce his candidacy or to allow his friends to present his qualifications to the public. General Hayes was at first extremely reluctant to permit the use of his name. While the duties of a Congressman were not particularly congenial to him, and he had no ambition for a prolonged career as a legislator, yet, as he had been elected to represent the Second District in Congress for two years, he did not feel it would be quite fair to his constituents to abandon the post they had given him to further his own political interests. On January 29 he wrote an Ohio friend as follows: —

Private and Confidential

WASHINGTON, D.C.,
29th Jany. 1867.

MY DEAR SIR, — I am this morning in receipt of yours of the 26th as to the next Union nomination for Governor.

Since General Cox's declination one or two persons, in a merely casual way, have spoken to me on the subject. Your letter contains the first and only serious suggestion of the sort I have received from Ohio. I therefore do not wish to speak now decisively, or for the public. I will mention a few things which strike me at first blush, one or the other of which will perhaps end the matter. Having been elected by the Union people of the Second District to an office which they knew I wanted, it would not be right to resign it without their approval. Again, I would not go into the state convention unless it was quite certain that I would be supported by the delegates of Hamilton County. And finally, I would not go into the contest with any other Union man of Hamilton County, for the support of the delegation of that county. In short, nothing but the general desire and approval of the party and its public men in the county would justify me in consenting to leave the office to which I have just been elected.

I prefer you would for the present keep this to yourself, with the understanding that I will write you fully, frankly, and definitely when I am a little better informed in the premises. — Sincerely,

R. B. HAYES.

WM. HENRY SMITH.

A few days later Mr. Hayes wrote the same correspondent as follows: —

Since writing you early last week, I have received a good many letters from Cincinnati, and the drift of them all is to confirm me in the correctness of my offhand impressions. I wish, therefore, to have it known that I decline to allow my name to go before the Union State Convention. Of course I feel flattered by the favorable way in which I have been named, and greatly obliged to my friends for their partiality. I would very much enjoy, I am sure, to make the canvass, and I do not pretend to be indifferent to the honor. If I had no place such as the one I now occupy I should quite willingly take the chances of getting a nomination. But under the circumstances, as I said in my former letter, I ought not to resign without the approval of the people who sent me here; and there is, judging by my correspondence, no general desire that I should do so. I shall write no letter for publication and of course want my decision made known without any "flourish of trumpets" or the assignment of reasons. This letter is marked "private" merely to indicate that I don't want it to be published.

At about the same time (February 2) Mr. Hayes wrote his uncle: —

I get letters about the governorship. It does n't worry me any, but I am really puzzled what to say. This is the truth as I now see it. I don't *particularly* enjoy congressional life. I have *no ambition* for congressional reputation — not a particle. I would like to be out of it creditably. If this nomination is pretty likely, it would get me out of the scrape, and after *that* I am out of political life decently. On the other hand, I ought not and will not resign my seat in Congress to be Governor unless the people of my district approve it. You see the case.

In spite of this decision in February to stay out of the race, the friends of Mr. Hayes continued to keep his name before the public. Of all the men that aspired to the nomination, or that were proposed for it, the opinion of the party leaders and of the party generally gradually became more and more convinced that General Hayes, with his reputation as a soldier, his record in Congress as a consistent supporter of the reconstruction measures, and his skill as a campaigner, would be best fitted to oppose the able and astute Thurman. Mr. Hayes himself finally yielded to the importunities of his friends and consented to appear as a candidate. The convention met at Columbus, June 19. It adopted a brief platform "fully endorsing" the reconstruction policy of Congress and declaring for "impartial manhood suffrage, as embodied in the proposed amendment to the state constitution." Mr. Hayes was nominated on the first ballot.

The issue between the two parties was thus simple and clean-cut, and national in its significance. Should the congressional mode of reconstruction, requiring the rebellious States to give guaranties for the future and placing them meanwhile under military rule, be condemned or approved? Should Ohio amend its constitution so as to extend the suffrage to negroes and deny it to deserters from the Union army, to Confederate soldiers, and to men that had fled the State to escape the draft?

That Mr. Hayes recognized that he had a hard fight before him, and one with extremely doubtful issue, is evidenced by a letter to his uncle immediately after his nomination. Referring to the midsummer meeting of Congress, which he was about to set out for, he said, "This is probably my last of public life." But he had no regrets for the step he had taken. He was not the kind of man to look back after he had put his hand to the plough. As soon as Congress adjourned (July 20) he resigned his seat and began to prepare for a vigorous speaking campaign. His first speech was made at Lebanon August 5, on the same day that Mr. Thurman opened his campaign at Waverly. These two speeches laid the lines on which the contest was principally waged. Mr. Hayes's speech presents so clear and admirable a review of the views and principles of the opposing parties, in dealing with the questions of the day growing out of slavery and the war of the Rebellion, that it is here given in full: —

Fellow Citizens, — President Lincoln began his memorable address at the dedication of the Gettysburg National Cemetery with these words: "Fourscore and seven years ago our fathers brought forth on this continent a new nation, conceived in liberty and dedicated to the proposition that all men are created equal."

This was Abraham Lincoln's opinion of what was accomplished and what was meant by the Declaration of Independence. His idea was that it gave birth to a nation, and that it dedicated that nation to equal rights.

Now, so far as the performance of duty in the present condition of our country is concerned, "this is the whole law and the prophets." The United States are not a confederacy of independent and sovereign States, bound together by a mere treaty or a compact, but the people of the United States constitute a nation, having one flag, one history, "one country, one constitution, one destiny." Whoever seeks to divide this nation into two sections — into a North and a South, or into four sections, according to the cardinal points of the compass, or into thirty or forty independent sovereignties, is opposed to the nation, and the nation's friends should be opposed to him.

Washington, in his Farewell Address, says: "The unity of government, which constitutes you one people, is also now dear to you. It is justly so; for it is a main pillar in the edifice of your real independence, the support of your tranquillity at home, your peace abroad; of your safety, of your prosperity, of that very liberty which you so highly prize. . . . The name of American, which belongs to you in your national capacity, must always exalt the just pride of patriotism more than any appellation derived from local discriminations. With slight shades of difference, you have the same religion, manners, habits, and political principles. You have, in a common cause, fought and triumphed together; the independence and liberty you possess are the work of joint counsels and joint efforts — of common dangers, sufferings, and successes."

The sentiment of nationality is the sentiment of the Declaration of Independence; it is the sentiment of the fathers; it is the sentiment which carried us through the war of the Revolution, and through the war of the late Rebellion; and it is a sentiment which the people of the United States ought forever to cultivate and cherish.

The great idea to which the nation, according to Mr. Lincoln, was dedicated by the fathers is expressed in the Declaration in these familiar phrases: "We hold these truths to be self-evident, that all men are created equal; that they are endowed by their Creator with certain inalienable rights; that among these are life, liberty, and the pursuit of happiness. That to secure these rights governments are instituted among men, deriving their just powers from the consent of the governed."

An intelligent audience will not wish to hear discussion as to the import of these sentences. Their language is simple, their meaning plain, and their truth undoubted. The equality declared by the fathers was not an equality of beauty, of physical strength, or of intellect, but an equality of rights. Foolish attempts have been made by those who hate the principles of the fathers to destroy the great fundamental truth of the Declaration, by limiting the application of the phrase "all men" to the men of a single race.

But Jefferson's original draft of the Declaration leaves no room to doubt what he meant by these words. The gravest charge he made against the King of Great Britain in the original draft of the Declaration of Independence was the following: "He has waged cruel war against human nature itself, violating its most sacred rights of life and liberty in the persons of a distant people, who never offended him, capturing and carrying them into slavery in another hemisphere, or to incur miserable death in their transportation thither. This piratical warfare, the opprobrium of infidel powers, is the warfare of the Christian King of Great Britain, determined to keep open market where MEN should be bought and sold."

In this sentence the word "men" is written by Jefferson in capital letters, showing with what emphasis he wished to declare that the King of Great Britain was making slaves of a people to whom belonged the rights of men.

Unfortunately for our country, that king, and others who "waged cruel war against human nature itself," had already succeeded in planting in the bosom of American society an element implacably hostile to human rights, and destined to become the enemy of the Union, whenever the American people, in their national capacity, should refuse assent to any measures which the holders of slaves should deem necessary or even important for the security or prosperity of their "peculiar institution."

I need not, upon this occasion, repeat what is now familiar history — how, by the invention of the cotton-gin, and the consequent enormous increase of the cotton crop, slave labor in the cotton States, and slave breeding in the Northern slave States, became so profitable that the slaveholders were able, for many years, largely to influence, if not control, every department of the National Government. The slave power became something more than a phrase — it was a definite, established, appalling fact. The Missouri controversy, South Carolina nullification, the Texas controversy, the adoption of the compromise measures of 1850, and the repeal of the Missouri Compromise in 1854, were all occasions when the country was compelled to see the magnitude, the energy, the recklessness, and the arrogance of the slave power.

Precisely when the men who wielded that power determined to destroy the Union it is not now necessary to inquire. Threats of disunion were made in the first Congress that assembled under the Constitution. Upon various pretexts they were repeated from time to time, and no one doubts that slavery was at the bottom of them. In 1833 General Jackson wrote to Rev. A. J. Crawford: "Take care of your nullifiers; you have them among you; let them meet with the indignant frown of every man who loves his country. The tariff, it is now known, was a mere pretext, . . . and disunion and a Southern Confederacy the real object. The next pretext will be the negro or slavery question." General Jackson was no doubt right as to the existence of a settled purpose to break up the Union, and to establish a Southern Confederacy, as long ago as 1832. But why was there such a purpose? On what ground did it stand?

Great political parties, whether sectional or otherwise, do not come by accident, nor are they the invention of political intrigue. A faction born of a clique may have some strength at one or two elections, but the wisest political wire-workers cannot, by merely "taking thought," create a strong and permanent party. The result of the Philadelphia Convention last summer probably taught this truth to the authors of that movement. Great political movements always have some adequate cause.

Now, on what did the conspirators who plotted the destruction of the Union and the establishment of a Southern Confederacy rely? In the first place, they taught a false construction of the National Constitution, which was miscalled States' rights, the essential part of which was that "any State of the Union might secede from the Union whenever it liked." This doctrine was the instrument employed to destroy the unity of the nation. The fact which gave strength and energy to those who employed this instrument was that in the southern half of the Union, society, business, property, religion, and law were all based on the proposition that over four millions of our countrymen, capable of civilization and religion, were, because of their race and color, "so far inferior that they had no rights which the white man was bound to respect." The practice, founded upon this denial of the Declaration of Independence, protected by law and sanctioned by usage, was our great national transgression, and was the cause of our great national calamity.

In a country where discussion was free, sooner or later, parties were sure to be formed on the issues presented by the slaveholders. The supporters of the Union and of human rights would band together against the supporters of disunion and slavery. For many years after the struggle really began, the issues were not clearly defined, and neither party was able to occupy its true and final position, or to rally to its standard all who were in fact its friends. Old parties encumbered the ground. Men were slow to give up old associations and leave the discussion of obsolete, immaterial, or ephemeral issues.

At last the crisis came. In 1860, Mr. Lincoln, who was unfriendly to slavery and faithful to the Union, was elected President. The party of disunion and slavery were prepared for this event. Their action was prompt, decisive, and defiant. They proceeded to organize Southern conventions, and formally to withdraw from the Union, and undertook to establish a new government and a new nation on the soil of the United States.

Prior to 1860 the party calling itself Democratic had gathered under one name and one organization almost the whole of the secessionists of the South, and a large body of the people of the North, many of whom had no sympathy either with secession or slavery. In 1860 the secessionists were so arrogant in their demands that the great body of the Democratic party in the North refused to yield to them, and supported Mr. Douglas in opposition both to Mr. Lincoln, and to the disunion and slavery candidate, Mr. Breckinridge. But it was well known that many leading Democrats who supported Mr. Douglas leaned strongly toward the Southern Calhoun Democracy, and that their sympathies were with slaveholding, or at least with slaveholders.

The evidence of this is abundantly furnished in their recorded opinions. The most distinguished and perhaps the most influential Democrat now actively engaged in politics in Ohio, who presided over and addressed the last Democratic State Convention held at Columbus, Mr. Pendleton, delivered a speech in the House of Representatives on the 18th of January, 1861.

You will recollect how far the slaveholders had progressed in their great rebellion at that date. Mr. Pendleton himself says: "To-day, sir, four States of this Union have, so far as their power extends, seceded from it. Four States, as far as they are able, have annulled the grants of power made to the Federal Government; they have resumed the powers delegated by the Constitution; they have cancelled, so far as they could, every limitation upon the full exercise of all their sovereign rights. They do not claim our protection; they ask no benefit from our laws; they seek none of the advantages of the confederation. On the other hand, they renounce their allegiance; they repudiate our authority over them, and they assert that they have assumed — some of them that they have resumed — their position among the family of sovereignties, among the nations of the earth. . . . To-day, even while I am speaking, Georgia is voting upon this very question. And unless the signs of the times very much deceive us, within three weeks other States will be added to the number."

Mr. Pendleton might also have said that prior to that date, forts, arsenals, dockyards, mints, and other places and property belonging to the United States, had been seized by organized and armed bodies of Rebels; the collection of debts due in the South to Northern creditors had been stopped; South Carolina had declared that any attempt to reënforce Fort Sumter by the United States would be regarded by that State as an act of hostility against her and equivalent to a declaration of war; the Star of the West, an unarmed vessel, with the American flag floating at her masthead, carrying provisions to the famishing garrison of Fort Sumter, had been fired on and driven from Charleston Harbor; in short, at that date the Rebels were engaged in actual war against the nation, and the only reason why blood had not been shed was that the National Government had failed in its duty to defend the nation's property, and to maintain the sacredness of the national flag.

At that crisis Mr. Pendleton delivered and sent forth a speech bearing this significant motto: "But, sir, armies, money, blood, cannot maintain this Union; justice, reason, peace, may." The speech was according to its motto. Accustomed as he is to speak cautiously, and in a scholarly and moderate way, we cannot be mistaken as to his drift. On the authority of the National Government he says: "Now, sir, what force of arms can compel a State to do that which she has agreed to do? What force of arms can compel a State to refrain from doing that which the State Government, supported by the sentiment of her people, is determined to persist in doing. . . . Sir, the whole scheme of coercion is impracticable. It is contrary to the genius and spirit of the Constitution."

These extracts sufficiently and fairly show Mr. Pendleton's notion of the duty and authority of the nation in that great crisis. He held the States' rights doctrines of Calhoun and Breckinridge, and not the national principles of Washington and Jackson.

As to the treatment of Rebels already in arms, and as to the "demands" of the slave power, consider this advice which he gave to Congress and the people: "If these Southern States cannot be conciliated;

if you, gentlemen, cannot find it in your hearts to grant their demands; if they must leave the family mansion, I would signalize their departure by tokens of love; I would bid them farewell so tenderly that they would be forever touched by the recollection of it; and if in the vicissitudes of their separate existence they should desire to come together with us again in one common government, there should be no pride to be humiliated, there should be no wound inflicted by my hand to be healed. They should come and be welcome to the places they now occupy."

Thus we see there were those who, with honeyed phrases and soft words, would have looked smilingly on, while the great Republic — the pride of her children, the hope of the ages — built by the fathers at such an expense of suffering, of treasure, and of blood, was stricken by traitors' hands from the roll of living nations, and while an armed oligarchy should establish in its stead a nation founded on a denial of human rights, and under whose sway south of the Potomac more than half of the territory of the old Thirteen Colonies — soil once fertilized by the best blood of the Revolution — should, for generations to come, continue to be tilled by the unrequited toil of slaves.

The best known, the boldest, and perhaps the ablest leader of the peace Democracy in the North is Mr. Vallandigham. He was Chairman of the Committee on Resolutions in the last Democratic State Convention in Ohio, and reported the present state platform of his party. He, probably, still enjoys in a greater degree than any other public man the affection and confidence of the positive men of the Ohio Democracy, who, from beginning to end, opposed the war. On the 20th of February, 1861, he delivered a speech in the House of Representatives in support of certain amendments which he proposed to the Constitution of the United States. In an appendix to that speech, he published an extract from a card in the Cincinnati *Enquirer* of November 10, 1860, from which I quote: "And now let me add that I did say, . . . in a public speech, at the Cooper Institute, on the 2d of November, 1860, that if any one or more of the States of this Union should at any time secede, for reasons of the sufficiency and justice of which, before God and the great tribunal of history, they alone may judge, much as I should deplore it, I never would, as a Representative in Congress of the United States, vote one dollar of money whereby one drop of American blood should be shed in a civil war. . . . And I now deliberately repeat and reaffirm it, resolved, though I stand alone, though all others yield and fall away, to make it good to the last moment of my public life."

Here was another strong man of large influence solemnly pledged to allow the Union to be broken up and destroyed, in case the Rebel conspirators chose that alternative, rather than forego their demands in favor of oppression and against human rights.

On the 23d of January, 1861, the Democratic party held a state convention at Columbus. Remember, at that date the air was thick with threats of war from the South. The Rebels were organizing and drilling;

arms robbed from the national arsenals were in their hands; and the question upon all minds was whether the Republic should perish without having a single blow struck in her defense, or whether the people of the loyal North should rise as one man, prepared to wage war until treason and, if need be, slavery went down together. On this question, that convention was bound to speak. Silence was impossible. There were present war Democrats and peace Democrats, followers of Jackson and followers of Calhoun. There was a determined and gallant struggle on the part of the war Democrats, but the superior numbers, or more probably the superior tactics and strategy, of the peace men triumphed.

The present candidate of the Democratic party for Governor of Ohio, Judge Thurman, a gentleman of character and ability, a distinguished lawyer and judge, and a politician of long experience, succeeded in passing through the convention this resolution: —

"*Resolved*, That the two hundred thousand Democrats of Ohio send to the people of the United States, both North and South, greeting; and when the people of the North shall have fulfilled their duties to the Constitution and to the South, then, and not until then, will it be proper for them to take into consideration the question of the right and propriety of coercion."

In support of this famous resolution, Judge Thurman addressed the convention, and, among other things, is reported to have said: "A man is deficient in understanding who thinks the cause of disunion is that the South apprehended any overt act of oppression in Lincoln's Administration. It is the spirit of the late Presidential contest that alarms the South. . . . It would try the ethics of any man to deny that some of the Southern States have no cause for revolution. . . . Then, you must be sure you are able to coerce before you begin the work. The South are a brave people. The Southern States cannot be held by force. The blacks won't fight for the invaders. . . . The Hungarians had less cause of complaint against Austria than the South had against the North."

When we reflect on what the Rebels had done and what they were doing when this resolution was passed, it seems incredible that sane men having a spark of patriotism could for one moment have tolerated its sentiments. The Rebels had already deprived the United States of its jurisdiction and property in about one fourth of its inhabited territory, and were rapidly extending their insurrection so as to include within the Rebel lines all of the slave States. The lives and property of Union citizens in the insurgent States were at the mercy of traitors, and the national flag was everywhere torn down, and shameful indignities and outrages heaped upon all who honored it.

This resolution speaks of fulfilling the duties of the people of the North to the South. The first and highest duty of the people of the North to themselves, to the South, to their country, and to God, was to crush the Rebellion. All speeches and resolutions against either the right or the propriety of coercion merely gave encouragement, "moral aid and comfort," more important than powder and ball, to the enemies of the nation.

Do I state too strongly the mischievous, the fatal tendency of these proceedings? The resolution adopted by the peace Democracy of Ohio is addressed in terms "to the people of all the States, North and South," and in fact was sent, I am informed, to the Governors of all the States. In the South, Union men were laboring by every means in their power to prevent secession. Their most cogent argument was that the National Government would defend itself by war against rebellion. To this, the Rebel reply was: "There will be no war. Secession will be peaceable. The peace party of the North will prevent coercion. If there is fighting, it will be as ex-President Pierce writes to Jefferson Davis, 'The fighting will not be along Mason and Dixon's line merely. It will be within our own borders, in our own streets.'"

For the evidence of the correctness of this opinion, the Rebels could point confidently to such speeches and resolutions as those we are now considering. Governor Orr, of South Carolina, in a recent speech at the Charleston Board of Trade banquet, is reported to have said: "I know there is an apprehension widespread in the North and West that, after the reconstruction of the Southern States, we shall fall into the arms of our old allies and associates, the old Democratic party. I say to you, gentlemen, however, that I would give no such pledges. We have accounts to settle with that party, gentlemen, before I, at least, will consent to affiliate with it. Many of you will remember that, when the war first commenced, great hopes and expectations were held out by our friends in the North and West that there would be no war, and that if it commenced, it would be north of Mason and Dixon's line, and not in the South."

Without pausing to inquire how much strength accrued to the Rebellion in its earlier stages by the encouragement it received from sympathizers in the North, let us pass on to the spring and summer of 1861, after the bombardment and surrender of Fort Sumter, and when the armies of the Union and of the Rebellion were facing each other upon a line of operations extending from the Potomac to the Rio Grande. The most superficial observer could not fail to discover these facts.

In the South, where slavery was strongest, the Rebellion was strongest. Where there were few slaveholders, there were few Rebels. South Carolina and Mississippi, having the largest number of slaves in proportion to population, were almost unanimous for rebellion. Western Virginia, eastern Kentucky, east Tennessee, had few slaves, and love of the Union and hatred of secession in those mountain regions was nearly universal.

The counterpart of this was found everywhere in the North. In counties and districts where the majority of the people had been accustomed to defend or excuse the practice of slaveholding and the aggressions of the slaveholders, there was much sympathy with the Rebellion and strong opposition to the war. Men who abused and hated negroes did not usually hate Rebels. On the other hand, antislavery counties and districts were quite sure to be Union to the core.

In Ohio, as in other free States, the Democratic party could not be led off in a body after the peace Democracy. Brough, Tod, Matthews, Dorsey, Steedman, and a host of Democrats of the Jackson school, nobly kept the faith. Lytle, McCook, Webster, and gallant spirits like them, from every county and neighborhood of our State, sealed their devotion to the Union and to true democracy with their life's blood.

They believed, with Douglas, in the last letter he ever wrote, that "it was not a party question, nor a question involving partisan policy; it was a question of government or no government, country or no country, and hence it became the imperative duty of every Union man, every friend of constitutional liberty, to rally to the support of our common country, its Government and flag, as the only means of checking the progress of revolution, and of preserving the Union of the States."

They believed the words of Douglas's last speech: "This is no time for a detail of causes. The conspiracy is now known. Armies have been raised, war is levied to accomplish it. There are only two sides to the question. Every man must be for the United States or against it. There can be no neutrals in this war — only patriots and traitors."

As the war progressed, the great political parties of the country underwent important changes, both of organization and policy. In the North, the Republican party, the great body of the American or Union party of 1860, and the war Democracy formed the Union party. The Democracy of the South, for the most part, became Rebels, and in the North those who did not unite with the Union party generally passed under the control and leadership of the peace Democracy.

At the beginning of the war, the creed of the Union party consisted of one idea — it labored for one object — the restoration of the Union. Slavery, the rights of man, the principles of the Declaration of Independence, were for the time lost sight of in the struggle for the nation's life. As late as August, 1862, President Lincoln wrote to Mr. Greeley: "My paramount object is to save the Union, and not either to save or to destroy slavery. If I could save the Union without freeing any slave, I would do it; and if I could save it by freeing all the slaves, I would do it; and if I could do it by freeing some and leaving others alone, I would also do that."

Slowly, gradually, after repeated disasters and disappointments, the eyes of the Union leaders were opened to the fact that slavery and rebellion were convertible terms; that the Confederacy, according to its Vice-President, Alexander H. Stephens, was founded upon "exactly the opposite idea" from that of Jefferson and the fathers. "Its foundations," said he, "are laid, its corner-stone rests upon the great truth that the negro is not equal to the white man; that slavery, subordination to the superior race, is his natural and normal condition." Mr. Lincoln and the Union party, struggling faithfully onward, finally reached the solid ground that the American Government was founded on the broad principles of right, justice, and humanity, and that, for this nation, "Union and liberty" were, indeed, "one and inseparable."

The leaders of the peace Democracy were for a time overwhelmed by the popular uprising which followed the attack on Fort Sumter, and were not able during the year 1861 or the early part of 1862 to mark out definitely the course to be pursued. But, like the Union party, they gradually approached the position they were ultimately to occupy.

Their success in the autumn elections of 1862 encouraged them to enter upon the pathway in which they have plodded along consistently if not prosperously ever since. Opposition to the war measures of Mr. Lincoln's Administration, and in particular to every measure tending to the enfranchisement and elevation of the African race, became their settled policy. By this policy they were placed in harmony with their former associates, the Rebels of the South. The Rebels were fighting to destroy the Union. The peace party were opposing the only measures which could save it. The Rebels were fighting for slavery. The peace party were laboring in their way to keep alive and inflame the prejudice against race and color, on which slavery was based.

The abolition of slavery in the District of Columbia, the repeal of the Fugitive Slave Law, Mr. Lincoln's proclamation of emancipation, in a word, every step of the Union party toward enfranchisement of the colored people, the peace Democracy opposed. Every war measure, every means adopted to strengthen the cause of the Union and weaken the Rebellion, met with the same opposition. Whatever Mr. Lincoln or Congress did to get money, to get men, or to obtain the moral support of the country and the world — tax laws, tariff laws, greenbacks, government bonds, army bills, drafts, blockades, proclamations — met the indiscriminate and bitter assaults of these men. The enlistment of colored soldiers, a measure by which between one and two hundred thousand able-bodied men were transferred from the service of the Rebels in cornfields to the Union service in battlefields — how Mr. Lincoln and the Union party were vilified for that wise and necessary measure! But worse, infinitely worse, than mere opposition to war measures, were their efforts to impair the confidence of the people, to diminish the moral power of the Government, to give hope and earnestness to the enemies of the Union, by showing that the Administration was to blame for the war, that it was unnecessary, unjust, and that it had been perverted from its original object, and that it could not but fail.

I need not go beyond the record of leaders of the Ohio Democracy of to-day for proof of what I am saying. Mr. Pendleton, usually so gentlemanly and prudent in speech, lost his balance after the victories of the peace Democracy in 1862. At the Democratic jubilee in Butler County over the elections, Mr. Pendleton is reported as saying: "I came up to see if there were any Butternuts in Butler County. I came to see if there were any Copperheads in Butler County, as my friends of the Cincinnati *Gazette* and *Commercial* are fond of terming the Democracy of the country. I came up to tell you that there are a good many of that stripe of animals in old Hamilton. I have travelled about the country lately, and I assure you there is a large crop of Butternuts everywhere; not only that, but the quality and character of the nut is quite as good as the quantity."

Of course Mr. Pendleton was applauded by his audience; and he returned to his place in the House of Representatives at Washington prepared to give expression to his views with the same plainness and boldness which marked the utterances of his colleague, Mr. Vallandigham.

On the 31st of January, 1863, he made an elaborate speech against the enlistment of negroes into the service of the United States, in which he said: —

"I should be false to you, my fellow Representatives, if I did not tell you that there is an impression, growing with great rapidity, upon the minds of the people of the Northwest that they have been deliberately deceived into this war — that their patriotism and their love of country have been engaged to call them into the army, under the pretense that the war was to be for the Union and the Constitution, when, in fact, it was to be an armed crusade for the abolition of slavery. I tell you, sir, that unless this impression is speedily arrested it will become universal; it will ripen into conviction, and then it will be beyond your power to get from their broad plains another man, or from their almost exhausted coffers another dollar."

In the same speech he says: —

"I said two years ago, on this floor, that armies, money, war cannot restore this Union; justice, reason, peace, may. I believed it then; I have believed it at every moment since; I believe it now. No event of the past two years has for a moment shaken my faith. Peace is the first step to Union. Peace is Union. Peace unbroken would have preserved it; peace restored will, I hope, in some time reconstruct it. The only bonds which can hold these States in confederation, the only ties which can make us one people, are the soft and silken cords of affection and interest. These are woven in peace, not war; in conciliation, not coercion; in deeds of kindness and acts of friendly sympathy, not in deeds of violence and blood. The people of the Northwest were carried away by the excitement of April and May. They believed war would restore the Union. They trusted to the assurances of the President and his Cabinet, and of Congress, that it should be carried on for that purpose alone. They trusted that it would be carried on under the Constitution. They were patriotic and confiding. They sent their sons, and brothers, and husbands to the army, and poured out their treasures at the feet of the Administration. They feel that the war has been perverted from this end; that the Constitution has been disregarded; that abolition and arbitrary power, not Union and constitutional liberty, are the governing ideas of the Administration. They are in no temper to be trifled with. They think they have been deceived. There is danger of revolution. They are longing for peace."

Need I pause to inquire who would receive encouragement, or whose spirits would be depressed, on reading these remarkable sentences? Imagine them read by the Rebel camp-fires, or at the firesides of the Rebel people. What hope, what exultation we should behold in the faces of those who heard them! On the other hand, at Union camp-fires, or by the loyal firesides of the North, what sorrow, what mortification, what depression such statements would surely carry wherever they were heard and believed!

The course of the peace Democracy of Ohio during the memorable contest of 1863, between Brough and Vallandigham, is too well known to require attention now. Judge Thurman was one of the committee who constructed the platform of the convention which nominated Mr. Vallandigham, and was the ablest member of the State Central Committee which had charge of the canvass in his behalf during his exile.

The keynote to that canvass was given by Mr. Vallandigham himself in a letter written from Canada, July 15, 1863. That letter contained the following: —

"If this civil war is to terminate only by the subjugation or submission of the South to force and arms, the infant of to-day will not live to see the end of it. No, in another way only can it be brought to a close. Travelling a thousand miles and more, through nearly half of the Confederate States, and sojourning for a time at widely different points, I met not one man, woman, or child who was not resolved to perish rather than yield to the pressure of arms, even in the most desperate extremity. And whatever may and must be the varying fortune of the war, in all which I recognize the hand of Providence pointing visibly to the ultimate issue of this great trial of the States and people of America, they are better prepared now every way to make good their inexorable purpose than at any period since the beginning of the struggle. These may be unwelcome truths; but they are addressed only to candid and honest men."

The assumption of the certain success of the Rebellion, and that the war for the Union would assuredly fail, was the strong point of these gentlemen in favor of the election of Vallandigham and the defeat of Brough. Fortunately, the patriotic people saw the situation from another standpoint, and under the influence of different feelings and different sympathies.

In the elections of 1863, the peace Democracy of Ohio and other States sustained defeats which have no parallel in our political history. But, notwithstanding their reverses, the year 1864, the year of the Presidential election, found the Ohio leaders possibly sadder, but certainly not wiser nor more patriotic than before.

At the National Convention at Chicago, in August, Mr. Pendleton was nominated for Vice-President, Judge Thurman was a delegate of the State of Ohio at large, and Mr. Vallandigham as a district delegate, and as a member of the committee on platform, was the author of the following resolution adopted by the convention: —

"*Resolved*, That this convention does explicitly declare, as the sense

of the American people, that, after four years of failure to restore the
Union by the experiment of war, during which, under pretense of military necessity, or war power higher than the Constitution, the Constitution has been disregarded in every part, and public liberty and private
rights have been alike trodden down, and the material prosperity of the
country essentially impaired, justice, humanity, liberty, and the public
welfare demand that immediate efforts be made for a cessation of hos-
tilities, with a view to an ultimate convention of all the States, or other
peaceable means, to the end that at the earliest practicable moment
peace may be restored on the basis of the Federal Union of the States."

This resolution does not seem to require explanation or comment.
But as General McClellan's letter accepting the nomination for President did not square well with this part of the party platform, Mr. Vallandigham, in a speech at Sidney, Ohio, September 24, 1864, explained
it at some length. In that speech, he said: —

"I am speaking now of the fact that this convention pronounced this
war a failure, and giving you the reasons why it is a failure. . . . What
has been gained by this campaign? More lives have been lost, more hard
fighting has been done, more courage has been exhibited by the Federal
as well as the Southern soldiers than in any former campaign, and what
has been accomplished? General Grant is nearer to Richmond, occupying a territory of perhaps eleven miles, which was not in the possession
of the United States when the campaign began, from City Point to the
suburbs of Petersburg. To secure that he gave up all the country from
Manassas down to Richmond and a large part of the Valley. . . . How
about the Southern campaign? General Sherman, through the courage
of the best disciplined, best organized, and most powerful army that has
been seen since the campaigns of the first Napoleon, has taken Atlanta
— a town somewhat larger than Sidney. It has cost him sixty thousand
men and four or five months of the most terrible campaign ever waged
on this continent or any other, or any other part of the globe. He occupies from two to five miles on each side of a railroad of one hundred and
thirty-eight miles in length. He has penetrated that far into Georgia.
What has been surrendered to obtain that? All of Texas, nearly all of
Louisiana, nearly all of Arkansas, Mississippi, Alabama, and a part of
Tennessee, which were in possession of the Federals on the first of May.
Kentucky has been opened to continual incursions of the Confederate
armies. All this has been surrendered in order to gain this barren strip
of country on the line of the railroad. The war, then, has been properly
pronounced a failure in a military point of view. The convention meant
that it has failed to restore the Union, and there is not a Republican in
the land who does not know it."

In the Sidney speech, Mr. Vallandigham says, also: —

"What will you have now? Four years more of war? What guaranties of success have you? Do you want two million more of men to go
forth to this war as the crusaders went to the sepulchre at Jerusalem?
The beginning of this Administration found us with very little debt,

comparatively no taxation, and peace and happiness among the States; and now look at the scene! Four more years of war, do you tell me, when the first four, with every advantage, has failed? Now, too, that the hearts of one half of the people are turned away from war, and intent upon the arts of peace? What will be the consequence? Four thousand millions more of debt, five hundred millions more of taxation, more conscriptions, more calls for five hundred thousand men, more sacrifices for the next four years. All this is what Abraham Lincoln demands of you in order that the South may be compelled not to return to the Union, but to abandon slavery."

All this logic, this eloquence, this taxing the imagination to portray the horrors of war, failed to deceive the people; Lincoln was reëlected; the war went on, and a few short months witnessed the end of the armed Rebellion, and the triumph of Liberty and of Union.

Now came the work of reconstruction. The leaders of the peace Democracy, who had failed in every measure, in every plan, in every opinion, and in every prediction relating to the war, were promptly on hand, and with unblushing cheek were prepared to take exclusive charge of the whole business of reorganization and reconstruction. They had a plan all prepared — a plan easily understood, easily executed, and which they averred would be satisfactory to all parties. Their plan was in perfect harmony with the conduct and history of its authors and friends during the war. They had been in very close sympathy with the men engaged in the Rebellion, while their sympathy for loyal white people at the South was not strong, and they were bitterly hostile to loyal colored people both North and South. Their plan was consistent with all this.

According to it, the Rebels were to be treated in the same manner as if they had remained loyal. All laws, state and national, all orders and regulations of the military, naval, and other departments of the Government, creating disabilities on account of participation in the Rebellion, were to be repealed, revoked, or abolished. The rebellious States were to be represented in Congress by the Rebels without hindrance from any test oath. All appointments in the army, in the navy, and in the civil service were to be made from men who were Rebels, on the same terms as from men who were loyal. The people and Governments in the rebellious States were to be subjected to no other interference or control from the military or other departments of the general Government than exists in the States which remained loyal. Loyal white men and loyal colored men were to be protected alone in those States by state laws, executed by state authorities, as if they were in the loyal States.

There were to be no amendments to the Constitution, not even an amendment abolishing slavery. In short, the great Rebellion was to be ignored or forgotten, or, in the words of one of their orators, "to be generously forgiven." The war, whose burdens, cost, and carnage they had been so fond of exaggerating, suddenly sank into what the Reverend Petroleum V. Nasby calls "the late unpleasantness," for which nobody but the abolitionists were to blame. Under this plan the States could soon reëstablish slavery where it had been disturbed by the war. Jefferson Davis, Toombs, Slidell, and Mason could be reëlected to their old places in the Senate of the United States; Lee could be reappointed in the army, and Semmes and Maury could be restored to the navy. Of course this plan of the peace Democracy was acceptable to the Rebels of the South.

But the loyal people, who under the name of the Union party fought successfully through the War of the Rebellion, objected to this plan as wrong in principle, wrong in its details, and fatally wrong as an example for the future. It treats treason as no crime and loyalty as no virtue; it contains no guaranties, irreversible or otherwise, against another rebellion by the same parties and on the same grounds. It restores to political honor and power in the Government of the nation men who have spent the best part of their lives in plotting the overthrow of that Government, and who for more than four years levied public war against the United States; it allows Union men in the South, who have risked all, — and many of whom have lost all but life in upholding the Union cause, — to be excluded from every office, state and national, and in many instances to be banished from the States they so faithfully labored to save; it abandons the four millions of colored people to such treatment as the ruffian class of the South, educated in the barbarism of slavery and the atrocities of the Rebellion, may choose to give them; it leaves the obligation of the nation to her creditors and to the maimed soldiers and to the widows and orphans of the war, to be fulfilled by men who hate the cause in which those obligations were incurred; it claims to be a plan which restores the Union without requiring conditions; but, in conceding to the conquered Rebels the repeal of laws important to the nation's welfare, it grants conditions which they demand, while it denies to the loyal victors conditions which they deem of priceless value.

In the meantime, President Johnson having declared that "the Rebellion, in its revolutionary progress, had deprived the people of the Rebel States of all civil government," proceeded by military power to set up provisional State Governments in those States, and to require them to declare void all ordinances of secession, to repudiate the Rebel debt, and to adopt the Thirteenth Amendment of the Constitution, proposed by the Union party, abolishing slavery throughout the United States. The peace Democracy opposed all conditions, and, instinctively unsound upon human rights, opposed the amendment abolishing slavery. The elections of 1865 settled that question against them, and deprived them of New Jersey, the last free State which adhered to their fallen fortunes.

At the session of Congress of 1865–66, the President, finding that his so-called State Governments in the Rebel States — created by military power alone and without the sanction of the legislative power of the Government — had accepted his conditions, insisted that those States were fully restored to their former proper relations with the general

Government, and that they were again entitled to representation in the same manner with the loyal States. This plan accorded with the wishes of all unrepentant Rebels, and as a matter of course received the support of their allies of the peace Democracy.

The Union party, at the sacrifice of all of the power and patronage of the Administration they had elected, firmly opposed and finally defeated this project. They required, before the complete restoration of the Rebel States, that the Fourteenth Amendment of the Constitution should be adopted, which was framed to secure civil rights to the colored people, equal representation between the free States and the former slave States, the disqualification for office of leading Rebels, the payment of the loyal obligations to creditors, to maimed soldiers, and to widows and orphans, and the repudiation of the Rebel debt and of claims to payment for slaves. On the adoption of this amendment turned the elections of 1866. After the amplest debates before the people the Union party carried the country in favor of the amendment, electing more than three fourths of the members of the House of Representatives. They also secured the adoption of the amendment in twenty-one out of the twenty-four States now represented, which have acted upon it by an average vote in the State Legislatures of more than four to one.

In striking contrast with this was the action of the Rebel States. Tennessee alone ratified the amendment. The other ten promptly and defiantly rejected it by an average majority in their State Legislatures of more than fifty to one. When, therefore, the Thirty-ninth Congress met in the session of 1866–67 they found the work of reconstruction in those ten States still unaccomplished.

Now, in what condition were those ten Rebel States? In the first place, all political power in those States was in the hands of Rebels, and for the most part of leading and unrepentant Rebels. Their Governors, their members of Legislature, their judges, their county and city officers, and their members of Congress, with rare exceptions, were Rebels. Such was their political condition.

What was their condition with respect to the preservation of order, the suppression of crime, and the redress of private grievances? After the suppression of the Rebellion the next plain duty of the National Government was to see that the lives, liberty, and property of all classes of citizens were secure, and especially to see that the loyal white and colored citizens who resided or might sojourn in those States did not suffer injustice, oppression, or outrage because of their loyalty. Loyal men, without distinction of race or color, were clearly entitled to the full measure of protection usually found in civilized countries, if in the nature of things it was possible for the nation to furnish it.

Inquiring as to the condition of things in the South, I waive the uniform current of information derived from the press and other unofficial sources from all parts of the South, and rely exclusively on the official reports of army officers like Grant, Thomas, Sheridan, and Howard —

officers of clear heads, of strong sense, and of spotless integrity, whose business it is to know the facts, and who all united in warning the nation that Union men, either white or colored, were not safe in the South.

General Grant says that the class at the South who "will acknowledge no law but force" is sufficiently formidable to justify the military occupation of that territory.

General Sheridan, in an official report, says the "trial of a white man for the murder of a freedman in Texas would be a farce; and, in making this statement, I make it because truth compels me, and for no other reason. . . . Over the killing of many freedmen nothing is done." General Sheridan cites cases in which our national soldiers wearing the uniform of the Republic have been deliberately shot "without provocation" by citizens, and the grand jury refused to find a bill against the murderers. Even in Virginia, General Schofield was compelled to resort to a military tribunal because "a gentleman" who shot a negro dead in cold blood "was instantly acquitted by one of the civil courts."

General Ord reports in Arkansas fifty-two murders of freed persons by white men in the past three or four months, "*and no reports have been received that the murderers have been imprisoned or punished.* . . . The number of murders reported is not half the number committed."

General Sickles says that in South Carolina, "in certain counties, such as Newberry, Edgecombe, and Laurens, so much countenance was given to outrages on freedmen by the indifference of the civil authorities and by the population, who made themselves accomplices in the crimes, that other measures became necessary."

In Mississippi, General Thomas calls attention to the legislation in regard to colored people. "It is oppressive, unjust, and unconstitutional." The laws as to buying real estate, bearing arms, making contracts, and the like, are of such a character "that the constitutional gift of freedom is not much more than a name."

General Sheridan, speaking of Louisiana, says: "Homicides are frequent in some localities. Sometimes they are investigated by a coroner's jury, which justifies the act and releases the perpetrator; in other cases, . . . the parties are held to bail in a nominal sum; but the trial of a white man for the killing of a freedman can, in the existing state of society in this State, be nothing more or less than a farce."

General Thomas, in February last, in relation to the display of the Rebel flag in Rome, Georgia, said: "The sole cause of this and similar offenses lies in the fact that certain citizens of Rome, and a portion of the people of the States lately in rebellion, do not and have not accepted the situation, and that is that the late civil war was a rebellion, and history will so record it. . . . Everywhere in the States lately in rebellion treason is respectable and loyalty odious. This the people of the United States who ended the Rebellion and saved the country will not permit; and all attempts to maintain this unnatural order of things will be met by decided disapproval."

Upon these official reports, showing not merely that atrocious crimes were everywhere committed against loyal people, but that the civil authorities did not even attempt to prevent them by the punishment of the perpetrators, it became the plain duty of Congress to adopt measures "to enforce peace and good order in the Rebel States, until loyal and republican State Governments could be legally established." How well this duty was performed will appear from a brief examination of the Reconstruction Acts which were passed by Congress in March last, and by the auspicious results which followed their adoption and execution.

By these acts, the ten Rebel States were divided into five military districts, subject to the military authority of the United States; and it was made the duty of the President to assign military officers, not below the rank of brigadier-general, to command each of said districts, and to detail a sufficient military force to enable such officers to perform their duties. The duties of military commanders were defined as follows, in the third section of the act: —

"SEC. 3. *And be it further enacted,* That it shall be the duty of each officer assigned as aforesaid, to protect all persons in their rights of person and property, to suppress insurrection, disorder, and violence, and to punish, or cause to be punished, all disturbers of the public peace and criminals; and to this end he may allow local civil tribunals to take jurisdiction of and to try offenders; or when, in his judgment, it may be necessary for the trial of offenders, he shall have power to organize military commissions or tribunals for that purpose; and all interference, under color of state authority, with the exercise of military authority under this act shall be null and void."

The act also sets forth the manner in which the people of any one of the Rebel States could form a state constitution, and the terms on which the State would be fully restored to proper relations with the Union. The most important provisions are those relating to the qualifications of voters and the one requiring the adoption of the amendment to the Constitution proposed by the Thirty-ninth Congress, known as Article Fourteen. The right of suffrage is given to all men of suitable age and residence, without distinction of race or color, except a limited number who are excluded for participation in the Rebellion.

In pursuance of these acts; the district of Louisiana and Texas was placed under the command of General Sheridan; Arkansas and Mississippi, under General Ord; Alabama, Georgia, and Florida, under General Pope; North Carolina and South Carolina, under General Sickles; and Virginia, under General Schofield. The merits of this plan are obvious.

(1) It places the Rebels again under the control of the power which conquered them, and of the very officers to whom they surrendered.

(2) It is well calculated to afford protection to all loyal people, white or colored, against those who would oppress or injure them on account of their loyalty.

(3) It places the new State Governments of the South upon the solid basis of justice and equal rights.

This plan received in Congress the support of many members of Congress who did not uniformly vote with the Union party, and was acceptable to some of its most distinguished adversaries. In the Senate, Reverdy Johnson, a Maryland Democrat, voted for it, and made effective speeches in its support. The loyal press of the North, without exception, upheld it.

In the South, its success was everywhere gratifying and unexampled. Its enemies had said that it would organize anarchy in the Rebel States — that it would immediately inaugurate a war of races between whites and blacks — and compared the condition of the South under it to the condition of India under English oppression, and to Hungary under the despotism of Austria.

But the course of the public press, and the conduct, the letters, and speeches of public men in the Rebel States, vindicated the wisdom and justice of the measure. I will quote only from Rebel sources.

In Virginia, the Charlottesville *Chronicle* addressed its readers as follows: —

"For WHITE FOLKS AND COLORED FOLKS. — Every colored person may now go where and when he pleases. He is a free man and a full citizen. This is not all; by another bound they have become voters. They will take part in the government of the country. No people was ever so suddenly, so rapidly lifted up.

"Shall we all live happily together, or shall we hate each other, and quarrel and bear malice?

"Let us all try and get on together. The land is big enough. Let the whites accommodate themselves to the new state of things Let them be polite and kind to all, and be always ready to accord to every man, whether white or colored, his full rights. We make bold to say that the behavior of the colored people of this State, since they were set free, has surprised all fair-minded white people. We do not believe the white people, under the same circumstances, would have behaved so well by twenty per cent. They have shown the greatest moderation. They have passed from plantation hands to freedom and the ballot without outward excitement."

The Richmond *Examiner*, the organ of the fire eaters, says of the colored people: —

"This class of our population, as a general thing, manifest a disposition to prepare themselves for the altered political condition in which the events of the past two years have placed them. The sudden abolition of slavery did not, as most persons expected, turn their heads. They have been, in the main, orderly and well behaved. They have not presumed upon their newly acquired freedom to commit breaches of the peace or to be guilty of any acts calculated to sow dissension between the two races. The utmost good feeling is felt by the white people of this city toward the negroes. There is not one particle of bitterness felt for them."

In South Carolina, Wade Hampton addressed a mixed assembly of whites and colored people at Columbia, in which he quoted from a former speech to his old soldiers: —

"There is one other point on which there should be no misunderstanding as to our position — no loop on which to hang a possible misconstruction as to our views — and that is the abolition of slavery. The deed has been done, and I, for one, do honestly declare that I never wish to see it revoked. Nor do I believe that the people of the South would now remand the negro to slavery, if they had the power to do so unquestioned.

"Under our paternal care, from a mere handful, he grew to be a mighty host. He came to us a heathen; we made him a Christian. Idle, vicious, savage in his own country, in ours he became industrious, gentle, civilized. As a slave, he was faithful to us; as a freeman, let us treat him as a friend. Deal with him frankly, justly, kindly, and, my word for it, he will reciprocate your kindness. If you wish to see him contented, industrious, useful, aid him in his efforts to elevate himself in the scale of civilization, and thus fit him not only to enjoy the blessings of freedom, but to appreciate his duties."

After stating the provisions of the "military bill," as he calls the Reconstruction Law, he said to the colored people: —

"But suppose the bill is pronounced unconstitutional; how then? I tell you what I am willing to see done. I am willing to give the right of suffrage to all who can read and who pay a certain amount of taxes; and I agree that this qualification shall bear on white and black alike. You would have no right to complain of a law which would put you on a perfect political equality with the whites, and which would put within your reach and that of your children the privilege enjoyed by any class of citizens."

In Georgia, the prevailing sentiment is indicated by the following. The Atlanta *New Era* says: —

"We freely accept the Sherman platform as the only means whereby to rescue the country from total destruction, and if we mistake not, our backbone will prove sufficiently strong to enable us to look the issue full in the face, without a shudder. It is our bounden duty, and that of every other patriot and well-wisher of the South, to at once signify an unconditional acceptance of the measures perfected by Congress for our restoration to the Union, and heartily coöperate with the United States authorities in securing that most desirable end."

The Augusta *Press*, alluding to the recent meeting of negroes at Columbia, South Carolina, and the fact that speeches were made by General Wade Hampton and others, states that —

"All good citizens all over the South entertain precisely the same kind feelings for the colored people that were exhibited by these eminent Carolinians, and it is unfortunate that these sentiments are not more widely manifested in meetings for public counsel with them. 'Representative men' in every community should be prompt and earnest in signifying their wish to coöperate with the colored people in the administration of the laws and the preservation of harmony and good will. To this end, we deem it our duty to urge that in every community public meetings be held, in which the two races may take friendly counsel together."

In Florida, Hon. S. R. Mallory, a former Democratic United States Senator, is reported to have said, at a large meeting composed of whites and blacks, in Pensacola, that —

"The recent legislation of Congress ought to be submitted to in good faith; that, as the negro was now entitled to vote, it was the interest of the State that he should be educated and enlightened, and made to comprehend the priceless value of the ballot, and the importance to himself and to the State of its judicious use.

"Let us fully and frankly acknowledge, as well by deeds as by words, their equality with us, before the law, and regard it as no less just to ourselves and them than to our State and her best interests to aid in their education, elevation, and enjoyment of all the rights which follow their new condition."

Governor Patton, of Alabama, says: —

"It seems to me that it is the true feeling of the Southern people to contribute their best influence in favor of an early organization of their respective States, in accordance with the requirements of the recent Reconstruction Act. Congress claims the right to control this whole question. In my humble judgment, it is unwise to contend longer against its power, or to struggle further against its repeatedly expressed will.

.   .   .   .

"The freedmen are now to vote the first time. We should cherish against them no ill-feeling. The elective franchise is conferred upon them; let them exercise it freely, and in their own way. No effort should be made to control their votes, except such as may tend to enable them to vote intelligently, and such as may be necessary to protect them against mischievous influences to which, from their want of intelligence, they may possibly be subjected. Above all things, we should discourage everything which may tend to generate antagonism between white and colored voters."

In Mississippi, Albert G. Brown, a former Democratic United States Senator, and a Rebel, says: —

"To those who think it most becoming men in my situation to keep quiet, I am free to say 'that is very much my own opinion.' As I speak reluctantly, you will not be surprised if I say as little as possible.

.   .   .   .

"The negro is a fixture in this country. He is not going out of it; he is not going to die out, and he is not going to be driven out. Nor is his exodus from the country desirable. I am frank in saying if they, every one of them, could be packed in a balloon, carried over the water, and emptied into Africa, I would not have it done, unless, indeed, it were already arranged that the balloon should return by the way of Germany, Ireland, Scotland, etc., and bring us a return cargo of white laborers. If the negro is to stay here, and it is desirable to have him do so, what is the duty of the intelligent white man toward him? Why, to educate him, admit him, when sufficiently instructed, to the right of voting, and as rapidly as possible prepare him for a safe and rational enjoyment of that 'equality before the law' which, as a free man, he has a right to claim, and which we cannot long refuse to give."

The Mississippi *Index* says: —

"There are some laws on our statute-book respecting negroes that are of no practical use, and will have to be done away with some day. The sooner we dispense with them the better. But in the matter of educating the negro we can accomplish more toward convincing the people of the North that we have been misrepresented and slandered than by legislative action. Let us take the work of education out of the hands of the Yankees among us. We can do this by encouraging the establishment of negro schools and placing them in the charge of men and women whom we know to be competent and trustworthy."

In Louisiana, General Longstreet, one of the most distinguished of the Rebel generals, says: —

"The striking feature, and the one that our people should keep in view, is that we are a conquered people. Recognizing this fact fairly and squarely, there is but one course left for wise men to pursue — accept the terms that are offered us by the conquerors. There can be no discredit to a conquered people for accepting the conditions offered by their conquerors. Nor is that any occasion for a feeling of humiliation. We have made an honest, and I hope that I may say, a creditable fight, but we have lost. Let us come forward, then, and accept the ends involved in the struggle.

"Our people earnestly desire that the constitutional Government shall be reëstablished, and the only means to accomplish this is to comply with the requirements of the recent congressional legislation.

.   .   .   .

"The military bill and amendments are peace offerings. We should accept them as such, and place ourselves upon them as the starting-point from which to meet future political issues as they arise.

"Like other Southern men, I naturally sought alliance with the Democratic party, merely because it was opposed to the Republican party. But, as far as I can judge, there is nothing tangible about it, except the issues that were staked upon the war and lost. Finding nothing to take hold of except prejudice, which can not be worked into good for any one, it is proper and right that I should seek some standpoint from which good may be done."

Quotations like these from prominent Democratic politicians, from Rebel soldiers, and from influential Rebel newspapers, might be multiplied indefinitely. Enough have been given to show how completely and how exactly the Reconstruction Acts have met the evil to be remedied in the South. My friend, Mr. Hassaurek, in his admirable speech at Columbus, did not estimate too highly the fruits of these measures. Said he: —

"And, sir, this remedy at once effected the desired cure. The poor contraband is no longer the persecuted outlaw whom incurable Rebels might kick and kill with impunity; but he at once became 'our colored fellow citizen,' in whose well-being his former master takes the liveliest interest. Thus, by bringing the negro under the American system, we have completed his emancipation. He has ceased to be a pariah. From an outcast he has been transformed into a human being, invested with the great national attribute of self-protection, and the reëstablishment of peace, and order, and security, the revival of business and trade, and the restoration of the Southern States on the basis of loyalty and equal justice to all, will be the happy results of this astonishing metamorphosis, provided the party which has inaugurated this policy remains in power to carry it out."

The peace Democracy generally throughout the North oppose this measure. In Ohio they oppose it especially because it commits the people of the nation in favor of manhood suffrage. They tell us that if it is wise and just to entrust the ballot to colored men in the District of Columbia, in the Territories, and in the Rebel States, it is also just and wise that they should have it in Ohio and in the other States of the North.

Union men do not question this reasoning, but if it is urged as an objection to the plan of Congress, we reply: "There are now within the limits of the United States about five millions of colored people. They are not aliens or strangers. They are here not by the choice of themselves or of their ancestors. They are here by the misfortune of their fathers and the crime of ours. Their labor, privations, and sufferings, unpaid and unrequited, have cleared and redeemed one third of the inhabited territory of the Union. Their toil has added to the resources and wealth of the nation untold millions. Whether we prefer it or not, they are our countrymen, and will remain so forever."

They are more than countrymen — they are citizens. Free colored people were citizens of the Colonies. The Constitution of the United States, formed by our fathers, created no disabilities on account of color. By the acts of our fathers and of ourselves, they bear equally the burdens and are required to discharge the highest duties of citizens. They are compelled to pay taxes and to bear arms. They fought side by side with their white countrymen in the great struggle for independence, and in the recent war for the Union. In the Revolutionary contest, colored men bore an honorable part, from the Boston massacre, in 1770, to the surrender of Cornwallis, in 1781. Bancroft says: "Their names may be read on the pension rolls of the country side by side with those of other soldiers of the Revolution." In the War of 1812 General Jackson issued an order complimenting the colored men of his army engaged in the defense of New Orleans. I need not speak of their number or of their services in the War of the Rebellion. The nation enrolled and accepted them among her defendants to the number of about two hundred thousand, and in the new Regular Army Act, passed at the close of the

Rebellion, by the votes of Democrats and Union men alike, in the Senate and in the House, and by the assent of the President, regiments of colored men, cavalry and infantry, form part of the standing army of the Republic.

In the navy, colored American sailors have fought side by side with white men from the days of Paul Jones to the victory of the Kearsarge over the Rebel pirate Alabama. Colored men will, in the future as in the past, in all times of national peril, be our fellow soldiers. Taxpayers, countrymen, fellow citizens, and fellow soldiers, the colored men of America have been and will be. It is now too late for the adversaries of nationality and human rights to undertake to deprive these taxpayers, freemen, citizens, and soldiers of the right to vote.

Slaves were never voters. It was bad enough that our fathers, for the sake of Union, were compelled to allow masters to reckon three fifths of their slaves for representation, without adding slave suffrage to the other privileges of the slaveholder. But free colored men were always voters in many of the Colonies, and in several of the States, North and South, after independence was achieved. They voted for members of the Congress which declared independence, and for members of every Congress prior to the adoption of the Federal Constitution; for the members of the convention which framed the Constitution; for the members of many of the state conventions which ratified it, and for every President from Washington to Lincoln.

Our government has been called the white man's government. Not so. It is not the government of any class, or sect, or nationality, or race. It is a government founded on the consent of the governed, and Mr. Broomall, of Pennsylvania, therefore properly calls it "the government of the governed." It is not the government of the native-born, or of the foreign-born, of the rich man, or of the poor man, of the white man, or of the colored man — it is the government of the freeman. And when colored men were made citizens, soldiers, and freemen, by our consent and votes, we were estopped from denying to them the right of suffrage.

General Sherman was right when he said, in his Atlanta letter, of 1864: "If you admit the negro to this struggle for any purpose, he has a right to stay in for all; and, when the fight is over, the hand that drops the musket cannot be denied the ballot."

Even our adversaries are compelled to admit the Jeffersonian rule, that "the man who pays taxes and who fights for the country is entitled to vote."

Mr. Pendleton, in his speech against the enlistment of colored soldiers, gave up the whole controversy. He said: "Gentlemen tell us that these colored men are ready, with their strong arms and their brave hearts, to maintain the supremacy of the Constitution, and to defend the integrity of the Union, which in our hands to-day is in peril. What is that Constitution? It provides that every child of the Republic, every citizen of the land is before the law the equal of every other. It provides for all of them trial by jury, free speech, free press, entire protection for life and liberty and property. It goes further. It secures to every citizen the right of suffrage, the right to hold office, the right to aspire to every office or agency by which the Government is carried on. Every man called upon to do military duty, every man required to take up arms in its defense, is by its provisions entitled to vote, and a competent aspirant for every office in the Government."

The truth is, impartial manhood suffrage is already practically decided. It is now merely a question of time. In the eleven Rebel States, in five of the New England States, and in a number of the Northwestern States, there is no organized party able to successfully oppose impartial suffrage. The Democratic party of more than half of the States are ready to concede its justice and expediency.

The Boston *Post*, the able organ of the New England Democracy, says: —

"Color ought to have no more to do with the matter [voting] than size. Only establish a right standard, and then apply it impartially. A rule of that sort is too firmly fixed in justice and equality to be shaken. It commends itself too clearly to the good sentiment of the entire body of our countrymen to be successfully traversed by objections. Once let this principle be fairly presented to the people of the several States, with the knowledge on their part that they alone are to have the disposal and settlement of it, and we sincerely believe it would not be long before it would be adopted by every State in the Union."

The New York *World*, the ablest Democratic newspaper in the Union, says: —

"Democrats in the North, as well as the South, should be fully alive to the importance of the new element thrust into the politics of the country. We suppose it to be morally certain that the new constitution of the State of New York, to be framed this year, will confer the elective franchise upon all adult male negroes. We have no faith in the success of any efforts to shut the negro element out of politics. It is the part of wisdom frankly to accept the situation, and get beforehand with the Radicals in gaining an ascendancy over the negro mind."

The Chicago *Times*, the influential organ of the Northwestern Democracy, says: —

"The word 'white' is not found in any of the original constitutions, save only that of South Carolina. In every other State negroes, who possessed the qualifications that were required impartially of all men, were admitted to vote, and many of that race did vote, in the Southern as well as in the Northern States. And, moreover, they voted the Democratic ticket, for it was the Democratic party of that day which affirmed their right in that respect upon an impartial basis with white men. All Democrats cannot, even at this day, have forgotten the statement of General Jackson, that he was supported for the Presidency by negro voters in the State of Tennessee.

"The doctrine of impartial suffrage is one of the earliest and most essential doctrines of Democracy. It is the affirmation of the right of every man who is made a partaker of the burdens of the State to be represented by his own consent or vote in its government. It is the first principle upon which all true republican government rests. It is the basis upon which the liberties of America will be preserved, if they are preserved at all. The Democratic party must return from its driftings, and stand again upon the immutable rock of principles."

In Ohio the leaders of the peace Democracy intend to carry on one more campaign on the old and rotten platform of prejudice against colored people. They seek in this way to divert attention from the record they made during the War of the Rebellion. But the great facts of our recent history are against them. The principles of the fathers, reason, religion, and the spirit of the age are against them.

The plain and monstrous inconsistency and injustice of excluding one seventh of our population from all participation in a Government founded on the consent of the governed in this land of free discussion is simply impossible. No such absurdity and wrong can be permanent. Impartial suffrage will carry the day. No low prejudice will long be able to induce American citizens to deny to a weak people their best means of self-protection for the unmanly reason that they are weak. Chief Justice Chase expressed the true sentiment when he said, "The American nation cannot afford to do the smallest injustice to the humblest and feeblest of her children."

Much has been said of the antagonism which exists between the different races of men. But difference of religion, difference of nationality, difference of language, and difference of rank and privileges are quite as fruitful causes of antagonism and war as difference of race. The bitter strifes between Christians and Jews, between Catholics and Protestants, between Englishmen and Irishmen, between aristocracy and the masses are only too familiar. What causes increase and aggravate these antagonisms, and what are the measures which diminish and prevent them, ought to be equally familiar. Under the partial and unjust laws of the nations of the Old World men of one nationality were allowed to oppress those of another; men of one faith had rights which were denied to men of a different faith; men of one rank or caste enjoyed special privileges which were not granted to men of another. Under these systems peace was impossible and strife perpetual. But under just and equal laws in the United States, Jews, Protestants, and Catholics, Englishmen and Irishmen, the former aristocrat and the masses of the people, dwell and mingle harmoniously together. The uniform lesson of history is that unjust and partial laws increase and create antagonism, while justice and equality are the sure foundation of prosperity and peace.

Impartial suffrage secures also popular education. Nothing has given the careful observer of events in the South more gratification than the progress which is there going on in the establishment of schools. The colored people, who as slaves were debarred from education, regard the right to learn as one of the highest privileges of freemen. The ballot gives them the power to secure that privilege. All parties and all public men in the South agree that, if colored men vote, ample provision must be made in the reorganization of every State for free schools. The ignorance of the masses, whites as well as blacks, is one of the most discouraging features of Southern society. If congressional reconstruction succeeds, there will be free schools for all. The colored people will see that their children attend them. We need indulge in no fears that the white people will be left behind. Impartial suffrage, then, means popular intelligence; it means progress; it means loyalty; it means harmony between the North and the South, and between the whites and the colored people.

The Union party believes that the general welfare requires that measures should be adopted which will work great changes in the South. Our adversaries are accustomed to talk of the Rebellion as an affair which began when the Rebels attacked Fort Sumter in 1861, and which ended when Lee surrendered to Grant in 1865. It is true that the attempt by force of arms to destroy the United States began and ended during the Administration of Mr. Lincoln. But the causes, the principles, and the motives which produced the Rebellion are of an older date than the generation which suffered from the fruit they bore, and their influence and power are likely to last long after that generation passes away. Ever since armed rebellion failed, a large party in the South have struggled to make participation in the Rebellion honorable and loyalty to the Union dishonorable. The lost cause with them is the honored cause. In society, in business, and in politics, devotion to treason is the test of merit, the passport to preferment. They wish to return to the old state of things — *an oligarchy of race and the sovereignty of States.*

To defeat this purpose, to secure the rights of man, and to perpetuate the National Union, are the objects of the congressional plan of reconstruction. That plan has the hearty support of the great generals (so far as their opinions are known) — of Grant, of Thomas, of Sheridan, of Howard — who led the armies of the Union which conquered the Rebellion. The statesmen most trusted by Mr. Lincoln and by the loyal people of the country during the war also support it. The Supreme Court of the United States, upon formal application and after solemn argument, refuse to interfere with its execution. The loyal press of the country, which did so much in the time of need to uphold the patriot cause, without exception, are in favor of the plan.

In the South, as we have seen, the lessons of the war and the events occurring since the war have made converts of thousands of the bravest and of the ablest of those who opposed the national cause. General Longstreet, a soldier second to no living corps commander of the Rebel army, calls it "a peace offering," and advises the South in good faith to organize under it. Unrepentant Rebels and unconverted peace Democrats oppose it, just as they opposed the measures which destroyed slavery and saved the nation.

Opposition to whatever the nation approves seems to be the policy of the representative men of the peace Democracy. Defeat and failure comprise their whole political history. In laboring to overthrow reconstruction they are probably destined to further defeat and further failure. I know not how it may be in other States, but if I am not greatly mistaken as to the mind of the loyal people of Ohio, they mean to trust power in the hands of no man who, during the awful struggle for the nation's life, proved unfaithful to the cause of liberty and of Union. They will continue to exclude from the administration of the Government those who prominently opposed the war, until every question arising out of the Rebellion relating to the integrity of the nation and to human rights shall have been firmly settled on the basis of impartial justice.

They mean that the State of Ohio, in this great progress, "whose leading object is to elevate the condition of men, to lift artificial weights from all shoulders, to clear the paths of laudable pursuits for all, to afford all an unfettered start and a fair chance in the race of life," shall tread no step backward.

Penetrated and sustained by a conviction that in this contest the Union party of Ohio is doing battle for the right, I enter upon my part of the labors of the canvass with undoubting confidence that the goodness of the cause will supply the weakness of its advocates, and command in the result that triumphant success which I believe it deserves.

Mr. Thurman, on the other hand, vigorously defended the course of the peace Democrats during the war, criticized Mr. Lincoln, asserted that there was "scarcely a provision of the Constitution" that had not been "shamelessly and needlessly trampled under foot" by the Republican Administration in the conduct of the war, which he averred had been unnecessarily prolonged for partisan reasons; insisted that the purpose of the war had been perverted from a contest to save the Union to a crusade to free the slave and to exalt the negro above the white man; and argued that the same spirit of defiance of constitutional rights and limitations which had pervaded the Republican party during the war was still controlling it in dealing with the problem of reconstruction — a spirit which if not rebuked would surely bring the nation to despotism and destruction. Fraught with dire disaster was the project of negro suffrage.

Other topics were introduced in the campaign — the burden of taxation, the danger and cost of a large standing army, the state of the finances, the manner of paying the public debt (the greenback heresy beginning to make its appearance). But all these questions General Hayes contended — and rightly — were of secondary importance, even where the parties differed in their views — as in many cases they did not — in regard to them. The question at this juncture of paramount importance was the complete rehabilitation of the Union on such terms as would guarantee its integrity in the future; as would establish it on enduring bases of right and justice; as would prevent the possibility of any new revival of the heresy of the right of secession. This paramount end could be attained, he argued, only by supporting the plan and policy of Congress, representing the party that had successfully reduced the Rebellion, and not by turning now to the party which in its obstinate adherence to the extreme States' rights doctrine and its insistence on a narrow and literal constitutionalism demanded the instant and unconditioned restoration of the Rebel States to full and equal relations in the Union.

These points were forcibly presented in a speech by Mr. Hayes at Sidney on September 4, in the course of which he said: —

All of the side issues presented are merely urged on the people to withdraw their minds from the great main issue which ought to engage the attention of the American nation. What is that great issue? It is reconstruction. That is the main question before us, and until it is settled, and settled rightly, all other issues sink into insignificance in comparison with it. Fortunately for the Union party of Ohio, events are occurring every day at Washington which tend more and more clearly to define the exact question before the people, showing that the main question is whether the Union shall be reconstructed in the interests of the Rebellion or in the interests of loyalty and Union; whether that reconstruction shall be carried on by men who, during the war, were in favor of the war and against the Rebellion, or by men who in the North were against the war, and who in the South carried on the Rebellion. On one side of this question we see Andrew Johnson, Judge Black, and the other leaders of the peace party of the North and the unrepentant Rebels of the South; and on the other side is the great War Secretary, Stanton, with General Grant, General Sheridan, General Thomas, General Howard, and the other Union commanders engaged in carrying out the Reconstruction Acts of Congress. This presents clearly enough the question before the people. General Grant, in one paragraph of his letter to the President, said to him: —

"General Sheridan has performed his civil duties faithfully and intelligently. His removal will only be regarded as an effort to defeat the laws of Congress. It will be interpreted by the unreconstructed element in the South — those who did all they could to break up this Government by arms, and now wish to be the only element consulted as to the method of restoring order — as a triumph. It will embolden them to renewed opposition to the will of the loyal masses, believing that they have the Executive with them."

This presents exactly the question before the people. We want the loyal people of the country, the victors in the great struggle we have passed through, to do the work; we want reconstruction upon such principles, and by means of such measures that the causes which made reconstruction necessary shall not exist in the reconstructed Union; we want that foolish notion of States' rights, which teaches that the State is superior to the nation — that there is a state sovereignty which commands the allegiance of every citizen higher than the sovereignty of the nation — we want that notion left out of the reconstructed Union; we want it understood that whatever doubts may have existed prior to the war as to the relation of the State to the National Government, that now the National Government is supreme, anything in the constitution or laws of any State to the contrary notwithstanding. Again, as one of the causes of the Rebellion, we want slavery left out, not merely in name but in fact, and forever; we want the last vestige, the last relic of that institution, rooted out of the laws and institutions of every State; we want that in the South there shall be no more suppression of free discussion.

I notice that in the long speech of my friend, Judge Thurman, he says that for nearly fifty years, throughout the length and breadth of the land, freedom of speech and of the press was never interfered with, either by the Government or the people. For more than thirty years, fellow citizens, there has been no such thing as free discussion in the South. Those moderate speeches of Abraham Lincoln on the subject of slavery — not one of them — could have been delivered, without endangering his life, south of Mason and Dixon's line. We want in the reconstructed Union that there shall be the same freedom of the press and freedom of speech in the States of the South that there always has been in the States of the North. Again, we want the reconstructed Union upon such principles that the men of the South who, during the war, were loyal and true to the Government, shall be protected in life, liberty, and property, and in the exercise of their political rights. It becomes the solemn duty of the loyal victors in the great struggle to see that the men who, in the midst of difficulties, discouragements, and dangers in the South were true, are protected in these rights. And, in order that our reconstruction shall be carried out faithfully and accomplish these objects, we further want that the work shall be in the hands of the right men.

Andrew Johnson, in the days when he was loyal, said the work of reconstruction ought to be placed absolutely in the hands of the loyal men of the State; that Rebels, and particularly leading Rebels, ought not to participate in that work; that while that work is going on they must take back seats. We want that understood in our work of reconstruction. How important it is to have the right men in charge of this work appears upon the most cursory examination of what has already been done. President Lincoln administered the same laws substantially, — was sworn to support the same Constitution with Andrew Johnson, — yet how different the reconstruction as carried out by these two men! Lincoln's reconstruction in all the States which he undertook to reorganize gave to those States loyal Governments, loyal Governors, loyal Legislatures, judges, and officers of the law. Andrew Johnson, administering the same Constitution and the same laws, reconstructs a number of States, and in all of them leading Rebels are elected Governors, leading Rebels are members of the Legislature, and leading Rebels are sent to Congress. It makes, then, the greatest difference to the people of this country who it is that does the work.

This, my friends, brings me to a proposition to which I call the attention of every audience that I have occasion to address, and that is this, that until the work of reconstruction is complete, until every question arising out of the Rebellion relating to the integrity of the nation and to human rights has been settled, and settled rightly, no man ought to be trusted with power in this country, who, during the struggle for the nation's life, was unfaithful to Union and liberty. That is the proposition upon which I go before the people of Ohio. At the beginning of the canvass, as I have said, the gentlemen who are engaged in advocating the claims of the peace party of Ohio did not desire to have this record discussed. I am happy to know by this long Wapakoneta speech of Judge Thurman that at last they have found it necessary to come to the discussion of the true question. Judge Thurman, in that speech, invites us to the discussion of it. He says: —

"I give all of them this bold and unequivocal defiance, that there is no one act of my life, or one sentence ever uttered by me that I am not prepared to have investigated by the American people; and I wish them to stand up to the same rule that I may see what is in their past record, and see how it tallies with what they say to the American people at the present time."

He proceeds to do this. He proceeds to examine the record of various gentlemen connected with the Union party. . . . I do not stop now to discuss the correctness of Judge Thurman's opinions as to the course of these men prior to the war. It is enough for me to say that the question I make — the question which the people of Ohio make — is, What was your conduct after it was found that there was a conspiracy to break up the Union, after war was upon us, and armies were raised — what was your conduct then? That is the question before the people. And I ask of an intelligent audience, What was the duty of a good citizen after that war for the destruction of the Government and the Union had begun? Need I ask any old Jackson Democrat what is his duty when the Union is at stake? In 1806, Aaron Burr proposed this matter to Andrew Jackson, of making a new confederacy in the Southwest. Jackson said: "I hate the Dons, and I would like to see Mexico dismembered; but before I would see one State of this Union severed from the rest, I would die in the last ditch." That was Jackson's Democracy.

Douglas said: "This is no time for delay. The existence of a conspiracy is now known; armies are raised to accomplish it. There can be but two sides to the question. A man must be either for the United States or against the United States. There can be no neutrals in this war — only patriots and traitors." There is the Douglas doctrine.

But I need not go back to Jackson and Douglas. I have the opinions of the very gentlemen who now lead the peace party on this subject. Let me read you a resolution, introduced and passed through a Democratic convention, in 1848, by Clement L. Vallandigham: —

"*Resolved*, That whatever opinions might have been entertained of the origin, necessity, or justice, by the Tories of the Revolutionary War, by the Federalists of the late war with England, or by the Whigs and Abolitionists of the present war with Mexico, the fact of their country being engaged in such a war ought to have been sufficient for them, and to have precluded debate on that subject till a successful termination of the war, and that in the meantime the patriot could have experienced no difficulty in recognizing his place on the side of his country, and could never have been induced to yield either physical or moral aid to the enemy."

I will quote also from Judge Thurman himself. In a speech lecturing one of his colleagues, who thought the Mexican War was unnecessary, he says: —

"It is a strange way to support one's country, right or wrong, to declare after war has begun, when it exists both in law and in fact, that the war is aggressive, unholy, unrighteous, and damnable on the part of the Government of that country, and on that Government rests its responsibility and its wrongfulness. It is a strange way to support one's country, right or wrong, in a war, to tax one's imagination to the utmost to depict the disastrous consequences of the contest; to dwell on what it has already cost and what it will cost in future; to depict her troops prostrated by disease and dying with pestilence; in a word, to destroy, as far as possible, the moral force of the Government in the struggle, and hold it up to its own people and the world as the aggressor that merits their condemnation. It was for this that I arraigned my colleague, and that I intend to arraign him. It was because his remarks, as far as they could have any influence, were evidently calculated to depress the spirits of his own countrymen, to lessen the moral force of his own Government, and to inspire with confidence and hope the enemies of his country."

He goes on further to say: —

"What a singular mode it was of supporting her in a war to bring against the war nearly all the charges that were brought by the peace party Federalists against the last war; to denounce it as an unrighteous, unholy, and damnable war; to hold up our Government to the eyes of the world as the aggressor in the conflict; to charge it with motives of conquest and aggrandizement; to parade and portray in the darkest colors all the horrors of war; to dwell upon its cost and depict its calamities."

Now, that was the doctrine of Judge Thurman as to the duties of citizens in time of war — in time of such a war as the Mexican War even, in which no vital interest of the country could by possibility suffer. . . . I propose to hold Judge Thurman to no severe rule of accountability for his conduct during the war. I merely ask that it shall be judged by his own rule: "Your country is engaged in war, and it is the duty of every citizen to say nothing and do nothing which shall depress the spirits of his own countrymen, nothing that shall encourage the enemies of his country, or give them moral aid or comfort." That is the rule. Now, Judge Thurman, how does your conduct square with it? I do not propose to begin at the beginning of the war, or even just before the war, to cite the record of Judge Thurman. I am willing to say that perhaps men might have been mistaken at that time. They might have supposed in the beginning a conciliatory policy, a non-coercive policy, would in some way avoid the threatened struggle. But I ask you to approach the period when the war was going on, when armies to the number of hundreds of thousands of men were ready on one side and the other, and when the whole world knew what was the nature of the great struggle going on in America.

Taking the beginning of 1863, how stands the conflict? We have pressed the Rebellion out of Kentucky and through Tennessee. Grant stands before Vicksburg, held at bay by the army of Pemberton; Rosecrans, after the capture of Nashville, has pressed forward to Murfreesboro, but is still held out of east Tennessee by the army of Bragg. The Army of the Potomac and the army of Lee, in Virginia, are balanced, the one against the other. The whole world knows that that exhausting struggle cannot last long without deciding in favor of one side or the other. . . . There is not a friend of freedom in all Europe who does not know that Lincoln and the loyal army are fighting in the cause of free government for all the world. Now, in that contest, where are you, Judge Thurman? It is a time when we need men and money, when we need to have our people inspired with hope and confidence. Your sons and brothers are in the field. Their success depends upon your conduct at home. . . .

Well, sir, in the beginning of that eventful year, there rises in Congress the ablest member of the peace party, to advise Congress and to advise the people, and what does he say? "You have not conquered the South. You never will. It is not in the nature of things possible, especially under your auspices. Money you have expended without limit; blood you have poured out like water."

Now, mark the taunt — the words of discouragement that were sent to the people and to the army of the Union: "Defeat, debt, taxation, sepulchres — these are your trophies. Can you get men to enlist now at any price?"

Listen again to the words that were sent to the army and to the loyal people: "Ah, sir, it is easier to die at home."

We knew that, Judge Thurman, better than Mr. Vallandigham knew it. We had seen our comrades falling and dying alone on the mountain-side and in the swamps—dying in the prison-pens of the Confederacy and in the crowded hospitals, North and South. Yet he had the face to stand up in Congress, and say to the people and the world, "Ah, sir, it is easier to die at home." Judge Thurman, where are you at this time? He goes to Columbus to the state convention, on the 11th of June of that year, as a delegate, as committeeman, and as an orator, and he spends that whole summer in advocating the election of the man who taunted us with the words, "Defeat, debt, taxation, sepulchres — these are your trophies."

In every canvass you know there is a keynote. What was the keynote of that canvass? Who sounded it? It came over to us from Canada. On the 15th of July, 1863, Mr. Vallandigham wrote, accepting the nomination of that convention of Judge Thurman's. He said, in his letter: —

"If this civil war is to terminate only by the subjugation or submission of the South to force and arms, the infant of to-day will not live to see the end of it. No; in another way only can it be brought to a close. Travelling a thousand miles and more, through nearly half of the Confederate States, and sojourning for a time at widely different points, I met not one man, woman, or child who was not resolved to perish, rather than yield to the pressure of arms, even in the most desperate extremity. And whatever may and must be the varying fortune of the war, in all of which I recognize the hand of Providence pointing visibly to the ultimate issue of this great trial of the States and people of America, they are better prepared now, every way, to make good their inexorable purpose than at any period since the beginning of the struggle."

That was the keynote of the campaign. It was the platform of the candidate in behalf of whom Judge Thurman went through the State of Ohio — all over the State — in July, August, and September, up to the night of the 12th of October, making his last speech just twenty-four hours before the glad news went out to all the world, over the wires, that the people of Ohio had elected John Brough by over one hundred thousand majority, in preference to the author of the sentiment, "Defeat, debt, taxation, sepulchres."

. . . .

This, my friends, is a part of that record which we are invited to examine by my friend Judge Thurman. I ask you to apply to it the principle that whoever, during the great struggle, was unfaithful to the cause of the country is not to be trusted to be one of the men to harvest and secure the legitimate fruits of the victory, which the Union people and the Union army won during the Rebellion. . . . When ought we to stop talking about that record, when leading men come before the people? Certainly not until every question arising out of the Rebellion, and every question which is akin to the questions which made the Rebellion, is settled. Perhaps these men will be remembered long after these questions are settled; perhaps their conduct will long be remembered. What was the result of this advice to the people? It prolonged the war; it made it impossible to get recruits; it made it necessary that we should have drafts. They opposed the drafts, and that made rioting, which required that troops should be called from all the armies in the field, to preserve the peace at home. From forty to a hundred thousand men in the different States of this Union were kept within the loyal States to preserve the peace at home. And now, when they talk to you about the debt and about the burden of taxation, remember how it happened that the war was so prolonged, that it was so expensive, and that the debt grew to such large proportions.

There are other things, too, to be remembered. I recollect that at the close of the last session of Congress, I went over to Arlington, the estate formerly of Robert E. Lee, and I saw there the great National Cemetery into which that beautiful place has been converted. I saw the graves of eighteen thousand Union soldiers, marked with white headboards, denoting the name of each occupant, and his regiment and company. Passing over those broad acres, covered with the graves of the loyal men who had died in defense of their country, I came upon that which was even more touching than these eighteen thousand headboards. I found a large granite, with this inscription upon it: —

"Beneath this stone repose the remains of two thousand one hundred and eleven unknown soldiers, gathered, after the war, from the field of Bull Run and the route to the Rappahannock. Their remains could not be identified, but their names and deaths are recorded in the archives of their country, and its grateful citizens honor them as of their noble army of martyrs. May they rest in peace. September, 1866."

I say to those men who were instrumental and prominent in prolonging the war, by opposing it, that when honeyed words and soft phrases can erase from the enduring granite inscriptions like these, the American people may forget their conduct; but I believe they will not do so until some such miracle is accomplished.

The contest was strenuously conducted from the day it was opened until the polls closed in October. Both candidates visited every quarter of the State and spoke daily, sometimes, indeed, three or four times in a single day. Each was assisted by the ablest speakers of his party in the State, and many brilliant orators came from other States to add their eloquence to the great debate. The whole country was interested because the contest was on national lines, and Ohio's verdict on negro suffrage would be significant of the opinion of the North on this absorbing question. Mr. Hayes was by no means sanguine of the result, but he did not shirk discussion of any pertinent topic, nor allow himself to be carried away into bitterness of denunciation of his opponent or to forget the amenities of dignified and decent debate — as did some of the orators who participated in the canvass. The Sunday before the election (October 6) he wrote this letter from Cincinnati to his uncle: —

My last speech of any consequence was made Friday night; one of the best I have made, and particularly with the best voice. It was rather queer. Governor Morton made a noble speech, but could not be heard by half his audience. I reached them all more easily than ever before.

It looks well here. We shall elect our county ticket and do well for the Amendment. But the Cary [1] affair is very much mixed. I shall not be surprised at any result. It has been badly managed — very.

I sent my card to Judge Thurman when he was here. He was not in his room. He afterwards sent me a note which I prize. He says: "Whatever the result, it is a great satisfaction to know that you and I have behaved like gentlemen and friends."

The result of the election was gratifying and disappointing alike to both parties. While Mr. Hayes and the rest of the Union state ticket were elected by a narrow margin (Mr. Hayes, who ran slightly ahead of the ticket, receiving a majority of 2983 in a total vote of 484,603), the Legislature, on which the election of a successor to Senator Wade would depend, was Democratic on joint ballot by eight votes,[2] and the suffrage amendment was rejected by a decisive majority. The election was so close that at first the Democrats were believed to have won a sweeping victory. The day after the election (October 9) Mr. Hayes wrote to his uncle: —

You need not be told how much the result of the election disappoints me. You know I will bear it cheerfully and with philosophy. It is, however, a puzzling thing to decide now what is next to be done. Assuming that I am beaten, which I do not doubt, I must choose my path anew. I will see you and talk it all over soon. No man in my place would probably have done differently — but the thing is over and now for a sensible future. I feel sorry for the boys — especially Birch. I hope your health is good and that you will borrow no trouble on account of this.

Mr. Hayes was inaugurated as Governor, January 13, 1868, when he made an address to the two houses of the Legislature. The retiring Governor, General Cox, whose administration he complimented, had already in his message set before the

[1] S. F. Cary, Labor candidate for Congress against Richard Smith, in the Second District, to fill the vacancy caused by Mr. Hayes's resignation.

[2] The Legislature elected Mr. Thurman, though throughout the campaign it had been assumed and expected that in case the Legislature should be Democratic, Mr. Vallandigham would be chosen.

Legislature the present condition and needs of the State. It was unnecessary, therefore, for him to go over that ground. Fortunately many questions that had long been subjects of commanding interest, relating to the state indebtedness and to internal improvements, had been solved or had been transferred to national consideration. "State taxation," he said, "was formerly the occasion of violent party contests. Now men of all parties concur in the opinion that, as a general rule, every citizen ought to be taxed in proportion to the actual value of his property, without regard to the form in which he prefers to invest it; and differences as to the measures by which the principle is practically applied rarely enter into political struggles in Ohio."

There was no need in his opinion of much legislation. "Excessive legislation," he declared, — and this was a thought to which he more than once recurred in later years, —"has become a great evil, and I submit to the judgment of the General Assembly the wisdom of avoiding it." But there was one topic on which he dwelt with especial emphasis, — the status of the negro in the State and the nation, — led to such expression because of the failure at the election of the Ohio constitutional amendment and because of the action already undertaken by the dominant party in the Legislature to rescind Ohio's approval of the Fourteenth Amendment. Mr. Hayes's words were: —

One important question of principle as old as our State Government still remains unsettled. All are familiar with the conflicts to which the policy of making distinctions between citizens in civil and political rights has given rise in Ohio. The first effort of those who opposed this policy was to secure to all citizens equality of civil rights. The result of the struggle that ensued is thus given by an eminent and honored citizen of our State: "The laws which created disabilities on the part of negroes in respect of civil rights were repealed in the year 1849, after an obstinate contest, quite memorable in the history of the State. Their repeal was looked upon with great disfavor by a large portion of the people as a dangerous innovation upon a just and well-settled policy, and a vote in that direction consigned many members of the Legislature to the repose of private life. But I am not aware that any evil results justified these apprehensions, or that any effort was ever made to impose the disabilities. On the contrary, the new policy, if I may call it so, has been found so consistent with justice to the negroes and the interests of the whites that no one — certainly no party — in Ohio, would be willing to abandon it."

An effort to secure to all citizens equal political rights was made in the State Constitutional Convention of 1851. Only thirteen out of one hundred and eight members in that body voted in its favor; and it is probable that less than one tenth of the voters of the State would then have voted to strike the word "white" out of the constitution.

The last General Assembly submitted to the people a proposition to amend the state constitution so as to abolish distinctions in political rights based upon color. The proposition contained several clauses not pertinent to its main purpose, under which, if adopted, it was believed by many that the number of white citizens who would be disfranchised would be much greater than the number of colored citizens who would be allowed the right of suffrage. Notwithstanding the proposition was thus hampered, it received 216,987 votes, or nearly forty-five per cent of all the votes cast in the State. This result shows great progress in public sentiment since the adoption of the constitution of 1851, and inspires the friends of equal political rights with a confident hope that in 1871, when the opportunity is given to the people, by the provisions of the constitution, to call a constitutional convention, the organic law of the State will be so amended as to secure in Ohio to all the governed an equal voice in the Government.

But whatever reasonable doubts may be entertained as to the probable action of the people of Ohio on the question of an extension of the right of suffrage when a new state constitution shall be formed, I submit with confidence that nothing has occurred which warrants the opinion that the ratification by the last General Assembly of the Fourteenth Amendment of the Constitution of the United States was not in accordance with the deliberate and settled convictions of the people. That amendment was, after the amplest discussion upon an issue distinctly presented, sanctioned by a large majority of the people. If any fact exists which justifies the belief that they now wish that the resolution should be repealed, by which the assent of Ohio was given to that important amendment, it has not been brought to the attention of the public. Omitting all reference to other valuable provisions, it may be safely said that the section which secures among all the States of the Union equal representation in the House of Representatives and in the Electoral Colleges in proportion to the voting population, is deemed of vital importance by the people of Ohio. Without now raising the grave question as to the right of a State to withdraw its assent, which has been constitutionally given to a proposed amendment of the Federal Constitution, I respectfully suggest that the attempt which is now making to withdraw the assent of Ohio to the Fourteenth Amendment to the Federal Constitution be postponed until the people shall again have an opportunity to give expression to their will. In my judgment, Ohio will never consent that the whites of the South, a large majority of whom were lately in rebellion, shall exercise in the Government of the nation as much political power, man for man, as the same number of white citizens of Ohio, and be allowed in addition thereto thirty members of

Congress and of the Electoral Colleges, for colored people deprived of every political privilege.

But in spite of Mr. Hayes's advice the Legislature promptly attempted to rescind the vote of the preceding Legislature approving the Fourteenth Amendment. Its action was duly certified to Congress and the Secretary of State, but was regarded by the federal authorities as nugatory. Indeed, at this session the Legislature devoted a large share of its attention to purely partisan efforts, especially to measures to prevent the voting of men with a "visible admixture of African blood." As the Governor of Ohio at that time possessed no veto power, Mr. Hayes was powerless even to check for reconsideration any measure that the small Democratic majority enacted.

Mr. Hayes took an active part in the national campaign of 1868, making many speeches in behalf of the election of General Grant. Immediately after the nomination of Horatio Seymour by the Democrats he wrote in his diary (July 9, 1868): —

Horatio Seymour nominated because
(1) He was more distinctly and decidedly committed against the greenback theory of Mr. Pendleton and the Western Democracy than any other man before the convention;
(2) He was by record more completely identified with the peace party than any man except Mr. Pendleton;
(3) He is for a reconstruction of the South which will be agreeable to the Rebels, and opposes the reconstruction which gives safety and power to the loyal.

In his speeches he made the most of Seymour's record during the war — his words and his acts, which, indeed, were not always consistently those of the avowed peace Democrat. "He frequently *said* things and several times *did* things which looked as if he meant to abandon the peace party and support the cause of his country. For this he was applauded, complimented, and flattered by the loyal press and by Stanton and other members of Lincoln's Administration. They hoped he would follow Dix, Dickinson, Griswold, and other New York war Democrats. And what they said is now paraded as the best claim of Mr. Seymour to the confidence of the country." But Mr. Hayes argued, from a review of Mr. Seymour's whole record during the period of the war, that such manifestations were the exception and not the rule of his course of conduct; and that, judged by all the facts of his public acts and utterances, he was — especially as compared with General Grant whose great services to the Union cause needed no comment — unfit to be trusted at such a juncture with the chief magistracy of the nation.

It was not till the session of the Legislature in November, 1868, that Governor Hayes had his first opportunity to address the Legislature officially on the interests of the State. His message on this occasion presented in brief and condensed form the financial condition of the State and pointed out the subjects demanding immediate attention with businesslike directness. The recommendations specially urged were, first, that provision be made for a "comprehensive geological survey of the State," and, second, that legislation be undertaken better to protect the purity of the ballot. On the latter subject Mr. Hayes said: —

The most important subject of legislation which, in my judgment, requires the attention of the General Assembly at its present session, relates to the prevention of frauds upon the elective franchise. Intelligent men of all parties are persuaded that at the recent important state and national elections great abuses of the right of suffrage were practised. I am not prepared to admit that the reports commonly circulated and believed in regard to such abuses would, so far as the elections in Ohio are concerned, be fully sustained by a thorough investigation of the facts. But it is not doubted that even at the elections in our own State frauds were perpetrated to such an extent that all good citizens earnestly desire that effective measures may be adopted by you to prevent their repetition. No elaborate attempt to portray the consequences of this evil is required. If it is allowed to increase, the confidence of the people in the purity of elections will be lost and the exercise of the right of suffrage will be neglected. To corrupt the ballot-box is to destroy our free institutions. Let all good citizens, therefore, unite in enacting and enforcing laws which will secure honest elections.

I submit to your judgment the propriety of such amendments to the election laws as will provide, first, for the representation of minorities in the boards of the judges and clerks of the elections; and second, for the registration of all the lawful voters in each township, ward, and election precinct, prior to the election. . . .

It is manifestly impossible, amid the hurry and excitement of an election, that the legal right to vote, of every person who may offer his ballot, should be fully and fairly investigated and decided. The experience of many of the older States has proved that this can best be done at some period prior to the election, so as to give to every legal voter, in an election precinct, an opportunity to challenge the claim of any person whose right is deemed questionable. Laws to accomplish this have been in force in several other States for many years, and have been carried out successfully and with the general approval of the people. Believing that an act providing for the registration of all legal voters is the most effective remedy yet devised for the prevention of frauds on the sacred right of suffrage, and that a registry law can be so framed that it will deprive no citizen, either native-born or naturalized, of his just rights, I respectfully recommend to your earnest consideration the propriety of enacting such a law.

CHAPTER XX

SECOND TERM AS GOVERNOR

SO successful and satisfactory was Mr. Hayes's first term as Governor that there was no opposition to his renomination. The state convention (June 23, 1869) made him the candidate by acclamation. It adopted a platform condemning the extravagance of the Democratic Legislature, commending the national Administration, and declaring in favor of the Fifteenth Amendment, providing for universal manhood suffrage. The situation, therefore, was not much different from that which confronted the parties in 1867, only now it was a national instead of a state constitutional amendment declaring for negro suffrage that was at stake. Governor Hayes appeared before the convention and accepted the renomination in a carefully prepared speech discussing the work of the Democratic Legislature and outlining the questions demanding the attention of the voters. In this speech he said: —

Twice since the organization of existing political parties the people of Ohio have trusted the lawmaking power of the State in the hands of the Democratic party. They first tried the experiment twelve years ago, and such were the results that ten years elapsed before they ventured upon a repetition of it. Two years ago, in a time of reaction, which was general throughout the country, the Democratic party, by a majority of the popular vote, having large advantages in the apportionment, obtained complete control of the Legislature in both of its branches. They came into power, proclaiming that the past ought to be forgotten; that old issues and divisions should be laid aside; that new ideas and new measures required attention; and they were particularly emphatic and earnest in declaring that the enormous burdens of debt and taxation under which the people were struggling made retrenchment and economy the supreme duty of the hour.

These were their promises, and the manner in which they were kept is now before the people for their judgment. Disregarding the well-known and solemnly expressed will of Ohio, they began the business of their first session by passing fruitless resolutions to rescind the ratification of the Fourteenth Amendment to the Constitution of the United States.

RUTHERFORD B. HAYES, 1869
While Governor of Ohio, 1868–1872

They placed on the statute-book visible admixture bills, to deprive citizens of the right of suffrage — a constitutional right long enjoyed and perfectly well settled by repeated decisions of the highest court having jurisdiction of the question.

They repealed the law allowing, after the usual residence, the disabled veterans of the Union army to vote in the township in which the National Soldiers' Home is situated; and enacted a law designed to deprive of the right of suffrage a large number of young men engaged in acquiring an education at "any school, seminary, academy, college, university, or other institution of learning." To prevent citizens who were deprived of their constitutional rights by these acts from obtaining prompt relief in the Supreme Court, they passed a law prohibiting that court from taking up causes on its docket according to its own judgment of what was demanded by public justice, in any case "except where the person seeking relief had been convicted of murder in the first degree, or of a crime the punishment of which was confinement in the penitentiary."

I believe it is the general judgment of the people of Ohio that the passage of these measures, unconstitutional as some of them are, and unjust as they all are, was mainly due to the fact that the classes of citizens disfranchised by them do not commonly vote with the Democratic party. The Republican party condemns all such legislation, and demands its repeal.

On the important subject of suffrage, General Grant, in his inaugural message, expresses the convictions of the Republican party. He says: "The question of suffrage is one which is likely to agitate the public so long as a portion of the citizens of the nation are excluded from its privileges in any State. It seems to me very desirable that this question should be settled now, and I entertain the hope and express the desire that it may be by the ratification of the Fifteenth Amendment to the Constitution."

.   .   .   .

But of all the pledges upon which the Democratic party obtained power in the last Legislature, the most important, and those in regard to which the just expectations of the people have been most signally disappointed, are their pledges in relation to financial affairs — to expenditure, to debt, and to taxation. Upon this subject the people are compelled to feel a very deep interest. The flush times of the war have been followed by a financial reaction, and for the last three or four years the country has been on the verge of a financial crisis. The burdens of taxation bear heavily upon labor and upon capital. The Democratic party, profuse alike of accusations against their adversaries, and of promises of retrenchment and reform, were clothed with power to deal with the heaviest part of these burdens, namely, with the expenditures, debts, assessments, and taxes which are authorized by state legislation. The results of their two years of power are now before the people. They are contained in the 65th and 66th volumes of the Laws of Ohio. Let any Republican diligently study these volumes, and he will fully comprehend the meaning of Job when he said, "Oh, that mine adversary had written a book." No intelligent man can read carefully these volumes, and note the number and character of the laws increasing the expenses and liabilities of the State and authorizing additional debts and additional taxation for city and village, for county and township purposes, without having the conviction forced upon him that the gentlemen who enacted these laws hold to the opinion that the way to increase wealth is to increase taxation, and that public debts are public blessings.

. . . . .

Now it is to be hoped, as to a considerable part of the local debts and local taxes authorized by the late Democratic Legislature, that the people will not be burdened with them. It is to be hoped that county commissioners, city councils, and other local boards, will show greater moderation and economy in the exercise of their dangerous and oppressive powers under the laws than was exhibited in their enactment. But, in any event, nothing is more certain than that the people of Ohio have great reason to apprehend that the evil consequences of these laws will be felt in their swollen tax bills for many years.

It is probable that many of the acts to which I have alluded, creating additional offices, incurring state liabilities, and authorizing local debts and taxes, were required by sound policy. But a candid investigation will show that the larger part of these enormous burdens of expenditure, debt, and taxation could and ought to have been avoided.

The last Legislature afforded examples of many of the worst evils to which legislative bodies are liable — long sessions, excessive legislation, unnecessary expenditures, and recklessness in authorizing local debts and local taxes. These evils "have increased, are increasing, and ought to be diminished." Let there be reform as to all of them. Especially let the people of all parties insist that the parent evil — long legislative sessions — shall be reformed altogether. . . .

It is said that one of the ablest Democratic members of the last Legislature declared at its close that "enough had been done to keep the Democratic party out of power in Ohio for twenty years." Let the Republican press and the Republican speakers see to it that the history of the acts of that body be spread fully before the people, and I entertain no doubt that the declaration will be substantially made good.

It is probable that the discussions of the present canvass will turn more upon state legislation and less upon national affairs than those of any year since 1861. Neither Senators nor Representatives in Congress are to be chosen. But it is an important state election, and will be regarded as having a bearing on national politics. The Republicans of Ohio heartily approve of the principles of General Grant's inaugural message, and are gratified by the manner in which he is dealing with the leading questions of the first three months of his Administration. . . .

On the great question of reconstruction, in what a masterly way and with what marked success has General Grant's Administration begun. Congress had fixed its day of adjournment, and all plans for reconstructing the three unrepresented States had been postponed until next December. At this juncture General Grant, on the 7th of April last, sent to Congress a special message recommending that before its adjournment it take the necessary steps for the restoration of the State of Virginia to its proper relations to the Union. . . . The message of the President was referred, in the House of Representatives, to the Committee on Reconstruction. That committee the next day reported a bill for the reconstruction of Virginia, and also of Mississippi and Texas. . . . It will be seen that by this bill the people of Virginia were to proceed in the work of reconstruction at such time as the President might deem best, and that such reconstruction in all its parts was to be on the basis of equal political rights. The constitution to be submitted was framed by a convention, in the election of which colored citizens participated, and of which colored men were members. The "registered voters" who are to vote on its ratification or rejection, and also for members of the General Assembly, for state officers, and for members of Congress, include the colored men of Virginia; and if the constitution is adopted, it secures to them equal political rights in that State. The remaining sections of the bill provide for the reconstruction of Mississippi and Texas on the same principles, and left the time and manner to the discretion of the President.

This bill was reported to the House of Representatives and unanimously agreed upon by a committee, of which four members were Democrats. The most distinguished Democratic Representatives of the States of New York and Pennsylvania advocated its passage. Out of about seventy Democratic members of the House, only twenty-five voted against it, and the only Democratic members from Ohio who voted on the passage of the bill, voted for it.

It thus appears that upon the recommendation of General Grant even the Democratic party of Ohio, by their Representatives in Congress, voted for equal political rights in Virginia, Mississippi, and Texas! And to-day the great body of the people of those States, Democrats and Conservatives as well as Republicans, have yielded assent to that great principle. In view of these facts I submit that I am fully warranted in saying that General Grant has begun the work of reconstruction in a masterly way and with marked success.

Again thanking you for the honor you have done me, I repeat, in conclusion, what I said two years ago. The people represented in this convention mean that the State of Ohio in the great progress, "whose leading object is to elevate the condition of men, to lift artificial weights from all shoulders, to clear the paths of laudable pursuits for all, and to afford all an unfettered start and a fair chance in the race of life," shall tread no more steps backward. I shall enter upon my part of the labors of the canvass believing that the Union Republican party is battling for the right, and with undoubting confidence that the goodness of the cause will supply the weakness of its advocates, and command in the result that triumphant success which it deserves.

The Democratic convention, which met two weeks later, condemned the Fifteenth Amendment, speaking with old-time vigor of the reserved rights of the States; pronounced the exemption of government bonds from taxation as unjust and intolerable, and declared: "That the claims of the bondholders, that the bonds which were bought with greenbacks, and the principal of which is by law payable in currency, should nevertheless be paid in gold, is unjust and extortionate; and, if persisted in, will inevitably force upon the people the question of repudiation." General W. S. Rosecrans was nominated for Governor, but on reflection he was unwilling to make the canvass on the reactionary platform which he was asked to approve. On his declination of the nomination the State Central Committee selected the able and accomplished George H. Pendleton to head the ticket.

The active speaking campaign, which was opened by Mr. Hayes at Wilmington, August 12, was conducted on the lines indicated by Mr. Hayes's speech of acceptance and by the portion of the Democratic platform above mentioned; state and national finances[1] and the Fifteenth Amendment commanding the greatest amount of attention. Mr. Pendleton argued forcefully and plausibly in favor of the partial repudiation of the war

[1] Mr. Hayes constantly pressed home on his audiences the extravagance of the Democratic Legislature in authorizing vast increases of local indebtedness. The following excerpt from his speeches shows his method of discussion: —

"The last Democratic Legislature acted as if it believed that *public debts* were public blessings. They could not easily increase the state debt, the state constitution plainly forbidding it — and yet they attempted that. In the Appropriation Bill of the last session the House, under the leadership of Judge Jewett, authorized bonds to be issued to pay the Morgan raid claims. The Senate struck it out and we are spared that dangerous precedent.

"But city debts, village debts, county debts, and township debts were authorized amounting in the aggregate to many millions.

"They did not wish to increase the taxes for state purposes, but for city and village and for county and township purposes they passed act upon act. If you wish to know the amount consult the laws, local and general, of the last two sessions — or, if they are not convenient, compare your tax bills of 1867 and 1868 with those of 1869 and 1870, and you will learn to your cost.

"But it is said the debts will not be contracted, the taxes will not be levied by cities and counties to the extent authorized by these laws. My observation is that city councils go to the limit always. This is not due to corruption. A rivalry is begotten between cities. Fine parks, workhouses, city halls, forums, etc., etc., are admired. All must imitate the finest. Your law expresses the legislative wisdom and will on the subject, and the average city councilman will act as if he were bound to obey it."

debt which its payment in greenbacks implied. But the sober second thought of the voters was proof against his eloquence. The Republicans regained control of the Legislature by a narrow margin and Mr. Hayes was reëlected by a small but increased majority.

When the Legislature assembled in January, 1870, Mr. Hayes was able, therefore, to present his second message to a friendly body. In this he renewed the recommendation of his previous message for improved election laws, asked for the repeal of the obnoxious partisan legislation of the preceding Legislature relating to the suffrage affecting negroes, inmates of the National Soldiers' Home, and students; and urged upon the Legislature the importance of voting to ratify the Fifteenth Amendment to the Federal Constitution. Further than this he dwelt at some length on the progressive increase of municipal taxation and debt and suggested the propriety of legislation to restrict the taxing and borrowing power of local authorities. He pointed out the urgent need of more humane methods in dealing with the State's prisoners, especially young men convicted of crime for the first time, with a view to reform rather than mere punishment. In this connection he commended the Irish convict system as worthy of study and possible adoption. The salutary influence of the newly created Board of State Charities in exposing abuses was emphasized; better provision was urged for caring for the insane; the immediate creation of a state home for the orphans of soldiers of the Civil War was, he argued, demanded in fulfilment of an obligation which the State ought not to be willing to shirk; and the hope was expressed that the establishment of a State Agricultural College, in accordance with the terms of the federal land grant accepted in 1864, should no longer be postponed.[1]

A few days later, January 10, Mr. Hayes was inaugurated for his second term as Governor. In his address on this occasion, he called attention to the opportunity to be presented the following year to vote for a convention to amend the constitution of the State and pointed out certain improvements which in his opinion should occupy the thought of the voters and those whom they should select for the high work of constitution-making. It is

[1] The Legislature embodied nearly all of the Governor's suggestions in laws.

significant, when one recalls the condition of public opinion and popular thought of the time, that the two subjects on which he laid most stress were reform of the civil service so as to base tenure of office on merit, and a return to the system of an appointive judiciary. Mr. Hayes's words were: —

For many years political influence and political services have been essential qualifications for employment in the civil service, whether state or national. As a general rule, such employments are regarded as terminating with the defeat of the political party under which they began. All political parties have adopted this rule. In many offices the highest qualifications are only obtained by experience. Such are the positions of the warden of the penitentiary and his subordinates, and the superintendents of asylums and reformatories and their assistants. But the rule is applied to these as well as to other offices and employments. A change in the political character of the executive and legislative branches of the Government is followed by a change of the officers and employees in all of the departments and institutions of the State. Efficiency and fidelity to duty do not prolong the employment; unfitness and neglect of duty do not always shorten it. The evils of this system in state affairs are, perhaps, of small moment compared with those which prevail under the same system in the transaction of the business of the National Government. But at no distant day they are likely to become serious, even in the administration of state affairs. The number of persons employed in the various offices and institutions of the State must increase, under the most economical management, in equal ratio with the growth of our population and business.

A radical reform in the civil service of the general Government has been proposed. The plan is to make qualifications, and not political services and influence, the chief test in determining appointments, and to give subordinates in the civil service the same permanency of place which is enjoyed by officers of the army and navy. The introduction of this reform will be attended with some difficulties. But in revising our state constitution, if this object is kept constantly in view, there is little reason to doubt that it can be successfully accomplished.

Our judicial system is plainly inadequate to the wants of the people of the State. Extensive alterations of existing provisions must be made. The suggestions I desire to present in this connection are as to the manner of selecting judges, their terms of office, and their salaries. It is fortunately true that the judges of our courts have heretofore been, for the most part, lawyers of learning, ability, and integrity. But it must be remembered that the tremendous events and the wonderful progress of the last few years are working great changes in the condition of our society. Hitherto population has been sparse, property not unequally distributed, and the bad elements which so frequently control large cities have been almost unknown in our State. But with a dense

population crowding into towns and cities, with vast wealth accumulating
in the hands of a few persons or corporations, it is to be apprehended
that the time is coming when judges elected by popular vote, for short
official terms, and poorly paid, will not possess the independence required to protect individual rights. Under the national Constitution,
judges are nominated by the Executive and confirmed by the Senate,
and hold office during good behavior. It is worthy of consideration
whether a return to the system established by the fathers is not the dictate of the highest prudence. I believe that a system under which judges
are so appointed, for long terms and with adequate salaries, will afford
to the citizen the amplest possible security that impartial justice will be
administered by an independent judiciary.

I forbear to consider further at this time the interesting questions
which will arise in the revision and amendment of the constitution.
Convinced of the soundness of the maxim that "that government is
best which governs least," I would resist the tendency common to all
systems to enlarge the functions of government. The law should touch
the rights, the business, and the feelings of the citizen at as few points as
is consistent with the preservation of order and the maintenance of justice. If every department of government is kept within its own sphere,
and every officer performs faithfully his own duty without magnifying
his office, harmony, efficiency, and economy will prevail.

Under the providence of God, the people of this State have greatly
prospered. But in their prosperity they cannot forget "him who hath
borne the battle, nor his widow, nor his orphan," nor the thousands of
other sufferers in our midst, who are entitled to sympathy and relief.
They are to be found in our hospitals, our infirmaries, our asylums, our
prisons, and in the abodes of the unfortunate and the erring. The
Founder of our religion, whose spirit should pervade our laws, and ani-
mate those who enact and those who enforce them, by his teaching and
his example, has admonished us to deal with all the victims of adversity
as the children of our common Father. With this duty performed, we
may confidently hope that for long ages to come our country will continue to be the home of freedom and the refuge of the oppressed.

Grateful to the people of Ohio for the honors they have conferred, I
approach a second term in the executive office, deeply solicitous to discharge, as far as in me lies, the obligations and duties which their partial
judgment has imposed.

In his message to the Legislature in January, 1871, Mr. Hayes
recurred to the ideas he had previously particularly emphasized,
namely, the inadvisability of much legislation; the need of greater
economy in public expenditure, of restriction in local taxing
power, of progressive improvement in prison discipline and reform methods, and of larger liberality in caring for soldiers'
orphans. Statistics showed, he noted, that in ten years state

taxes had increased 33 per cent; local taxes 170 per cent. The increase of local taxes had been far greater than the growth of the State in wealth and population. Probably no single remedy would cure the evil. He said: —

Much, however, can be accomplished by wise legislation. . . . Local authorities should be empowered to levy no higher rate of taxation than is absolutely required for practical efficiency under ordinary circumstances. In extraordinary cases general laws should provide for the submission of the proposed tax or assessment to the people to be affected by it, under such regulations that it cannot be levied unless at least two thirds of the taxpayers approve the measure.

One of the most valuable articles of the present state constitution is that which prohibits the State, save in a few exceptional cases, from creating any debt, and which provides for the payment at an early day of the debt already contracted. I am convinced that it would be wise to extend the same policy to the creation of public debts by county, city, and other local authorities. The rule "pay as you go" leads to economy in public as well as in private affairs; while the power to contract debts opens the door to wastefulness, extravagance, and corruption.

In the early history of the State, when capital was scarce and expensive public works were required for transporting the products of the State to market, public debts were probably unavoidable; but the time, I believe, has come when not only the State, but all of its subordinate divisions, ought to be forbidden to incur debt. . . .

It would promote an economical administration of the laws if all officers, state, county, and municipal, including the members of the Legislature, were paid fixed salaries.

Under existing laws a part of the public officers are paid by fees and a part by fixed annual salaries or by a *per diem* allowance. The result is great inequality and injustice. Many of those who are paid by fees receive a compensation out of all proportion to the services rendered. Others are paid salaries wholly inadequate. For example, many county officers and some city officers receive greater compensation than the judges of the Supreme Court of the State. The salaries paid to the judges ought to be increased; the amount paid to many other public officers ought to be reduced. To do justice, a system of fixed salaries, without fees or perquisites, should be adopted. . . . To remove all ground of complaint, on account of injustice to present incumbents, the new system should apply only to those elected after its adoption.

The subjects dealt with at greatest length and with most emphasis by Mr. Hayes in his message of January, 1872, on the eve of his retirement from the capital, were the railway problem as related to the State and the need of devising some method of checking the growing corruption of local administration. Regarding the railways, he said: —

The importance of wise legislation on the subject of railroads, in a State having the geographical position which belongs to Ohio, cannot be overestimated. . . . Last year they [the railways] carried twelve millions of passengers, and their gross receipts exceeded thirty millions of dollars.

All of the just powers of the corporations which conduct this immense business are derived from the laws of the State. If these laws fail to guard adequately the rights and the interests of our citizens, it is the duty of the General Assembly to supply their defects. Serious and well-grounded apprehensions are felt that in the management of these companies, which are largely controlled by non-residents of Ohio, practices, not sanctioned by the law, nor by sound morality, have become common, which are prejudicial to the interests of the great body of the people, and which, if continued, will ultimately destroy the prosperity of the State.

Regarding railroads as the most useful instrumentality by which intercourse is carried on between different sections of the country, the people do not desire the adoption of a narrow or unfriendly policy toward them. But it should be remembered that these corporations were created, and their valuable franchises granted by the Legislature to promote the interests of the people of the State. No railroad company can sacrifice those interests without violating the law of its origin. It is not to be doubted that the authority of the General Assembly is competent to correct whatever abuses have grown up in the management of the railroads of the State.

Mr. Hayes cited the official reports of the State Commissioner of Railroads and Telegraphs, to show that in many respects, relating to rates, speed regulations, stock-watering, and the like, the railways of the State were guilty of constant violation of the laws, and he came to this conclusion: —

The interests involved are of such magnitude that all legislation ought to be based on the fullest and most accurate information which a careful investigation can furnish. I, therefore, recommend that a commission of five citizens, of whom the railroad commissioner shall be one, be organized, with ample powers to investigate the management of the railroad companies of the State, their legal rights, and the rights of the State and its citizens, and to report the information acquired, with a recommendation of such measures as the commission shall deem expedient.

In regard to the other topic mentioned Mr. Hayes said: —

One of the most difficult and interesting practical problems which now engages the thoughts of the American people is how to maintain economy, efficiency, and purity in the administration of local affairs, and especially in the government of towns and cities, without a departure from principles and methods which are deemed essential to free popular government. Many of the most important functions of government are in the hands of the local authorities. They are directly charged with the expenditure of large sums of money, with the protection of life and property, and with the administration of civil and criminal justice. These duties, in one way or another, touch nearly and constantly the interests and feelings of every citizen. Upon their faithful performance depends the prosperity, happiness, and safety of the community. It is true that as yet Ohio is happily, in a great measure, free from the operation of causes which in the commercial metropolis of the country recently led to such extraordinary corruption in the government of that city. But those causes do not belong alone to the great cities of the East. They are already at work in our midst, and they are steadily and rapidly increasing in power. No political party is altogether free from their influence, and no political party is solely responsible for them. We have laws prohibiting almost every conceivable official neglect and abuse, and penalties are affixed to the violation of those laws which cannot be regarded as inadequate. The difficulty is to secure their enforcement. Those whose duty it is to detect and prosecute are often interested in maintaining good relations with the wrongdoers. The contractors for public work and supplies not infrequently have a community of interest with those who are the agents of the public to let and superintend the performance of contracts. Where these abuses exist there is apt to be a large circle of apparently disinterested citizens, who labor to conceal the facts and to suppress investigation.

What the public welfare demands is a practical measure which will provide for a thorough and impartial investigation in every case of suspected neglect, abuse, or fraud. Such an investigation, to be effective, must be made by an authority independent, if possible, of all local influences. When abuses are discovered, the prosecution and punishment of offenders ought to follow. But even if prosecutions fail in cases of full exposure, public opinion almost always accomplishes the object desired. A thorough investigation of official corruption and criminality leads with great certainty to the needed reform. Publicity is a great corrector of official abuses. Let it, therefore, be made the duty of the Governor, on satisfactory information that the public good requires an investigation of the affairs of any public office or the conduct of any public officer, whether state or local, to appoint one or more citizens who shall have ample powers to make such investigation. If by the investigation violations of law are discovered, the Governor should be authorized, in his discretion, to notify the Attorney-General, whose duty it should be, on such notice, to prosecute the offenders. The constitution makes it the duty of the Governor to "see that the laws are faithfully executed." Some such measure as the one here recommended is necessary to give force and effect to this constitutional provision.

Thus, in reference to both these problems, which in later years have bulked so large in the thought of the American people and in the activities of state and national legislators, Mr. Hayes was prompt in grasping the need of remedial legislation; but he desired to have this result from a thorough knowledge of the facts and conditions that made it necessary.

Throughout his incumbency of the Governor's office, Mr. Hayes's state papers — inaugural speeches, messages, and proclamations — were distinguished for their conciseness, .their directness, and their businesslike quality. There was in them no "playing to the galleries," and they reveal no conscious effort to increase his personal political prestige. Rather they leave the reader with the impression that the author, as the head of the State Government, was desirous only of bringing about such changes in the laws and the activities of the Commonwealth as should increase the efficiency of the State Government and should redound to the greater glory of the State. He was firmly convinced — as what thoughtful man is not? — that state legislatures pass too many laws — unnecessary, ill-digested, of ephemeral impulse and quality. Always he deprecated this tendency and warned against it. Further he had an old-fashioned abhorrence of public debts,[1] lightly incurred, and of heavy taxation. So, he constantly exerted his influence in favor of economy of public expenditures not only of the state revenues, but especially in the minor subdivisions of the State. It was his idea that a community did best to live within the limits of its annual income, which should not be a burdensome exaction upon the property and industry of its citizens, and that debt — a draught on the future — should be incurred only to meet some pressing need or to provide some essential permanent improvement in whose benefit the long future would share.

The wide range of Governor Hayes's interest, the broad scope of his statesmanship, becomes manifest, when one summarizes the principal measures which he advocated and which, for the

---

[1] "It is perhaps a hobby with me, but I do hate debt, and I am opposed to authorizing it except as a *dernier ressort*." (From letter, August 27, 1869, to Julius O. Converse, Chardon, Ohio.)

most part, were adopted by the Legislature and carried into effect. He always stood for simple manhood suffrage and for a liberal attitude toward all classes of citizens in the exercise of the right to vote. Naturally, therefore, he advocated in his first campaign for Governor the adoption of the amendment to the state constitution providing for negro suffrage, though friends warned him not to be insistent, and though, no doubt, his advocacy lessened his chance of election and lowered the majority by which he was chosen. This amendment failed, but Governor Hayes had no regrets for his course and never doubted the ultimate prevalence of the principle it embodied. Again, in 1869, he urged the adoption of the Fifteenth Amendment to the Federal Constitution which placed negro suffrage under the protection of the fundamental law of the nation. This the Ohio Legislature in the session of 1870 sanctioned, much to Mr. Hayes's satisfaction.[1] Further, he favored the repeal of the notorious "visible admixture" law, which, however, had been pronounced unconstitutional, and he obtained legislation restoring to men in the National Soldiers' Home and to students in college the right to vote in the Home and college precincts.

Mr. Hayes recommended in his messages, and used his influence to obtain from the Legislature, action providing for minority representation on boards of election — a provision of such obvious importance and of so general acceptance now that it is hard to think it should ever have been lacking in any State. He also favored minority representation on boards of trustees of state institutions and appointed Democrats to boards, even where the law did not require such action and in the face of violent opposition from his fellow Republicans.[2] In the appointment

---

[1] The Legislature was so evenly divided that the vote for the Amendment stood, Senate, ayes 19, noes 18; House, ayes 57, noes 55. The change of a single vote in either house would have been fatal.

[2] For example, he placed a Democrat on the board of the new Home for Soldiers' Orphans. To a man who violently criticized the appointment he wrote: —

COLUMBUS, O., 19th Apr., 1870.

O. H. BOOTH, Esq.,
    MANSFIELD, O.

MY DEAR SIR, — I am in receipt of yours of the 18th. You are totally mistaken in my character when you say that you presume what you have written will not disturb me in the least. I assure you I feel keenly the disappointment and

of judges, when that duty devolved upon him, he took counsel
of the leaders of the bar in the jurisdiction involved and named
the men that the majority of the bar approved. He spoke on all
proper occasions in behalf of civil service reform to the end that
fitness and not partisan service should be the determining factor
in the appointment and retention of public officers. And in this
respect, too, he showed his faith by his works, by refusing to dis-
miss a worthy State Librarian to make room for a Republican
aspirant for the position. To the latter, Dr. George R. Morton,
of North Bass, he wrote: —

The present incumbent of the librarianship is a faithful, painstaking
old gentleman with a family of invalid girls dependent on him. His
courtesy and evident anxiety to accommodate all who visit the library
have secured him the endorsement of almost all who are in the habit of
using the books, and under the circumstances I cannot remove him. Old
association, your fitness, and claims draw me the other way, but you
see, etc., etc.

A measure of large scientific and industrial importance, which
owed its adoption largely to Mr. Hayes's intelligent insistence,
was the act providing for a thorough geological survey of the
State. The appointment of the geologist for this work was entrusted to the Governor, and he promptly selected Professor
J. S. Newberry, of Columbia College, a man of eminent scientific
attainments. Under Professor Newberry's efficient direction the
survey was rapidly but carefully prosecuted; the reports were
published in several volumes, giving for the first time full and

censures of my Republican friends in Mansfield, and feel vexed that you can so
write. I would not be just to myself not to say this.

I wrote the facts to Mr. Hedges and others [who had protested against the
appointment]. They are simply: 1st, All friends of the Home agreed that there
should be a Democratic representative on the Board. 2d, For three weeks I
named Colonel Burns to all who conversed with me (his name having been suggested to me by a friend of the Home) on the subject of the appointment, and all
spoke of him as a proper man if a Democrat was to go on the Board. You are in
error in saying I set aside anybody. No other Mansfield man was named.

Six good men are on the Board and I hope Colonel Burns will turn out less
objectionable than you anticipate. If I have made a mistake, it has been done
with the best of motives and in accordance with the views of many of our best
men. I hope you and my Mansfield friends will see in the facts room for a charitable construction of my act. If not, one thing is sure, when you come to dispense
patronage, you will agree with me that it is no easy job to do satisfactorily. All
this is confidential. — Sincerely,

R. B. HAYES.

accurate information regarding the many and varied mineral resources of the State. It would be difficult if not impossible to estimate how much this survey has done in stimulating the development of the coal, stone, and clay industries of Ohio.

Governor Hayes gave much and serious thought to the development and improvement of the State's penal and benevolent institutions. In this work he was laying the foundation of knowledge and enlightened philanthropy displayed in his later career in his large efforts in the interests of prison reform. He labored in behalf of improved prison discipline, of enlarged prison accommodation, and of a graded system among the prisoners. He was instrumental in the establishment of a Girls' Reformatory; of a Home for Soldiers' Orphans;[1] of provision being made for the care of the chronic insane. After the burning of the insane hospital at Columbus, he exerted his influence to have the new hospital built outside the city; and further it was due to his advocacy

---

[1] The Home for Soldiers' Orphans at Xenia was started first by private effort, in which Mrs. Hayes shared enthusiastically, and was supported by voluntary contributions. This was in 1869. Meetings in its behalf were held in various cities at which Governor Hayes appeared and pleaded the cause of the orphans. In a letter of January 21, 1887, to a Mrs. Harrison, Mr. Hayes, recounting the history of the Home, wrote: "The first public affair of the voluntary Home was the holiday celebration the 26th December, 1869. Mrs. Hayes, with Mrs. Lovejoy, of Columbus, to make this enjoyable for the orphans, ransacked the city of Columbus for money, books, gifts, etc., etc. . . . There were then between forty and fifty children in the Home. The gathering on this occasion gave to the institution great prestige. . . . The next year (1870), after the State had adopted the institution and Dr. Griswold was superintendent, the number of orphans had greatly increased." The contest in the Legislature over the adoption of the Home by the State was, as a memorandum in Mr. Hayes's handwriting records, "bitter, close, and doubtful. Mrs. Hayes exerted all her influence with her friends, especially in the Senate, and was very anxious and energetic. The bill making the Home a state institution was passed by one majority. In April, 1870, the last night of the session, the Home was defeated practically for several hours. The Senate by a tie vote refused to confirm the nominees of Governor Hayes for the Board of Managers. This was by reason of the absence of Senator Gatch, of Greene County, who had gone home believing all was safe. Governor Hayes sent word to Senator Potts and others that if they could keep the Senate in session a few hours, he would get Senator Gatch from his home. Potts sent the Governor soon after the following note: 'Goepper is making a Dutch speech (in Dutch). We have them in a deadlock and they can't get out until Gatch comes. Will you send to the depot and bring him forthwith?' Goepper spoke in German, French, and English several hours, until just at daylight a locomotive brought Gatch from Xenia. The Board was then confirmed and the Home was safe. Hon. Michael Goepper was a patriotic German from Cincinnati and a warm friend of Mrs. Hayes."

that the Board of State Charities, with its beneficent powers of supervision and suggestion, was thoroughly established and sustained. In this connection, too, may be noted his interest and influence in the establishment of the State University by the use of the funds derived from the sale of the lands given by the National Government for that purpose. In the organization of the board of trustees for the university politics was eschewed by Mr. Hayes. "Gentlemen were selected," as he wrote some time later, "either of known liberal views, or men of such character and influence selected as would strengthen the institution. The plan was not thought to be feasible by many of its well-wishers, who were consulted, but perseverance and good judgment, it is believed, will yet be able to smooth all difficulties and establish at Columbus an institution worthy of the State, and worthy to be the head of the educational system of the State."

Mr. Hayes was never engaged in more congenial employment than when he was busied in preserving memorials of the earlier days, of the struggles and sacrifices of pioneer times. Everything relating to the settlement and progress of the country, and especially of his own State, was of interest to him. Doubtless his service on the Library Committee of Congress had enlarged his conception of the importance of collecting and preserving the materials of history. To the end of his life he never ceased to increase his own collection of Americana nor lost interest in the accumulation of the data of local history. It was only natural, therefore, that as Governor he should do all in his power to further the acquisition of historical documents and other memorials for the State. Through his efforts the papers of General Arthur St. Clair, of great historical value, were purchased;[1] a collection of sketches, letters, and other manuscripts illuminative of pioneer conditions was obtained; the portraits of the Governors of Ohio were acquired;[2] a memorial to Lincoln and the Ohio soldiers was

[1] In accomplishing this and similar work Mr. Hayes was assisted by the zealous and intelligent efforts of William Henry Smith, Secretary of State of Ohio during the first year of Mr. Hayes's incumbency of the Governor's office. The St. Clair papers were published in two volumes, a few years later, having been carefully edited and annotated by Mr. Smith.

[2] No funds were provided for this purpose by the General Assembly. Mr. Hayes obtained some portraits by applying to the relatives of the early Governors. Where expense was involved he drew upon the contingent fund. In three

placed in the State Capitol;[1] and a collection undertaken of objects and casts of objects made by the mound-builders. This was the beginning of the remarkable collection of objects from the mounds of Ohio now gathered in the State Museum at Columbus, the archæological interest and value of which can hardly be overestimated.

All through the years that Mr. Hayes was Governor, he was in constant requisition for speeches on all kinds of occasions — civic celebrations, old soldiers' gatherings, receptions, dedications of public monuments, and the like. On most occasions it was Mr. Hayes's custom to make very brief addresses, oftentimes with slight preparation; but the reports of such speeches preserved in the newspapers of the day give evidence that his utterances were seldom if ever of a purely perfunctory character. Even in his briefest speeches there was an appropriateness of sentiment which gave them a distinctive quality. But frequently the speeches were carefully prepared beforehand, and these, while never notable for rhetorical grace, were characterized by a fitness for the particular occasion, a soundness of views, and a wholesome manliness of expression which lift them far above the commonplace. Significant examples of these speeches are all that can be given. In a speech at Youngstown, July 4, 1868, in anticipation of the erection of a monument to commemorate the soldiers from that region that had perished in the Civil War, Mr. Hayes said: —

We build a monument in honor of the men who died in the war for the Union. They went out to do battle with the only enemy that could put our nation in jeopardy, even for an instant. Separated by broad oceans from every rival power, our nation was impregnable to foreign assault. From the days of Washington, our danger had been the prevalence of a false theory of the Constitution which might some day be carried into

years he succeeded in getting portraits of all who were ever elected Governor of the State and of all the acting Governors except two.

[1] "I did an unusual, and, I think, meritorious thing last night. Tom Jones's Memorial to Lincoln and the Ohio soldiers was to be inaugurated in the rotunda of the Capitol. I presided. I had a fairish little opening speech, which with my good lungs I could make go off well. But there were three speakers to give addresses. I knew that the little, pretty, pet things to be said were not numerous, and that my speech would more or less interfere with the success of theirs. I accordingly swallowed my speech and introduced the various actors without an extra word. Who has beaten this?" (Diary, January 20, 1871.)

practice. That theory was that the Union under the Constitution was created by the States, each acting in a sovereign capacity, and that any State might rightfully withdraw from, and thereby destroy, the Union. The opposite theory is that the Constitutional Union, in the language of Washington, "makes us one people." These soldiers gave their lives that the people of the United States might have "one country, one Constitution, one destiny." If their warfare had failed, this generation would probably have seen the great central belt of this continent divided into hostile nations, — no man knows how many, — each with its separate government, its standing army, its arsenals, its forts, and its camps. Our people, so full of enterprise, energy, and courage, would have been compelled to make war their study and their business. Whatever evil belongs to a condition of war, its military courts and commissions, its taxes, etc., its drafts, its idleness, ignorance, vice, and crime, its sacrifices, privations, and sufferings; — all of those, if the war for the Union had failed, would have been part of the familiar daily life of our people, until, as a refuge from war, lawlessness, and anarchy, they would gladly have sunk into the repose of a military despotism. The men we would honor to-day have given the last full measure of devotion to save from such a fate the precious inheritance won by our fathers. . . . The first great purpose, then, of the monument we build is to expound to all who behold it, as long as it shall endure, the true principles of the Constitution on the unity of the people of the United States. . . .

All monuments in honor of the soldiers who fell in the struggle are at the same time monuments to national unity, to impartial liberty, and to universal education. They teach the world that North America belongs to the Stripes and Stars, that under them, no man shall wear a chain, and that every child of the Republic shall have a fair chance to grow to the full stature of a mental and moral manhood. . . .

In other times and other lands monuments have seldom been built in memory of subordinate officers or of private soldiers. Great leaders are remembered and honored while they live, and after death, power, fortune, and rank are the inheritance of their children. Too often their brave followers, with their families, the public danger having passed away, are forgotten or neglected. . . . It has often been said that in our army the bayonets could think. Unfortunately, the sword was not always in the hand of a wise and trustworthy thinker. . . . The courage of citizen soldiers depends more upon their personal character, their patriotism, their manhood, and their faith in the goodness of their cause.

On a somewhat similar occasion, some time subsequently at Toledo, Mr. Hayes used this language: —

This celebration needs little explanation and no apology. It has its origin in a sound and healthy sentiment. It gratifies the noblest feelings of the best side of human nature. We know very well that what we may do and say cannot reach those who are gone. We are here to share in these ceremonies because God hath so fashioned us that it is good for us to take part in them. We are here to endeavor to express and to feel what it is natural for us to express and to feel in the contemplation of great sacrifices for country and for liberty. . . .

Good men and women do not need to be told that admiration, gratitude, and everlasting remembrance are due to all men who with unselfish courage, in obedience to their convictions of duty, devote their lives to the right side of a great cause. Mere daring in the presence of the last enemy, under any circumstances, commands a degree of respect. Even the intrepidity of the guilty in the very act of crime will win admiration. But if to courage is added conscience — if a man goes to his death bravely from a sense of duty, blinded and mistaken although he may be, he has the sympathy of every true and noble heart. Old John Brown and Stonewall Jackson are to be reckoned heroes for all coming time. We do not stop to inquire as to their clearness of vision. We accept as true that they did their duty as it was given them to see it, and we yield them the homage to which they are entitled.

January 20, 1870, the members of the Legislature of Kentucky and other distinguished citizens of that State visited Cincinnati and were entertained by a banquet in the evening at the Burnet House. The toast "Kentucky and Ohio" was responded to by Governor Hayes in these words: —

Ohio and Kentucky; Kentucky and Ohio. How well these names sound together. The early history of Ohio is inseparably blended with the early history of Kentucky. At the beginning, Kentucky, first settled, was most populous, and most powerful; Ohio, in every moment of alarm and peril, appealed to her sister State, and never appealed in vain. That history alluded to here, so familiar, so hackneyed, we know it by heart. Our favorite Governor, Corwin, in his eloquent speeches, in his conversation still more eloquent and still more epigrammatic, made us familiar with the history of his native State.

Why, I remember again and again to have heard him, fond as he was, you know, of illustrating everything by reference to Scripture, declare to great audiences in Ohio that never, since the dispersion on the plains of Shinar, was a people more truly and literally cradled in war than this same gallant people of Kentucky. In childhood they fought the savages of the Northwest, by the side of their mothers and their sisters in their dwellings. In their youth and in their manhood, they fought them upon the battlefield and in the ambuscade. "Go," said he, "and trace the path of any savage incursion in early times, and you shall find it marked with Kentucky blood. Wander over any of the battlefields which rescued this Northwest from the savages, and you shall find the whitened bones of Kentucky's sons."

In early times, then, my friends, Kentucky and Ohio were of one mind and one heart. Later, in 1824, aye, and in 1844, when the great statesman of Kentucky was put up for the high office of the nation, Ohio rallied to his support with the same zeal and heartiness that did Kentucky. [Cheers — "Henry Clay."] Aye, Henry Clay. It is not among the least of the pleasant recollections of my life that I cast my first vote for Henry Clay, of Kentucky.

And you reciprocated; for, when, in 1836 and 1840, the pioneers of the West selected her favorite soldier and statesman, General Harrison, to be the Executive of this nation, he found his heartiest support and largest majority in the State of Kentucky.

But now, my friends, if in latter days alienation, dissensions, estrangements, and hostility have arisen between us, it was from causes outside either of Kentucky or Ohio — causes which neither Ohio nor Kentucky, nor both united, could possibly control.

But now all that is past, causes and all. No more division, no more separation, to the last syllable of recorded time. God grant that, as the ancient friendship between Kentucky and Ohio depended upon and arose out of a community of toils, sufferings, hardships, and dangers that they endured for each other, that again that ancient accord and harmony may return by reason, perhaps, we may say, of the community of interests and participation in common enterprises, and the enjoyment of the same common prosperity. I believe this is destined to be our future history. I believe that the reviving harmony and friendship is destined to increase; and God grant that it may last forever and ever.

In April, 1870, the colored people met at Columbus to celebrate the adoption of the Fifteenth Amendment, when Governor Hayes made this short but striking address: —

Fellow Citizens, — We celebrate, to-night, the final triumph of a righteous cause, after a long, eventful, and memorable struggle. The conflict, which Mr. Seward pronounced "irrepressible," at last is ended. The house which was divided against itself, and which, therefore, according to Mr. Lincoln, could not stand as it was, is divided no longer; and we may now rationally hope that, under Providence, it is destined to stand — long to stand the home of freedom, and refuge of the oppressed of every race and of every clime!

The great leading facts of the contest are so familiar that I need not attempt to recount them. They belong to the history of two famous wars — the War of the Revolution and the War of the Rebellion — and are part of the story of almost a hundred years of civil strife. They began with Bunker Hill and Yorktown, with the Declaration of Independence and the adoption of the Federal Constitution. They end with Fort Sumter and the fall of Richmond, with the Emancipation Proclamation and the antislavery and equal rights amendments to the Constitution of the nation. These long and anxious years were not years of unbroken, ceaseless warfare. There were periods of lull, of truce, of compromise. But every lull was short-lived, every truce was hollow, every compromise, however pure the motives of its authors, proved deceitful and vain. There could be no lasting peace until the great wrong was destroyed, and impartial justice established.

The history of this period is adorned with a long list of illustrious names — with the names of men who were indeed "Solomons in council and Samsons in the field." At its beginning there were Washington, Franklin, and Jefferson, and their compeers, and in the last great crisis Providence was equally gracious, and gave us such men as Lincoln, and Stanton, and George H. Thomas. All who bore their part in the great conflict, may now with grateful hearts rejoice that it is forever ended.

The newly made citizens who seem to carry off the lion's share of the fruits of the victory — it is especially fitting and proper that they should assemble to congratulate each other, and to be congratulated by all of us that they now enjoy for the first time in full measure the blessings of freedom and manhood.

Those also who have opposed many of the late steps in the great progress — it is a great satisfaction to know that so large a number of them gracefully acquiesce in the decision of the nation.

The war of races, which it was so confidently predicted would follow the enfranchisement of the colored people — where was it in the elections in Ohio last week? In a few localities the old prejudice and fanaticism made, we may hope, their last appearance. There was barely enough angry dissent to remind us of the barbarism of slavery which has passed away forever. Generally throughout the State, especially in the cities of Cincinnati, Cleveland, Columbus, Dayton, and Toledo, where the new element is large, those who strove to avert the result over which we rejoice, leaders as well as followers, were conspicuous in setting an example of obedience to the law.

Not the least among the causes for congratulation, to-night, is the confidence we have that the enfranchised people will prove worthy of American citizenship. No true patriot wishes to see them exhibit a blind and unthinking attachment to mere party. But all good men wish to see them cultivate habits of industry and thrift, and to exhibit intelligence and virtue; and at every election to be earnestly solicitous to array themselves on the side of law and order, liberty and progress, education and religion.

Let them do this, and we may confidently expect that, in the judgment of history, the Fifteenth Amendment will take rank with the Declaration of Independence and the Emancipation Proclamation.

In 1871, Mr. Hayes was urged by many of his personal and political friends to stand for a third term. But that would have been for him to violate the unbroken precedent of the State, even had he not earnestly desired to return to private life. He

therefore promptly and emphatically refused to allow his name
to be used as a candidate, and General Edward F. Noyes was
nominated by the Republicans as his successor. The Democrats
nominated Colonel George W. McCook, on a platform which
accepted the war amendments to the Federal Constitution as
accomplished facts, while "denouncing the extraordinary means
by which they were brought about." This platform became
known as "the new departure," and was much ridiculed by
Republican orators in the campaign that followed. Mr. Hayes
made many speeches during the canvass in defense of Republican policies and in favor of the election of General Noyes who
was chosen, October 10, by a majority of 20,000. Governor
Hayes's speech at Zanesville, August 24, 1871, presents clearly
and vigorously the issues of the campaign and the position of the
Republican party of that period. It is here given in substantial
fulness: —

The change of principles which a majority of the late Democratic
State Convention at Columbus decided to make, commonly called "the
new departure," lends to the pending political contest in Ohio its chief
interest. Indeed, there is no other salient feature in the Democratic
platform. Resolutions in the usual form were adopted on several other
political topics; but the main discussion, and the absorbing interest of
the convention, was on the question of accepting as a finality the series
of Republican measures which is generally regarded as the natural and
legitimate result of the overthrow of the Rebellion, and which is embodied in the last three amendments to the Constitution.

Certain influential Democratic leaders in Ohio had become satisfied
by the repeated defeats of their party that no considerable number of
Republicans would ever aid the Democratic party to obtain power until
it fully and explicitly accepted in good faith, as a final settlement of the
questions involved, the leading Republican measures resulting from the
war. They were convinced that Republicans generally regarded these
measures of such vital importance that, until they were irrevocably
established, other and minor questions would not be allowed to divide
that great body of patriotic people who rallied together in support of the
Government during its struggle for existence. The important principles
which Republicans claim should be accepted as settled are: —

(1) That the national power is the supreme power of the land, and
that the doctrine that the States are in any proper sense sovereign,
including as it does the right of nullification and secession, is no longer
to be maintained.

(2) That all persons born or naturalized in the United States, and
subject to their jurisdiction, are citizens thereof, and entitled to equal

rights, civil and political, without regard to race, color, or condition.

(3) That the public debt resulting from the war is of binding obligation, and must be fully and honestly paid.

Mr. Vallandigham, with that boldness and energy for which he was distinguished, undertook the task of forcing his party to take the position required to make success possible in Ohio. In this work, he was encouraged, and probably aided, by the counsel and advice of that other eminent Democratic leader, Chief Justice Chase. The first authentic announcement of the new movement in Ohio was made by the Montgomery County Democratic Convention, held at Dayton, on the 18th day of May last. The speech and resolutions of Mr. Vallandigham in that body contained much sound Republicanism. He still clung to a general assertion of the States' rights heresy, but accepted the last three constitutional amendments "as a settlement, in fact, of all the issues of the war," and "pledged" the Democratic party to the faithful and absolute enforcement of the Constitution as it now is, "so as to secure equal rights to all persons, without distinction of race, color, or condition." On the subject of the national debt, and of currency, he was equally explicit. He declared "in favor of the payment of the public debt at the earliest practicable moment consistent with moderate taxation; that specie is the basis of all sound currency; and that true policy requires a speedy return to that basis as soon as practicable without distress to the debtor class of people."

Surely, here was a long stride away from the Democracy of the last ten years, and toward wholesome Republican ideas. If a Democratic victory could be gained by adopting Republican principles, the framer of the Dayton platform was not lacking in political sagacity. Unfortunately for the success of the scheme, no Ohio Democrat of conspicuous position, except Mr. Chase, is known to have approved Mr. Vallandigham's resolutions as a whole. The Chief Justice wrote to Mr. Vallandigham the well-known letter of May 20, in which he warmly congratulated him on the movement which was to return "the Democratic party to its ancient platform of progress and reform."

This was perfectly consistent with the previous opinions and public conduct of Mr. Chase. He had supported the three amendments to the Constitution, and notwithstanding the censure of his Democratic associates, he had been signally active and influential in procuring the ratification by Ohio of the Fifteenth Amendment. In addition to this, he was probably the only prominent Western Democrat who was for the payment of the public debt in coin, and in favor of a speedy return to specie payments.

When the convention assembled, on the 1st of June, neither the talents and energy of Mr. Vallandigham nor the great name and authority of the Chief Justice were sufficient to carry through in all its parts the Dayton programme. The financial resolutions were stricken out and the oft-defeated greenback theory, slightly modified, was inserted in its place. Other important paragraphs of Mr. Vallandigham were also omitted, in which "secession, slavery, inequality before the law, and political inequality" were described as "belonging to the dead past" and "buried out of sight." This left as the new departure two resolutions, which were adopted only after strong opposition: —

"1. *Resolved, by the Democracy of Ohio,* That denouncing the extraordinary means by which they were brought about, we recognize as accomplished facts the three several amendments to the Constitution, recently adopted, and regard the same as no longer political issues before the country.

"2. . . . The Democratic party pledges itself to the full, faithful, and absolute enforcement of the Constitution as it now is, so as to secure equal rights to all persons under it, without distinction of race, color, or condition."

The Democratic managers claim that by this movement they have taken such a position that, at least equally with the Republicans, they are entitled to the confidence and support of the early and earnest friends of the principles of the three recent constitutional amendments. They claim at the same time, in the same breath, that they are entitled also to the confidence of the Democratic people whom they have hitherto taught that the amendments were ratified by force and fraud; that they are revolutionary and void, and that they are a dangerous departure from the principles of the fathers of the republic, and destructive of all good government.

Now, the important question presented is, whether it is safe and wise to trust these amendments for interpretation, construction, and execution to the party which, from first to last, has fiercely opposed them. The safe rule is, if you want a law fairly and faithfully administered, intrust power only to its friends. It will rarely have a fair trial at the hands of its enemies. These amendments are no exception to this rule.

What the country most needs, and what good citizens most desire in regard to these great measures, is peace — repose. They wish to be able to rest confidently in the belief that they are to be enforced and obeyed. They do not want them overthrown by revolutionary violence or defeated by fraud. They do not wish them repealed by constitutional amendments, abrogated by judicial construction, nullified by unfriendly legislation, state or national, or left a dead letter by non-action on the part of lawmakers or executive officers. Has the time come when the country can afford to trust the Democratic party on these questions? Consider the facts.

The new departure is by no means generally accepted by the Democratic party, and where accepted the conversion is sudden and recent, and against the protest of a large element of sincere and inflexible Democrats.

The only State touching the borders of Ohio which has been reliably Democratic for the last five years is Kentucky. She sends to Congress

an undivided Democratic delegation of two Senators and nine Representatives. At the late election, notwithstanding the heroic efforts of her
Republicans under the splendid leadership of General Harlan, the Democratic organs are able to rejoice that they still hold the State by from
thirty to forty thousand majority. Where did the Democrats of Kentucky, in their canvass, stand on the new departure? They marched in
the old Democratic path. They turned no back somersault to catch
Republican votes. On the very day that the Ohio Democracy were
wrangling in convention over the bitter dose, Governor Leslie, addressing the Democracy of Lewis County, said: "As to the new amendments,
I am out and out opposed to them. I care not who in Indiana, Ohio, or
elsewhere may be for them. Those amendments were engrafted upon
the Constitution of the country, and proclaimed to the country as part
and parcel of the Constitution by force and by fraud, and not in the
legitimate way laid down in the Constitution: Ten States of this Union
were tied hand and foot, and bayonets were presented to their breasts
to make them consent against their will to the passage of these amendments. The procuring of these amendments was a fraud upon this people, and upon the people of the whole United States, and having been
thus obtained, I hold that they ought to be repealed. There may be
some Democrats who are not for their repeal, but the great body of our
party is for it."

The Democratic candidate for Lieutenant-Governor, Mr. Carlisle,
was equally decided. Said he: "In the first place, I do not think that the
resolution passed by the Ohio Democracy, declaring that these Constitutional amendments are no longer political issues before the country,
will have the effect which they appear to have supposed it would. Instead of withdrawing them as subjects of political discussion, it will give
them far more prominence than they ever had heretofore, and they will
be confronted with them throughout the entire canvass. The only way
in which any question can be withdrawn from the arena of political
discussion is for both parties to ignore it altogether. This cannot be
done as to these amendments, because they present real living issues, in
which the people feel a very deep interest. They are not dead issues,
and politicians cannot kill them by resolutions. The Ohio Democrats
seem to recognize this to some extent at least, for they have simply
attempted to turn the discussion away from the validity and merits of
the amendments themselves to the question of their construction. In
this I think they have made a grievous mistake."

In Indiana, the last authoritative Democratic utterance on this subject, was the passage, in January last, by the Senate of that State, of
the following resolution, offered by Mr. Hughes, every Democrat supporting it: —

"*Resolved*, That Congress has no lawful power derived from the
Constitution of the United States, nor from any other source whatever,
to require any State of the Union to ratify an amendment proposed
to the Constitution of the United States as a condition precedent to

representation in Congress; that all such acts of ratification are null and void, and the votes so obtained ought not to be counted to affect the rights of the people and the States of the whole Union, and that the State of Indiana protests and solemnly declares that the so-called Fifteenth Amendment is not this day, nor ever has been in law, a part of the Constitution of the United States."

It is not necessary to go to neighboring States for Democratic authorities, to show how far the new departure is from modern Democracy. When this question was last debated before the people of Ohio, the Democratic position on the principle of the Fifteenth Amendment, and on its constitutional validity, if *declared* adopted, was thus stated: —

Speaking of the principle of the amendment, Judge Thurman said: "I tell you it is only the entering wedge that will destroy all intelligent suffrage in this country, and turn our country from an intelligent white man's government into one of the most corrupt mongrel governments in the world."

On its validity, if declared adopted, General Ward said: "Fellow citizens of Ohio, I boldly assert that the States of this Union have always had, both before and since the adoption of the Constitution of the United States, entire sovereignty over the whole subject of suffrage in all its relations and bearings. Ohio has that sovereignty now, and it cannot be taken from her without her consent, even by all the other States combined, except by revolutionary usurpation. The right to regulate suffrage as to the organization of its own government, and the election of officers under it, is an inalienable attribute of sovereignty, which the State could not surrender without surrendering its sovereign existence as a State. To take from Ohio the power of determining who shall exercise the right of suffrage is not an amendment of the Constitution, but a revolutionary usurpation by the other States, in no wise constitutionally binding upon her sovereignty as a State."

These opinions are still largely prevalent in the Democratic party. When a new departure was announced at Dayton, the leading organ of the party in this State said: "There are matters in the Montgomery County resolutions which, it is very safe to say, will not receive the approval of the state convention, and which should [not receive its endorsement. They have faults of omission and commission. They evince a desire to sail with the wind, and as near the water as possible without getting wet. The Democracy everywhere believe that the Constitution was altered by fraud and force, and do not intend to be mealy-mouthed in their expression of the outrage, whatever they may agree upon as to how the amendments should be treated in the future, for the sake of saving, if possible, what is left of constitutional liberty."

After the scheme was adopted in convention, the common sentiment was well expressed by the editor who said that "the platform was made for present use, and is marked with the taint of insincerity."

The speeches of Colonel McCook and other Democratic gentlemen exhibit, when carefully read, clearly enough the character of the new departure.

. . . .

These paragraphs furnish no adequate reply to the questions which an intelligent and earnest Republican, who believes in the wisdom and value of the amendments, would put to these distinguished gentlemen, when they ask him for his vote. He would ask: "If the Democratic party shall obtain the controlling power in the general Government, in its several departments, executive, legislative, and judicial, and in the State Governments, what would it do? Would it faithfully execute these amendments, or would it not rather use its power to get rid of them — either by constitutional amendment, by judicial decision, by unfriendly legislation, or by a failure or refusal to legislate?" Before the new departure can gain Republican votes, its friends must answer satisfactorily these questions. The speeches I have quoted fail to furnish such answers. Colonel McCook objects to the Fifteenth Amendment, because "it contains a provision intended to confer power upon Congress which is dangerous to the liberties of the country." Now, what is this dangerous provision? It reads: "Section 2. The Congress shall have power to enforce this article by appropriate legislation." Each of the three recent amendments contains a similar provision. Without this provision, they would be inoperative in more than half of the late Rebel States. The complaints made of these provisions warn us that in Democratic hands the legislation required to give force and effect to these provisions would be denied.

But the most significant part of these speeches are the passages which refer to the repeal of the amendments. Mr. Hubbard [chairman of Colonel McCook's first meeting] said: "We don't surrender the right to make such returns to the old Constitution as we may deem expedient. It is a future question that we are not bound to discuss." Colonel McCook says: "How can I answer for all the future? How can I tell what the Democracy of New York or any other State may do?" Mr. Hunt [candidate for Lieutenant-Governor] says: "The fact that they have been declared a part of the Constitution does not preclude any legitimate discussion as to their expediency. Proper action will never be barred." The meaning of all this is that the Democratic party will acquiesce in the amendments while it is out of power. Whether or not it will try to repeal them when it gets power is a question of the future which they are not bound to discuss. Or, as another distinguished gentleman has it, this question is "beyond the range of profitable discussion." In reply to these gentlemen, the well-informed Republican citizen when asked to vote for the new departure, is very likely to adopt their own phraseology, and to say, "Whether I shall vote your ticket or not is a question of the future which it is not now proper to discuss — it is beyond the range of profitable discussion"; and if he has the Democratic veneration for Tammany Hall, he will say, with Colonel McCook, "How can I tell what the Democracy of New York may do?"

Notwithstanding the decision of the late convention, it is probable that the real sentiment of the Democracy of Ohio is truly stated by the Butler County *Democrat:* —

"Our position, then, is, that while we regard the so-called amendments as gross usurpation and base frauds — not a part of the Federal Constitution *de facto* nor *de jure* — and, therefore, acts which are void, we will abide by them until a majority of the people of the States united shall, at the polls, put men in power who shall hold them to be null and of no effect. We adhere strictly, on this point, to the second resolution of Hon. L. D. Campbell, adopted at the Democratic convention held in this county last May; and to refresh the minds of our readers we reproduce it here: —

" '2. That now, as heretofore, we are opposed to all lawlessness and disorder, and for maintaining the supremacy of the Constitution and laws as the only certain means of public safety, and will abide by all their provisions until the same shall be amended, abrogated, or repealed by the lawfully constituted authorities.' "

The new departure has certainly very little claim to the support of Republican citizens. What are its claims on honest Democrats?

Colonel McCook, to make the new departure palatable to his Democratic supporters, tells them that a repeal of the Fifteenth Amendment would fail of its object. That the right to vote, once exercised by the black man, cannot be taken away. Is this sound either in law or logic? By the Fifteenth Amendment no State can deny the right to vote to any citizens on account of race or color. Suppose that amendment was repealed; what would prevent Kentucky from denying suffrage to colored citizens? Plainly nothing. And in case of such repeal it is probable that in less than ninety days thereafter every Democratic State would deny suffrage to colored citizens, and the great body of Democratic voters would heartily applaud that result. The truth is, no sound argument can be made, showing or tending to show that the new departure is consistent with the Democratic record. Hitherto Democracy has taught that, as a question of law, the amendments were made by force and fraud, and are therefore void; that, as a question of principles, this is a white man's government, and that to confer suffrage on the colored races — on the African or Chinaman — would change the nature of the government and speedily destroy it. Now the new departure demands that Democrats shall accept the amendments as valid, and shall take a pledge "to secure equal rights to all persons, without distinction of race, color, or condition." Sincere Democrats will find it very difficult to take that pledge, unless they are now convinced that their whole political life has been a great mistake.

When an individual changes his political principles — turns his coat merely to catch votes — he is generally thought to be unworthy of support. I entertain no doubt that the people of Ohio, at the approaching election, will, upon that principle, by a large majority, condemn the Democratic party for its bold attempt to catch Republican votes by the new departure.

The last few days of Mr. Hayes's service as Governor were marked by an episode which throws strong light on his character for straightforwardness in politics and his loyalty in friendship. John Sherman's term as United States Senator was about to expire. He was a candidate for reëlection and the Republicans were in control of the Legislature. But Mr. Sherman was by no means the unanimous choice of the party, and he had many active opponents among the Republican members of the Legislature. There were several aspirants for Mr. Sherman's place, and Mr. Hayes was besought to allow his name to go before the Republican caucus. Indeed, early in 1871 he had been solicited to enter the race; but after thirteen years of official life, during the greater part of which his salary had been insufficient to meet his living expenses, he felt that he must return to private life, attractive as a seat in the Senate would be. He thought, too, that Mr. Sherman deserved reëlection. He therefore had resisted the importunities of his friends and now again refused to entertain the question.[1] Meanwhile, as soon as the members of the Legislature assembled at Columbus, the Democratic legislators who were most eager to prevent Mr. Sherman's return to the Senate quickly let it be known that they were willing to join with the recalcitrant Republicans and cast their votes for Mr. Hayes. All that was necessary to insure the success of the scheme was the permission of the Governor to the use of his name. This without the slightest hesitation he sturdily and steadfastly refused. Writing to his uncle, January 3, 1872, he said: —

Everything for two days or three has been absorbed in the senatorial fight. I am squarely out of it. It has seemed, and still seems that I could command the place by entering the contest. But I have steadily refused. I could not consent, even if I wanted it, in the way proposed. The requisite number of Republicans to elect, added to the Democrats, would stay out of caucus if I would consent to be elected that way. This is the only condition, my consent to be elected. The upshot will be, I think, that Sherman will be nominated and elected. It is rather pleasant to be so endorsed by one's opponents. But, etc., etc., etc.

The next day, January 4, Mr. Hayes put an end as he thought to all possible manipulation in his behalf by obtaining

---

[1] December 28, 1871, he wrote William Henry Smith: "I shall *not* go before the caucus — shall not be a candidate under any circumstances."

the publication in the *Ohio State Journal* of a brief editorial paragraph which read: —

It is well known, and we speak by authority, that Governor Hayes has not been and will not be a candidate for Senator, either in or out of caucus.

To this paragraph, as preserved in his scrapbook, Mr. Hayes appended this note: —

I wrote the above and published it the first chance after it became apparent that I was to be supported merely to defeat the nominee of the Republican caucus, and at a time when it seemed to me certain that I would be elected if I would consent to an election under such circumstances.

But in spite of this, and even after Mr. Sherman had received the caucus nomination and the vote had been taken in the separate houses of the Legislature, a Republican State Senator and a Representative called on Mr. Hayes at his house late at night and tried to persuade him to allow them to vote for him in the joint session. Enough Republicans, they assured him, were still so opposed to the election of Mr. Sherman that they would turn to him if he would consent to an election. They were confident that after a few ballots, when it became apparent that Mr. Sherman could not be chosen, the Republicans would come to him, and they added: "The man now elected Senator over the caucus will be the next President of the United States." But Mr. Hayes refused to be tempted, declaring that with his ideas of duty he could not honorably consent and would not. The Senator said it was strange to see the Senatorship refused with the Presidency in prospect. Later that same night Mr. Hayes was roused from a sound sleep by another friend who came to him with a similar plea and with an even stronger assurance that if he would give the word the Senatorship would be his. Again he resisted the temptation, saying: "I can't honorably do it and there is no use talking. It is settled and has been for weeks." The visitor replied: "Well, if you say *that*, I must give it up. I admire your principle, but John Sherman would n't do it." [1]

The conclusion of Mr. Hayes's term was celebrated by a reception given by Mr. and Mrs. Hayes to the new Governor (General

[1] Diary.

Noyes) and his wife attended by the state officers, the members of the Legislature, and many others. His first day of release from official duties gave him an unwonted sense of relief and exhilaration. He wrote his uncle, January 9: —

I feel foolishly happy this, my first day of freedom. For a week or two past, there has been a feeling with me that something might happen to cast a shadow on the four years of good fortune in the Governor's office. Besides, I was hurried with perplexing business to the last moment. To-day I am independent. Our big reception went off nicely. Everybody says pleasant things. It looks as if I might have been Senator. My refusal gives me position, and, true or not, the common remark is that I am the most esteemed of the Governors within the memory of people living. But enough of this vanity.

And two days later: —

It seems good to be no man's servant — to be the equal of the best in rights, at least.

PREPARATIONS were immediately made to return to Cincinnati — still Mr. Hayes's nominal residence, though he had spent little time there since he entered the army in 1861. He was cordially welcomed by his old friends and neighbors. February 4, he wrote his uncle: "I shall enjoy life here, but more and more I am satisfied with my final decision on two points — *public life* and my *permanent residence in future.*"

It was his purpose to abandon politics, to give up all thought of further political preferment, and, as soon as his affairs at Cincinnati could be put in proper shape, to make his permanent home at Fremont. There cannot be the slightest doubt of the sincerity of his determination to quit public life — so many and emphatic are the expressions in his diary and his letters [1] of this settled purpose. But his perennial interest in public affairs — in the current of political discussion, in the fortunes of the party with which he had so long been identified — was in no degree abated. Only now he regarded himself rather as a disinterested observer of the course of events.[2] However, quite against his

---

[1] For example, in a letter to Joseph A. Joel (an old comrade), of New York, of May 29, 1871, Mr. Hayes wrote: "I am looking forward to a release from public life, and to freedom, as hopefully as a schoolboy to his coming vacation, or a soldier to a furlough. I retire absolutely. I shall make no attempt to go higher. If I ever accept public employment again, it will be incidental and for special reasons." Many letters before this and subsequent to it contain similar expressions. A letter to Murat Halstead, of December 29, 1871, had this postscript: "My intention is to quit the struggle for political promotion and at the end of my present term to go into private life. I don't want to quit with friends accusing me of blind partisanship. I don't want any friend to take back his uttered opinions, but perhaps the fact here stated may influence the expression of them. Hence this P.S."

[2] "Having resolved to quit the race for political promotion, I can now look at the current events in political affairs without the bias created by personal interest. The Senatorship to be decided this year in Ohio seems to be as likely to fall to me, if I enter the struggle for it, as to any other Republican. But the great questions which have so occupied my thoughts and enlisted my feelings — the great questions of freedom for the slaves and the unity of the nation — liberty

will and inclination, he soon found himself involved in the
activities of the national campaign of 1872.[1] General Grant's
first term as President, beginning under the happiest auspices,
had gradually increased in unpopularity until a considerable element of the Republican party, guided by leaders of conspicuous
ability, undoubted patriotism, and sincerity of purpose, had
become completely alienated and saw no hope for a betterment
of conditions except in direct opposition to the reëlection of
Grant. The Liberal Republican movement, as it was called, was
early in 1872 in full swing. Wisely directed, and solidly supported by the Democrats, Mr. Hayes was disposed to believe
that it might be successful in its purpose. But he saw little
prospect of the necessary unity of action. April 30 he wrote his
uncle from Cincinnati: —

The city is filling up with Liberals. No doubt the number here is
largely greater than the constituency they represent requires. But I am
satisfied that the opposition to Grant, *if it could be united*, would carry
the country. But the prospect of such unity does not strike me as
probable. The leading candidates are Adams and Judge Davis. Adams
would carry off more Republicans than any other man; but would not,
I think, get a solid Democratic support. In fact, I suspect they would
repudiate him. Judge Davis would be dropped by a large share of the
Liberal Republicans. But as he would probably get the solid Democratic
vote he would be very formidable. But I need not speculate about it.

and nationality — are now settled. No political or party resolutions can unsettle
the established facts that all men are to have in this country equal civil and
political rights and that the United States form one people — one nation.

"The small questions of to-day about taxation, appointments, etc., etc., are
petty and uninteresting. I cannot consent, after having borne my part in the
glorious struggle against slavery during the last seventeen years, now to endure
the worry and anxiety belonging to political life for the sake of the honors of
office merely, and without subjects interesting me deeply involved in the struggle.
I do not expect or desire to withdraw from all interest and participation in passing events. It is simply I am out of the race for promotion. I am not a candidate,
and shall avoid being made one, for the Senatorship, or for any other high
office." (Diary, March 16, 1871.)

[1] January 2, 1872, General John Pope wrote Mr. Hayes: "I am glad to hear
that you feel so much relief in retiring from office, but your resolution to take no
further conspicuous part in public affairs is not accepted with so much satisfaction, even if you had the power to carry it out. Men like you are too much
needed in public affairs to be permitted thus to escape the bondage of public
life, and whilst I have no doubt at all that your personal happiness would be
greatly promoted by leaving public life, if you can do so without regret, . . . yet
I do not for a moment believe that the people will permit you to withdraw from
what they consider a duty to the country." ˙

The affair is as well understood abroad as it is here. A new man in such cases is always a possibility. I am glad to be out of such a muss.

With the nomination of the brilliant but erratic and impracticable Horace Greeley, a man most offensive to the Democrats though they accepted him as their candidate, Mr. Hayes was at first not confident of results, but inclined to think that the movement would be a failure and was convinced that it deserved to fail. In his diary, May 6, three days after the nomination of Greeley, he wrote: —

I am not confident of results. If the Democrats adopt Greeley as their candidate he may win, and win by a large majority. The people are sick of politics — ready for change and may break in any new direction. Yet I rather incline to the opinion that the Democrats will find a dissent in their own ranks, when they take up Greeley, which they can't control — a dissent strong enough to let Grant keep the chair. A queer result it is! Free traders nominate their bitterest and most formidable foe. A party whose strength is mainly in the German element, which is clamorous against temperance fanaticism, nominate the author of that fanaticism. Democrats are required to support a man who said that he would go for Grant in preference to any Democrat. "Anything to beat a Democrat" has been, and was up to the day of his nomination, his lifelong motto.

Against his preferences, Mr. Hayes was made one of the delegates at large to the Philadelphia Convention which renominated Grant. On his return from the convention, in which he served on the platform committee, he wrote his uncle, June 10, from Delaware, Ohio, where his family was spending the heated period: —

I returned from the Philadelphia Convention yesterday. It was completely successful in all respects. It was united, harmonious, and the most enthusiastic convention any of us ever saw. The recent vindictive attacks on General Grant have created a strong reaction in his favor, which accounts for the unexpected feeling in his behalf — I mean the unlooked-for enthusiasm.

Disturbing reports of the number of disaffected Republicans in Ohio and neighboring States came to him in the next few weeks and caused him alarm. July 17 he writes in his diary: —

Altogether it is plain to my mind that Greeley will win, if the Democrats support him with their whole force. I think they can't do it, but I fear it. I fear that the thing is in great doubt; but I have seen too little to be positive. I must say that I have just now a feeling that Greeley will be elected.

But a month later, after he had entered the campaign and been somewhat about the State, he wrote: "I now think Grant's election quite certain."

Meanwhile, his old friends of the Second Congressional District were bombarding him with letters, soliciting him to allow them to nominate him again for Congress. To all his correspondents he sent an emphatic "out of the question." He had no desire to return to Congress, and had given assurances to prospective candidates for the nomination that he would not enter the race. He declared, therefore, that he could not under any circumstances allow his name to be used against them. He could see only one contingency which would induce him to change his mind, — and this contingency he refused to give any expression to lest his expression be used to bring the contingency about, — namely, that it should be the general wish of the Republicans and of the candidates themselves that he should be nominated. But even in that event the nomination would be against his preference. In spite, however, of his protests the Congressional Convention, August 6, in his absence from the city, nominated him on the first ballot and with manifestations of great enthusiasm and elation. The announcement of the convention's action was conveyed to him in a dispatch from Richard Smith, editor of the Cincinnati *Gazette*, who added: "We assured Republicans that Governor Hayes never retreated when ordered to advance." Even then Mr. Hayes sought to decline the honor, but he reluctantly yielded his preferences on the receipt of a petition, numerously signed by influential Republicans and independent voters of the district, urgently soliciting his acceptance of the nomination. His feeling is clearly indicated by a letter, dated Delaware, Ohio, August 10, to General M. F. Force, of Cincinnati: —

Returning from Fremont last night I found your dispatch of the 7th. On hearing of the nomination, and long before the convention adjourned, I sent dispatches to Smith, of the *Gazette*, and William E. Davis, explicitly declining to accept. There would have been time after the receipt of the dispatches to nominate another. I am now placed in a position where to withdraw might be injurious to the cause. I shall

probably stand. But I wish to be uncommitted until I come down
and see how it is. Many reasons, mostly of a private nature, make the
thing distasteful. But I feel pleased by what you and others say, and
I shall not worry about it any more. It annoyed me for a time. I will
come down and stop at the Gibson House Wednesday afternoon. Hope
to see you that evening.

Mr. Hayes made a vigorous canvass of his district, speaking
constantly during the five weeks immediately preceding the
election, though most of the time he was suffering from an inter-
mittent fever. He found from the start that he was engaged in
a losing battle. After a week of effort he wrote (September 8)
to his uncle: —

I have stood the first and worst week's work well. The result here is
more doubtful than I supposed. The Greeley strength is in my district.
I feel it the truth that Greeley ought to be beaten, and I strike him in
every speech. This drives the Greeley men from me. I shall not be surprised at defeat. But we gain steadily. I think Grant's election almost
sure. Four weeks and I am free. I enjoy this.

The kind and quality of the speeches made by Mr. Hayes in
this campaign are sufficiently indicated by excerpts from the
carefully prepared address which he made at Glendale, in the
first week of his canvass, namely, on September 4. He said: —

In the present condition of the country, two things are of vital importance — peace and a sound financial policy. We want peace —
honorable peace, with all nations; peace with the Indians; and peace
between all the citizens of all the States. We want a financial policy so
honest that there can be no stain on the national honor and no taint
on the national credit; so stable that labor and capital and legitimate
business of every sort can confidently count upon what it will be next
week, the next month, and the next year. We want the burdens of taxation so justly distributed that they will bear equally upon all classes of
citizens in proportion to their ability to sustain them.

We want our currency gradually to appreciate until, without financial shock, or any sudden shrinkage of values, but in the natural course
of trade, it shall reach the uniform and permanent value of gold. With
lasting peace assured, and a sound financial condition established, the
United States and all her citizens may reasonably expect to enjoy a
measure of prosperity without a parallel in the world's history. . . .

Notwithstanding the predictions of our adversaries, that to confer
political rights upon colored people would lead to a war of races, white
people and colored people are now voting side by side in all of the old
slave States, and their elections are quite as free from violence and

disorder as they were when the whites alone were the voters. In a word, peace prevails in the South to an extent which, under the circumstances, the ablest statesmen among our adversaries three years ago pronounced impossible. The watchword of the Republican party four years ago was, "Let us have peace." A survey of every field where the public peace was then imperilled, of our affairs with foreign nations, with the Indians, and in the South, shows that the pledge implied in that famous watchword has been substantially made good, and that if the people continue to stand by the Government the peace we now enjoy will be continued and enduring.

Our financial affairs, four years ago, were of a condition that filled the minds of our ablest public men with anxiety and alarm. . . . The financial situation in 1868, according to these gentlemen [Mr. Thurman and other eminent Democratic statesmen], was a great debt steadily increasing, excessive taxation, enormous expenditure, and an impoverished people. Their remedy was to elevate the Democratic party to power, and to pay off the bonded debt with greenbacks. The majority of the people did not like the remedy. General Grant was elected, a Republican Congress was elected, and Governor Boutwell became Secretary of the Treasury. Instantly the country felt the change. . . .

Since General Grant became President taxes have been abolished which produced annually $130,460,580. If no taxes had been repealed, the reduction of the debt under Grant would have exceeded $650,000,-000 in three years and a half.

Our currency, which is of uniform value throughout the United States, has steadily appreciated until the total increase in its value is about $140,000,000, and the fluctuations in the premium on gold are comparatively slight.

The credit of the National Government has improved, and it can borrow funds to carry the debt at lower rates of interest than ever before.

. . . .

Four years ago, and three years ago, the ablest debaters among our adversaries were accustomed to speak of the country as on the brink of ruin. They said that "the people were in distress, in want, and impoverished; that the national burdens amounted to virtual confiscation, and that the people were daily growing poorer and poorer." They declared that to continue Republican rule would complete the destruction of the country. The Republican rule has been continued, and what do we see? A prosperity the like of which is not found anywhere else on earth. More miles of railroad are building, more dwellings, shops, and houses of every kind are in course of erection than ever before. Population is increasing, wealth is increasing, and in every foreign land the man who would improve his condition is hopefully looking to America.

I do not wish to be understood as holding that all the blessings which a country enjoys are due to good government. I would not so exaggerate the functions of government. Our great prosperity is the result of the inherent and reliable resources of the country, and depends largely on the natural wealth of the nation, which is daily more and more developed by the enterprise and industry of the people. But the sound financial policy of the Government has contributed important elements to that prosperity. The great Cincinnati Exposition of which we are all so proud, and which will do so much for this city and for this part of the United States, could not have been successfully inaugurated if the financial schemes of our adversaries had been adopted by the Government.

There are several questions relating to the present and the future which merit the attention of the people. Among the most interesting of these is the question of civil service reform.

About forty years ago a system of making appointments to office grew up, based on the maxim, "To the victors belong the spoils." The old rule, — the true rule, — that honesty, capacity, and fidelity constitute the highest claim to office, gave place to the idea that partisan services were to be chiefly considered. All parties in practice have adopted this system. Since its first introduction it has been materially modified. At first, the President, either directly or through the heads of departments, made all appointments. Gradually, by usage, the appointing power in many cases was transferred to members of Congress — to Senators and Representatives. The offices in these cases have become not so much rewards for party services as rewards for personal services in nominating and electing Senators and Representatives. What patronage the President and his Cabinet retain, and what offices Congressmen are by usage entitled to fill is not definitely settled. A Congressman who maintains good relations with the Executive usually receives a larger share of patronage than one who is independent. The system is a bad one. It destroys the independence of the separate departments of the Government, and it degrades the civil service. It ought to be abolished. General Grant has again and again explicitly recommended reform. A majority of Congress has been unable to agree upon any important measure. Doubtless the bills which have been introduced contain objectionable features. But the work should be begun. Let the best obtainable bill be passed, and experience will show what amendments are required. I would support either Senator Trumbull's bill or Mr. Jenckes's bill, if nothing better were proposed. The admirable speeches on this subject by the Representative of the First District, the Honorable Aaron F. Perry, contain the best exposition I have seen of sound doctrine on this question, and I trust the day is not distant when the principles which he advocates will be embodied in practical measures of legislation. We ought to have a reform of the system of appointments to the civil service, thorough, radical, and complete.

The duties levied under our present tariff laws were largely adopted during the war when all home productions were burdened with heavy taxation under the internal revenue laws. All tax laws, whether internal revenue or tariff, were then regarded as war measures. Now that war expenditures are happily ended and the internal taxes abolished, our tariff laws need extensive revision. In all changes of laws affecting the business of the country a prudent legislator will move cautiously. When capital has been invested and labor employed in the faith of existing laws, the importance of stability is not to be overlooked. Reductions should be gradual and moderate. Violent and sweeping changes of laws affecting the business of the country should be avoided. But where inequality has crept into the laws it is never too early to begin to head the ship in the right direction. The tariff laws now contain many inconsistencies and inequalities. Duties are levied which cost more to collect than the revenue they produce. All such ought to be abolished. Some duties, now that the internal revenue taxes are repealed, amount to jobs in favor of special interests, and increase to the consumer the cost of the dutiable articles far beyond the revenue realized by the Government. In some cases the duties upon articles deemed necessaries are greater than upon luxuries. On all these heads revision and correction are demanded. Upon this subject each Representative is accustomed, more, perhaps, than on any other, to regard the particular interests of his own constituents. In the needed revision of the tariff laws it will be the special duty of the Representative to see that the wishes and interests of his own constituents are fully and fairly represented. The question is not a party question and cannot be made one. The Democrats have ignored it in their national, state, and congressional platforms, and on all sides they are supporting candidates for Congress without regard to their opinions on this subject.

. . . .

The salient features of the pending Presidential canvass are the abandonment by the Democratic party of its old principles, the adoption of a Republican platform, the laying upon the shelf of its tried and heretofore trusted leaders, and the nomination of Mr. Greeley, who has yet to cast his first vote for a Democratic ticket. It is now certain that this movement does not mean the dissolution of the old Democratic party or the formation of any new party. The Democratic party has its national, state, district, and county conventions and organizations, and proposes to go forward to a Democratic victory or defeat, as in former years. It admits by its action that a Democratic victory can't be gained either on Democratic principles or with Democratic candidates. The Republican administration of General Grant has been so successful that the present Democratic leadership admits that a Democratic victory, pure and simple, is impossible. But it hopes that, screened by a Republican platform and the name of Mr. Greeley, it can win a victory for the Democratic organization. What would such a victory signify? Whom will such a victory bring into power? Who surround Mr. Greeley? Who nominated him? These questions are important when we consider the peculiarities of Mr. Greeley's character. One of his ablest supporters in the East, Mr. Samuel Bowles, of the Springfield *Republican*, over his own signature used this language about him, since his nomination: —

"But, with his usual perversity of temper and openness to flattery, Mr. Greeley will probably continue to give his faith and attribute his success to those who fawn upon him that they may use him, and to slander and abuse those braver and truer friends who dare to expose these creatures to him and the world, and tell him the truth that he needs to hear, even if he does not like it.   SAMUEL BOWLES."

Mr. Greeley's nomination was not the work of such Democrats as John Quincy Adams, Judge Thurman, Mr. Pendleton, Senator Buckalew, or Senator Hendricks. It was plainly the work of the New York City politicians and the Confederates of the South. It was not the best elements of the Democratic party which led in this movement. The Cincinnati *Commercial* said truly, in reply to the Mobile editor, that the nomination of Mr. Greeley was due to the Confederates. Mr. Samuel Bowles said, "The South decided it." New York City and the South head the column. The Tammany politician is apt to have his eye on the Treasury, and the Southern Democrat has not forgotten the lost cause.

There is nothing in Mr. Greeley's character or opinions to relieve the well-founded apprehensions which his doubtful surroundings excite. His notions of finance are familiar to all. He would resume specie payments immediately by posting over the door of the Treasury a notice that "specie payments are resumed." "The way to resume," he says "is to resume." If he could have his way he says he would put a duty of one hundred dollars per ton on pig iron. He was the special champion of the law to put a stop to gold gambling in 1864, which was repealed after two weeks of signal failure. In 1867, he said, "we believe in taxing so as to pay the debt in ten years."

He would extend the sphere of government farther than any other public man in America. He holds that the hand of power may beneficially meddle with the business, the interests, and the habits of every citizen. Power is never safe in the hands of such a man.

. . . .

General Grant, by the admission of his most formidable adversary in Ohio, "has made a safe sort of President." Under him we have had, and we shall have, a sound financial policy — sound because it is based on common sense, on the laws of trade; and, above all, because it is honest. Under him we have had, and we shall have, peace — peace that will last, because it stands on the sure foundation of liberty for all, equality for all, and justice for all.

In other speeches Mr. Hayes urged that Mr. Greeley had never been regarded as possessing the qualities of an able statesman. Lacking firmness, soundness of judgment, and knowledge of men (Mr. Hayes argued), he had never received high office or important nominations from his own party. During forty years' activity in politics, his highest recognition had been a fragment of one term in Congress. He owed his adoption by the Democrats to a bargain in the Cincinnati Liberal Republican Convention;

Brown and Blair struck hands with Fenton and Tammany. The men of character, of reputation for integrity and ability, all opposed him. The Ohio delegation — the best in the convention — were solid against him. He was a candidate of the Democratic party because the leaders of the Tammany Ring believed they could use him as a mere cat's-paw. The absurdity of his candidacy was made manifest when it was recalled that he had stood for every measure that the Democrats had most stoutly opposed and condemned; not merely before the war but since. He had been a fanatical supporter of prohibitory liquor legislation; he was an extreme protectionist; and he had defended with all his power the Republican reconstruction measures and all the associated legislation. And even now, according to the high authority of one of his most distinguished supporters, Senator Sumner, he had not in the least changed his most radical views on the race question. The Greeley movement bore a strong resemblance to the Johnson movement of 1866. The Democrats sustained Johnson, not because they admired or loved him, but because they hoped he would be a good club to beat the Republicans with. The Republicans that adhered to him did so mainly for selfish reasons. So now the Democrats could not at heart trust Greeley, always their bitter enemy, nor could the Republicans that were supporting him, knowing his impractical qualities, have confidence in his statesmanship.

While throughout the canvass Mr. Hayes felt that the Republicans were constantly gaining, even in the face of the opposition of most of the papers of Cincinnati, as Greeley's weakness was pointed out and especially as it was made manifest by Greeley's own speeches,[1] yet he had faint hope that sufficient headway would be made in his district to overcome the formidable Liberal Republican defection and give him success in October. On the eve of the election (October 6) he wrote his uncle: —

I still expect defeat. Of course, I would prefer it to be otherwise, but it is of small consequence. I look for victory in the State and in other States.

Mr. Hayes's prediction was verified by the event in both

[1] "Greeley's speeches must surely weaken him and destroy what chances he had. He left yesterday for Louisville and must continue to make mistakes." (From Letter to Sardis Birchard, September 22.)

respects. The day after the election (October 9) he wrote his uncle: —

You will know of our Waterloo defeat in Cincinnati long before this reaches you. It is complete and overwhelming. So complete that it leaves no personal sting. In fact my share in it is rather pleasant. I am largely ahead of my ticket. At the close of the polls my election was conceded at the *Enquirer* office. I met no one who doubted it. I seemed to be the only one who appreciated the load, and I was surprised at its size. The slips I enclose show how well it leaves my record. I have no regrets.

The result of the Presidential business is most happy. We can rejoice over *that*.

He had run much ahead of his ticket, however, thus justifying the assertions of his friends that his nomination would strengthen the Republican cause. While Mr. Eggleston in the First District suffered an adverse majority of 3569 votes, Mr. Hayes was defeated by only 1502 votes. The strain of the canvass in his fevered condition left Mr. Hayes so weakened that he could take little further part in the Presidential campaign, going to Fremont to recuperate and not returning to Cincinnati until the eve of the election. The morning after the balloting (November 6) he wrote his uncle: —

I hope the rainy, raw weather has left you well enough to enjoy the great victory of yesterday. It is indeed a happy and glorious result. It was amazing to see how the immense crowd at the *Gazette* office stood in the mud enjoying the news as it poured in from eight to eleven o'clock.

And that evening at a great meeting called to celebrate the overwhelming victory of Grant at the polls, Mr. Hayes made the following felicitous little speech: —

Fellow Citizens, — I am very grateful for this hearty greeting. I am glad to have an opportunity to say a few words to this vast multitude of happy and enthusiastic Republicans. You will perhaps better appreciate my feelings if I remind you that about four weeks ago in the Second Congressional District I was badly snowed under, and that by reason of that circumstance — a circumstance which I assure you was entirely beyond my control — I was compelled to explore the head waters of that doleful stream, so much dreaded by aspirants for political office — the head waters of Salt River; and you perhaps know that by the rules established for governing the emigrants to that region, all who arrive there are compelled to remain until they are redeemed by a political victory of their friends in the county whence they came. Bearing this fact in mind you can imagine the feelings of the Republicans who in October were sent up Salt River as they read the bulletins in the *Gazette* office windows last evening. Those bulletins relieved us of our disability and entitled us to rejoice with you to-night.

And in all soberness there is great cause for rejoicing. We rejoice that the land of William Penn, by 100,000 majority, has proved worthy of her great founder. We rejoice that our own State of Ohio stands firmly by the most eminent man who was ever born upon her soil. We rejoice that the American people have sustained a man of great deeds and great services rather than a man whose greatness is chiefly in words and promises. We rejoice that the people have sustained the party which for twelve years has done so much to preserve the prosperity, the good name, the liberty, and the union of the nation. We rejoice that they have condemned the coalition between fragments of the old parties formed in May last — a coalition having few principles and no history which any rational man would wish to have remembered.

But I must not make a speech. This is not an occasion for speech-making. It is an occasion for rejoicing, for songs, and for music, and above all for gratitude to the Giver of all good that our Government for four years longer has been entrusted to safe hands.

President Grant, desirous of recognizing Mr. Hayes's efficient services in the campaign and at the same time of strengthening the public service, urged Mr. Hayes to accept the office of Assistant United States Treasurer at Cincinnati. But Mr. Hayes could not be induced to abandon his purpose to return to private life. Early in 1873 he bade permanent farewell to Cincinnati and removed his family to Fremont,[1] taking possession of the substantial brick house in Spiegel Grove which his uncle had built for him some years before, and which with the grove was now deeded to him. Here was his home for the remainder of his life. He at once set about beautifying the great place by opening vistas where the growth of forest trees was dense and with fresh plantations of trees and shrubs. At the same time he was encouraging his uncle to present a park and a library to the town. He soon became interested in real estate development at Toledo,

[1] "Our return, or rather my return and our settlement at Fremont will date from May 3, 1873. I left Fremont for Cincinnati in 1849 and now come back, having achieved as much as I expected, or even hoped by my life in Cincinnati, with kindly feelings towards all the world, to spend the closing years in the home of my youth, and the favorite resort of my childhood. Let me resolve to lead a good and useful life — characterized by kindness, friendliness, and liberality." (Diary, May 2, 1873.)

as the following letter of April 25, 1873, to General Force indicates: —

I am getting into my new way of life and find myself rather too busy, if I am to find any fault with it. The business is to buy, improve, and sell real estate in Toledo and thereabouts. The gentlemen for and with whom I act, have invested about one hundred thousand dollars at Toledo since I came up, and our talk is of drainage, dock lines, streets, alleys, roads, fillings, and excavating. Pleasant enough it is, and I hope remunerative.

Another thing is more interesting. Uncle has decided to give in land about thirty-five or forty thousand dollars to establish a free library here. Buckland and others with myself will be trustees. We block it out this way: (1) Seven to ten thousand dollars for a building — the ground will come from the town; (2) ten thousand dollars' worth of books to start; (3) the rest, fifteen to twenty thousand dollars, for a fund. The building also to be a place for pictures, relics, pioneer doings, etc., etc. I want your thoughts on all of these things. We will have plenty of time. The land is not sold and some will not sell readily at our figures at present. *Our* hobby will be one of the hobbies I will run in the library. The two questions are, What sort of a house? — What shall it be? And the other, What list of books to begin with? We are just in the first of it, and shall *do* nothing for some time.

Mr. Hayes felt that he was now completely and finally out of public life, so far as participation in official affairs was concerned. Henceforth he was to devote himself to his family and his private interests; to his home, his friends, and his books.[1] The new mode of life was altogether agreeable to him. But in January, 1874, it was clouded for a time by a great sorrow. His uncle Sardis Birchard,[2] who had been, his whole life long, father, counsellor, and most loyal friend to him, after years of declining health came peacefully to the end of his long and useful life. He came of sturdy, God-fearing New England stock. Left an orphan at the age of twelve, he went to live with his sister Sophia, just married to Rutherford Hayes. With the Hayes family he came to Ohio in 1817, and on the death of his brother-in-law in 1822 he at once assumed the character of protector and guardian of his sister and her children. In early manhood he

---

[1] "One of my pet schemes for the future will be to form, to collect a complete library of Ohio books — books relating to the State. I may *hope* at least for twenty years of life. In that time I may gather what in the State Library, or other fit place, will be of much interest." (Diary, January 11, 1872.)

[2] Born July 15, 1801; died January 21, 1874.

fixed his home at Lower Sandusky (Fremont), where thenceforward he always lived. He never married, but found ample outlet for his affectionate nature in fraternal oversight of his sister and in guiding and protecting her son and daughter and their children. His nephew Rutherford was his particular care and the source of his greatest pride; from him he received unvarying filial respect and love. Always between the two the closest relations of affection and sympathy were maintained and in periods of separation letters were constantly exchanged. Mr. Birchard was active, enterprising, and successful in business, accumulating a considerable estate, mostly in lands, the greater part of which he left to his nephew. He was universally respected by his friends and neighbors for his integrity and business acumen; a thoroughly good citizen in his public spirit, in his fulfilment of public duties, and in his church relations, giving liberally to Christian causes. The city of Fremont was enriched by him by the gift of a public park and a public library, both of which bear his name, as does also one of the principal avenues of the city, heavily shaded with great trees such as he loved. Mr. Hayes, writing to General Force of his uncle's closing hours, adds these words of eloquent simplicity: —

He was gifted with many unusual and beautiful traits and had almost nothing but good in his character. We yet feel lonely and sad without him. At the same time it is a happiness to think of his release in so pleasant a way. He could joke and be serious by turns to the close. He felt confident of meeting his friends again beyond.[1]

The death of his uncle placed many and large responsibilities upon the shoulders of Mr. Hayes. Upon him devolved the execution of his uncle's will. That instrument had been drawn some time before the final summons came to its maker. It did not contain the provision for the proposed library,[2] steps toward the

[1] Mr. Hayes's old friend and classmate, Guy M. Bryan, of Texas, who had known Mr. Birchard well, wrote Mr. Hayes: "I have your letter announcing the death of your uncle. My old friend and a man I *loved*. A pure man and a good friend. He lived a long life, was useful and blessed. I am glad you and your family were with him months before he died and that his last days were passed in the bosom of your family. I am sad at his death, but I feel that an upright man has passed away and will receive his reward hereafter, as it is allotted to the good and just in this life."

[2] Mr. Hayes at once made a will, making provision for the library in case of his demise before his uncle's plans could be carried out. This was one of the

creation of which had already been taken. Moreover, on his deathbed Mr. Birchard had thought of many other minor gifts, — making an appreciable sum in the aggregate, not included in his will, — which he desired to make. All these Mr. Hayes carefully noted down and religiously carried into effect. But Mr. Birchard's estate consisted almost wholly of lands in and about Fremont and Toledo. While these lands had large prospective value, they could at the time be sold, if at all, only at a serious sacrifice. Business and industry were in a state of severe depression as a result of the disastrous financial panic of the preceding year. Moreover, Mr. Hayes had himself, in association with friends, made considerable investment in land and lots at Duluth, which was most seriously affected by the collapse of Jay Cooke and Company who had been its chief financial sponsors. He had, as already noted, been making similar investments at Toledo. On these investments he still owed much money and felt himself constrained to assume still further obligations to relieve one of his associates, who had become financially embarrassed by reason of losses through the great Chicago conflagration. It was necessary, therefore, for Mr. Hayes, in order to pay the bequests and to make the gifts directed by his uncle, to encumber the estate at a high rate of interest and to assume a depressing burden of indebtedness.[1] He preferred, for the sake of the good name of his uncle, to fulfil as promptly as possible all the benefactions he had been charged with, even though some of them had been made contingent on the sale of certain lands at a specified valuation. The result was that Mr. Hayes found himself for many months absorbed in business cares, not unattended with more or less anxiety. But he lost no buoyancy of spirit; he gave much time and thought to the purchase of books for the new library, installed in temporary quarters until a building could be erected on the site of old Fort Stephenson which the city had bought;[2] he went on with his improvements at Spiegel

documents photographed by Democratic agents who visited Fremont in 1876 to search for materials to be used *against* Mr. Hayes in the Presidential campaign.

[1] "I am largely in debt, and so, busy is no word for it." (Letter to General M. F. Force, April 27, 1874.)

[2] "The work I have been engaged in for several weeks seems now complete or near completion. When Uncle Birchard decided to adopt my suggestion to establish a free library in Fremont, it seemed to me that it should occupy the

Grove; and he found time to keep up his investigations of local history and to continue his general reading.[1]

While so much absorbed in his business affairs and his domestic concerns, Mr. Hayes did not cease to take an interest in current political topics. He was keenly observant of the activities of the state administration and of what was going on at Washington; and he was reaching conclusions in regard to the solution of the still perplexing Southern problem which showed his independence of thought and his statesmanlike wisdom and foresight. In the state campaign of 1873 and the congressional canvass of 1874, he made some speeches, but did not play a conspicuous part.

site of old Fort Stephenson and that by appropriating part of the library fund towards the purchase money the town would be willing to furnish enough to buy the whole for a park. The owner, Mr. Leppelman, asked eighteen thousand dollars for the property. This was a great price. The people generally approved of the purchase. But in a quiet way there was strong opposition. Some opposed it because they did n't want Leppelman to make a speculation. The exorbitant price was the ostensible reason for opposition. . . . One [man] secretly opposed because it would be an honor to uncle. Finally the Council refused to pay eighteen thousand dollars and offered fifteen thousand dollars. Leppelman refused the offer. The proposition was likely to fail. The majority of Council wanted it to fail. I consulted all of the trustees — told them I did not mean to fail and proposed to offer Leppelman three thousand dollars if he would accept the fifteen thousand dollars offered by the City Council. It was agreed I might do so on my individual responsibility, with the understanding that the trustees would hold me harmless, out of the library fund. I made the offer to Leppelman. He agreed to it. The Council were taken by surprise by his acceptance, and after some trouble the bonds of the town were authorized and I now think the fort is safe in the hands of the public. Mayor Dickinson told me it had to be done promptly or it would have failed. . . . " (Diary, September 13, 1873.)

[1] "I am reading between-times *Noctes Ambrosianæ*. Years ago I worried over it. But now it is delightful." (Letter to General Force, April 27, 1874.)

CHAPTER XXII

IN 1871, as already recorded, General Edward F. Noyes had been elected Governor on the Republican ticket by a substantial majority. Governor Hayes had contributed all within his power to bring about that result — his own efficient administration during two terms being a strong argument for a continuance of his party's control of the State. General Noyes's administration was praiseworthy and in 1873 he was renominated. The Democrats nominated the aged William Allen, an uncle of Senator Thurman, who for more than a quarter of a century had been out of politics.[1] Candidates were nominated also by the Prohibitionists and by a convention of disaffected Democrats and Liberal Republicans; these fusionists declaring that both the old parties had " outlived the issues in which they had their origin and had outlived their usefulness."

After a spirited contest, the election resulted in the choice of Allen for Governor by a plurality of 817 votes, while all the Republican candidates for the other state offices won by small pluralities. The minor parties cast between them something over twenty thousand votes and there was a falling off, as compared with the previous year, of fifty-two thousand Republican and thirty-seven thousand Democratic votes. The Democrats gained a majority in both branches of the Legislature, thus insuring the reëlection of Senator Thurman. The Republicans naturally were much chagrined at the loss of the governorship by so small a margin.

In 1874, as so widely throughout the country, the Democrats carried Ohio; electing the Secretary of State and certain other officers by a plurality of more than seventeen thousand votes.

---

[1] Allen was elected to Congress by a majority of one vote at the age of twenty-five in 1832. He entered the Senate in 1837 and served two terms, when he retired from politics. One paper spoke of him in 1875 as "that marvellous relic of a bygone era of statesmanship."

At the same time they elected thirteen out of twenty Congressmen, just reversing the proportion of two years before.

Meanwhile Governor Allen was conducting the affairs of the State acceptably and was winning popularity by his insistence, in his messages and public utterances, on reduction of taxes and greater economy of public expenditures. The outlook for a Republican victory in 1875 was, therefore, most gloomy, and the Republican leaders began early to canvass the situation in the hope of nominating a candidate for Governor that could "redeem" the State. The two successful campaigns of General Hayes against the two ablest and most popular Democratic leaders, Thurman and Pendleton, could not fail to be recalled. No man in Ohio had ever been chosen Governor for the third time. The precedents were all against a third nomination. But the situation from a party standpoint was desperate, and the more all its elements were considered the clearer it seemed to the wiser party leaders that, if there was any hope of success for them, it lay in placing at the head of their ticket the name of the man who had proved his skill as a campaigner against the strongest and most adroit champions of Democracy, and who as Governor had stood for all that was progressive, businesslike, and economical in administration. How general and spontaneous this sentiment was, became manifest when on March 25, on the invitation of the State Central Committee, a large number of Republican politicians from various parts of the State met at Columbus for consultation in regard to the approaching campaign. While no formal expression was recorded, the day's conference showed that all the men present were of one mind in the belief that Mr. Hayes was the man to nominate, and in the desire that he should be the candidate. The publication of a report of this meeting, expressive of the feeling that pervaded it, was received with acclaim by Republicans of the State and induced many to write Mr. Hayes urging him to come to the rescue of the party. All this came as a surprise to Mr. Hayes in his retirement at Fremont. March 28 he writes in his diary: —

The independence of all political and other bother is a happiness. The Republican caucus at Columbus last Thursday, according to report, was unanimously for me for Governor. A third term would be a distinction — a feather I would like to wear. No man ever had it in Ohio. Letters tell me I am really wanted. But the present condition of my money matters requires attention. The chance of an election is not good. More important still, I do not sympathize with a large share of the party leaders. I hate the corruptionists of whom Butler is leader. I doubt the ultra measures relating to the South, and I am opposed to the course of General Grant on the third term, the civil service, and the appointment of unfit men on partisan or personal grounds. I would n't hesitate to fight a losing battle, if the cause was wholly and clearly good, and important. I am not sure that it is in all respects what it should be; and as to its importance I am more than in doubt. Hence I have said decidedly *no* to all who have approached me.

In spite of his "decided no" the agitation in his favor continued with slight abatement. To Major Bickham, of the Dayton *Journal,* he wrote April 14: —

I am in receipt of your favor of the 12th as to the governorship. What you say is very gratifying. It is too flattering, of course, but I like it. . . . I wish I could. I like the place — would take it again if it was open to me. I don't care for the chances of defeat. I have tried *that* two or three times, and it don't hurt me. I have written a good many letters on this subject and have invariably said "No" decisively, on account of my affairs. Private reasons alone. If I were with you, face to face, I could give you what would, I know, be regarded by you as controlling as it is by me. The mere business, pecuniary part, I have named to many. There is another thing I do not write about. I am on the way fairly to freedom. A year or two will, I am confident, do it. Therefore, Major, I can't consent. *This is final;* and you may in the briefest way, without flourish, let it be known that on account of private affairs, I am not in the list.

On the same day he wrote in his diary: —

I am still importuned in all quarters to consent to run as Republican candidate for Governor. Several suggest that if elected Governor now, I will stand well for the Presidency next year. How wild! What a queer lot we are becoming! Nobody is out of the reach of that mania.

And a few days later, April 18: —

The talk about my candidacy for Governor rather grows in spite of my repeated refusals. I regret this, flattering as it is to my self-esteem. I don't wish to say, against a general and urgent request, "No," with due emphasis. It looks like a lack of appreciation of the good opinion of the party and a want of gratitude for past favors. The prospect of an election seems to me to be not good. The third term talk, the Civil Rights Bill, the partisan appointments of the baser sort, in other words, the Butlerism of the Administration, are all bad and weights on us.

Meanwhile many Republicans, reluctantly accepting Mr. Hayes's declination as final, suggested the nomination of Judge Alphonso Taft, of Cincinnati, and began an active canvass in his behalf. Ex-Senator Wade was urged by many, and other names of less importance were also proposed. But everywhere the feeling that Mr. Hayes was the one man for the occasion prevailed and continued to find expression. As one paper said, there was "a widespread and persistent popular disposition to refuse to give him up as a candidate"; and the Toledo *Commercial*, endorsing these words, declared "that few public men have been permitted to respond to a more general or more earnest call for personal sacrifice"; and added: "We are sure that we speak the unanimous sentiment of the Republicans of Ohio when we ask that gentleman to reconsider his decision." But Mr. Hayes remained unshaken in his determination, especially after Judge Taft became an aspirant for the nomination. On the eve of the convention, May 31, he made this entry in his diary: —

I am still importuned to allow my name to be used for Governor. I am no less averse to-day than at the beginning. If Judge Taft and others should withdraw, and the convention generally should insist on my candidacy, I shall not refuse. This is not likely to happen. A general demand by the party that has honored me so often, I regard as a command which I must obey. If, notwithstanding my declination and known preference, the members of the convention with substantial unanimity insist on the use of my name, I shall regard their wish as a command and obey it. If the friends of Judge Taft or of other candidates still present their names, I will under no circumstances be a candidate against them. In that event my name must unqualifiedly be withdrawn.

But Mr. Hayes's preference, his positive and repeated refusal to be considered as a candidate, were disregarded by the convention. The party insistently demanded his leadership and would not be denied. The story of the nomination is best told in Mr. Hayes's own words: [1] —

I was nominated for Governor yesterday at Columbus. I persisted in declining to the last. The leading other candidate before the convention, Judge Taft, of Cincinnati, is an able and good man. But he had such a record on the Bible question in the schools that his nomination was impossible. I did all I could to remove the prejudice against him and to aid in his nomination. I sent to Richard Smith, a leader in the struggle for Judge Taft, the following dispatch: "I cannot allow my name to be

[1] Diary, June 3.

used in opposition to Judge Taft. He became a candidate after I declined. He is an able and pure man and a sound Republican. I would not accept a nomination obtained by a contest with him"; and another as follows to Charles Foster: "I have stated to everybody that I would not consent to go into a contest. I do not want it and would not accept if nominated in opposition to Judge Taft."

I was nominated notwithstanding — 396 for me, 151 for Taft. The nomination on motion of a friend of Taft, Major Bickham, was made unanimous. At first, I wrote a dispatch declining. Then came a dispatch from the secretary of the convention, stating that on behalf of his father, Charles P. Taft had moved my nomination by acclamation and that it was splendidly carried. I then sent the following: "In deference to the wish of the convention, I yield my preference and accept the nomination." The substance of all this is that I did all I could to prevent my own nomination and to aid Taft. Taft being even then so far short of a nomination, and in view of the decided wish of the convention and the injury my declination would do the party, I gave up my own preference and declared purpose, and accepted.

Some facts should be added which Mr. Hayes's modesty forbade him to record. Both his dispatches given above were known to all the delegates. Moreover, the delegates were perfectly cognizant that for months Mr. Hayes, by private letters and public announcements, had repeatedly given unequivocal expression of his desire to remain in retirement. But the temper of the convention was shown unmistakably, when, in defiance of his wishes, his name was presented by Mr. Eggleston. The delegates broke out into such tumultuous and long-continued cheering that Mr. Eggleston could not proceed with the speech he had intended to make. It was evident that no speech was necessary. Again Mr. Foster asked the delegates to hear the dispatch that Mr. Hayes had sent him; and Major Bickham warned them that Mr. Hayes would not accept the nomination. But Mr. Eggleston declared that when the people of Ohio should command, Mr. Hayes would obey the call. Then the balloting proceeded with the result recorded above. The announcement of the vote was signalized by "a tremendous demonstration of approval." Again, when Mr. Charles P. Taft, on behalf of his father, moved that the nomination be made unanimous, "the delegates rose to their feet *en masse* and waving their hats uttered three lusty cheers"; and when at last Mr. Hayes's dispatch of acceptance was received it was welcomed with "a deluge of approbation."

The Cincinnati *Times* declared: "Never since the nomination of Abraham Lincoln, at Chicago, in 1860, has any convention, we venture to say, been a scene of such intense and prolonged enthusiasm as that which followed the nomination of Governor Hayes."

The nomination was received by the Republican press and people of the State with enthusiastic approval and elation. "You were nominated by the people," wrote Major McKinley, "and it could not be helped. Never did I witness such enthusiasm for a leader as burst forth for you. It was spontaneous and uncontrollable." The nomination attracted attention and commendation throughout the country. Here was an encouraging instance of a return to the older and better political custom of the country. Manipulation and wire-pulling had been flouted; self-seeking politicians had been sent to the rear; the voice of the people themselves had been heeded, and the office had sought the man. "For a party thus to crowd honors," said the Cincinnati *Gazette* (whose editor had stanchly favored the nomination of Judge Taft) the day after the convention, "upon a man against his private wish — thus to insist that he, of all others, is the one to lead them to victory — is not only a magnificent tribute to his worth, but it carries us back to the golden days of the Republic, when the office sought the best man, instead of the man seeking the best office." Expressions of a similar character from the newspaper comment of the day could be indefinitely multiplied. Opposition papers in Ohio sought to arouse disaffection in the Republican ranks by trying to make it appear that Mr. Hayes had been untrue to Judge Taft.[1] But a plain statement of the facts, the action of Judge Taft himself in the convention, and his instant and cordial approval of the nomination, as shown in a speech made by him on the very evening of convention day, completely frustrated this attempt. June 5 Mr. Hayes writes in his diary: —

[1] This attempt gave Mr. Hayes some annoyance. June 14 he wrote a friend regretting that the Ironton *Journal* had misrepresented his course; denying that he was in any way responsible for the candidacy of Judge Taft and reiterating that he had steadfastly refused to allow his name to be used against Taft. But he declared: "I do not want to go into print about it. The sooner we drop all discussion as to matters prior to the convention and go into the fight as it stands, the better."

I am overwhelmed with correspondence by mail, telegraph, etc., etc., congratulating me on my nomination,[1] and the manner of it. The newspapers show that it was done in a way never before seen in Ohio, and rarely if ever anywhere. It is reading that would turn a head not *firm and level.* I have just written my competitor — if it is proper to call a man my competitor with whom I in no way competed and to whom I gave a hearty support from the beginning: —

Private   FREMONT, O., 5 June, 1875.

MY DEAR SIR, — I write to thank you in the sincerest and heartiest way for your action on my nomination. It gave me very great and much needed relief. On getting the secretary's first dispatch I was sorely perplexed. To refuse would offend and disappoint friends to whom I was under many obligations. I wrote a dispatch declining, and was considering it with a friend, when the second dispatch from the secretary announcing the motion of Mr. Charles P. Taft came and decided the question. I am confident you would regard my course as fully justifying your friendly act and speech, if all I have said and done since this affair arose were fully before you. — Sincerely your friend,

R. B. HAYES.

HON. A. TAFT, CINCINNATI.

The platform adopted by the convention was briefer and more concise than usual. As to national questions its most important pronouncements, for that time, were an emphatic declaration against the third term, about which the country was genuinely apprehensive, and this resolution in relation to public finances:—

That policy of finance should be steadily pursued which, without unnecessary shock to business or trade, will ultimately equalize the purchasing capacity of the coin and paper dollar.

On state issues the two salient resolutions were: —

We stand by free education, our public-school system, the taxation of all for its support, and no division of the school fund.

That the power of municipal corporations to create debts should be restricted, and local and other expenditures should be so reduced as to diminish taxation.

Of these two state resolutions the former was to play the more important part in the campaign. It owed its adoption to the

---

[1] These congratulatory messages were not confined to Ohio and Ohio men, but came from all parts of the country. For example, Mr. Blaine wrote (June 11): "I congratulate you very cordially and I congratulate the Republicans of Ohio still more, for I have no doubt that you can poll a larger vote than any other man that could have been named. And as to winning, that is a necessity. 'Success is a duty,' and I believe you always do your duty."

passage by the Democratic Legislature at the recent session of what was known as the Geghan Law, opening the penal and benevolent institutions to the ministrations of Catholic priests for such of the inmates as were of Catholic antecedents. Besides this there was widespread and growing agitation in the country on the part of the Catholic clergy against the common schools as godless; the mere reading of the Bible at the opening of schools was being forbidden in many cities; and the Catholic clergy and press in various parts of the country were beginning to demand a division of the public-school money for the support of their parochial schools. The Democrats, with whom the Catholics were at that time predominantly affiliated, deprecated public discussion of the problem presented and were inclined to listen to the Catholic demands. But discussion could not be checked, and the public prints of the day show that it was conducted with much heat and acrimony on both sides; and that the Protestant masses were alarmed lest a fatal blow should be struck at the great system of free public schools which they believed — and justly — to be not only a distinctive feature of American civilization, but also the most powerful influence in assimilating the children of immigrants to American ideals of life and in preserving the foundations of American liberty and democracy.

The Ohio Democratic Convention, which met June 17, renominated Governor Allen by acclamation. For Lieutenant-Governor it nominated Samuel F. Cary, of Cincinnati, a notorious champion of the fiat-money heresy. Its platform condemned "the contraction of the currency, . . . with a view to the forced resumption of specie payment," as fraught with disaster, and demanded "that this policy be abandoned, and that the volume of currency be made and kept equal to the wants of trade." It demanded also that "all the national bank circulation be promptly and permanently retired, and legal tenders issued in its place"; and that "the Government should make its legal tenders receivable for all dues" except where forbidden by contract obligations. And it upbraided the Republican Convention for seeking to make an issue of the school question, as "a base appeal to sectarian prejudices," declaring for a "purely secular education at the expense of the taxpayer," without any possible division of the school fund among religious sects.

The Republican pronouncement on the school question had thus forced the Democrats to take an equally decided stand; but the Republicans maintained that the action of the Democrats in passing the Geghan Bill, together with the tone of the Catholic organ of Cincinnati, spoke louder than the words of their convention; and that it was high time, at the very beginning of the attack of the Catholic hierarchy on the school system, to face the question and to declare unequivocally for the maintenance of free schools in unimpaired strength and usefulness.

The two great issues of the campaign, therefore, were the integrity of the national credit and the integrity of the free schools; and both were of national interest. Naturally the greater interest attached to the former issue. In the East the Democrats had for the most part stood for a sound financial policy. But this year the Democrats of Pennsylvania had followed their brethren in Ohio in glorifying the greenback as a panacea of hard times and industrial depression and in denouncing the national banks. In both States the contest was clean-cut between the advocates of honest money and the misguided and mistaken — though, doubtless, in most cases, honestly deluded — devotees of the "rag baby"; which was the happy contemporary personification of the fiat-money heresy. The country at large watched this contest with intense interest, regarding it as the preliminary skirmish to the Presidential campaign to be fought the following year. It was hoped that Republican success would stamp out forever the agitation in favor of partial repudiation by cheapening the currency. How vain that hope was, years of subsequent agitation proved. It was feared that Democratic success would portend control of the next National Democratic Convention by the friends and champions of a debased and depreciated circulating medium, as well as reënforced efforts in Congress to retard the resumption of specie payments.

Mr. Hayes was prompt to recognize the nature and vast importance of the combat [1] in which he was to engage, and he

---

[1] Three weeks after his nomination, being serenaded at the home of General Mitchell in Columbus, Mr. Hayes made this brief speech: —

"If it shall turn out that the party in power are opposed to a sound, safe, stable currency, I have no doubt that in October the people will make a change. If it shall turn out that the party in power were guilty of gross corruption in the legislative department, and that when that corruption was exposed the majority

did not underestimate the strength of his opponents, nor the plausibility of their arguments when skilfully presented to the unthinking masses, who felt the pressure of hard times and were eager to accept any remedy that promised relief. He began at once to make preparation for his campaign work, proposing to throw himself into it with all the ardor and energy that its great significance demanded. June 8 he wrote Major Bickham: —

Thanks for your paper of yesterday, and still more for your efforts to get me out of this scrape before I was in, and now to carry me through successfully. It is well and gratifying to have the convention facts fully and authentically set forth. I read the article [1] with much interest. Hereafter we can afford to let bygones go, and seek discussion only with the common adversary. I am, perhaps, under a delusion, but I still hope to be supported by Halstead. At any rate, being on the track, I now want to win, and am willing to do my share of the solid work required to do it. It is of the first importance to nominate in the counties, and organize early. For the topics of the canvass, and bringing them before the people, the press is *the means*. Meetings and speeches are less important, relatively, than ever before. They come in too late ; and in a day of enterprising newspaper men they are merely stale repetitions of the press. Meetings and speeches, like the election itself, are the results of what the press has already done.

I judge from several paragraphs that you regard the subserviency of the Democratic party to Catholic designs as the salient feature of the canvass. It is certainly so in popular estimation in this quarter. If you have leisure to give me a brief note on this head, it will be useful. What I have said about meetings and speeches is not with a view to shirk labor. I am ready to do all that may be reasonably expected. But early and earnest discussion by the press is, I am sure, far more effective.

To General Garfield, June 28, Mr. Hayes wrote: —

Our contest will be a hard one. We must have a great deal of work done to redeem the State. Our organization must be reconstructed and

shielded those who were implicated, I have no doubt the people will make a change. If it shall turn out that the party in power yielded to the dictation of an ecclesiastical sect, and through fear of a threatened loss of votes and power has suffered itself to be domineered over in its exercise of the lawmaking power, there ought to be, as I doubt not there will be, a great change. If it shall turn out that the party in power is dangerously allied to any body of men who are opposed to our free schools, and have proclaimed undying hostility to our educational system, then I doubt not the people will make a change in the administration."

[1] An editorial in the Dayton *Journal* plainly setting forth the facts of the nomination and Mr. Hayes's attitude thereto, and conclusively refuting the charge of disloyalty to Judge Taft.

meetings held everywhere. Your ideas as to our true policy are precisely mine. We must attack. Their scheme for inflating our irredeemable currency is bad enough; but there are debtors and speculators in large numbers in Ohio who want it. They are not all Democrats. We shall lose some votes on this question. The Catholic question is also interesting the people very much. This seems to be thus far almost wholly favorable.[1]

July 10 he wrote again to Major Bickham: —

We must not let the Catholic question drop out of sight. If they do not speak of it, we must attack them for their silence. If they discuss it or refer to it, they can't help getting into trouble. We can't, I think, do better than to stick to the texts — *honest money, and no sectarian interference with the schools.*

The active speaking of the campaign began the last of July and was continued without intermission up to the day of election. Mr. Hayes spoke in all parts of the State. The two "texts" were throughout the principal topics discussed, but more and more the stress was laid upon the first, and a battle royal was waged in behalf of sound finance.

Senator Thurman, himself a sound-money man, disappointed his better friends and evoked wide criticism by his demagogic championship of the Ohio platform. "Minor differences," he urged in a speech at Mansfield, must be conceded to secure the success of the party. The platform, he declared, "nowhere says that the greenback should be irredeemable." "And then as to inflation the platform does not expressly demand more currency. It says 'that the volume of currency should be made and kept equal to the wants of trade.' To him who believes that the present volume is sufficient, it means no inflation, for in his mind it is already quite equal to the wants of trade. To another man who thinks that more currency is needed, it does mean inflation." But the real Democratic prophets were Governor Allen and General Cary. They confidently expected to sweep everything before them and make Ohio Democratic by a majority of

---

[1] Mr. Garfield had written: "Let me suggest that we will gain far more than we can lose, even on the score of public policy, by pressing our views of finance boldly and aggressively, as against the wretched and dishonest scheme of the Democracy. We have a few soft-money men who will be hurt by it, but we shall gain far more than our loss on that score. I think now is our time to cripple the Democracy for next year. Even if they should win this campaign, it will hopelessly divide them in the next year's Presidential campaign."

sixty thousand. The friends of sane government everywhere were apprehensive because an unlimited issue of paper money was such "a taking idea." "If Allen be elected," the Chicago *Times* declared, "the immediate effect is very sure to be a prodigious rise in the threatening and dangerous tidal wave of inflation and repudiation."

Feeling ran high in the State as the canvass proceeded. The people were roused to a pitch of interest and enthusiasm seldom experienced except in a Presidential year.[1] The eyes of the nation were upon the contest and the papers throughout the country watched its varying phases with constant attention. The Ohio leaders of both parties were enlisted in the canvass and their efforts were supplemented by prominent political orators from other States. Nothing was left undone by either party to attain success. Both parties recognized that the issue was doubtful; but the Democrats, in view of their victory of the year before and because of the hard times and the apparent popularity of their appeal for more money, felt the greater confidence in their chance of success.

Mr. Hayes and Senator Sherman opened the campaign at Marion, Lawrence County, on the 31st of July. The issues were squarely met by Mr. Hayes in a carefully prepared speech which presented in succinct form the line of argument which, with many variations and constant change of illustration and manner, he pursued in his many subsequent speeches. After a brief reference to the records of the parties, Mr. Hayes said: —

Let us now proceed to the consideration of some of the questions which engage the attention of the people of Ohio. The war which the Democratic party and its doctrines brought upon the country left a large debt, heavy taxation, a depreciated currency, and an unhealthy condition of business, which resulted two years ago in a financial panic and depression, from which the country is now slowly recovering. With this condition of things the Democratic party in its recent state convention at Columbus undertook to deal.

The most important part — in fact, the only part — of their platform in Ohio this year which receives or deserves much attention, is that in which is proclaimed a radical departure, on the subject of money, from the teachings of all of the Democratic fathers. This Ohio Democratic

---

[1] "*Portsmouth, 3 Aug.* — Had a fine meeting. Numbers, enthusiasm, and other cheering indications. Nothing better since 1866. It is like a Presidential year." (Diary.)

doctrine inculcates the abandonment of gold and silver as a standard of value. Hereafter gold and silver are to be used as money only "where respect for the obligation of contracts requires payment in coin." The only currency for the people is to be paper money, issued directly by the general Government, "its volume to be made and kept equal to the wants of trade," and with no provision whatever for its redemption in coin. The Democratic candidate for Lieutenant-Governor, who opened the canvass for his party, states the money issue substantially as I have. General Cary in his Barnesville speech, says: —

"Gold and silver when used as money, are redeemable in any property there is for sale in the nation; will pay taxes or any debt, public or private. This alone gives them their money value. If you had a hundred gold eagles, and you could not exchange them for the necessaries of life, they would be trash, and you would be glad to exchange them for greenbacks or anything else that you could use to purchase what you require. With an absolute paper money, stamped by the Government and made a legal tender for all purposes, its functions as money are as perfect as gold or silver can be."

This is the financial scheme which the Democratic party asks the people of Ohio to approve at the election in October. The Republicans accept the issue. Whether considered as a permanent policy or as an expedient to mitigate present evils, we are opposed to it. It is without warrant in the Constitution, and it violates all sound financial principles.

The objections to an inflated and irredeemable paper currency are so many that I do not attempt to state them all. They are so obvious and so familiar that I need not elaborately present or argue them. All of the mischief which commonly follows inflated and inconvertible paper money may be expected from this plan, and in addition it has very dangerous tendencies, which are peculiarly its own. An irredeemable and inflated paper currency promotes speculation and extravagance, and at the same time discourages legitimate business, honest labor, and economy. It dries up the true sources of individual and public prosperity. Overtrading and fast living always go with it. It stimulates the desire to incur debt; it causes high rates of interest; it increases importations from abroad; it has no fixed value; it is liable to frequent and great fluctuations, thereby rendering every pecuniary engagement precarious and disturbing all existing contracts and expectations; it is the parent of panics. Every period of inflation is followed by a loss of confidence, a shrinkage of values, depression of business, panics, lack of employment, and widespread disaster and distress.

The heaviest part of the calamity falls on those least able to bear it. The wholesale dealer, the middleman, and the retailer always endeavor to cover the risks of the fickle standard of value by raising their prices. But the men of small means and the laborer are thrown out of employment, and want and suffering are liable soon to follow.

When Government enters upon the experiment of issuing irredeemable paper money there can be no fixed limit to its volume. The amount will depend on the interest of leading politicians, on their whims, and on the excitement of the hour. It affords such facility for contracting debt that extravagant and corrupt government expenditure are the sure result. Under the name of public improvements, the wildest enterprises, contrived for private gain, are undertaken. Indefinite expansion becomes the rule, and in the end bankruptcy, ruin, and repudiation.

During the last few years a great deal has been said about the centralizing tendency of recent events in our history. The increasing power of the Government at Washington has been a favorite theme for Democratic declamation. But when, since the foundation of the Government, has a proposition been seriously entertained which could confer such monstrous and dangerous powers on the general Government as this inflation scheme of the Ohio Democracy? During the war for the Union, solely on the ground of necessity, the Government issued the legal tender, or greenback currency. But they accompanied it with the solemn pledge in the following words of the Act of June 30, 1864: —

"Nor shall the total amount of United States notes issued or to be issued ever exceed four hundred millions, and such additional sum, not exceeding fifty millions, as may be temporarily required for redemption of temporary loans."

But the Ohio inflationists, in a time of peace, on grounds of mere expediency, propose an inconvertible paper currency, with its volume limited only by the discretion or caprice of its issuers, or their judgment as to the wants of trade. The most distinguished gentleman whose name is associated with the subject once said: "The process must be conducted with skill and caution, . . . and by men whose position will enable them to guard against any evil"; and using a favorite illustration he said: "The Secretary of the Treasury ought to be able to judge. His hand is upon the pulse of the country. He can feel all the throbbings of the blood in the arteries. He can tell when the blood flows too fast and strong, and when the expansion should cease." This brings us face to face with the fundamental error of this dangerous policy. The trouble is the pulse of the patient will not so often decide the question as the interest of the doctor. No man, no Government, no Congress, is wise enough and pure enough to be trusted with this tremendous power over the business and property and labor of the country. That which concerns so intimately all business should be decided, if possible, on business principles, and not be left to depend on the exigencies of politics, the interests of party, or the ambition of public men. It will not do for property, for business, or for labor to be at the mercy of a few political leaders at Washington, either in or out of Congress. The best way to prevent it is to apply to paper money the old test sanctioned by the experience of all nations — let it be convertible into coin. If it can respond to this test, it will, as nearly as possible, be sound, safe, and stable.

The Republicans of Ohio are in favor of no sudden or harsh measures.

They do not propose to force resumption by a contraction of the currency. They see that the ship is headed in the right direction, and they do not wish to lose what has already been gained. They are satisfied to leave to the influences of time and the inherent energy and resources of the country, the work that yet remains to be done to place our currency at par. We believe that what our country now needs to revive business and to give employment to labor, is a restoration of confidence. We need confidence in the stability and soundness of the financial policy of the Government. That confidence has for many months past been slowly but steadily increasing. The Columbus Democratic platform comes in as a disturbing element, and gives a severe shock to reviving confidence. The country believed, and rejoiced to believe, that Senator Thurman expressed the sober judgment of Ohio, when he spoke last year in the Senate on this subject. The Senator said March 24, 1874: —

"Never have I spoken in favor of that inflation of the currency, which, I think I see full well, means that there shall never be any resumption at all. That is the difference. It is one thing to contract the currency, with a view to the resumption of specie payment; it is another thing neither to contract nor enlarge it, but let resumption come naturally and as soon as the business and production of the country will bring it about. But it is a very different thing, indeed, to inflate the currency with a view never in all time to redeem it at all. And that is precisely what this inflation means. It means demonetizing gold and silver in perpetuity, and substituting a currency of irredeemable paper, based wholly and entirely upon government credit, and depending upon the opinion and the interests of the members of Congress and their hopes of popularity, whether the volume of it shall be large or small. That is what this inflation means. Sir, I have never said anything in favor of that. I am too old-fashioned a Democrat for that. I cannot give up the convictions of a lifetime, whether they be popular or unpopular."

April 6, when the Senate inflation bill was debated, he said: —

"It simply means that no man of my age shall ever again see in this country that kind of currency which the framers of the Constitution intended should be the currency of the Union; which every sound writer on political economy the world over says is the only currency that defrauds no man. It means that so long as I live, and possibly long after I shall be laid in the grave, this people shall have nothing but an irredeemable currency with which to transact their business — that currency which has been well described as the most effective invention that ever the wit of man devised to fertilize the rich man's field by the sweat of the poor man's brow. I will have nothing to do with it."

How great the shock which was given to returning confidence by the Democratic action at Columbus abundantly appears by the manner in which the platform is received by the Liberal and the English and the German Democratic press throughout the United States. The Liberal press and the German press, so far as I have observed, in the strongest terms condemn the platform. They speak of it as disturbing confidence, shaking credit, and threatening repudiation. A large part of the Democratic press of other States is hardly less emphatic. It would be strange, indeed, if this were otherwise. In Ohio, less than two years ago the convention which nominated Governor Allen resolved, speaking of the Democratic party, that "it recognizes the evils of an irredeemable paper currency, but insists that in the return to specie payment care should be taken not to seriously disturb the business of the country or unjustly injure the debtor class." There was no inflation then. Now come the soft-money leaders of the Democratic party, and try to persuade the people that the promises of the United States should only be redeemed by other promises, and that it is sound policy to increase them.

The credit of the nation depends on its ability and disposition to keep its promises. If it fails to keep them, and suffers them to depreciate, its credit is tainted, and it must pay high rates of interest on all of its loans. For many years we must be a borrower in the markets of the world. The interest-bearing debt is over seventeen hundred millions of dollars. If we could borrow money at the same rate with some of the great nations of Europe, we could save perhaps two per cent per annum on this sum. Thirty or forty millions a year we are paying on account of tainted credit. The more promises to pay an individual issues, without redeeming them, the worse becomes his credit. It is the same with nations. The legal-tender note for five dollars is the promise of the United States to pay that sum in the money of the world, in coin. No time is fixed for its payment. It is therefore payable on presentation — on demand. It is not paid; it is past due; and it is depreciated to the extent of twelve per cent. The country recognizes the necessities of the situation, and waits, and is willing to wait, until the productive business of the country enables the Government to redeem. But the Columbus financiers are not satisfied. They demand the issue of more promises. This is inflation. No man can doubt the result. The credit of the nation will inevitably suffer. There will be further depreciation. A depreciation of ten per cent diminishes the value of the present paper currency from fifty to one hundred millions of dollars. Its effect on business would be disastrous in the extreme. The present legal tenders have a certain steadiness, because there is a limit fixed to their amount. Public opinion confides in that limit. But let that limit be broken down and all is uncertainty. The authors of this scheme believe inflation is a good thing. . . . The platform means inflation without limit; and inflation is the downward path to repudiation. It means ruin to the nation's credit, and to all individual credit. All the rest of the world have the same standard of value. Our promises are worthless as currency the moment you pass our boundary line. Even in this country very extensive sections still use the money of the world. Texas, the most promising and flourishing State of the South, uses coin. California and the other Pacific States and Territories do the same. Look at their condition. Texas and California are not the least prosperous part of the United

States. This scheme cannot be adopted. The opinion of the civilized world is against it. The vast majority of the ablest newspapers of the country is against it. The best minds of the Democratic party are against it. The last three Democratic candidates for the Presidency were against it. The German citizens of the United States, so distinguished for industry, for thrift, and for soundness in judgment in all practical money affairs, are a unit against it. The Republican party is against it. The people of Ohio will, I am confident, decide in October to have nothing to do with it.

Since the adoption of the inflation platform at Columbus, a great change has taken place in the feelings and views of its friends. Then they were confident — perhaps it is not too much to say that they were dictatorial and overbearing toward their hard-money party associates. There was no doubt as to the intent and meaning of the platform. Its friends asserted that the country needed more money, and more money now. That the way to get it was to issue government legal-tender notes liberally. But the storm of criticism and condemnation which burst upon the platform from the soundest Democrats in all quarters has alarmed its supporters. Many of them have been seized with a panic, and are now utterly stampeded and in full retreat. They say that they are not for inflation, not for inconvertible paper money, and that they never have been. That they look forward to a return of specie payment, and that it must always be kept in view. Why, what did they mean by their platform? Did they expect to make money plenty by an issue of more coin? Certainly not. By an issue of more paper redeemable in coin? Certainly not. They expected to issue more legal-tender notes — notes irredeemable and depreciated. But public opinion, as shown by the press, is so decidedly against them, that Ohio inflationists now begin to desert their own platform. Even Mr. Pendleton is solicitous not to be held responsible for the Columbus scheme. He says: "I speak for myself alone. I do not assume to speak for the Democratic party. Its convention has spoken for it," and proceeds to interpret the platform as if it were for hard money.

Senator Thurman did not so understand it. He thought the hard-money men were beaten and felt disappointed. It now looks as if General Cary might be left almost alone before the canvass ends. If Judge Thurman could get that convention together again, it is evident that he could now in the same body rout the inflationists, horse, foot, and artillery. Nothing but a victory in Ohio can put inflation again on its legs. Let it be defeated in October, and the friends of a sound and honest currency will have a clear field for at least the life of the present generation.

Passing then to questions of state interest, Mr. Hayes said: —

Altogether the most interesting questions in our state affairs are those which relate to the passage, by the last Legislature, of the Geghan Bill and the war which the sectarian wing of the Democratic party is now waging against the public schools. In the admirable speech made by

Judge Taft at the Republican State Convention, he sounded the keynote to the canvass on this subject. He said, "Our motto must be universal liberty and universal suffrage, secured by universal education." . . .

If Republicans acting on the defensive discuss the subject, and express the opinion that the Democratic party can't safely be trusted, they are denounced in unmeasured terms. General Cary calls them "political knaves" and "fools" and "bigots." But it is very significant that no Democratic speaker denounces those who began the agitation. All their epithets are levelled at the men who are on the right side of the question. Agitation on the wrong side — agitation against the schools may go on. It meets no condemnation from leading Democratic candidates and speakers. The reason is plain. Those who mean to destroy the school system constitute a formidable part of the Democratic party, without whose support that party, as the Legislature was told last spring, cannot carry the county, the city, nor the State.

The sectarian agitation against the public schools was begun many years ago. During the last few years, it has steadily and rapidly increased, and has been encouraged by various indications of possible success. It extends to all of the States where schools at the common expense have been long established. Its triumphs are mainly in the large towns and cities. It has already divided the schools, and in a considerable degree impaired and limited their usefulness. The glory of the American system of education has been that it was so cheap that the humblest citizen could afford to give his children its advantages, and so good that the man of wealth could nowhere provide for his children anything better. This gave the system its most conspicuous merit. It made it a republican system. The young of all conditions of life are brought together and educated on terms of perfect equality. The tendency of this is to assimilate and to fuse together the various elements of our population, to promote unity, harmony, and general good will in our American society. But the enemies of the American system have begun the work of destroying it. They have forced away from the public schools, in many towns and cities, one third or one fourth of their pupils and sent them to schools which, it is safe to say, are no whit superior to those they have left. These youth are thus deprived of the associations and the education in practical republicanism and American sentiments which they peculiarly need. Nobody questions their constitutional and legal right to do this, and to do it by denouncing the public schools. Sectarians have a lawful right to say that these schools are "a relic of paganism — that they are godless," and that "the secular school system is a social cancer." But when having thus succeeded in dividing the schools, they make that a ground for abolishing school taxation, dividing the school fund, or otherwise destroying the system, it is time that its friends should rise up in its defense.

We all agree that neither the Government nor political parties ought to interfere with religious sects. It is equally true that religious sects ought not to interfere with the Government or with political parties. We believe that the cause of good government and the cause of religion both suffer by all such interference. But if sectarians make demands for legislation of political parties, and threaten that party with opposition at the elections in case the required enactments are not passed, and if the political party yields to such threats, then those threats, those demands, and that action of the political party become a legitimate subject of political discussion, and the sectarians who thus interfere with the legislation of the State are alone responsible for the agitation which follows.

And now a few words as to the action of the last Legislature on this subject. After an examination of the Geghan Bill, we shall perhaps come to the conclusion that in itself it is not of great importance. I would not undervalue the conscientious scruples on the subject of religion of a convict in the penitentiary, or of any unfortunate person in any state institution. But the provision of the constitution of the state covers the whole ground. It needs no awkwardly framed statute of doubtful meaning, like the Geghan Bill, to accomplish the object of the organic law....

If the Geghan Bill is merely a reënactment of this part of the bill of rights, it is a work of supererogation, and it is not strange that the Legislature did not, when it was introduced, favor its passage. The author of the bill wrote, "The members claim that such a bill is not needed." The same opinion prevails in New Jersey, where a similar bill is said to have been defeated by a vote of three to one. But the sectarians of Ohio were resolved on the passage of this bill. Mr. Geghan, its author, wrote to Mr. Murphy, of Cincinnati: "We have a prior claim upon the Democratic party. The elements composing the Democratic party in Ohio to-day are made up of Irish and German Catholics, and they have always been loyal and faithful to the interests of the party. Hence the party is under obligations to us, and we have a perfect right to demand of them, as a party, inasmuch as they are in control of the State Legislature and State Government, and were by both our means and votes placed where they are to-day, that they should, as a party, redress our grievances."

The organ of the friends of the bill published this letter, and among other things said: "The political party with which nine tenths of the Catholic voters affiliate on account of past services that they will never forget, now controls the State. Withdraw the support which Catholics have given to it and it will fall in this city, county, and State, as speedily as it has risen to its long-lost position and power. That party is now on trial. Mr. Geghan's bill will test the sincerity of its professions."

That threat was effectual. The bill was passed, and the sectarian organ therefore said: "The unbroken solid vote of the Catholic citizens of the State will be given to the Democracy at the fall election."

In regard to those who voted against the bill, it said: "They have dug their political grave; it will not be our fault if they do not fill it. When any of them appear again in the political arena, we will put upon them a brand that every Catholic citizen will understand." No defense of this conduct of the last Legislature has yet been attempted. The facts are beyond dispute. This is the first example of open and successful sectarian interference with legislation in Ohio. If the people are wise, they will give it such a rebuke in October that for many years, at least, it will be the last.

But it is claimed that the schools are in no danger. Now that public attention is aroused to the importance of the subject, it is probable that in Ohio they are safe. But their safety depends on the rebuke which the people shall give to the party which yielded last spring at Columbus to the threats of their enemies. It is said that no political party "desires the destruction of the schools." I reply, no political party "desired" the passage of the Geghan Bill; but the power which hates the schools passed the bill. The sectarian wing of the Democratic party rules that party to-day in the great commercial metropolis of the nation. It holds the balance of power in many of the large cities of the country. Without its votes, the Democratic party would lose every large city and county in Ohio and every Northern State. In the Presidential canvass of 1864, it was claimed that General McClellan was as good a Union man as Abraham Lincoln, and that he was as much opposed to the Rebellion. An eminent citizen of this State replied: "I learn from my adversaries. Whom do the enemies of the Union want elected? The man they are for, I am against." So I would say to the friends of the public schools: "How do the enemies of universal education vote?" If the enemies of the free schools give their "unbroken, solid vote" to the Democratic ticket, the friends of the schools will make no mistake if they vote the Republican ticket.

In other speeches Mr. Hayes emphasized the fact of sectarian interference with politics, elections, and legislation, as well as sectarian attacks on the public schools. There was a sectarian newspaper press and there were sectarian military organizations, equipped at the expense of the State. "And all these dangerous influences," he declared, "derive increased power from the fact that they belong to the sectarian wing of the Democratic party." "The initial steps towards a union of Church and State have already been taken. The history of all modern nations is full of warning against such attempts. Look at Germany, at Italy, at Belgium, and heed the warning they give." But, he said: "We mean to maintain the present American system of education by means of free schools, established and supported at the public expense. We mean to oppose the establishment of a system for the education of the youth of the State in the peculiar doctrines of any religious sect, in whole or in part, at the public expense. We believe that the separation of Church and State is best for the Church and best for the State, and that this separation requires also the separation of the public schools from all sectarian control. Popular education is the brightest star in our civil firmament, and we do not want it blotted out or its lustre dimmed by sectarian interference." "Democrats oppose discussion, agitation of this topic. So they did of the slavery question. But the enemies of the free schools discuss it. They in a solid body vote with reference to it. Republicans say, the demand is made now, the debate has begun. All is not safe unless the people act — unless they vote. When great questions are at stake, are agitated, are debated, the party which says, 'Don't reply, don't debate, don't agitate; there is no danger; all is well; don't reply! We are sound, but we deprecate discussion'; — the party that takes that position is already at the halfway house; they are *en route* for the camp of your adversary. They can't be trusted. They must be voted down." In this insistence on the duty of the people to rebuke any and every assault, open or covert, on the integrity of the public-school system, "we make no complaint, no attack on the faith or mode of worship of anybody." "We say simply to all sects, hold what faith you will, worship as you please; but when it comes to the public schools, intended for all, supported by the taxes of all, we say to them, hands off."

In discussing the financial question Mr. Hayes laid repeated stress on the inconsistency of the Democratic platform and plea for inflation and an irredeemable currency with previous declarations of the party in Ohio. Senator Thurman was in principle and profession utterly at variance with his party friends in their present declaration despite his advocacy of the party ticket. The New York Democracy was for sound money and an honest payment of the national debt, as were the Democrats generally in the commercial and industrial East. "The Democratic financial scheme," Mr. Hayes conceded, "may seem plausible, to have advantages, even to Republicans." But he further said: —

To such I want to present its objectionable character as a disturber, as a destroyer of confidence — as a present and as a future cause of perplexity if Ohio sustains it. It can't be carried out. The Democracy themselves will stamp it out. It is an impossible scheme. Its success in Ohio will not establish it. The healthful business reaction may be checked by it, but as a practical measure, it is dead from the start. . . .

They say they will "demonetize" gold and silver. That is, under their system, in the United States at least, coin shall no longer be money. This as a permanent policy. Why, they might as well tell us that coal shall no longer be fuel; that flour and beef and pork shall no longer be food.

We must march towards specie payments or away from specie payments. Our permanent policy must look towards the return or away from it. The path that leads away from specie resumption is a path that leads to ruin, to extravagance, to speculation, to crisis after crisis, to bankruptcy, to repudiation.

A greenback is a promise to pay money. Let me ask, to pay what money? Why, the money of the world, coin — gold and silver. Now, either it is intended to keep that promise, at some day in the future, or it is the intention not to keep it. The day is coming when you must gather in the gold and silver to redeem, and when that day comes, the pinch comes, the crisis comes, and the more greenbacks you have out, the closer the pinch, the greater the crisis, the sorer will be the troubles of business and the distresses of labor.

Then we will not redeem. We will repudiate. No; we now have another device. We will say *that is money which the Government makes money.* We will no longer issue promises, we will drop greenbacks, we will print paper, saying that the United States *declares this is a dollar,* and everybody shall take it as such except the bondholders. If that is money which Government makes money, why tax the people for the expenses of the Government? Why not abolish all taxes? Why not make money when it is wanted and all the Government wants? Oh, yes, but then we would soon *have too much.* Too much? Can you have too much of so good a thing as money? Did you ever have too much? or you, or you, sir? No, we all see that Government cannot make that money which is merely paper. Gold and silver are worth as much before it is stamped as it is after. But paper to have a permanent value must be a promise to pay money, and a promise that is redeemed.

This brings us to the test, and the only true test of the amount of money which — the volume of promises which — Government can issue: How many can you redeem? To make your promise of uniform and permanent value, you must redeem it, or at least must be able and willing to redeem it. Like the promise of a State, of a county, of a city, of an individual, it must be redeemable in coin at the will of the holder. If you have more than this, it is no longer a safe, a stable, a sound currency.

The value [of the greenbacks] depends on the credit of the United States — the ability to pay, and the willingness to pay. But it is a broken promise. Therefore it is depreciated. Now the effect of issuing more broken promises would be to depreciate them more.

A favorite illustration of Mr. Pendleton's is: "The wise financier at the head of the Treasury will have his hand on the pulse of trade; he will issue the currency as the condition of his patient requires — no more, no less." But the truth is that the pulse of the doctor, not of the patient, will at last decide it. His condition and interests will be more important to him than the condition and interests of the country.

What a concentration of power, what a centralization of power, when the purse and the credit of the nation, when the business of all — of sections, of States, of individuals — are in the hands of the power at Washington! The welfare of every section, its business and prosperity, of every State, of every individual, will be at the mercy of the power at Washington. The honesty or corruption, the wisdom or folly to be found there, will control everything. The business of the country must not be dealt with as a sick patient whose doctors at Washington are to control and dose and diet. The number and character of those doctors, liable to change, do not give warrant of stability and health. The business of the country would then depend on political considerations, political interests and ambitions. This is precisely what honest business wishes to avoid. It prefers to be conducted and controlled exclusively by business interests and business considerations. What it asks of Government and politics is to be let alone.

The present greenback currency has had these great advantages. It was a war measure, justified by the war alone, to end with the necessity of the war. The faith of the nation is pledged to a limited issue, and the redemption is sure to take place at an early day.

Government paper, stamped paper, has no real value. It depends on Congress, on the elections. Repeal the Legal Tender Act and it is trash. But gold does not *represent* value; it is value.

While Mr. Hayes laid the principal stress upon the two great questions, sound money and the integrity of the free public schools, he did not neglect the discussion of other topics of interest to the voters of the State. For the first time, he would say, since the present division of parties the public affairs of Ohio, state and local, had now for about two years been administered by the Democratic party. And what was the result? Coming into power after great professions of reform intentions, yet "by the judgment of Democrats themselves the Democratic party had signally failed as a party of reform." Instead of adhering to the principles of civil service reform to which it had committed itself in 1872, "it turned its back on the Republican reformers who had joined it, repealed the old laws, and entered upon the work of reorganizing the state institutions," which were confessedly well managed. Every place possible was seized as spoils — even and notoriously the Soldiers' Orphans' Home. And what scandal followed! No Republican or independent who would examine this subject could doubt how to vote.

The voters should note, too, the condition of affairs in the leading cities of Ohio under Democratic control.

How best to govern cities and towns, [Mr. Hayes proceeded] without a departure from the methods and principles of free government, is one of the most difficult and important problems before the American people. Neither of the political parties can justly claim to have approached its solution. In the cities and towns we see debts increasing, taxes increasing, and corruption increasing. Without doubt public improvements are also going on, but it may well be doubted whether they keep pace with the increase of debts and taxes. Indeed, what are called improvements are too often the opportunities of rogues. . . .
When the great frauds in the city of New York were discovered, the party which had ruled the State and city were driven from power. The example is a good one. In Ohio the laws which govern cities and define and limit the powers of their various departments depend on the Legislature. The action of the city governments under those laws depends on the city rulers. If one party controls the city government and the other party the State Government, there may be doubt as to where the chief responsibility rests. It may be a question whether the fault is in the laws of the State, or in the action of the city authorities under the laws. But where both the city and State Governments are in the hands of the same political party, there can be no doubt of the justice of holding that party responsible for city misgovernment. With this safe rule as a guide, go to the leading cities and towns of the State. Take, for example, the chief city of the State. It is fully in possession of Democratic officials and under the laws of a Democratic Legislature. . . . It is quite safe to say that well-informed persons in that city, not implicated in its government, with great unanimity assert that it is now worse governed than ever before. . . . The truth is, Democratic reform, as our Liberal Republicans have found out, is not a success.

But as the campaign became more and more animated and the minds of the people seemed to be given up to the all-engrossing topic, General Hayes paid less attention to other subjects and elaborated on the disastrous effects of an unlimited issue of irredeemable currency. His speeches were usually concise, but on occasion, as at Dayton August 25, he devoted two hours to a discussion of the financial issue. The proposition of the Democrats "was the violation of the national faith and the destruction of national credit." "More money is the cry of the speculators in distress." "The Government has no warrant of law to issue money that is not convertible into the coin which is the money of the world." These and other striking sentences were accompanied by apt illustrations and plain arguments founded upon law and experience. But at no time did he fail to realize that the contest was a close and desperate one. The talk of the opposition was plausible and was addressed to those who were in debt and who wanted better times. "With a stamped paper currency," said Cary, "made a legal tender in all cases, we have a currency as nearly perfect as possible." This was supported by William D. Kelley, of Pennsylvania, who, as the champion protectionist, was sent into the mining and iron districts to arouse the laboring and artisan classes against the banking system and the proposed resumption of specie payments — to which the industrial evils were attributed. Mr. Kelley spoke to men who wanted work, and to whom the whole subject of finance was a mystery. The capitalists, he declared at Youngstown, "had better pause before reducing the working people to the last measure of despair." The question recurs in every such contest, Who is the true friend of the poor man, he who would pay him a dollar good the world over, or he who would pay him in an irredeemable currency of uncertain value?

The importance of the issue brought into the State in support of the Republicans such able political orators as Carl Schurz, Senator Morton, and Stewart L. Woodford. Whether one considers the issues involved, the character and ability of the speakers engaged, or the brilliant part taken by the press, this campaign was doubtless one of the most important, from an educational standpoint, in American political history. But no one could feel assured as to its result. How doubtful Mr. Hayes was a few days before the election is manifested by a letter to Mrs. Hayes, written September 19 at Youngstown: —

This is Sunday morning before breakfast. I had a fine meeting in a beautiful opera house last night. Here I am received by 23ders [members of his old regiment] and all, Democrats, bolters, etc., etc., with a friendship apparently most hearty. The "Hard Times and Plenty of Money to cure it" is here hurting us badly. Since the Maine election I have felt that we might be beaten in Ohio, perhaps badly. But it has good compensation for me. That awful bug of the Presidency is in many minds wherever I go. Ben Wade and H. B. Payne, Democratic M.C. from Cleveland, both told me seriously that my election would surely put me ahead of all competitors. So, defeat will be a relief from a terrible trouble and worriment. You will be a philosopher over this result, as I am. It looks to me a great deal that way. If people ask you what I say as to prospects, say to them that I am enjoying fine meetings, but say nothing about chances; that is important. . . . I see that the part I have taken in this famous contest will leave me, even if defeated, in a more conspicuous and influential position than I have ever had before. Our friends are warm and zealous.

Mr. Hayes spoke practically every day except Sundays, from the date of his opening speech at Marion on July 31, until the Saturday before election, October 9, when he closed his canvass at Oberlin. He made in all more than fifty speeches.[1] His letters and brief entries in his diary show that he maintained his vigor throughout the strenuous days of travel by all sorts of conveyance, the frequent receptions, the varied accommodations of his night sojourns, and all the other incidents that mark a trying political campaign. He was home at Fremont on election day (October 12) when he wrote in his diary these words; —

Election day! The weather is perfect. Spiegel Grove, my home, never looked so beautiful before. I am as nearly indifferent, on personal grounds, to the result of this day, as it is possible to be. I prefer success. But I anticipate defeat with very great equanimity. If victorious I am likely to be pushed for the nomination for President. This would make my life a disturbed and troubled one until the nomination, six or eight months hence. If nominated, the stir would last until November, a year hence. Defeat in the next Presidential election is almost a certainty. In any event, defeat now returns me to the quiet life I sought in coming here.

The large considerations of country, patriotism, and principle find little place in a deliberation of this question. The march of events will carry us safely beyond the dangers of the present questions.

The next entry in the diary is under date of October 17: —

Elected; a pleasant serenade from my neighbors; a day of doubt and anxiety as to the result. It looked on Thursday as if the Democrats were bent on counting me out. All right, however. Now come papers from all the country counties urging me for the Presidential nomination.

Mr. Hayes was elected by a plurality of 5544 votes. All the other Republican state candidates were successful and the Republicans gained a majority in both houses of the Legislature. The significance of the victory was recognized by the press of the

---

[1] The impression made by his campaigning was well summed up by the Mansfield *Liberal* a few days after the election: "He never lost his balance, never slopped over, never made a false move. From the beginning to the end, although he was speaking every day, he never said a single word which any one cared to have him recall. . . . A better tactician never headed a party ticket."

country and evoked much comment, coupled with commendation of Mr. Hayes's character and the fearless quality of his campaign oratory. *Harper's Weekly*, which had followed the Ohio canvass with unremitting attention, in its leading editorial article of October 30 declared: —

The result in Ohio is very much more than a Republican partisan victory. It has a significance which is obvious. The Republican defeats of last year were, as we insisted at the time, not an indication of the deliberate preference of the country for the Democratic party, but a stern call to Republicans to mend their ways. . . . Comprehension, confidence, and courage — the courage that enabled the Ohio Republicans to take the most uncompromising position for hard money and against inflation; the courage to dare and bear the taunt of inconsistency; the courage to trust the intelligence and common sense of the people, and not to treat them as children and puppets; the courage to appeal to the loyalty of 1861 and the war, and to the love of order, of honesty, of liberty, and of human and constitutional rights in the popular heart — these are what we need.

In Pennsylvania the same issue of sound money or inflation was the paramount topic of the campaign. After Mr. Hayes's successful canvass and election the urgent call came to him from Governor Hartranft, who was a candidate for reëlection, to come to Pennsylvania and lend his assistance there to the cause he had so ably presented and defended in Ohio. With characteristic modesty he at first declined the invitation, but so insistent was the solicitation that he reluctantly yielded. He was in Pennsylvania some ten days, speaking at Philadelphia, Bethlehem, Easton, Allentown, Oil City, and other places. Everywhere he was warmly welcomed. In Philadelphia he participated in a great procession in celebration of the Ohio victory. The leading men of the State and prominent citizens in the towns he visited vied with one another in doing him honor and paying him attention. More than once he was introduced to his audiences with some reference to the probability of his nomination and election the next year to the Chief Magistracy of the nation. Papers and politicians were satisfied that his clear and straightforward speeches against the "rag baby" contributed materially to the success of the Republican cause.[1] The State, which had gone

[1] "The speech of Governor Hayes last night has had an excellent effect. If he could multiply himself by fifty and make two or three such addresses in every county in the State before election, the inflation candidate would be buried under

Democratic the year before, returned to its old allegiance, and Governor Hartranft was reëlected, though by a majority much smaller than he had commanded three years before.

Mr. Hayes spent the months of November and December quietly at Fremont busied with his large correspondence, relating largely to his prospective candidacy for the Presidency, and with the preparation of his inaugural address. Early in January he went to Columbus, where on the 10th he for the third time with becoming ceremony took the oath as Governor of the Commonwealth. His record in the diary of this event reads: —

The weather cold and windy but bright. A handsome display of military. Governor Allen and I rode together. He is aged, but full of spirits and vim; talked cheerfully and well. It all passed off pleasantly.

Mr. Hayes's address on this occasion was like all his state papers in his former incumbency of the Governor's office, marked by brevity and simplicity of expression. "Questions of national concern" he refused to discuss, as inappropriate to the occasion; neither did he propose to give any extended survey of the State's condition and needs; Governor Allen had presented this in his annual message a few days before. But one or two topics he did wish to emphasize. While under the operation of the sinking fund the debt of the State was being steadily diminished, municipal indebtedness, expenditures, and taxation were rapidly increasing. This, he insisted, was "certainly a great evil." "How to govern cities well," he continued, "consistently with the principles and methods of popular government, is one of the most important and difficult problems of our time. Profligate expenditure is the fruitful cause of municipal misgovernment. If a means can be found which will keep municipal expenses from largely exceeding the public necessities, its adoption will go far toward securing honesty and efficiency in city affairs. In cities large debts and bad government go together. Cities which have the lightest taxes and smallest debts are apt, also, to have the purest and most satisfactory governments."

a majority of forty thousand. . . . His vigorous, honest, common-sense way of handling the currency question is exceedingly effective. . . . Governor Hayes rarely speaks over half an hour, but in that short time he covers the whole financial ground. His delivery is deliberate, though never halting; his manner dignified, though familiar, and his presence magnetic." (Reading, Pennsylvania, dispatch of staff correspondent of New York *Tribune*, October 27.)

This was not a mere local question. All the people of the State were deeply interested. They must share the burden in part at least. Experience had shown that, while necessarily large discretion must be left to the local authorities, this should be carefully restricted. In his opinion, "if the rule of the state constitution, which forbids all debts except in certain specified emergencies, is deemed too stringent to be applied to local affairs, the Legislature should at least accompany every authority to contract debt with an imperative requirement that a tax sufficient to pay off the indebtedness within a brief period shall be immediately levied, and thus compel every citizen who votes to increase debts to vote at the same time for an immediate increase of taxes sufficient to discharge them." "Let a requirement analogous to this [the sinking fund provision of the state constitution] be enacted in regard to existing local indebtedness; let a judicious limitation of the rate of taxation which local authorities may levy be strictly adhered to, and allow no further indebtedness to be authorized except in conformity with these principles; and we may, I believe, confidently expect that within a few years the burdens of debt now resting upon the cities and towns of the State will disappear, and that other wholesome and much-needed reforms in the whole administration of our municipal government will of necessity follow the adoption of what may be called the cash system in local affairs."

Among the most interesting duties of the Legislature were those relating to the care of dependent and criminal classes of the State. In 1867 the Legislature had created a Board of State Charities with authority to supervise the State's penal and benevolent institutions and to submit recommendations of improvement. The board had done efficient and valuable service. But in 1872 the law creating the board had been repealed, without, as it was believed, due consideration. Now he urged that the board be reëstablished. He also emphasized Governor Allen's recommendation that proper provision be made for an adequate exhibition of the State's resources and accomplishments at the approaching centennial celebration at Philadelphia; urged the Legislature to make its session short, and to "avoid all schemes requiring excessive expenditure whether State or local"; and ended with a graceful compliment to the retiring Governor.

The sound, practical sense of the address, expressing principles which it may be said, in passing, wise statesmanship now generally recognizes and seeks to enforce, received wide commendation [1] and added fresh impetus to the growing repute of its author.

The Legislature heeded the Governor's recommendation and promptly revived the Board of State Charities, with the Governor as an *ex-officio* member. It repealed the Geghan Law which had evoked so much criticism during the campaign of the previous year, made many changes in the manner of controlling the state institutions, and passed several laws limiting the taxing and debt-creating powers of municipalities.

Meanwhile the Governor was busied with an enormous correspondence relating to the possibility of his candidacy for the Presidency — about which he refused to become excited or anxious — and with the exacting routine duties of his office. These involved the appointment of men to fill many offices and places on boards and commissions. His aim was, while not ignoring political considerations, to select men known to be fitted for the duties they were expected to perform. There is no evidence that any appointments were made for the purpose of "building up a machine," or with a view to affecting men's attitude in the approaching Presidential contest. Writing of this feature of the Governor's duties in his diary, April 11, 1876, Mr. Hayes says: —

I have made the last appointments for this session of the Legislature. Some mistakes have been made, but on the whole I have been fortunate. One or two things I must bear in mind. No man should be finally determined on until the people where he resides have been heard from, *after he is seriously talked of, or nominated for the place.* The saying, that "no man knows what can be said against him until he is a candidate for office," has a wise side to it. I named a Democrat of excellent character for trustee of [the] Dayton Hospital for the Insane. Straightway it appeared he had been a bitter Copperhead during the war. Another, a gallant soldier and fine gentleman, was no sooner named than it was notorious that he was a shameless libertine.

As in his previous service as Chief Executive of the State, Mr.

[1] One enthusiastic correspondent, George W. Jones, of Cincinnati, wrote the Governor: "Plain and simple — that's the talk for the people. Grand old Saxon words, more full of sound, singing emphasis than all the modernized construction."

Hayes was extremely careful and conscientious in the exercise of the pardoning power. He laid down for himself these salutary rules for his guidance and control: —

1. Grant no pardon and make no promises on the first presentation of a case. Take time before deciding, or even encouraging the party.

2. If two or more are concerned in the crime, consider the cases of all together. One is often called the dupe until he is pardoned; then the other becomes dupe and the pardoned man the leader.

3. Pardon no man who is not provided with employment, or means of subsistence.

4. Pardon no man unless some friend is ready to receive him as he comes from the prison.

5. Of course, the judge, the prosecuting attorney, and some intelligent citizen of sound sense should be heard from in all cases.

These rules may be departed from in cases requiring it, but let them always be considered before the pardon is granted, or any committal had.

To these rules he adhered with substantial steadfastness, but giving always the benefit of the doubt to the side of mercy. Regularly in the cases of men that he pardoned who had committed crime under the influence of intoxicating liquor, the pardon was made conditional on their future total abstinence from the use of intoxicants. If this condition was broken, the man was returned to the penitentiary to serve out the remaining portion of the term of imprisonment to which he had been sentenced.

In spite of the exciting Presidential canvass of 1876, and his own enthralling interest in the outcome, Mr. Hayes remained steadily at his post in the executive chamber of the Ohio capitol and neglected no duty appertaining to his office. When the Legislature reassembled on January 2, 1877, the entire country was in a fever of doubt and controversy over the disputed election. Governor Hayes must have labored under prodigious temptation in preparing his annual message to the Legislature, to make at least some passing allusion to the topic of universal interest and anxious discussion; the topic, too, which must have been uppermost in his thought. The people had rather expected that he would take advantage of this public and official occasion to give some expression to his views on questions of national concern. But with singular self-restraint and wisdom, Mr. Hayes confined his message absolutely to matters of state interest. Indeed, the message contains not the slightest intimation of the momentous controversy, whose decision would mean so much to its author, which was engrossing the public mind.[1]

A brief summary of this message must suffice. In spite of the laws passed at the last session, the aggregate debt of Ohio municipalities had increased fifty per cent in the last year. The Governor therefore repeated and amplified the views on this subject that he had expressed a year before in his inaugural address. One reason he believed for the extravagance and inefficiency of city governments lay in the application to them of national politics.

There is no more reason [he declared — and what thinking man shall dispute his declaration?] for the antagonisms of political parties in municipal government than in a bank or a railroad company. Municipal governments are organizations designed chiefly for the better protection of property and person, and the better management of schools and charities. In the administration of such governments all honest, industrious citizens have an identical interest. The coöperation of a moderate proportion of the best citizens in any city in Ohio, with the determination expressed by them that good men from all political parties, or no political party, shall administer its affairs, and that unfit men, of any party, shall not hold its offices, would soon secure a good municipal government. Such a government calls for the best work of the best men, and neither party alone can furnish it. The improvement of our municipal government, generally, would constitute one of the best possible guaranties of an efficient civil service upon a large scale.

The Governor took pride in the admirable character of the state exhibit and in the large success of Ohio exhibitors at the Centennial Exposition; he spoke in praise of the activity of the reconstituted Board of State Charities; he recommended a further appropriation to insure a completion of the enlarged report of the geological survey of the State, inaugurated during his first term as Governor; he urged upon the Legislature the passage of a registry law, to the end that fraudulent voting should be reduced; and, in the interest of economy, he recommended the submission to the people of an amendment to the constitution

---

[1] "Upon the whole, this modest message is businesslike, free from flourish and flurry, and reveals an utter unconsciousness in the author of being to-day the most conspicuous and interesting character on the continent." (New York *Times*, January, 1877.)

making the date of the state election the same as that of the national election.

This was the final official utterance of Mr. Hayes as Governor to the Legislature and people of Ohio. On the 1st of March he resigned his office to become Chief Magistrate of the nation.

CHAPTER XXIII

THE MONTHS BEFORE THE CONVENTION OF 1876

FOR the first time since 1860 the Republican nomination for the Presidency was in 1876 not a foregone conclusion. Mr. Lincoln's second nomination was inevitable, as were also the two nominations of General Grant. The logic of the situation made any other result inconceivable, and there was practically no contest, though Mr. Chase and his friends flattered themselves that there might be. But in 1876 no Republican leader towered so high above his fellows as to rouse in the popular consciousness of the party an overwhelming demand for his selection. The sentiment of the party and the condition of the country had opened the way for a real contest, and the rivalry of ambitious leaders for the supreme party honor began early to develop and constantly increased in scope and intensity.

Moreover, the party approached the contest with many misgivings and with much apprehension.[1] Long continuance in undisputed possession of power had weakened the coherence of the party. The great moral impulse to which it owed its origin had abated in fervor with the practical righting of the wrongs and the solution of the problems to which it was directed; with rising doubts in the popular mind of the entire wisdom of prevailing policies, and question of the perfect integrity and unselfish devotion to the public welfare of many of the leaders that held high if not commanding positions in the party counsels. The loosening of political morals which seems inevitably to attend prolonged exercise of unchecked power, especially in a

[1] "If we look for the causes which have reduced the Republican party to its present doubtful condition, we can easily find them. One, of limited scope, is the hard times; the other, and the efficient cause, is impatience with what may best be described as a low, personal, selfish, intensely partisan character of administration, which fosters such iniquities as the Credit Mobilier, the moiety system, the salary grab, the enormous whiskey and Indian frauds, questionable transactions of all kinds involving high officers and an apparent disregard of them, a despotic party control by the officeholding interest, and a contemptuous violation of solemn party pledges." (*Harper's Weekly*, December 25, 1875.)

period of civil convulsion and war, — the supreme energies being directed toward the one great end, to the subordination or neglect of minor considerations however intrinsically important, — had continued and culminated under General Grant's headship of the nation. Many and substantial as were the achievements of his Administration, yet its lustre was sadly dimmed by the revelation of scandal after scandal in the public service, involving men of party prominence, some even in the Cabinet, in sordid corruption and shameless betrayal of trust. General Grant, as a military commander, seemed to possess unerring insight and judgment in selecting his lieutenants for important posts, and in directing and controlling their movements. He came to the White House with absolutely no experience or knowledge of the methods and demands of civil rule.[1] Conscientious and patriotic, as undoubtedly he was in the full implication of these epithets, his judgment was frequently at fault in the selection of men for high office; his reliance on the advice of self-seeking politicians who courted his favor was too unqualified, and his personal loyalty to men he counted his friends, even after their public dereliction became known, provoked serious censure and uncharitable condemnation. Moreover, he was quick to take offense at public men who criticized a policy on which his heart was set; as witness his determined hostility to Senator Sumner after the latter's opposition to his unfortunate Santo Domingo annexation scheme. So the Administration came widely to be thought of as too much enveloped in the atmosphere of personal government;[2] while the abuses of patronage and the vast increase of the civil service, wholly dominated by favoritism and

[1] "It was my fortune, or misfortune, to be called to the office of Chief Executive without any previous political training. From the age of seventeen I had never even witnessed the excitement attending a Presidential campaign but twice antecedent to my own candidacy, and at but one of them was I eligible as a voter." (From Grant's last annual Message.)

[2] "The truth is undeniable that ten years ago the Republican party had the fairest opportunity that was ever offered to a political organization. Is it any less true that this year its only chance of success lies in its power to persuade the country that it is not hopelessly corrupt? The President must bear his share of the responsibility for this lamentable result. The very fact that his administration has been peculiarly a personal government — that he has regarded his office as a reward given to him for his great services, and not as a trust to be administered for the common welfare — exposes him to stronger condemnation." (George William Curtis, in *Harper's Weekly*, March 25, 1876.)

partisan politics, had begun to awaken popular indignation and to quicken the demand for radical reform in administrative methods.

Besides all this, the condition of the South was a constant source of irritation and discussion. The wild orgies of negro Legislatures, under the guidance of unscrupulous whites, largely adventurers from the North, appalled and disgusted the sober sense of the country. The cruel and murderous barbarities of the Kuklux Klans, with which local authority was unwilling or unable to cope, evoked mingled feelings of amazement and righteous wrath, and led to passionate demands for national interference. Partisan feeling, on the one side, doubtless exaggerated, on the other side, doubtless belittled, the extent and enormity of the atrocities that were committed. But making all allowance for the passion and misrepresentation of the time, one cannot to this day read the remaining record of carpetbag corruption and Kuklux savagery without tingling shame and hot resentment. But gradually thinking men of the North were more and more becoming weary of the eternal Southern question. More and more they were coming to realize that it was principally, if not essentially, a domestic problem; that sooner or later the Southern people must work out their own salvation or go their own course to degradation and disorder. State Governments sustained or bolstered up by federal bayonets could not go on forever. And so the demand was increasing in volume, not only from the entire Democratic party, but likewise from far-seeing and patriotic Republicans, for the withdrawal of the federal troops from the Southern States and for a complete cessation of federal interference in the domestic affairs of the South. Only so, such Republicans thought, could fuller reconciliation now be hastened, and the party be strengthened to deal with the new questions that demanded consideration. The rights of the negroes had been established by the nation, as far as it was practicable, by the three great amendments. Adjustment of the practical relations of the races within the States must be left largely to the States themselves and to the beneficent influence of time, of public opinion, of social and moral forces. However, a large proportion, perhaps the dominant proportion, of the Republican party still favored the policy toward the South that had so long been pursued.

Another thing that contributed to the anxiety felt by thoughtful Republicans at the prospect of the party was the financial and industrial condition of the country. Years of rapid expansion in industry and railway construction, coupled with feverish speculation and extravagance of life, had suddenly been checked by the financial crisis of 1873. The "hard times" and depression which resulted from this had not yet ceased to be felt. For the first time since the Republicans had come into power, the Democrats in the election of 1874 had gained control of the House of Representatives and had reduced considerably the Republican majority in the Senate. Monetary heresies, attractive in their appeal to the unthinking masses who felt the pressure of the financial stringency, had been espoused by the principal leaders of the Democratic party, especially in the West and South, and were shrewdly presented as an easy way to alleviate the burden of debt, national and private, and to quicken the sluggish current of industry. Some Republicans of commanding influence, like Senator Morton, wavered in their allegiance to sound finance and scrupulous maintenance of the public faith. Apprehensive of the kind of financial legislation likely to be attempted by the new Congress, the Republicans of the Forty-third Congress, early in January, 1875, performed a duty long neglected and, until that time, apparently impossible because of wide diversity of opinion, by passing a law providing definitely for the resumption of specie payments January 1, 1879, and giving the Secretary of the Treasury abundant authority to make the law effective. But this law only added fuel to the flames of Democratic cheap-money advocacy, as soon appeared in the state campaigns of Ohio and Pennsylvania of that year. The part played by Mr. Hayes in combating the error and winning a victory for sound money has already been recounted. But the error was so insinuating in its appeal, and the margin of victory was so slight, that Republicans could not help feeling nervous regarding the influence on the course of political events which this heresy, in connection with all the causes of dissatisfaction with the party in power, might still exert.

On the other hand, the Democrats were better organized, were more harmonious among themselves, despite wide differences of opinion on finance, were more ably led, and were more confident of success than at any time since the obscuration of the party in 1860. Conditions pointed indubitably to their nomination of the adroit and resourceful New York statesman who had won high popular regard by his masterly skill in helping to smash the infamous "Tweed Ring," though he had long affiliated with Tweed in party politics,[1] and by his course as Governor against the almost equally rapacious and odious "Canal Ring."

In the preliminary canvass for the Republican nomination four men early became conspicuous and active. Of these by far the most popular was the brilliant, versatile, and magnetic James G. Blaine, of Maine. Devoted to his fortunes with ardent loyalty were hosts of able party leaders in nearly all parts of the country, while among the masses of his party he commanded a fervor of popularity such as no other man since Henry Clay's demise had been able to inspire. Some shadow rested on his reputation for scrupulous exclusion of personal interests from his activity as a legislator which caused many thinking people to doubt his absolute probity of character, and led vastly more to question the advisability of his nomination at such a crisis in the party's history. Moreover, by his overweening ambition, and by his merciless power of caustic characterization and denunciation in the heat of debate, he had made bitter and aggressive enemies within the party ranks.

One of these enemies, implacable in his hostility, was now a competitor for the party's favor. This was the imperious and arrogant Roscoe Conkling, of New York, famous for the brilliancy of his political oratory; famous for his stalwart devotion to General Grant and the defense of the Administration;[2] famous for his sole and absolute mastery of the party machinery in his own State; and famous, above all else, for his dominating and supercilious personality. Outside his own State he had many admirers but few friends. Whatever influence President Grant

---

[1] "During all Tweed's ascendancy and control in the Democratic party of the State, Mr. Tilden, as Democratic chairman, gave the weight of his name and official action to Tweed's nominations." (*Harper's Weekly*, July 15, 1876.)

[2] "No Republican has been so signally identified with the Executive at every point and in every detail as Senator Conkling." (*Harper's Weekly*, March 11, 1876.) Again two weeks later the same paper speaks of Mr. Conkling as "the cleverest and most unshrinking courtier of an Administration under which the Republican party has been well-nigh ruined."

could exert in the contest, however, it was well understood would be used in his behalf. He would, moreover, go to the convention with the largest single delegation; and one which, if he could not himself be nominated, would with few exceptions yield unquestioning deference to his will.

Worthier than either of these two, so far as force of character and achievement go, was Oliver P. Morton, the great war Governor of Indiana, and for many years one of the commanding figures in the Senate.[1] His fame rested on a more solid basis than theirs; on the actual accomplishment of arduous tasks; on proved executive ability of the highest order; on recognized capacity for constructive statesmanship. He was wise in counsel, skilful in political strategy, bold and daring in attack. He was dowered with superb moral courage, was animated by pure and unselfish patriotism, was scornful of all that savored of self-seeking. The freedmen had no more untiring friend and champion; the Republican party no more devoted adherent to its principles and purposes; the Democratic party no more persistent critic or determined antagonist. But there were grave intimations regarding his private character, and already for years his physical powers had been undermined; so that while his intellectual vigor showed no impairment, even his most devoted friends and followers, when judgment for the moment could control their zeal, must have doubted the advisability of pressing his candidacy.

Last of the four was Benjamin H. Bristow, of Kentucky, a comparatively new man in the arena of national politics. He had risen suddenly into conspicuous public favor and fame by his course as Secretary of the Treasury in pursuing and prosecuting with righteous and relentless vigor, in defiance of all clamor that he was "hurting the party," the members, however prominent, of the malodorous and widely ramified whiskey conspiracy. His zeal in this procedure had made the impression that he was some way superior to the Administration of which he was a part; that he more than any one else was imbued with reform purposes. It

---

[1] After a visit at Washington in June, 1870, Mr. Hayes wrote in his diary, July 1: "The great statesman at Washington now is Governor Morton. He is a strong, logical debater, who has the faculty of putting an argument in a way that is satisfactory to the best minds, and at the same [time] is understood and appreciated by the most ignorant."

was known that entire harmony between him and the President no longer existed and his early retirement from the Cabinet was predicted, much to the chagrin of the better friends of the Administration.[1] The Republican critics of Grant and "Grantism," the men in the party that saw most clearly the imperative need of reform in the civil service and in administrative methods, thought they discovered in Bristow the man best fitted to lead the forces of reform and eagerly attached themselves to his standard. With them were most of the Republicans that had been prominent in the futile Liberal Republican movement of 1872. That all these men greatly overestimated the ability of Mr. Bristow, his subsequent inconspicuous career seems clearly to demonstrate.

Behind each of these men was an energetic organization of friends and supporters, actively engaged in a propaganda in his behalf. Through the press and by means of personal representatives, efforts were put forth to urge his claims and to win the allegiance of state organizations and individual delegates. The longer this rivalry continued the more partisan the followers of each aspirant became and the stronger their hostility to all the others. More and more it became apparent that the adherents of each candidate would turn to any one of the other three with emotions of extreme repugnance, and that then they would give him only halting and half-hearted support.

Thus naturally a condition was developing, such as has appeared not infrequently in American politics, favorable to the exaltation of some strong man, from a doubtful and important State, unencumbered by entangling alliances with any one of the fighting factions, but sustaining kindly relations with all. Mr. Hayes was not blind to the situation, but serenely watched the course of events, not overanxious as to its outcome; content, indeed, as he had ever shown himself with whatever fate should have in store for him.

Senator Sherman, who had himself been suggested as a possible candidate, was among the first of the leading statesmen of

---

[1] "Every honest man in the country must hope that the rumors of the retirement of Secretary Bristow, at the request of the President, are untrue." (*Harper's Weekly*, March 11, 1876.) Mr. Bristow resigned from the Cabinet immediately after the Cincinnati Convention, being virtually forced out.

the party to divine the probable course of the various movements within the party and to express the opinion that the nomination of Mr. Hayes would be wisest for the party and best for the country. This opinion was set out in a letter from Mr. Sherman, bearing date of January 21, 1876, to a member of the Ohio Senate. Mr. Sherman described the strong qualities in Mr. Hayes's character, reaching this climax: "He is fortunately free from the personal enmities and antagonisms that would weaken some of his competitors, and he is unblemished in name, character, or conduct." Mr. Sherman urged that Ohio should "give Governor Hayes a united delegation instructed to support him in the National Convention, not that we have any special claim to have the candidate taken from Ohio, but that in General Hayes we honestly believe the Republican party of the United States will have a candidate for President who can combine greater popular strength and greater assurance of success than other candidates, and with equal ability to discharge the duties of President of the United States in case of election. Let this nomination be thus presented, without any wire-pulling or depreciation of others, and as a conviction upon established facts, and I believe Governor Hayes can be and ought to be nominated."

The advice of the last sentence was altogether in accord with the predilections of Mr. Hayes and with the counsel and course of his closest friends. It correctly describes in brief the anteconvention conviction and activities of the advocates of Mr. Hayes's nomination.

There is no evidence that Mr. Hayes of himself had ever nursed the hope or entertained the ambition of some day becoming President. The self-revelatory confidences entrusted on occasion to his diary betray no intimation that such an aspiration had ever tinged his day-dreams or haunted his sleeping hours. The earliest suggestions of the thought by friends or admirers made no impression on his mind except as evidence of flattering regard, pleasing to his self-esteem, to be sure, but not to be allowed in any way to disturb his serenity or to affect his conduct. The very first mention of him as a man on whom the nation might well at some time bestow the highest honor, was made at Cincinnati, on the eve of his second election as Governor, in October, 1869. Governor Hayes spoke that night in the

Seventeenth Ward Wigwam. Mr. S. F. Covington presided at the meeting and in introducing Mr. Hayes, proposed his nomination for the Presidency. The incident passed without comment or report, being taken as the exuberance of an admiring neighbor; it was only recalled later when the prediction it embodied was in process of verification.[1]

In November, 1871, to some correspondent whose name is not preserved that had written him in regard to the Presidency, Mr. Hayes replied: —

If I thought there was the slightest danger of so obscure a personage as I being attacked with that wretched mania, an itching for the White House, I would beg for the prayers of your church for my deliverance.

And yet in the following month some correspondent of the New York *Tribune* wrote that paper advocating his nomination in place of General Grant; and in January, 1872, the Republican members of the Ohio Legislature, as we have already seen, that were opposed to the reëlection of Senator Sherman, insistently urged Mr. Hayes to accept election to the United States Senate through a coalition of the anti-Sherman Republicans and the Democrats, by assuring him that such an election — a triumph of independence over machine methods — would so impress the country as to insure his nomination for the Presidency. To all such appeals, as it will be remembered, Mr. Hayes resolutely turned a deaf ear.[2]

---

[1] August 21, 1876, Mr. Covington wrote a friend who was at the meeting and recalled the incident: "It seemed to be almost a farce to introduce Governor Hayes to that audience. He knew many of them quite as well as I did, and they all knew him and honored him. If you will remember, I referred briefly to his residence in this city, to the fact of his having been City Solicitor, having served in Congress, his brilliant military career, and his record as Governor; stated that in every position he had occupied, whether civil or military, he had met the most sanguine expectations and hopes of his friends; that on the following day he would be reëlected Governor, and by the time he had given to the people of Ohio all the service they would have a right to ask of him, the people of the nation would demand his service as President and make him the successor of General Grant. That latter thought came to me as I was speaking. Was it not prophecy?"

[2] A local poetaster, in the Columbus *Gazette*, on Mr. Hayes's retirement from the Governor's office, ended a sonnet with these verses: —

> "Oh, may it be thy set is brief; and like the Sun
> Rise thou again — thy light to fill the sky —
> A brighter course of glory still to run, —
> Till millions now unborn shall hail thy name,
> In ages yet to come with glad acclaim!"

When Mr. Hayes retired to Fremont in the spring of 1873, there can be no doubt that in all sincerity he had abandoned every thought of further political or official preferment. Leaders of public opinion and friends that had followed his career, with intelligent appreciation of the qualities of his character, deprecated his decision and could not be convinced to accept it as final; and political influences were steadily at work, which, with the definiteness of fate, forced him, in 1875, against his will and preferences, to return to the hazards of the political arena; to accept once more the leadership of his party in Ohio and to fight to a successful conclusion the doubtful battle in behalf of sound money and unimpaired maintenance of the national faith. He foresaw at once, as has already been recorded, but evidently with more of misgiving than elation, that his success in the Ohio canvass — certain under the circumstances to attract the attention of the nation — would lead inevitably to serious consideration of him for the Republican nomination to the Presidency in the following year. But he records his meditations on the subject as impersonally as though he were writing of the chances and prospects of a friend or even an utter stranger. Long practical experience and acute observation of American political influences and the currents of popular opinion had taught him so well to estimate accurately their force and direction that he could foresee as clearly the probable effect of their operation in his own behalf, as though he were an altogether disinterested looker-on. But he made no conscious effort to stimulate these influences or to control these currents toward himself. He was content, absolutely, to leave the event to the future — doing simply with all his might the duty that lay next. In his campaign for the governorship one can detect not the least evidence of any subconsciousness even that perhaps the supreme honor of the nation might be dependent on his efforts; that therefore he should be cautious in the opinions he expressed and should be careful not to give offense to any large class of voters. Far from that, he discussed the topics of the day with the utmost vigor, evading no pertinent question, was unsparing in his denunciation of the greenback heresy, with which many Republicans also were infected, and steadfastly combated the Catholic attacks on the common-school system.

Mr. Hayes was not alone in apprehending the implication of his nomination and prospective election as Governor. Political leaders and personal friends, not only in Ohio, but in other States, wrote him predicting that if Ohio returned him to Columbus, the White House would be within his grasp the following year. And so shrewd a political observer as the independent but erratic editor of the New York *Sun* declared, in an editorial article of June 26, long before the active canvass had begun, "If General Hayes should be elected Governor of Ohio by a rousing majority, he would take a place in the Republican list" of candidates. As soon as the result of the Ohio election was known, numerous papers in the State placed his name at the head of their columns as their candidate; and innumerable letters and dispatches of congratulation poured in upon the newly elected Governor hailing him as the President that should be. In his ten days of campaigning in Pennsylvania, immediately following his election, his probable candidacy for Presidential honors was more than once proclaimed by speakers in his presence.

The metropolitan press was also prompt to recognize the significance of Mr. Hayes's election as affecting his future prospects. For example, the New York *World*, two days after the Ohio election, declared that it "prognosticates no good to any of the Republican Presidential candidates, who have been heretofore prominent in the field. It brings forward at once into the front rank a new candidate with portentous claims. Governor Hayes has suddenly assumed the leading position in his party. . . . It will not be easy even for Governor Hayes to make headway against the general drift of Grant and his Administration. But he will certainly be urged to undertake the task." A few days later the Boston *Herald* said: "He is a man whom ' it will do to tie to,' and . . . we are not sure but the Republicans and honest men of the country could go farther and fare worse than if they looked to him as a leader, capable, willing, and courageous enough to lead them in their onset upon the incompetents and corruptionists of the present Administration." The Springfield *Republican* promptly proposed Hayes and Woodford for the ticket, and this suggestion was widely discussed and commended by Republican papers throughout the country.

On Mr. Hayes's return from Pennsylvania he found an accumulation of letters bearing upon this subject. One that is fairly representative in tone and character may well be quoted in part. It was from Mr. Hayes's old friend, General M. F. Force, of Cincinnati, and was written October 18. It contained these paragraphs: —

When I wrote last I said Judge Taft would not be nominated, that you would be nominated, and that Mr. Delano would leave the Cabinet.

These are all accomplished and I now write to congratulate you upon your election. I do not congratulate you upon obtaining an office you did not covet, but on being leader in a struggle that the whole country watched with breathless interest and a victory which is of importance to the nation.

And now for the after-fruits. It is natural that you should now be spoken of for the Presidency. When you finished your speech at Marietta, General T. C. H. Smith said you were his candidate for the Presidency. Mr. Hook in the first speech he made nominated you. I discouraged talking about it in Ohio, lest somebody's susceptibilities might be touched in advance. But to friends at the East I wrote you would be the next Governor of Ohio, and the next President of the United States.

In this matter you, of course, must be passive. The rule is almost without exception that a man who seeks the Presidency never gets it, and Morton, Conkling, and Blaine, who might as a means of defeating each other in the end unite on you, would fight against you, if you should become too prominent before the convention meets.

To this letter Mr. Hayes replied November 2: —

. . . I can't realize the "after-point."[1] There is enough of it brought to my notice in a multitude of ways to make me think of it. I heard but little of it in Pennsylvania. It will perhaps die out with the subsidence of the interest in the recent election. In any event, I mean not to mix in it, or heed it — to go right along as if no such talk existed. I . . . feel as you do that the future success of the Republicans in Ohio and the nation is exceedingly doubtful, with the prospect of a national victory rather against us. . . .

To other correspondents letters of a similar tenor were written.[2] He was determined to go forward in the execution of the duties

---

[1] So Mr. Hayes wrote it, evidently misreading General Force's word.

[2] To one man he wrote: "Content with the past, I am not in a state of mind about the future. It is for us to act well in the present. George E. Pugh used to say, 'There is no political hereafter.'" This letter found its way into print and went the round of the press — affording a striking contrast to the solicitous activity of the acknowledged aspirants for the nomination.

to which the voters of Ohio had chosen him, undisturbed in mind or purpose by the promptings of his friends or by aspirations for higher place. In his inaugural address as Governor he refrained pointedly from any discussion of national issues, making absolutely no play calculated to attract the attention of the nation in his direction, and he entered upon the duties of his office as though these were his sole care, albeit letters relating to the Presidency kept pouring in upon him and frequent callers interrupted his official tasks, intent on discussing the prospects of his nomination. In his diary, February 15, Mr. Hayes records: —

Since I came to Columbus, six weeks ago, there has been no day in which I have not had letters and visits on the subject of my nomination for the Presidency. Many days' there is a succession of callers at my office on this topic. I say very little. I have in no instance encouraged any one to work to that end. I have discountenanced all efforts at organization or management in my interest. I have said the whole talk about me is on the score of availability. Let availability do the work, then.

This was written a few days subsequent to the publication of Senator Sherman's letter, which has already been spoken of above. The day after this letter was known in Chicago (January 26), William Henry Smith, at that time general agent of the Western Associated Press, wrote Mr. Hayes, informing him that General Sheridan was heartily in his favor, and analyzing the currents of party opinion in the Northwestern States, and concluding with this remarkable forecast: —

As to the situation in general: The ticket and platform should be of such character as to give the Republicans New York, Pennsylvania, and Indiana, or the first two certainly. This ticket would do it: Hayes and Wheeler.

Senator Sherman's letter was published everywhere and attracted general attention and comment.[1] Its sentiments were

---

[1] George William Curtis, in *Harper's Weekly*, spoke of this letter as "very significant." While Mr. Curtis deprecated the nomination of a candidate on the score of availability alone, he went on to say: "We are speaking in general and impersonally, for all we know of Governor Hayes is most creditable. He has beaten before the people, in turn, the leader of every faction of the Democratic party in Ohio, and his hold upon the confidence of his fellow citizens is plainly very strong. Three facts show that he is already among the most prominent of the probable candidates. First, the date of the Ohio state election and the immense advantage of a Republican victory at that time; then the meeting of the

seconded a few days later in a brief letter by General Sherman; and more and more the wisdom of Mr. Hayes's nomination, and the political advantages likely to flow therefrom, found lodgment in the public mind and elicited discussion in the public prints. Correspondents of metropolitan newspapers began to appear at Columbus, seeking interviews with the Governor and writing to their papers elaborate accounts of Mr. Hayes's personal characteristics, and of his manner of meeting men and dealing with the affairs of his office. Try as they might, however, they were unable to draw from him any acknowledgment that he was an active candidate for the nomination, or to betray him into any indiscretion of commitment as among the contesting leaders in the race. The special correspondent of the New York *Times* (at that time one of the most ably conducted Republican papers of the country), who notes incidentally that he "had known Mr. Hayes for twenty years or more," wrote, February 24: —

> Governor Hayes did not in the long interview depart in the slightest degree from his fixed policy of saying little and doing less in reference to his chance for the Presidency.... Concerning his candidacy for the Presidency, he said it was a matter with which he had not had, and did not intend to have, anything to do. It was an office, he thought, which no citizen should seek.

The accuracy of this quotation is confirmed by Mr. Hayes's letters written at this period. To General Garfield he wrote under date of March 4: —

> *Private.*
> MY DEAR GENERAL, — I have your note of the 2d. I am kept busy with callers, correspondence, and the routine details of the office, and have not, therefore, tried to keep abreast of the currents of opinion on any of the issues. My *notion* is that the true contest is to be between inflation and a sound currency. That the Democrats are again drifting all to the wrong side. We need not divide on details, on methods, or time when. The previous question will again be irredeemable paper as a

convention at Cincinnati, which will give him, what has been shown to be very advantageous, the pressure of local public opinion and of personal influence in his favor; and then the frank declaration of a leader like Senator Sherman, who is usually overcautious. His prompt and positive expression of preference must be considered not as his own only, but as that of a powerful opinion in the Western States — an opinion of which we have already had private intimation from other States than Ohio. The Senator's letter will be of great service if it should encourage other leaders to speak as frankly and forcibly."

permanent policy, or a policy which seeks a return to coin. My opinion is decidedly against yielding a hair's breadth.

We can't be on the inflation side of the question. We must keep our face firmly in the other direction. "No steps backward" must be something more than unmeaning platform words.

"The drift of sentiment among our friends in Ohio," which you inquire about, will depend on the conduct of our leading men. It is for them to see that the right sentiment is steadily upheld. We are in a condition such that firmness and adherence to principle are of peculiar value just now. I would "consent" to no backward steps. To yield or compromise is weakness, and will destroy us. If a better resumption measure can be substituted for the present one, that may do. But keep cool. We can better afford to be beaten in Congress than to back out.

I do not write letters to be shown, or used in any way, on political questions, but this much I may say to you. Do not quote me.

I note what you say on the personal aspect of our politics, and assure you that I feel the compliment implied very sensibly.[1]

---

[1] General Garfield's letter to which Mr. Hayes replied was: —

Personal.   WASHINGTON, D.C., March 2, 1876.

MY DEAR GOVERNOR, — It is becoming evident that we shall soon be called upon to confront the question of what shall be done with the Specie Resumption Act. The Democracy started out with strong declarations in favor of a sound currency, saying that they would show that they were hard-money men and sounder than the Republicans on that question. The election of Kerr was a triumph of the hard-money wing of that party ; the appointment of his committees was in the same line of policy. But it is evident that the soft-money element of that party has been making progress steadily since the first day of the session and I shall not be surprised if they succeed in bringing the House to a vote on the naked question of a repeal of the Resumption Act. In the meantime the soft-money men of our own party have not been idle. They have said but little in the House and we have been able to hold our minority in very good shape thus far. Still, men throughout the country who are in debt or engaged in speculation, have been aggressively clamorous in their efforts to make a diversion in our ranks, and I see there are many grounds for the fear that a considerable Republican vote will be thrown with the soft-money Democrats whenever the issue is fairly made in the House.

Will you please tell me what appears to be the drift of sentiment among our friends in Ohio on this question? How far, if at all, would it be wise for us to consent to a modification of the Resumption Act? If, by repealing the date we could obtain a certain method which would bring us to specie payments, would such a policy be safe? Some of our friends here are taking that view of the case and urging it as a wise policy in view of our safety at the coming election.

Of course I will quote nothing you write unless you are willing I should do so; but I ask your opinion mainly for my own guidance in considering the question.

It seems to me we have been gaining on the Democracy ever since the session began, and I apprehend no serious obstacle in the way of our success unless it be the financial question. My own opinion is that an appeal to what is true and honest is always safest; still we want to put the issue in the best shape.

I am greatly gratified at the way you are bearing yourself during these

This letter brings out in the clearest light the sturdiness of Mr. Hayes's convictions on the question of the public finances. With party friends wavering in their adherence to the established policy and with the possibility of the Presidential nomination gleaming before his vision, he was unwilling to consider any compromise of the party's position. It must not yield a hair's breadth; it must not take a single backward step.[1]

A few days later (March 9) to a former comrade in the Twenty-third Regiment, Captain D. K. Smith, of Mantzville, Missouri, he wrote: —

Your note of the 6th is received. We are no doubt entering on a doubtful political contest. Whoever may be the candidate, his election can only be secured by "solid work." Both parties are injured by what is going on at Washington. Both are, therefore, more and more disposed to look for candidates outside of that atmosphere. It is very gratifying, whatever may be the event, to be so heartily supported by the men with whom I served.

I do not wish my friends to do any pushing. I shall continue to avoid everything of the sort.

preliminary months of platform and President making. I have believed from the beginning that your friends ought not for some time yet to make an aggressive fight, nor involve you in any antagonism. But we should give you the solid vote of the Ohio delegation and await the break up which must come as the weaker candidates drop out.

I shall try to attend the state convention if possible. Our people desire me to be a delegate from our county and I think I shall go.

So far as I know, the Republican delegation here in Congress are unanimously your friends.

Mrs. Garfield joins me in kindest regard to Mrs. Hayes and yourself. — Very truly yours,

J. A. GARFIELD.

GOVERNOR R. B. HAYES,
COLUMBUS, OHIO.

[1] His inflexible attitude in this respect is shown by the following letter, two weeks later, to Senator Sherman: —

EXECUTIVE DEPARTMENT, STATE OF OHIO.
COLUMBUS, 20 Mch., 1876.

MY DEAR SIR, — There cannot be the least danger that our Committee will be so weak as to lean towards unsoundness on the money question. I have heard no one suggest that we should be *less* explicit than we were last year, and my preference decidedly is, that if we change, it be in the direction of resumption. My views are so exactly expressed in your note that I do not enlarge. If consulted, I shall advise accordingly. But *do come out if practicable.* I am confident we shall be sound as coin. — Sincerely,

R. B. HAYES.

HON. JOHN SHERMAN.

The deep-seated dissatisfaction among the more thoughtful Republicans with existing political conditions and the urgency of the demand for reform were reflected early in April by the appearance of a call for a free conference to be held in New York, "to consider what may be done to prevent the national election of the centennial year from being a mere choice of evils." This call bore the signatures of William Cullen Bryant, Theodore D. Woolsey, Alexander H. Bullock, Horace White, and Carl Schurz; men whose distinction for civic virtue and disinterested patriotism could not fail to impress the country with the seriousness of their purpose. When men like these were moved by the "widespread corruption in our public service which threatened to poison the vitality of our institutions"; by "the uncertainty of the public mind and of party counsels as to grave economical questions involving the honor of the Government"; and by "the danger that an inordinate party spirit" by machine methods might "monopolize political power for selfish ends"; to seek by counsel with men of similar conviction to make effective protest against the ruling influences of the party, the significance of their action could not be obscured by the sneers of the politicians that they were impracticable visionaries. The conference met at the Fifth Avenue Hotel on May 15, with men of the highest character in attendance from every important Northern State. President Woolsey was made the presiding officer, and a committee on business, with Carl Schurz as chairman, was appointed. This committee submitted an "address to the American people," written substantially by Mr. Schurz, which the conference accepted and approved. The address denounced in the most vigorous language the spoils system and the corruption in the public service, declaring it to be "the first duty of the American people to reëstablish the moral character of the Government by a thorough reform." Finally it proclaimed: —

The abolition of class legislation and of special privileges in the Government, and the adoption of equal suffrage and eligibility to office, without distinction of race, religious creed, property, or sex.

These declarations, which, even the blindest of party workers could not fail to see, gave correct voice to the sentiments of a very considerable portion of the rank and file of the Republican party, were a plain warning that the nomination of either

Blaine, Conkling, or Morton would greatly weaken the party's hope of success. And so, undoubtedly, this conference had its influence in preparing the way for Mr. Hayes's success at Cincinnati.

The following entries in the diary fully reveal alike the course of political activity in Ohio and the trend of Mr. Hayes's inmost thoughts during the weeks preceding the convention: —

March 21. — The last week a large number of the counties have elected delegates to the state convention. Several counties have not expressed a preference on the Presidential [nomination], but the most of them have passed resolutions in favor of me. It is likely that all of the counties have sent delegates who are favorable. Certainly none are avowedly opposed. There is a sentiment for Bristow as a second choice. His war on the whiskey thieves gives him prestige as the representative of reform. I am not sure but he would be the best candidate we could nominate. I am sure I prefer him to any other man.

It will be a small disappointment for me to give up my chances. With so general an expression in my favor in Ohio, and a fair degree of assent elsewhere, especially in States largely settled by Ohio people, I have supposed it was possible that I might be nominated. But with no opportunity, and no desire, to make combinations or to lay wires, I have not thought my chance worth much consideration. I feel less diffidence in thinking of this subject than perhaps I ought. It seems to me that good purposes, and the judgment, experience, and firmness I possess, would enable me to execute the duties of the office well. I do not feel the least fear that I should fail.

This all looks egotistical, but it is sincere. On the other hand, I do not desire the place with any strong or uneasy feeling. I shall accept the result which now seems probable without any bitterness. If Bristow is nominated, I shall give him hearty support in speeches and otherwise.

April 2. — On the 29th ult. the Republican State Convention of 750 delegates was held. It declared by a unanimous vote that I was the choice of the Republicans of Ohio for President. They *instructed* the senatorial delegates and requested the district delegates "to use their earnest efforts to secure his nomination." This is certainly very flattering. It was done with enthusiasm and in earnest.

From the beginning I have done nothing directly or indirectly to bring about this result. I have discouraged rather than encouraged "the Hayes movement."

And now for the future. I would be glad if now I could in some satisfactory way drop out of the candidacy. I do not at present see what I can do to relieve myself from the embarrassment of the position I am in. It does not greatly disturb me. My usual serenity carries me along. But I would like to be out of it. I will think about it.

April 11. — . . . In politics I am growing more indifferent. I would like it, if I could now return to my planting and books at home. I wrote the following letter to one of the delegates,[1] supposed to lean toward Blaine, in reply to his note on the subject: —

COLUMBUS, 6 April, 1876.

MY DEAR SIR, — I am exceedingly obliged for your very satisfactory letter. A press of business has prevented an earlier reply. Having done absolutely nothing to make myself the candidate of Ohio, I feel very little responsibility for future results. When the state convention was called it seemed probable, that if I encouraged my friends to organize for the purpose, every district would elect my decided supporters. But to make such an effort in my own behalf, to use Payne's phrase on repudiation, " I abhorred."

Being now in the field without any act of my own, I have no uneasy ambition to remain a candidate. I think I have a right, however, to considerate treatment at the hands of the Ohio delegation. If I am to be voted for at all, and as long as I am to be voted for at all, may I not reasonably expect the solid vote of Ohio? Whenever any considerable number of the delegation thinks the time has come to withdraw my name, it ought to be promptly done. I can speak of this, I think, with a judgment as impartial as if it were the case of another man. I am not solicitous to be a candidate for nomination, nor for the nomination itself. I agree with you that Mr. B.'s [Blaine] course with you was very handsome.

You may show this note to Mr. Garretson, but it is, of course, not for publication. — Sincerely,

R. B. HAYES.

May 7. — The Ohio friends think our prospect at Cincinnati grows daily better. General Garfield writes me the following which I prize more than the prospect of success, if I can continue to deserve it: —

"I repeat with more emphasis than before what I said in my last letter to you that we are all delighted with the sensible and masterful way in which you are bearing yourself during the chaotic period of President-making. You are gaining strength every day with our most thoughtful people."

To which I reply: "I value the compliment in your closing paragraph. It has been my desire to deserve it. Not to lose my head, and to get through without doing or saying anything unjust, or even uncharitable, toward competitors or their supporters, has been my ambition in this business. If I am successful in this, the adverse result which I anticipate, will not give me a moment's uneasiness."

May 19. — Nothing new in the political way of special personal interest. I still think Blaine is so far ahead in the number of delegates he

---

[1] This was Edwin Cowles, editor of the Cleveland *Leader.*

has secured and is securing that his nomination is not improbable. He has not been greatly damaged by the investigations. As a candidate before the people his newly acquired wealth, his schemes for getting the nomination, and his connection with money interests depending for success on legislation, will damage him. But with two or three hundred delegates in his favor, will not all of the loose odds and ends gravitate to him? It so seems. If he fails, the next is a combination for selfish ends to make a candidate among the friends of the leading candidate. This would not be in my favor. My independent position, aloof from bargaining, puts me outside of the list from whom the managers will select. It is only in the contingency of a union between those who look for availability in the candidate, and those who are for purity and reform in administration, that I am a probable nominee.

I write to Sherman to-day as follows: —

COLUMBUS, O., 19 May, 1876.

MY DEAR SIR, — It would specially gratify me if you would attend the Cincinnati Convention. I do not mean to depart from the position I have taken to remain perfectly passive on the nomination. But it is fair to assume that the time may come when I ought to be withdrawn. To be able to act on this, and other possible questions, it is important for me that I have friends of experience and sound judgment on the ground by whom I can be advised of the exact condition of things, and of the proper course to be taken. I have consulted with the delegate from my own district and town, General Buckland, more freely than with any other member of the delegation and regard him as a friend in whom I can confide unreservedly. — Sincerely,

R. B. HAYES.[1]

HON. JOHN SHERMAN.

May 21. — I have a friendly note of the 18th from Secretary of War, Judge Taft, in which he says: "I am no prophet in such confused elements of calculation, but it really seems to me that your chances are

---

[1] To this letter Mr. Sherman replied from Washington (May 22): —

"I do not see how I could attend the Cincinnati Convention with any influence or power to aid you or I would go. The critical moments will be in the convention, and delegates will naturally be restive under any interference with them by outsiders. My appearance there at all, when rejected as a delegate, would naturally be commented on, and destroy any influence I could exert out of the State. As to your nomination, I feel that it ought to be made and that there is a fair chance that it will be made. Your strength is in being in reserve when the strong antagonisms among other candidates will make your nomination not only natural and proper, but the strongest that can be made. So it has always appeared to me.

"The course you have pursued has been the proper one. Your friends ought quietly and firmly to ask for you, and abide the inevitable second choice of the delegates. . . . I now regret that I had not been formally a candidate for delegate and elected, but it is too late now. I can only do what I can for you here and by conversation with and correspondence with people from different States."

stronger than those of any other man. I mean that, taking into view such elements of calculation as exist and are appreciable, the probabilities are in your favor. . . . I should feel that it was another strong point gained for Ohio if it should come to you."

Judge Dickson (W. M.), of Cincinnati, asked me a question or two, put him by an Eastern correspondent. I replied. It turns out the correspondent was George William Curtis. Judge Dickson now sends me the following reply of Curtis to his (the judge's) note sending my letter. —

> West New Brighton,
> Staten Island, New York,
> 17 May, 1876.

My dear Sir, — I am exceedingly obliged for your note and the letter of Governor Hayes which you have kindly sent me. I have read it, you will easily believe, with very great interest, and with equal satisfaction that I obeyed the impulse to ask you the questions. That it is the reply to a letter so frank as you state yours to have been is only the more agreeable, for it places him in a most manly and simple position.

His chances seem to me daily to improve, for the feeling among the friends of other candidates is becoming so positive that I feel as if some compromise were probable. Yet the real compromise candidate is Blaine. The extremes are Bristow and Conkling. The friends of the latter, however, would very much prefer Hayes to Blaine. But might accept B. if they could do no better. I have never doubted that Conkling would be the final machine candidate, and very strong for that reason. But he would be so distasteful to all but the regulation Republicans that I cannot but hope even his supporters will see it as you see. They are making great efforts to unite the New York press upon him. But New England is strong against him. . . .

May 25. — I to-day received from Judge Dickson my letter to him, which he sent to Curtis and which was as follows: —

> Columbus, 3 May, 1876.

My dear Judge, — Returning after a few days' absence at Fremont I find your letters of the 27th and 29th. You evidently understand the situation as well as any one who is writing or talking on the subject. You are unquestionably correct in assuming that your Eastern correspondent is not personally acquainted with me. Having thus far avoided all complications, committals direct or indirect, — having in short been a mere looker-on as you are, — I do not now expect to change my course, or to give assurances of any sort. Your conjectures or views, as given in the copy, show plainly enough that you understand me so well that for your satisfaction nothing from me is required. You speak of management by my friends securing results. I think I can see that part of it impartially. If anything depends on management I suspect my chances may be set down at zero. The best I can look for is that the march of events may be allowed to go along undisturbed by friendly management, either wise or otherwise.

In any event, your letters interest me and oblige me. I class you, as a political writer, with our best men. With good health, you would, if you had chosen that path, [have] ranked with George William Curtis and our other great political writers — (if there are others abreast of Mr. C.), but God disposes. — Sincerely,

R. B. HAYES.[1]

HON. W. M. DICKSON.

[1] The letters of Judge Dickson, bearing upon this correspondence, are so interesting and throw such vivid light on the current of contemporary political opinion, as well as on Mr. Hayes's character, that they are worthy of preservation in full: —

CINCINNATI, OHIO,
April 27th, 1876.

MY DEAR SIR, — I have for many years past had a friendly correspondence with a man of eminence of the East, a member-elect to the Cincinnati Convention, and one who will have as large an influence as any other member. You know, and I doubt not admire him. In writing to him recently I had occasion to speak of you and seem to have used the words "good and true."

To-day I received a letter from him in which he inquires: "You say that Hayes is good and true. But if Conkling and Cameron should throw their force for him would he have force enough not to be their man if elected ?"

I enclose herein a copy of my answer to the question. [The enclosure was: "I answer yes. If I understand him, he would not consciously nor unconsciously be any man's man. This is not his character. He is self-poised and self-reliant, unobtrusive, and repelling intrusion. His aim would be to deal fairly with each of the divisions of his party, giving due weight and patronage to each, and always in the disposition of patronage selecting the best men in each division. He would not fully meet the wishes of advanced reformers, but he would in this respect perhaps do as much as the country would bear. I think his chief excellence is in his intuitive perception of what at the moment is practicably attainable. He would immensely raise the standard of official qualification. All this I say from my knowledge of his general character and without any communication with him directly or indirectly."] The author did not expect his words would be seen by you — and in giving them to you (even anonymously) I do not know that I do right. But my motive is my excuse. I want you to see where your danger is and, for the good of my country, what you must avoid if you become President. This I have no doubt you would do anyhow, but no harm can come of my calling your attention to the matter.

But let this be for yourself alone. I explain my position. Of the candidates now before the public I prefer personally you. But I desire the success of the party above all else. There is force in the point that Bristow can carry the independent vote and thus the election. This has great weight with me; for it looks as if he would be forced aside by opposing elements. Then would come your opportunity. The danger then is that Morton or Conkling may win. You perhaps alone can prevent this, which, I think, would be fatal to the party. I wish you, therefore, to be strong with the Bristow and Blaine men. I think you will pardon my candor, and this intrusion.

I leave to your judgment whether you should answer me and shall not

That Mr. Hayes refused to become excited or anxious as the date of the convention drew near is shown by a letter to William Henry Smith, dated May 31. In this he wrote: —

I am growing more indifferent to the result as the time of the issue approaches. This makes it easy for me to keep myself clear of complications. You have noticed the Boston *Herald* talk of my preference for

misinterpret your silence. But I think you know me well enough to know that your answer would be used only as you wished. I go further: if you should deem it proper that it should reach my correspondent, it would be as safe with him as with you. He has not at all the power to dictate the nominee of the convention; but it is a question whether that nominee could be elected without his support. He is above all office-seeking. A political like a military campaign is a complex web. I expose to you one thread. — Truly yours,

W. M. DICKSON.

GENERAL R. B. HAYES.

CINCINNATI, OHIO,
April 29th, 1876.

MY DEAR SIR, — I write to make an explanation of one sentence in my letter of yesterday. I believe I wrote that you knew my correspondent. I do not know that you know him personally but you know him by reputation as you know Tilden or other public men. I say this because you may think if he knows you he ought not to have made that inquiry about you. I take it from his letter that his mind is turning towards you, regretfully it may be, from another; still, turning.

The situation seems to me to be thus. If the Republican party makes a nomination that will secure the coöperation of the independents, its success is assured and the country is safe for another four years. If they do not make this nomination and the Democracy improve the opportunity by the nomination of Tilden or even Davis, they will win. To be more concrete, if the Republican party nominates Morton or Conkling it will fail. If it nominates Bristow it will succeed.

Now I think the independents will turn favorably towards you, and if there is judicious management on the part of your friends they can be brought to you — Bristow failing. My mite I am contributing to that end.

Cut off forever by broken health from personal aspirations, I yet take an interest in public affairs. The situation has one advantage, I see things in a light uncolored by personal hope or fear. — Most truly yours,

W. M. DICKSON.

GENERAL R. B. HAYES.

CINCINNATI, OHIO,
May 19th, 1876.

MY DEAR SIR, — It is now proper for me to disclose to you my correspondent. I do it by sending to you his letter in reply to one from me inclosing to him your letter. Please return me his letter; he has returned to me your letter. Of course I advised him that you wrote me in ignorance of my correspondent.

The frankness on my part to which he refers, is that I advised him that I had written you that I inclined to Bristow as the man who would get most votes. I did it because I wished to be perfectly honest with you. My dear sir, I did this once before. Mr. Lincoln and I married cousins; he and his had spent weeks at

Blaine. The whole paragraph is a sheer fabrication. John Q. Smith, the supposed authority for the statement, writes me that he said nothing of the sort.

My correspondents all give the same flattering report — sinister news does n't reach me.

I am pleased to think that I am so untouched by this whole business. I say to the Ohio delegates that my name ought not to be thought of

my father-in-law's house; he had spent a week with me; we often corresponded. Yet when I wrote him that my obligations and situation made it my duty to support Chase first, Mr. Lincoln never forgave me, and soon after our relations ceased forever. I never saw him after he went to Washington except at a distance — never spoke to him again. I thought you were more magnanimous, and it has done no harm.

I think the Schurz meeting was Bristow's chance. That meeting makes it a point of honor with all regular "machine" Republicans, not to stultify themselves by acquiescing in the virtual charge that they are all rascals. The nomination of Bristow would seem to mean that. But it is useless to prophesy. Conkling does not seem as dangerous to us as to Curtis, but he may be. No doubt many of Morton's men would go to him.

But if you are to become President I shall have accomplished my purpose, as I wrote Curtis, if I shall have been the means of putting you and him thoroughly *en rapport*. I think him a great and good man. And now, if you become President, let me add, be President, in the sense of doing what you think is right, in appointing the best men to office — without a thought as to whom it hurts or as to its effects on the next election.

Without reference to yourself — is there danger of the nomination of Conkling? I do not think him a bad man; do think him a much better man than some of the Schurz meeting, but he is fatally unpopular and his nomination would be defeat. We must conciliate the independents, meaning thereby men within and without the party who seek reform. As things now stand Bristow does this best, you next best. The capacity of the Democrats to help us is simply prodigious. Witness the Ewing demonstration. What a great name Tom Sr. and Jr. have; yet on the great questions, the great crises, both have been uniformly wrong. Old Tom, alone of men, asked Lincoln to withdraw his Emancipation Proclamation.

But the son will hardly rule at St. Louis. Tilden, I think, will be the man. New York will say to the South, give us the man and we will furnish the money. But enough and more. — Most truly yours,

W. M. Dickson.

Avondale,
May 23rd, 1876.

My dear Sir, — At your request I return you herewith your letter of 3rd inst. It is a good letter and has done you no harm, whatever the future may have in store for you. It would be pleasant for me to keep it, but if you desire otherwise you need not return it.

I quite agree with you that the moral tone of our public life will not suffer in a comparison with the past, if you will make two exceptions. I think you must exclude the carpetbag representation of the South and Grant's pet appointees. These are indeed exceptional and, as I hope, soon to pass away. Excluding these

unless it will promote harmony and the prospect of success; that it should be withdrawn the moment the condition of things makes it, in their judgment, desirable.

And during all these weeks preceding the date fixed for the convention the increasing bitterness of rivalry among the leading candidates was more and more creating a situation in which the sober second thought of the party was coming to acknowledge the inadvisability of nominating any one of them, and bringing more men of discernment to see in Mr. Hayes the man most likely to profit by the factional differences. This situation was clearly perceived and admirably set forth in an editorial of May 9 in the independent New York *Sun* (Charles A. Dana) which declared: —

All the signs continue to point to the nomination of Governor Hayes of Ohio as the Republican candidate for President. Mr. Hayes became known throughout the country by his brilliant success in defeating

elements there has been great improvement in the moral character of our public men, even in our own time. Thirty years or less ago, public men were notoriously unchaste and almost professional gamblers, without loss of caste.

The public offices were filled with the relatives and retainers of public men as a *matter of course*. What Grant has done in this respect was then done with common approbation. In Kentucky the offices were filled with the relatives of Crittenden, and in Indiana by the relatives of the Brights. You know more about Ohio than I do. There were then no investigating committees, or, I doubt, not even Belknap's offense would have been exposed.

I remember as a little boy, the Government bought a site for a public building in New York for $160,000, — bought it of a brother of Jesse Bright, who had made a timely contract for its purchase for $80,000, [and] sold it to the Government for twice that and brought to Madison $80,000 in gold, a goodly sum in those days. I was a little boy when this occurred, and may be mistaken in the facts, but am not mistaken in this fact, that I heard the matter then greatly talked about and never heard one word of reproach to the Brights. It was thought to have been a smart thing and good for Madison.

I readily believe both Pendleton and Schenck when they express surprise that any one should think they had done wrong. Old Tom Corwin would have done what Schenck did in a moment. Nor did it ever occur to Pendleton that there was anything wrong in him turning his aristocratic social position to account. That has been his stock in trade for many years, and while toadies throng about him why not use it?

There is an evident determined office-holding movement to put in Conkling. Surely it can't win. Between that and the people's movement for Bristow is the tug of war. Can either win? And if not, who? You. But it is a lottery. Can you be composed? I could not. — Most truly yours,

W. M. DICKSON.

Hon. R. B. HAYES.

Governor Allen in the state election in Ohio last year. Previous to that time, but little had been heard of him outside of the State; but that event at once made him conspicuous and marked his name upon the list of candidates for President.

Greatly to his advantage, however, it did not render him so prominent as to excite those antagonisms and animosities which necessarily rise up against the foremost men on the stage of public life. . . . Each of the more celebrated aspirants, and their friends with them, would rather have him than either of their immediate rivals. He will be nominated, if such be his fate, as Lincoln was nominated in 1860, or Pierce in 1852, or Polk in 1844. He is that kind of a neutral man who is always taken when the powerful chiefs can only succeed in foiling each other.

Though he stands in this neutral and secondary position, Governor Hayes is far from being an inferior or unworthy character. He is a man of talent; he is a gentleman; he is rich and independent; he served with credit as a soldier in the war, and his record as Governor of Ohio is without flaw or spot; he would make a very fair President for ordinary times.

Those who intend to vote the Republican ticket under any circumstances may about as well make up their minds that Rutherford B. Hayes is the man who will receive their suffrages.

In his policy as Governor, Mr. Hayes did not allow the Presidential possibilities to interfere in any particular with the prompt performance of what he believed to be his duty. About the middle of April serious disorder occurred, as the result of a strike of coal miners, in Stark and Wayne Counties. Without a moment's hesitation, when it was apparent to the Governor that the local authorities were unable to cope with the situation, he issued a proclamation warning the rioters that he would, "to the extent of the powers vested in him, aid the civil authorities to protect laborers in their right to work and property-owners in the use and possession of their property, and would employ all lawful means to bring to justice whoever violates these sacred rights of citizens." No fear of the effect of his action, as the Chicago *Tribune* at the time remarked, on the labor-union votes could deter him, affording, as the same paper said, a "refreshing contrast to the gingerly course of the Pennsylvania authorities in dealing with their strikes." As the disorder continued after the issuance of the proclamation, Governor Hayes promptly ordered militia to the centres of disturbance, under command of Adjutant-General Wikoff, and retained them there until the leading rioters had been indicted and placed under arrest and normal conditions were restored. The Governor kept in close touch with General Wikoff, writing him at Masillon on May 8: —

DEAR GENERAL, — I still feel that there is doubt as to the sufficiency of your force. Be sure to have it ample. If you call out too many men, I will be responsible, but if you fail for want of enough, it will be your fault. It now looks as if this trouble would last a long time. I wish you to make preparations to hold your men in camp at and near Masillon until all danger of lawless violence is at an end; therefore let your arrangements be of a more permanent character; let it be understood that you mean to stay until lawlessness ceases, or is plainly controllable by the civil authorities. — Sincerely yours,

R. B. HAYES.

Further, he directed the attorney-general to assist the prosecuting attorney of Stark County in procuring the indictments against the rioters and likewise to appear at the trial and aid in prosecuting the cases with all severity. The result was that defiance and riotous violation of the law were soon brought to an end.

CHAPTER XXIV

NOMINATED FOR PRESIDENT

EARLY in the year the Republican National Committee decided on Cincinnati for the convention city. It was understood that this choice was due to the influence of the friends of Mr. Morton and of Mr. Bristow, as Cincinnati would be easy of access for enthusiastic supporters of each man from his home State, and the friends of neither at the time apparently regarded the candidacy of Mr. Hayes as a serious factor in the situation. But it was soon seen and admitted that whatever advantage there might be in the location of the convention would be most likely to accrue to Mr. Hayes.

During all the months preceding the date fixed for the convention, Mr. Hayes, as we have seen, remained practically aloof [1] from the preliminary contest. Without effort or influence on his part the Ohio state convention had unanimously declared for him; had instructed the delegates at large and requested the district delegates to work in his behalf. After this action he felt, as he wrote one of the delegates, that he should "reasonably expect the solid vote of Ohio" as long as there appeared to be any likelihood that the nomination might come to him. At the same time, as it was now settled that his name should be presented to the convention, he became interested in the organization of the delegates and in the choice of the man who should propose his name; but without the slightest desire to dictate to his friends or too insistently to express his preferences.

The date of the convention was fixed for June 14. Up to the very day of its assembling there was, as *Harper's Weekly*

---

[1] May 22, three weeks before the convention, the special correspondent of the New York *Herald* wrote: "I found Governor Hayes busy signing papers in his private office, and when I subsequently left him, it was with the conviction that for a Presidential candidate he was the most unconcerned one I ever met. . . . There was none of that nervous evasiveness about him in the presence of an interviewer peculiar to most candidates. He talked of the situation as unreservedly as if he had no more concern in it than the questioner, and this was very refreshing."

correctly stated, "universal agreement that the result was incalculable." By Saturday, June 10, most of the Ohio delegates and many other stanch friends of Mr. Hayes were on the ground. Mr. Hayes himself remained quietly at his post in Columbus. That evening he wrote in his diary: —

The members and others interested are assembling at Cincinnati preparatory for the convention. Up to this time, the course of the canvass, so far as I am concerned, has been agreeable. My friends have been quiet. Those of other candidates have generally treated me well. The Vice-Presidency seems to be conceded to me on all sides, or nearly so. I have seen evidences of a desire to give me the second place on the ticket from Conkling, Blaine, and Bristow men. Morton is so near to us that it would hardly do for his friends to suggest an Ohio candidate for Vice, and yet even they occasionally suggest. The balloting among the readers of the New York *Witness*, a Presbyterian paper of large circulation, puts me at the head of the poll for Vice-President. This is all flattering and gratifying. However, the thoughts of my friends are on the first place. My chances there are merely probabilities. Yet there are some encouraging facts. I seem to be the second choice of many of the leading supporters of other candidates — ex-Vice-President Hamlin of Maine, President White (A. D.) of New York, and others.

Members of the Ohio delegation to the number of twenty-five assembled Saturday afternoon for an informal conference. Governor Noyes, who acted as chairman, opened the meeting by declaring that the people of Ohio were for Hayes and that it was the duty of the delegation to stand by him until he was nominated. He then called on the delegates one after another for an expression of opinion. Without exception they declared their concurrence in Mr. Noyes's views. One or two men who were known to favor Blaine or Morton for second choice asserted that they would vote with the rest of the delegation "as long as there was a ghost of a chance." At the same time the delegates and friends of Mr. Hayes began in an earnest and discreet way to move about among the delegations from other States. Wherever they went they made friends and were careful to provoke no hostility.

On Monday the delegation held two meetings. On motion of Senator Wade, Governor Noyes was made permanent chairman.[1]

[1] As showing the spirit that animated Mr. Hayes's friends in their devotion to his interests, the following portion of a letter written to Mr. Hayes by Governor

With one exception the delegates all renewed their purpose of fealty to Mr. Hayes. The one recalcitrant read a speech expressing preference for Mr. Bristow, though ready to vote for Mr. Hayes on the first ballot. Subsequently in the day he regretted the haste with which he had spoken. Cheering reports were coming to the delegation from representative men of other States. While it was manifest that Mr. Blaine commanded the greatest single following, and his friends were boasting that he would be nominated on the first ballot, the Hayes men were confident that his strength was exaggerated, and that the bitter rivalry of the other leading candidates would prevent a sufficient accession of votes to crown his ambition. From New York leaders came the encouraging advice to the Ohio men by all means to keep their candidate in the field to the last. Moreover, it developed that Mr. Hayes was pretty generally the second choice of all factions, and that, in case of the nomination of any other man for first place, he would receive the second place without contest.

It is unnecessary here to recite the story of the convention in great detail. The convention was opened by Governor E. D. Morgan, long the Chairman of the Republican National Committee, with a speech emphasizing the importance of the duties to be performed. The three last conventions had been little else

Noyes on June 1 is significant: "Now, as to who shall present your name. I have been written to by various parties, and spoken to by two or three delegates, and have always said that your name should be presented by the person you might select. I shall neither feel slighted nor hurt if that person is Senator Wade or any other. Possibly it would be better for Mr. Wade to do it, as he is broadly known, has a national reputation, and, I am informed, is heartily for you. There are two men in the delegation, and very likely more, but two, at least, Eggleston and Bickham, who will not want me to do it. It is not worth the while to have any divisions, and my friends (who I think constitute a majority of the delegation) I will take care shall not feel offended. I have some reason to think that an effort has been made to create the impression that you preferred Mr. Wade for chairman. I do not think so, as I presume you care but little about it, and it is a matter really of little consequence. Of course the chairman, whoever he is, will present your name, and it would be seconded from some other State. I cannot and will not enter into any controversy about so small a matter, and unless the delegation should be nearly unanimous, I should not desire the position. If your wishes were known, that would probably determine the matter, but I appreciate the embarrassment such expression would occasion you. I shall be satisfied with anything, but am inclined to think it would be better, all things considered, to settle on Mr. Wade, who has age, experience, and reputation; and I have so said to several of the delegates and your friends."

than ratification meetings to confirm decrees already made by the people. But this year it was different. There was no man to whom the unerring finger pointed as the only candidate. But the man selected, whoever he should be, should be a man committed to the cause of economical administration and civil service reform, "not only by his expressed opinions, but also by his public life and conduct." Theodore M. Pomeroy, of New York, was made temporary chairman. He reviewed briefly the achievements of the Republican party, declaring its immediate duty to be "to establish on sure foundations and make secure for the coming ages the fruits of the war, debt, and taxation through which the present had been achieved." Thereupon the various committees were selected, and, while the committee on permanent organization was deliberating, the convention listened to the reading by George William Curtis of an address from the Republican Reform Club of New York, declaring emphatically for the resumption of specie payment and urging the necessity of civil service reform; and to speeches from various party leaders, including General Logan, Governor Hawley, Governor Noyes, and Frederick Douglass. On the report of the committee, Edward McPherson, of Pennsylvania, took the platform as permanent chairman, and the convention adjourned till the following morning.

The next day was devoted to the reception of and debate on the reports of the committees on credentials and platform, and to the speeches of nomination. The platform, reported by Governor Hawley, of Connecticut, contained seventeen planks. Of these the most important were those relating to the South, to the financial situation, and to the reform of the civil service. The first of these declared "it to be the solemn obligation of the legislative and executive departments of the Government to put into immediate and vigorous exercise all their constitutional powers for removing any just causes of discontent on the part of any class, and for securing to every American citizen complete liberty and exact equality in the exercise of all civic, political, and public rights." The second asserted: "Commercial prosperity, public morals, and national credit demand that the [promise for the redemption of the United States notes in coin] be fulfilled by a continuous and steady progress to specie payments." The third declared: "The invariable rule in appointments should have reference to the honesty, fidelity, and capacity of the appointees, giving to the party in power those places where harmony and vigor of administration require its policy to be represented, but permitting all others to be filled by persons selected with sole reference to the efficiency of the public service, and the right of all citizens to share in the honor of rendering faithful service to the country."

The minor planks promised prosecution of those who betrayed public trust; condemned the grant of public money to sectarian schools; approved of the tariff, "adjusted to promote the interests of American labor and advance the prosperity of the whole country"; opposed further land grants to corporations; urged the modification of treaties so as better to protect the rights of foreign-born citizens; recommended an investigation by Congress of the effect of Chinese immigration on the moral and material interests of the country; paid a meaningless compliment to the woman suffragists; demanded the suppression of polygamy in the Territories; insisted that the pledges to the soldiers be fulfilled; deprecated "all sectional feelings and tendencies"; denounced the Democratic party and Congress roundly for their recent performances; and spoke a good word for General Grant's Administration. The platform as a whole, neither in form nor in vigor of expression, could be considered a very impressive document.[1]

The platform having been adopted the way was open for the nomination of candidates on the call of the roll of the States. The candidates were named in the following order: Marshall Jewell, of Connecticut; Oliver P. Morton, of Indiana; Benjamin H. Bristow, of Kentucky; James G. Blaine, of Maine; Roscoe Conkling, of New York; Rutherford B. Hayes, of Ohio; and John F. Hartranft, of Pennsylvania. Mr. Jewell and Governor Hartranft were believed to be nominated principally for the

---

[1] An indication of contemporary Republican opinion of the platform is afforded in a letter to Mr. Hayes from Washington, June 22, by Charles Nordhoff, the well-known journalist: "Our platform is certainly thin and weak; and is so thought here by our own people. I wish it might happen that you would delay your letter of acceptance until after the St. Louis Convention, and then speak your mind freely on resumption, etc. But on such matters, which have necessarily a *political* side, I am not fit to advise."

purpose of holding the delegations of their States together in the early stages of the balloting and without any serious expectation or hope of their 'success. Mr. Morton's name was presented by Colonel R. W. Thompson, famous in the Middle West for his political oratory, in a brief but effective summary of Mr. Morton's achievements and qualifications. "He had been equal to every crisis during the darkest hours of our Rebellion; equal to every crisis since that darkness had been dispelled." The nomination was seconded by Governor P. B. S. Pinchback, a colored delegate from Louisiana. John M. Harlan, later and for many years a distinguished Justice of the Supreme Court, proposed the name of Mr. Bristow, as a man who, from his whole career and especially from his conduct of the Treasury Department, was best fitted to "combine with enthusiasm all elements of opposition to the Democratic party." General Harlan was followed in seconding speeches by Luke P. Poland, of Vermont, George William Curtis, of New York, and Richard H. Dana, of Massachusetts. Mr. Curtis spoke most eloquently and forcibly of all, commending General Bristow as the man of all others to lead in the work of reform essential to the perpetuation of the party and to the security of the country. Robert G. Ingersoll, of Illinois, named Mr. Blaine in a speech, which, for sheer eloquence and electrical effect on the audience, has probably never been surpassed in any national convention. Every sentence was calculated to rouse interest or to excite enthusiasm. In the speech occurred the phrase which ever afterward was associated with Mr. Blaine's name. "Like an armed warrior," he said, "like a plumed knight, James G. Blaine marched down the halls of the American Congress and threw his shining lance full and fair against the brazen foreheads of the defamers of his country and the maligners of his honor." Mr. Blaine's nomination was seconded by Henry M. Turner, of Georgia, a flowery colored orator. Stewart L. Woodford, of New York, alone spoke for Mr. Conkling, as the special champion of General Grant. New York, he declared, honored all the candidates already before the convention, "but," with evident allusion to Mr. Blaine, he said, "let us not nominate with our hearts but with our heads. This is not a time for the Republican party to endanger all the interests committed to its care in a moment of emotional insanity."

When the roll-call of the States proceeded and Ohio was reached, Edward F. Noyes took the platform and spoke as follows: —

Gentlemen, — On behalf of the forty-four delegates from Ohio, representing the entire Republican party of Ohio, I have the honor to present to this convention the name of a gentleman well known, and favorably known, throughout the country; one held in high respect, and much beloved, by the people of Ohio; a man who, during the dark and stormy days of the Rebellion, when those who are invincible in peace and invisible in battle were uttering brave words to cheer their neighbors on, himself, in the forefront of battle, followed his leaders and his flag until the authority of our Government was established from the Lakes to the Gulf, and from the river round to the sea. A man who has had the rare good fortune since the war was over to be twice elected to Congress from the district where he resided, and subsequently the rarer fortune of beating successively for the highest office in the gift of the people of Ohio, Allen G. Thurman, George H. Pendleton, and William Allen. He is a gentleman who has somehow fallen into the habit of defeating Democratic aspirants for the Presidency, and we in Ohio all have a notion that from long experience he will be able to do it again. In presenting the name of Governor Hayes, permit me to say we wage no war upon the distinguished gentlemen whose names have been mentioned here to-day. They have rendered great service to their country, which entitles them to our respect and to our gratitude. I have no word to utter against them. I only wish to say that General Hayes is the peer of these gentlemen in integrity, in character, in ability. They appear as equals in all the great qualities which fit men for the highest positions which the American people can give them. Governor Hayes is honest; he is brave; he is unpretending; he is wise, sagacious, a scholar, and a gentleman. Enjoying an independent fortune, the simplicity of his private life, his modesty of bearing, is a standing rebuke to the extravagance — the reckless extravagance — which leads to corruption in public and in private places.

Remember now, delegates to the convention, that a responsible duty rests upon you. You can be governed by no wild impulse. You can run no fearful risks in this campaign. You must, if you would succeed, nominate a candidate here who will not only carry the old, strong Republican States, but who will carry Indiana, Ohio, and New York, as well as other doubtful States. We care not who the man shall be, other than our own candidate. Whoever you nominate, men of the convention, shall receive our heartiest and most earnest efforts for their success. But we beg to submit that in Governor Hayes you have those qualities which are calculated best to compromise all difficulties, and to soften all antagonisms. He has no personal enemies. His private life is so pure that no man has ever dared to assail it. His public acts throughout all these years have been above suspicion, even. I ask you

then if, in the lack of these antagonisms and with all of these good qualities, living in a State which holds its election in October, — the result
of which will be decisive, it may be, of the Presidential campaign, — it
is not worth while to see to it that a candidate is nominated against
whom nothing can be said, and who is sure to succeed in the campaign.

In conclusion, permit me to say that, if the wisdom of this convention
shall decide at last that Governor Hayes's nomination is safest and is
best, that decision will meet with such responsive enthusiasm here in
Ohio as will insure Republican success at home, and which will be so far-
reaching and wide-spreading as to make success almost certain from the
Atlantic to the Pacific.

Mr. Hayes's nomination was seconded by Senator Wade in a
short and incisive speech. He declared him to be "well known
by all the Republicans of Ohio and respected by all the Democracy of Ohio"; "a gentleman about whom nothing can be said
to his discredit." A delegate from Missouri and a delegate from
West Virginia also spoke in his favor. The nomination of Mr.
Hayes was received by the convention with much applause;
not so much, to be sure, as had been given to Mr. Morton, Mr.
Bristow, and Mr. Blaine. It was evident to all observers that the
galleries were filled most numerously with Bristow and Blaine
men. But the friends of Mr. Hayes were enough in number and
enthusiasm to make an impression of his popularity.

It was already nearly dark when the nominating speeches
were brought to a conclusion by Mr. Bartholomew, of Pennsylvania, presenting the name of Governor Hartranft. An adjournment was therefore made until the following morning, much to
the chagrin of Mr. Blaine's supporters, but to the satisfaction of
the followers of all the other candidates, who felt somewhat apprehensive lest, under the immediate spell of Colonel Ingersoll's
fervid periods, the convention might be "stampeded" for Mr.
Blaine. A night of reflection, they thought, would clear the
atmosphere of that danger.

At a little before eleven o'clock the next morning the balloting
began. The first ballot showed Mr. Blaine far in the lead, though
not so far as his more sanguine friends had confidently predicted
he would be. Out of the 756 votes of the convention, he received
285, from 36 different States and Territories; Mr. Morton was
second, with 125 votes from 13 States and Territories; Mr.
Bristow third, with 113 votes from 19 States and Territories; Mr.

RUTHERFORD B. HAYES, 1876

When Candidate for President

Conkling fourth, with 99 votes from 10 States — 69 of them from New York; Mr. Hayes fifth, with 61 votes from 9 States. Mr. Hartranft received only the 58 votes of his own State; Mr. Jewell 10 of the 12 votes of Connecticut and 1 from Alabama; and Mr. Wheeler, whose name had not been placed in nomination, 3 votes from Massachusetts. Mr. Jewell's name was now withdrawn and the votes of Connecticut were distributed among the other candidates, most of them going to Bristow.

As soon as the result of the ballot was declared, a second ballot was ordered. While it was proceeding, on the announcement by the chairman of the Pennsylvania delegation of 58 votes for Hartranft, 4 delegates from Pennsylvania appealed to the chair, protesting that the announcement was not correct; that they desired to be counted as voting for Mr. Blaine, but that under the unit rule adopted by the delegation their votes were being cast for them against their will. The chair ruled that every delegate, regardless of any caucus action of his delegation, had the right to vote as he wished and to have his vote so recorded; and he directed that the vote from Pennsylvania be set down as 54 for Hartranft and 4 for Blaine. An appeal was taken from this decision of the chair and an acrimonious dispute arose over the question of a state convention's right or the right of a caucus to bind the individual members of a delegation. At last the chairman declared that the entire controversy was out of order while the roll-call of the States was in progress, and the roll-call was resumed. On its conclusion the debate on the question was renewed and continued with much vigor and heat for some time. Finally the question, "Shall the ruling of the chair," as above stated, be sustained, was put. The chair was sustained by a vote of 395 to 353. The convention at Chicago, four years later, followed this precedent and took similar action. And thus was settled for all time, so far as Republican conventions go, that every delegate is an absolutely free man, at liberty to vote his own individual convictions and preferences, unbound by instructions, uncontrolled by caucus dictation, except in so far as he chooses to acquiesce therein. He comes into a convention to do what in his judgment the needs of the occasion demand; and no party authority or discipline can be invoked to determine his action against his will.

The second ballot showed many small changes of votes, but resulted in a net gain to Mr. Blaine of 11 votes, making his total 296; Morton had 120; Bristow, 114; Conkling, 93; Hayes, 64 (a gain of 3); and Hartranft, 63. On the third ballot Blaine's vote fell to 293; Bristow and Morton changed places, the former receiving 121 votes, the latter, 113; Conkling dropped to 90; Hartranft advanced to fifth place with 68 votes; and Hayes again gained 3 votes. On the fourth ballot Blaine lost 1 vote, Conkling lost 6, Hartranft gained 3, and Hayes gained 1, his total now being 68. On the fifth ballot Blaine lost 6 votes, making his total 282; Bristow fell back to 114; Morton to 95; Conkling to 82; and Hartranft to 69. The others' losses went to Hayes, who now appeared as third in the contest with a total of 104 votes. The sixth ballot placed Hayes in second position. The figures were: Blaine, 308; Hayes, 113; Bristow, 111; Morton, 85; Conkling, 81; Hartranft, 50.[1]

The seventh ballot was decisive. The pronounced increase of Mr. Hayes's vote on the fifth ballot marked the beginning of the drift to his standard. Michigan cast its solid vote (22) for him,[2] having given him only 5 votes before, and North Carolina gave him 12 of her 20. On the sixth ballot North Carolina gave 12 votes to Blaine and only 1 to Hayes; and Blaine's decided gain of 36 votes — the first gain he had made since the second ballot — and the effort of Mr. Blaine's partisans to give this gain factitious

---

[1] William A. Wheeler, of New York, was voted for on each of the ballots except the last, receiving three votes on the first and two on every other. Elihu B. Washburne, of Illinois, was voted for on every ballot except the first and the last, receiving three votes on the second; one on the third; three on the fourth and fifth; and five on the sixth ballot.

[2] William A. Howard, chairman of the Michigan delegation, in announcing the vote rose on his crutches and said: "There is a man in this section of the country who has beaten in succession three Democratic candidates for President in his own State, and we want to give him a chance to beat another Democratic candidate for the Presidency in the broader field of the United States. Michigan, therefore, casts her twenty-two votes for Rutherford B. Hayes, of Ohio." This was the signal for a wild uproar. "Anything like the scene that followed," wrote the correspondent of the London *Times*, "I had never, I think, witnessed. . . . The Michigan vote being at once recognized as the first anti-Blaine blow, set more than half the delegates themselves into a state of the most frantic commotion, and the *claqueurs* (most of them Bristow partisans) being more ready to yell for the 'coming man' than for their falling favorite, the uproar was something 'terrific.' Three long salvos of applause were given before order could be restored."

importance by cheering, which failed, however, to be taken up very strongly by the galleries, brought the leaders of the opponents of Mr. Blaine to hurried consultations. It was evident, when the seventh ballot began, that the crisis was at hand. The first States called showed less scattering of their votes. Alabama, which on the previous ballot had given Blaine 15, Bristow 4, and Hayes 1, now gave Blaine 17 and Bristow 3; Arkansas, which had given Blaine 1 and Morton 11, now just reversed its vote; California, which had given Blaine 6, Conkling 2, and Hayes 4, now divided its vote equally between Blaine and Hayes; Colorado, Connecticut, and Delaware voted as before; Florida was now solid for Blaine, instead of dividing equally between him and Morton; Georgia now gave Blaine 17 and Hayes 7, whereas before Blaine had 9 and Hayes none, the other votes going to Conkling, Morton, and Bristow; Illinois gave Blaine 2 more votes and Hayes 1 less, making its vote, Blaine 35, Bristow 5, and Hayes 2.

Then, when Indiana was called, the clear purpose of the forces allied against Blaine was made apparent to the dullest apprehension. The chairman of the Indiana delegation, Will M. Cumback, announced the withdrawal of Mr. Morton's name from further consideration and declared the vote of Indiana, which up to that time had been given solidly for Morton, as 25 for Hayes and 5 for Bristow.[1] Iowa and Kansas followed, voting solidly for Blaine. Then, speaking for Kentucky, Mr. Harlan withdrew the name of Mr. Bristow and gave the State's 24 votes to Hayes. Indiana then sought to give the 5 votes it had cast for Mr. Bristow to Hayes, but under the rules of the convention this was declared out of order. Louisiana divided now, 14 for Blaine and 2 for Hayes, whereas before it had given the former only 6, the latter none. Maine and Maryland were solid for Blaine as before; Massachusetts, 5 for Blaine and 21 for Hayes, an increase for the latter of 2 votes; Michigan again solid for Hayes; Minnesota again gave Blaine 9, but cast its other vote for the first time for Hayes; Mississippi was now solid for Hayes, though before it had

[1] The London *Times* correspondent wrote: "I must leave to the imagination of your readers here and hereafter — to the end of the chapter — the scene which followed, lest time and my vocabulary should both fail me. They have only to picture from four to five thousand persons, one moment seated in solemn silence to hear a vote given, the next jumping, yelling, stamping, waving arms and hats as if suddenly stricken with raving madness, and the thing is done."

given him only 4 of its 16 votes; Missouri now gave Blaine 20 and Hayes 10, a gain for the former of 2, for the latter of 8; Nebraska was again solid for Blaine, but Nevada was solid for Hayes, having before given him only 1 vote; New Hampshire again gave Blaine 7, but transferred its other 3 votes from Bristow to Hayes; New Jersey voted as before, Blaine 12, Hayes 6.

And now came New York. What would the Empire State do? No one could believe that many of Mr. Conkling's friends would turn to his bitter enemy — not even if his success was certain. And the vote justified this belief. Of the 70 votes of the great Commonwealth Mr. Hayes received 61, Mr. Blaine only 9. North Carolina followed, now casting its full vote for Hayes as, of course, did Ohio. Then came Oregon true, as from the start, to Blaine. And the Blaine men still were pinning large hopes on Pennsylvania. If its 58 votes went in a body to Blaine, he might still win the prize that seemed to be slipping from his grasp. But hope fled when Don Cameron, speaking for the great State, withdrew Governor Hartranft's name and declared the vote. The delegates divided almost equally, giving Blaine 30 and Hayes 28. The roll was quickly completed, Blaine receiving a total from the remaining States and Territories of 66 votes, as compared with 70 votes on the sixth ballot, and Hayes obtaining 76 votes, as against 21 before. On the announcement of the result of the ballot, — Hayes, 384; Blaine, 351; Bristow, 21, — Mr. Frye, of Maine, seconded a motion to make Mr. Hayes's nomination unanimous and the vote was given with loud acclaim.

The ticket was thereupon promptly completed by the nomination for Vice-President of William A. Wheeler, of New York. Mr. Wheeler had long been one of the trusted and influential leaders of his party, not only in his own State, but in its national councils. In his service in Congress he had gained an enviable reputation for sturdiness of character and for conservative views of public questions.[1] Like Mr. Hayes he was of Vermont family and antecedents.

Thus the disciplined and highly organized cohorts of "the

[1] Mr. Wheeler had attracted nation-wide attention and commendation in 1875 by the practical good sense and wise statesmanship displayed by him in formulating the plan, which became known as the "Wheeler Compromise," for settling the distressing political disputes, tantamount almost to civil war, existing in Louisiana.

Plumed Knight" had been routed by the combined forces [1] of the allies, who had accepted as their leader a tried and tested man, to be sure, but a man who had relied not at all on organization to win position; a man who had displayed no eager desire for exaltation; a man who had remained, apparently unconcerned, at his post of duty, serenely awaiting the decree of Fate; a man, however, whose career and character, coupled with the chance of his location, were such as to justify wise party leaders in their confidence that his selection would most easily and most surely allay factional feeling, and bring all elements of the party strength into harmonious relation and stir them to aggressive activity. The stars in their courses were fighting for him!

Already sufficient time has elapsed to render calm judgment possible. Whoever will consider the condition of national politics

[1] William Henry Smith, who was present and active at the convention, wrote Mr. Hayes, June 21, in praise of the high skill and zeal displayed by the leader of the Ohio delegation and other Ohio men. He adds: "But it was of first importance to have such a leader as Edward F. Noyes. Better management I never saw. It was able, judicious, untiring, unselfish, inspiring, adroit. If there was a mistake made I did not discover it. The disloyalty attempted on the part of one or two well-known Ohioans in the interest of Blaine was anticipated and cleverly disarmed. The general seemingly never slept. His eyes were everywhere and discipline was preserved with as much vigor as on the field of battle. He comprehended fully the situation and inspired the confidence of the men of New England, New York, Kentucky, and Indiana. His personal friendship for Generals Bristow and Harlan did not, as some mischief-makers asserted would be the case, lessen his loyalty to you, but served an important purpose at a critical moment. If I had more time I could give you a perfect history of General Noyes's management, and I must let these few words suffice at present — and after all what more could I say? — his conduct was that of a noble, chivalrous, honorable gentleman."

Edwin Cowles, editor of the Cleveland *Leader*, wrote Mr. Hayes after the convention (June 27): "The Ohio delegation did nobly. We all formed ourselves into a mutual admiration society as soon as you were nominated. But to be candid, I felt almost conscience-smitten at my having apparently gone back on Blaine, after having announced to him three years ago in his library that I was going to trot him out for the Presidency and fight for him to the bitter end. But then I am reassured when I bear in mind that he agreed with me that I should vote for you as long as there was a chance for you, and then after that chance disappeared, to vote for him. He is a noble fellow and the best abused man in America. I know you would not blame me for feeling as I do toward that man when it is considered what my personal relations were with him, that I was among the first to propose that he should run for the Presidency long before I had the pleasure of making your acquaintance; consequently *my heart* was for him, but *my head* was for you. My duty to the great cause, to the Republican party, and my belief in your popularity and fitness for the office of President was what governed me at the convention."

at that period, in a judicial spirit, disabusing his mind of personal
predilections or antipathies; whoever will justly appraise the
characters and qualities of the chief aspirants for the nomination,
not forgetting the affiliations by which they were known, or the
antagonisms they had roused, or the doubts about their integrity or political wisdom that had penetrated the public mind,
can hardly fail to reach the conviction that in the choice of Mr.
Hayes the convention came to the wisest conclusion possible —
wisest on the score of party expediency and wisest for the future
welfare and harmony of the country.[1] Especially will this be the
case if one will regard the facts in the light of subsequent history.

The morning of that eventful day at Cincinnati Mr. Hayes at
Columbus wrote in his diary: —

This is the third day of the convention at Cincinnati. My friends
were there a week ago to-night. One whole week of convention work.
At the adjournment last night all was ready to begin the balloting. At
ten this morning the decisive balloting begins. Early in the struggle
my friends were very hopeful. But on the 13th, Blaine became decidedly the prominent man — his prospects deemed almost a certainty.
There has been a gradual change on the 14th and 15th, and now it seems
something more than a possibility that he will fail. If he fails my
chance as a compromise candidate seems to be better than that of any
other candidate. So we are now in suspense. I have kept cool and unconcerned to a degree that surprises me. The same may be said of Lucy.
I feel that defeat will be a great relief — a setting free from bondage.
The great responsibility overpowers me. That is too strong. It sobers
me. It is a weight, but not overpowering. I shall try to do in all things,
more than ever before, if nominated, precisely the thing that is right —
to be natural, discreet, wise, moderate, and as firm in the right as it is
possible for me to be. And in this spirit I await the event.

In that spirit he did await the event. While the balloting was
proceeding at Cincinnati he remained in his office at Columbus
all day, quietly viewing the situation and receiving callers, apparently as unconcerned as any man in the room. Not till the result

[1] Senator Sherman, writing to Mr. Hayes, June 19, to congratulate him, said:
"With me the process seemed like demonstration — your nomination being the
inevitable sequence of facts that forbade the nomination of certain prominent
candidates and pointed to your nomination. The gallant fight made by Blaine
excited the greatest enthusiasm and for a few days seemed to make his nomination certain. But the prudent hesitation of a majority of the delegates secured
what long ago seemed to me to be the logic of events, and now there is a general
and hearty acquiescence in the simple truth that the nominations made are the
wisest and best that could be made."

of the sixth ballot was announced did he betray marked interest. That, he thought, was a clear indication that Mr. Blaine would be nominated on the next ballot. When a bulletin of the final ballot was received, he exhibited no signs of nervousness. He was, indeed, as a man present at the time afterward said, "the only perfectly cool and composed person present." His first thought was that there might be an error in the report and he asked to see the figures. But presently a dispatch came which settled all doubt; and then people, irrespective of party affiliations, began to throng the room with enthusiastic congratulations. He could only express his thanks for the good will that was manifested.[1]

The next day after the nomination the committee designated by the convention, headed by Mr. McPherson, visited Columbus and gave Mr. Hayes formal notification of the convention's action. Mr. McPherson, speaking for the committee, said: —

Governor Hayes, — We have been deputed by the national convention of the Republican party, holden at Cincinnati on the 14th of the present month, to inform you officially that you have been unanimously nominated by that convention for the office of President of the United States. The manner in which that action was taken, and the response to it from every portion of the country, attest the strength of the popular confidence in you and the belief that your administration will be wise, courageous, and just. We say, sir, your administration, for we believe that the people will confirm the action of the convention, and thus save the country from the control of the men and the operation of the principles and policy of the Democratic party. We have also been directed to ask your attention to the summary of Republican doctrine contained in the platform adopted by the convention. In discharging this agreeable duty we find cause of congratulation in the harmonious action of the convention; and in the hearty response given by the people we see the promise of assured success. Ohio, we know, trusts and honors you. Henceforth you belong to the whole country.

[1] Writing in his diary April 28, 1878, on the return of himself and Mrs. Hayes from a four days' visit to Philadelphia, when they were the recipients of marked attentions, Mr. Hayes said: "Perhaps most notable was the reception given to Lucy at the Academy of Fine Arts, Friday evening. . . . I this morning asked Lucy how she felt as the central figure of such a fairy scene. 'Oh,' said she, 'humble. I always feel humble on such occasions. I enjoy them very much, but am humbled by them.' This reminds me of my feeling at the great moment of my life, when I heard I was nominated at Cincinnati. I felt a sense of responsibility — a sobered feeling. It was my feeling that with soundness of judgment, with a cheerful and elastic temper, with firmness, with an honest purpose to do right, and with some experience in affairs, I could do well in the place."

Under circumstances so auspicious, we trust you will indicate your acceptance of the nomination.

To these words Mr. Hayes replied: —

Gentlemen, — I have only to say in response to your information that I accept the nomination. Perhaps at the present time it would be improper for me to say more than this, although even now I should be glad to give some expression to the profound sense of gratitude I feel for the confidence reposed in me by yourselves and those for whom you act. At a future time I shall take occasion to present my acceptance in writing, with my views upon the platform.

Mr. Hayes's comment in his diary on his nomination is characteristically brief and modest. Sunday, June 18, he writes: —

I have had no time to write since my nomination on the seventh ballot about 4 P.M. on the 16th, Friday. Friday has been a lucky day for me before! My deepest emotions were on receiving Blaine's dispatch of congratulation. It for a few moments quite unmanned me. And then Shoemaker's dispatch, wishing that Uncle Birchard was alive.

And five days later this: —

The nomination has been well received. The best people, many of them heretofore dissatisfied with the Republican party, are especially hearty in my support. I must make it my constant effort to deserve this confidence.

Mr. Hayes's brief statement correctly summarized the tone of public expression, at any rate, of Republican papers and of the more intelligent members of the Republican party, as well as of a decided majority of the independent leaders, regarding the nomination. This is clearly shown by reference to the files of newspapers of the day and by examination of the innumerable letters and dispatches of congratulation and friendly advice that thronged in upon the candidate. At the same time the Democratic papers of greatest perspicacity and sobriety of judgment were prompt to recognize the political strength of the Cincinnati ticket.

Mr. Hayes during this period, despite the adulation and deference now shown him, bore himself with the same modesty and poise that had characterized him throughout the months preceding the convention.[1] He had been summoned by his party to the

---

[1] The impression made by Mr. Hayes's demeanor on visitors in the days succeeding the nomination is indicated by the dispatches sent to various papers by

greatest position it could give; he would devote all the strength he possessed, without pose or pretense, to the conscientious fulfilment of the new duties placed upon him; neither overwhelmed by their magnitude nor elevated in conceit by any new sense of his own greatness.

A week after his nomination Mr. Hayes visited his home at Fremont, when the citizens of the place, without regard to party affiliations, gave him a welcoming reception which deeply touched his heart. The city was decorated and illuminated and large delegations of citizens came from the neighboring cities and towns to share in doing honor to the candidate. In reply to the address of congratulation Mr. Hayes said: —

Mr. Mayor, Fellow Citizens, Friends, and Neighbors, — I need not attempt to express the emotions I feel at the reception which the people of Fremont and this county have given me to-night. Under any circumstances, an assemblage of this sort at my home to welcome me would touch me, would excite the warmest emotions of gratitude; but what gives to this its distinctive character is the fact that those who are prominent in welcoming me home, I know, in the past, have not voted with me or for me, and they do not intend in the future to vote with me or for me. It is simply that, coming to my home, they rejoice that Ohio, that Sandusky County, that the town of Fremont, has received at that national convention high honor; and I thank you, Democrats, fellow citizens, independents, and Republicans, for this spontaneous and enthusiastic reception.

I trust that in the course of events the time will never come that you will have cause to regret what you do to-night. It is a very great responsibility that has been placed upon me — to be a representative of a party embracing twenty millions of people — a responsibility which I know I am not equal to. I understand very well that it was not by reason of ability or talents that I was chosen. But that which does rejoice me is that here, where I have been known from my childhood, there are those that come and rejoice at the result. . . .

Forty-two years ago my uncle, Sardis Birchard, brought me to this place, and I rejoice, my friends, in the good taste and good feeling which have placed his portrait here to-night. He, having adopted me, brought me to Fremont. I recollect well the appearance of the then

special correspondents who flocked to Columbus. Among many statements of similar purport, the following from the correspondent of the New York *Herald* may be cited: "He makes a good impression upon visitors of every class, taking quite easily the very prevalent assumption that he is for the moment public property, yet not especially making any virtue of his freedom in this respect; indeed, it is not perceptible that the fact of his nomination has even rippled the surface of his public life, or changed in any respect the even tenor of his way."

Lower Sandusky, consisting of a few wooden buildings scattered along the river, with little paint on them, and these trees none of them grown, the old fort still having some of its earthworks remaining, so that it could be easily traced. A pleasant village this was for a boy to enjoy himself in. There was the fishing on the river, shooting water-fowls above the dam, at the islands, and the lake. Perhaps no boy ever enjoyed his departure from home better than I did when I first came to Fremont.

But now see what this town is — how it has grown. It has not increased to a first-class city, but it has become a pleasant home; so pleasant, so thriving, that I rejoice to think that whatever may be the result next fall it will be pleasant to return to it when the contest is over. If defeated, I shall return to you oftener than if I go to the White House. If I go there I shall look forward with pleasure to the time when I shall be permitted to return to you, to be a neighbor with you again. And really we have cause to be satisfied with our home and the interests which the future has in store for us here. Larger cities always have strife and rivalry, from which we are free; and yet we are well situated between two commercial centres, the Eastern and Western, between which is the great highway of the world, and we cannot but partake of their prosperity. Over the railroad passing through this place, or near it, will pass for all time to come the travel and trade of New York and San Francisco, of London and Pekin. . . . Those of our friends who travel in Europe return sometimes dissatisfied, because there is a rawness in this country not seen in England and the older countries of Europe. But then the greatest happiness, as all of us know, in preparing a garden or a home is to see the improvements growing up under our hands. This is what we enjoy; and the change in Fremont from the time I first knew it till to-day gives me very great pleasure.

There is another change which gives rise to mournful reflections. When I came here in the year 1834, I became acquainted with honored citizens who are no longer living. . . . Of all those I remember seeing on that first visit, not one is with us to-night. All who came with me, my uncle, my mother, and my sister, are gone. But this is the order of Providence. Events follow upon one another as wave follows wave upon the ocean. It is for each man to do what he can to make others happy. This is the prayer and this is the duty of life. Let us, my friends, in every position, undertake to perform this duty.

For one, I have no reliance except that which Abraham Lincoln had when, on leaving Springfield, he said to his friends: "I go to Washington to assume a responsibility greater that that which has been devolved upon any one since the first President, and I beg you, my friends and neighbors, to pray that I may have that Divine assistance, without which I cannot succeed, and with which I cannot fail." In that spirit I ask you to deal with me. If it shall be the will of the people that this nomination shall be ratified, I know I shall have your good wishes and your prayers. If, on the other hand, it shall be the will of the people that another shall assume these great responsibilities, let us see to it that we who shall oppose him give him a fair trial.

My friends, I thank you for the interest you have taken in this reception, and that you have laid aside partisan feeling. There has been too much bitterness on such occasions in our land. Let us see to it that abuse and vituperation of the candidate that shall be named at St. Louis do not proceed from our lips. Let us, in this centennial year, as we enter upon this second century of our existence, set an example of what a free and intelligent people can do. There is gathered at Philadelphia an assemblage representing nearly all the nations of the world, with their arts and manufactures. We have invited competition, and they have come to compete with us, and with each other. We find that America stands well with the works of the world, as there exhibited. Let us show, in electing a Chief Magistrate of the nation — the officer that is to be the first of forty or forty-five millions — let us show all those who visit us, how the American people can conduct themselves through a canvass of this kind. If it shall be in the spirit in which we have met to-night, if it shall be that justness and fairness shall be in all the discussions, it will commend free institutions to the world in a way which they have never been commended before. . . .

About the middle of the war, General Sherman lost a boy, named after himself, aged about thirteen years. He supposed that he belonged to the Thirteenth Infantry, and when they went out to drill and dress parade, he dressed in the dress of a sergeant and marched with them. But he sickened and died. The regiment gathered about him, for he was to them a comrade — dear as the child is loved by men who are torn away from the associations of home. General Sherman, the great soldier, was touched by it. He said it would be idle for him to try to express the gratitude which he felt; but he said they held the key to the affections of himself and family, and if any of them should ever be in need, if they would mention that they belonged to the Thirteenth Infantry at the time his boy died, they would divide with him the last blanket and last morsel of food. It is in this spirit that I wish to express my thanks to the people of Fremont for the welcome they have given me. I bid you, my friends, good-night.

The first subject to engross Mr. Hayes's attention after his nomination was the preparation of his formal letter of acceptance, and to this in the next three weeks he gave profound thought and deliberation. The amount of advice showered upon him in personal letters and by the public prints in this connection can hardly be overestimated. The mails were so burdened that had he undertaken carefully to read, much less to ponder, all the suggestions that were given him, he would have had neither time nor strength for any other consideration. But valuable as much of the advice was, Mr. Hayes was not greatly in need of it, and it is doubtful whether either his views or his manner of expressing them was much, if at all, affected thereby.[1] He had strong and clear convictions on the issues of the day that he believed to be of paramount importance, and he knew how to set these views forth in a simple and cogent manner which had the unmistakable ring of settled judgment and complete sincerity. The letter of acceptance was as follows: —

COLUMBUS, OHIO, July 8, 1876.

GENTLEMEN, — In reply to your official communication of June 17, by which I am informed of my nomination for the office of President of the United States by the Republican National Convention at Cincinnati, I accept the nomination with gratitude, hoping that, under Providence, I shall be able, if elected, to execute the duties of the high office as a trust for the benefit of all the people.

I do not deem it necessary to enter upon any extended examination of the declaration of principles made by the convention. The resolutions are in accord with my views, and I heartily concur in the principles they announce. In several of the resolutions, however, questions are considered which are of such importance that I deem it proper to briefly express my convictions in regard to them.

The fifth resolution adopted by the convention is of paramount interest. More than forty years ago a system of making appointments to office grew up, based upon the maxim, "To the victors belong the spoils." The old rule, the true rule, that honesty, capacity, and fidelity constitute the only real qualification for office, and that there is no other claim, gave place to the idea that party services were to be chiefly considered. All parties in practice have adopted this system. It has been essentially modified since its first introduction. It has not, however, been improved. At first the President, either directly or through the heads of departments, made all the appointments, but gradually the appointing power, in many cases, passed into the control of members of Congress. The offices in these cases have become not merely rewards for party services, but rewards for services to party leaders. This system destroys the independence of the separate departments of the Government. It tends directly to extravagance and official incapacity. It is a temptation to dishonesty; it hinders and impairs that careful supervision and strict accountability by which alone faithful and efficient

[1] Writing to Carl Schurz, June 27, about his letter he had said: "One other suggestion let me now submit to you. I really think that a President could do more good in one term if untrammelled by the belief that he was fixing things for his election to a second term, than with the best intentions could be done in two terms with his power embarrassed by that suspicion, or temptation during his first four years. Our platform says nothing on the subject. I am averse to adding topics; but could I not properly avow my own view and purpose on this head?"

public service can be secured; it obstructs the prompt removal and sure punishment of the unworthy; in every way it degrades the civil service and the character of the Government. It is felt, I am confident, by a large majority of the members of Congress to be an intolerable burden and an unwarrantable hindrance to the proper discharge of their legitimate duties. It ought to be abolished. The reform should be thorough, radical, and complete. We should return to the principles and practice of the founders of the Government — supplying by legislation, when needed, that which was formerly the established custom. They neither expected nor desired from the public officers any partisan service. They meant that public officers should give their whole service to the Government and to the people. They meant that the officer should be secure in his tenure as long as his personal character remained untarnished and the performance of his duties satisfactory. If elected, I shall conduct the administration of the Government upon these principles, and all constitutional powers vested in the Executive will be employed to establish this reform. The declaration of principles by the Cincinnati convention makes no announcement in favor of a single Presidential term. I do not assume to add to that declaration; but believing that the restoration of the civil service to the system established by Washington and followed by the early Presidents can be best accomplished by an Executive who is under no temptation to use the patronage of his office to promote his own reëlection, I desire to perform what I regard as a duty in now stating my inflexible purpose, if elected, not to be a candidate for election to a second term.

On the currency question I have frequently expressed my views in public, and I stand by my record on this subject. I regard all the laws of the United States relating to the payment of the public indebtedness, the legal-tender notes included, as constituting a pledge and moral obligation of the Government, which must in good faith be kept. It is my conviction that the feeling of uncertainty inseparable from an irredeemable paper currency, with its fluctuations of value, is one of the great obstacles to a revival of confidence and business, and to a return of prosperity. That uncertainty can be ended in but one way — the resumption of specie payments. But the longer the instability of our money system is permitted to continue, the greater will be the injury inflicted upon our economical interests and all classes of society. If elected, I shall approve every appropriate measure to accomplish the desired end; and shall oppose any step backward.

The resolution with respect to the public-school system is one which should receive the hearty support of the American people. Agitation upon this subject is to be apprehended, until, by constitutional amendment, the schools are placed beyond all danger of sectarian control or interference. The Republican party is pledged to secure such an amendment.

The resolution of the convention on the subject of the permanent pacification of the country, and the complete protection of all its citizens in the free enjoyment of all their constitutional rights, is timely and of great importance. The condition of the Southern States attracts the attention and commands the sympathy of the people of the whole Union. In their progressive recovery from the effects of the war, their first necessity is an intelligent and honest administration of government which will protect all classes of citizens in their political and private rights. What the South most needs is peace, and peace depends upon the supremacy of the law. There can be no enduring peace if the constitutional rights of any portion of the people are habitually disregarded. A division of political parties resting merely upon sectional lines is always unfortunate and may be disastrous. The welfare of the South, alike with that of every other part of this country, depends upon the attractions it can offer to labor and immigration, and to capital. But laborers will not go and capital will not be ventured where the Constitution and the laws are set at defiance, and distraction, apprehension, and alarm take the place of peace-loving and law-abiding social life. All parts of the Constitution are sacred and must be sacredly observed — the parts that are new no less than the parts that are old. The moral and material prosperity of the Southern States can be most effectually advanced by a hearty and generous recognition of the rights of all, by all — a recognition without reserve or exception. With such a recognition fully accorded it will be practicable to promote, by the influence of all legitimate agencies of the general Government, the efforts of the people of those States to obtain for themselves the blessings of honest and capable local government. If elected, I shall consider it not only my duty, but it will be my ardent desire, to labor for the attainment of this end.

Let me assure my countrymen of the Southern States that if I shall be charged with the duty of organizing an administration, it will be one which will regard and cherish their truest interests — the interests of the white and of the colored people both, and equally; and which will put forth its best efforts in behalf of a civil policy which will wipe out forever the distinction between North and South in our common country.

With a civil service organized upon a system which will secure purity, experience, efficiency, and economy, a strict regard for the public welfare solely in appointments, and the speedy, thorough, and unsparing prosecution and punishment of all public officers who betray official trusts; with a sound currency; with education unsectarian and free to all; with simplicity and frugality in public and private affairs; and with a fraternal spirit of harmony pervading the people of all sections and classes, we may reasonably hope that the second century of our existence as a nation will, by the blessing of God, be preëminent as an era of good feeling and a period of progress, prosperity, and happiness.

Very respectfully, your fellow citizen,

R. B. HAYES.

To THE HONS. EDWARD McPHERSON, WM. A. HOWARD, JOS. H. RAINEY, AND OTHERS, *Committee of the National Republican Convention.*

In form, in temper, in appropriateness of phrasing, and in perspicacity and directness, this letter might well be taken as a model for documents of its sort. With unerring insight Mr. Hayes placed the stress on the three subjects which more than all others were uppermost in men's minds and which more than all others were of immediate and pressing importance. First in his estimation — at least he gave it the prominence of first consideration — was the subject of civil service reform, the need of which had been brought home to men's thoughts with increasing force by reason of the manifold abuses and betrayals of faith of the last few months. It would be difficult for the most skilful writer or reformer to set forth the evils of the spoils system in so few words as Mr. Hayes used with equal comprehensiveness and force. And those who knew or chose to inform themselves of Mr. Hayes's conduct as Governor were aware that the ideas and purposes which Mr. Hayes so admirably set forth in words were reënforced and emphasized by the practice of his official life. As a corollary to his pronouncement of his views on the subject of the pressing need of reform in the civil service was Mr. Hayes's announcement of his "inflexible purpose" not to seek or to accept a second nomination in case he should be elected. The platform, to be sure, had nothing to say in favor of a single Presidential term, and he would not venture to add to what it said. To one who read between the lines, however, it was apparent from his form of expression that he himself believed that a single Presidential term would give added strength and independence to the executive authority, and that its establishment in our system of government was something to be desired. It is a subject on which we shall hear more from him in the years to come. For the present it was enough for him to give as a sufficient reason for his personal determination his belief that the civil service could most easily be restored to its ancient sensible status by an Executive who was under no temptation to use the patronage to promote his own reëlection. This declaration was crowning proof of the sincerity of his purpose in the furtherance of reform.[1]

[1] The civil service reformers were more than pleased with Mr. Hayes's words. Richard H. Dana, Jr., wrote from Boston August 10: "On the point of civil service reform you have done the best service that has been done yet. You have done what our platform failed to do, and our politicians here failed to say in

Secondly, he gave added force and vigor to the not entirely satisfactory platform declaration in regard to the resumption of specie payments. The platform failed to declare in set terms in favor of the Resumption Act already on the statute-books, making only the vague declaration above set out. Debate arose in the convention over this plank, an amendment to the platform committee's report having been proposed. But the convention was too timid, it would appear, to declare itself except in general terms of righteous purpose, and so refused to change or to add to the committee's resolution. Mr. Hayes in his letter left no doubt that he would adhere to the views he had already expressed on this subject. His campaign for the governorship the previous year had been fought on the hard-money basis. He had declared already: "Certainly I am not in favor of the repeal of the Resumption Act, unless something is substituted that will more effectually bring about specie payments as soon as the time prescribed in that act."[1] That declaration was virtually implied in his letter by his assertion: "I stand by my record on this subject," and by his unqualified pledge: "If elected, I shall approve every appropriate measure to accomplish the desired end, and shall oppose any step backward." The country was left in no ambiguity as to his position and purposes. The letter could not be interpreted in one way in a hard-money constituency and in another way in a community where heretical monetary doctrines were popular. In Mr. Hayes's opinion, as he had written to General Garfield in March, the Republican party could better afford to be beaten in the fight for sound money than to back out.

In regard to the Southern problem Mr. Hayes wrote without passion or acrimony; pointing out the need of complete peace, complete supremacy of the law, and the protection of the rights of all citizens as prerequisites to the moral and material prosperity of the South as well as to the general welfare of the country. And he assured the South if he came to the headship of the country that his best efforts would be directed to the end of wiping

terms, — either from not having thought deep enough or from lack of civic courage, — you have said what you mean by civil service reform. You have put your finger on the spot where the disease lies, and stated what is to be done. I regard all generalities about good men in office, faithful performance of their official duties, etc., as cant which any one may sing."

[1] Columbus correspondence of Cincinnati *Commercial*, May 8, 1876.

out all distinction between North and South. To appreciate the full force of this part of Mr. Hayes's letter, one needs to revive one's memory of the rancor of feeling and expression in relation to all Southern topics which was at that time the prevailing characteristic of most Republican newspaper discussion in the North. This had been deepened by the foolish violence and virulence which in the late session of Congress had marked many of the speeches of the "Rebel brigadiers" who were asserting their dominance of the House of Representatives. It required large political foresight and moral courage of a high order for the Republican candidate for the Presidency in 1876 to approach the Southern question calmly and discuss it in a judicial and optimistic spirit.

The letter made a most favorable impression upon the country. It gave the people of other States than Ohio, which knew him well, material for measuring the quality of the man who had been preferred by the Republican Convention to the more prominent leaders of the party. The better papers of the country, whatever their political preferences, recognized its force and its sincerity, acknowledging that the candidate had added strength and definiteness to the unsatisfactory platform declaration regarding the resumption of specie payments; that he had spoken boldly and to the point on the reform of the civil service; and that his treatment of the Southern question transcended partisan expression and revealed the patriot and statesman. The independent press was particularly pleased with the letter and was prepared now to accept the Republican candidate, not only without misgiving, but with large satisfaction. The only discordant notes were from men who were themselves wavering in their monetary views or who were apprehensive that the manly outspokenness of Mr. Hayes on resumption would deter Republican voters weak in the faith; and from the "practical politicians," who were inclined to regard the possibility of civil service reform, in the famous phrase of Governor Allen, as a "d——d barren ideality."[1] The prevailing opinion of the letter of

---

[1] The immediate impression of the letter in Washington is reflected in a letter from that city to Mr. Hayes, July 10, from Charles Nordhoff, who wrote: "1. The letter is an eminent success. The best men in Congress speak the most highly of it, as honest, frank, square, and in every way strong and satisfactory. 2. As

sober-thinking Republicans, was that expressed by the New York *Times*, at that time the ablest exponent, of the daily press, of Republican doctrines. It said: —

It is the manly, frank, and explicit declaration of a sincere and able man. It is not the letter of a partisan, a trimmer, an aspirant for office who wishes to avoid criticism by evading an expression of his views and purposes, or, in any sense, the letter of a negative man. General Hayes professes nothing, conceals nothing, shuns nothing for the purpose of winning support or propitiating possible opponents. Such as he is he paints himself, and without any pretensions to sincerity, stamps every word with the cogent emphasis of simple and unreserved honesty. There is no more trace of double-dealing than of timidity in what he says. He would not deny that he desires an election with the earnestness which an honorable ambition kindles in every man conscious of capacity for public service; but the election must come to him from a constituency which is neither uninformed nor misinformed concerning the principles he holds and the general objects he would, if elected, pursue. Modestly but fully he lays these before his fellow citizens, and leaves with them the duty of choice, which cannot, so far as he is concerned, be a blind one.[1]

Meanwhile the Democratic National Convention had met at St. Louis, June 28, and nominated Samuel J. Tilden, of New York, and Thomas A. Hendricks, of Indiana, for President and Vice-President. It adopted a prolix and highly rhetorical

you probably supposed, there is an undercurrent of dissatisfaction among the 'machine' men about the civil service paragraphs. Logan says it's d——d stuff; Morton, words to the same effect; Allison thought it a little impracticable; and so on. *Per contra*, Charles Foster, Pierce (Mass.), and a great lot of others — the bone and sinew of the party in the House — are in the greatest delight about that part. 3. The Democrats generally thought the whole letter very shrewd and adroitly calculated to capture everybody. That is the sum [of] opinions as I gathered them for you to-day. It is a success. Eminently so."

[1] George William Curtis in *Harper's Weekly* (July 29, 1876) said: "[The letter] is thoroughly satisfactory. Clear, sagacious, and courageous, no one can read it without the conviction that it is the word of a man who fully comprehends the political situation, and whose sympathies and purposes are those of all patriotic citizens. It is not the utterance of a dextrous politician, intended to mean all things to all men. It is the declaration of an honest and experienced public man with no embarrassing record. It appeals to the general intelligence and patriotism of the country. . . . If any voter has felt that he did not know the Republican candidate, he will feel so no longer. His character and career are the earnest that his letter says only what he thinks and means."

W. D. Howells wrote, July 13: "I can't forbear telling you how much I like your letter of acceptance. It's the manliest thing done in politics since the Declaration, on which it's an improvement in some respects."

platform, written, as it was understood, by Mr. Manton Marble, a brilliant journalist of New York, in consultation with Mr. Tilden. The platform [1] in its "vast wash of words," as George William Curtis characterized it, arraigned the Republican party and the Grant Administration in perfervid phrase for all the crimes in the political category, and in strident periods demanded reform in all the ways of government, "measures and men." It devoted several paragraphs to the financial problem, full of glittering generalities and nebulous promises, embedded in which, however, was the single specific demand for the repeal of the Resumption Act — the one measure which fixed a definite time in the near future for resumption and provided ample authority for its execution. It spoke in eloquent sentences in favor of a thorough reform of the civil service system; but the neglect of any Democrats in any State where they were in power to show any practical interest in this reform and the recent performance of the Democratic majority in the House of Representatives in dismissing all Republican employees of the House, however efficient or however humble their station, and replacing them with Democrats, could not fail to make men doubt the sincerity of the platform's eloquence.

Mr. Tilden's letter of acceptance was dated July 31. It followed the manner of the platform in length, in fervor of rhetoric,

[1] Mr. Blaine's analysis of the platform is fairly accurate: " It was marked by the language of an indictment, and contained the extended argument of a stump speech. Its one pervading thought, emphasized in resonant phrase, iterating and reiterating, 'that reform was necessary,' was an additional proof of its origin. But with all its effusiveness of expression, it lacked definiteness in the enunciation of principles. Only two or three propositions upon pending issues were explicitly set forth. It accepted the constitutional amendments; denounced 'the present tariff levied upon nearly four thousand articles as a masterpiece of injustice, inequality, and false pretense'; demanded that 'all custom-house taxation should be only for revenue'; and then addressed itself to a somewhat vituperative arraignment of the Republican party." (*Twenty Years in Congress*, chap. xxv.)

But writing to Mr. Hayes soon after the St. Louis convention (July 6), Joseph Medill, the able editor of the Republican Chicago *Tribune*, said: "Tilden, in writing his platform, — for I assume it is his composition in the main, — has seized upon the omission in the Republican platform in respect to reform, retrenchment, official purification, etc., to produce a striking contrast between the platforms; and he has immensely strengthened his party and his chances thereby, and generally reconciled the 'soft shells' to his hard-money notions because of his loud reform proclamation. He has also furnished them texts on which to preach innumerable sermons during the campaign."

and, on the financial situation, in vagueness of utterance. He was quite as sure, however, as the platform that the Resumption Act was a "hindrance" "to the speedy resumption of specie payments" and should be repealed, to give way to "a judicious system of preparation" for resumption without naming a precise day for its consummation. It was manifest that, hard-money man as he was, he was striving with all the resources of his adroit political skill so to express himself and so to defend the financial plank of the platform as not to offend the financial heretics of the West and the South whose prejudices had been deferred to in draughting the platform and in placing Mr. Hendricks on the ticket.

July 8 Mr. Hayes wrote in his diary: —

The nomination of Tilden makes doubtful the States of New York, New Jersey, and Connecticut.

I have prepared a bold and honest letter of acceptance. It will offend some and cool the ardor of others; but it is sound, and I believe will be strong with the people. At any rate, it is the true course.

Our adversaries reckon on a *united South*. This is their hope. We must meet them on this.

They are under the same leadership which for fifteen years has been on the wrong side of every question.

CHAPTER XXV

THE PRESIDENTIAL CAMPAIGN OF 1876

IT is not necessary to describe the campaign that followed with great particularity. The Democratic party managers were bold and aggressive, ably counselled throughout the campaign by the shrewdness and political acumen of their sagacious candidate.[1] The recent administration of public affairs, the whole mass of phenomena succinctly characterized as "Butlerism" and "Grantism," offered abundant opportunities for criticism and attack. The slogan of the Democrats was "Tilden and Reform," and the drift toward the Democrats on the part of independent voters, disgusted with the scandals brought to light in the government service and dissatisfied with the tameness of the Cincinnati platform, was too evident to be ignored. This drift was measurably checked by the vigor and straightforwardness of Mr. Hayes's letter on the essential issues pressing for settlement, reënforced as his utterance was by widening public knowledge of his sincerity and strength of character. The Democrats were more hopeful, more confident of success than in any Presidential contest since that of 1856. The Republicans were much demoralized and less buoyant in spirit; for the first time in a national campaign they found themselves rather on the defensive than steadily leading the attack. Try as they might, they could not escape the consciousness that the issue of the present conflict was clouded with grave uncertainty.

[1] Mr. Wheeler wrote Mr. Hayes, July 1: "I am afraid some of our friends are underrating the strength of Tilden. He is a wonderful organizer and manipulator, has large wealth and is utterly unscrupulous in its use." — During the campaign, Mr. Tilden spent much of his time at his home in New York City, so as to be in close touch with the Democratic managers, giving them the benefit of his large knowledge and experience of political organization and campaign methods. His course, which at that time was thought not to be in keeping with proper aspiration for the highest office in the land, subjected him to much criticism. Ex-President Woolsey, of Yale University, in a public address at New Haven, gave voice to the widely felt judgment when he said: "I feel that Mr. Tilden has sought the office with uncommon anxiety. I don't remember of any President who seems to me to have pursued his object, so far as I can understand, with greater assiduity, greater ability, and determination than he has shown."

Mr. Hayes himself took no active part in the campaign, though he was kept informed of its progress by frequent communications from the secretary of the National Committee and from other leaders closely connected with the Republican organization or active in the campaign.[1] There was, of course, a constant stream of visitors at his office, newspaper editors and correspondents, prominent politicians from all parts of the country, and men from various walks of life, who called to pay their respects or to volunteer advice. All these brought information or indulged in speculation and surmise. Furthermore, Mr. Hayes was the recipient of innumerable letters [2] from far and near, not only from acquaintances and men that stood for something in the party councils, but also from strangers of high and low degree, eager to express approval or criticism, to give intelligence, or to make suggestion. To many of these letters he replied, but usually with utmost brevity. It was still thought not quite dignified for a candidate for the Presidency to appear upon the campaign hustings. What he had to say was understood to be expressed in his letter of acceptance and in the record of his past achievements. Neither had it become the custom, which was established a few years later, for frequent delegations of citizens from places near or remote to visit the home of the candidate to do him honor and to draw from him some expression on the topics of the campaign. With the exception of two brief visits to the Centennial Exposition at Philadelphia, one shortly after his nomination, the other in October, on "Ohio Day," and then in his capacity as Governor, not as candidate, Mr. Hayes remained in Ohio, and for the most part in his office at Columbus, throughout the period from the date of his nomination until after the election.[3]

---

[1] Between him and the chairman of the National Committee no letters at all passed.

[2] Among his correspondents were George William Curtis, Carl Schurz, E. D. Morgan, William Henry Smith, J. A. Garfield, John Sherman, Oliver P. Morton, Murat Halstead, and hosts of other prominent Republicans.

[3] "During all the campaign his conduct has been that of a quiet, self-respecting gentleman. He is Governor of the State of Ohio, and his official residence is at Columbus. There he has remained, with the exception of the time given to two official visits to Philadelphia, tranquilly engaged in the discharge of his duties. His 'canvass' and the management of its details have been in the hands of his friends. As he did not intrigue and plan for the nomination, so he was content to await the event of the election with the same dignity and self-respect. In

Zachariah Chandler, long a Senator from Michigan, but at that time Secretary of the Interior, was selected as chairman by the Republican National Committee. Doubtless a much wiser selection could have been made. Mr. Hayes would have preferred his friend General Noyes; [1] but his wishes were not consulted. The majority of the committee belonged to the old régime. There was no question of Mr. Chandler's ability and sagacity as a political manager; but he had long been identified with the little group of "Grant Senators" of whom the country was weary; and now being a member of President Grant's Cabinet, he laid himself and the party organization open to the criticism of being too much under the control or influence of the Administration, whose faults were largely responsible for the critical plight of the party.[2]

all this the contrast between the two candidates has been extraordinary. . . . He [Mr. Hayes] has been a true representative of the good old cause; pure, honorable, sagacious, self-respecting, and self-restrained; a true type of the best American citizen — an American gentleman without fear and without reproach." (George William Curtis, in *Harper's Weekly*, November, 1876.)

[1] "When I found that both Cornell and Chandler (Zach) wanted the chairmanship of the National Committee, I did not deem it best for Hayes that I should be a candidate, though Hayes wanted me to have it. I did not make known Hayes's wish to the committee, but told all who approached me that it was not best in any way I should have it." (From letter of Edward F. Noyes, July 13, to William Henry Smith.)

Wilson J. Vance, Washington correspondent of the Cincinnati *Commercial*, writing from Washington, July 11, to Mr. Halstead, said: "The selection of a man who was not identified so entirely and completely with Grant and Grantism as Chandler is, would have been a reassuring circumstance to a great many liberal voters, who were puzzled to know precisely how much of a party man Governor Hayes is. But the administration influence was all cast for Chandler, as was also the entire Blaine strength. The Hayes men, in the restricted sense of the term, were completely overslaughed and had no sort of a show for their white alley. The question whether they are to be kept under, during all of the approaching campaign, or not, is one of considerable importance. 'The Hayes men, in the restricted sense of the term,' comprise the original Hayes men, the Bristow men, a few of the Morton men, and fewer of the Conkling men — in brief, the real reform element of the party."

[2] Carl Schurz, in a letter to Mr. Hayes, July 15, voiced the reform sentiment regarding Mr. Chandler's headship of the committee: "But one of the worst things done yet is the election of Secretary Chandler to the chairmanship of the National Committee. It is in the highest degree improper on principle that a man who wields the patronage and influence of one of the departments of the Government, should also be the manager of a party in a campaign, and it seems utterly impossible that a member of General Grant's Administration, who is universally known as a strenuous advocate of the same vicious civil service system which your letter condemns and proposes to abolish, should be the manager of a campaign in which the reform of the civil service is one of the principal issues.

Moreover, Mr. Chandler's official duties made such demands on his time and strength that he could not give to the direction of the campaign the undivided attention which a survey of the political conditions of the country should have convinced all the members of the committee was more than ever desirable that year. The country would assuredly have been more favorably impressed with the genuineness or efficiency of the reform spirit, which brought about the nomination of Mr. Hayes and which permeated his letter of acceptance, if a man not conspicuously associated with the prevailing order of things had been placed at the head of the campaign work. While certain men recognized and admitted the purity of Mr. Hayes's intentions and the wholesome quality of his purposes, they found the firmest ground for opposition in doubt whether he would be able to resist the influences that had controlled the Grant Administration and brought it into popular disrepute.[1] But the mass of progressive Republican leaders, the majority of those who had been influential in the Liberal Republican movement of four years before, — men like George William Curtis and Carl Schurz, — abating no whit of their condemnation of the abuses and corruptions which had scandalized Republican rule in recent years, still believed and urged that there was vastly greater hope for genuine administrative reform with a sincere man like Mr. Hayes in the White House, backed by the powerful forces of reform within the Republican party with which he was affiliated and to which he owed his elevation, than with a trimmer and politician, however able, like Mr. Tilden, supported and sustained by a party

Several Republican papers, seeing the absolute incongruity of this arrangement, have already taken up the matter and are urging Chandler to decline the appointment. This, I suppose, he will not heed, unless some extraordinary influence be brought to bear upon him. What that influence should be, I confess I do not know. I feel that it would be a delicate matter for you to interfere directly; but something should be done or the management of the campaign will be the most glaring satire on civil service reform imaginable."

[1] Charles Nordhoff, the distinguished journalist, wrote Mr. Hayes, October 15, from his home near New York: "What is most often, and very frequently expressed to me, who am known to be friendly to you, is a fear that, granting your good intentions, you may in fact, if elected, be a mere prisoner in the hands of the men who are now carrying things with so high a hand; that the Chandlers, Mortons, Logans, and Butlers will justly say that they showed their hand clearly, and you were elected on a coercion and revolutionary policy, to which the country committed itself."

eager for the spoils of office and unsympathetic with reform — a party which for long years had been in the wrong on the great fundamental questions of nationality. Moreover, what prospect of sound financial legislation, of an early return to specie payments, could there be from a party which demanded the repeal of the Resumption Act and which was overwhelmingly affected by the cheap-money fallacy? It was on the basis of these considerations principally, the peril of entrusting the National Government to the men that had sought to destroy it and to their Northern sympathizers — the men that had questioned and criticized and condemned all the measures made necessary by the Rebellion for the preservation and rehabilitation of the nation, the fear that Democratic success would further postpone efforts for administrative reform, and dread of reckless cheap-money agitation and legislation, that the appeal was made to the more intelligent and conservative voters to continue the Republican party in power.

Of course, as is invariably the case in American politics, the personal qualities, characteristics, and careers of the rival candidates, as well as the record of their public achievements, were exploited and discussed by the press and the campaign speakers, with much partisan exaggeration, hasty inference, uncharitable conclusions, and at times reckless disregard of truth. Lieutenant-Governor Dorsheimer, an intimate friend and adviser of Mr. Tilden, was authority for the statement that the Democratic National Committee employed men to search the life and record of Mr. Hayes — in the hope, no doubt, of discovering some act or expression or course of conduct which might be turned to his discredit. But Mr. Dorsheimer acknowledged that the search was fruitless. Numerous tales, to be sure, derogatory to his personal integrity found their way into print; numerous distortions or perversions of his public acts were set forth under screaming headlines by the Democratic newspapers; but in all cases these publications proved less than a nine days' wonder when the absurd falsity of the one sort was demonstrated, or a plain and straightforward statement of the facts in the other sort was presented. As one paper at the time happily said, all the efforts of partisan and press to find something in Mr. Hayes's career to smirch his character had resulted in showing that the only mud that had ever clung to Hayes's garments was that which he had gained in plunging under fire through the morass at Winchester, leading his command to glorious victory.

After the publication of newspaper articles charging Mr. Tilden with persistent evasion of the full payment of the national income tax, men were sent to Fremont to scrutinize the tax records of Sandusky County.[1] As a result of this scrutiny a sensational article appeared in Democratic papers, with plentiful use of headlines and italics, which sought to show that Mr. Hayes in his tax return had omitted taxable credits, aggregating several thousand dollars, and that he had grossly undervalued horses and carriages and other possessions, and even failed altogether to include a piano! Here at last was a complete answer to the Republican criticism of Mr. Tilden for his income-tax dereliction. But a rigid examination and analysis of the facts, with knowledge of the Ohio tax law, quickly revealed, first, that no taxable credits had been omitted; second, that at the time the tax return was made Mr. Hayes did not own a piano; and third, on the testimony of his friends and neighbors (some of whom were Democrats, indignant at unfair campaign methods) who were competent from personal knowledge to express a judgment, that far from undervaluing horses and vehicles, etc., Mr. Hayes had actually given them a value in excess of what they could be sold for.[2] So this wonderful "answer" to the allegations touching the income-tax record of Mr. Tilden fell to the ground.

---

[1] Search was also made of Mr. Hayes's income-tax returns, his income in the period of the tax being only his official salary. Mr. Hayes comments in his diary, September 14, as follows: "As an offset to what is said of Governor Tilden's income returns, mine have been examined. It appears that in 1868 and 1869 I made none at all. No doubt all I made are substantially accurate. If none were made in the two years named, it was because my attention was not called to the matter — a mere oversight. My taxable income in those years did not exceed $1500 or $2500. If no return can be found and no payments [were] made, there is due from me the tax on that amount, and it will be paid. If no returns were made in the two years 1868 and 1869, it was because no returns were called for. I had left Cincinnati December, 1867, and had my domicile at Columbus — my permanent residence still remaining at Cincinnati."

[2] "The truth is my property returns were full, honest, and if in error at all as to values, they were placed above the actual cash values. My extravagancies, if I have any, run to books, and to trees, flowers, and other improvements of my place. I had nothing in the way of furniture, horses, or equipages that were more than barely decent. But it is easy to talk of expensive horses, carriages, etc., etc.

Two or three baseless stories were revived or started charging Mr. Hayes with having retained for his own use money that fell into his hands while in the military service. One story was to the effect that a private of the Twenty-third Regiment, named Leroy, just before the battle of Winchester had given General Hayes eight hundred or one thousand dollars for safe keeping, to be sent to his mother in case he fell. Leroy was killed in the battle. In 1869 Mr. Hayes, while making his second canvass for Governor, received letters from Leroy's father, living then in Wisconsin, making the charge above stated, and demanding the money. Mr. Hayes wrote the man at once that there was absolutely no basis in fact for his claim; that he was either himself deceived or was seeking blackmail. At the same time Mr. Hayes had the official records examined and obtained information from comrades of young Leroy. All this showed that the soldier could not possibly have had any such sum of money at the time, — indeed, that he owed money, — and that whatever was due him at the time of his death in bounty and back pay had been duly paid to his mother. Again in the campaign of 1875, Leroy, the father, sought to blackmail Mr. Hayes. His efforts having failed, he now peddled his vile story to the Chicago *Times*, which gave it large space and prominence. But the Chicago *Tribune* at once published the real facts and added much information about the blackmailer himself. He was a characterless pettifogger, who many years before the war had abandoned his wife and family in Ohio and had left a trail of lies and debt and dishonor wherever he had lived in Illinois and Wisconsin.

A somewhat similar story was started in West Virginia — that the money in the possession of a deserter and spy who was tried

As to wealth, my property is almost entirely real estate. The rest, bank and other stocks, taxed in the name of the corporation. You may feel safe that in all this there is no damaging *fact*. And whenever the truth can be known, as it is at my home, there will be nothing in it to relieve the case against Tilden, whatever that may be. . . . I do not wish to weary you with this. But it concerns my character for common honesty in ordinary life, and I confess that I am interested more in that than in that which touches my prospects of political advancement. . . . Let me assure you that my stakes as set in the letter will stand. If elected you can trust me to adhere to the text. No political, no partisan duty (if such things can be called duties) — at any rate, no partisan or personal service shall be required, or allowed to be required, of public officers." (From letter of Mr. Hayes to Carl Schurz, September 6, 1876.)

by drumhead court-martial and shot [1] was turned over to General Hayes and never accounted for. The fact was that the money which had come to the scamp as bounty was never in General Hayes's hands, but was used to obtain another recruit for the Twenty-third Regiment.

These campaign slanders gave Mr. Hayes little concern, though he was somewhat annoyed by the last, as it impugned his integrity as an officer and a gentleman. He refreshed his memory of the court-martial and attendant circumstances by correspondence with other officers who were present and knew the facts and prepared a statement of the case in the form of an interview, which, however, was never given to the press. He preferred personally to avoid making any public statement or explanation, whatever the papers might print.[2]

Persistent effort was made, late in the campaign, to inflame the foreign vote against Mr. Hayes by charging that he was

[1] "The case was a remarkable one on account of the coincidences which led him to his fate. In the fall of 1863 he came in Rebel uniform into the Union lines in the Kanawha Valley, claiming to be a Union man who had been forced into the Rebel army. Subsequently he enlisted in Company D, Twenty-third Ohio. Soon after he became sick and was in hospital a month or two. Next he deserted, taking with him arms and equipment with watches and pistols that he stole from his comrades. Afterward, May 9, 1864, he was taken prisoner, with arms in his hands, fighting in the Rebel ranks at Cloyd Mountain, was recognized by Twenty-third men who were detailed to guard prisoners, and finding he was discovered managed to escape in the night. In August afterwards a squad of recruits and drafted men and substitutes was brought to the Twenty-third Regiment from Ohio while the regiment was camped at Monocacy Junction, August 5, 1864. Among them this Rebel deserter, Union deserter, and spy and bounty-jumper was discovered. The facts were reported to General Crook's headquarters. His adjutant-general, Captain J. L. Bottsford, ordered a drumhead court-martial to meet immediately. . . . The man was tried, found guilty, and sentenced to be shot. He confessed that after his escape in June, 1864, he went down the Kanawha to Ohio and became a bounty-jumper; that he had received a number of times bounties from localities and perhaps individuals and had deserted; was prevented from doing it on this occasion by the recent order which required that recruits should be receipted for at their regiments before payment of bounties; that he had money, about four hundred dollars, received for bounties he had jumped, and two watches. . . . After the trial, members of the court-martial, on talking it over, concluded, as the bounty money of the Rebel spy and deserter was received . . . to furnish a soldier for the Twenty-third Regiment, that it ought to be used to get another recruit for the same regiment. . . . I have always supposed that this was accordingly done with the money." (Diary, August 19, 1876.)

[2] "I have not wished to make any denials of any falsehood over my own signature — to leave my friends to deal with all such affairs." (Diary, August 19.)

committed to the principles of the American Alliance, an organization, as it appeared, which favored the restriction of the right of suffrage to native-born citizens. This charge had a colorable basis, sufficient for the partisan press on which to erect a vast fabric of accusation and demagogic appeal, but one that quickly crumbled when subjected to the acid test of plain common sense. It seemed that at a meeting of the Grand Council of the Alliance, held at Philadelphia July 4, resolutions were adopted, opposing Roman Catholic influence in politics, commending the public-school system, urging friendlier relations between North and South, favoring a sound currency and a speedy return to specie payments, and endorsing the nomination of Messrs. Hayes and Wheeler. The resolutions contained not one syllable reflecting on foreign-born citizens or implying opposition to their possession of the franchise. A copy of these resolutions reached Governor Hayes's office in the mass of mail that was daily received. It came under the eye of Mr. Hayes's private secretary and was acknowledged by him in a letter which was hardly more than perfunctorily polite — precisely as innumerable other communications were acknowledged. Doubtless if the secretary, Mr. Alfred E. Lee, had known exactly what the foundation principles of the American Alliance were, or had been more astute, he would have referred this particular set of resolutions to Mr. Hayes before writing his letter. But the resolutions contained nothing to which any sound-money Republican could object, and Mr. Lee made the usual polite but noncommittal acknowledgment.

The Republican managers were somewhat apprehensive of what effect the Democratic use of this episode might have. But Mr. Hayes was not disturbed. To William Henry Smith, under date of October 5, he wrote: —

Touching Lee's letter to the secretary of the American Alliance I write these observations: —

1. It was written without my knowledge before or after. I never heard of it until now. Lee had a general authority to reply to letters of congratulation and tenders of support — "suitable acknowledgments" merely.

2. I see nothing damaging, specially, in the letter if we don't write it into importance. It approves and endorses nothing.

3. The resolutions it replies to in acknowledging are eight in number, adopted at Philadelphia July 4 and 5, and are all such as

Republican foreigners, not Catholics, approve. You have seen the resolutions.

4. The whole affair is to put us on the defensive and will fail if we are not led off by it. Three of our most intelligent Germans speaking of it (Cincinnati Germans) say it will not hurt a particle; that Republican Germans do not mind such roorbacks, etc., etc.

5. The drift of the canvass is plain. The people *do dread* a victory for the united South. They see in it continued trouble — nullification of the Amendments, Rebel claims and schemes, etc., etc., etc., — and I think anything which withdraws attention from this issue to merely personal matters is a mistake. The school issue, the civil service issue, the currency issue, etc., are all in point and good, but merely personal issues may well be dropped with a few words of denunciation.

We see encouragement here and it increases daily.

While Mr. Hayes at the time this letter was written saw signs of encouragement and was hopeful of the result, yet during the canvass he had many hours of misgiving and doubt. At no time was he oversanguine. Long before the nomination, as it will be recalled, he had thought that the chances of Republican success were precarious; and he was too keen and dispassionate an observer of the course of political events, too susceptible to the currents of public opinion, to be carried away by the unreasoning confidence of enthusiastic partisans or the undoubting hopefulness of stalwart supporters. He was too experienced in feeling the force and direction of public opinion, of estimating the strength and quality of appeals to the popular sentiment and prejudice, to fail to realize the weaknesses of the Republican situation or to underestimate the attractiveness of the large but vague promises of bettered conditions which the Democrats so insistently and stridently proclaimed. He was not surprised, therefore, to hear from Senator Morton in the middle of August that things political in Indiana boded ill for the Republican party. In his diary, August 13, he records: —

Last night with Attorney-General John Little I met Senator Morton at Bradford Junction, on his request, to talk over the political situation. We rode together to this place [Columbus] . . . and reached here at 12.45 A.M. after an interview of three hours. Governor Morton regards the situation as grave; that if Indiana is Democratic in October our chance is not one in ten of success in the country in November; that if we carry Indiana in October, our chances of carrying the country in November are forty-nine in fifty; in short, that we lose the Presidency in November if we lose Indiana in October. He thought it his duty to state to me the condition and prospects — that we ought to face it. He detailed the figures of elections in Indiana since 1860. He showed the closeness of the State. Also referred to the Greenback party — its organization, growing strength, and the fact that it drew four fifths of its voters from our side. I said: "And now the remedy." He, after some further talk, said: "*Money and speakers.* Money to pay men to travel and organize — to print and circulate documents," etc., etc. To my question, how much is needed to do the work required to carry the State, he replied one thousand dollars to a county will do it, or ninety-four [two] counties, one hundred thousand dollars. I asked how much is generally used. He replied: "Four years ago we had from outside of the State fifty-five thousand dollars." As to speakers he named Judge Kelley, Robert G. Ingersoll, Carl Schurz, Gibson, Sheridan, and perhaps others. Others to be seen or written to on the money question are Governor Morgan, Mr. [blank], of Boston, and perhaps others.

On the whole his talk was not encouraging. The use of money I have little faith in,[1] and I am confident no such large sum can be raised.

I mean to go through cheerfully and firmly and with clean hands. If defeated, there will be no bitterness in the disappointment and I shall have my self-respect and an approving conscience.[2]

4 P.M. I just wrote General Buckland, who is enjoying the Centennial, the following honest words: "You are to be envied. Now that the flush of gratification upon the nomination is about at an end, I begin to prefer the independence of a private citizen. If the result leaves me so I will be the most contented defeated Presidential candidate, having any prospects, that was ever voted for."[3]

[1] How scrupulous Mr. Hayes was in avoiding any use of money in campaign times is shown by a letter to W. J. Troy, of Columbus, Ohio, written at Fremont June 14, 1875, shortly after his third-term nomination for Governor. The letter follows: —

"DEAR SIR: — Your note and the newspaper slip came duly. Both show you to possess education and talents. The sketch of your history is interesting and is well calculated to enlist sympathy in your behalf. If I were not a candidate, it is altogether possible that your appeal for pecuniary aid would be favorably considered. But a little reflection will, I am confident, lead you to see that, under the circumstances, it is altogether out of the question. Sound men of all parties are coming to the conclusion that the use of money by candidates, except in the recognized public way for legitimate expenses, is a great evil that ought to be abated. Believing this myself, I must say no, hoping your cool judgment will approve the decision."

[2] "We should cultivate a hopeful tone. Men in the right can afford to be cheerful even if the outlook is gloomy." (From letter of Mr. Hayes to Carl Schurz, August 30, 1876.)

[3] The same day he wrote Mrs. Hayes: "Last evening I went with Attorney-General Little to near the west line of the State to ride back with Governor Morton. We left about 6 P.M. and were at home about midnight. Morton is vigorous but has aged, and looks more like Nast's unfavorable cartoons than I had supposed. Mrs. Morton is a good woman. She is at his side looking out for all

It was notorious that money was used in Indiana that year, as in former and subsequent campaigns, in liberal sums by both parties for more or less legitimate purposes. The impression of the time was that the Democratic "war chest" was rather more abundantly supplied from the East than was the Republican; but it seems not unlikely that whatever money could accomplish on the one side was practically offset by similar accomplishment on the other, and that the final result would not have been appreciably different if both parties in the State had been left by the national organizations to depend wholly upon their own resources.[1] The fact was that Indiana, while a close State, was at that time Democratic, being especially carried away by the inflation doctrine which Mr. Hendricks steadfastly championed. Indeed, so popular was this doctrine in the State that Mr. Morton himself had not been entirely proof against its insinuating appeal. Moreover, the presence of Mr. Hendricks's name on the national ticket roused the Democrats to even more than their usual efforts; — and Indiana had long been famous for the unremitting energy, the persistent fierceness, with which political contests were habitually conducted. But much as Mr. Hayes was impressed by Senator Morton's analysis of the Indiana situation, he could not agree with Mr. Morton in thinking that Indiana's adverse vote in October would be a sure presage of national defeat in November. It would, to be sure, have a depressing effect, probably, indeed, out of proportion to its true significance, especially in the

dangers, cheerful and intelligent. He is not overconfident of Indiana, but will work well. When I am alone I always wish I was a quiet private citizen again. But it will soon be if we are beaten. I almost hope we shall be. Independence is such a comfort and blessing."

[1] But Senator Morton wrote Mr. Hayes after the October election: "I attribute our defeat chiefly to the disbursement of large sums of money at different points on the day of the election and employed generally in this way: They would pick out men who are Democrats, generally working men from the shops or loafers, and agree to give them five or ten dollars for their services on the day of the election to work for the Democratic ticket, generally with conditional contracts to give them a certain sum, say two or five dollars, for every additional vote they will get from the Republican party. This converts the men who are employed into bribers and tricksters, and they are turned loose to work upon such men as they can influence in any way, exerting every effort to bring out the vote and to make votes. The men thus employed also, in many cases, become repeaters, being paid for every time they vote, as if they had secured a convert from the Republican party. The process is simple but powerful, and will be employed in every State in the North which they hope to carry in November."

East. It was, therefore, wise to endeavor to prepare the public mind against the inconsiderate acceptance of the notion that Indiana's vote in October would be a decisive indication of what the nation would do in November. In this spirit Mr. Hayes on September 9 wrote this letter to William Henry Smith: —

Your letter of the 6th is very encouraging, and most interesting. I wish to make a suggestion which I deem important. If you agree with me, you may see a way to do what is requisite. It is common to say, "If Indiana and Ohio go right in October," "If Indiana is for us," etc., etc., thus hinging all on Indiana. Now, Indiana is a Democratic State. Emigration of Republicans West and the Greenback heresy have made it so. Until within a fortnight, I have seen small chance of carrying it. The chances are still greatly against us. The true pivot is New York. Let us therefore prepare our friends and the public not to be disheartened if Indiana is wrong — especially our friends in the East. *October will not decide the election unless* BOTH *Ohio and Indiana go the same way.* This is the truth. We ought to see that it is so understood everywhere.

A few days later (September 16) Mr. Hayes wrote to Mr. Edwards Pierrepont, American Minister at the Court of St. James, the letter which follows: —

I have yours of the 31st. At this time the tide is with us — at least, this is the opinion of our friends generally. I think it is so. In Ohio the contest in October will be close. The Greenback Democracy made the state ticket of the party and will support it heartily. The Tilden Democracy will support it for the effect on November. In November Greenback Democrats in considerable numbers will vote for Cooper, and others for Hayes. They hate Tilden because he tried to beat Allen last year.

Indiana leans to the Democracy. It is owing to emigration West that Ohio and Indiana are not Republican. Catholics are taking the places of Republican farmers and soldiers. But if the tide is as our friends think, we shall pull through.

The point you make as the controlling idea of the canvass is rapidly becoming the one topic of the press and of speakers. It *does* tell.[1]

---

[1] Mr. Pierrepont had written: "The election of Tilden secures the power to the South. Tilden could not resist it even if he desired. As you know, it is all idle to expect that any man elected by Southern votes will not be ruled by Southern influences. The nomination of Seymour raises the old war issue in New York, and the war issue cannot be and ought not to be kept out of this contest. The success of the Democratic party now is the success of those who opposed the war and who believe that the South ought to be paid for their slaves. I cannot doubt that the people will awake to the real danger and when the time comes rise in their might as they did four years ago."

Meanwhile Mr. Hayes had taken occasion to let the members of the National Committee know that he meant precisely what he had written in his letter of acceptance in regard to civil service reform, as the following communication clearly indicates: —

Private   COLUMBUS, O., 8 Sept., 1876.

MY DEAR SIR, — I send you a slip,[1] cut from an Eastern newspaper, on the subject of assessments upon official salaries for political purposes. It is charged that this is done by authority of the National Committee. My views as to what ought to be required of officeholders are set forth in my letter of acceptance and are no doubt sufficiently well known. But I think it is proper to say to the committee that if assessments are made as charged, it is a plain departure from correct principles, and ought not to be allowed. I trust the committee will have nothing to do with it. — Sincerely,

R. B. HAYES.

HON. R. C. McCORMICK,
    Secretary Republican National Committee.

Here was a plain and unequivocal expression of what the reformers of that time declared, and what all thinking men now

---

[1] Carl Schurz in more than one letter had directed Mr. Hayes's attention to this subject, giving him specific information which corroborated the substantial accuracy of newspaper assertions. In a letter, dated New York, September 5, Mr. Schurz quoted from a letter he had received from a friend of his in the Treasury Department, giving details of the methods employed in collecting two per cent of officials' annual salaries, and added: "It is the old story, only a little worse, if possible. Certainly this will not do in a campaign which is run on your letter of acceptance. It is a mockery of civil service reform. General McCormick, the secretary of the National Republican Committee, with whom I spoke about assessments in a general way, — not having received the letter from Washington when I saw him, — tells me that if assessments are levied, it is done without his knowledge; that probably Mr. Chandler, who scarce ever shows his face here and does not otherwise trouble himself about the management of the campaign, makes these operations at Washington his special business. . . . You will admit that such practices cannot go on without scandal and disgrace, but I apprehend nobody can stop them but yourself." — Already, some weeks before this (July 24), Mr. Hayes had written Mr. Schurz: "I think the assessment business will not be pushed by our committee; beyond that, I do not see how I can act efficiently. We can (and are doing it) commit the party to the right doctrines by resolutions of clubs, meetings, and the like, until there will be left no basis for the objectors. But I suspect the main thing is to be like flint when action is had. A good degree of stubbornness at the start, I have great faith in. I read the articles in the *Nation*. The trouble is not, it seems to me, the real intrinsic difficulty of doing the right thing, but it has been that those whose duty it was to act did n't believe in, or care for, the work. On a small scale I have tried it. It was curious to see the horror of friends when I announced quietly that I meant to appoint at least one Democrat on every state board. But the thing once done soon became easy and a matter of course."

Private

Columbus, O.
24 July 1876

My dear Sir:

I think the assessment business
will not be pushed by our Committee, beyond
that, I do not see how I can act efficiently.
We can, (and are doing it.), commit the
party to the right doctrines by resolutions
of clubs, meetings, and the like, until
there will be left no basis for the objectors.

But I suspect the main thing is to be
like flint when action is had. A good degree
of stubbornness at the start. I have great faith
in. I read the articles in the Nation. The
trouble is not, it seems to me, the real intrinsic
difficulty of doing the right thing, but it
has been that those whose duty it was to
act didn't believe in, or care for, the
work. On a small scale I have tried it. It
was amusing to see the horror of friends when I
announced quietly that I meant to at least one
about
Democrat on every State Board. But this

thing once done, soon became easy as a matter of course. — Just now our Tilden people seem hereabouts to be drooping. Their currency muddle - Hendricks & &c disturb them. I really don't see what their worry means, but that there is a worry is plain enough. —

Don't work too hard until this tournée matter leaves us. I inherit a Presbyterian fatalism. We shall go through, if we are to do it. —

With many regards

R B Hayes

Gen C. Schurz
& &c

recognize, to be the only correct attitude of mind toward this subject. But it was an unusual and advanced position for any man in active public life to assume in that year of grace.[1] The great majority of men in high office, or desirous of high office, of both parties practically approved, even if they did not openly defend, the law-defying practice of levying, for campaign purposes, assessments, proportioned somewhat to salaries, upon all public officeholders of their party faith. Long after an aroused public opinion had forced the adoption of most stringent laws to protect the employees of the Government from this party imposition, the practice was continued by one evasion of law or another; and even to this day, despite the agitation and condemnation of all these years, there can be no doubt that the pressure of campaign managers for "voluntary contributions" is oftentimes tantamount, in the minds of the victims, to a forced levy; and so we have still virtually, though of course not so extensively nor flagrantly as in the earlier times, the "plain departure from correct principles" which Mr. Hayes was among the first of active statesmen to recognize and emphatically to condemn.

While Mr. Hayes took so little part in the conduct of the canvass, it is evident from his diary and letters that, however successful he was in maintaining his serenity and equipoise of demeanor, he still at times keenly felt the strain of the campaign. September 24 he wrote in his diary: —

I am looking anxiously forward to the end of the contest. It is now almost one hundred days since the nomination, and only about forty-five to the election. The general drift of the campaign has been rather favorable to our side for some weeks past. The Greenback heresy in Indiana and Ohio is likely to cause those States to do badly in October. If there was no election before the final vote in November I should feel very confident of a favorable result. But our friends East and elsewhere count on more favorable results in Ohio and Indiana than are likely to occur. We shall be much stronger at the Presidential elections in both States. But the discouraging effect of defeats in October is sure to hurt us. Our adversaries are to be correspondingly encouraged. The truth is, time and money would be saved if all elections

[1] A month before this (August 10) Mr. Hayes had expressed himself on this subject quite as emphatically in a letter to William Henry Smith: "I hate assessments. They are all wrong, and are sure to do more harm than good. Officeholders, like other people, should be left free to contribute or not as they choose."

in Presidential years were fixed for the same day. It should be done.[1]

"I am prepared for either event," I can again repeat. To go into the great office will be a sore trial. Health, comfort, happiness, all imperilled if not sacrificed. I shall find reasons enough for satisfaction with the result if I am defeated. If elected, the firmest adherence to principle, against all opposition and temptations, is my purpose. I shall show a *grit* that will astonish those who predict weakness.

October 4, he wrote: —

Birthday; fifty-four years of age. The good omen of the day is that Colorado, the first State to elect electors (or rather a Legislature that will elect electors), has been carried by the Republicans. "First gun for Hayes" is the headline in the *Journal*.

I called on Blaine at Ewing Miller's. He looks well — is clearheaded, prompt, and quick-witted, with no trace that I detect of his great calamity. He is hopeful and friendly. I called with him on Mrs. Ben Smith, on Lucy, and at my office. We met Wayne McVeagh. He has almost precisely my views and hopes as to the South. By conciliating Southern whites on the basis of obedience to law and equal rights, he hopes we may divide the Southern whites and so protect the colored people.

The October elections in Indiana and Ohio went precisely as Mr. Hayes had expected. For three months he had been predicting that Ohio would go Republican and Indiana Democratic. Ohio gave a Republican plurality of 8839, in the case of the man that attracted the largest vote; Indiana, a Democratic plurality of 5084. Mr. Hayes was therefore not in the least disappointed or cast down by the result. He was convinced that Ohio would do still better for the Republicans in the national election; and the plurality in Indiana was so small that he had hopes for a reversal of judgment in November. His feeling was fully expressed in the following letter to the secretary of the National Committee: —

Personal.   COLUMBUS, O., 14 Oct., 1876.

MY DEAR SIR, — The elections have gone just about as I anticipated in these two States. Our majority in Ohio on the true test is about 9000. It is made up by handsome gains in the rural districts which overcome losses in the cities. The reliable Republican counties have given their full

---

[1] Mr. Hayes, in his annual message to the Legislature a few months later, recommended that this change be made. Ohio finally, in 1885, by a constitutional amendment adopted the national election date for all state elections.

high-tide majorities. The cities like Springfield, where business and manufacturing are prosperous, have done well. Our losses are in cities and towns where the hard times pinch. All of the non-Catholic foreigners, Germans, Welsh, etc., etc., have stood by us except the trading classes in Cincinnati, who feared a loss of Southern trade; and even there I doubt if we lost in the foreign Republican vote. I infer from this that a full vote makes Wisconsin ours beyond all question. We shall double our majority here in November without effort.

Indiana is surely now a doubtful State. We have a fair fighting chance to carry it, a much better chance than we had to carry it in October. I do not write of the East. You understand about the situation there. In the South, if we have a prospect to carry any States, we must look after North and South Carolina, Florida, Mississippi, and Louisiana.

Another matter I would like to hear from you about. Ohio Republicans, interested in the Centennial, want an Ohio day, and wish me to be present — next week or the week after. Should it be encouraged?

Know-Nothing charges made by the Democrats, the people here care nothing about. It is perfectly well known that I do not favor the exclusion of foreigners from the ballot or from office, and that *I do oppose* Catholic interference and all sectarian interference with political affairs — and especially with the schools. This last point is influential — particularly with non-Catholic foreigners. It has not, I suspect, been sufficiently urged in the canvass. But I need not take up your time with these rambling speculations. The contest is now with the East. The inflation States have done better for the hard-money candidates than you had a right to expect. Now let the hard-money States do as well, and we are safe. — Sincerely,

R. B. HAYES.

Gov. R. C. McCORMICK, etc.

The vote in Ohio was peculiarly gratifying to Mr. Hayes, as justifying the confident predictions of his supporters at the Cincinnati Convention. October 15 he wrote in his diary: —

The October elections leave the result of the Presidential contest still in doubt and to be decided by New York in November. That Ohio has done so well is a great satisfaction. My friends urged as one of their strongest arguments for my nomination that Ohio was a doubtful State; that its loss in October would be fatal; that no man named except myself could surely carry it in October; that with me as the candidate success in Ohio in October was assured; that I always had carried it, and would do so again. After all this, the loss of Ohio in October would have been a sore mortification. We had at the head of our ticket a good soldier and citizen, but one who was mixed up with the temperance crusade, which was so hateful to all Germans and to many others. He was a load — a heavy load to carry. But our prominent

Germans, brewers and others, behaved admirably, nobly, and we are safe! I can bear defeat in November far more philosophically than I could have borne the loss of Ohio in October. My own ward, town, county, and congressional district did well — indeed, very handsomely. This is gratifying. Endorsed by my State and home, I feel gratified by the result.

Mr. Hayes's temper of mind and thought in the last few days of the campaign is distinctly manifested by the following entries in his diary: —

Oct. 22, 1876, Sunday. — Only two Sundays more before the Presidential election. I am surprised whenever I think of it to find myself so cool — so, almost, indifferent about it. It would be a calamity, I am sure, to give the Democrats the Government. But public opinion, the press, the march of events, will compel them to do better than their character and principles indicate. Here is our safety. Public opinion, the fear of losing the public confidence, apprehension of censure by the press, make all men in power conservative and safe. On personal grounds I find many reasons for thinking defeat a blessing. I should stand by my letter; I should hew to the line; but what conflicts and annoyances would follow! I do not fear my pluck or constancy a particle. But to be deceived by the rogues — to find many a trusted reformer no better than he should be, here would be humiliations and troubles without end.

The huge registration in New York City looks sinister. It seems to look to our defeat in that State. Another danger is imminent — a contested result. And we have no such means for its decision as ought to be provided by law. This must be attended to hereafter. We should not allow another Presidential election to occur before a means for settling a contest is provided.

If a contest comes now it may lead to a conflict of arms. I can only try to do my duty to my countrymen in that case. I shall let no personal ambition turn me from the path of duty. Bloodshed and civil war must be averted if possible. If forced to fight, I have no fear of failure from lack of courage or firmness.

Oct. 29, Sunday. — Returned last night from Ohio Day at the Centennial. It was an enthusiastic and prodigious crowd which greeted me. I managed to shake some four thousand people by the hand and to make half a dozen speeches from steps, windows, and roof of the Ohio building, without saying anything that I regret — without "slopping over." . . .

I return feeling that with the probabilities of fraud and violence — fraud North, violence South — the chances are that we shall lose the election. My *luck* is the other way. But I have made a good fight — sound letter to stand on — judicious course of conduct throughout — my head steady and level up to this time. Let me keep it so ten days longer.

Mr. Hayes had been doubtful of the propriety of visiting Philadelphia, lest it should be thought by the censorious that he was seeking to gain some political advantage thereby. He only consented to go, and then accompanied by Mrs. Hayes and a party of personal friends, after he had consulted more than one of his confidential advisers.

The contemporary record of Ohio Day, as preserved in the daily papers, shows that Mr. Hayes was as usual most modest in his report of his reception, and proves likewise that he, indeed, did not "slop over" in his speeches. A dense throng surrounded the Ohio Building before the appearance of Mr. Hayes's party. "Everybody seemed determined to see the next President if he perished in the attempt, and the crushing, pushing, cheering, and the general enthusiasm, was quite alarming." When Governor Hayes "appeared at the east portico such a roar of greeting swelled up as could be heard half a mile off." [1] Having been briefly introduced by General Hawley, speaking in behalf of the managers of the exhibition, Governor Hayes made a short speech in which he dwelt principally on the qualities of Ohio and the share of its people in the great Centennial Exposition. There was no reference in the speech to politics, but it ended with these patriotic words: —

This Centennial Exhibition is now near its close. It will not be forgotten. It will pass into history. It will live in the minds of our countrymen, linked with recollections of the fathers whose work it has so fitly commemorated. We hope, nay, we confidently believe, that the influence of this celebration will be to extend and perpetuate the principles of our Revolutionary ancestors and to give increased assurance to all mankind that the new nation, brought forth on this continent a hundred years ago, is destined under Providence long to remain the home of freedom and the refuge of the oppressed.

After the speech people flocked through the building for hours to shake hands with Governor Hayes. From time to time, in response to the insistent clamor of the cheering crowds outside, Mr. Hayes would show himself at window or balcony, more than once uttering a few pleasant words in response to the enthusiastic

[1] Special dispatch, October 26, New York *Times.*

demand for a speech. At intervals, when he was resting for a brief period from the handshaking, he had opportunity to converse with party leaders, like Governor Hartranft, of Pennsylvania, and Mr. E. D. Morgan, Republican candidate for Governor of New York. In the evening the Union League Club honored him with a brilliant reception attended by hundreds of the prominent citizens of Philadelphia and by distinguished public men and politicians from other parts of the country. The impression made by Mr. Hayes on all who met him — most of them for the first time — was altogether favorable. The comment of the Philadelphia *Press* was: —

Affability and straightforwardness mark every movement. His face betrays a reserve of modest power. . . . No average reader of human character who felt the earnest grasp of Rutherford B. Hayes's strong hand, or noted his voice, expression, and manner, could fail to perceive that there is something in the man that accounts for the threefold honors conferred upon him by his own great State, and that inspires the confidence of the people.

The latter part of Mr. Hayes's entry in his diary is evidence that the party leaders, with whom he had confidential discussions of the political outlook, must have been far from sanguine of success. Mr. Hayes continued despondent in mind, but altogether serene and composed in demeanor up to the day of election. He wrote in his diary: —

November 1, 1876. — The contest is close and yet doubtful, with the chances, as I see them, rather against us. So small a loss as the defeat in Hamilton County [Cincinnati] in October may have made the difference between victory and defeat. A few hundred votes improvement there would have given our friends the prestige of victory in Ohio and throughout the country. Our loss was due to bribery and repeating. The hard times, if we are beaten, may be assigned as the great and sufficient cause. All crimes are increased by hard times. It is especially so with crimes against the ballot-box. It is easy to hire men desperate with want to vote contrary to their convictions, and even to become repeaters. Hard times — there is the ultimate cause of our danger. We shall be beaten if at all by crime — by bribery and repeating North, and violence and intimidation in the South.[1]

[1] September 12, Judge Taft, the Attorney-General, had written Mr. Hayes from Washington: "The consultation with Republicans from the Southern States has very much absorbed my attention of late. The wrongs the Republicans of the South are suffering are incredible. It is a fixed and desperate purpose of

November 5, Sunday, 1876. — The election is only a day or two off, and I find myself strangely calm and indifferent about it. I shall read Mr. Andrews's address, and other matter, as much interested in what I am doing as usual. It now looks as if the chance of my election was improving, and as if Republican success was not improbable.

I make a list of States to be counted certain for us as follows (necessary to a choice 185): —

Maine	7
New Hampshire	5
Vermont	5
Massachusetts	13
Rhode Island	4
Pennsylvania	29
Ohio	22
Michigan	11
Illinois	21
Minnesota	5
Iowa	11
Nebraska	3
Kansas	5
Colorado	3
	144

Probably Republican —

Wisconsin	10
California	6
South Carolina	7–23
	167

This leaves 18 required to elect out of the following doubtful States: —

New Jersey	9
Nevada	3
Florida	4
New York	35
Indiana	15
North Carolina	10
Louisiana	8
Connecticut	6
Oregon	3
	93

the Democratic party in the South that the negroes shall not vote, and murder is a common means of intimidation to prevent them. The tyranny is so terrible, of the whites, that Republicans dare not publish the murders which are committed nor testify to the facts in court. I suppose that nothing can be effected in Mississippi to prevent fraud. All the machinery of the State Government is in the hands of the Democrats, and the intimidation is exercised to keep the negroes from registering, and then they would count them out however great the Republican majority should be. In South Carolina, in Florida, and in Louisiana, and in North Carolina we shall try to protect the negroes. What success we shall have I cannot tell."

November 7. — *Dies iræ !* A cold but dry day; — good enough here for election work. I still think Democratic chances the best. But it is not possible to form a confident opinion. If we lose, the South will be the greatest sufferer. Their misfortune will be far greater than ours. I do not think a revival of business will be greatly postponed by Tilden's election. Business prosperity does not, in my judgment, depend on government so much as men commonly think. But we shall have no improvement in civil service — deterioration rather, and the South will drift toward chaos again.

Mr. Hayes did not go home to vote. He felt a delicacy about casting his ballot even indirectly for himself. He had never done that in all his political experience. But, on the other hand, he could not vote for his opponent, because to do that would have been to vote against his principles.

CHAPTER XXVI

THE DISPUTED ELECTION

THE long controversy over the disputed election of 1876, with its nation-wide discussion, its angry disputation, and its rancorous recrimination, forms an important and most interesting chapter in the history of American institutions. Its peaceful solution, by resort to extraordinary and unprecedented means,[1] and the ready if not satisfied acquiescence of all parties in the settlement, are a lasting tribute alike to the Anglo-Saxon genius for self-government, to the vitality of the American constitutional system, and to the practical good sense and patriotism of the American people in meeting a grave emergency and abiding faithfully by the duly attained decision. It is still too soon probably for any sincere student of that period to divest himself entirely of partisan prepossessions in approaching the facts or appraising their significance. Without elaboration or argument, the writer desires to say that, as a result of his prolonged study of the conditions and contentions of the time, he is thoroughly convinced that in the final arbitrament essential justice and right prevailed, and that the best interests of the country in all its parts were served. He ventures the prediction that more and more this will come to be the judgment of impartial historians.

It is not appropriate in the biography of Mr. Hayes to follow the controversy in its infinitude of details. That belongs to the general history of American politics.[2] Little more is required here than to set forth Mr. Hayes's personal relations to the great dispute, and to describe his personal conduct and public bearing in those trying and tumultuous times.

When Mr. Hayes retired late on election night, it was with the impression that the vote had gone against the Republican party

---

[1] "There are no analogies for it in our Constitution or in our laws or in our history." (From speech of Senator Morton on Commission Bill during debate in the Senate, January, 1877.)

[2] The subject has been carefully and judiciously treated by Paul Leland Haworth in his volume, *The Hayes-Tilden Disputed Election of 1876.*

and that a majority of the Tilden electors had been chosen. He
had spent the evening, which was raw and disagreeable, at his
home in company with Mrs. Hayes and a small group of interested friends, among them the correspondent of the Chicago *Tribune*. Dispatches reporting the progress of the count throughout
the country were delivered at the house as fast as they were received by the telegraph company. Particular interest centred
naturally on the reports from the doubtful Northern States,
especially those from New York, as Mr. Hayes had felt that New
York's vote would be decisive of the contest. When it became
evident that the Democratic vote in New York City and Brooklyn was too great to be overcome by the Republican majority in
the rest of the State; that New Jersey and Connecticut had, as so
often, followed New York's lead; and that Indiana had failed to
reverse its October verdict, Mr. Hayes was forced to share the
opinion of Republican disaster, reached by most newspapers
and public men of the country that night; leaving out of account
for the moment the fact that from large parts of the country,
especially in the South and the Far West, the returns were too
meagre to warrant confident prognostication of the result.[1]

During the evening Mr. Hayes maintained his habitual serenity and cheerfulness, discussing and appraising the varying
phases of the returns with sagacious understanding and imper-
turbable impartiality. He retired soon after midnight, disappointed, naturally, but not unduly dejected by his supposed
defeat. He was at his office in the State House at the customary
hour on the following morning, ready to attend to the routine
of his duties. But the stream of callers, friends, politicians, and
newspaper correspondents, and the suspense and excitement of
the day, as later election dispatches alternately raised fresh hopes

[1] "The facts are that on the morning after the election, when the returns from
many States were not known, and could not possibly be known, the vote of certain States was put down for Mr. Tilden. For a few hours it was assumed that he
was elected. But a few hours later showed, what might have been easily enough
foreseen, that as the returns could not have been known when the result was
announced, the true result might turn out to be different from the announcement. . . . There was not a day within the month after the election on which it
was possible to form a proximately fair judgment of the actual situation in the
disputed States." (George William Curtis in *Harper's Weekly*, December 23,
1876.) — The New York *Herald* and the New York *Times* of November 8, however, declared the result in doubt.

or caused renewed depression, completely occupied his time and thought. His manner during the day, however, was such that "the ordinary habitué of the Capitol could not tell from his appearance whether he was a candidate for any office or not. He received those who called in his usual cordial manner, and was very unconcerned, while the greatest office on the American continent was trembling in the balance." [1] Late in the afternoon a dispatch reached Columbus from New York reporting that that State had, after all, gone Republican by 29,000. As this false rumor spread abroad a wildly excited throng quickly filled the streets, and presently, as by a common impulse, started with tumultuous shouts for Mr. Hayes's house. In response to prolonged and insistent demands, Mr. Hayes appeared at the door and spoke substantially as follows: —

Friends, — If you will keep order for one half minute I will say all that it is proper to say at this time. In the very close political contest, which is just drawing to a close, it is impossible, at so early a time, to obtain the result, owing to the incomplete telegraph communications through some of the Southern and Western States.

I accept your call as a desire on your part for the success of the Republican party. If it should not be successful, I will surely have the pleasure of living for the next year and a half among some of my most ardent and enthusiastic friends, as you have demonstrated to-night.

Earlier in the day he had talked freely with political friends and with the correspondent of the Cincinnati *Times.* He could see little hope of success, despite some encouraging dispatches, and he deprecated holding out false hopes. Then, after rallying his companions on their despondent looks,[2] he added: —

By the way, I do not think it is right to joke over this matter. I don't care for myself; and the party, yes, and the country, too, can stand it; but I do care for the poor colored men of the South. I do not fear that

---

[1] *Ohio State Journal*, November 9.

[2] The feeling of Mr. Hayes's personal friends is well expressed in a letter of Mr. Stanley Matthews of November 9: "I seemed all day to walk through the valley of the shadow of death. I felt as if a great conspiracy of ignorance, superstition, and brutality had succeeded in overthrowing the hopes of a Christian civilization as represented and embodied in the Republican party. You once said in a speech that the cause of the Republican party was the cause of righteousness. I never believed it so thoroughly as I have done since it appeared that that cause may have been lost. I sincerely hope that the later and more encouraging news may be verified and that our fears may be removed. I shall rejoice with joy unspeakable and full of gladness."

business will be greatly disturbed by Mr. Tilden's election. Trade governs itself. Capitalists may just at present say we won't lend money, but it will be only a nine days' wonder, which will wear away as soon as they recover from the chagrin of defeat. Business will, I think, go on as usual. I do not think parties responsible for financial depression. We see the troubles they have had in Germany and Austria. If any part of the country suffers or remains at a standstill, it will be the South under the new régime. Northern men can't live there and will leave, and immigration into the States will cease. But, as I said before, I do pity the poor black men of the South. The result will be that the Southern people will practically treat the constitutional amendments as nullities, and then the colored man's fate will be worse than when he was in slavery, with a humane master to look after his interests. That is the only reason I regret that the news is as it is.[1]

These remarks were widely discussed by the press. Papers of all shades of political opinion commended the spirit that

---

[1] November 15, Samuel McKee, who had served in Congress with Mr. Hayes, a native Kentuckian, and at that time a prominent lawyer in Louisville, wrote Mr. Hayes: —

"I am firmly convinced that a Democratic success would result in the removal of thousands of Republicans from the Southern States and an abandonment by them of all they have rather than remain in peril of their lives; and to starve. They are now ostracized in business, socially, and to a very large extent religiously, and professional men are only employed by these people because of their superior merit, as is the case sometimes; or because it is believed they could secure a more advantageous hearing in our federal courts, when these courts are controlled by Republicans. They are so constituted themselves that they think a Republican official won't do a Democrat justice unless the Democrats are represented by a friend of the court politically. It is a sad commentary on their intelligence, but it is true, and comes of their training. For myself I would be a freeman in speech, in thought, and act, and starve, rather than shut my mouth at their bidding and grow fat off of their gains; and if this calamity befalls us, I can sell what little I have here at a sacrifice and in another part of the Republic where all men are not 'knaves,' because they express their thoughts differently from the dominant class, with the talent God has given me, and with his blessing of health continued, I can and will live by my own honest toil. But all can't do this. Thousands can do nothing but submit. They can't go away, and they submit rather than die."

Letters of similar purport came from leading Republicans in other Southern States. On the other hand, Mr. Hayes's old friend Guy M. Bryan, writing from Galveston, December 10, said: "So far as the negro is concerned, it is a great misfortune to the country, to the interests of society at the South, and to the negro himself that he is not left to the management of the Southern people, instead of to designing and selfish people who teach him that they [the Southerners] are his enemies. As to Northern men living in the South, they are and would be as safe there as they could be in the North if they deported themselves properly. If I were to go North and so act as to make myself offensive to the people I was among, I doubt not I should receive the treatment I merited."

prompted them, though Democratic editors took exception to his apprehension regarding the South. The next few days duplicated practically the experiences of Wednesday; only that more and more correspondents appeared at Columbus, trying by all means to obtain expressions of opinion or comments on the progress of events, as the "visiting statesmen" [1] were hurrying to the contested Southern States to witness the official count by the Returning Boards. It was some days before Mr. Hayes began to admit to himself that the confidence in his election, which his stanchest partisans had entertained from the start, might have substantial basis. On the Saturday following the election he wrote in his diary: —

The election has resulted in the defeat of the Republicans after a very close contest. Tuesday evening a small party assembled in our parlor to hear the news. . . . The first dispatch was from Rutherford [his son, at Cornell] showing a majority of [blank] in Ithaca, New York, a gain of [blank] over Grant in 1872. We all felt that the State of New York would decide the contest. Our last dispatches from our committee in New York were very encouraging — full of confidence. Mr. A. B. Cornell, chairman of the New York State Committee, said in an experience of ten years he had not seen prospects brighter on the eve of an election. But we all knew — warned by the enormous registration in the cities of New York and Brooklyn and other facts — that we must not count confidently on carrying the State. The good omen from Ithaca was accepted with a quiet cheerfulness.

Almost at the same instant came a gain of 36 in Ballville, the township nearest my own home. This was good. Then came, one at a time, towns and precincts in Ohio. The comparison was made with the vote in 1875 instead of with the vote of October last. This was confusing. But soon we began to feel that Ohio was not doing as well as we had hoped. The effect was depressing. I commanded without much effort my usual composure and cheerfulness. Lucy felt it more keenly. Without showing it, she busied herself about refreshments for our guests, and soon disappeared. I found her soon after abed with a headache. I comforted her by consoling talk. She was cheerful and resigned, but she did not return to the parlor.

Without difficulty or much effoit I became the most composed and

---

[1] Among those asked by the President to go to Louisiana was Senator Sherman who records (*Recollections*, vol. I, p. 554): "I at once started for New Orleans, stopping on the way at Columbus to confer with Governor Hayes, who said he wished I would go to New Orleans and witness the count, but expressed, in the strongest language, his opposition to any movement on the part of any one to influence the action of the Returning Board in his favor. He said if Mr. Tilden was elected he desired him by all means to have the office."

cheerful of the party. At [blank] P.M., or thereabouts, we heard that in some 200 precincts of New York City Tilden had about 20,000 majority, which indicated 50,000 in the city. The returns received from the rural districts did not warrant the belief that they would overcome such a large city majority. From that time I never supposed there was a chance for Republican success.

I went to bed at 12 to 1 o'clock. Talked with Lucy, consoling her with such topics as readily occurred of a nature to make us feel satisfied on merely personal grounds with the result. We soon fell into a refreshing sleep and the affair seemed over. Both of us felt more anxiety about the South — about the colored people especially — than about anything else sinister in the result. My hope of a sound currency will somehow be realized; civil service reform will be delayed; but the great injury is in the South. There the amendments will be nullified, disorder will continue, prosperity to both whites and colored people will be pushed off for years.

But I took my way to my office as usual Wednesday morning, and was master of myself and contented and cheerful. During the day the news indicated that we carried California — some of the other Pacific States; all New England, except Connecticut; all of the free States West, except Indiana; and it dawned on us that with a few Republican States in the South, to which we were fairly entitled, we would yet be the victors.

From Wednesday afternoon the city and the whole country has been full of excitement and anxiety. People have been up and down several times a day with the varying rumors. Wednesday evening, on a false rumor about New York, a shouting multitude rushed to my house and called me out with rousing cheers. I made a short talk. From that time the news has fluctuated just enough to prolong the suspense and to enhance the interest. At this time the Republicans are claiming the election by one electoral vote. With Louisiana, South Carolina, and Florida we have carried 185. This creates great uneasiness. Both sides are sending to Louisiana prominent men to watch the canvassing of the votes. All thoughtful people are brought to consider the imperfect machinery provided for electing the President. No doubt we shall, warned by this danger, provide, by amendments of the Constitution, or by proper legislation, against a recurrence of the danger.

The next day Mr. Hayes wrote: —

The news this morning is not conclusive. The headlines of the morning papers are as follows: The *News*, "Nip and Tuck"; "Tuck has it"; "The Mammoth National Doubt"; — and the *Herald* heads its news column, "Which?" But to my mind the figures indicate that Florida has been carried by the Democrats. No doubt both fraud and violence intervened to produce the result. But the same is true in many Southern States.

We shall, the fair-minded men of the country will, history will hold that the Republicans were by fraud, violence, and intimidation, by a nullification of the Fifteenth Amendment, deprived of the victory which they fairly won. But we must, I now think, prepare ourselves to accept the inevitable. I do it with composure and cheerfulness. To me the result is no personal calamity.

I would like the opportunity to improve the civil service. It seems to me I could do more than any Democrat to put Southern affairs on a sound basis. I do not apprehend any great or permanent injury to the financial affairs of the country by the victory of the Democrats. The hard-money wing of the party is at the helm. Supported, as they should be and will be, in all wise measures, by the great body of the Republican party, nothing can be done to impair the national credit or debase the national currency. On this, as on all important subjects, the Republicans will still hold a commanding position. We are in a minority in the Electoral Colleges: we lose the Administration. But in the former free States — the States that were always loyal — we are still in a majority. We carry eighteen of the twenty-two and have 200,000 majority of the popular vote. In the old slave States, if the recent amendments were cheerfully obeyed, if there had been neither violence nor intimidation nor other improper interference with the rights of the colored people, we should have carried enough Southern States to have held the country and to have secured a decided popular majority in the nation. Our adversaries are in power, but they are supported by a minority only of the lawful voters of the country. A fair election in the South would undoubtedly have given us a large majority of the electoral votes, and a decided preponderance of the popular vote.

I went to church and heard a good, strong, sensible sermon by Critchfield's son-in-law. After church and dinner I rode with General Mitchell and his children over to Alum Creek and around past the place of my old friend Albert Buttles. We talked of the Presidential question as settled, and found it in all respects well for me personally that I was not elected. On reaching home at Mitchell's, we found my son Webb with the following dispatch from Governor Dennison, a prudent and cautious gentleman, which seems to open it all up again: —

WASHINGTON, D.C., Nov. 12, 1876. Rec'd at Columbus 2.05 P.M.
To GOVERNOR R. B. HAYES: —
You are undoubtedly elected next President of the United States. Desperate attempts are being made to defeat you in Louisiana, South Carolina, and Florida, but they will not succeed.
W. DENNISON.

(In the evening I asked if there were objections to publishing this dispatch. About 10 P.M. reply came, "No objections.")

As Mr. Hayes had made no effort to obtain the nomination, as he had taken no active leadership in the conduct of the

campaign, so now he refrained from suggestion or advice to the
party authorities or political leaders that were convinced of his
election and were sparing no proper effort to prove to the country
that their contention was right.[1] He went on quietly doing his
duty as Governor, content as ever to await without undue anxiety
the destiny of larger responsibility or of shattered hopes that the
future must soon declare for him.[2] The impression he created on

[1] "While I believe that with a fair election in the South, our electoral vote
would reach 200, and that we should have a large popular majority, I am yet
anxious, as you are, that in the canvassing of results there should be no taint of
dishonesty. I have had no part in sending leading men South. If you at any
stage of the proceedings feel like going to Louisiana, it would gratify me if you
go. Hewitt's men are many of them ex-Republicans, and of course bitterly prejudiced against their late associates." (From letter of Mr. Hayes to Carl Schurz,
November 13, 1876.)

[2] That this demeanor accorded with what those who knew him best expected
of him is evident from a letter of November 14 written him by a warm personal
friend and admirer, Mr. R. C. Anderson, of Dayton: "Day and night the streets
have been in a regular turmoil. Nothing has been talked or thought about but
news from the South. Business came to a standstill and the ruin or the salvation
of the country seemed to depend upon the returns of four or five States. I have
never seen anything like it since the war, and it recalled the incidents of that
excited period more vividly than I deemed possible to a political struggle. I
firmly believe that you are fairly and honestly President of the United States.
Whether you are or not, I know that you ought to be and that this opinion is
shared by the best and purest men in the country. Another thing I know, and
it fills me with pride to reflect, that your conduct through the whole canvass,
with all its temptations, has been such as to challenge the respect and admiration
of your opponents, and that malignity and mendacity have failed to find or
fasten a flaw in your character or put the slightest stain on your good name.
Whatever the issue of the business may be (and I trust to God it will be favorable
to you), hereafter your name will from one end of the country to the other be
remembered with veneration and love — become in the mouths of all good men
'familiar as household words.' As for myself I could not feel more pride in or
affection for you were you not only President of the United States, but ruler of
the rest of the world. Your worth depends neither upon success nor defeat, and
I am sure that you have the magnanimity neither to be unduly elated by the one
nor unreasonably depressed by the other, and that the qualities which so eminently fitted you for a position of such high trust will enable you to accept either
issue with philosophical resignation."

A letter from General J. D. Cox of the same date said: "I maintain strong
hopes that all will come out well and am coolly but determinedly ready to do
whatever is necessary to support the right. As we will not knowingly impose a
wrong on others, so we will not bear it ourselves. But we need to have the justice
of whatever may be done in Louisiana or other States so clear that we may appeal
to any candid arbiter for the approval of our course."

Mr. Hayes maintained his dignified course through all the exciting months
that followed, winning thereby the growing respect and approval of the country.
For example, apropos of the Bar Association banquet which he attended at

visitors at the Capitol in these days of intense excitement and
uncertainty is made vividly manifest by a special dispatch from
Columbus of November 15 to the Cincinnati *Gazette.* The correspondent describes the frantic but futile efforts of the metropolitan papers to draw Mr. Hayes into the controversy, and even
to get expressions of opinion from Mrs. Hayes and the sons, and
then adds: —

> Meanwhile, could the anxious inquirers see the subject of their in-
> quisitive zeal they would certainly laugh at themselves. His days are
> passed in his usual routine of executive business and home life, and if
> indications are anything, he is the calmest man in the country. His
> regular habits appear the same, and he evidently enjoys a calm domestic
> life like any other good husband and father. . . . Let us say, once for
> all, that Governor Hayes believes in the American people, and their
> capacity for self-government; and accordingly he is not prophesying
> evil concerning the present imbroglio. Whatever is done in Louisiana
> will be done according to law, and he has no doubt the people will ac-
> quiesce whether it elect him or Governor Tilden.

The same issue of the *Gazette* that records the paragraph just
quoted gives also an account of an official visit of Mr. Hayes with
the Board of State Charities to the State University at Athens.
While at Athens several gentlemen called on the Governor, when
he frankly discussed the political situation. He had no doubt
that if a fair vote and a fair count were had he was elected. It
was suggested, on the basis of newspaper talk, that perhaps some
elector might solve the perplexing situation by voting regardless

Cincinnati, February 10, the *Enquirer* said: "His modest manner and unosten-
tatious address always make him friends. . . . Throughout all the trying hours
since and before the election Governor Hayes has done nothing to forfeit the
respect of his fellow citizens." And George William Curtis, in *Harper's Weekly,*
March 17, 1877, writes: "The attitude of Mr. Hayes during the long uncertainty
since the election has been as dignified and self-respectful as it was during the
campaign. He has never shown an 'uncommon anxiety' for the Presidency. . . .
He has undoubtedly greatly won upon the confidence and respect of the country
since the election. Before that time he was a party candidate, and was viewed
only as a partisan. But his moderation and good sense, his total freedom from
anxiety, and unaffected and simple devotion to his duty under unprecedentedly
trying circumstances, leave him in a most favorable light. It would be unkind to
Mr. Tilden to compare his attitude throughout with that of Mr. Hayes. It has
been that of an old politician dextrously pulling wires to secure a great office;
and the full light that has been turned upon his canvass shows at the very last his
nephew and confidential secretary telegraphing from his house an agreement to
buy an electoral vote."

of his obligation to the party which had elected him.[1] To this
one of the callers said: "No man in this country has courage
enough to accept the office of President if elected by such a vote;
and by courage I mean hardihood, bravado, wickedness, and all
the qualities requisite to such an act." Whereupon, as the dispatch continues: —

Governor Hayes very promptly, but quietly said: "I know one man,
certainly, who has not." Enlarging upon this idea, he said: "Any man
fit to be President, or even a candidate of a great party for the office,
would prefer to be 'counted out by fraud, rather than counted in by
fraud, of which there is a reasonable suspicion." The self-possession,
coolness, modesty, and freedom from excitement or agitation of Governor Hayes are most remarkable. He talks of the situation as though
he had no interest in the result, beyond that of any other citizen.

This remark of Mr. Hayes found wide currency and was used
as a text by papers friendly to Mr. Tilden on which to base
homilies addressed to Mr. Hayes, urging him at once to assert
his manhood, declare his belief in the election of his rival, and
announce that he could not and would not abide by the decision

---

[1] Some way it got noised about that James Russell Lowell was the elector that
was to be guilty of this act of perfidy — a thing quite inconceivable to a man of
his probity of character. In a letter to Mr. Hayes of May 26, 1877, the great poet
and scholar referred to the calumny in these words: —

"I may fairly plead for a few minutes of your attention as an Elector who
voted for you with both his eyes and ears open and who was the innocent nucleus
of a comet with a tremendous tail to it that made a day's sensation in the newspapers. At the time I thought silence imposed on me by my own self-respect, but
I may be allowed to say to *you* that, if I had ever had any doubt between the
candidates, I should have resigned my place at once. In accepting it I took pains
to say that I had satisfied myself that the Republican candidates (I used the
plural out of courtesy, but of course meant you) represented honestly certain
principles. I never saw any reason to change my mind, and your course as President has justified me. In common with all right-minded men, to be sure, I was
shocked at the unwise and inhuman turn given to the canvass by the selfish
parasites of our political system, but as my opinions are from long habit apt to
be opinions and not forms of words, I did not lose my faith in *you* because men in
whom I never had any faith disgusted me. I expected nothing else of them, but I
did expect something else of you and I was right. I received letters of counsel,
warning, encouragement, deprecation, and even menace from all parts of the
country, but I am happy to say that from my own district there never came a word
either orally or in writing. Where I was best known I was least doubted. The
only thing that for a moment ruffled my composure was when I read in the newspapers that Mr. H. W. Beecher had been pleased to say that 'one of the Massachusetts electors was suspected.' I am not used to associate myself with such an
epithet, and *he*, of all men, might have been chary of it."

of the authorities legally charged with the duty of canvassing the vote in the disputed Southern States, in case that decision were in his favor. Of course, such an abdication, under all the circumstances as they appeared at the time, was wholly inconceivable on the part of a strong and conscientious man like Mr. Hayes. It was with him not at all a question of personal triumph or of the gratification of personal ambition. He had not sought the nomination; he had not striven with feverish assiduity to win the election; when it seemed that Mr. Tilden was elected he was, so far as he was personally concerned, completely reconciled to his lot. But he had no right to consult his own preferences; he had, without personal solicitation, been selected by his party, to whose fundamental principles he was attached with fervent ardor, to be its leader; the continuance of that party in the control of the National Government he unreservedly believed was highly important, if not, indeed, essential, to the best welfare of the country; the men of largest wisdom and experience in the management and direction of the party — men of unquestioned patriotism and probity of character — were convinced that the election rightfully had gone in his favor; the lawfully constituted authorities were engaged in the performance of the duties for which they were created — in determining on the evidence presented what, under the law, the true vote of the States in controversy was; for him, a thousand miles away and with only the flying and discordant voices of the press to give him information, to prejudge the case and abandon his post, would have been an act, not of magnanimity and high courage, but rather of cowardice and pusillanimity; of disloyalty to his party and discredit to his country. The only proper course for him, as it was for Mr. Tilden, — leaving aside all thought of personal preference, — for the sake of his party and for the sake of the peace, the welfare, and the satisfaction of the nation, was to wait for the orderly processes of the constituted authorities to determine the facts of the election and then to accept the result. He was not and could not be the judge in his own case; no, not his own case, the case of the American people. His personal fortunes were a mere incident in the great controversy, and so he steadfastly regarded them. What, under the law, was the voice of the American people on November 7, 1876? That was what was to be determined; to be determined, not by him, not by newspaper clamor, not by partisan assumption or prejudice, not by sentimental appeal, but by the orderly methods and instrumentalities which the legislative power of the States, whose votes were in dispute, had created for that purpose. Either he was elected or he was not elected. If he was duly declared elected by the powers which alone had the authority to make that declaration, what possible right could he have to refuse to abide by the decision? What could have resulted except confusion and disaster to the country? If he was duly declared not elected, why, the matter was ended and there should be no railing at fortune, no personal lamentation because of defeat.

Gradually, as more definite information came to Mr. Hayes from the South, especially in private letters from competent and trustworthy observers,[1] he began to reach the conviction that the true voice of the disputed States had declared for the Republican party. For example, November 23 John Sherman wrote him from New Orleans: —

My dear Sir, — I have not written you sooner, for the progress of our visitation will be known to you through the papers sooner than from my letters, and the telegraph office here is more public than a

---

[1] General Garfield wrote him from New Orleans: "Of the justice of our claim, I have no doubt; though I fear it will be impossible for our Northern people to understand how difficult a thing it is for anything like regularity and order to be brought out of such chaos as this in a few days. They must be patient and let the mill of the law grind out its grist. Nearly all of us [the visiting statesmen] have abstained from writing you partly because we did not want you annoyed by the details of the contest, and partly because we were not always sure that our letters would pass to you undisturbed."

· On December 1, Aaron F. Perry, of Cincinnati, wrote from Washington: "I write now to say that I find here more deliberate attention to pending election difficulties than I expected. There is great activity of telegrams, legal opinions, and Cabinet consultations. More is known here of details than I have seen in the papers. Circumstances are known which show some of the rulings not arbitrary as they would appear by the papers. I think more deliberate consideration to questions of law is given than our friends generally suppose. The spirit also appears to be temperate and reasonable. Errors may be made, but I think not purposely. At the present moment everything looks well for your election, and it is looked for with confidence and yet with a proviso for unforeseen contingencies. I have no time for details. I thought you would be glad to know how much careful consideration the subject receives; and that the strong hand is not intended to be shown except in support of law and preservation of order; nor is it intended to encourage any arbitrary or unlawful counts. But if it shall be found that you are lawfully elected, it is intended that you shall be inaugurated and the law enforced."

sheriff's sale. We sometimes hear of private telegrams before they are delivered. The action of the Returning Board has thus far been open and fair and only confirms the general result known before. . . .

We are now collecting the testimony as to the bulldozed parishes. It seems more like the history of hell than of civilized and Christian communities. The means adopted are almost incredible, but were fearfully effective upon an ignorant and superstitious people. That you would have received at a fair election a large majority in Louisiana, no honest man can question; that you did not receive a majority is equally clear. But that intimidation, of the very kind and nature provided against by the Louisiana law, did enter into and control the election, in more election polls than would change the result and give you the vote, I believe as firmly as that I write this. The difficulty of gathering this testimony and putting it in the legal form has been very great, but I believe has been fully met.

The whole case rests upon the action of the Returning Board. I have carefully observed them, and have formed a high opinion of Governor Wells and Colonel Anderson. They are firm, judicious, and, as far as I can judge, thoroughly honest and conscientious. They are personally familiar with the nature and degree of intimidation in Louisiana. They can see that the intimidation, as organized, was with a view of throwing out Republican parishes rather than endangering Democratic parishes. Our little party is now dividing out the disputed parishes, with the view of a careful examination of every paper and detail. Many are impatient of the delay, and some have gone home. We will probably be able to keep about ten here. . . . We are in good hope and spirit. Not wishing the return in your favor, unless it is clear that it ought to be so, and not willing to be cheated out of it, or to be "bulldozed" or intimidated, the truth is palpable that you ought to have the vote of Louisiana, and we believe that you will have it, by an honest and fair return, according to the letter and spirit of the law of Louisiana.

To this Mr. Hayes replied: —

COLUMBUS, O., November 27, 1876.

MY DEAR SIR, — I am greatly obliged for your letter of the 23d. You feel, I am sure, as I do about this whole business. A fair election would have given us about forty electoral votes at the South — at least that many. But we are not to allow our friends to defeat one outrage and fraud by another. There must be nothing crooked on our part. Let Mr. Tilden have the place by violence, intimidation, and fraud, rather than undertake to prevent it by means that will not bear the severest scrutiny.

I appreciate the work doing by the Republicans who have gone South, and am especially proud of the acknowledged honorable conduct of those from Ohio. The Democrats made a mistake in sending so many ex-Republicans. New converts are proverbially bitter and unfair towards those they have recently left.

I trust you will soon reach the end of the work, and be able to return in health and safety. — Sincerely,

R. B. HAYES.

And yet, so far as Mr. Hayes was personally concerned, he felt, as he wrote Mr. Schurz, that "to be counted out would be a relief." On Thursday, November 30, Thanksgiving Day, he wrote in his diary: —

The Presidential question is still unsettled. For more than two weeks it has seemed almost certain that the three doubtful States would be carried by the Republicans. South Carolina is surely Republican. Florida is in nearly the same condition, both States being for the Republicans on the face of the returns, with the probability of increased majorities by corrections. Louisiana is the State which will decide. There is no doubt that a very large majority of the lawful voters are Republicans. But the Democrats have endeavored to defeat the will of the lawful voters by the perpetration of crimes whose magnitude and atrocity has no parallel in our history. By murder and hellish cruelties they at many polls drove the colored people away, or forced them to vote the Democratic ticket. It now seems probable that the Returning Board will have before them evidence which will justify the throwing out of enough to secure the State to those who are lawfully entitled to it.[1]

On the following day the diary records: —

Colonel Roberts, of the New Orleans *Times*, wanted an interview with me. Had lunch at Comly's. After lunch he said he called on me

[1] A letter from George A. Sheridan, dated New Orleans, November 21, to Mr. Hayes had said: "Counting the ballots as cast would be in my judgment as great an infamy as was ever perpetrated. Our election law is a very stringent one, its stringency necessitated by the lawless character of a large portion of our population. Applying the provisions of our law to the recent election in this State will give you the electoral vote. You are, of course, posted by the papers as to the extent and character of the intimidation practised in this State in the recent election. The press has not overstated the matter. The Returning Board will do its duty and throw out parishes and polls where intimidation prevented a fair election. Under the law they are *compelled* to do this. In my judgment an honest, fair interpretation of the law leaves them no alternative. In equity and law you are entitled to Louisiana, and your conscience will assure you, upon a full examination of the case, that its electoral vote is as lawfully and legitimately yours as the electoral vote of Ohio. Matters are quiet here. The Democrats are settling down to the conviction that you will get the vote of Louisiana. I do not apprehend trouble. There will be no outbreak here because these people know in their hearts that the election was one of violence upon the part of the Democrats, and it will be very hard, I think impossible, to make them put their lives in peril for what they know to be a wrong."

to give me the views of Lamar, of Mississippi, General Walthall, ditto, Wade Hampton, of South Carolina, and probably Gordon, of Georgia. "You will be President. We will not make trouble. We want peace. We want the color line abolished. We will not oppose an Administration which will favor an honest administration and honest officers in the South. We will favor measures to secure the colored people all of their rights. We may not, and probably will not, leave the party of opposition, but such an Administration as you will have we can support as men of the opposite party can. We want nothing of you in the way of promise or pledge."

This was the substance. I replied by saying I was gratified to know it; that my letter of acceptance covered the whole ground; that it meant all it said and all that it implied. This was the substance. In case of my election there will be further conference, and I hope for good results.

A newspaper correspondent sent a highly imaginative report of this interview to the Cincinnati *Enquirer*, asserting that Mr. Hayes had spoken disparagingly of certain Republican leaders of the South, and had criticized severely certain features of President Grant's Southern policy and certain of his Southern appointees, and declaring that he had given Colonel Roberts assurances of his desire to coöperate with the conservative Democratic leaders of the South and to divide the government patronage with them, impliedly in return for their support. This report was widely copied by other papers and provoked much discussion, though its absurdity and falsity were promptly declared by the *State Journal*, at the house of whose editor the conversation had taken place, and it was completely disproved by Colonel Roberts's version of the interview. The mischievous purpose of the report was manifestly to seek to excite disaffection or indifference in President Grant's mind toward the interests of his prospective successor. But this effort completely failed. Even without contradiction from an authoritative source, all who knew Mr. Hayes's temper of mind, his habitual reticence of judgment or commitment until all pertinent facts were in his possession, must have recognized the weird inconsonance of the report with the whole course of conduct that Mr. Hayes had consistently pursued throughout the campaign.[1]

[1] The New York *Times*, Sunday, December 10, advised its readers to reject any reports purporting to give the words or opinions of Mr. Hayes unless such reports were in harmony with his known characteristics; "otherwise they are

Sunday, December 3, three days before the Electoral Colleges were to meet and cast their votes, Mr. Hayes, despite what Colonel Roberts, a Democrat, had said to him, was inclined to believe that Louisiana might have to be yielded to the Democrats. That day he wrote in his diary: —

Various indications lead me to think that in Louisiana the report of the Returning Board will probably be unfavorable. No doubt a fair election would have carried the State for the Republicans. But it is possible that the wrong cannot lawfully be corrected by the Returning Board. But suppose they do correct without sufficient warrant of law. The returns will be made to the President of the Senate, and on their face the Republicans will have a majority. Suppose a way is found to go behind those returns by the Senate. Should not in that event the whole case be gone into? Should not the equitable result be reached? Not only throw out the Democratic majorities where violence procured them, but count in fairly the honest Republican majorities which were prevented by lawlessness?

But assurances were given him the next day which left no doubt in his mind of the justice of the Republican cause. Tuesday, December 5, he writes: —

Yesterday Elwood E. Thorne and Francis A. Stout, of the Republican Reform Club of New York, came here and had an interview with me. The purport of their communication, written and oral, was that New York was lost by coldness and neglect (perhaps treachery) on the part of the New York managers of the canvass — meaning Cornell [and] some of the Federal officers, generally, I suppose, friends of Conkling.[1] Their

likely to be as the wild vagaries of a dream." Readers should remember that "Governor Hayes is a reticent, self-restraining, self-contained man. He listens well, weighs and often refutes what is said, and mentally takes the measure of all who approach him. He is a singularly well-poised man, free absolutely from hobbies, vanities, or affectations; and hence never loses his balance. His tongue, unlike his mind, is not active, and is under the most perfect government." The *Times* further specifies, with amplification on each particular, that "he is an exceedingly cautious man," "an extremely judicious man," "a remarkably well-informed man," and, finally, "a public man of firm, resolute will."

[1] Apropos of this visit General Garfield wrote Mr. Hayes from Washington, December 9: "I think you ought to know that a persistent attempt has been made to lead the President to believe that you were going to ignore his friends in such a way as to imply a censure upon his Administration. I suspect that a part of this impression has come from the two New York gentlemen (Messrs. Stout and Thorne) who visited you the day we saw you. They came on to this city with us. I am informed that one of them has reported that they said to you: 'You are probably aware that Senator Conkling did nothing to aid your election'; and that you answered: 'I received no help either from him or his friends'; and that they express their satisfaction with the prospect that the Senator and such as he will

facts were not very conclusive, but tended to show a lack of hearty support.

In the afternoon a number of Republicans who had been in New Orleans to witness the proceedings of the Returning Board, on the invitation of the President or of the National Republican Committee, stopped here on their return East. Senator Sherman, General Garfield, Eugene Hale, of Maine, Mr. Stoughton and General Van Alen, of New York, and General White, of Indiana County, Pennsylvania, constituted the party. Cortlandt Parker did not stop, but returned with this party.[1] They called on me at my office about 3 P.M., General Comly and Webb being present. They spread before me very fully the condition of things in Louisiana, and the action of the Returning Board. They emphatically endorsed the general fairness and honesty of the Board's conduct. They said it was the opinion of all of the Republicans who went down to New Orleans that the Republican ticket was lawfully and honestly entitled to be declared elected. That largely more parishes and polls ought to be thrown out for violence and intimidation than were necessary to elect the whole Republican ticket, state and national; that a fair election would have given the Republicans not less than thirteen to fifteen thousand majority; that the intimidation was deliberately planned and systematically executed by means of rifle clubs organized in the parishes selected for the process of intimidation known as "bulldozing." I asked each of the gentlemen for his individual views. All concurred in saying in the strongest terms that the evidence and law entitled the Republican ticket to the certificate of election, and that the result would in their opinion be accordingly. They spoke highly of Wells and Anderson, and frankly of the two colored men.[2]

be ignored during your term. Now, I have no idea that anybody has any authority to speak for you on these topics. But I will say that Senator Sherman and I were not favorably impressed with the discretion of these gentlemen from their talk on the journey."

[1] In a letter to Mr. Hayes, dated Newark, December 5, Mr. Parker explained that a professional engagement compelled him to forego stopping at Columbus. He added: "I beg leave to add that if the count finally reported by the Returning Board in Louisiana shall entitle the Republican electors to their certificate, you need have no scruples against their vote. I attended almost all the sessions of the Board. They were especially fair and open. Technicalities received no favor. I acquainted myself likewise, so far as the nature of things permitted, with the evidence upon the subject of intimidation. No one except returning officers can speak as to the extent to which this evidence is applicable. I can only say that if the testimony I have not seen is like that which I have been made acquainted with, the exclusion of any votes affected will be justifiable, and that the conduct of the Board shows them to be men in whose judgment and desire to do right full confidence may be placed. The law of Louisiana as to this matter is the law of the Union. The Board is vested by that law with full jurisdiction in the premises. And from what I have seen of them, I shall be ready to acquiesce as readily in their decision; while all must allow, I suppose, that it is legally final."

[2] The members of the Returning Board.

After this conversation, Mr. Hayes was not surprised the next evening, while he and Mrs. Hayes were entertaining the members of the Ohio Electoral College and other friends, to receive dispatches from New Orleans advising him that the Republican electors of Louisiana had been declared elected. As the Returning Boards of South Carolina and Florida had reached a similar result, and as the Democratic effort to seize one electoral vote in Oregon could not in reason succeed, the Electoral Colleges on December 6 gave Mr. Hayes a total of 185 votes; Mr. Tilden, 184. During that day and evening Mr. Hayes heard directly from every Republican State except four, among the latter Oregon, about which he felt some solicitude.[1] December 7 he writes: —

. . . This morning Isaiah, our colored man, when he came in to build the fire, laid the *State Journal* on our bed. He lighted the gas and I read the telegraphic accounts showing how Governor Grover of Oregon had refused to commission Watts, the Republican elector, an ex-postmaster, and had given the certificate of election to Cronin, the highest Democratic elector; and how he, Cronin, had *met* as the college, and elected two Republicans to fill the two vacancies created by the refusal of the Republicans, two of whom were commissioned, to act or meet with him; and how *this* college met and cast two votes for Hayes and Wheeler and one for Tilden and Hendricks; — thus giving in the nation to Hayes and Wheeler 184 electoral votes and to Tilden and Hendricks 185 votes, and in this way electing the latter President and Vice-President. The two regularly commissioned Republican electors met. Watts the postmaster resigned, was reëlected, and *this* college gave Hayes and Wheeler the three votes of Oregon, making their aggregate 185, and thus electing them, if this vote is treated as the true one.

Here is the danger: A contest ruinous to the country — dangerous, perhaps fatal, to free government — may grow out of it. I would gladly give up all claim to the place if this would avert the evil, without bringing on a greater calamity. I am determined that no selfish ambition or interest shall influence my conduct in the face of these tremendous events. Whatever, on the whole, is best for the country, that I will do, if I can know it, regardless of consequences to myself. I shall keep cool — master all tendencies that may lead me astray, and endeavor to act as Washington would have acted under similar circumstances.

My wife feels some disappointment; is unhappy on account of the consequences of our defeat to the poor colored people of the South; but

[1] "I am overwhelmed with callers congratulating me on the results declared in Florida and Louisiana. I have no doubt that we are justly and legally entitled to the Presidency. My conversation with Sherman, Garfield, Stoughton, and others settled the question in my mind as to Louisiana." (From letter of Mr. Hayes to Carl Schurz, December 6, 1876.)

on personal grounds is contented, and will without effort show her usual cheerfulness. We shall both bear this new responsibility with composure. Our friends will suffer more than we shall, whatever the suspense or the final result.[1]

Further consideration evidently convinced Mr. Hayes that he had taken the Oregon intrigue much too seriously, for the very next day he writes: —

The Oregon fraud appears to have been carried out in so bungling a way that it is not likely to do more than complicate matters. Indeed, it now looks as if it would damage our adversaries in the public judgment without in any manner injuring us. The fraud is so transparent, palpable, and disgraceful that it is not impossible that it will be thrown aside without dissent from any quarter.

But the voting of the Electoral Colleges did not settle this historic controversy. It flamed more fiercely if possible than ever. In each of the disputed States contesting electors were commissioned by one authority or another. These went through the form of voting, and their votes, bearing some kind of official attestation, were forwarded, with circumspect conformity to legal requirements, to the President of the Senate at Washington. The clamor of indignant Democratic newspapers and orators filled the air, and threats of a resort to arms to enforce their asserted rights began to be heard. As soon as Congress assembled committees were appointed by both houses to proceed to the disputed Southern States and investigate the facts and conditions of the election and the actions of the Returning Boards. The results of these investigations cover endless pages of official reports. Question at once arose, too, in public discussion and in Congress, as to how the electoral vote was to be canvassed and counted and the result declared. In what way were the contesting returns to be dealt with? How was it to be determined which returns from each disputed State were the true returns? Here was matter for limitless controversy, for the widest variety of opinion and suggestion. The supreme interest of the nation was

[1] "One thing you can count on, I mean to do my duty, uninfluenced by selfish ambition or interest. I feel very strongly that in the presence of the tremendous dangers now threatening us we should all try to be deliberate and calm — not hasty to condemn or to act — remembering always what an unmixed evil civil war is." (From letter to Carl Schurz, December 7, 1876.)

involved; the very fate of free institutions seemed to be at stake. It is no wonder that public sentiment fluctuated from day to day as the great debate went on in every coterie of men and at every fireside in the land; no wonder that the country was in a state of suspense, of agitation, of alarm. It was a situation to tax the wisdom, the patience, and the patriotism of all able and conscientious statesmen.

The appeal to the Constitution and the precedents of all former Presidential elections was neither conclusive nor convincing. The Constitution merely orders that "The President of the Senate shall, in the presence of the Senate and House of Representatives, open all the certificates, and the votes shall then be counted." Were the two houses to be present simply as spectators or witnesses of the count, or were they entitled to some voice in the proceeding? Did the President of the Senate have sole right and power to determine which of two or more certificates from any State was to be accepted and counted, without possibility of challenge or appeal? There were many men that held steadfastly to that position. But the practice of Congress at previous epochs militated against this narrow interpretation of the ambiguous constitutional mandate. It had been customary for Congress, at the approach of each quadrennial count of the electoral votes, to adopt a joint rule of procedure governing the manner of that august function of state. Such rules had recognized the right of the houses of Congress to determine questions in dispute. But in no case had any action taken under such rules of procedure had the least effect on the result. In all previous cases, under any rules or no rules, the choice and voice of the voters was so clearly expressed that the count of the electoral votes by the President of the Senate, in the presence of the two houses of Congress, had been little more than a formal and ceremonial proceeding. But now conditions were altogether different. The Presidency hung upon a single electoral vote. The Senate was Republican; the House, Democratic — both in actual numerical majority and by States. Under the joint rule which had been in force at the three last counts, it was obvious, human nature and partisan spirit being what they are, that the Republicans would inevitably lose the Presidency. Naturally, therefore, the Republican Senate would not consent to a renewal of the joint rule of

FREDERICK T. FRELINGHUYSEN   OLIVER P. MORTON

GEORGE F. EDMUNDS

THOMAS F. BAYARD   ALLEN G. THURMAN

THE SENATORS

SAMUEL F. MILLER   STEPHEN J. FIELD

NATHAN CLIFFORD

WILLIAM STRONG   JOSEPH P. BRADLEY

THE SUPREME COURT JUSTICES

THE ELECTORAL COMMISSION

EPPA HUNTON   J. G. ABBOTT
          HENRY B. PAYNE
GEORGE F. HOAR   JAMES A. GARFIELD

THE REPRESENTATIVES

recent canvasses.[1] If the President of the Senate had exclusive and final authority to accept or to reject certificates according to his own single judgment, then it was thought indubitable that the votes for Mr. Hayes from every disputed State would be counted. It is apparent that there were here the elements of a situation that afforded ample opportunity for earnest and sincere argument on all sides, as well as abundant scope for the play of selfish purposes and personal ambitions. But it was the very kind of situation that demanded wise compromise and patriotic accommodation — even to the extent of straining, if need were, the limits of constitutional authority. Otherwise civil strife and anarchy, and the possibility of the wreck of the ship of state, whose peaceful progress the Constitution was intended to insure, loomed ominous on the country's horizon.

While this momentous debate was going on throughout the land, and the leaders in Congress of both parties were seeking a solution of the tremendous problem which confronted the country, Mr. Hayes continued to maintain his equanimity and to pursue the even tenor of his way; in outward bearing no more interested, apparently, in the outcome than any other high-minded and patriotic citizen. About the middle of December he made a visit to his friend, R. C. Anderson, in Dayton.[2] In the evening a salute of one hundred and eighty-five guns was fired in his honor and a large number of people serenaded him. When he appeared, the people pressed forward to grasp his hand, while the band played and fireworks illuminated the sky. Then, when the personal greetings were over, Mr. Hayes mounted a chair and spoke to the throng in these words: —

My Friends, — I will not detain you longer than four or five minutes. I am here on a short visit to your beautiful city of Dayton, not on any political mission, or to talk on any of the political questions of the memorable canvass that has just closed. I understand that these greetings

[1] This was the famous Twenty-second Joint Rule. The Senate in January, 1876, long before the beginning of the Presidential campaign, had refused, after long debate, to readopt this rule.

[2] "*Columbus, December 16, 1876.* — We returned last night from Dayton. . . . At Dayton I made an offhand talk which seemed to be successful. Several hundred people shook hands with a gushing sort of enthusiasm and I was visited by many of the best people. . . . At Springfield the people, especially the workingmen, turned out in great force. I spoke from the rear of the car until the train moved on." (Diary.)

here to-night are not so much in honor of myself as on account of the peculiar interest that is felt in the present condition of the country. In the excitement that has pervaded the country before and since the election, people of ardent temperament have said and done things that are indiscreet. But as the excitement subsides, we begin to return to our better wisdom and judgment. I have too much faith in the saving common sense of the American people to think they desire to see in their country a Mexicanized government.

Whatever may be the result at which the lawful authorities shall arrive, you and I will quietly submit; and I have sufficient respect and confidence in the great majority of the opposite party to believe that they will do the same. I was glad to see in a paper this evening an article from the London *Times* respecting the condition of this country. "Such a state of affairs," it said, "could not occur anywhere else in the world. The entire area of the country agitated by the uncertain issue of the political struggle, yet not one shot fired, not one man killed, no breaches of the peace."

We have seen this centennial year the wonders of our growth displayed in the exhibition of agricultural and mechanical arts, and we are now afforded an opportunity of giving to the world an example of the value of a republican government. In speaking to you this evening, I have referred without previous thought to what must have occurred to every one of us standing here, and I take my leave of you with most sincere acknowledgment of this expression of your friendship and good will.[1]

During all these excited weeks Mr. Hayes was the recipient of innumerable letters from personal friends and party leaders of all parts of the country giving him assurances of continuing loyalty, expressing unvarying confidence in the righteousness of the official decisions in his behalf in the disputed States, and imparting information regarding public opinion and the efforts that were making to insure the establishment of his right to the Presidency. To many of these letters Mr. Hayes replied briefly, constantly disavowing any purpose or intention of seeking himself by suggestion or committal to control or influence the evolution by Congress of special legislation or instrumentalities for dealing with the crisis. He himself was convinced, as were many of his intimate

---

[1] The Dayton *Democrat*, criticizing the taste of the demonstration, especially the salute of one hundred and eighty-five guns, still was constrained to say: "And it is not out of courtesy, but simply out of a regard to truth, that we here say that we know of no Republican statesman in the land whom we think so worthy to be President (*if he were elected*) as Governor Hayes; and no man, *in any party*, upon whose personal integrity and patriotic intentions the people could rely with more profound confidence."

friends and advisers, and, indeed, a large proportion of the Republican party, that the simple injunction of the Constitution was sufficient; that it gave the President of the Senate plenary authority to open the certificates, decide, in case of duplicate or triplicate certificates, which were the authentic returns, count the vote, and declare who was elected. He could not believe that serious resistance would be made to such exercise of authority or that trouble would ensue.[1] But a calm review of all the facts of the situation — of the vast divergencies of opinion among statesmen and publicists as well as the people at large, of the heated condition of the public mind — leaves little doubt that a decided majority of the people of the country would have regarded such a disposition of the case as highly arbitrary; as the exercise by the President of the Senate of a questionable authority, whose existence was utterly denied by the powerful Democratic majority of the House of Representatives; and that consequently resentment at defeat by means or methods which they believed in defiance alike of the Constitution and of fair dealing would have been likely to stir the Democrats, leaders and masses, to resistance and civil strife.[2] It was altogether better that extreme partisan counsels gave way to a larger and more liberal view; and that the joint committee of the two houses of Congress, composed of some of the ablest leaders of both parties, which was entrusted with the task, was able to devise a plan of adjustment which was accepted by Congress and which appealed to the conservative sense of the country — eager for relief from the suspense of uncertainty and for assurance of a peaceful settlement — as fair and reasonable.

During this time, too, many men of distinction journeyed to Columbus to consult with Mr. Hayes on the political situation,

[1] December 29, Mr. Hayes wrote Mr. S. Shellabarger, a former member of Congress from Ohio and an eminent lawyer: "I wish in strict confidence to say that in case our adversaries go to law with us, I shall want you to assist the Attorney-General. Let your thoughts dwell on the points that may be raised either to question our rights or simply to perplex and annoy us.

"One other matter. My judgment is that neither House of Congress, nor both combined, have any right to interfere in the count. It is for the Vice-President to do it all. His action is final. There should be no compromise of our constitutional rights. We should firmly insist upon them.

"Again allow me to assure you that I am in no way committed as to persons or policies. No one is authorized to commit me. I shall remain free to the end."

[2] Consult James Ford Rhodes's *History of the United States*, vol. VII, chap. XLIV.

to volunteer advice, or to seek to elicit from him some intimation
of his purposes and policy, or some encouragement for themselves
in their political activity or aspirations. Mr. Hayes, in his diary,
December 17, preserves a record of such a visit in the following
entry: —

Yesterday Colonel Albert D. Shaw, Consul at Toronto, came from
Washington to talk with me about affairs there, and my purposes as to
persons and policies.[1] He is a friend of Senator Conkling, and seemed

[1] Mr. Hayes had been prepared for this interview by the following letter: —

U.S. SENATE CHAMBER, WASHINGTON,
December 12, 1876.

MY DEAR SIR, — I this evening gave to Colonel Albert D. Shaw, of New York,
now Consul-General at Toronto, a letter of introduction to you, and now write
you in advance of its presentation my reasons for giving it, and the probable
nature of the interview Colonel Shaw will seek with you. The letter was written
at the request of Mr. Cameron, Secretary of War, and of Mr. Platt, member of
Congress from New York, and after interviews with them. A studied effort has
been made by influential men, mainly of the Democratic party, to poison the
mind of Senator Conkling against you and your Administration, partly by assertions that you will be under the influence of Carl Schurz and Mr. Curtis whom he
regards as his enemies, and partly by representations that you will be personally
unfriendly to him because he was not active in your support and for other reasons. I have felt safe in saying that, while you have a friendly feeling for Schurz
and Curtis and appreciate their support, that this will not in the least induce you
to ignore the merits, ability, and just influence of Conkling as a leading prominent Republican Senator, nor make you a party to personal antagonism or
enmity to him; and that you know, as I do, that his physical condition last fall
would not justify his taking a more active part in the canvass. This is perfectly
manifest now, for his physical strength is much broken, and by reason of this he
is more easily moved by such suggestions.

Colonel Shaw is his intimate personal friend, and so is Mr. Platt, and yours
also. Cameron is very active and influential in calming these incipient jealousies
with a view of a united, hearty coöperation of all Republicans here in your inauguration and installation in office. With this brief statement you will see the
importance of assuring Colonel Shaw that you will come into the Presidential
office with a determination to do exact justice to all without fear, favor, or prejudice, and the alleged hostility to Conkling has no foundation whatever. He is
undoubtedly a man of great ability and influence and we do not want either his
opposition or cold reserve.

I write you this, not to commit you in any way by pledge or promise, but to
explain why I regard my introduction of Colonel Shaw, not as a matter of form,
but of great importance in removing doubts and discontents which otherwise
might develop into serious opposition. — Very truly yours,

JOHN SHERMAN.

To this letter Mr. Hayes replied, December 16: "Thanks for your favors.
Touching the business of Mr. Shaw, I am free absolutely from committals as to
persons or policies. People who talk to me are listened to respectfully, and I talk

to be on intimate terms with the Secretary of War [Don Cameron] and others in high places. He talked forcibly and with much feeling. He fears that the apprehension that I am in the hands of the reform element of the Republican party will lose me in the Senate the friendship and support of enough Senators in the approaching struggle in the Senate to change the result of the Presidential election, and bring in Mr. Tilden. Mr. Conkling has been committed against our present views on some of the legal questions now before the country — notably, as I infer, on the right of the Senate and House to pass on the returns of the Electoral Colleges. The Southern Republican Senators are afraid they will be ignored as "carpetbaggers" or otherwise objectionable under the Hayes policy of conciliation. Names were not mentioned, but Spencer, of Alabama, Dorsey, of Arkansas, Clayton, and Conover seemed to be the Senators Colonel Shaw was thinking of.

I told Colonel Shaw I had concluded that I ought to take no part in the pending contest in Washington, that I should probably make no declaration of policy and no committal as to members of my Cabinet until the result was announced in February. That I stood on my letter. That as to Southern affairs it plainly indicated what I thought desirable. That the Southern people must obey the new amendments, and give the colored men all of their rights; that peace in that country could only be had in this way; that prosperity would come to the South with immigration from the North and from Europe; that to get this, people must feel as free to go to the South as they now do to go to Kansas or Nebraska; that I had no private views or pledges to give; that what I said to him I said publicly, and to all who called on me and desired to know my views.

He showed the reasons why Mr. Conkling took no active part in the canvass, that his health was broken, and his eyes required that he should remain in a dark room. He explained the bad faith of Curtis [1] towards Conkling; of Bristow towards Conkling and Grant; of Morgan towards Conkling, etc., etc. He urged the appointment of Conkling (or rather of his being offered the appointment) as Secretary of State. Spoke well of Platt, of Morrill, of Maine, of [the] Secretary of War, and in disparagement of Chandler, Blaine, and Jewell.

Although I gave him no pledges, and merely said as to appointments I would try to give first consideration to the claims of all sections of the Republican party, he seemed to be pleased with what I told him. He

quite freely up to the point of my letter and other public utterances, but I have no *private* utterances for any of my visitors. I have no prejudices which will prevent me from listening to suggestions impartially. I mean to keep myself free as long as practicable, and to hear in a friendly spirit all that may be offered. I do not like to mention names, but this disposition *extends to all*. My desire is to do all I can to have a strong, wise, and successful Administration. All personal considerations must yield to this. I want to hear from you fully, freely, and confidentially."

[1] George William Curtis was the only delegate from New York at the Cincinnati Convention who refused to vote for the nomination of Mr. Conkling.

evidently came with a desire to be pleased, and left professing to think he could remove difficulties at Washington.[1]

Certain of Mr. Hayes's closest political advisers were of the opinion that either Mr. Hayes should go to Washington himself, or that he should have there some intimate or confidential friend who should be able, without committing him in any way, to speak authoritatively for him, or in his behalf, when any question of immediate concern should arise in the constantly shifting discussions and conferences relating to the Presidential succession.[2] To one of these advisers, Governor Dennison, at that time one of the Commissioners of the District of Columbia, Mr. Hayes wrote December 17: — [3]

I am exceedingly obliged for your valuable letters. It seems to me desirable that I should remain quietly in Ohio, committing myself to no person or policy beyond that which the public may fairly infer from my

[1] Another visit is described in the diary, December 30, as follows: "The political event of the week is the visit made me by Judge T. J. Mackey, of Chester, South Carolina, with a letter from General Wade Hampton. Mackey is a fluent and florid talker. His representations are such as lead one to hope for good results by a wise policy in the South. The letter is not of much importance, except as it indicates General Hampton's views of duty in case of armed resistance by the Democrats. I have a dispatch from C. P. Leslie as follows: 'I warn you to beware of Tom Mackey. . . . He is a first-class fraud . . . , etc., etc.' This is a specimen of the Southern complications."

[2] Senator Sherman, in a letter dated Washington, December 9, wrote Mr. Hayes: "There is a strong feeling in certain quarters here that you should come to Washington in an informal way with a view to conferences as to some important points. My judgment has not inclined me as yet to the necessity or propriety of it, but it may be that events will occur to render it expedient for you to come, of which you will be advised in time. Please turn it over in your mind, so as to be prepared if the request should be sent you. In case you come it would be better for you to stay with me, rather than at the President's or at a public house, but of this I will advise you further."

[3] Governor Dennison had written, December 9. A portion of his letter read: "I have no fear of the President; at the same time, I think he made a mistake in giving Hewitt a wholly private audience. But it has occurred to me that no injury could result from an early visit here of General Comly or some other Ohio friend, whom the country regards as having your confidence, to talk as he might think prudent, to the President and all others, on any matter; to remove any misapprehensions, if any he might find here, affecting your purposes. Of course, he would not speak under any special authority, only from his general knowledge of your feelings and methods of doing things. If he come it may be well for his mission to be known only to himself and you. General Comly or any other Ohio friend's visiting here will surprise nobody. I have not mentioned to any one my purpose to write you. And shall not do so. It will be as well for you to throw this letter in the fire after reading it."

letter and other published and authorized utterances. Believing firmly that I have been honestly and legally elected, I propose to wait contentedly for the issue. If the result is changed by violence, fraud, or treachery, I shall suffer less than my friends — less than the country, and I may truly say I shall suffer chiefly on their account.[1]

Two weeks later, December 31, Mr. Hayes wrote to Mr. J. A. Kasson, member of Congress from Iowa: —

I still think I ought to leave Washington well alone. I have many friends in that city who can of their own motion speak confidently of my ways of thinking and acting. An authorized representative could remove some troubles that you now see; but only think of yet greater troubles he might create.

I like to get your suggestions, and am interested in the facts you give. Do not misconstrue my silence if in the hurry of the time I fail to reply.[2]

[1] How Mr. Hayes's course of conduct impressed the country at this period is indicated by a letter to him from J. W. Forney, the famous Philadelphia journalist. He wrote: "I cannot refrain the expression of my frank opinion in regard to the good example you are setting the country in this painful interval. A political experience of more than a generation of time justifies me in the observation that nothing is doing more to relieve the country from its trying suspense than your moderation. . . . We are fortunate in the blunders of our antagonists; and I read in the signs of the times the rapid cessation of all those doubts and fears which have troubled our timid friends. Oregon has been a rare magician. Colorado also. These two States, in which the Democrats have made two cardinal mistakes, are doing more for us than anything except the Democratic division on the Twenty-second Rule. Such papers as the *Nation* are coming around to reason under these influences, and even the London papers are affected by the same argument and impressed by the gentleness and modesty of your example."

[2] Mr. Kasson had written first: —

WASHINGTON, D.C.,
Confidential. December 17, 1876.
DEAR GOVERNOR HAYES, — I take the liberty of expressing the wish that some confidential friend of yours could be here during the remainder of this winter. Some gentleman who can keep counsel, and who can also, if the emergency arises, have some intercourse with the Southern elements of the Democracy. General Bristow, if he could be persuaded to come, might be of great service. I cannot, in a letter, explain to you the situation as I comprehend it. I think, however, that these two premises may be assumed: 1. That 185 votes will be ascertained and counted by the Senate for you, followed by the declaration of your election as President. 2. That our security against the subsequent election of Tilden by the House is to be found in a division of sentiment in the Democracy, led by Southern Representatives.

The basis of this division exists in the indisposition of a large part of the South to become again embroiled in national disorder, and in their wish to recover intelligent white rule in the South. To give them this need not involve the sacrifice of the constitutional rights of the negro, nor should it. Nor will they demand it. They also perceive an opportunity to reëstablish a cordial union with the North, which is Republican, and end forever the old strife.

On the same day he wrote to General Noyes: —

Something like your views as to a friend or friends at Washington has been mentioned by a good many. There are two sides to it. It seems

It is necessary to make an effort to organize this element to make it effective; nor do we yet know its present or possible extent. It is wise, at least, to foster it, and to give an orderly and peaceful alternative to their thought.

Some friend of yours, disconnected from congressional life, and not provoking Democratic prejudices, could ascertain whether any reliance can be placed on the sentiment I have mentioned, and whether that, added to the more conservative Democracy of the Senate, is likely to be able to save the country from the shame of a Mexican contest over the Presidency. He would be able, also, to indicate the probable spirit of your Administration, if not its policy, touching questions which most concern the South.

I have advised our side of the House to abstain from provoking debate on the Presidential question, so as to leave time for partisan fires to die out, and for the intervention of peaceful sentiments. I believe in a peaceful solution, but am not free from anxiety about the issue.

Very truly, your friend and obedient servant,

JOHN A. KASSON, M.C.

To that letter Mr. Hayes replied expressing his disinclination to interfere, whereupon Mr. Kasson wrote the following letter, to which Mr. Hayes's letter given in the text was in reply: —

CLARENDON HOTEL, NEW YORK CITY,
December 27, 1876.

DEAR GOVERNOR, — Yours of the 21st was forwarded to me here, and just received. Undoubtedly freedom from committals, ante-official, both to persons and policies, is not only expedient but right in itself. My suggestion did not intend any variation from that rule. My desire was for the presence of a trusty friend, whose ears would be more open than his mouth, and whose candor would induce frankness of expression in response to questioning suggestions. I do not think any one contemplates agreements for mutual considerations. I have seen no disposition for what is called bargaining. It is rather inquiry into probable future action, not involving pledges.

Each day appears to diminish the spirit of disorder. Frelinghuysen's notion is that under the constitutional power to give effect to the provisions of the Constitution by legislation, we may enact a mode of counting votes; and in case of conflicting, or alleged invalid, certificates of Electoral Colleges, we may create a final tribunal, *ad hoc;* as, for example, a Board composed of President of Senate, Speaker of House, and Chief Justice of Supreme Court. Some such solution will be offered to the new conference committee.

By the way, Randall outraged us in the minority appointments on that committee, not a Republican *lawyer* among them. The logical position of our Democratic House in monstrous; thus the Constitution gives the right to the House to elect when no one has majority of votes cast. The House says it, by itself, has the right to reject the votes of States which give that majority. That is, the body which, in a certain contingency, has the right to make a President has also the right to make the contingency!

Such a doctrine would forever rob the people and the Electoral Colleges of their constitutional functions at the will of the House. — Very sincerely yours,

JOHN A. KASSON.

to me that Comly and Shellabarger and Dennison can give such facts about my general ways of thinking and action as will accomplish all that is right and practicable.[1] I am in the habit of saying that we can better afford defeat by the knavery of the adversary or the crotchets or treachery of friends than success by intrigues. Of course, I understand you to mean that we must have men at Washington prepared to defeat the corrupt practices of our adversaries. For this purpose the gentlemen I name can be useful, and other of our friends who may be in Washington can lend a helping hand. This must be left to volunteers. For me to select and send to Washington a *representative* would in my judgment be a mistake. Think of it. I will *hear* and *heed*, but you have my decided impressions.[2]

Influences of every sort were busy at Washington working upon the sentiment and opinions of members of Congress. Personal ambitions and antipathies were affecting the views and attitudes of some men. This is made evident by the tone of Colonel Shaw's conversation, related above, and by numerous expressions in letters to Mr. Hayes from his correspondents at the Capital. Mr. Tilden and his able lieutenants were active, day and night, with argument, promises, and intrigues, to incite disaffection and distrust in the Republican ranks and to rouse their own followers to aggressive assertion of their claims; to a determination to enforce them at all hazards. The conservative business interests of the country were becoming restless at the long-continued uncertainty of affairs; and apprehensive of the threatened confusion and disorder which the 4th of March might precipitate upon the country, and were urging Congress to adopt

[1] Already a few days before (December 25), Mr. Hayes had written John Sherman: "You know my general course of conduct. It has always seemed to me wise, in case of decided antagonisms among friends, not to take sides — to heal by compromise, not to aggravate, etc. I wish *you* to feel authorized to speak in pretty decided terms for me whenever it seems advisable — to do this not by reason of specific authority to do it, but from your knowledge of my general methods of action." — About this time General Comly visited Washington at President Grant's request. He had a long and confidential talk with the President setting forth Mr. Hayes's attitude as he understood it. He had also many conferences with Republican leaders with a view to reassuring Southern Republican Senators and others. On his return to Columbus he made a long written report to Mr. Hayes of his efforts and of his impressions of the condition of affairs at Washington.

[2] A letter of precisely similar purport was written the same day also to William E. Chandler, which had this postscript: "You now see the troubles which an authorized friend could remove. If you had such a friend in Washington, what other and greater troubles might you not see?"

some method or measure which would insure a peaceful solution
of the national controversy.[1] Discreet friends of Mr. Hayes held
frequent conferences with the more conservative Democratic
Senators from the South, especially those of Whig antecedents,
emphasizing Mr. Hayes's good intentions toward the South, as
set forth in his letter of acceptance and as could clearly be inferred from his pacific character, and encouraging them to resist
any radical or revolutionary action in connection with the count.
In this endeavor Colonel A. J. Kellar, editor of the Memphis *Avalanche*, who had long labored for purer and more liberal political
methods in Tennessee, took the most active and effective part.[2]
Efforts also were successfully made by some of Mr. Hayes's more
enthusiastic but less prudent friends to enlist the services of
Thomas A. Scott, the most powerful railway manager of the
day,[3] to exert his persuasive powers with Southern members
of Congress and Southern business men to reconcile them to
the Republican succession; and it was sought to have Mr.
Hayes commit himself as favoring government aid in building
the Texas-Pacific Railway which was at that time seeking a
subsidy. But Mr. Hayes had no faith in such methods and refused to make any commitments. Writing to William Henry
Smith, December 24, he said: —

Enclosed I return you the letters. I do not wish to be committed to
details. It is so desirable to restore peace and prosperity to the South
that I have given a good deal of thought to it. The two things I would
be exceptionally liberal about are education and internal improvements
of a national character. Nothing I can think of would do [so] well to

---

[1] General Garfield wrote from Washington, December 12: "In the meantime
two forces are at work. The Democratic business men of the country are more
anxious for quiet than for Tilden, and the leading Southern Democrats in Congress, especially those who were old Whigs, are saying that they have seen war
enough, and don't care to follow the lead of their Northern associates who, as
Ben Hill says, were 'invincible in peace and invisible in war.' After my speech
to-day on the point of order as to the validity of the Joint Rule, Hill came to me
and said: 'You are clearly right, and I don't intend to follow our people in this
sort of reckless warfare.'"

[2] "You never did a more important act than when with your friend you sent
Colonel Kellar here. He was just the man needed to reach the Southern men,
and he came at the very time he was most wanted. He merits great praise."
(General H. V. Boynton, in letter from Washington, February 18, 1877, to
William Henry Smith.)

[3] President of the Pennsylvania Railway system.

promote business prosperity, immigration, and a change in the sentiments of the Southern people on the unfortunate topic. Too much
politics, too little attention to business, is the bane of that part of
our country.

There is no doubt that most Republicans thought that any
proposed compromise, which should limit or qualify the full
authority which they believed the Constitution conferred on the
President of the Senate to count the electoral votes, would work
to their disadvantage. On the other hand, it is certain that the
Democrats believed that such a compromise would make possible the establishment of their claims. It is not surprising, therefore, that practically all the opposition to a compromise measure
came from the Republican press and from Republicans in Congress. It is not surprising that while most of the Republican
leaders that favored compromise did so from purely patriotic
motives, — from the conviction that otherwise the peace and
prosperity of the country would be imperilled, — others were
believed to act from motives that were not wholly disinterested.

At this juncture, in reply to a letter from Senator Sherman,[1]
Mr. Hayes clearly set forth his view: —

[1] The letter is as follows: —

U.S. SENATE CHAMBER,
WASHINGTON, Jan. 3, 1877.

To GOVERNOR HAYES: —

MY DEAR SIR, — Some matters have transpired here that I think you ought
to know. The formation of the Senate committee on counting the electoral vote
gave us great solicitude, but the Vice-President, after consulting many Senators,
thought it best to put Mr. Conkling in the place of Logan. My judgment was
against it, but when pretty generally concurred in I did not feel justified in
objecting further. The committee is now sitting daily. I have heard from the
most reliable sources some indications of an unfavorable character, which I am
only at liberty to communicate to you in like confidence. Mr. Conkling has
openly stated in the committee his position that the President of the Senate has
no right *to count* the votes, and that, as the case stands, he will not vote that you
have either Florida or Louisiana. He may vote to allow the Supreme Court to
pass upon these questions. This develops a danger that I anticipated, but perhaps it is no greater with him on the committee than in the Senate. This brings
up directly the question whether we ought not promptly to agree to refer, by
proper legislation, in the nature of an appeal, to the Supreme Court or to a tribunal composed of the President of the Senate, Speaker, and Chief Justice, all the
legal questions that may arise in the progress of the count. I would like very
much your opinions or impressions on this matter, not only for my own but for
the information of others. Comly is here. — Very truly yours,

JOHN SHERMAN.

Confidential.   COLUMBUS, O., Jan. 5, 1877.

MY DEAR SIR, — I have your note of the 3d. I do not wish to influence the action of our friends, and do not volunteer opinions. But *you* have a right to my opinion. I believe the Vice-President alone has the constitutional power to count the votes and declare the result. Everything in the nature of a contest as to electoral votes is an affair of the States. The rest is a merely ministerial duty. Therefore it is not right in my judgment for Congress to interfere. — Sincerely,

R. B. HAYES.

HON. JOHN SHERMAN,
      U.S. SENATE.

P.S. I would like your opinion and Senator Morton's on resigning as Governor before the count in February. It would be a decided announcement of my own opinions as to the result of the election. I can do it with great satisfaction whatever the probable action of the two houses, if it is thought advisable. — H.[1]

Undoubtedly the view here expressed is correct. The States have sole power and right to appoint the electors and to determine all contests relating to their appointment. That is the view which in the end prevailed; that is the view now universally accepted. But in case of two or more certificates of returns, forwarded in proper form from a State to the President of the Senate, who was to determine which certificate was the authentic one and was to be counted? That was the crux of the dispute; and those who contended that Congress should have some voice in the determination seemed to have much the best of the argument.

On the same day of the letter to Mr. Sherman, Mr. Hayes wrote in his diary: —

My advices are that the result of the action of the Senate will depend on the report the committee of the Senate makes on the election in Louisiana. This seems not to be in much doubt; but there is enough to leave me in a state of suspense. I must therefore prepare for either event. The Cabinet is the 'chief work, next the inaugural. As to the address, I wish to repeat my letter of acceptance on, 1, currency and national faith; 2, on civil service reform; 3, on the South. I must urge a liberal policy towards the South, especially in affording facilities for education, and encouraging business and immigration by internal improvements of a national character.

How little disposed Mr. Hayes was, however, to insist on his

---

[1] Mr. Sherman replied at once advising against the resignation.

opinion or to impose it on others, appears from a letter of January 17 to Carl Schurz. He wrote: —

MY DEAR GENERAL, — I returned late last night and find your letter. I have no time to reply suitably this morning, but hasten to assure you that nobody is authorized to represent me on the subject of the count. I have thought it fitting that I should let that matter well alone. Of course I have opinions. But I shall abide the result. No one ought to go to war or even to law about it. I am free to say *to you* that I concur with Kent.[1] But others, abler to judge, think otherwise, and I recognize their right as good Republicans so to think. Many good Republicans think that the interests of the party will be promoted by Tilden's success. I can see many reasons for this opinion.

In the absence of congressional action the Vice-President should count and declare. I am not favorably impressed with having it decided by lot. But I beg you to believe me sincere when I say that I take no part in this and shall quietly await the event.[2]

[1] "The Constitution does not expressly declare *by whom* the votes are to be counted and the result declared. In the case of questionable votes and a closely contested election, this power may be all-important; and I presume, in the absence of all legislative provision on the subject, that the President of the Senate counts the votes and determines the result, and that the two houses are present only as spectators, to witness the fairness and accuracy of the transaction, and to act only if no choice be made by the election." (Kent's *Commentaries*, vol. i.)

[2] Mr. Schurz replied at length, January 21. In the course of his letter he said: "I think there is no man in the country who would be more heartily congratulated upon its passage [the Electoral Commission Bill], if it does pass, — which I can scarcely doubt, — than yourself. My reasons are these : If the Board of Arbitration established by the bill decides in your favor, no man will be able to say that you were put into the Presidency by mere partisan action. The result of the great contest will not only be submitted to by the whole people, but all the good citizens will unite in defending it, as brought about by the fair and impartial judgment of the highest tribunal in the land, against what clamor may still be raised against it by extreme partisans. The latter will then appear as wanton disturbers of the public repose. And even if the Board should decide against you, you would be saved from the mortifications and disappointments which would inevitably follow a decision in your favor brought about by a proceeding which would be looked upon, not only by Democrats, but by a very large number of Republicans, as an unscrupulous stretch of party power for selfish party interest; and so the counting and declaring of the vote by the Senate would undoubtedly be regarded. Your name would not be associated in our history with one of the most dangerous precedents of party action. The Conference Bill may not be perfect; it may provide for a proceeding of an extra-constitutional character, although I think its constitutionality can be defended on solid ground; but it has the great virtue of removing a question, the manner of whose decision may furnish a precedent fraught with the most precarious consequences for the future of the Republic, from the theatre of excited and apparently selfish partisan strife; of insuring the country a Government whose legitimacy will stand above serious dispute and of restoring confidence and repose to the public mind. It is no wonder that, some

There is a contingency which I must be prepared for. I must consider, if not write, an inaugural, and consider, if not appoint, a Cabinet. On these points I am glad to hear from all my friends. I had a good talk with General Cox at Toledo Saturday.

Write often and fully. — Sincerely,

R. B. HAYES.

The same day the diary records: —

Wheeler, Chandler (William E.), and others write that Conkling is decidedly hostile, and that he has enough followers to pass through the Senate a compromise measure. The effect of this is to change the result in all probability. Well, I am personally content. I must go on to the end, and in the meanwhile prepare for either event.

In the Senate, on January 18, Senator Edmunds, on behalf of the Joint Committee of fourteen, submitted the bill for the creation of the Electoral Commission, together with the report of the committee. This report, which set forth admirably but concisely both the difficulties which the committee had faced in its task and the merits, as it believed, of the conclusion it had reached, after long and conscientious consideration, in the bill now presented, was signed by every member of the committee,[1] except Senator Morton who remained irreconcilably opposed to any compromise.[2] The practical unanimity of the committee as well as the

political circles excepted, the people should have welcomed it with such a preponderance of sentiment as a measure of relief."

[1] The Senate members of the committee were Messrs. Edmunds, Morton, Frelinghuysen, and Conkling, Republicans; and Messrs. Thurman, Bayard, and Ransom, Democrats. The House members were Messrs. Payne, Hunton, Hewitt, and Springer, Democrats; and Messrs. McCrary, Hoar, and Willard, Republicans.

[2] Two days after the Commission Bill was introduced, Mr. Hayes wrote John Sherman, who was opposed to the measure: "Your views of the compromise are also mine. I prefer not to be quoted. I do not desire to influence the decision by Congress. But the bill seems to me to be a very dangerous violation of the Constitution. I agree with you also that the true appeal is to the Supreme Court, according to the accustomed rules and principles of law, by *quo warranto*, or otherwise. . . . I write this for your eye alone, believing that *you* are entitled to my opinions. I do not wish them to be used to influence anybody."

January 25 he wrote Garfield: "I have not replied before to your esteemed favor of the 19th because I did not want to even seem to wish to influence the action of Congress on the subject of the count. Good Republicans differ as to the bill of the Conference Committee. I see, or think I see, constitutional objections to it. Certainly I prefer any plan which leaves the decision to the Supreme Court. But now that it is before the country, with many Republicans committed to it, the question is a different one from what it was when it was before the committee as an original proposition. There ought to be full argument before the Commission.

sobriety of its report could not fail to exercise potent influence alike on Congress and on public opinion generally. In a word the committee declared: —

This bill, then, is only directed to ascertaining, for the purpose and in aid of the counting, what are the constitutional votes of the respective States; and whatever jurisdiction exists for such purpose, the bill only regulates the method of exercising it.

The debate which followed laid special emphasis upon this point — that the proposed Commission would have and could exercise no greater power in determining the questions that should be submitted to it than that already possessed under the Constitution by the two houses of Congress. Whatever jurisdiction over the electoral count Congress possessed, the Commission would possess and only that.[1]

The Senate passed the bill by a vote of 47 to 17, 10 members being absent. The majority was made up of 21 Republicans and

Argument on all questions — their powers, the true principles of the Constitution, and the substantial equities. If this is not sufficiently provided for, it is worthy of consideration whether amendments should not be made to secure it. Do not understand me as wishing to influence you for or against the bill. I understand you are fully decided on your course."

He wrote Carl Schurz, January 23: "No doubt the compromise will pass and I hope it will turn out well. I shall do nothing to influence the result. The measure is, as you say, 'extra-constitutional.' I am not disposed to look anxiously for constitutional objections when an important good is to be accomplished. With me the chief objection is the usurpation of the Presidential power of appointment which it involves. Congress, as my 'letter' intimates, has done this too much in the past."

[1] "In framing this act the two committees carefully and intentionally refrained from changing in any way any law then existing that might affect either way the fundamental merits of the existing controversy; and so, when the bill was under debate in the Senate, and Mr. Morton, a member of the committee, who did not concur in its report or in the passage of the bill, moved to amend the same by providing 'That nothing herein contained shall authorize the said Commission to go behind the finding and determination of the canvassing or returning officers of a State authorized by the laws of the State to find and determine the result of an election for electors,' I moved to amend the amendment so as to make it declare that the Commission should have authority to go behind the returns. The purpose of my motion was to make it impossible that any inference should exist from Mr. Morton's proposition being rejected that the Commission should be granted by the act any authority either way that did not already exist. I, of course, voted against my own amendment and only one Senator voted for it. The amendment of Mr. Morton was defeated by a majority of more than two to one. Thus the bill passed without any amendment at all." (Ex-Senator George F. Edmunds, in *Century Magazine*, June, 1913.)

26 Democrats. Of those voting against the bill all but one (Eaton, of Connecticut,) were Republicans.[1]

In the House, which took up the bill on January 25, the strongest argument in favor of passing the measure was made by Mr. Abram S. Hewitt, of New York, a member of the Joint Committee, and a close friend of Mr. Tilden. He pointed out the consequences which he believed inevitable — and his position in the party councils (chairman of the Democratic National Committee) gave his words additional weight — in the absence of the proposed legislation. "The President of the Senate would count the votes for Hayes, and he would be inaugurated by the use of the army. But the House would not be silent and passive spectators. They would insist on their right to participate in the count. They would count the votes of Florida and Louisiana for Tilden and Hendricks and declare them elected. Thus there would be two Presidents claiming each to be lawfully chosen. The logical result would be civil war with all its horrors. The end no man could foresee, save refuge sooner or later under an imperial ruler. But the committee had formed a plan absolutely fair between the two political parties, which meant the supremacy of the civil over the military power."

In conclusion Mr. Hewitt said: —

No man can predict who will become President by virtue of its operation, but all men can predict that it will be the man who is *lawfully* entitled to be President. If the law should violate the equity of the case, it is ground for the amendment of the law, but not of rebellion against its decrees. . . . It means the preservation of the autonomy of the States, and the right of the people therein to regulate and administer their local affairs, without any interference from any quarter. Lastly, it means oblivion of all the bitterness of the past, security for the present, hope for the future.

The House passed the bill by a vote of 191 to 86, 14 not voting. Of the majority, 159 were Democrats and 32 Republicans; of the minority, all but 18 were Republicans.

Thus, while both parties shared equally in the draughting of

[1] After the passage of the bill by the Senate Mr. Sherman, who had opposed the bill, wrote Mr. Hayes, January 26: "Still, it is the surrender of a certainty for an uncertainty, with the advantage that the decision of the tribunal, whatever it should be, will be peacefully acquiesced in. . . . Your quiet, reserved course is universally commended, and I close with the hope that even the bill, which I feared so much, may make your 'calling and election sure.'"

the bill, and the bill could not have been passed by the Senate without the coöperation of the Republicans, the measure after all owed its existence and support much rather to the Democrats than to the Republicans. In the entire Congress only 19 Democratic votes were recorded against it and few Democratic voices were raised in opposition to its passage. But Republican after Republican argued against its adoption, and 84 Republicans expressed their disapprobation of it by their votes. With such practical unanimity of Democratic sanction of this plan of settling the electoral dispute, the Democrats of the nation, leaders and masses, were under compelling moral obligation to accept in good faith any decision, though adverse to their contentions, that the Electoral Commission should render.

The President promptly signed the bill, notifying the Senate of his action in a message to that body on January 29. After reviewing the conditions, which to his mind made action by Congress imperative, he concluded his message with these wise and reassuring words: —

The country is agitated. It needs and it desires peace, and quiet, and harmony, between all parties and all sections. Its industries are arrested, labor unemployed, capital idle, and enterprise paralyzed, by reason of the doubt and anxiety attending the uncertainty of a double claim to the Chief Magistracy of the nation. It wants to be assured that the result of the election will be accepted without resistance from the supporters of the disappointed candidates, and that its highest officer shall not hold his place with a questioned title of right. Believing that the bill will secure these ends, I give it my signature.

Mr. Hayes followed the progress of the debate in Congress on the Commission Bill with intense interest. As already set forth, his opinion was adverse to the propriety or the need of any legislation; least of all of an extraordinary character. The measure when proposed seemed to him exposed to constitutional objections. Sunday, January 21, he writes in his diary: —

The compromise reported by the Joint Committee seems to be a surrender, at least in part, of our case. The leading constitutional objection to it, perhaps, is that the appointment of the Commission by Act of Congress violates that part of the Constitution which gives the appointment of all other officers to the President. To this it will possibly be replied that the members of the Commission are not officers — that they are analogous to referees and master commissioners, to advisory boards, or committees. But is this true? Their decisions stand unless both houses of Congress concur in overruling them. If the Commission decides to throw out the vote of Mississippi, the vote of that State will be lost if *one* House concurs. If the Commission decides that Cronin's vote for Tilden shall be counted, it will be counted if the House alone concurs. The Commission is analogous to inferior tribunals. Its decisions are binding unless the superior tribunal overrules them by a concurrent vote of both houses. The President of the Senate and the Senate may be overruled by the Commission and the House. Surely the members of such a commission are officers. Their appointment by Congress is a usurpation of the Presidential authority. If the bill has not a two-thirds vote in both houses, the President's veto ought to prevent it from becoming a law.

The next most important objection to the bill is that if passed it may turn out to be an act to prevent the counting of the electoral vote. There can be no count if the Commission refuses or fails to act. This power to prevent a decision is a power far above any power belonging to Congress, master commissioners, advisory boards, or committees.

January 26 Mr. Hayes wrote: —

The compromise bill for counting the Presidential vote passed the Senate by 47 to 17. More Republicans supported it than voted against it. The Democrats all voted aye except Eaton, of Connecticut. Its passage by a like majority in the House is probable. What Congress and the popular sentiment approve is rarely defeated by reason of constitutional objections.

I trust the measure will turn out well. It is a great relief to me. Defeat in this way, after a full and public hearing before this Commission, is not mortifying in any degree, and success will be in all respects more satisfactory. I have not tried to influence the opinions or actions of anybody on the bill.

Before another Presidential election this whole subject of the Presidential election ought to be thoroughly considered, and a radical change made. It is probable that no wise measure can be devised which does not require an amendment of the Constitution. Let proposed amendments be maturely considered. Something ought to be done immediately.

On the same day Mr. Hayes wrote to Judge Alphonso Taft, the Attorney-General, as follows: —

I am obliged for your valued letter. The bill in relation to the election will become a law. Of course, with so strong a vote in its favor, the President will promptly sign it. I have not attempted to influence the result and shall not. If the principles of Mr. Frelinghuysen's speech are adopted by the Commission, our success is almost certain. I take it our friends will see that we are ably and wisely represented both *on* and *before* the Commission. This is the next point of interest.

The law provided for a Commission of fifteen members, five to be elected by each House of Congress by *viva voce* vote and five to be justices of the Supreme Court. Of the last, four were designated by the Act itself, two being Democrats and two Republicans. These four were to select the fifth. It had been the general supposition or tacit understanding that the fifth justice was likely to be Judge David Davis, who was regarded as an independent in politics.[1] But just at this juncture, a coalition of independents and Democrats in the Illinois Legislature, which had been in a deadlock over the choice of a United States Senator (certain Republicans refusing to vote for the reëlection of Senator Logan), elected Judge Davis to the Senate, and so he was considered ineligible for service on the Commission. There was much speculation and solicitude on all sides as to which one of the other four justices should be chosen. When the announcement was made, January 31, that the choice had fallen upon Mr. Justice

---

[1] The public prints of the day and private letters voiced this understanding. It is expressed, for example, in the following letter: —

WASHINGTON, D.C.,
January 20, 1877.

DEAR GOVERNOR, — I write briefly. You have read the "compromise" which amounts to the giving a certainty for an uncertainty. What will be its fate the future can only determine. The impression yesterday, after the reading of the report, seemed to be that it will pass the two houses. But it will be opposed by some of our leading friends and, rumor says, by some of the opposition. What the President will do no one knows. I send the leader in this morning's *National Republican*. Whether it had any inspiration from the White House I don't know. My instincts are all opposed to the measure. I have not, however, examined it carefully. Waite, Sherman, Taft, and I talked it over last night at the Chief Justice's house. Sherman is opposed to it; so Taft; and the Chief Justice listened attentively to all that was said. I have had several conversations with him on the general subject and am sorry he is not to be on the Commission, if the compromise be adopted. I don't mean that the two Republican judges selected are not reliable, but I have not talked with either of them. It looks as if Davis may be the fifth judge, and as to him I will say, that I have more confidence in him than our friends here generally have. I can't well explain on paper; still, I would feel easier as to him, if he had had less to do with the Democracy than he has had. I have no authority to say what he will probably do, if on the Commission. My opinion is formed on what I have heard he has said generally on the Presidential question.

Suppose the President would veto the bill? What then?

There are many matters connected with this whole affair I would like to talk over with you, but can't well write about. — Truly yours,

W. DENNISON.

GOVERNOR HAYES.

Bradley, the Republican leaders believed that the chances of a decision in consonance with their interpretation of the powers of the Commission were decidedly favorable.

Mr. Hayes, writing in his diary, January 31, says: —

The Commission seems to be a good one. At 2 P.M. Webb [his son] announced, "The judge, it is Bradley. In Washington the bets are five to one that the next [President] will be Hayes!"

But I am in no way elated. I prefer success. But I am clear that for our happiness failure is to be preferred. I shall await the event with the utmost composure. If the result is adverse, I shall be cheerful, quiet, and serene. If successful, may God give me grace to be firm and wise and just — clear in the great office — for the true interest of all the people of the United States!

On Thursday, February 1, the count of the electoral votes began, the States being called in alphabetical order. When Florida was reached, contesting certificates were presented and all the papers in the case were referred to the Electoral Commission.[1] Elaborate arguments were presented for and against the power of the Commission to "go behind the returns" which consumed several days. The Commission decided by a strict party vote that it had no such power; that the action of the duly constituted state authorities, within the time specified by law, was final in determining who were the properly chosen electors; and that it had no authority to inquire into the methods pursued in such determination or to take cognizance of any subsequent action or reversal of its decision by a State.[2]

[1] The members of the Commission were Justices Clifford (President), Field, Miller, Strong, and Bradley; Senators Edmunds, Morton, Frelinghuysen, Bayard, and Thurman; Representatives Abbot, Hunton, Payne, Garfield, and Hoar.

[2] The general principle was best laid down later by the Commission in the South Carolina decision: "There exists no power in this Commission, and there exists none in the two houses of Congress, in counting the electoral vote, to inquire into the circumstances under which the primary vote for electors was given. The power of the Congress of the United States in its legislative capacity to inquire into the matters alleged, and to act upon the information so obtained, is a very different one from its power in the matter of counting the electoral vote. The votes to be counted are those presented by the State, and, when ascertained and presented by the proper authorities of the State, they must be counted."

The New York *Nation* (February 22, 1877), which was inclined to the view that the equities favored the Democrats, declared: "If the Commission had decided to 'go behind the returns,' to the extent asked for by the Democrats, . . . it would have prepared the way for endless complications at future elections, and perhaps for the conversion of the Presidential election into a farce. We should have had to prepare ourselves for 'double returns' from two thirds of the States and a fight

Probably no one to-day who has a proper conception of the just powers or rights of the States, who understandingly considers the limits of their autonomy under the Federal Constitution, doubts that the judgment of the majority of the Electoral Commission was absolutely sound and correct; that any other judgment would have been in serious derogation of the dignity and integrity of state authority. Even if he should believe that this judgment involved a violation of the equity of the case (which, of course, the author does not believe), he must still acknowledge that it was faultless in principle. The wonder must always be that the Democrats, who have ever professed themselves the truest and sturdiest defenders of the rights of the States, should, in their eagerness to attain their immediate end, have been willing to desert their historic position and sanction the invasion of state authority by the federal power.

As the result of its decision the Commission, February 9, reported to the President of the Senate that the electoral votes of Florida should be counted for Hayes and Wheeler. As the Senate concurred in this decision the votes were so counted.[1] The count proceeded, the papers from each disputed State being referred in order to the Commission and the decision in every instance following the precedent set in the Florida case.[2] It was not till the

in Congress over the vote in each State, which would have caused the count to last for a year, and would, every fourth year, have inflicted a season of complete paralysis on business."

[1] Mr. Hayes's comment on the Florida decision in his diary, February 8, follows: "Yesterday the Electoral Commission decided not to go behind the papers filed with the Vice-President in the case of Florida. The question was well argued on our side. Judge Matthews was notably able and successful. Mr. Evarts's argument was worthy of his fame. I read the arguments in the *Congressional Record* and can't see how lawyers can differ on the question. But the decision is by a strictly party vote — eight Republicans against the seven Democrats. It shows the strength of party ties. The general situation is now regarded as much more favorable to us, and now our friends are very confident of success." — The next day Mr. Hayes records: "I hear from [blank] of Steubenville, that Eli T. Sheppard, being unwell, kept his bed in a hotel at Washington, while Jere Black discussed with his callers in a room separated from that of S. by a door, [thus hearing] the loud talk in Black's room on the situation. Black said: 'God damn them, they will beat us and elect Hayes; but we shall give them all the trouble we can!'"

[2] The following letter to Mr. Hayes gives a vivid contemporary impression of the tense feeling at Washington during the count: —

1333 G St., Washington, D.C.,
February 18, 1877.

Dear General, — Since I wrote you we have passed through the "Louisiana

early morning of March 2 that the count was completed and the
result declared. While the Democrats, after the Florida decision,
could hardly have entertained much expectation of success, they
contested every case with the utmost vigor, and as they saw
every hope gradually vanishing, the more impulsive of them were
disposed to resort to dilatory tactics and even attempted a filibuster,[1] — which was steadfastly opposed by Speaker Randall[2]
and the leading Democratic members from the South,[3] — so
as to delay the completion of the count beyond the 4th of March.

experience." The trial — the awaiting the "verdict" — the attendance upon
the announcement of the decision of the Commission and the resulting scenes of
excitement and indignation were affairs of strange and most transcendent interest. But they are already, apparently, about past; and the quickness with which
they all subsided, and were lost in this great ocean of ours, furnishes a remarkable
indication as to what an ocean it is; and as to how prodigious those currents are
which sweep on and on forever, unchecked, and almost undisturbed by the most
momentous events transpiring on its vast surface.

Of course, you are kept incessantly informed about what is occurring, and is
likely to occur; and it is because I know you are overwhelmed with "information," that I have deemed it best to trouble you but little with statements about
our trial. We all think the case virtually decided, and that the Democracy will
make little further fight. Your inauguration will be peaceful and I trust auspicious. And now, my dear friend, may Heaven attend you in the most momentous
duties about to come to you; and if you can only contribute to the restoration of
our Government, and its methods and administrative processes, to the conditions pointed out in your letter of acceptance, — especially in regard to the civil
service, — then will your Administration pass into our history as an epoch — a
rescue of the Republic from impending disaster.

But when I began I had not the slightest idea of what I was about to write —
so, good-bye, and God bless and uphold you. — Yours faithfully and ever,

S. SHELLABARGER.

[1] W. D. Bickham, editor of the Dayton *Journal*, writing to Mr. Hayes from
Washington, February 14, 1877, said: "I *know*, by authority not to be committed
to writing, that Tilden intends that his friends shall filibuster to prevent a completion of the count. That *was* his *intention* Sunday. I *know also by testimony*
that the New York *Sun* articles generally, for some time past, have been submitted to him in proof."

[2] "Read last evening the speeches on Randall. His greatest act was in 1877—
holding the scales even in carrying out the Electoral Commission's decision."
(Diary, May 16, 1891.)

[3] "In all the debates in the House over the Presidential dispute, ever since the
election, the Southern members have been foremost in supporting a policy of
peace and moderation; they held the violent Northern Democrats in check in the
earlier days of the controversy; they threw their influence in favor of the plan of
arbitration; they helped to pass it; and since the decision has gone against them
they have counselled a cheerful submission and have discountenanced all schemes
for 'filibustering' or delay or resistance." (*The Nation*, February 22, 1877.)

But just what they expected to gain by that procedure it is difficult to surmise.

These Southern leaders were doubtless fortified in their opposition to the attempted filibuster by assurances received from close friends of Mr. Hayes that he would abide by the full implication of his letter of acceptance in dealing with the South. Senator Gordon and Congressman John Young Brown, of Kentucky, called on Congressman Charles Foster, of Ohio, on February 26. Mr. Young reminded Mr. Foster that he "had been voting against all dilatory motions and had in a speech advocated the inflexible execution of the Electoral Bill"; and that he intended to continue doing so whatever other Southern members might do; that his course had evoked much criticism from his friends in Kentucky; and that he "desired a written assurance from him that the policy of Mr. Hayes would be as indicated" in the speech Mr. Foster had made in Congress a few days before. Mr. Foster replied that he had a letter from Mr. Hayes approving his speech and that he would give him the written assurance he requested. He consulted with Stanley Matthews and the next day gave Mr. Brown the following joint letter: —

WASHINGTON, February 27, 1877.

GENTLEMEN, — Referring to the conversation had with you yesterday in which Governor Hayes's policy as to the status of certain Southern States was discussed, we desire to say that we can assure you in the strongest possible manner of our great desire to have him adopt such a policy as will give to the people of the States of South Carolina and Louisiana the right to control their own affairs in their own way, subject only to the Constitution of the United States and the laws made in pursuance thereof, and to say further that from an acquaintance with and knowledge of Governor Hayes and his views, we have the most complete confidence that such will be the policy of his Administration. — Respectfully,

STANLEY MATTHEWS,
CHARLES FOSTER.

To the HON. JOHN B. GORDON
and the HON. JOHN YOUNG BROWN.

Mr. Brown gave copies of the letter to several Southern men with authority to use them as they thought best. Moreover, acting on the suggestion of the call of Senator Gordon and Mr. Brown, Mr. Foster arranged for a conference with other Southern

members of Congress that same evening. Mr. Foster's account
of this conference at Wormley's Hotel follows: —

During the final hours of the count under the Electoral Bill, several
Southern gentlemen who opposed a filibustering movement were solicitous that they should have definite assurances from Mr. Hayes as to his
Southern policy. An informal meeting was arranged, at which were present as friends of Mr. Hayes Messrs. Sherman, Garfield, Dennison,
Matthews, and myself. The object of the meeting was simply to arrive
at a better understanding in regard to the policy of the incoming
Administration. They, on their part, did not claim that the assurances
they asked for were to determine their action as to carrying out the
provisions of the Electoral Bill. They desired them as a guaranty to
their people that they acted in good faith. To this end they desired that
Governor Hayes give them only such guaranties as he had already
given to his own friends.

In reply it was stated by us that it would be improper and indelicate
at this time for Governor Hayes to give any assurances foreshadowing
his policy. We felt, however, fully justified in stating, from our knowledge of the views and intentions of Governor Hayes, that his policy
would be to favor local self-government and home rule in the South. We
gave no assurances as coming directly from Mr. Hayes. We simply
stated our belief as to his course, based upon communications from and
conversations with him. Whatever may have been said with regard to
the withdrawal of troops was simply in the nature of a belief that such
would be the result of the policy which we believed the President would
adopt.[1]

The country gave a sigh of relief when the result was declared.
Even the bitterly disappointed Democrats were glad the agony
was over. Only here and there were heard faint murmurs of a
disposition to resent and resist the decision by force. The Commission had accomplished the purpose for which it had been created; it had secured a peaceful settlement of a dispute which
threatened the stability of the Government.[2] It had determined,

[1] Interview in Fostoria (Ohio) *Review*, March 23.

That the friends of Mr. Hayes were abundantly justified in their assurances to
the Southern gentlemen is proved by the following extract from a letter of Mr.
Hayes to Senator Sherman, of February 15: "Boynton writes to Smith that an
assurance that my views on the Southern question are truly set forth in my letter,
with such additions as I could properly make, would be useful. I prefer to make
no new declarations. But you may say, if you deem it advisable, that you *know*
that I will stand by the friendly and encouraging words of that letter and by all
that they imply. You cannot express that too strongly."

[2] "*Harper's Weekly* held then and holds now that there had been so much intimidation, bribery, fraud, and suppressions that it was absolutely impossible to

as Mr. Hewitt predicted that it would, who was *"lawfully* entitled to be President." The Democrats, who had had the largest share in its creation, could not with any respect for consistency "rebel against its decree." And be it said for the great body of them, that, even if they still felt that the victory fairly belonged to them, they accepted the arbitrament as final, in the spirit of loyal and patriotic Americans.[1]

It is always confidently assumed by Democratic critics of the decision of the Electoral Commission that had the Commission decided that it was authorized "to go behind the returns," Mr. Tilden would have become President.[2] But that is pure

know what the vote really was, and that under the circumstances the only way to avoid civil convulsion was to agree upon such scheme of settlement as was adopted. Its adoption and the peaceful carrying out of the decision, was one of the greatest triumphs of patriotism in our annals." (George William Curtis, in *Harper's Weekly*, June 23, 1888.)

[1] As Secretary Evarts said, in a speech at Cooper Union, New York, October 24, 1878: "By an exhibition of wisdom and courage, by a comprehensive and circumspect estimate of the gravity of the situation, the people of the country exhibited a control over themselves in an emergency of this kind — certainly unforeseen and wholly unprovided for — that bespoke the greatness of the nation in a civil capacity, as the record of the civil war had proclaimed its greatness as a military nation. . . . When both sections, both parties, resorted to a method of final settlement that should be of debate and of reason, of judgment and of decision, the unanimous applause alike of the nations that had admired our scheme of free government, and nations that dissented from it, went up that the final trial of the American people had carried them safely through; and henceforth, in peace or war, there was no problem too great for them to solve."

[2] In the *Century Magazine* for May, 1913, Mr. Henry Watterson, the brilliant editor of the Louisville *Courier-Journal*, who was a member of Congress during the electoral dispute and a leader in Democratic counsels, has a discursive article on "The Hayes-Tilden Contest for the Presidency" which starts off by asserting: "The time is coming, if it has not already arrived, when among fair-minded and intelligent Americans there will not be two opinions touching the Hayes-Tilden contest for the Presidency in 1876–77, — that both by the popular vote and a fair count of the electoral vote Tilden was elected and Hayes was defeated, — but the whole truth underlying the determinate incidents which led to the rejection of Tilden and the seating of Hayes will never be known." But Mr. Watterson presents no facts to sustain his assertion. In the next following number of the same magazine, ex-Senator George F. Edmunds, the last surviving member of the Electoral Commission, replies to what he calls Mr. Watterson's "rather astonishing article." He declares: "I believe that the time *has* come when among fair-minded and intelligent Americans who will investigate the public and printed documents and papers in existence on the subject, there will be few divergent opinions touching the justice and lawfulness of the election of Mr. Hayes. They will find that he was lawfully elected and instituted to the office by fair and lawful means." Further he says: "He [Mr. Watterson] imputes to the members of the

assumption. What would have followed would have been a prolonged contest before the Commission, involving the presentation of an infinite amount of detailed information, affidavits, and testimony regarding the elections in the disputed States, and extended arguments by the opposing counsel, and then a finding in each case by the Commission as to which one of the various sets of certificates was the proper one and was to be counted. No one can possibly be assured that after such hearings the majority of the Commission would in any single case have decided in favor of the Tilden certificate. It is conceivable, of course, that it might have done so, but the author believes that this is altogether improbable. To him it seems beyond doubt that if the Commission had proceeded in that manner the final result would have been precisely the same. But meanwhile the country would have continued in depressing uncertainty, with increasing bitterness of partisan recrimination and disputation. There is no reasonable probability that the labors of the Commission could have been completed before the 4th of March; and the nation would thus have been confronted with an interregnum, the consequences of which the mind shudders to contemplate.

There is absolutely no more ground for charging the Republican members of the Commission with having been dominated solely by partisan considerations than for making the same charge against the Democratic members. All the members of the Commission were men of the highest character, men of unblemished reputation, and of eminent ability. It is impossible to believe that any one of them consciously acted in the matter except in accordance with what he conscientiously believed to be right and just. The Republicans adopted one theory of the power of the Commission (the right theory, the author believes, the true

Republican party at that time officially or otherwise connected with public affairs the crime of bribing the state canvassing boards of the disputed States 'at least in patronage, to make false returns in favor of the Republican electors.' As one of the few survivors of that stormy time, as the *last survivor* of the members of the select committees of the two houses who conducted the passage of the Electoral Bill, and as the last survivor of the members of the Electoral Commission, I feel bound to repel the imputation as wholly groundless. In all our frequent consultations during the whole time there never was a proposal, suggestion, or hint of ours, or on the part of any one of us, resorting to bribery in any form, or of promise of office or other benefit, or influencing or trying to influence any of the canvassing boards or other state officials to depart from their lawful duty."

THE ELECTORAL COMMISSION IN SESSION

historic Democratic theory of constitutional interpretation), the Democrats, another theory. The difference was fundamental. It is not singular in view of all the circumstances of the case that party lines were thus sharply drawn. Every member, whether Republican or Democrat, must have felt a subconscious compulsion to support the theory which his party believed to be the right and true one. Had any single commissioner of either party given his voice to the opposing theory, the imagination falters in contemplating the odium and obloquy that would have been his portion from his fellow partisans for the remainder of his days. What the Republican Senators who refused to vote for the impeachment of Andrew Johnson suffered in cruel despite would not have been a circumstance to what such a man might reasonably have expected.

For some reason the Democratic critics of the Commission's decision conceived that special and particular responsibility rested on Mr. Justice Bradley, because he was the last man selected. But he had no other or greater responsibility than each and every other member of the Commission. If it be assumed that the decision was made without regard to right or reason, but solely on partisan grounds, it was no more the duty of Judge Bradley to rise above partisanship than it was the duty of every other member. Nor is there, so far as the author knows, any sound basis for the Democratic assumption that if Judge Davis had been the fifteenth man the decision would have been different. Certain it is that while the Commission was sitting Judge Davis in conversation with friends approved its action. William Henry Smith, who knew Judge Davis well, writing to Mr. Hayes, from Chicago, February 17, 1877, had this to say: "Judge Davis has been spending three days in this city. You will be pleased to hear that he most heartily approves the action of Judge Bradley. He says no good lawyer, not a strict partisan, could decide otherwise." [1]

Mr. Hayes himself never had any doubt, after he was informed

[1] "The day after the inauguration of Hayes my kinsman, Stanley Matthews, said to me, 'You people wanted Judge Davis. So did we. I tell you what I know, that Judge Davis was as safe for us as Judge Bradley. We preferred him because he carried more weight.' The subsequent career of Judge Davis in the Senate gives conclusive proof that this was true." (Henry Watterson, in *Century Magazine*, May, 1913.)

concerning the elections and the election laws in the disputed States, that he was not only legally but equitably entitled to the Presidency. Writing, February 16, 1885, to the Honorable Hugh Campbell, at that time the United States District Attorney of Dakota, Mr. Hayes said: —

I have never had any doubt as to the legality or the fairness of the final result in 1876. Garfield, Sherman, and other gentlemen of high character who visited Louisiana to observe the count, personally assured me in the strongest terms that my equitable as well as legal right to the vote of that State was beyond all question.

More than this, one of the ablest and most influential Democrats in the country, who was perfectly familiar with the inner history of the whole affair on the Democratic side, told me that no intelligent or candid man of his party could claim the election for the Democratic party if he conceded the validity of the Fifteenth Amendment. Said he: "If the negro vote is entitled to be considered, you should have had more States than were counted for you." No doubt this is true.[1]

Again in his diary, December 10, 1886, Mr. Hayes wrote: —

Evarts, Sherman, McCormick, and others recently talked on the "Fraud issue," which a faction of the Democratic party still harp upon. My notions of it are clear and decided.

1. In 1876 the Republicans were equitably entitled to the advantages of the Fifteenth Amendment under which, if it had been obeyed and enforced, they would have had *a majority of the popular vote of the country, and at least 203 electoral votes to Tilden's 166.* This includes Louisiana, Florida, Mississippi, Alabama, and South Carolina among the Republican States.

2. If the States which equitably belonged to the Republicans, but which were claimed by the Democrats, are excluded from the count, namely, Alabama, Mississippi, Louisiana, and Florida, — that is, if only

[1] "To continue with a word the disputed election of 1876. Washington McLean, proprietor of the Cincinnati *Enquirer*, a firm Democrat, of large ability and influence, a Warwick in his party, never taking office, said to me often, 'Oh! we all agree that if the Fifteenth Amendment is to be regarded, you were clearly entitled to the place.' 'No man of sense can deny that we nullified that in the election.' 'The negroes were kept from the polls by our people deliberately — and we in the North looked on with approval.'

"The truth [is], the Republicans were clearly entitled to Mississippi, Alabama, and other States that were counted for Tilden.

"If all the States in which fraud and force controlled were thrown out and not counted at all, the Republicans would have had a clear and decided majority, and if all the States whose legal and constitutional votes were Republican had been so returned, Tilden would have [been] beaten [by] about forty votes in the electoral colleges." (Diary, February 4, 1892.)

the States are counted about which no ground of dispute existed, — the vote would have stood, Republican 173, Democratic 166.

3. When the disputed election came before Congress the Democratic party decided to leave the question to the Electoral Commission. Mr. Tilden advised his friends to support the measure. This is clearly stated by Governor R. C. McCormick. He says that Senator Thurman was so advised by Mr. Tilden. After the result unfavorable to the Democrats was announced, doubts of Mr. Tilden's position were first heard of. Governor McCormick is the son-in-law of Judge Thurman and likely to know the facts.

4. In 1880 the question was practically settled, in all fairness, by the action of the Democratic party and the people. The Republicans nominated General Garfield. He was identified in many ways with the result of 1876, as declared in favor of the Republicans. He was one of the visiting statesmen who supervised the count in Louisiana. He reported to General Hayes, and officially to President Grant, that the Republicans were legally and equitably entitled to the Presidency.

He was by a unanimous vote of the House of Representatives made one of the Electoral Commission, and as such judge, under oath, found in favor of the Republicans, when his vote if cast for the Democrats would have given them the victory. In the canvass of 1880 this was made a point against him, but the people elected him in spite of the fraud cry.

But still more cogent was the action of the Democratic party. They declined to take issue with the Republicans in their nomination. They declined to nominate Mr. Tilden against General Garfield. This, it may be said, was because, after the Potter Committee and the cipher dispatches, Mr. Tilden was no longer an available candidate. But there was Mr. Hendricks who as Vice-Presidential candidate might well be nominated for the first place if Mr. Tilden was unavailable. Or Judge Thurman, one of the Electoral Commission, or Mr. Bayard, ditto, if nominated, might have "saved the fraud issue."

That the whole question was given up is shown by the editor of the *Courier-Journal*, Mr. Watterson, in his article on Mr. Tilden. He says: (quote). [Mr. Hayes failed to insert quotation.] The nomination of Hancock was a most significant yielding of the question. Pending the count he wrote to General Sherman: (quote). [Quotation again lacking.]

When the result was declared, he was perhaps the first army officer in full uniform, having come on his own motion from New York to Washington to attend the inauguration, immediately after the ceremony, to call on President Hayes and to congratulate him. He belonged to that wing of the party who agreed with Vice-President Hendricks, Alex. H. Stephens, and the great body of the party that General Hayes's title was perfect. The Democratic party, by nominating Hancock and refusing to nominate Tilden, or any one identified with the maintenance of the fraud issue, against Garfield, who was fully identified with every essential step in the series of events which gave the Republicans the victory in 1876-77 [abandoned the fraud issue].

Those who were closely connected with the declaration of the result in 1876-77 retain the confidence of the people.

Mr. Evarts, the leading counsel for the Republicans, after serving as Secretary of State in the Hayes Administration, has been chosen Senator for six years by New York. Mr. Sherman, who was a visiting statesman to supervise the count in Louisiana, after serving as Secretary of the Treasury in the Cabinet of President Hayes, is the Senator of Ohio, and by the vote of the Senate of the United States is presiding officer of that body.

Numerous other entries in the diary are of similar purport; but Mr. Hayes never throughout his life entered into any public discussion of the matter.

END OF VOLUME I

DATE DUE